THE LETTERS OF
ROBERT FROST
VOLUME 2

THE LETTERS OF
ROBERT FROST

VOLUME 2 · 1920–1928

EDITED BY

Donald Sheehy

Mark Richardson

Robert Bernard Hass

Henry Atmore

THE BELKNAP PRESS OF HARVARD UNIVERSITY PRESS

Cambridge, Massachusetts

London, England

2016

Library of Congress Cataloging-in-Publication Data
Frost, Robert, 1874–1963.
  [Correspondence]
  The letters of Robert Frost / edited by Donald Sheehy, Mark Richardson,
  and Robert Faggen.
      v. cm
  Includes bibliographical references and indexes.
  Contents: Volume 1. 1886–1920
  ISBN 978-0-674-05760-9 (v. 1)
  1. Frost, Robert, 1874–1963—Correspondence.   2. Poets, American—20th
century—Correspondence.   I. Sheehy, Donald Gerard.   II. Richardson, Mark,
1963–   III. Faggen, Robert.   IV. Title.
  PS3511.R94Z48 2014
  811'.52—dc23
  [B]
                                                                    2013015203

Contents

FEBRUARY 1920–SEPTEMBER 1921

*I took out an accident policy limited to death by boiling in a sap
pan, swore off on baths, and took up my new life as a farmer
to-day by absentmindedly boring a hole clear through a two foot
maple tree and out onto the other side. "Amatoor!" all the little
leaves began to murmur. "Book farmer!" Leaves is of course an
anachronism—that well known figure of speech. There werent
any leaves as yet.*

        —Robert Frost to Louis Untermeyer, March 21, 1920

SEPTEMBER 1921–MAY 1923

*Wait till I get wisdom; wait till I sell out and move to "the place
of understanding" by which Solomon (or was it David?) must
have meant Chicago—the Middle West anyway.*

        —Robert Frost to Van Wyck Brooks, September 4, 1921

MAY 1923–SEPTEMBER 1925

*I shall have to stay here in New England for one place wherever
else I may manage to be in September. That's clear now. And
the reason is that from an unnatural curiosity about education
and its problems I've just been getting myself freshly involved in*

*the affairs of Amherst College. I couldn't stand by and let it be
said of the poor thing that it was no longer a place for rebels.
How would you like it said of you that you were no longer a
place for rebels?*

— *Robert Frost to Lew Sarett, August 1923*

OCTOBER 1925–JUNE 1926
*Well, old friend, we are going to be where we shall see a lot of
each other again. I shall count on you more than on anyone else
to help me find out how to make the most of what the University
has given me. We must conspire to manage me with the wisdom
of the serpent.*

— *Robert Frost to Morris Tilley, November 10, 1924*

JUNE 1926–DECEMBER 1928
*You know how acute our homesickness always is: and to what
mental turns it spurs us. I suppose our realest anguish ensues
from our being caught on what looks like touring at all. We
ought not to be in France after all we have said from the
platform and the throne against tourism literal and metaphorical. By metaphorical I mean in Survey courses in education. . . . Think of me sightseeing in spite of all the protective
laziness I have developed on principle against it. I deserve to be
punished. Upon my soul I never saw anything to match this
summer Paris for ugliness not even a White Mountain resort.
We're catching it. But never mind. As I say we deserve it. You
may say another time we'll know better. Not necessarily. We're
not the kind that can be taught. We know instinctively all we
are going to know from birth and inexperience.*

— *Robert Frost to his daughter Lesley, September 1, 1928*

Preface

"If you want to find out your real opinion of anyone," Arthur Schopenhauer remarked, "observe the impression made upon you by the first sight of a letter from him." After years of "opening" and reading Frost's letters and with years of doing so still ahead, we have each come to realize—and admitted somewhat sheepishly to each other—that it is still rather exhilarating to read them for the first time. The news may be dated and the ink faded, but the work of editing never gets old because the sensibility that informs the correspondence remains so capable of surprising us with its expansiveness, its agility, and its mastery of tone and phrase. At their frequent best, Frost's letters are performances as interesting for *how* they say as for *what* they say. The accumulated correspondence reveals a mind remarkable for its range of reference, its feats of association, its intricacies of argument, its inherent sense of decorum but also its exuberance. To read Frost's letters is to be made always aware of the poetic cast of his thought, of the constant incipience of metaphor, of the figurative mind at work and play.

In prefatory remarks to the first volume of these letters, we dwelt briefly on the damage done to a collective sense of Frost as a human being—as a son, a brother, a husband, a father, a grandfather, a friend, a neighbor, a colleague, a teacher, an artist, and a public figure—by Lawrance Thompson's three-volume "official" biography. Collecting and editing a person's correspondence is always to some degree an effort to reintroduce the writer by offering ready access to an extensive body of thoroughly annotated primary documents. For us, there is a particularly appropriate poetic justice in giving Frost a second chance to make a first impression by providing readers of these letters an opportunity to encounter him verbatim in the course of daily life without editorial selection, interpretation, evaluation, or tendentious narratives and indexes. Letters, along with memoir and accounts by witnesses, are the raw material of biography, and we believe that Frost—as can anyone—can be best and justly served only by a fresh encounter with, and an unmediated impression taken from, the actual evidence of his life.

The present volume contains 569 letters, nearly two-thirds of which are collected here for the first time. Written at an average rate of nearly six per week, they allow us to track Frost's career fairly closely through the eight years this volume covers. In editing these letters we have constrained our enthusiasms, abjured interpretation and extrapolation, and striven to keep the annotations free of evaluation. Annotating Frost's letters, as the sheer number of our notes suggests, is an educational enterprise from which one never really "commences." We have endeavored to be thorough, but though we freely admit to exhaustion, we make no claim to exhaustiveness. Some allusions we likely missed, and certain persons or events referred to in the letters have remained elusive despite our best efforts.

Written during a period in which Frost's stature as one of America's leading poets was confirmed by the critical and popular reception accorded three new volumes—*New Hampshire* (1923), *Selected Poems* (1923), and *West-Running Brook* (1928)—the letters in this volume reveal an artist confident in his powers and seeking to expand his range. Solicited by editors, lecture bureaus, and literary societies, cultivated by his publisher, and pursued by prestigious academic institutions, Frost had achieved the kind of success he had described in a letter to John Bartlett in November 1913, as he was working on his second book, *North of Boston* (London, 1914), which in its 1915 American edition would become a best seller: "There is a kind of success called 'of esteem' and it butters no parsnips. It means a success with the critical few who are supposed to know. But really to arrive where I can stand on my legs as a poet and nothing else I must get outside that circle to the general reader who buys books in their thousands. I may not be able to do that. I believe in doing it—dont you doubt me there. I want to be a poet for all sorts and kinds" (*LRF-1*, 154). Along with the buttered parsnips had come ever-increasing demands upon his time and attention that competed not only with the obligations of family life but with the writing of poetry itself. Fame brought unwanted levels of public scrutiny, and the entanglements of academic politics could occasionally turn from irritating distraction into deep and enervating distress.

Finding a balance between the private and the public self, between the pull of family and the haul of work, between desire and obligation, is the essential drama of nearly every life, and Frost's is no exception. What makes this life exceptional, of course, is the poetry that rises from it. In the eight years of life recorded in the letters of this volume, Robert Frost experiences a full share of sorrow and joy, of doubt and certainty, of anxiety and hope, of frustration and success. But in a way no one but he himself would ever have predicted, he was finally enjoying the career he had imagined. "My dream would be to get the thing started in London," Frost had written to Ernest Silver in December 1913, "and then do the rest of it from a farm in New England where I could live cheap and get Yankier and Yankier" (*LRF-1*, 165). A decade later, in the title poem of a volume for which he would win his first Pulitzer Prize in 1924, Frost closed by wishing playfully for a future he was already living.

> *I choose to be a plain New Hampshire farmer*
> *With an income in cash of, say, a thousand*
> *(From, say, a publisher in New York City).*
> *It's restful to arrive at a decision,*
> *And restful just to think about New Hampshire.*
> *At present I am living in Vermont.*

Abbreviations

ABW: *A Boy's Will,* Robert Frost. London: David Nutt, 1913.

ACL: Amherst College Library, Amherst, Massachusetts.

AFR: *A Further Range,* Robert Frost. New York: Henry Holt, 1936.

Alger: Private collection of Pat Alger, Nashville, Tennessee.

ALS: Autograph letter, signed.

ALS-photostat: Autograph letter, signed, photostat.

Arkansas: University of Arkansas, Fayetteville, Arkansas.

Bates: Bates College, Edmund Muskie Archives and Special Collections.

Bowdoin: Bowdoin College, George. J. Mitchell Department of Special
Collections and Archives, Brunswick, Maine.

Brown: John Hay Library, Special Collections, Brown University, Providence, Rhode Island.

Bryn Mawr: Bryn Mawr College Library Special Collections, Bryn Mawr,
Pennsylvania.

BU: Boston University, Howard Gotlieb Archival Research Center.

Cardiff: Cardiff University Library Archive, Cardiff, Wales.

Chicago: University of Chicago, Special Collections Research Center,
Chicago, Illinois.

Columbia: Columbia University Libraries, New York.

CPPP: *Robert Frost: Collected Poetry, Prose and Plays,* ed. Richard Poirier and
Mark Richardson. New York: Library of America, 1995.

CPRF: *The Collected Prose of Robert Frost,* ed. Mark Richardson. Cambridge,
MA: Harvard University Press, 2007.

DCL: Dartmouth College Library, Hanover, New Hampshire.

EY: Robert Frost: The Early Years, 1874–1915, Lawrance Thompson. New York: Holt, Rinehart and Winston, 1970.

FL: The Family Letters of Robert and Elinor Frost, ed. Arnold Grade. Albany: State University of New York Press, 1972.

Gloucester: Gloucester Archives, United Kingdom.

Harvard: Harvard University Archives and Special Collections, Cambridge, Massachusetts.

Hopkins: Johns Hopkins University, Special Collections and Archives, Baltimore, Maryland.

HRC: Harry Ransom Center, University of Texas at Austin.

Huntington: Huntington Library, Pasadena, California.

Illinois: Rare Book and Manuscript Library, University of Illinois at Urbana-Champaign.

Indiana: Indiana University, Ruth Lilly Special Collections and Archives, Bloomington, Indiana.

Jones: Jones Library, Amherst, Massachusetts.

La Crosse: Murphy Library, University of Wisconsin-La Crosse.

LoC: Library of Congress, Washington, DC.

LRF-1: The Letters of Robert Frost, Volume 1: 1886–1920, ed. Donald Sheehy, Mark Richardson, and Robert Faggen. Cambridge, MA: Harvard University Press, 2014.

LY: Robert Frost: The Later Years, 1938–1963, Lawrance Thompson and R. H. Winnick. New York: Holt, Rinehart and Winston, 1966.

Mass. Hist.: Massachusetts Historical Society, Boston.

MI: Mountain Interval, Robert Frost. New York: Henry Holt, 1917.

Miami, Ohio: Miami University, Walter Havighurst Special Collections, Oxford, Ohio.

Middlebury: Middlebury College Libraries, Middlebury, Vermont.

Minnesota: University of Minnesota Archives, Elmer L. Andersen Library, Minneapolis, Minnesota.

Morgan: Morgan Library and Museum, New York.

NB: North of Boston, Robert Frost. London: David Nutt, 1914.

NBRF: The Notebooks of Robert Frost, ed. Robert Faggen. Cambridge, MA: Harvard University Press, 2006.

Newberry: The Newberry Library, Chicago, Illinois.

NH: New Hampshire, Robert Frost. New York: Henry Holt, 1923.

Northwestern: Northwestern University Library, Special Collections, Evanston, Illinois.

NYPL: New York Public Library, New York.

NYU: Fales Library and Special Collections, New York University.

Penn: University of Pennsylvania, Rare Book and Manuscript Library, Philadelphia, Pennsylvania.

Phillips Exeter: Phillips Exeter Academy, Class of 1945 Library, Exeter, New Hampshire.

Plymouth: Plymouth State University, Lamson Library, Plymouth, New Hampshire.

Princeton: Princeton University, Firestone Library, Princeton, New Jersey.

Private: Privately held.

RFJB: Robert Frost and John Bartlett: The Record of a Friendship, Margaret Bartlett Anderson. New York: Holt, Rinehart and Winston, 1963.

RFLU: The Letters of Robert Frost to Louis Untermeyer, ed. Louis Untermeyer. New York: Holt, Rinehart and Winston, 1963.

RFSC: Robert Frost and Sidney Cox: Forty Years of Friendship, ed. William R. Evans. Hanover, NH: University Press of New England, 1981.

Rollins: Rollins College, Olin Library, Winter Park, Florida.

S.C. Hist.: South Carolina Historical Society, Charleston, South Carolina.

SIUE: Southern Illinois University Edwardsville, Lovejoy Library, Illinois.

SL: Selected Letters of Robert Frost, ed. Lawrance Thompson. New York: Holt, Rinehart and Winston, 1964.

SLU: St. Louis University, Special Collections and Archives, St. Louis, Missouri.

Southern California: University of Southern California, Special Collections Department, Doheny Memorial Library, Los Angeles, California.

TG: Telegram.

TL: Typed letter.

TL-C: Typed letter, copy.

TLS: Typed letter, signed.

Trinity: Trinity College, Watkinson Library, Hartford, Connecticut.

Tulsa: University of Tulsa, Special Collections and Archives, McFarlin Library, Tulsa, Oklahoma.

UFL: University of Florida, George A. Smathers Libraries, Gainesville.

UM: University of Michigan Library, Ann Arbor.

UNH: University of New Hampshire, Douglas and Helena Milne Special Collections and Archives, Durham, New Hampshire.

UVA: University of Virginia Library, Charlottesville.

Vassar: Vassar College, Catherine Pelton Durrell Archives and Special Collections Library, Poughkeepsie, New York.

Vermont: University of Vermont Libraries Special Collections, Baily/Howe Library, Burlington, Vermont.

Wagner: Horrmann Library, Wagner College, Staten Island, New York.

Wellesley: Wellesley College, Special Collections, Margaret Clap Library, Wellesley, Massachusetts.

Wesleyan: Wesleyan University, Olin Library Special Archives and Collections, Middletown, Connecticut.

Wisc. Hist: Wisconsin Historical Society, Madison.

WRB: West-Running Brook, Robert Frost. New York: Henry Holt, 1928.

Yale: Yale University, Beinecke Library, New Haven, Connecticut.

YT: Robert Frost: The Years of Triumph, 1915–1938, Lawrance Thompson. New York: Holt, Rinehart and Winston, 1970.

Editorial Principles

The Letters of Robert Frost, of which this volume is the second of five, is without precedent. All of the poet's letters of which we have a record—including the 569 letters collected here, more than 350 for the first time—will now be presented in a single, uniform edition, consistently and fully annotated, with fidelity to the manuscripts and typescripts from which they derive. Like the first volume in this edition, *The Letters of Robert Frost, Volume 1: 1886–1920,* the present volume is considerably more extensive than Lawrance Thompson's *The Selected Letters of Robert Frost.*[1] Yet it takes the reader only from February 1920 to December 1928, shortly after Frost's fifth book, *West-Running Brook,* appeared, when the poet had lived but fifty-four of the eighty-eight years that were to be his lot.

---

1. Thompson includes a number of letters written by persons other than Frost. We do not print incoming correspondence, although on occasion we quote from it in annotations. Were we to include even a modicum of incoming letters, the edition, already slated for five volumes, would overflow its banks. For the same reason we typically do not reprint enclosures, including fair copies of poems, when these are not integral to a given letter, although we usually describe them. One exception is Frost's March 21, 1920, letter to Louis Untermeyer, the bulk of which is in fact a poem, introduced into the record just after the salutation, and followed by talk of religion. Another is a document Frost sent to Untermeyer on February 12, 1923. Untermeyer brought it into his *The Letters of Robert Frost to Louis Untermeyer* (New York: Holt, Rinehart, and Winston, 1964), although it is in fact the text of a poem (with a few notes added): "The Star-Splitter"—the preparation and publication of which is discussed in several *other* letters, and which we here complement with an illustration drawn from its first appearance in *Century Magazine.* What constitutes a "letter" is not always easy to determine. For example, Frost had a habit of inscribing books in quasi-epistolary ways. We take a practical approach: the letters reprinted here are almost always conventionally "epistolary" in nature. One more thing bears mentioning. Publication of the present edition, as it unfolds, will bring to light additional letters held in private hands or in archives where they have gone un-catalogued. *The Letters of Robert Frost, Volume 1: 1886–1920* has already brought a handful of such letters to our attention. An appendix to the last volume of the edition will present all the letters we become aware of after the publication of the preceding volumes.

Our edition provides verified transcripts of the letters, gathered from more than ninety archives and private collections. The majority of Frost's handwritten letters, and nearly all of his typed ones, exist in a form common to letter writing of the period: date and place of inditing in the upper-right-hand corner of the first page; salutation below and to the left; body of the letter following in conventionally paragraphed form, with lineation determined by the size of the paper, and with text flowing from sheet to sheet, or, on pre-folded stationery, from first page to second page, and then to the back of the first page, and so on; and with a signature following the whole with a customary, if often whimsical, valediction. When Frost adds a postscript, he does that, too, in the usual way, below the signature—although sometimes in the margins, if he has run out of space at the bottom of the concluding sheet. In other words, the disposition of the text on the pages of Frost's manuscript and typescript letters is almost never a significant feature of their meaning. For these reasons we have produced not type facsimiles but clean transcripts of the letters. We concentrate entirely on the intended content of the original. When Frost makes a correction in a letter, he does so by striking out a word and continuing, or by striking out a word or phrase and inserting a correction interlinearly. Our practice, unless special circumstances apply, is to produce the single text that any corrections present in the document plainly require. When Frost inserts, say, the conjunction "that" interlinearly, we simply produce the sentence as he intended it to read without the special markings (carets or arrows, for example) that he employed to make it read that way. However, there are a few instances where the look of the manuscript becomes an interesting component of its meaning, and in each instance we have noted the fact. See, for example, Frost's July 23, 1920, letter to Louis Untermeyer, and the annotations that accompany it. The facsimile of the original is printed as an illustration on page 78. We have also left telegrams in ALL CAPS to distinguish them visually on the page.

We have, within limits, adopted a policy of silent correction. When Frost has unintentionally repeated a word—for example, when he carries a sentence over from one sheet to the next, or from the front of a sheet to the back—we have omitted the repetition, as in this February 28, 1925, letter to Wade Van Dore, about the latter's poems: "Let me keep track of you in these paths. I've been looking again and I find much of this really lovely and original—underivative:—I was was sending it back but I believe unless you demand it I will keep it to show to a friend or two. Send me more as you get on, poet." Rather than have the text read "I was was [sic] sending it back," we omit the duplicate word. We also correct silently those few occasions on which Frost drops a letter from a word in ways uncharacteristic of his manuscripts generally, as in an October 1924 letter to George Roy Elliott: "Miss Millay is a great audience-killer. Boys and girls equally fall for her charm. She loses nothing of course with them by her reputation for dainty promiscuity. She only trades on that to the extent of here and there a whimsical hint. She is already a love-myth. I dont have to tell you how much I admire he [*sic*] less flippant verse." We supply the missing letter so that the last sentence reads: "I admire her less flippant verse." The same practice applies to the following sentence from a May 5, 1924, letter to Lincoln MacVeagh: "It looks as if I were coming down with Elinor to read a poem from some one of my four book [*sic*] to the P.E.N. Club of which I am told I am an honorary member." We correct the phrase to read "some one of my four *books*." We also add quotation marks or parentheses when Frost uses the opening punctuation mark but forgets to close it, as in this March 21, 1920, letter to Untermeyer:

> "Spring," I say, returneth and the maple sap is heard dripping in the buckets (allow me to sell you a couple). (We can quote you the best white first-run sugar at a dollar a pound unsight and unseen—futures.)"

We supply the missing quotation mark ("returneth . . .) silently, instead of bracketing it (["]returneth). When Frost sets off parenthetical text with a comma and then neglects to close it with one, we correct that silently, too, as in a June 26, 1920, letter to Carl Van Doren: "I came in my recent wanderings on G. R. Elliot [*sic*], the critic who wrote so acceptably of me in The Nation and took him to friend." We supply the comma after "The Nation" so as not to hobble the reader, and insert [*sic*] so as to register the misspelling ("Elliot" for Elliott). Our aim is to rectify manifestly inadvertent slips of the pen, while reserving *sic* within brackets for the many occasions on which this or that irregularity is actually a characteristic feature of Frost's handwritten prose.

Another category of silent intervention concerns the date and place where each letter was written. More or less coincident with his move to Ann Arbor in September 1921, Frost began, though inconsistently, to give his address and the date on which he was writing below the signature, rather than at the head of the letter. We have standardized all letters, placing the address and date always at the head, unless special circumstances make placement below the signature an expressive element of the letter in question.

At times, Frost favors spellings that are long since out of use and that may not be registered in the *Oxford English Dictionary*. He writes, in a February 26, 1925, letter to Bernice Lurie, who helped the family arrange for housing in Ann Arbor when Frost accepted his second appointment there: "We think that that small house would be just the thing to complete and save the poem—if poem our life is going to be out there. . . . Will you just give me two or three weeks to make sure that I can have it with a perfectly clear conscience? I know [Marion LeRoy] Burton would have been entirely on my side in living where I could live freeest." "Freeest" can be found in books printed in the eighteenth and nineteenth centuries, although "freest" is now standard. It is not clear that Frost spells in error, so we do not insert [*sic*]. Cases of this kind are quite rare, and are always noted. One more example will serve to illustrate our practices, this time from a June 25, 1925, letter to MacVeagh: "I'm too played out to travel anywhere right now. But can't you come up here for a few days? You'll find me annointing my wouds on a a warm rock from which is a view of the young growing orchard you dug so many holes for two years ago." The last sentence we render as follows: "You'll find me annointing [*sic*] my wounds on a warm rock . . ." The first misspelling, "annointing," is of a type common in Frost's letters: the incorrect use of double consonants. But the second misspelling, "wouds," is not at all characteristic, given that "woud" cannot be made to sound like "wound"; we amend it. And we remove the duplicate article "a."

A final sort of editorial intervention occurs when an accidentally omitted word might better be added as a marked correction, as against a silent one; we use brackets to indicate that we have added it. In a May 10, 1926, letter to George Roy Elliott, Frost writes, in connection with the salary Amherst College has offered him: "The five thousand is a lot for ten weeks. I'm satisfied with the amount. What I am after is detachment and long times alone rather than money. Nobody knows how much less money I have taken in late years than I could have. Enough is enough. So say I and all my family fortunately agree with me. For at least one or two of them less is enough than for me. There's where my real success lies, if [I] may be accused of having any, in being so uncursed in my family." We supply the dropped pronoun to ease the reader through that last sentence, while making it clear that a correction has been made. The same rule applies to Frost's letter of about April 30, 1925, to Julia Patton, where a preposition is inadvertently omitted: "Thanks for the pleasant time you gave me and I wonder if the enclosed books would mean anything as remembrances from me to any [of] your girls or fellow teachers."

Frost uses apostrophes inconsistently and haphazardly; one may often find both "don't" and "couldnt" within a single sentence. Editors of Frost's letters have respected these inconsistencies for decades, and so do we. We have indicated or left untouched most misspellings of proper names, supplying an explanatory note where the error might lead to confusion.

Headnotes to the letters identify the recipient; indicate with an abbreviation whether the letter is an autograph letter signed (ALS), or a typed letter signed (TLS), and so on; and then give the location of the archive now holding the manuscript, or an indication, where needed, that it remains in private hands. Headnotes also register all cases where the dating of a letter is editorially supplied. The "Abbreviations" section provides a key to all abbreviations used in the book, in addition to the ones already mentioned. When Frost has dictated a letter to someone else (to his daughter Lesley, for example), this, too, is indicated either in the headnote or a footnote, as convenience dictates. For the most part, we rely on footnotes to identify—when identification proved possible; in a few cases it did not—persons, poems, and events alluded to or mentioned in the letters. Our purpose is to provide on each page, alongside each letter, all information about it that a reader may require. Sometimes we repeat footnotes concerning persons already identified, when a reader might need a reminder. At the back of the book, a "Biographical Glossary" of all letter recipients is provided, both as an aid to memory and as a resource for better understanding the wide range, in vocation and experience, of the more than 160 correspondents in the present volume. Readers will also find a detailed chronology covering Frost's life from February 1920 through December 1928, including apposite passages from the letters to give the chronology color (a practice consistent with the chronology in *The Letters of Robert Frost, Volume 1: 1886–1920*).

THE LETTERS OF

ROBERT FROST

VOLUME 2

Introduction

In the summer of 1921, Robert Frost accepted a position at the University of Michigan. President Marion LeRoy Burton had tendered an extraordinary offer, partly at the suggestion of the poet and dramatist Percy MacKaye, who held a similar post at Miami University in Oxford, Ohio, under President Raymond M. Hughes. Frost was to be, for a year, Fellow in Creative Arts on a stipend of $5,000, a sum provided by the former governor of Michigan, Chase Salmon Osborn.[1] The fellowship carried no formal teaching responsibilities. It was decidedly unconventional.

In announcing the appointment, Burton acknowledged that some might regard the enterprise with skepticism. "Michigan has a vision," he said, "and is about to try a unique experiment, which the educational world, and the doubting world will, each in its own way, watch closely, the one hoping to approve, the other ready for the opportunity to scoff."[2] Given the opportunity to scoff, the *Washtenaw Post*, a paper serving the German-American community in southeast Michigan, duly seized it. "Robert Frost, called 'the best loved of New England's poets,' is in Ann Arbor for a year, by invitation of the University of Michigan," an October 27 editorial noted. "He is not asked to do anything, not even twirl his thumbs, if he does not so desire. And for his presence he is presented with [an] honorarium of $5,000. Mr. Frost may be

---

1. $5,000 in 1921 had the buying power of $66,232 in 2016.

2. "Poet Frost Brings Creative Art to Students of U of M," *Detroit Free Press*, Sunday, September 18, 1921.

worth it. Far be it from the Washtenaw Post to question the wisdom of President Burton and the U. of M. board of regents," the paper added sarcastically. "[Frost's] presence may be such an inspiration that some of the 11,000 students here may blossom out into writers of verse that will stir the world as did that marvelous poem entitled: 'Down Went McGinty to the Bottom of the Sea,' or 'Silver Threads Among the Gold,' or 'Tommy Trott's Toothsome Tomato.'"[3]

Had he seen what Frost said of his new position to Louis Untermeyer in a letter dated November 23, the *Post*'s editorialist would have been neither mollified nor enlightened:

> To some I am known as the Guessed of this University because I came as a riddle and was so soon solved. The fact that I was so soon found out is uppermost in some minds. In other minds what I was found out to be is uppermost, namely a radiator of the poetic spirit. To them I am known as the Radiator. I differ from other radiators not only in what I have to radiate but also in where I have to work. Other radiators have to heat a room. I am expected to do something else to all out of doors. I only tell you to clarify my own mind. If it has come to this here let us face it. If I could will my job to you as Roosevelt willed Taft the Presidency I sure would. I find I do my best work on a diet of soft coal or carbide and water.

Frost isn't gloating at having won an easy chair. He's responding to publicity *about* his new position, much of it amusing, often at his expense. The riddle of his function at Michigan had in fact been formulated and solved, though in differing, often incompatible, ways. We have no reason to suppose Frost ever saw an item in the *Evening Kansas-Republican,* published five days before he wrote Untermeyer on November 23, but it wouldn't have surprised the radiant Guessed of Michigan. It was typical of articles in papers from coast to coast: "[Robert Frost] is employed by the University of Michigan at a salary of $5000 a year to reside at the College campus. He has no classes but is to come in contact with students simply to radiate inspiration." The International

---

3. "Silver Threads Among the Gold," a popular song composed in 1873 (lyrics by Eben E. Rexford, music by Hart Pease Danks), became a standard in the repertoire of barbershop quartets. "Down Went McGinty" is an Irish folk and drinking song. "Tommy Trott's Toothsome Tomato" is apparently an alliterative spoof; we have been unable to track it down.

News Service syndicated an article that popped up, even as Frost arrived on campus, in papers from North Carolina to Pennsylvania to California, under varying headlines, such as "FOUND—SOFTEST JOB IN WORLD: POET TO GET $5,000 FOR YEAR'S GENTLE INFLUENCE ON STUDENTS AT MICHIGAN UNIVERSITY; HE CAN LOAF." "Discovered—the world's softest job," the article begins. "Robert Frost, New England poet, has it. All he has to do is to live in Ann Arbor, Mich., and let his artistic influence flow out over the campus and through the academic corridors of the University of Michigan. For this he receives $5,000 a year! And he doesn't have to instruct a single class in the art of making 'blue' and 'you' rhyme, with the correct number of feet to a line." After this little spree, the article correctly observed that "the new venture . . . created a sensation in academic circles," and cited the conflicting opinions of eminent educators in Chicago: " 'The experiment represents an interesting return to the patronage system of artists which broke down about one hundred and fifty years ago. It will be a great thing for Michigan'—Dean P. H. Boynton of the University of Chicago." His colleague, Professor C. H. Judd, disagreed: "I think it would do the institution more good if the poet would give instruction in the form of regular class work." Professor C. F. Taeusch of Northwestern took a more worldly view: "Many men are hindered by classes. It's only a scholarship plan for professors instead of students."[4]

Reading Frost's letters from fall 1921 through spring 1922, we do well to bear in mind the nature and extent of the publicity that attended his new appointment. One editorialist, syndicated by the Chicago News Service, called the $5,000 salary "rather unpoetic." Even so, the *Des Moines Register* for December 11, 1921, declared that "the founding of this fellowship and its acceptance by a poet of Frost's international reputation adds recognition and impetus to a movement begun by Percy Mackaye [sic] and President Hughes of Miami." Frost was "to have no academic duties," true. But word was out by December "that a club of young writers [had] already grown up about him." In fact, certain members of the Whimsies, a student literary society, had adopted him—Yuki Osawa and Stella Brunt in particular.[5] With his help, they coordinated,

---

4. *The Morning News* (Wilmington, Delaware), Friday, September 16, 1921.

5. Remarkable women, both of them. After graduating from the University of Michigan summa cum laude in 1922, Stella Brunt (1894–1988) returned to the university for an MA in medieval studies, which she received in 1930, and was adopted by Chase Osborn, the man who had underwritten Frost's first fellowship. She then collaborated on a number of books with Osborn. A year after his wife, Lillian Gertrude Osborn, died,

in concert with the Ann Arbor branch of the American Association of University Women, a series of readings in the spring of 1922 that brought the poets Padraic Colum, Carl Sandburg, Louis Untermeyer, Amy Lowell, and Vachel Lindsay to campus. The series drew thousands of students, members of the faculty, and townspeople, and was widely regarded as a success.[6]

The *News Star* of Monroe, Louisiana, had run an op-ed on September 6, 1921, when Frost was still in Vermont packing his bags: "As it might seem unkind, perhaps unjust, perhaps undignified, to insinuate, with a smile or a chuckle, that paying Mr. Frost $5,000 a year as poet ex-officio specially assigned to the theoretical department of rhyme and refinement, would be an advertising expense item, the faculty could not construe as unethical the impassioned statement that the exploitation will be worth far more than the outlay. As an inspirer of free publicity for the university Mr. Frost inactively will earn in a few weeks much more than his salary." The conclusion drawn befits a proper southern newsman: "President Burton's innovation may mark the passing of football and other rough sports and the beginning of an Orlandoan era" that would "jingle and rhythm the work of the student body." Felicitously, with his reference to Orlando, the Louisiana editorialist lit upon the hero of the very play, *As You Like It,* most often echoed in Frost's letters, and by spring 1922 his prognostications were in some measure borne out. Addressing a meeting of Michigan alumni in Louisville, Kentucky—in a word, fundraising, with his "poet ex-officio" as a featured attraction—President Burton wondered aloud who was the more popular man on campus, Frost or legendary Michigan football coach Fielding Harris Yost. His remarks were quoted by *The Michigan Daily,* which observed that, although Burton had spoken "in a spirit of fun," there was a good deal of truth in what he said: "The interest in literature and in any pursuit which deals with the arts" had become "widespread" at Mich-

---

Chase, on a single day, April 9, 1949, had the adoption annulled and then married Stella. The next day he died. In 1978 the University of Michigan awarded Stella Osborn an honorary doctorate in letters. Yuki Osawa (1896–1988) was born in Seattle to Japanese immigrants. At Michigan, she befriended her classmate Stella (their extensive correspondence is held now at the Bentley Historical Library), joined the Whimsies, and worked with Frost (see page 235, note 103, for more about her).

6. The crowd attending Amy Lowell's reading on May 4, 1922, packed Hill Auditorium, then the largest venue on campus, seating more than four thousand. For a detailed account of Frost's years in Ann Arbor, see Robert M. Warner, *Frost-Bite & Frost-Bark: Robert Frost at Michigan* (Ann Arbor: Bentley Historical Library, 1999).

igan, the unsigned editorial said, largely due to "the stimulating influence of Robert Frost."[7]

The letters collected in this volume reveal just how much Frost did, and just how early he did it, to fashion the kinds of institutional support accorded creative writers in the second half of the twentieth century, support that continues to the present day. He accomplished this in part by negotiating remarkable positions for himself as a poet much more than as a teacher at Michigan and then at Amherst in the early to mid-1920s. He did it also at the Bread Loaf School of English, at the Institute for Modern Literature at Bowdoin College (1925), in residencies at Wesleyan College and elsewhere, and, after 1926, at the Bread Loaf Writers' Conference, the early success of which his presence did much to assure. The letters and telegrams gathered here show Frost not only haggling out the best terms possible for himself as Fellow in the Creative Arts at Michigan, but also, after he left the position, ensuring that the fellowship survived him by conferring with administrators and faculty members as to suitable candidates. Other letters show him working outside the classroom with the young poet Wade Van Dore, whose first book, *Far Lake* (1930), Frost helped him assemble and bring into print. Gathered here, too, are letters of advice to other writers and to young scholars about the art of poetry.[8]

Of course, the provision of "education"—even if only by "radiation," or presence—was more than an enterprise from which Frost drew a living. It hit home, and was integral to his life. In mid-November 1925, from Ann Arbor, Frost wrote a remarkable letter to his eldest child, Lesley, then in Pittsfield, Massachusetts, where she had opened a bookstore with her sister Marjorie in 1924. The letter is worth dwelling on here for what it both states and intimates

---

7. *The Michigan Daily*, April 21, 1922. Frost was so pleased in his happy rivalry with Yost that he asked Dorothy Dunbar Bromley, a publicist at Henry Holt and Company, to feed tales about it to the press (see Frost to Bromley, June 11, 1922). Lawrance Thompson offers a gloss on the affair: "When asked to comment, Frost said he was willing to demonstrate which man [he or Coach Yost] had the stronger drawing power. He would wait until the next football game, and would schedule for that same Saturday afternoon a Robert Frost reading in Hill Auditorium. On that afternoon, he declared, the stadium would be filled and nobody would be in the Hill auditorium, 'not even myself, because I'll be at the football game'" (*YT*, 183–184).

8. See, for example, Frost's letters to an unidentified Miss O'Brien, June 11, 1922; to John Freeman, November 5, 1925; to B. F. Skinner, April 7, 1926; to Clarence Cline, May 9, 1927; and to Walter Evans Kidd, October 28, 1927.

about his ventures in education, and about the Frost family dynamic as the children entered adulthood. The letter also merits detailed discussion because, like most of the letters in this volume, it has never before been collected.[9]

Frost replies, in part, to news about his first grandson, Prescott Frost (the one-year-old son of his son Carol and Lillian Labatt), which Lesley and Marjorie had relayed in letters to their parents. Frost touches first on education and then moves, in a way that doesn't quite register as a change in topic, to family matters—his own, and those of a colleague at the University of Michigan. For the Frosts, education had always been a family affair. His children generally shared their father's ambivalent attitude toward educational institutions. For the most part they had been taught at home, in ways that made little distinction between educating and rearing a child, or between lessons and play.

Frost opens with a cocksure piece of advice intended for a young man, most likely Harold Newman, who had two months earlier entered Amherst College: "The proper study of the school boy is his professors, you tell Harold from me. He knows as much already. He will only need to be reminded of it to be made ashamed." Repurposing a line from Pope's *Essay on Man*—"The proper study of mankind is man"—Frost utters a truth unacknowledged in much high-minded talk about liberal education, talk of the kind he came to scorn while on the faculty at Amherst during the presidency of Alexander Meiklejohn. "And knowledge of professors isn't enough," Frost adds; "it is necessary to remain while in college not above using that knowledge. That is to say, in college you must play college. It is really a very much more human and a very much less intellectual game than some of us are prone to fear." We are here let in on a Frost family secret. College is a *more* "human game" than most "fear" it is. Administrative and professorial parties to higher education—certainly the deposed President Meiklejohn—prefer not to think of it as a thing one *plays*.[10] It is too seldom observed that the academic side of college is also a "game." Saying so to Lesley is as much a reminder as a proposition. As letters to her in this volume and in *The Letters of Robert Frost, Volume*

---

9. We thank Elinor Wilbur, Lesley's eldest daughter, for making a copy of the letter available. (Lawrance Thompson quotes it in part in *YT* [613–614], although to purposes different from ours.)

10. Amherst's Board of Trustees forced Meiklejohn out in 1923. For further details, see Frost's July 20, 1923, letter to Morris Tilley, and his August 12, 1924, to Louis Untermeyer; the entry for Meiklejohn in the index directs readers to additional letters concerning the affair.

1: 1886–1920 make plain, Lesley never learned—or perhaps never deigned—to "play college," whether in the classrooms of Barnard or on the tennis courts at Wellesley. Or, for that matter, on the campus at Michigan, where she took enough courses, and saw enough of the Alpha Phi sorority, to be put off.[11] Harold Newman, by contrast, "played" Amherst sparklingly well, winning honors in almost every subject he studied and graduating near the top of his class—accomplishing, with ease, what a Frost had never really sought to accomplish. Later in the letter Frost speaks of the academy as if it were Masonic in its obscurity: "I wonder how these scholars recognize each other when they meet. By what signs. Accuracy is a word they traffic in. I ask for the deadliest accuracy in a comparison. It must prick something. There are all sorts of ways of saying Hell! Say it with the mouth pulled open downward and somewhat to one side. You three girls can practice till you get something satisfactorily tired and disgusted."[12] If Lesley took this as reassurance that her father didn't know how to play college any better than his daughter did, she would not have been far wrong. Education by poetry and metaphor ("I ask for the deadliest accuracy in a comparison")—and not done chiefly within institutions—had become a Frost family creed.[13]

---

11. In another letter collected here for the first time, written in February 1922, Frost says this to Harriet Moody, a close family friend on whom he could rely to take his remarks in the right spirit: "I'm bringing Lesley [to Chicago] instead of Elinor. Don't forget. I wouldnt have you take Lesley for Elinor. She calls for entirely different treatment. That is to say, she can be treated worse, though I shouldn't say there weren't bounds beyond which bad treatment ought not to go even in her case, young and tough as she is and of small account to her father." Frost adds, "If it could be arranged, I should like to leave her a little while with you in Chicago for the good you would do her. The poor kid is rather sick of this institution and that through no fault of hers. She's had splendid marks and liked seventy five percent of her teachers. But my line of talk isnt calculated to make her like any institution. You know how I'm always at it against colleges, in a vain attempt to reconcile myself with them. The part of them which the youngsters are most free in or where they could be most free, their own so-called activities, they are the most slavish and conventional in. . . . You needn't tell poor dear Martha, but its [*sic*] Alpha Phi that has done for Lesley's love of Ann Arbor." Moody's friend, Martha Foote Crow (1854–1924), assistant professor of literature at the University of Chicago, was among the seven founding members of Alpha Phi in 1872.

12. Lesley, Marjorie, and their friend Mary Ellen Hager, in Pittsfield.

13. See two books by Lesley Lee Francis (Lesley Frost's second daughter): *You Come, Too: My Journey with Robert Frost* (Charlottesville: University of Virginia Press, 2015), and *Robert Frost: An Adventure in Poetry* (Piscataway, NJ: Transaction, 2004).

Then the father moves right ahead, taking Edward Gibbon as his text:

> I wish I could transcribe for you the complaint of Gibbon in his
> Autobiography against the Oxford of his time. One of his tutors
> was so bad that he shields him with a blank for his name. His
> other was nothing. There was no oversight to keep him from any
> excess mental physical or moral. Before anybody knew it he had
> become a Roman Catholic and had to be expelled from Magdalen.
> Just think of the neglect that would let a boy of sixteen wander so
> far in the mind as to arrive at a belief in transubstantiation. Gibbon
> never forgave them. But I don't know. We owe the best parts of
> the Decline and Fall to Gibbon's education having gone wrong at
> that point. Couldn't we lay down the general rule that where edu-
> cation goes wrong just there it is most educative. But again I don't
> know.

What Frost gives Lesley might as well be a transcription, so close does he hew
to the text of the autobiography.[14] "Such almost incredible neglect [as he suffered at Oxford] was productive of the worst mischiefs," says Gibbon. "The
blind activity of idleness urged me to advance without armour into the dangerous mazes of controversy; and at the age of sixteen, I bewildered myself
in the errors of the church of Rome." He embraced "the superior merits of
celibacy, the institution of the monastic life, the use of the sign of the cross,
of holy oil, and even of images, the invocation of saints, the worship of relics,
the rudiments of purgatory in prayers for the dead, and the tremendous mystery of the sacrifice of the body and blood of Christ, which insensibly swelled
into the prodigy of transubstantiation." Gibbon was expelled from Magdalen
and, at his father's direction, completed his education in Lausanne, ended his
flirtation with Catholicism (his father threatened to disinherit him if he didn't),
and returned to the Anglican fold. But during his five-year exile in Switzerland Gibbon developed the interests, and the mastery of Latin, that allowed
and inclined him to write *The Decline and Fall of the Roman Empire*. Here, surely,
was an example of how an education is "most educative" when it "goes wrong,"
an example sufficient to warrant a "general rule."

And yet Frost's certainty in his premises deserts him. "But I don't know."
"But again I don't know." Which leads him to a second illustration of a young

---

14. Frost occasionally assigned the book to students.

man's education "gone wrong," this time drawn from acquaintance, not literary history. At issue now is the suicide, in March 1925, of the son of an Ann Arbor colleague. Frost alters the point in hand so as almost entirely to conflate "education" with "the proper training of a child in the way he should go"—a queer phrase for an unnerving course of events. We can be fairly sure Lesley knew some of the backstory, given how economically her father makes his point. He could write in this confidential way to few other correspondents:

> I'll never forget the day when a dozen of us were telling each other exactly as if we knew what was the proper training of a child in the way he should go and I was suddenly aware and by something in my manner made everybody else aware that we had Mrs Patterson in our midst whose highly educated son had just broken an uncommon family pride by jumping into the ocean from a liner and drowning himself to rectify the mistake of his second marriage. From sheer embarrassment before God I said for all of us What are we talking about all so self-assured?

Frost refers, here, to George Washington Patterson IV (1893–1925), son of the University of Michigan professor of engineering and dean, George Washington Patterson III (1864–1930), and Merib Susan (Rowley) Patterson (the "Mrs Patterson" mentioned in the letter). After four brilliant years at Yale, Patterson served with distinction in World War I and was awarded the Croix de Guerre. His first marriage ended in 1921 with the premature death of his wife, Suzette Parker Ryerson Patterson, who had also been awarded the Croix de Guerre for her service in the ambulance corps. In July 1924, he married again, this time to Grace Virginia Pomeroy Hendrick, a New York socialite. The *New York Times* printed articles about Patterson's suicide that quoted Grace's father, the eminent chemist Ellwood Hendrick, to the effect that the second marriage had nothing to do with the suicide.[15] Hendrick's detailed public statement was ornamented with speculation, scraps of dialogue, gossip, off-the-rack psychology, and anecdote—stuff that would have interested and mortified Frost in equal measure ("We did not hear of his disappearance until Saturday, when his Chinese servant came to our house and said: 'Mr. Patterson, he no come back'"). Patterson's parents, on sabbatical in Europe at the time,

---

15. The articles appeared on March 15 and 16, 1925.

weren't available to reply to Hendrick's statement (with which, Frost's letter implies, they firmly disagreed).[16]

In any case, the indelible scene Frost recalls—"I'll never forget the day"—has a certain Jane Austenian quality: a man (Frost) suddenly becomes aware that a casual conversation to which he is party has turned to a topic that will inadvertently pain some *other* party to it; and he catches himself becoming aware in such a way as to make *others* aware—including Mrs. Patterson—*that he has become aware,* which only compounds the embarrassment. The result? Frost's recourse, if he reports the incident accurately, is to a public confession that he, and the rest of them, had been carrying on in thoughtless vanity: "From sheer embarrassment before God I said for all of us *What are we talking about all so self-assured?*"

There is a lot in Frost's 1925 letter, and behind and around it: the unhappy, dire vicissitudes of marriage (a widower remarries, and badly); the shattering of parental hopes, and also of a not undue sense of family pride; the spectral presence of depression and madness in the suicide (all the more keenly felt if one considers the coverage the *New York Times* accorded the affair); the public airing of such family matters as Frost always strove to keep private (which the Pattersons had been unable to do, while Ellwood Hendrick, their dead son's second father-in-law, held forth in the *Times*); the follies of pedagogy, which become, by the merest act of extrapolation, also the follies of parenting. To whom other than Lesley could Frost have conveyed this scene of so highly particular an embarrassment, with its several implications? Who other than she could have understood its larger meaning to the Frost family?

"What are we talking about all so self-assured?" It isn't hard to imagine what Frost might have had in mind (but didn't burden Lesley with), besides the misfortune that had befallen the Pattersons: the death in 1885 of his own father, a man of thwarted ambition, and the straits in which that event left Belle Moodie and her young children; Frost's tentative months at Dartmouth in the fall of 1892, and the uncertainties and humiliations that followed his

---

16. According to Hendrick, Patterson labored under an "inferiority complex," a term then newly minted in English out of Freudian brass. Hendrick stated further that Patterson had suffered a bout of "suicidal mania" after the death of his first wife, and called Patterson's suicide note "hysterical and maudlin." Patterson's body was never found. He was the last of four generations of George Washington Pattersons. The first (1799–1879) was a New York state congressman and lieutenant governor, whose father, Thomas, had fought in the Revolution.

impetuous departure from the college as he shifted from job to job, anxious that Elinor might never marry him; his own tragicomic flirtation with suicide in the Dismal Swamp in 1894, when he thought Elinor had rejected him; the deaths in early childhood and infancy of his son Elliott, in 1900, and daughter Elinor Bettina, who lived only three days in 1907; the death of his sister-in-law's child, which blighted her marriage; the fate of his sister Jeanie, since 1920 confined to the Maine Insane Asylum; the increasingly frail health of his youngest daughter, Marjorie, whose illness would soon darken the household for months (as the letters gathered here attest); the emotional struggles of his middle daughter, Irma, who had already shown symptoms of the dangerous instability that would overtake her in the 1930s and 1940s;[17] and his ongoing worry that his often contrary and incommunicative son Carol, Prescott's father, was still uncertain about "the way he should go" in life.

As the letter continues, what might first seem a commonplace grandfatherly sentiment becomes startlingly salient, as we hold the fate of Mrs. Patterson's son in mind. Beginning a new sheet, but immediately following the embarrassed admission of how little we know about "the proper training of a child in the way he should go," Frost turns his thoughts to the grandchild whose education had just begun. In what amounts to prayer, however unorthodox, he asks that the boy be protected from error. Though masked in playfulness, the depth of his feeling and the sincerity of his plea are evident:

> Mama was saying she hoped no mistakes would be made in the education of such a cute little fellow as Prescott (We'd just been reading yours and Marj's letters). Amen says I. You hear that, God? We are saying we hope no mistake will be made in the education of Prescott Frost South Shaftsbury Vermont U.S.A. on the Earth. A word to the All-wise should be sufficient. There's nothing we can do about it if you ignore the hint. We are not threatening to stop going to church. (We've pretty well stopped already.) We were just discharging any responsibility we might be supposed to have in

---

17. Frost had written to Lesley in October 1920, when Irma was headed for New York to study art: "You may have to live with Irma a few days alone before Mama or I come down. Please take the way with her that will keep the peace. Remember that her strictness is part of her nature. Don't try to make her over. Some of it she will outgrow, but not all of it even by the time she is eighty. It has its beauty if you know how to look at it. When you find it a little agressive [sic], you can disregard it." Like her aunt Jeanie, Irma would later in life fall prey to schizophrenia.

holding you to what we admit is almost entirely your own business.
No disrespect intended. We believe in you. Go in and win. At any
rate do the best you can. We are with you at every opening we
see in your fight against the Older God—I mean Chaos Chronos
Column (Newspaper) Saturn Satan or whatsoever alias he turns up
under.

Two questions immediately arise. Did Frost have occasion enough to relay
these sentiments directly to Carol, and had Carol ever confided his hopes and
fears for Prescott to him ("We'd just been reading yours [i.e., Lesley's] and
Marj's letters")? For all the apple orchards they planned out and laid in together
on the South Shaftsbury farm, relations between Frost and his only surviving
son were never so confident and close as those he enjoyed with his eldest and
youngest daughters: the first he often addressed as he would a peer; regarding
the second he could be tender to the point of heartbreak. Consider how he
would but five months later put off a request his friend and fellow poet Witter
Bynner had made for a preface. "Dear Witter," Frost wrote on April 5, 1926,
from Ann Arbor, some seven hundred miles from where Marjorie lay in distress: "For my part, my daughter, the best poet in the family, has been dangerously ill for twelve weeks now, my wife is prostrated and my heart indisposed
to prefaces." What follows—this letter, too, has never before been collected—
reads as if anxiety had unhinged him: "In the last homecoming to roost, the
exigencies of the irresponsible are more ruthless than the most military of
law and order. But I forgive you them even as I hope to be forgiven a murder
I once did.[18] The question is what am I going to do for you," Frost adds, and
then writes as peculiar a pair of sentences as a reader is likely to find in this
volume: "This is the twilight of the mind—before God it is. I'll go out to
grass at a word in the wrong key." In more practical terms, Frost responded
to the crisis by resigning a lifetime appointment at Michigan after a single
year and moving back to Vermont so he and Elinor could remain near the
children. In 1926, he returned under new terms to Amherst College.[19]

---

18. Likely a reference to the guilt Frost still felt in connection with the death of his
first child, Elliott, in 1900. Worries that the death was occasioned by a delay in seeking
proper medical advice vexed the young father. Marjorie's precarious health may well
have reopened the old wound.

19. Some letters suggest that Frost may have preferred the bustling state university—a
coeducational institution with some twelve thousand students at that date, and a rich
and diverse faculty—to the all-male, small, and rather clubby Amherst College. In any

No letters from his father to Carol dating to this period are known to survive. Lingering between them still were memories of Carol's precipitous, wordless departure from Ann Arbor in the spring of 1922, after a dustup with his father over a $35 rooster. Carol had simply walked out of the house on 1523 Washtenaw Avenue and vanished into the night. He turned up some days later in South Shaftsbury, keeping farm alone—a fact of which Frost and Elinor were made aware only by a phone call from Marjorie, not Carol, who kept his counsel. The son and father had grown increasingly opaque to one another. Writing some two years later to John Bartlett about another of Carol's sudden departures, Frost begins in jocularity and ends in bewilderment: "I wish it was Elinor and I seeing you about now [in Colorado] instead of them two irresponsible wastrels our son and [daughter-in-law Lillian] hell bent for California. . . . Carol is a curious boy. I wonder if this expedition of his is to spy out a new country to live in. He wouldn't say so if it was and it may not be." A "curious" boy. Frost uses the word in senses now largely obsolete: cautious, peculiar, anxious, difficult to satisfy and to know.[20]

---

case, the letters show that during the 1920s he hardly spent a week in the town of Amherst when not required to. He wrote his friend Morris Tilley, professor of English at the University of Michigan, on December 15, 1923, after returning to Amherst: "If someone had asked me to give one seminar a week out there [at Michigan] as long as I wanted to stay for 5000 a year I should have taken him up. I liked the folks. I made more and closer friends than I ever did before." He wrote to John Bartlett in May 1926: "We're going east again said the pendulum. This was no go this year, or rather it was too much go and what wasnt go was come. Marjorie's long illness (means more than sickness) kept Elinor with her in Pittsfield Mass and me commuting for months. Every week or so I would run the water out of the pipes and leave the house here to freeze. It wasnt exactly in the contract [with the University of Michigan] that I should be away all the time and I wasn't quite all. I'm not going to try to keep it up here with the children back there and such things likely to happen again." He added: "You've got adopted and adapted out there [in Colorado]. But me, I'm sort of a Yank from New England. I want to get back, if its [*sic*] just the same to everybody. Nothing's invidious about my preference. I like Michigan people and I like Michigan. Only only. / Best love to you all. / Ever yours in everything."

20. Another letter illuminates the often abortive nature of Frost's efforts to communicate with his son. In December 1925, with Carol suffering from a respiratory ailment, Frost wrote to Bartlett from Ann Arbor about the possibility that his son might move from Vermont to Colorado to improve his health: "We wrote to Carol at about the same time we were writing to you. At about the same time you were answering, Carol apparently wasn't. Don't you get too ready to have him for Christmas company. He will be moved to act slowly if at all. . . . His heart is in his Vermont projects, the flower garden and the orchard. It will come hard for him to break off and start all over. He has something

Whatever the case, midway through the letter to Lesley, as he launches his prayer, Frost appears, for a moment, as much to address the daughter he believes in—and who had been the object of considerable fatherly advice during her own vagrant education—than any special Providence, in relation to which the letter seems as wary as it is wry. The language of parenting and of prayer—however humorous the latter may be—all but merge here, quite as if Frost had said to Lesley: "We were just discharging any parental responsibility we might be supposed to have in holding you or any of our children to what we admit is almost entirely your and their own business, Lesley. No disrespect intended. We believe in you. Go in and win. At any rate do the best you can. We are with you at every opening." Frost would have himself and his wife overheard by their eldest daughter—who would know how to take it—speaking of her and Prescott as if to God, or, what is more to the point, addressing God as if he were a child in whose prospects Frost had a parent's interest.

And then there are the many poems devoted to themes touched on in this letter about the more painful uncertainties (mutatis mutandis). Among those Frost had already written and published are "A Prayer in Spring" ("Oh, give us pleasure in the flowers today; / And give us not to think so far away / As the uncertain harvest . . ."); "Rose Pogonias" ("We raised a simple prayer / Before we left the spot / That in the general mowing / That place might be forgot . . ."); "October" ("O hushed October morning mild, / Thy leaves have ripened to the fall; / Tomorrow's wind, if it be wild, / Should waste them all"); "Reluctance" ("Ah, when to the heart of man / Was it ever less than a treason / To go with the drift of things, / To yeild with a grace to reason, / And bow and accept the end / Of a love or a season?"); "Home Burial" (passim); "An Old Man's Winter Night" ("One aged man—one man—can't keep a house, / A farm, a countryside . . ."); "The Exposed Nest" ("We saw the risk we took in doing good, / But dared not spare to do the best we could / Though harm should come of it . . ."); "The Hill Wife" ("Sudden and swift and light as that / The ties gave, / And he learned of finalities / Besides the grave"); and "Nothing Gold Can Stay" (the title alone says it).

Other poems yet to be written or published on these themes are too numerous to cite. We may content ourselves with one, which recasts the excla-

---

of my father [William Prescott Frost Jr.] in him that won't own up sick. . . . But never mind. He may listen to us in the long run. He may sooner than I expect. Anyway we had to make a beginning with him. . . . More soon when I hear from Carol. This is just to thank you for your letter, you old friend."

mation that was in Frost and in the situation with Mrs. Patterson on that Ann Arboreal day he'd never forget: "The Peril of Hope."

> *It is right in there*
> *Betwixt and between*
> *The orchard bare*
> *And the orchard green,*
>
> *When the boughs are right*
> *In a flowery burst*
> *Of pink and white,*
> *That we fear the worst.*
>
> *For there's not a clime*
> *But at any cost*
> *Will take that time*
> *For a night of frost.*

Or, to put it another way (and with no dark pun on "frost"): "From sheer embarrassment before God I said for all of us What are we talking about all so self-assured?" *Spes alit agricolam, spes alit poeta*—Hope sustains the farmer; hope sustains the poet. Well, yes, but also no. Hope can manifest itself as a disease state; it must be managed. A man comes "out of the trees," slaughters your horse at a blow, and vanishes; the "night [draws] through the trees / In one long invidious draft"—and what you do when that happens is simply take it and "walk the rest of the way" "through a pitch-dark limitless grove."[21]

The scene Frost recalls for Lesley—the scene in which he "became aware" of Mrs. Patterson and her dead son, and by his awareness made others aware that he was aware—works right in there betwixt and between where we fear the worst. Frost writes it with a discernible wince. The Pattersons had *endured* the worst, as would Frost also, in his education of his son Carol "in the way he should go." So, yes: "What are we talking about all so self-assured?" That's a real plea—and a throwing up of the hands in self-reproach. It comes with no small measure in it of the futility of too many of our home enterprises, as Robert Burns knew:

---

21. Notably, in *In the Clearing* (1962), Frost places between "The Draft Horse"—quoted here—and "The Peril of Hope" a poem titled "Ends," which concerns the collapse of a marriage: "Oh, there had once been night the first, / But this was night the last." See *CPPP*, 454–456.

But Mousie, thou art no thy-lane,
In proving foresight may be vain:
The best laid schemes o' Mice an' Men
                Gang aft agley,
An' lea'e us nought but grief an' pain,
        For promis'd joy!

Still, thou art blest, compar'd wi' me!
The present only toucheth thee:
But Och! I backward cast my e'e,
        On prospects drear!
An' forward tho' I canna see,
        I guess an' fear!

Belle Moodie read that to her son Rob in her Scottish brogue. He devoted a
lifetime—one sometimes feels inclined to say—to rewriting it in other words,
even as his own career unfolded so brilliantly, as if by "best laid scheme,"
throughout the 1920s, such that, by the time his fifth book, *West-Running Brook,*
appeared in November 1928, Frost had negotiated a new contract with Henry
Holt and Company that would be the envy of any poet: 15 percent royalties
on the first 5,000 copies of the new book, and 20 percent on all copies sold
thereafter, and a $2,000 advance against it all; a fine-press limited edition to
be issued alongside the trade edition; a new *Selected Poems* (also released in
November 1928); a monthly stipend of $250, to be paid through 1933; and, to cap
it off, a *Collected Poems* scheduled for release in 1930 and, in 1929, a gift of stock
in the firm (preferred and common shares). Nothing "gang agley" on the business front. On other fronts, however, the Frost family prospects were neither
clear nor secure.

Late in 1925, as we've seen, Marjorie's health went agley in the gravest of
ways; she would never fully recover. The hope to restore her led Frost and
Elinor—in the fall of 1928, as *West-Running Brook* went to press—to peril a European trip with Marjorie that they had, year after year, been compelled to
defer. But as the letters dating from autumn 1928 show, the sojourn in France
did little to bring Marjorie around, or to relieve the anxieties about her that
had brought her mother to the brink of nervous prostration.[22] After an often

---

22. Frost wrote to his friend Jack Haines from Paris on August 28: "Thus far I have
nothing to report of this expedition but bad. We came to France in the hope that it might
improve our invalid Marjorie by awakening an interest in her to learn the French lan-

melancholy tour of England and Ireland to see old friends and acquaintances, Robert and Elinor recalled Marjorie from France, where she'd remained in the care of friends, and the family hastily took ship from Southampton for New York. Frost's way of putting it to his English friend John Freeman—in another letter gathered here for the first time—is instructive: "It had to be sometime if it was ever going to be. So we bought a boat on the evening of one day and took the cold plunge into the Atlantic on the morning of the next," he wrote from the ship on November 19. "The abruptness made it easier to break with you all. And we had got it up for a new superstition that it would be good luck not to be too long about picking and choosing the boat. We took the first boat we happened on. . . . After all we don't know yet what is or isnt lucky," he added, striking a Burnsian note. "We ran right out of Cherbourgh [sic] into a hundred-and-fifty mile gale that knocked her nose in and brought us to a standstill for three hours a thousand miles from anywhere." "It was the same gale that seems to have been killing people in England," Frost said.[23] "It scared the sea sickness out of us to lie so mysteriously dead in those wind-flayed hills and hollows. We wondered if we had stopped at the port of missing ships and if all the strange pale faces appearing from everywhere weren't ghosts that had come on board." A haunted letter—by no means to be taken in jest—from a man who'd just revisited the old family haunts in London and Gloucestershire, where Frost had, with uncanny felicity, launched his career in 1913 and 1914. Only fourteen years had passed, but the family's English interval now lay somewhere ages and ages *thence.* And when the three Frosts returned, more exhausted than refreshed, to South Shaftsbury and Pittsfield, they found that Lesley's marriage to Dwight Francis—effected in September, while the Frosts were abroad—was already in danger of failing.

The November 1925 letter to Lesley is representative of the volume in which it now first appears in full. The better part of the correspondence gathered here concerns education, in all of its phases: Frost's several appointments at

---

guage. That hope has failed and the disappointment has been almost too much for Elinor on top of everything else she has had to bear for the last two years. I cant tell you how she has lost courage and strength as I have watched her. She is in a serious condition—much more serious at this moment than Marjorie. We ought by right to abandon our campaign and baggage and retreat to America. But that seems too cruel to contemplate with nothing done, none of our friends seen that we wanted to see and have been wanting to see so long."

23. A powerful Atlantic gale killed some thirty-eight people, most of them in England, in mid-November 1928.

the University of Michigan and at Amherst College, posts negotiated always with an eye toward the family's fortune and misfortunes; and, most notably in the last three years covered in these pages, the health and welfare of Robert and Elinor Frost's children and grandchildren. On that front, what awaited them all in the 1930s, to be covered in the next volume of this edition, would tax the capacity for rightly getting it down in prose of even so gifted a writer of letters as Robert Frost. "An forward tho' I canna see, / I guess an' fear!"

I

"Book Farmer"

February 1920–September 1921

I took out an accident policy limited to death by boiling in a sap
pan, swore off on baths, and took up my new life as a farmer to-day
by absentmindedly boring a hole clear through a two foot maple tree
and out onto the other side. "Amatoor!" all the little leaves began to
murmur. "Book farmer!" Leaves is of course an anachronism—that
well known figure of speech. There werent any leaves as yet.

      —Robert Frost to Louis Untermeyer, March 21, 1920

[To Lesley Frost. No year is supplied in the heading, but internal evidence indicates 1920; the great winter storm of 1920 lasted four days, February 4–7. ALS. UVA.]

Franconia N.H.

February 8 (circa)[1] [1920]

Dear Lesley:

I write this snowed in by the greatest snow-storm of all time with very little hope of ever mailing it. We are running short of food fuel and water. How long we can last we are not experienced enough in rationing to calculate. (We could last longer of course if Marjorie would eat less.) Rescuing parties have been by with teams of six and eight horses, but these are merely local and neighborly: they are satisfied if they push the snow a little from our doors: they are not intended to establish communication with the outside world. Everybody is frightened but Marjorie [and Carol {and Irma (and Mama)}][2] who doesn't know enough isn't, I fear, tall enough to appreciate the seriousness of snow actually half way up our windows. She coolly, nay freezing coldly, calls for paints and brushes and sits down at a window, that has to be shoveled open for her, to do Lafayette in oils. The picture is now declared done and we are justified in saying of it that the only way it betrays the anxiety under which the artist worked is in the coloring of the sky which is very much

---

1. The day and month are in RF's hand, as is the "circa." The letter appears to have been written a day or two prior to the eighth (by which time the storm had abated).

2. Brackets, parentheses, and curled brackets in the original.

too dark a blue; and this is partly attributable to the scarcity of white paint in
the house owing to our having been robbed during our absence of a whole
can of it as well as a Stilson wrench and probably other things we sha'n't miss
till we happen to need them as much as Margeries [*sic*] sky does the white paint
(I should say so!). In several ways the picture is a success at least as an expression and record of our present plight if not as a lasting work of art that the
artist will look with favor on when she knows more. The cloud cap is the more
real that you cant be sure it may not be a cap of drifting snow. She had fortunately enough white paint to do this in white rather than blue or yellow. On
the whole then it is a meritorious performance that does great credit to our
resources when you consider how far we are and how cut off from an artists
supply store not to say an ordinary hardware store. You will enjoy looking at
it in the heat of summer if you havent forgotten by then that it was done of
and in extreme winter conditions.

Meanwhile (convenient transition word!) I wish you would call up
Raymond and tell him from me (what possibly he knows) that there hasnt
been a drop of water in his and my water works all winter and what he
probably ought to know, I wouldn't on the present showing go ahead and
spend any more money on the water in that place. What's the use of har-
nessing water that isn't there. Tell him my advice is to stop where he is and
wait. He must do as he pleases of course. But tell him I wanted him to have
my opinion. Will gathers from the talk he overhears between Reed and the
contractor's boss that Raymond has already spent more than his estimated $15,000 and the building not over two thirds done.[3] His road is going
to cost him a lot more before he can enjoy it. He has spent nearly a thousand
on the water and nothing so far to show for it. I'd feel sorry for him if he wasn't
in the profession of being sorry for other people. Don't tell him much. Just say
I don't want to see him venture any more money on that spring that, maybe,
isn't a spring.

---

3. Raymond Holden (1894–1972), a family friend and aspiring poet, had, in 1919, purchased the upper half of RF's property in Franconia for $2,500 and begun to build a house
there. See *YT*, 136–145. "Will": Willis E. Herbert (then a teenager), nephew of the man
from whom RF had purchased the Franconia farm in 1915 (also named Willis E. Herbert).
"Reed": likely Burton J. Reed, a forty-four-year-old lumber dealer in Franconia in 1920.

I think I told you Louis got me to get Whicher to find Sasoon [*sic*] fifty dollars for appearing before the class I surrendered to Whicher on leaving.[4] It was all very personal. Sassoon didn't want much money. What he wanted was a chance to meet boys and men when his prospects seemed bad for seeing anything in this country but girls and women's clubs. Louis was very earnest and personal about it. The next we knew Whicher was hearing from Pond the agent instead of Sassoon himself.[5] Not a word from Sassoon to Whicher who I had told Sassoon would entertain him. And Pond's tune was this: Fifty would do for talking to the class but Amherst was a good way off and couldn't Mr Whicher make it a hundred and fifty for a class talk and a talk to the whole college. To hell with such doings. Louis says Whicher ought not to have minded. Louis means well enough but how is Sassoon any different in this episode from the other Englishmen we complain of. It's a joke. I don't suppose Sassoon thought [so]. The English ought to be taught to be careful over here.

Black's The Great Desire is really a full book. Except that [it] doesn't go reeling along with emotion it reminds me of Changing Winds.[6] The method is like that of Changing Winds. It's a good way to get a lot in. It is charged with the good American prejudices that will save us if we are saved. Black has evidently listened to all this foreign talk against our differences in law and custom from Europe. To be sure we use quarters where England uses shillings; we have a written constitution where they have none; we let our children run around more unattended by nurses; we drink less than they do; and so I might go on. I dont say who the differences are in favor of from God's point of view. From England's I expect them to be in favor of the English. From America's I think I am safe in saying they are in favor of the Americans. You'll enjoy the wisdom of the book.

---

4. British poet Siegfried Sassoon (1886–1967), who spoke at Amherst at the request of George Whicher (1889–1954), professor of English there. RF had resigned his professorship at Amherst only a week or two earlier.

5. James Burton Pond Jr. (1889–1961), head of the Pond Lyceum Bureau in New York, which booked a number of writers, American and British, for lectures. Pond inherited the business from his father (also named James Burton), who had managed Mark Twain, Booker T. Washington, Winston Churchill, Arthur Conan Doyle, and Frederick Douglass, among other luminaries.

6. The author, editor, and photographer Alexander Black published a novel entitled The Great Desire in 1919 (New York: Harper and Brothers). St. John Greer Ervine's novel Changing Winds had been published in 1917 (New York: Macmillan).

I'm sick enough of that wild crowd to settle in Maine rather than in Connecticut.[7] Their hearts may be in the right place and so may some of their other organs but they have no brains.

> Affectionately
>
> Papa.

[*To Arthur H. Quinn (1875–1960), professor of English and Dean of the College at the University of Pennsylvania. Date derived from internal evidence. ALS. Private.*]

> [Franconia, NH]
>
> [circa February 9, 1920]

Dear Mr Quinn:

Suppose I take for my subject What's New in Poetry. I could make it Three or Four Realities.[8] I leave it to you to choose.

I shall get into Philadelphia Friday morning in time for lunch and perhaps a little rest before performing.[9] Shall I look you up at the University?

Trust your cold has left you.

Here's looking forward.

> Always yours sincerely
>
> Robert Frost

---

7. RF would soon begin (in the spring and summer) to hunt for a new house and farm, Franconia winters having proved too hard on the family's health.

8. RF had been giving lectures on "Vocal Reality" (among other topics) during the winter of 1919–1920. See RF to Untermeyer, October 15, 1919: "no one succeeds in any of the arts without observing at least some one of the various realities. That's the way he gets his originality whatever it comes to. He may be as romantic as a girl of eighteen in subject matter and in vocabulary: you'll find him trying to make it up to you in vocal reality or some other reality. He must get back to the source of sanity and energy somewhere. Every form of romance is but an exhalation from some form of reality. The common speech is always giving off, you and I know how, the special vocabulary of poetry. The same thing happens with the tones of every day talk. They have emanations of grandeur and dignity and reverence and heroism and terror" (*LRF-1*, 711; see also *LRF-1*, 708–709, 726).

9. The talk was given on February 13. RF had mentioned a visit to New York—presumably to occur just after the talk—in a January 18, 1920, letter to Lesley: "Can you wait to decide [whether or not to go to France] until I am down on the fourteenth of February?" (*LRF-1*, 728).

[To Anita P. Forbes (1889–1965), a teacher at Hartford (Connecticut) Public High School and editor of Modern Verse, British and American *(New York: Henry Holt, 1921). ALS. Private.]*

Franconia N.H.

March 7 1920

My dear Miss Forbes:

I am of course going to let you have those two poems anyway, but suppose I pretend to bargain with you for them.[10] Don't you think if you got those two of your own choosing without money and without price, you ought to be willing to take one more of my choosing to go with them? It could be any one of several I would name in order of my preference: Going for Water, Mowing, To the Thawing Wind or October.[11] (They are all in A Boy's Will.) They represent a side of my work I hate to see overlooked. And don't you think I ought to be consulted in my prejudices a little if not as the author of the poems, then as one who has taught poetry (and other things) all the way up through all the grades from the lowest primary through college? You can form some idea of my judgement when I tell you that it coincides exactly with yours as far as you go in your selections. I only ask you to go a little further.

In getting permission from Henry Holt & Co please say that you have mine.

Sincerely yours

Robert Frost

[To George R. Elliott (1883–1963), a professor at Bowdoin and, later, Amherst, whom RF mistakenly addresses here as "Mr. Young." At some point, Elliott himself added a handwritten note to the letter, in clarification: "I had invited him [RF] to teach in Bowdoin during my sabbatical. GRE." ALS. ACL.]

Franconia N.H.

March 8 1920

Dear Mr Young:

Your letter is just here in the first mail in four days. I make such haste as the winter permits in answering you.

---

10. The two poems in question are "After Apple-Picking" and "Birches," both included in *Modern Verse*.

11. Forbes selected "To the Thawing Wind."

Any journey from home this month looks impossible. I'm down with the bad cold that's going round and I'm a slow recoverer.

Has it positively to be this month? Somebody must be found to take care of the class I suppose. Except for that I don't see why I should be expected to come to Bowdoin when you are away. You couldn't ask me over toward the middle or end of April now could you? If not I shall just have to send you a poem or two in manuscript and ask you to call it square till I can have you to see us on the farm some day not too distant.

What you wrote for me in The Nation made me feel that I had formed a new tie in the world.[12]

Always yours sincerely
Robert Frost

[To Lesley Frost. At the top left of the first page RF has written "Check enclosed" and, down the left margin, "Manuscript in big envelope mailed with this." ALS. UVA.]

Franconia N.H.
March 11 1920

Dear Lesley:

Two doubts in sending this precious stuff: will it ever reach you? will you have time to do it in type?[13] You dont mention having had a couple of poems from me lately. It makes me afraid they got lost. We don't seem to know what bundles you speak of sending.

Don't let this MS out of your hands and don't let the typewritten copies go to Harpers till I say the word. I may want to see them.

I'm thinking I ought to get seven or eight hundred dollars for the lot. I shall have settled some things with Wells by the time you are ready with these.[14]

---

12. See George R. Elliott, "The Neighborliness of Robert Frost," *The Nation,* December 6, 1919, 713–714.

13. Lesley often typed RF's manuscripts at the time.

14. Thomas Bucklin Wells (1876–1944), vice president of Harper and Brothers and editor of *Harper's* magazine. The transaction had been long in progress. See RF's January 28, 1920, letter to Lesley: "Joseph Anthony [in the publicity department at Harper and Brothers] seemed an able-minded boy when I talked with him here [in Amherst]. He ought to go a long way. He said there was no immediate rush for the poems for Harper's. Wells is out of the office for the moment and no one else ought to have the handling of

The way to settle these radicals is to confuse them by quoting them to each other—I shouldnt stick at a little misquoting if it was for the purpose of teasing. You should have said to that fool girl "One of my friends who edits the Liberator says—" and then given her any old wild stuff to mix her up.[15] Tell em you are not interested in the things they are going to change. You are willing they should change them. But there must be some things they havent time or inclination to change. You'd like to ask for the humble job of holding on to those while they are changing the others. You could hold some of them in your lap—the lap dogs and the cats for example. I don't suppose there is any scheme on foot to alter the cats and dogs. If your function is simply to hold on to what they don't want to change I dont see how that makes you either a conservative or a radical. To Hell with their inability to think.

Make the poems look as well as possible. Correct my slips in spelling and make none yourself.

Affectionately
Papa

[To Louis Untermeyer (1885–1977), American poet, anthologist, critic, and editor. ALS. LoC.]

Franconia N.H.
March 12 [1920]

Dear Louis:

Honestly and truly this is what I dreamed last night. I'm not to blame for what I dream I hope.

I dreamed I had just been dining late at a conservatives [*sic*] who had made me a little uncomfortable by treating me as a radical—a little uncomfortable, not very. (You can't find anybody in these times who isn't more or less flattered by being regarded as a radical.) I was standing on the street corner waiting for the last car when who should walk up to me out of the darkness

---

them. I shall send them to you to copy when I have regarded them a little longer. Overhauling them has stopped me writing new ones for the moment" (*LRF-1*, 729).

15. Founded by Max and Crystal Eastman in 1918, *The Liberator* was the premier socialist magazine of its day, succeeding *The Masses*, which the federal government had shut down in 1917, due to its vocal opposition to the war effort. Louis Untermeyer was a contributing editor.

to tell me the last car had gone more than an hour ago but you looking pretty well considering you looked for all the world in every detail like Martha Foote Crowe [*sic*].[16] The likeness was so exact that I don't know how I knew it was you except by the Current Opinion that you held devoutly to your breasts like a prayer book.[17] The next thing I remember we were away forward in a debate in which I was trying hard to establish to the tune of

> *"Watchman watchman dont take me*
> *Take that nigger behind the tree*
> *He stole gold and I stole brass,"*[18]

that I was neither a radical nor a conservative. I had a strange inward assurance that I was making my position perfectly clear because I was speaking in a form of regular verse more or less acceptable to both radicals and conservatives. I wish I could reproduce the verse here out of the dream, but it seems to have got away from me. The important thing is my argument. "Madman" I said, meaning of course Madam, "I am willing that you should change everything in the world that you want to change. You can hand me a list at any time and I will cheerfully subscribe it. (English use of the verb acquired from much reading of English authors.) But surely there are some things you have neither strength nor inclination to change. Now all I ask is the humble job of being allowed to hold on to the things you don't want changed. There must be some?" I pressed you. "Aren't there?"

---

16. Martha Foote Crow (1854–1924), at the time dean of women at Northwestern University in Chicago and an associate of Harriet Moody's, a close Frost family friend.

17. A magazine then published in New York, edited by Edward Jewitt Wheeler (1859–1922), president of the Poetry Society of America.

18. From a folk song that exists in a number of iterations. The song was familiar enough to be quoted as "an old cry" in an anonymous February 11, 1895, article in the *Indianapolis Journal*: "It is a common experience with officers of the law that whenever an offender is arrested, or 'pinched,' as we say in police circles, he at once says: 'Why did you arrest me; there is A or B, who is just as guilty as I and you have not arrested him.' It is the old cry of 'Watchman, watchman, don't take me, take that negro behind the tree.'" In a Folkways Records recording of *"When I Was a Boy in Brooklyn"* (FW-03501/FG-3501, 1961), Israel Kaplan recalls it as a common taunt in New York City during World War I:

Watchman, watchman, don't catch me;
Catch the feller behind the tree.
He stole copper, I stole brass;
Watchman, watchman, kiss my ass!

"I spuzso," you conceded reluctantly as if one didn't know what they would be and wouldn't delay the action to find out then.

"In the general rush of change with almost everything going, I should think there would be danger that some things would be carried away that even the wildest revolutionary would be sorry to see carried away. Well then that's where I come in. Delegate me to hold on to those. 'Here hold these,' you could say. You would find me so serviceable that never again would you hurt my feeling by calling me a conservative. I should count my life not spent in vain if I were permitted to sit and hold in my lap just one thing that conservatives and radicals were alike agreed must be saved from being changed by mistake in the general change of other things. I am interested in what is to stay as it is; you are interested in what is not to stay as it is. We can't split on that difference. We operate in mutually exclusive spheres from which we can only bow across to each other in mutual appreciation. If I am a conservative it is the kind of conservative you want in your pay to take care of what you don't want to take with you. And just so if I am a radical it is the kind you can have no kick against because I let you take with you all you care to load up with. The fact is I am neither a conservative nor a radical and I refuse henceforth to be called either. I am a strainer: I keep back the tea leaves and let the tea flow through."

At this point you began to show signs of wanting to go back and reconsider something you had been led by my eloquence in my own desperate defence to pass over too easily.

"Let's see," says you, "what some of these things are you might be trusted to hold while the rest of the world went forward."

"Or backward. Drive 'em in any direction you please. If the flame has got to be bent, I don't care which way it bends. My interest is to keep the candle from going over."

"You sound to me suspiciously open-minded. Don't care, do you, whether we drive the world forward or backward. Think us capable of driving it backward?"

"Dont get mad."

"It shows the prejudice I have suspected you of, against reform and reformers."

"How so?" I asked to give you the trouble of putting an elusive thought into words.

"But now I want the more to know what the things are you would hold in your lap."

"You wouldn't mind my holding a lap-dog surely. You weren't thinking of altering all the lap-dogs, I hope? Or I might hold a cat. You werent thinking of altering all the tom cats?"

I looked, and if you yourself weren't changing! A curtain descended: there was a confused noise as of scenery being shifted; the curtain rose, and you stood revealed in appearance intermediate between Jessie Rittenhouse and Harriet Monroe.[19]

"Any thing personal intended by 'cats'?" you said.

And then a voice that was unmistakably Jeans[20] said wearily "Louis, Louis come to yourself."

"Coming," said a voice just as unmistakably yours, shrill but far away as from the inmost inwards of yourself. Very ventriloquial.

The place seemed to be in Brookline.

It was unlabelled except for a street sign which read Heath Road.[21]

I vow I have given it exactly as I dreamed it especially the last part of it where I wasn't laboring under the temptation of stretching it to use up the note paper I happened to have in the house. You ought to know how accurate it is. Where were you on the night of March 11? Can you bring anyone to swear that you couldn't have been on the streets with Martha Foote Crowe [*sic*], Jessie Rittenhouse, and Harriet Monroe?

I stick to the position I dreamed I took. It looks to me fairly tenable. You want to blow the candle to see if it won't give more light. All right let me hold the candle so you can give all your attention blowing it carefully so as not to blow it out. And let me hold the matches too so that if you should blow it out we could form a society to relight it. (Just made it last the paper out.[22])

Everly yours
Robert Frost

---

19. Jessie Belle Rittenhouse (1869–1948), poet and anthologist, and a founder and secretary of the Poetry Society of America; Harriet Monroe (1860–1936), founder and editor of *Poetry*.

20. Jean Starr Untermeyer (1886–1970), Louis's wife.

21. Heath Street runs through Brookline, Massachusetts.

22. That is, the stationery he used.

[To Lesley Frost. A portion of the letter is missing. The context provided by other letters—and by newspaper articles about the 1920 sugar season in New Hampshire— places this one in mid-March. ALS. UVA.]

[Franconia, NH]

[mid-March 1920]

[. . .] I have decided not to go at Wells for the big money but for another kind of thing entirely.[23]—I really want him to give me a send off by printing five or six poems in a bunch. They will be as follows and in this order

Fragmentary Blue Place for a Third

Good-bye and Keep Cold

An Empty Threat Two Look at Two

For Once Then Something.

So hold these six ready to send in the minute you hear from me.

The sap started yesterday. Some of the buckets are nearly full. Carol and I principally Carol are going to do one mans share of the sugaring this year. You can stock up with sugar and hand the girls cakes of it in place of arguements [*sic*] for or against God, Hoover, Womens Suffrage, Soviets, Sedition Laws, the Treaty Drinkwater or the Pine Tree Blister.[24] "What have you to say to this," you can ask and get them out a cake.

---

23. Again, Thomas B. Wells, editor of *Harper's,* which would publish four poems by RF in its July 1920 issue: "Fragmentary Blue," "Good-bye and Keep Cold," "Place for a Third," and "For Once, Then, Something." All were collected in *NH,* where "An Empty Threat" and "Two Look at Two" appeared for the first time.

24. RF's catalog of topics for "arguments" to be settled with (Carol's) maple sugar cakes is a lark. As for "the Treaty Drinkwater": assuming, as the phrasing suggests, that RF did not omit a comma, we cannot rule out that RF conflates two public controversies then being "argued" about, "for or against": the punitive Treaty of Versailles (1919) and Prohibition (hence, perhaps, "Drinkwater"), which had gone into effect in January 1920. The two were often mingled in public debate. German Americans typically opposed both the treaty and Prohibition. During the war, the Anti-Saloon League lobbied the Senate to investigate prominent brewers as "alien enemies" under the "sedition laws" RF mentions earlier in his catalog. The English poet John Drinkwater, an acquaintance of RF, had lately enjoyed considerable success when his play *Abraham Lincoln* (1918) opened in New York in 1919. Whether he figures in the mischief, other than as a ready vehicle for a pun, is impossible to say. In American parlance at the time, "John Drinkwater" was the type of the prohibitionist, just as "John Barleycorn" was of the inebriant. The "Pine Tree Blister"—an invasive fungus (*Cronartium ribicola*) indigenous to Eurasia—had made its

Yes I think Mrs Clark at the Sunwise Turn must have doubted my cold and swollen jaw.[25] She thinks if I'm as cold by nature as they tell about catching cold couldnt make me enough worse so that I'd know the difference. But I was utterly unpresentable. Still I might have tried to set out and got as far as Littleton if Mama hadnt stopped me.

Affectionately

PAPA

[To Lesley Frost. The letter is undated, the first page or pages missing. RF's reference to house hunting in Connecticut with Warren R. Brown, a real estate agent and family friend in Amherst, suggests it was written in March 1920.[26] ALS. UVA.]

[Franconia, NH]

[mid-March 1920]

[. . .] We laughed over the account of it all in The Post: the hypocracy[27] of making the decision of the judges so unanimous: and the idiocy of calling the first poem at once so original and so like Amy and Carl.[28] I should suppose it very likely that the four "honorable mentions" meant that the judges each picked a different pair

---

way, via imported plants, into North America in the early twentieth century; by 1911 it was killing off white pines throughout New England. In 1920 the federal government ordered that all plants in the genus *Ribes* (host to the fungus, including gooseberry and currant bushes) be quarantined on import into the United States.

25. Arnold Grade explains: "RF's reference is apparently to a broken engagement at Madge Jenison's Sunwise Turn Bookshop in New York City. She later authored *Sunwise Turn: A Human Comedy of Bookselling* [New York: E. P. Dutton] (1923)" (*FL,* 83).

26. In a letter Grade dates March 1920, Elinor Frost writes to Lesley: "We are <u>not</u> settling down to stay in Franconia all summer. Papa is going down the last week of April to make a determined hunt for a farm in western Connecticut. Mr. Brown, in Amherst, the real estate man, you know, is going to drive papa all around in his car" (*FL,* 87).

27. A spelling found in books printed in the nineteenth century.

28. Amy Lowell and Carl Sandburg. The account to which RF refers is likely that on page 1 of the *Barnard Bulletin* for March 5, 1920, headlined "Results of the Bear Poetry Contest." Six poems were recognized, with a first prize, a second prize, and four honorable mentions awarded. One honorable mention was for "English Daisies," a sonnet by "Leslie [*sic*] Frost '21." The winning poem, "Texas," by Jewel Wurtsbough (also in the class of 1921), was written in free verse. The contest judges were Charles Sears Baldwin, professor of rhetoric at Yale; John Erskine, professor of English at Columbia; and Walter Prichard Eaton, a drama critic and later a professor of playwriting at Yale.

for the first two and compromised with Erskine by letting his pair win if he would let theirs be given some credit. Erskine said that the moral of it was that Barnard should have some more money for teachers' salaries.

Too bad I couldn't get down to see you. I doubt if I shall get down in April either; though I shall be within a hundred miles of you farm-hunting in Connecticut. Brown (W. R. of Amherst) is going to carry me round in his automobile.

I have a half wild impulse to go the other way, though, into Maine. There's a little 3,000 population town of small industries (snow shoes, toys etc) called Norway over there among lakes and about forty miles from Portland. I shall probably not settle down anywhere else till I have had a look round it anyway. I suppose it is foolish to get too far away from our markets both for poetry and for farm produce.

To Hell with the Untermeyers if they don't ask you to see them. They are busy every minute they are awake talking of fame. They don't think of it any more than they talk of it because they talk of it all the time. The absurdity of it never strikes them. Dont think you are under one least single obligation to seek them. All I think is we must have no trouble or break with them after what has passed between us. Louis means to be a good backer. It's funny to watch him, though, when its a question of Edward Thomas. He parts company with me there. He refuses to like Thomas' poetry and he refuses to like my poetry to Thomas.[29] Funny world.

> Affectionately
>
> Papa

Just happened to run across this by Daniel Webster: "I had not then learned that all true power in writing is in the idea not in the style, an error into which ars rhetorica, as it is usually taught, may easily lead stronger heads than mine."[30] Ideas ideas ideas. Of course emotional ideas. Senses and sentiments are what to get after.

Carol will send a five pound can of sugar tomorrow.

---

29. RF refers to his poem "To E.T.," written in memory of Thomas and published first in the *Yale Review* in April 1920, where an essay by George Whicher, "Edward Thomas," accompanied it. Untermeyer's article on Edward Thomas appeared in the *North American Review* in January 1919. RF was chagrined to find that Untermeyer mentioned him as often as he did Thomas, and that Untermeyer claimed, with regard to Thomas's first volume, that "the genius, the influence, the inflection, even the idiom, of Robert Frost, can be found in almost all of these English pages. The book itself, with its logical dedication, is a tribute to Frost the person as much as Frost the poet" (263).

30. The remark, from Webster's *Autobiography,* is often quoted.

[*To Marion Elza Dodd (1883–1961), cofounder, with Mary Byers, of the Hampshire Bookshop in Northampton, Massachusetts. Enclosed with the letter was a copy of "Good-bye and Keep Cold," first published in* Harper's *in July 1920 and later collected in NH. ALS. ACL.*]

Franconia NH.

March 17 1920

My dear Miss Dodd:

This is the poem I promised you when I was in Amherst but put off sending till I could send it from a safe distance.

With best wishes for the enterprise

Sincerely yours

Robert Frost

You'll notice [I] put "browse" in company that won't allow it to be mis-pronounced.[31]

[*To Helen Alison Fraser Penniman (1882–1964), a Baltimore socialite, daughter of British diplomat Gilbert Fraser, and wife of Nicholas Penniman, a wealthy manufacturer. She was also a theater critic and for forty years the moving force behind Baltimore's Vagabond Players (founded in 1916; one of America's oldest "little theaters"). RF's stage directions in the letter indicate that the play in question is* A Way Out *(1917), which premiered at the Northampton Academy of Music on February 24, 1919. Despite Penniman's interest in the play, there is no record that the Vagabond Players staged it. ALS. UVA.*]

Franconia N.H.

March 17 1920

My dear Mrs Penniman:

It grieves me many times more than it possibly can you that I haven't answered your letter long before this because I am many times more the loser than you if my delay keeps you from using my play. By all means use it if you like. What I get for it is not important for the present. Some day I hope to make money with plays. Till then—

Let me ask that you will try to have the two characters pretty well matched and your light low enough for the last part of the scene.

Sincerely yours

Robert Frost

----

31. In "Good-bye and Keep Cold," RF rhymes "browse" with "house," "mouse," and "grouse."

[To Lesley Frost. ALS. UVA.]

Franconia N.H.

March 18 1920

Dear Lesley:

Do you suppose it would be safe for me not to see the manuscript again before it goes to Harpers?[32] You're not afraid you may have misread my hand writing seriously somewhere. If you think I ought to see it why don't hesitate to send it back. Only be very sure to send it in a good envelope and insure it for fifty dollars. Things do get lost. We have never seen the drawing paper you sent Irma.

The magazines came all right. Muzzey makes me like him.[33] The trouble with most people we know is, as he says, that they may be very good at catching on to the very latest style in thought but they never even think of such a thing as wanting to set the style themselves as Lenine[34] has set it for so many millions. They have never even tasted the pleasure of starting an idea for themselves however small. They look on ideas as things to take up with and subscribe. They value themselves on the number they have heard of and the radicality of the ones they go partizan for. College is where you are in the way of keeping up on ideas; certain courses in college are where you are more in the way of keeping up. The poor things have been allowed to think that declaring for a more or less new idea is the same as thinking. It would be hard to explain to them what thinking is unless you could catch them sometime

---

32. See RF to Lesley Frost, March 11, 1920.

33. The historian David Saville Muzzey (1870–1965). See his untitled omnibus review of new books on the Bolsheviks and the Russian Revolution, published in *Political Science Quarterly* (December 1919), and in which he writes: "Although but two years have passed since Lenine and Trotzky put an end to the Kerensky regime and gained control of what remnants of organized government there were left in Petrograd and Moscow, the literature on Bolshevism is already extensive. It is almost entirely polemic or apologetic, too, as might be expected in view both of the fateful crisis for Russian democracy in the Bolshevist dictatorship, and of the challenge to the democracy of the world in the tyranny of the 'purged' Soviet. We have impassioned pleas for the old order, like the Princess Radziwill's *The Firebrand of Bolshevism*, salutations of the new order, like Professor Ross's *Russia in Upheaval* or mere diatribes against the disorder, like Charles Edward Russell's *After the Whirlwind* and William Roscoe Thayer's *Volleys from a Non-Combatant;* and we have ardent apologetics on the other side, ranging from the products of Lenine's own prolific brain to the chirpings of the parlor Bolshevists of New York and Chicago" (654–655).

34. A spelling often used at the time.

in the act of thinking. They must think accidentally sometimes. We all start accidentally and unconsciously. We grow in the power to think as we become aware of ourselves or have ourselves pointed out to ourselves by circumstances and by other people. I suppose it starts too in the realm of plain observation, that is outward observation. From there it goes on to inward observation. There is sight and there is insight. You learn first to know what you see and to put fresh words on it: you learn second to know what you feel and put fresh words on it. That's the whole story. I don't believe there's anything in literature that that doesn't cover.

Would you have time to make a copy of Place for a Third and send it to G. R. Elliott, Founders Hall, Haverford, Pennsylvania? It would have to reach him there on the 25th, that is not later than the 25th. Just scribble on the bottom of the MS that I asked you to send it.

I haven't heard from Joseph Anthony this week.[35] I wonder if he thinks the track is clear to go ahead.

I am suffering from a loss of interest in revolutions. I'd like to tie together by the tail a couple going in opposite directions and see if it would result in a standstill. Theoretically it ought to. Something up in Germany.[36] We had been watching the stars pretty closely and we hadn't noticed anything out of the usual. Perhaps we should have watched the papers. It just shows how easy it is to look in the wrong place for a thing. Hope nobody escaped unhurt. Up with the Kaiser next I suppose.

Affectionately

Papa.

Did I make those lines in An Empty Threat read
No
There's not a soul
For a windbreak
Between me and the North Pole.[37]
Be sure it's that way.
Letter just came from Joseph. Will send letter for Wells by next mail.[38]

---

35. On the staff in the publicity department at *Harper's*.

36. Events surrounding the March 1920 Kapp-Lüttwitz Putsch, aimed at overthrowing the Weimar Republic.

37. As to phrasing, the lines are exactly as published in *NH*, although there they are punctuated differently.

38. Thomas B. Wells.

[To George R. Elliott. ALS. ACL.]

Franconia N.H.

March 20 1920

Dear Mr Elliott:

Worse conscience than you need have had! I wasn't liking you because you had liked everything I had written but because you seemed to have read nearly everything I had written. More than anyone else you made your case out of chapter and verse.[39] I had begun to be afraid certain things that had been said about me in the first place (and in praise, mind you) by people who had hardly taken the trouble to read me would have to go on being said forever. You broke the spell. You took a fresh look, and the fun of it is your report, based so evidently on your own observation uninfluenced by anything Ford Hueffer[40] set going, confirms me in some of my better suspicions of myself.

Moreover I think it cant be presuming too much on your criticism to conclude from it that we are more or less sympathetic in our view of things; in other words if in these bad days I propped your mind so also you might be expected to prop mine.[41]

I have asked my daughter at Barnard to send you a copy of one of my less amiable poems in character called Place for a Third.[42] I'm sending herewith several shorter ones I like better myself. The time draws near publishing again. I shall let a few out into the magazines this year and next year book a good

------

39. In his (Elliott's) "The Neighborliness of Robert Frost."

40. British novelist Ford Madox Hueffer (1873–1939), who changed his surname from Hueffer to Ford in 1919. In his "Mr. Robert Frost and 'North of Boston,'" published in the *Outlook* for June 27, 1914, Hueffer had remarked that RF's "vers libre . . . was an excellent instrument for rendering the actual rhythms of speech." Although Hueffer's purpose was laudatory, RF was at pains to insist that he had no interest in free verse.

41. See Matthew Arnold's sonnet "To a Friend," written for Arthur Hugh Clough:

Who prop, thou ask'st, in these bad days, my mind?—
He much, the old man, who, clearest-soul'd of men,
Saw The Wide Prospect, and the Asian Fen,
And Tmolus hill, and Smyrna bay, though blind . . .

These lines concern Homer, believed to have been born in Smyrna.

42. See RF's foregoing letter to Lesley Frost.

many. These enclosed need not be returned. Carol (one of my children) has made the copies for you.

Always yours sincerely
Robert Frost

[*To Louis Untermeyer. ALS. LoC.*]

Franconia NH
March 21 1920

Dear Louis:

Is it nothing to you that no longer than ten years ago I was writing town poems[43] like this:

The Parlor Joke

You wont hear unless I tell you
How the few to turn a penny
Built complete a modern city
Where there shouldn't have been any
And then conspired to fill it
With the miserable many.

They drew on Ellis Island.
They had but to raise a hand
To let the living deluge
On the basin of the land.
They did it just like nothing
In smiling self-command.

---

43. "Town poems": a term often applied to the urbane poetry of the Augustan period, and associated with Juvenal's third satire, as in Samuel Johnson's "London: A Poem in Imitation of the Third Satire of Juvenal" (1738), the epigraph for which, taken from Juvenal, reads: "*Quis ineptæ / Tam patiens Urbis, tam ferreus ut teneat se?*" ("For who can be so tolerant of this monstrous city, who so iron-willed as to contain himself?" [trans. J. D. Fleeman in *Samuel Johnson: The Complete English Poems* (New Haven, CT: Yale University Press, 1971)]). RF chose "The Parlor Joke" for inclusion in the first edition of Untermeyer's *A Miscellany of American Poetry* (New York: Harcourt, Brace and Howe, 1920). It is also collected in *CPPP*, 516–518.

If you asked them their opinion
They declared the job as good
As when to fill the sluices
They turned the river flood;
Only there they dealt with water
And now with human blood.

Then the few withdrew in order
To their villas on the hill
Where they watched from easy couches
The uneasy city fill.
"If it isn't good," they ventured
"At least it isnt ill."

But with child and wife to think of
They werent taking any chance.
So they fortified their windows
With a screen of potted plants,
And armed themselves from somewhere
With a manner and a glance.

You know how a bog of sphagnum[44]
Beginning with a scum
Will climb the side of a mountain;
So the poor began to come
Climbing the hillside suburb
From the alley and the slum.

As the tenements crept nearer,
It pleased the rich to assume,
In humorous self-pity,
The mockery of gloom
Because the poor insisted
On wanting all the room.

And there it might have ended
In a feeble parlor joke,
Where a gentle retribution

---

44. Peat moss.

Overtook the gentlefolk;
But that some beheld a vision:
Out of stench and steam and smoke,

Out of vapor of sweat and breathing
They saw materialize
Above the darkened city
Where the murmur never dies
A shape that had to cower
Not to knock against the skies.

They could see it through a curtain,
They could see it through a wall,
A lambent swaying presence
In wind and rain and all,
With its arms abroad in heaven
Like a scarecrow in a shawl.

There were some who thought they heard it
When it seemed to try to talk
But missed articulation
With a little hollow squawk
Up indistinct in the zenith
Like the note of the evening hawk.

Of things about the future
Its hollow chest was full;
Something about rebellion
And blood a dye for wool[45]

---

45. RF worked as a light trimmer replacing carbon rods in arc lamps in the Arlington Woolen Mill in Lawrence, Massachusetts, in 1893–1894. Two other poems, which he left unpublished, arose from what he saw there, "The Mill City" and "When the Speed Comes" (*CPPP*, 509, 511). And although RF here dates his "parlor joke" to 1910, he would also have recalled the violent Bread and Roses Strike in Lawrence in January–March 1912, in which workers, most of them immigrants, led by the Industrial Workers of the World, protested pay cuts that the "Wool Trust" had implemented in response to a state law mandating a fifty-four-hour workweek for women and children. In fact, RF had attended school with John Breen, a member of the Lawrence school board charged with having planted explosives in a plot to discredit the workers. See RF to Rowell, June 15, 1912 (*LRF-1*, 64–65). For more on RF and his years in Lawrence see Donald G. Sheehy, "'Stay

And how you may pull the world down
If you know the prop to pull.

What to say to the wisdom
That could tempt a nations fate
By invoking such a spirit
To reduce the labor-rate!
Some people don't mind trouble
If it's trouble up-to-date.

Patented 1910 by R. (L.) Frost

Elinor has just come out flat-footed against God conceived either as the fourth person seen with Shadrack Meshack and Tobedwego in the fiery furnace or without help by the Virgin Mary.[46] How about as a Shellean [*sic*] principal or spirit coeternal with the rock part of creation, I ask. Nonsense and you know its [*sic*] nonsense Rob Frost only you're afraid you'll have bad luck or lose your standing in the community if you speak your mind. "Spring," I say, "returneth and the maple sap is heard dripping in the buckets (allow me to sell you a couple[47]). (We can quote you the best white first-run sugar at a dollar a pound unsight and unseen—futures.)" Like a woman she says Pshaw. You know how a woman says Pshaw—you with your uncanny knowledge of your own wife. I took out an accident policy limited to death by boiling in a sap pan, swore off on baths, and took up my new life as a farmer to-day by absentmindedly boring a hole clear through a two foot maple tree and out onto the other side.[48] "Amatoor!" all the little leaves began to murmur. "Book

---

Unassuming': The Lives of Robert Frost," in *The Cambridge Companion to Robert Frost*, ed. Robert Faggen (New York: Cambridge University Press, 2001), 7–34.

46. See the Book of Daniel, chapters 1–3, for the story of Shadrach, Meshach, and Abednego (not "To-bed-we-go," as RF jokingly has it).

47. See *Alice in Wonderland*, chapter 5, "Advice from a Caterpillar":

"In my youth," said the sage, as he shook his grey locks,
"I kept all my limbs very supple
By the use of this ointment—one shilling the box—
Allow me to sell you a couple?"

48. RF was sugaring with his son, Carol.

farmer!" Leaves is of course an anachronism—that well known figure of speech. There werent any leaves as yet.

Think it over and do as the last line of Drummonds famous poem [illegible][49]

R.F.

[*To Henry Reynolds Johnson (1868–1959), who, along with his brother, the writer Clifton Johnson, had opened Johnson's Bookstore in Springfield, Massachusetts, in 1894. A local landmark, it closed in 1998 after being in business for 104 years. ALS. Vassar.*]

Franconia N.H.
March 27 1920

Dear Mr Johnson:

In my anxiety to do enough for you, I am afraid I may have done too much. Try not to mind. I promise to do less next time. I always preach restraint and often practice it.

We have had bad luck in not meeting at Amherst. Someday we must deliberately look for each other there or somewhere else.

With good wishes
Sincerely yours
Robert Frost

---

49. Untermeyer accurately describes the few words that follow as "an undecipherable scrawl" (102). RF refers to the last lines of "Saint John Baptist," by William Drummond (1585–1649), which would have been familiar to him as the poem that closes Book One of Palgrave's *Golden Treasury*:

> All ye whose hopes rely
> On God, with me amidst these deserts mourn,
> Repent, repent, and from old errors turn!
> —Who listen'd to his voice, obey'd his cry?
> Only the echoes, which he made relent,
> Rung from their flinty caves, Repent! Repent!

*[To Wilbur Rowell (1862–1946), Massachusetts attorney, banker, and judge; executor
of RF's grandfather's will. ALS. UVA.]*

Franconia N.H.

March 31 1920

Dear Mr Rowell:

This is no worse than I have been expecting.[50] The last time we saw Jean
she came to us at Amherst a fugitive from a mob that was going to throw her
into a mill-pond for refusing to kiss the flag.[51] The war was just ending and
she was actually in tears for the abdicated Emperor. Nothing she said or did
was natural. I should have had her examined by an alienist then if I had known
how to manage it without disturbing her. Looking back I can see that she
hasn't been right for years. She has always simply dismayed the children with
her wild talk.

As you say the question is What can we do for her. I am made bold by your
use of the word "we" to ask if I can come to you for advice before I go to encounter the authorities at Portland. It's a kind word and I appreciate it. It means
more trouble for you where you have already had so much.

Jean was born in Lawrence in 1877[52] but was never settled to live there except for the ten years from 1890 to 1900. Her mother was settled there from
1890 to 1900. Her father grew up and came of age there, but spent the last ten
years of his life in San Francisco—1874 to 1885 to be exact. Might she possibly
have a claim on New Hampshire through me? I have had a residence in New
Hampshire for twenty years.

------

50. On March 25 Jeanie Florence Frost (1876–1929), RF's sister, had been arrested in
Portland, Maine, for disturbing the peace; she was pronounced insane by local authorities. RF oversaw her commitment to the Maine Insane Asylum in Augusta, where she
lived until her death in 1929. See Rowell to RF, March 29, 1920: "Last Thursday morning
the Police Department of Portland, Maine, telephoned me to say that they had Jeanie
Frost in confinement and that she was demented. They wanted me to come there and
take her off their hands. This I declined to do. I have neither the authority nor the means
to take care of her. . . . I have paid her during the year $300 [from her annuity] so that there
is little less than nothing available for her now. . . . Was she born in Lawrence [Massachu-
setts], and were her father and mother residents of Lawrence? I wonder if she has lived
long enough in any one place of late to gain a settlement" (*SL*, 245).

51. See *LRF-1*, 691–692.

52. Although the Frost family lived in San Francisco at the time, Jeanie Florence Frost
was born in Lawrence on June 25, 1876 (not 1877, as RF has it here), while her mother and
RF, then two years old, were visiting her paternal grandfather.

If no state will have her and I haven't the means to have her taken care of in a private institution, what happens then? I am too shaken at the moment to know what to propose. It may not be an incurable case. My hope is that what has been pronounced insanity may turn out no more than the strange mixture of hysteria and eccentricity she has shown us so much of. If so, she might be perfectly manageable at large in the company of somebody like Louise Merriam. But I should want them to come to rest somewhere and should feel obliged to contribute a little to make it possible for them to. I wish I knew where to find Louise Merriam.[53]

We are just back from Amherst and in here where letters seem forever in reaching us. Will you wire at my expense if you wish to see me to instruct me as to how I shall approach the Portland police without assuming more responsibility than I am equal to? I may say that there isn't the haste that there would be if my personal attendance could do anything to soothe or comfort Jean. It's a sad business.

Sincerely yours

Robert Frost

---

53. Jeanie's long-time companion, Louie Merriam (whose first name RF here misspells). Born in 1871, she was five years Jeanie's senior. She grew up in or near Methuen, Massachusetts (census records place her there in 1880). The Frost family settled in that part of the state in 1885 when they returned from San Francisco after William Prescott Frost Jr. (1850–1885), RF's father, died. Merriam met Jeanie in the early 1890s, when Jeanie's and RF's mother Belle Moodie taught school in Methuen. In 1910, Jeanie and Louie shared a household in Monmouth, New Jersey (the census lists Jeanie as "head" of the household, Merriam as her "partner," and designates both as "teacher"). When Jeanie entered the University of Michigan in 1916—see LRF-1, 498–499, 603–604—Merriam accompanied her for at least part of her two-year enrollment. Census records taken on January 3, 1920, place her and Jeanie as boarders at the farm of Quincy B. Nash in Sullivan, New Hampshire (with both listed as teachers). But by March of that year Jeanie had evidently moved up to or near Portland, where she was arrested. As for where Merriam was on March 31, 1920: in Maine (as RF would soon discover), having arranged for Jeanie to be released into the custody of a doctor. In the early 1950s, Merriam exchanged a handful of letters with RF (held now at DCL), recalling the events of 1920 and several visits to Jeanie in Augusta during the ensuing decade. Merriam also reports having slapped RF in the face when he turned up in Portland in 1920. She died in Billerica, Massachussetts, on April 28, 1962.

[To Louis Untermeyer. ALS. LoC.]

Franconia N.H.

April 12 1920

Dear Louis:

I must have told you I have a sister Jeanie two or three years younger than myself. This is about her. It is not a story to tell everybody; but I want you to hear it if only so that you will understand why I am not as gay as I have been in my recent letters.

The police picked her up in Portland Maine the other day insane as nearly as we can make out on the subject of the war. She took the police for German officers carrying her off for immoral use. She took me for someone else when she saw me. She shouted to me by name to save her from whoever she thought I was in person.

I was prepared for this by what I saw of her a year ago (a year and a half ago) when she came to us at Amherst, a fugitive from a mob in a small town fifty miles away who were going to throw her into a mill pond for refusing to kiss the flag. She got Hell out of the war. She turned everything she could think of to express her abhorrence of it: pro-German, pacifist, internationalist, draft-obstructor, and seditionist.

She has always been antiphysical and a sensibilitist.[54] I must say she was pretty well broken by the coarseness and brutality of the world before the war was thought of. This was partly because she thought she ought to be on principle. She has had very little use for me. I am coarse for having had children and coarse for having wanted to succeed a little. She made a birth in the family the occasion for writing us once of the indelicacy of having children. Indelicacy was the word. Long ago, I disqualified myself for helping her through a rough world by my obvious liking for the world's roughness.

But it took the war to put her beside herself, poor girl. Before that came to show her what coarseness and brutality really were, she had been satisfied to take it out in hysterics, though hysterics as time went on of a more and more violent kind. I really think she thought in her heart that nothing would do justice to the war but going insane over it. She was willing to go almost too far to show her feeling about it, the more so that she couldn't find anyone who would go far enough. One half the world [*sic*] seemed unendurably bad

---

54. In "New Hampshire," RF applies this term to himself; he never chose to clarify it in print.

and the other half unendurably indifferent. She included me in the unendurably indifferent. A mistake. I belong to the unendurably bad.

And I suppose I am a brute in that my nature refuses to carry sympathy to the point of going crazy just because someone else goes crazy, or of dying just because someone else dies. As I get older I find it easier to lie awake nights over other people's troubles. But thats as far as I go to date. In good time I will join them in death to show our common humanity.

Always yours
Robert Frost

[To George Whicher (1889–1954), American scholar and educator. ALS. ACL.]

Franconia N.H.
April 12 1920

Dear George:

I had rather you heard it from me than in round about ways from other people that my sister has at last gone clearly insane. She took the Portland police who picked her up on the streets for German officers who wanted to carry her off for immoral use. She didn't know me when she saw me. It seems as if the poor girl had tried being everything, pro-German, pacifist, internationalist, draft-obstructor, and seditionist as a protest against the war; only to decide in the end that nothing would do her feelings justice but going insane. I dont know that I blame her. I admire the courage that is unwilling not to suffer everything that everyone is suffering everywhere. She has always been a sensibilitist and has now gone the way of the sensibilitist to the bitter end. It is a coarse brutal world, unendurably coarse and brutal, for anyone who hasn't the least dash of coarseness or brutality in his own nature to enjoy it with.

I don't know yet what hope there is for her, but it looks small.

I think of you more than I write to you. It wont be long before I see you again.

Ever yours
Robert Frost

[To Lesley Frost. ALS. UVA.]

Franc

April 23 '20

Dear Lesley:

Raymond buys the rest of the farm for another twenty-five hundred to avoid the risk of my having to mortgage it to Louis to raise money for the next farm.[55] Louis has pressed me so hard to lend me money on this one that I could hardly keep from suspecting him of wanting to get a foot hold here. I dont think Raymond would have minded that if he hadnt been afraid it mightnt end with Louis. The accepted theory is that the beginning of Jews is never the end of them. He would have brought others in his wake—or might have. My memory would have been execrated here if I had started a Jewish colony on the slope of Sugar Hill. It was only right anyway before I let Louis gain so much as a mortgage on the place to give Raymond the chance to take up the option he had on it. So we are out of Franconia before you kids have ever climbed Mt Washington.

I am almost sorry to be avoiding Raymond's society in this way. He has been good to us in spite of what we say. Carol likes him. They have been shooting woodchucks with the two rifles the last two or three afternoons. But Raymond makes himself almost too much one of the family. He walks in on us when we are eating and is in and out all day. You can imagine the effect on Mama when she is lying around half sick unable to get meals she can invite him to. He coolly waves a box of lunch he has brought down from Pecketts so we wont have to take care of him when I say we can't and propose sending him to Herberts.[56] I tell him all right let him spread his lunch on our table with ours and we will eat together. The darndest mix up! Irma stays in her room while it lasts. Mama swears. She thinks she knows how he regards us that he treats us so informally not to say rudely. I'm only puzzled. I doubt if he means much harm. I think the benefits will about even up if I introduce him to Harcourt.[57] He can't exactly despise us. Still we couldnt live so close to him.

---

55. For details about Raymond Holden's purchase of the Franconia property, see *YT*, 136–145.

56. Peckett's-on-Sugar-Hill Inn was a posh White Mountain resort in Franconia. RF had purchased his farm from the Herbert family.

57. Alfred Harcourt (1881–1954), RF's editor at Henry Holt and Company until 1919, when Harcourt left to found his own firm, Harcourt, Brace and Howe. The Macmillan

Wells offered me two hundred for the four poems Fragmentary Blue, Place for a Third, Goodby and Keep Cold, and For Once Then Something.[58] I took it to have a long thing over. It was about a dollar and a half a line which though less than it might have been was more than I have had before I think. I'm sorry Joseph Anthony is leaving me to the other people there. He's sure to be bettering himself though. He is going to take time to write another novel before he hires out again isn't he?[59]

Don't have Jean's troubles much on your mind. We will do all we can for her short of darkening our lives with what we are not to blame for. She is where she is for treatment. When she is well enough we will propose putting her on a small place somewhere (not near us) with Louie Merriam; and they can keep hens and bees together. That's when she gets better if she gets better. She has about ten or twelve hundred dollars left which can go toward making her position more respectable in the hospital. We'll keep track of her and see that she's not treated unkindly.

I wish we could have a farm on the edge of a river town where the boats went up and down—down to towered Camelot.[60] I wonder if Wilkinson will be free after May 4 for a ride up Burrough's way. I have put the search for a Connecticut farm in W. R. Brown's hands and shall have to let him go ahead

---

Company—not Henry Holt or Harcourt, Brace and Company—issued Holden's first book of poems, *Granite and Alabaster*, in 1922.

58. Again, Thomas B. Wells of Harper and Brothers. See RF to Lesley Frost, January 28, 1920. The poems here mentioned appeared in *Harper's* in July 1920.

59. Joseph Anthony worked in the publicity department at *Harper's*. He was indeed at work on another novel: Henry Holt and Company published *The Gang* in 1921. (Holt had published Anthony's first novel, *Rekindled Fires*, in 1918.) Anthony would also publish a substantial article on RF in the *New York Times* on July 4, 1920, which amounted to a review of the poems RF has just mentioned. Titled "Robert Frost, Realist and Symbolist," and based on conversations with the poet (and perhaps also with Lesley), the article tells us something about how RF managed his public persona: "It may be in place to point out that publication has always been incidental with Robert Frost—something that, in the midst of creative work and a unique range of interest in life, seems almost an interruption. . . . Mr. Frost is almost completely devoid of what Louis Untermeyer calls the 'cacoethes scribendi,' which might be termed the cosmic urge to print." The letters in the present volume show how wrong, on one or two counts, Anthony is, and yet what he says accurately reflects how RF wished to be seen. Later in the article, Anthony asserts—again, contrary to the evidence—that RF "shuns literary almost as much as pseudo-literary gatherings."

60. RF quotes from part 1, stanza 4, of Tennyson's "The Lady of Shalott."

with it. I'll write to Wilkinson that if Brown finds nothing we want I'll take the road with him. I'm afraid I've lost Wilkinson's letter with the address.[61]

Take care of your fingers.

No Hoover this year.[62]

Fishing season seven days off.

Took sugar pails down on Monday.

Be sure to see a ball game or two.

Good luck in tennis.

Louis clamors about Miscellany.[63]

All his ideas echo Sassoon at present.

Saw some good poetry by a Nora May French.[64]

Overall craze hasn't struck farms yet.[65]

Mosher gave me his reproduction of the first edition of Leaves of Grass.[66]

Davy Todd went up to get near view of Mars today.[67]

Raymond's water works cause anxiety.[68]

Spring peepers been going five nights.[69]

---

61. Warren R. Brown, a real estate agent in Amherst, was a family friend. We have been unable to identify Wilkinson and Burroughs.

62. Indeed, although Herbert Hoover would be placed in nomination at the Republican National Convention in June, he would not run in 1920. Warren G. Harding (1865–1923) was the standard-bearer.

63. See RF to Untermeyer, April 28, 1920.

64. Nora May French (1881–1907), a California poet and member of the bohemian literary circles of San Francisco.

65. A sharp deflationary depression befell the United States from January 1920 to July 1921.

66. Bibliophile and publisher Thomas Bird Mosher (1852–1923), whom RF had known for more than a decade (twelve of RF's letters to him are printed in *LRF-1*). Mosher lived in Portland, Maine, and gave RF a copy of his 1921 facsimile edition of Whitman's *Leaves of Grass* while RF was in Maine seeing to his sister Jeanie's affairs (RF spent a night at Mosher's place; see *YT*, 558). It was on this visit and others made that spring that RF saw the "beautiful farms" subsequently mentioned in the list.

67. David Peck Todd (1855–1939), a noted American astronomer. From 1881 to 1917, he was a professor of astronomy and director of the observatory at Amherst, a facility that he designed.

68. See RF to Lesley Frost, February 8, 1920.

69. Common name for *Pseudacris crucifer* (also known as *Hyla crucifer*), a small chorus frog, familiar to Lesley from her childhood in Derry. See RF's poem "Hyla Brook" (*CPPP*, 115–116), where their chirping is also dated, correctly for the region, to April. Hyla Brook was the name the family bestowed on a stream that ran through the farm at Derry.

Mr. Parker wanted to know if I would take principalship of Dow Academy at a price.[70]

Pretty damned English number of Yale Review.[71]

Louie Merriam writes to say that I now live surrounded by geese.[72]

Sonora would be a sonorous republic.[73]

Whom did you address Place for a Third to?[74]

I think I gave you the wrong name.

The Meiklejohns will spend next year in Italy.[75]

Beautiful farms cheap in Maine. Too far off.

---

70. Dow Academy, founded in 1884 by Moses A. Dow, was a preparatory school in Franconia, New Hampshire. Both W. F. Parker and Osman Parker served on the board of trustees.

71. In addition to RF's poem in memory of Edward Thomas ("To E.T."), the April 1920 number of the *Yale Review* included poems by the English poets Alfred Noyes, John Drinkwater, and Robert Nichols; a quasi-ethnographical essay called "The Anglo-American Entente," by George McLean Harper; an essay on "The English Actor of To Day," by A. B. Walkley; an essay on Edward Thomas by RF's friend and colleague George Whicher; an essay on Benjamin Disraeli; and reviews of a book by the English poet John Masefield and a book about Charles Dickens and his circle.

72. Merriam meant (if she said this) that RF was surrounded by dupes or fools (*OED*, goose: "a simpleton"). Doubtless the letter concerned Jeanie's psychotic break and hospitalization, and RF's handling of both. When Jeanie was arrested, Merriam presented herself to local authorities and asked that Jeanie be released into her custody. They refused, awaiting word from next of kin. In a letter to Wilbur Rowell, Merriam professed no trust in RF and offered to take Jeanie with her to Boston. Indeed, she secured Jeanie's release from the police into the care of a doctor in West Pownal, Maine, which is where RF found her when he arrived in the state and, on the advice of the doctor the police had first consulted, had her committed. See *YT*, 123–134.

73. Opposition to the new revolutionary government in Mexico City was strong in the northwest province of Sonora. On April 23, 1920, supporters of General Alvaro Obregon in Sonora drafted the so-called "Plan de Agua Prieta," repudiating the Mexican president, Venustiano Carranza.

74. Likely George R. Elliott. See RF to Lesley Frost, March 18, 1920.

75. President Alexander Meiklejohn of Amherst had announced that he and his wife, Nannine, would depart for a seven-month sabbatical in Italy in August 1920. This irritated the college trustees, who had launched a $3 million capital campaign and expected the president to take part in it. His refusal to do so exacerbated his already tense relations with the trustees, a tension that would lead to his forced resignation in 1923. See Adam R. Nelson, *Education and Democracy: The Meaning of Alexander Meiklejohn, 1872–1964* (Madison: University of Wisconsin Press, 2001), 102.

Just digging our parsnips and salsify.[76]
Is Chapin happy about the book?[77]
Cant be many weeks before we see you.

> Affectionately
>
> Papa

[To George R. Elliott. ALS. ACL.]

> Franconia N.H.
>
> April 27 1920

My dear Elliott:

I wonder if you have had the poems I sent you long enough to have come round to my way of thinking, that Good-bye and Keep Cold is probably the best of the lot. Let's see, I sent you three, and the one in blank verse, Place for a Third made four. Your sepulcral [*sic*] silence on this last is not I hope to be taken as too adverse. You got a copy of an early draught with some rough-nesses on it I had as soon you hadn't seen. I want to crowd it out of your mind with the better version I am enclosing, and then hear what you have to say sometime.

I return to the magazines with a group in Harpers in July: Fragmentary Blue, Place for a Third, Good-bye and Keep Cold and For Once Then Something. It is so long since I printed anything I feel as if I were about to begin all over again. For Once Then Something is calculated to tease the metrists,[78] Fragmentary Blue my personal friends who want to stop my writing lyrics. So be prepared. Perhaps I may as well send you copies of them, if you'll be-lieve that it isnt more than ten times in a life time that I come at anyone with manuscript this way. Try not to feel overwhelmed.

Mind you I dont insist on my lyrics—I dont insist on anything I write ex-cept as continuing to write it may be regarded as a gentle form of insistance [*sic*]. I find I dont get over liking the few lyrics I ever really liked in my first

---

76. Salsify (*Tragopogon porrifolius*) is a vegetable whose root and leaves can be used for cooking purposes. It is also known as white salsify, goatsbeard, vegetable oyster, and the oyster plant.

77. James Chapin (1887–1975) had illustrated the second (limited) American edition of *NB* in 1919.

78. The poem is in hendecasyllabics.

book, To the Thawing Wind, Reluctance, Mowing, October, My November Guest, Going for Water and one or two others I can't stop to look up the names of. The one I called Storm Fear is interesting as it shades off into the nearly lyrical that you allow me in.

But's [sic] let's not take trouble to agree on me in particulars.

My chief object in writing this is to say I am to be in Augusta Saturday[79] and may call you up by telephone from there to see if we couldn't meet in Portland or somewhere Saturday night. I shall be on my way to Boston for an evening with Copelands boys Monday.[80]

Sincerely yours
Robert Frost

[To Lesley Frost. The closing page (or pages) of the letter has not survived. ALS. DCL.]

Franconia N.H.
April 27 1920

Dear Lesley:

I'm sorry you've put yourself through the Latin. I don't know why I had you do it or let you. You have hardly met a decent person connected with the subject. You have found the subject itself as you might expect from the people that teach it, empty. I might have known all this beforehand but I didn't know it as well as I know it now that I've had the benefit of your experience. I have learned a lot from the way you have been treated. I hope you have learned you should catch yourself before you get any more out of sorts with the mock-English bitch and manage to end the term at ease and smiling.[81] Or if you think of any dramatic way of spitting on her course and getting out right now, I'm for it. I'm as bad tempered these days as you can possibly be.

Of course you understand where the pinch comes on Joseph Anthony. He thinks he got me in for the beggarly two hundred. But he didn't. I got myself

---

79. May 1, on another visit to Jeanie.

80. Charles Townsend Copeland, professor of English at Harvard. RF gave a talk to his class on May 3.

81. RF may be referring to Gertrude M. Hirst (1869–1962). A classicist born in Yorkshire and educated at Cambridge before she completed her PhD at Columbia, she joined the Barnard faculty in 1901 and retired as a full professor in 1943. For more on Lesley's education in Latin, see *LRF-1*, 589–591, 596–597.

in for it. I would have liked two dollars a line for the name of it, but I was about ready to publish [. . .]

[To Louis Untermeyer. Heading and date supplied by Untermeyer. ALS. LoC.]

[Franconia, NH]
[April 28, 1920]

Dear Louis:

The way it stands now I am in four deep with Harpers and I'm not sure that isn't four deeper than I wish I were in. The four are Fragmentary Blue, Place for a Third (namely Eliza), Goodbye and Keep Cold, and For Once Then Something (formerly Wrong to the Light).[82] What do you want of me for the Misc?[83] To tell you the truth I am feeling recessive for me and don't seem to know how I come to be publishing anything anyway. First you propose having I forget what and then A Parlor Joke and then A Star in a Stone Boat and then The Runaway: meaning that as a friend you are going to be delighted with anything I give you no matter how damaging it may prove to me as an author and to you as an editor. You know you old skeezicks you never managed to dislike heartily any poem I ever wrote except the one to E. T. and that is complicated with the war in such a way that you are afraid it may be a tract in favor of heroism. (But it isnt.) I hear you were down on the Cape seeing Comrad Aching and I almost hope you found there what will make it easy to go without anything from me. Sarah [*sic*] you say is hastening East with a trunk full of Lyrics to My Husband In Different Places, Buenos Aires, Rosario Punta Arenas etc. Carl has brought forth a mountain.

I'll tell you what puts me off the game a whole lot. It's the state of my affairs with publishers. MacVeagh spoiled all with Heinemann by making over-

---

82. Published in *Harper's* in July 1920. "Eliza" is the "third" in "Place for a Third."

83. In 1920 Untermeyer began publishing anthologies titled (with slight variations over the years) *A Miscellany of American Poetry,* for which the poets included their own selections from their newest work. Editions of the *Miscellany* (the first three published by Harcourt and the last by Granger) appeared in 1920, 1922, 1925, and 1927, with RF contributing poems for all but the 1925 edition. For the 1920 edition, RF ultimately chose "Plowmen," "Good-bye and Keep Cold," "The Runaway," "The Parlor Joke," "Fragmentary Blue," and "The Lockless Door." Sara Teasdale (1884–1933) (who had recently married), Conrad Aiken ("Comrad Aching"), and Carl Sandburg—mentioned later in the letter—also contributed poems. For details, see *RFLU,* 103–104.

tures to Mrs Nutt without consulting him.[84] Heinemann is put out and I am disappointed. My troubles over there arent ended and my troubles here are pretty well begun. Whats the use of writing stuff that I don't know who is to own in England or America. I am going to write drama after this and let poetry go to hell. But I don't say I will stay out of your Misc if I am committed. One poem more or less in print can't make much difference either way.

May see you in N.Y. before long or on neutral ground between there and here.

Whicher was wholly enthusiastic about Sassöon [sic].[85] You never saw my pome [sic] on The Importance of Being Versed in New England Ways. It ends:

> But one had to be versed in New England Ways
> Not to believe the Phoebes wept[86]

> To our better acquaintance!
> Robertus

[To Carl Van Doren (1885–1950), professor of English at Columbia and literary editor for The Nation from 1919 to 1922. Date and place derived from the coding on the telegram. RF was in Winsted, Connecticut, scouting out possible houses to buy; he passed through Cornwall Bridge, Connecticut, on the same trip. TG. Princeton.]

> [Winsted, CT]
> [May 10, 1920]

MR CARL VANDOREN

    OFFICE OF THE NATION NYC

CAN YOU HELP ABOUT ANY CORNWALL PLACE WIRE MY EXPENSE CORNWALLBRIDGE [sic] MONDAY OR TUESDAY

    ROBERT FROST

---

84. Lincoln MacVeagh succeeded Alfred Harcourt as managing editor at Henry Holt and Company in 1919. William Heinemann would soon become RF's British publisher; David Nutt, operated by Mrs. Alfred Nutt (widow of the firm's founder), had been his first.

85. See RF to Lesley Frost, February 28, 1920.

86. An early version of the closing lines of "The Need of Being Versed in Country Things."

[To Louis Untermeyer. ALS. LoC.]

Franc again

May 14 1920

Dear Louis

You know you can have anything you want of mine. The Harpers Group would be out in July. What do you say to waiting for the two in that you seem to like Goodbye and Keep Cold and Fragmentary Blue? A good story has attached to the Goodbye one. A friend of mine an unsophisticated farmer and real estate agent at Amherst handed a copy of it to the pomologists of the Agricultural College of Massachusetts to pass judgement on its pomological content. Their report was that pomologically it was all right, but poetically not: they would rewrite it and make a better poem of it. Thus I get it on all sides now-a-days! How would it be to hold the Misc till we get the agriculturalist's version to go with mine? At least it would be one more poem to help fill my allotted space.[87]

You did well not to send the thankless Bodenheim to Europe.[88] You have enough uses for your money taking mortgages on my next farm without patronizing poetry as she is written out of focus by the villain of the Village. Have no compunction.

I am just back from as far south as New Milford where I had a good talk with Lesley and had half a mind to summon you as per your promise of a recent letter. If I am that far down again next week land-looking as before would it be too much to call you to look at the property I am thinking of buying? Anyway hold yourself ready to be talked to on the telephone. Take a lozenge to clear your throat.

I have three or four houses on the possible list—one at Monson Mass, one at West Springfield Mass, one at Winsted Conn and one at New Milford. The call of three is pretty much.[89]

---

87. The real estate agent is Warren R. Brown. For an account of this "pomological" affair, which RF often retailed in readings, see *YT*, 560. Needless to say, the agriculturalist's version of "Good-bye and Keep Cold" did not make it into Untermeyer's *Miscellany*.

88. The poet Maxwell Bodenheim (1892–1954), the self-styled "Greenwich Village Villon." On the matter of the mortgage, see RF to Untermeyer, April 23, 1920.

89. RF ultimately chose a house in South Shaftsbury, Vermont. It is now the Robert Frost Stone House and Museum.

I got horribly kicked round for me as I rode. The agents, taking me for I don't know what, descended on me with loud lies to pick my bones. Little they suspected that it was the other way about and I was gluttonously picking theirs for literary purposes. I have an old poem on a real estate agent that only wants a little more material to finish it and make it marketable. I'm not sure that they haven't supplied it.

Tell Jean safety first:[90] always ascribe any offensive [*sic*] I seem to say to the Frostian humor: I am always joking. I don't believe I can have told her not to write to Elinor, but if I did say not to of course I must have been having my little joke however private. We folks are not going to go back on you folks intentionally. It rests with you not to let us do it unintentionally.

But I'll whisper you something that by and by I mean to say above a whisper: I have about decided to throw off the light mask I wear in public when Amy is the theme of conversation.[91] I dont believe she is anything but a fake, and I refuse longer to let her wealth, social position, and the influence she has been able to purchase and cozen, keep me from honestly bawling her out—that is, where I am called on to speak: I shant go out of my way to deal with her yet awhile, though before all is done I shouldn't wonder if I tried my hand at exposing her for a fool as well as fraud. Think of saying that as the French have based their free verse on Alexandrines so she has based her polyphonic prose on the rhythms of the periodic sentence of oratory.[92] She couldn't get away with that if she hadn't us all corralled by her wealth and social position. What

---

90. Jean Starr Untermeyer, Untermeyer's wife.

91. Amy Lowell.

92. Lowell discusses her "polyphonic" prose in several places. See the preface to her *Can Grande's Castle* (New York: Macmillan, 1918): "In the preface to *Sword Blades and Poppy Seed,* I stated that I had found the idea of the form [i.e., polyphonic prose] in the works of the French poet, M. Paul Fort. But in adapting it for use in English I was obliged to make so many changes that it may now be considered as practically a new form. The greatest of these changes was in the matter of rhythm. . . . Every form of art must have a base; to depart satisfactorily from a rhythm it is first necessary to have it. M. Fort found this basic rhythm in the alexandrine. But the rhythm of the alexandrine is not one of the basic rhythms to an English ear. . . . There appeared to be only one basic rhythm for English serious verse: iambic pentameter, which, either rhymed as in the 'heroic couplet' or un-rhymed as in 'blank verse,' seems the chief foundation of English metre. It is so heavy and so marked, however, that it is a difficult rhythm to depart from and go back to; therefore I at once discarded it for my purpose. Putting aside one rhythm of English prosody after another, I finally decided to base my form upon the long, flowing cadence of oratorical prose" (xi–xii).

could "periodic" have to do with it. Periodic sentences have no particular rhythm. Periodic sentences are sentences in which the interest is suspended as in a plot story. Nonsense and charlatanry—that's all that kind of talk amounts to. I'm sure she guessed without looking it up that there must be something recurrent like beat or pulse implied in periodic. She knew ladies were periodic because they recurred monthly. She's loony—and so periodic by the moon herself. Feeling as I do you don't think it would be honester for me to refuse to be bound between the covers of the same book with her do you?

I wish you could see the mts now. Every one wears one great white mountain birch laid out giantesque in the ravine system on its side like a badge of the north country. I don't know that that is any inducement to you to come up.

Ever yours

Robert Fross

Please let me know to onct[93] if nearly all this meets with your approval.

[*To Wilbur L. Cross (1862–1948), professor of English at Yale and editor of the* Yale Review. *ALS. Yale.*]

Franconia NH.

May 15 1920

Dear Mr Cross:

I should have answered your letters sooner, but I have been busy retiring from education. I discovered what the Amherst Idea was that is so much talked of, and got amicably out.[94] The Amherst Idea as I had it in so many words from its high custodian[95] is this: "Freedom for taste and intellect." Freedom from what? "Freedom from every prejudice in favor of state home church morality, etc." I am too much a creature of prejudice to stay [and]

---

93. Dialect form of "once." See Noah Webster, *Dissertations on the English Language* (Boston: Isaiah Thomas, 1789): "In the middle states also, many people [say] oncet and twicet. This gross impropriety [has] prevalence among a class of very well educated people; particularly in Philadelphia and Baltimore" (111).

94. RF resigned his position at Amherst in February 1920.

95. Presumably Alexander Meiklejohn.

listen to such stuff. Not only in favor of morality am I prejudiced, but in favor of an immorality I could name as against other immoralities. I'd no more set out in pursuit of the truth than I would in pursuit of a living unless mounted on my prejudices. There was all the excuse I needed to get back to my farming. Hocking says if I probed any college to its inmost idea I couldn't teach in it. But by any college Hocking means simply Harvard. The trouble with Hocking is he belongs at Yale where he formed himself in the plastic age. He will never be happy anywhere else. Neither will Mrs Hocking.[96]

But why these confidences in a letter to one who has never shown the least curiosity in my hearing about Amherst? What I set out to tell you was that having kicked myself free from care and intellectuality, I ought to find time to polish you off the group of poems I had in mind to offer you—perhaps A Star in a Stone-boat and two or three short poems. Do you think you could stand an unrelated group such as Harpers is about to publish?[97] My plan would be to return to print hurling fistfulls right and left. You may not be willing to fall in with anything so theatrical. I wonder if I know you well enough to ask you to let me wait till some number when the poverty of your material would thrust me automatically into the place of prominence in your make-up. Of course there might never be such a number. I could wait a year to see; and then if there wasn't—You let me know some time when you are not too well off for poetry or prose. No hurry.

> Always yours
> Robert Frost

---

96. William Ernest Hocking (1873–1966), professor of philosophy at Harvard, whom RF and his family befriended in 1915. His wife was Agnes (O'Reilley) Hocking. Hocking taught at Yale from 1908 to 1914, during which time he published his first major book, *The Meaning of God in Human Existence* (New Haven, CT: Yale University Press, 1912). For discussion of the latter, see *LRF-1*, 277–278.

97. For the group in *Harper's,* see notes to RF's March 18, 1920, letter to his daughter Lesley.

[To Louis Untermeyer. Date supplied by Untermeyer. ALS. LoC.]

Franconia, Last Moments

[June 3] 1920

Dear Louis:

All right then if you have a thousand dollars you can lend me please send it with your blessing to my brand new address Monson (MONSON) Mass. some day this week.[98] I may have to ask you for some more in a month or so. The thousand will fix me up for the present. Gee I'm blue over this move to new scenes and neighbors. Encourage me in it as you always have in all things.

You'd think you might let me see some of the poems the rest of you are filling the Misc with.[99] Are any of them half bad?

I am afraid I am trying to write too many plays at once for the good of the novel I am also writing.[100] Never mind. It gives me a feeling of business if not of art. I wish I could throw style over: I seem slowed up by it. I dont know how it is with you.

Be as good as it is in your nature to be.

Yours ever

Robert Frost

[To John Gould Fletcher (1886–1950), American poet, later associated with the Fugitive-Agrarian school. ALS. Arkansas.]

Franconia N.H.

June 3 1920

Dear Mr Fletcher:

Why didn't you tell me more about those friends over there I haven't seen since nineteen-fifteen. Jack Haines[101] probably speaks of me as faithless. But I'm not. I think of him all the time when I'm awake and part of the time when

---

98. RF had been house hunting in Monson. He did not, however, buy a property there. He soon returned the loan unused.

99. See notes to RF's April 28, 1920, letter to Untermeyer.

100. No manuscript or typescript of a novel by RF has survived and no plays dating from this period, although fragments of dialogue (perhaps drafts of plays) are scattered throughout RF's notebooks.

101. John W. Haines (1875–1966), a Gloucestershire friend of RF's from his time in England.

I am asleep. I'm just a bad letter-writer—that's all. I must send him the E.T. poem if you think it will help him forgive me for the letters I haven't written.[102]

Thanks for taking the poem you took to exemplify me to the English. It belongs to the English anyway. I wrote it in England about some English elms at our house, the Gallows, in Gloucestershire where we lived with the Abercrombies a while after the war started.[103]

So you are just back from seeing Monroe [*sic*] plain.[104] I can't call what you make me feel homesickness, because the Poetry Bookshop isn't home though I once lived there for a week with my whole family; but the wish I have to see the old place amounts almost to homesickness.

Can't we see each other for a talk about such things sometime?

Ask Conrad Aiken to let me know where he keeps himself any more, will you?

Sincerely yours
Robert Frost

[To Louis Untermeyer. ALS. LoC.]

Franconie[105]
June 19–20 1920

Dear Louis:

You remember the thousand dollars you lent me late week before last. Well I always meant to repay you in full, but as day after day dragged by and my position seemed no stronger financially, I began to despair of ever being able to repay you even in part. I did my best to believe that as it is more blessed to give than to receive, so, obviously, it must be more blessed to receive than to give back. In vain. Nothing would comfort me. My New England upbringing had put me beyond help of such sophistries. Life was becoming serious, not

---

102. "To E.T.," RF's elegy for Edward Thomas; published in the *Yale Review* in April 1920.

103. "The Sound of the Trees," collected in *MI*.

104. Harold Monro (1879–1932), proprietor of the Poetry Bookshop in London and publisher of *Poetry and Drama*.

105. French spelling of the German region Franken, the central-southern region of Germany, after which Franconia was named.

to say a burden under the weight of owing you so much when suddenly I had a saving thought, which was to apply the thousand dollars you had lent me in paying it back. Luckily I had the thousand intact. Isn't it funny? We have had one of the great affairs of the purse that will go jingling down through Am Lit—and all in the space of ten days elapsed time and neither of us one cent the worse off for the experience. In the supreme hour of trial you proved generous—you gave me all you had offered—and I proved grateful and honorable—I paid you back with thanks. We are out of the woods where we can crow. When we ask ourselves, as we must in our position, what boshterity will say of us in this transaction, we know beforehand what it will say. It will say that we were both perfect. Even our wives will say no less I think. Hurrah for our wives!

Suppose in my agony of debt I had sought forgetfulness like a drunkard by plunging deeper into debt and tried to borrow, say, of Harcourt Brace and Howe of Henry Holt and Company or both together, how would I have stood with boshterity? Thats what you have to think of.

> *O Thyme whose vurdicks mock our own*
> *The only righteous judge art thou.*[106]

I have decided several things that I will tell you about later. One of them is that I will probably go further off for my farm and fare cheaper. This came to me a trifle suddenly the day I got to Monson. The object in life is hard to keep in mind. I let it slip sometimes, but never for long—never for good and all any way. In this instance it is apples bees fishing poetry high school and nine or ten rooms. Nothing else matters. Nearness to no particular city matters. Farming in style doesn't matter. Open fireplaces don't matter. Neither does my next book (as book). It would be interesting to make a list of all the things that don't matter and that I mean to consider less and less. We could have a bonfire and a ceremonial burning of them all some night when you come to see us in the Aroostook.[107] The United States wouldn't be on the list. Wouldn't be, I say. I can promise to stay on this side of the Canadian line. I think too I can promise to keep out of teaching for a while, though I have had several invitations to come back to it since I pulled out of Amherst.

---

106. Adapted from the last stanza of "On a Bust of Dante," by Thomas William Parsons (1819–1892).

107. The northernmost county in Maine.

Fishing bees poetry apples nine rooms and a high school! All of which we now think are within our unaided means. So I am enclosing your thousand dollars, old friend, with a thousand thanks for the support it gave me when I was ambitious for a business farm at a business distance from big cities. Saved in time!

Ever thine
Robbered Frossed

[*To Louis Untermeyer. Date derived from postmark. ALS. LoC.*]

Franconie
[June 25, 1920]

Dear Louis:

You got the check yesterday I trust and here's the proof today.[108] You must forgive the delay with both: I had been scattering myself all over the Six States—literally: I pared my fingernails in Winsted Conn, had my hair cut in Portland Maine and a tooth out in Brattleboro Vt. Nothing but the Last Resurrection will ever reassemble the disjected members. In the disintegration of body and soul you cannot blame me if I neglected my friends.

The proof only just came forward from Monson and I hasten to give it a dab and return it to you. No time to read anybody's but my own. Your Tadpole got me by the tail and twisted it.[109] There seem to be eleven poets where there were ten. Is Fletcher the new one? Glad he's in. Couldn't you let Kreymborg make the twelfth?[110] Then we would all be poets in a friendly dozenship and could sign ourselves.

Yours dozenly
R.F.

---

108. Proofs for *A Miscellany of American Poetry;* see the notes to RF's April 28, 1920, letter to Untermeyer.

109. Untermeyer's poem "Boys and Tadpoles."

110. Alfred Kreymborg did not, in fact, appear in this *Miscellany;* the eleven poets therein anthologized are, in alphabetical order, Conrad Aiken, John Gould Fletcher, RF, Vachel Lindsay, Amy Lowell, James Oppenheim, E. A. Robinson, Carl Sandburg, Sara Teasdale, Jean Starr Untermeyer, and, of course, Untermeyer himself.

[To Carl Van Doren. ALS. Princeton.]

Franconia N.H.

June 26 1920

Dear Mr Van Doren:

Nothing came of my day in the Cornwalls, though I looked as high as your village on the plateau and as low as the villages on the river.[111] The country was right, but there was no house or farm to our measure. I don't know that there is anywhere. I have had a fruitless hunt thus far. But never mind, I have learned more of small town New England than Timothy Dwight and more of the nature of real estate agents than they have to know of human nature to do business.[112] And Franconia will do a while longer as an enforced residence.

I dont forget your having spoken for a poem when I should have one to print with people in it. When I should have one, have one to print, have one to print with people in it—three conditions. I for my part might be willing to waive all but the second for the editor of such an unagricultural journal as The Nation who can honestly say he has followed the plough twenty-five miles in a day.

I came in my recent wanderings on G. R. Elliot [*sic*], the critic who wrote so acceptably of me in The Nation, and took him to friend.[113] Could you find me a spare copy of the number his criticism appeared in? I have lost the only copy I had.

Always yours sincerely

Robert Frost

[To Harriet Moody (1857–1932), American educator, entrepreneur, and patron of the arts. ALS. Chicago.]

Franconia N.H.

June 26 1920

My dear Harriet Moody:

I never forget old friends; so you needn't be so reproachfully silent about it. What keeps me from writing to them is that I forget their street numbers.

---

111. See the notes to RF's May 10, 1920, telegram to Van Doren.

112. Timothy Dwight IV (1752–1817), theologian, president of Yale College (1795–1817), and poet of the so-called "Hartford Wits" school.

113. George R. Elliott; see RF's March 20, 1920, letter to him (and notes).

Why don't you live decently in a small town where you don't need a street number to be found? It goes against me to have to write a letter as I write this without knowing where it's going to and what's to become of it. I only do it to be able to say I have done my duty.

I wonder if you are wondering off there what I have decided about the farm at West Cummington.[114] How shall I decide about anything at my age. I have kicked myself out of Amherst with some finality. But perhaps you haven't heard what I have been doing: For the moment I have ceased from teaching forever or until I shall begin to grow hungry again for food. Manly has asked if I will give a course in prosody some term at Chicago.[115] That would be, not next year, but the year after, as I understand it, by which time I ought to begin to grow hungry again for food (as distinguished from truth). So I shall probably take him up, though as yet I haven't given him his answer any more than I have you yours about the farm.

To be right the farm at West Cummington would have to give us a summer and winter house of not less than nine rooms and a high school within two miles. I'm afraid it cant be made out or made to do either. And it seems a pity. I'm particularly sorry because I dont see but that it makes it necessary for you to sell there and buy a sugar orchard farm somewhere in New Hampshire or Vermont with us where we can all go into the fancy sugar business together.[116]

If this seems to offend against friendship, please remember that I should probably see more of you in one term of lecturing at Chicago than in a cycle of farming at West Cummington. Really now shouldn't I?

And if you are still unplacated, here are a few poems in manuscript enclosed to make a bad matter worse.[117]

Are you coming this way this summer?

Always yours faithfully
Robert Frost

---

114. In 1914 Moody bought the William Cullen Bryant Homestead in Cummington, Massachusetts, which she then had dismantled and moved to its present location, on the road between Pittsfield and Northampton. She had advised RF about farms in the area.

115. John Matthews Manly (1865–1940), a noted Chaucerian and former army intelligence cryptographer, was head of the English department at the University of Chicago from 1898 to 1933.

116. A jest, but not an impertinent one: Moody owned and operated a successful catering business. She launched her Home Delicacies Association in 1890, and, by 1911, had opened a branch in London. In 1920 she opened Le Petit Gourmet, a restaurant, in Chicago.

117. The enclosure was separated from the letter; we do not know which poems RF sent.

[To John Gould Fletcher. ALS. Arkansas.]

Franconia N.H.

June 26 1920

Dear Fletcher:

I am well-content to be accepted on such terms. Thanks particularly for what you said about dialect and about my other-than-New-England poetry. But thanks for everything.[118]

I should be tempted to thank you too for your fairness to Ezra, if it were any of my business.[119] A lot of us owe him a lot for where we are and the least we can do him in squaring accounts is an occasional justice when it comes natural.

Now more than ever I think we ought to see something of each other before you go back. You'd be welcome with us here. But if this is too far to come, perhaps we could arrange to meet somewhere half way.

Sincerely yours

Robert Frost

[To Otto Manthey-Zorn (1879–1964), professor of German at Amherst and RF's friend since 1917. ALS. ACL.]

Franconia N.H.

June 28 1920

Dear Zorn:

Every time I set out farm hunting I planned to bring up in the end at Amherst to relieve you of the furniture and get my instructions how to behave and vote while you are absent in Germany.[120] But as each trip came to nothing,

---

118. Fletcher had written about RF in "Some Contemporary American Poets," *The Chapbook: A Monthly Miscellany* (London: The Poetry Bookshop, May 1920)—a wide-ranging essay that also treats E. A. Robinson, Amy Lowell, Edgar Lee Masters, Vachel Lindsay, Conrad Aiken, and Wallace Stevens (among others).

119. Ezra Pound (1885–1972), American poet, whom RF came to know during his time in England (Pound favorably reviewed both *ABW* and *NB*).

120. RF had stored furniture from his Amherst house with the Manthey-Zorns when he abruptly departed Amherst in February 1920. Manthey-Zorn's sojourn in Germany from June 1920 to January 1921 resulted in his *Germany in Travail* (Boston: Marshall Jones, 1922).

I put off till the next my final visit to Amherst, till now most of the time is used up and most of my car-fare too and [I] don't know what to say about either you or the furniture. Just like me. I suppose it wouldn't do—it would sound outrageous—to wish you could run up here on your increased salary which we have read so much about in the papers and set in with me for a forty-eight hour talk. There are a lot of things I'd like to ask you before you are in a position to know the answers. But probably you have asked yourself most of them. As I am inclined to imagine it from here you are going to an overwhelmingly new experience. But probably it wont seem so very different from life as it goes everywhere—breakfast dinner and supper—roads and pavements outdoors and chairs and beds indoors. There will be the little tell-tale incidents that you will get something out of because you will be looking for them. Those will be the best, the most fun anyway, because the most personal. And there will be the heaped up statistics that almost anybody can get at even from this distance and that everybody is pawing and pulling and hauling to make them mean what he pleases. You'll suffer the same old mental strain in inference-making, the same old sense of bamboozlement we have here and now on the eve of punishing the democratic party for the sins of the author of the fourteen points.[121] That anyway wont be any different in Germany. You'll make your own inference and say what you think, all the time wishing to the devil inside that it was what you positively knew. I don't believe things will be very different in Heaven even.—Yes they will.

If I can't see you again, good voyage to you this way by letter. I'll often wish I could be with you, but should wish it more if I thought I could help you understand a world turned upside-down. I have half a mind to enclose a poem on my inability to understand things for you to remember me by.

Best wishes to the family.

Always yours
Robert Frost

---

121. Woodrow Wilson delivered his "Fourteen Points" address—a declaration of principles that must underlie any lasting peace, as he understood it—before the United States Congress on January 8, 1918. RF saw the 1920 presidential election campaign between the Republican Warren G. Harding and the Democrat James M. Cox (1870–1957) as a referendum on Wilson's handling of peace negotiations with Germany and his support for the League of Nations.

[To Louis Untermeyer. ALS. LoC.]

Franconia N.H.

July 12 1920

Dear Louis:

   Has Merrill Root been so foolish as to mention my name or the name of Amherst to make way for his poetry anywhere?[122] You have something more than any resemblance you see in his poetry to connect him with me. The last I saw of his poetry it was pretty much his own and what wasn't his own wasn't mine I'm sure. I won't believe he has been coming under my influence after having got out from under my shadow. He never was a member of my class of geniuses anyway. I had him in an enormous crowd I read Gammer Gurton's Needle[123] with and he has perhaps called at the house half a dozen times. I count him a friend, and just for that reason I have left him to break in among you poets without my doubtful help. Now that two or three of you have noticed him of your own motion I should think I could speak without prejudice to his chances. He's not in the same classification with Raymond Holden whom I throw out the window onto your spear points.[124] I'm pretty sure he's a poet. It would please me a lot if you should see it as I see it. Max Eastman's[125] good opinion ought to weigh with you if Harriet Monroe's doesn't. I say no more. But I think you ought to make your half-inclination whole and go in for Root, or rooting for Root, a little. He's some sort of a homely devil of perversity that should commend itself more to you than to me. His father is a poor preacher and Merrill is himself a Quaker preaching, though not ordained, in orthodox pulpits. I don't know how he gets by in any pulpit with the radical stuff that froths out of him. He had his troubles as a conscientious objector before the fact, if you are not too tired of the breed.

   But Raymond Holden. They say we poor expect the rich to consider the poor but when we are asked to consider the rich, we start talking a priori. One of the books I am writing at this moment is to be called On Looking into

---

   122. Edward Merrill Root (1895–1973), poet and, later, educator and anti-Communist polemicist; he had studied under RF at Amherst.

   123. RF taught the play, one of the earliest extant comedies in English, at Amherst.

   124. Raymond Holden, a man of some means, had purchased RF's property in Franconia (see *YT*, 136–145). His first book of poems, *Granite and Alabaster*, appeared in 1922 (New York: Macmillan).

   125. Max Eastman (1883–1969), American critic, journalist, and poet.

the Rich. Won't I consider them though! I count myself peculiarly qualified for looking into them by my freedom from prejudice against them. Neither they nor their trappings make me the least bit embarrassed self-conscious or unhappy with the bitches and sons of bitches. I have come right up to them and looked in without fear and without even dislike. I believe I honestly liked them not only for themselves but for their money before I looked into them. I was just the one for doing them justice I should say. But what have I seen in them? Well the book tells that. Buy the book.

Yours everly

Robert Frost

You are the first person I have mentioned Merrill Root to in any terms.

[*To Wilbur Rowell. ALS. UVA.*]

Franconia N.H.

July 16 1920

Dear Mr Rowell:

There is not the least reason why you should do anything about the money before the notes you speak of fall due.

You ought not to have to be bothered with Jean's small bills. I wonder if I couldn't take the money from you in a lump and pay it out to the Hospital at Augusta as it is called for at the rate of six dollars a week as I understand it. Would that protect me? It hardly seems worth while for me to be made her guardian to handle the little money that is left. But you know better than I what is safe and proper.

I have been over twice to see Jean, and should have been oftener if the journey weren't so long and expensive. When I was with her she was nearly rational—not quite. But she is in a semi-violent ward and the doctors tell me she is noisy and destructive at times. Her general health is bad. I should think she might not live long. Whether she is as happy as may be where she is I don't quite make out. She expressed to me a wish to stay and "take the treatment." She shows a disposition to run away, though, that deprives her of the freedom that milder cases have of walking in the yard. The doctors say she must have been years in reaching her present state. I thought you might like to know how it is with her. She speaks with the greatest appreciation of your kindness to her.

Sincerely yours

Robert Frost

[To Lola Ridge (1873–1941), Irish American poet, editor, and political activist. We have been unable to locate the manuscript, which was sold off in 1957. We rely instead on a typed copy made at the time of the sale—by Robert Black, a rare book dealer—and held now at ACL.]

Franconia, N.H.

July 17, 1920

Dear Lola Ridge:

Some one wrote me from a department of The New Republic the other day that if I didn't subscribe after all he had urged me, he should begin to have his doubts about how seriously I took the job of being a citizen. But if he had taken his job of being an advertiser a little more seriously he would have known that in the current number of The New Republic at that moment he had an "argument" to bring me to terms better than any unveiled threat.[126] What could I have answered if he had come at me this way: Confess that you didn't know that The New Republic was right now full of your praises as sung by your friend Lola Ridge and you wouldn't have known to thank her if I hadn't told you? Then he would have had me for a life subscription, I should have been so ashamed to think what had nearly come of my not keeping up with the paper. I am afraid there is not the close connection it is maliciously whispered there is between the editorial and the business departments of our best magazines.

It was only by accident and no thanks to him that I learned what you had been doing to encourage me. Friends had been supposing in their letters that I must like the nice things being said about me lately but not till yesterday did any one tell me where so I could look the nice things up.[127]

Nice things is not the right name for such criticism.

No one has been so poetical about my poetry as you are in the passages about the little natures that whimper and look from side to side and about the snow-touched leafless trees under the clouded winter sky.[128] Your power

---

126. RF refers to Ridge's article about him: "Covered Roads," *New Republic*, June 23, 1920, 131–132.

127. Possibly Untermeyer, to whom RF also wrote on July 17 and who appears to have been an acquaintance of Ridge's (see *LRF-1*, 642).

128. See the following passages from Ridge, "Covered Roads": "His less traveled road led to no poetical Coney Island of pyrotechnics and scenic surprises. It meandered over snowed-in countrysides and stopped at lonely farmhouses, where life, cornered and whimpering to itself, glanced piteously from side to side. . . . His book, North of Boston,

lies in no very different direction from mine. You would do the people of this country, if not the things, better than I.

I am venturing out with a little of the little I have written while I was at Amherst and (as you may have heard) I have left Amherst to write a little more.[129] I think I <u>show</u> as sufficiently reckless for my years to be printing new poetry at the exact moment when you are speaking so beautifully of my old poetry. The main thing is to look reckless—and then try to feel as reckless as you look.

I wonder what you have been about. I suppose scattered poems in the magazines where I wouldn't see them. When will they appear in the next book where I would see them?[130]

> More than ever your friend for this,
>
> Robert Frost

[To Sidney Cox (1889–1951), American scholar and critic, teaching at the University of Montana at Missoula at the time. RF enclosed typescripts of several poems: "Plowmen," "Fire and Ice," "The Onset," "A Star in a Stone-Boat," "Two Look at Two," and "Silver Lizards" (the working title of "A Hillside Thaw"). ALS. DCL.]

> Franconia N.H.
>
> July 17 1920

Dear Sidney:

I trust you know I think of you away off out there at least a thousand times to every once I write to you.

You tell me about yourself when you write and I'll tell you about myself now.

I've kicked myself out of Amherst and settled down to revising old poems when I am not making new ones. I published a set of four in the July Harpers which you may or may not have seen. I'm sure you liked them in either case because they were mine. I shall enclose with this a few more. Try them on the baby and if they do no harm it will prove that my work ought to have

---

suggests a forest of leafless trees lightly silvered with snow. The still whiteness of snow pervades all his work."

129. "Fragmentary Blue," "Place for a Third," "Good-by and Keep Cold," and "For Once, Then, Something" were published in the July 1920 issue of *Harper's*.

130. Ridge's second volume of verse, *Sun-Up and Other Poems,* was published by B. W. Huebsch in 1920. She had been placing poems in *The New Republic, Poetry, Playboy* (the literary magazine that ran from 1919 to 1924), and *Others.*

been included in a recent anthology of verse for children that I hear it was left out of.[131] Never mind. The main thing is that you like your job in Montana or you would have written to me to complain of it. Teaching is all right and I dont mean to speak of it with condescension. I shall have another go at it before the last employe[132] is fired. I believe in teaching but I dont believe in going to school. Everyday I feel bound to save my consistency by advising my pupils to leave school. Then if they insist on coming to school it is not my fault: I can teach them with a clear conscience.

We seem on the point of leaving Franconia. The hawser is cast off in fact, though we lie still against the wharf. They say when you run away from a place it is yourself you are generally running away from and that goes with you and is the first thing you meet in the next place you turn up. In this case it is frosts we are running away from and Frosts can hardly help going with us since Frosts we are ourselves. If you ever see any talk of me in print you may notice that it is my frostiness that is more and more played up. I am cold, snow-dusted and all that.[133] I can see that I am in a way or I would write to my best friends oftener. Don't say amen to that too fervently if you don't want to hurt my feelings and your own prospects.

My best to the whole family of you.

> Always yours
> Robert Frost

[To Wilbur L. Cross. ALS. Yale.]

> Franconia N.H.
> July 17 1920

Dear Mr Cross:

Of course use the poem to Edward Thomas as you propose. Anything you can say or do to keep him from being forgotten helps me pay the debt of friend-

---

131. Cox's son Arthur Macy Cox had been born on May 2, 1920. The "anthology" is likely Roger Inchen, ed., *One Thousand Poems for Children* (Philadelphia: Jacobs, 1920).

132. Not an error, but a variant spelling of "employee."

133. A reference not only to Ridge's "Covered Roads" but also to Theodore Maynard's "Snow the Predominant Note in Frost's Poetry," *New York Tribune*, June 27, 1920. For more about the latter, see RF's September 4, 1920, letter to Braithwaite and the notes thereto.

ship I owe him. Do you think it would be better to give his name in full in-stead of just his initials when you reprint the poem in a book without the ac-companying essay?[134]

Coming with a group of poems for The Review soon.[135] One or two more last looks at them and I should be as ready as I'll ever be to part with them.

Sincerely yours

Robert Frost

Thanks for your interest in Place for a Third.[136]

R.F.

[*To Louis Untermeyer. ALS. LoC.*]

Franconia N.H.

July 17 1920

Dear Louis:

If you have enough poems like The New Adam and A Marriage[137] to make up a volume without the help of anything else of any other kind, you can set yourself so far apart from anyone else that you wont even need boundary lines let alone stone walls to mark you off. I dont know where else to look for that full-savoring sensuousness of thirty years that ploughs where twenty years used to tickle. It would be one thing to do and of course you would do it well. Why plan to have a little of everything (as I'll bet you do) in your next book. Why not hew to the idea of your title however small a book it leaves you for a dollar and a half? Don't have the The Pollywog in it for instance. Save the Pollywog to go with the The Frog when you shall write it.

---

134. Cross had asked permission to reprint "To E.T." under the title "To Edward Thomas" in *American and British Verse from the Yale Review* (New Haven, CT: Yale Univer-sity Press, 1920). George Whicher's essay "Edward Thomas" had accompanied RF's poem in the April 1920 issue of the *Yale Review.*

135. "A Star in a Stone-Boat," "The Onset," and "Misgiving," all published in the *Yale Review* in January 1921.

136. In the July number of *Harper's.*

137. Both appeared in Untermeyer's *Miscellany* (1920), as did Untermeyer's "Boy and Tadpoles" ("The Pollywog," as RF here calls it) and "Intercession" (mentioned later). In the rest of the letter, RF reviews other contributors to the book, which had yet to appear. See the notes to RF's June 25, 1920, letter to Untermeyer.

Intercession is the lovely one of the lot. But I don't know that you want to be encouraged to be lovely in that sense. Being lovely might interfere with being energetic, which is what you always give the effect of being at your best even in such a thing as The Pollywog. And no matter whom you translate he comes through you energized and more energetic than he went in. It would be foolish not to reckon with that and not make yourself out of what you are.

While I am about it I may as well have my shot at the other contributors to your Misc. When shall I listen to anything I like better than The Long Hill and The Water Lilies.[138] The perfect accent. And neither of them the least bit wrested to bring in Sappho or the bursting heart. You must forgive me for liking these two poems about as well as anything you have in the book.

Vachel I don't have to deal with because these poems have been withdrawn. I tried to read his Golden Whales aloud in company last night.[139] It failed to get me by the hyperbolics.

All I want to say about Amy is she had better enquire of the Smithsonian Institute if the Indian or any other American but H.D. (and shes an expatriate) wails in the two separate vowels "a" and "i" after the Greeks.[140] Her poem on the resolute young men you can't have too much of in this world[141] reminds me of one on A Pair of Pants a lady of Europe wrote before the war made atrocities popular. She was said to dance it out as Duncan was then dancing verse.[142] It went:

---

138. Both by Sara Teasdale.

139. Printed not in Untermeyer's *Miscellany* but as the title poem to Vachel Lindsay's *The Golden Whales of California and Other Rhymes in the American Language* (New York: Macmillan, 1920).

140. RF refers to the last (and by far the longest) of Amy Lowell's poems in the *Miscellany*: "Funeral Song for the Indian Chief Blackbird, Buried Sitting Upright on a Live Horse on a Bluff Overlooking the Missouri River." It begins: "He is dead / Our Chief. / Aï! Aï! Aï! Aï!" H. D.: American poet Hilda Doolittle (1886–1961), then living in England.

141. "New Heavens for Old," with such Whitmanesque lines as these:

Young men with naked hearts jeering between iron house-fronts,
Young men with naked bodies beneath their clothes
Passionately conscious of them,
Ready to strip off their clothes,
Ready to strip off their customs, their usual routine,
Clamouring for the rawness of life,
In love with appetite . . .

142. Isadora Duncan (1877–1927).

"We women are restricted to a glance
At where the virile member bags the pants."

I only remember the authoress wasn't Felicia Hemans.[143] Anyway Amy is more exciting when she calls for young men not incapable than when she takes five hundred thin lines to bury an Indian Chief on horseback. No to her. The Chief is buried all right.

Carl's idiom and lingo would be enough if there was nothing else in the book. He's a box of pen points. Gimme Aprons of Silence; Crapshooters; Man, the Man Hunter; Blue Island Intersection; and Pencils.[144]

Robinson the cunning devil isn't forgetting his effects when he pretends to have only the one small poem to be lost among our many. I'd like to punish him for his selfish calculation if I could see where to strike. But I don't unless it is his calling the sunset a sound for the rhyme.[145]

Fletcher is a whole lot better than I expected him to be. I have mixed him up too much with Amy to be fair to him.

There's a lot of good in Aiken. Maybe it's all good (though never the thriller that The Morning Song of Senlin is); but it is too formidable, especially for leading off with.[146] Our misfortune more than his that his name begins with an A. You couldn't get him further into the book by arranging us in some other order on some other principle? Beans is a good Boston subject, and the beans are the best part of the poem.[147] Wouldn't I be likely to say so?

---

143. Hemans (1793–1835) was among the most widely read British poets of her day. The joke is about the impossibility of a nineteenth-century British female poet, of such unimpeachable rectitude, discoursing of "virile members."

144. All collected in the *Miscellany*.

145. E. A. Robinson's sole contribution to the *Miscellany* was the short lyric "Dark Hills"; RF refers to the second line and its partner in rhyme, line 4 ("Where sunset hovers like a sound / Of golden horns that sang to rest / Old bones of warriors under ground").

146. Conrad Aiken's long poem "First Movement from 'The Pilgrimage of Festus'" led the book (part 3 of which RF has in mind in speaking of "beans": "Festus, planting beans in the early morning. . . ." etc.); Untermeyer had reprinted Aiken's "Morning Song from 'Senlin'" in his popular anthology *Modern American Poetry* (New York: Harcourt, Brace and Howe, 1919).

147. Boston had been known to the rest of the nation as Bean Town since 1907, when, in promotion of an event called "Old Home Week," the city distributed stickers bearing an image of two hands clasped above a pot of beans. Men in the shipping trade had called Boston Bean Town since the seventeenth century.

James should have read again what Korah said to Moses and then written his denunciation of Woodrow.[148] "You take too much upon seeing all the congregation (namely the Senate) are holy every one of them and the Lord is among them: wherefore then lift you up yourself above the congregation of the Lord?" "Is it a small thing that thou hast brought us up out of a land that floweth with milk and honey to kill us in the wilderness except thou make thyself altogether a prince over us?" You remember what happened to Korah and his friends and his wives and his sons and his little children. I was brought up on that.

There remains only Jean to speak of. Why will she let the spirit be dragged down sick by the sick body.[149] If the spirit were sick in its own right I shouldn't be preaching this sermon. But it is the body uttering its sickness through the spirit—I can tell by the sound. I suppose I should distrust any sickness of the spirit as from the body unless I knew for certain that the body had a clean bill of health from the medical dept. A sick spirit in a sound body for me. It's a personal preference I am expressing. No doubt a sick spirit in a sick body has its honor and its reward. So much for the subject matter apart from the poeticality of the poetry. Of course I know the poems are truthful close and workmanlike.

If it were My Misc I'm pretty sure I would jumble the poetry in it. I'd begin with a real lady say Jean or Sara go over us once in one order and then in another. It would look less like the Georgians and it would get rid of Aiken's solid thing lying across the threshold.

Thanks from the heart for "Shin-leaf."[150] Some day when you have given me up as cold and ungrateful I shall requite it.

Ever yours

Robert Frost

Have you had a "bid" to a South Sea Island party to include Clarence Darrow, Frank Harris, Somebody Russell, Mary Pickford, Me and Edith Thomas? It is to raise vanilla and forget civilization at least till after election.[151]

R.

---

148. James Oppenheim's study in verse of Woodrow Wilson, "The Man Who Would Be God"; for Korah and Moses, see Numbers 16.

149. RF appears to have in mind the first of Jean Starr Untermeyer's contributions to the *Miscellany,* a long poem titled "Three Dreams."

150. Untermeyer had dedicated "Shin-Leaf" to RF. It also was in the *Miscellany.*

151. See Untermeyer's lengthy note of explanation (*RFLU,* 114–115), which begins: "During the summer of 1920, several writers received letters from a Mr. H. G. Rinehart

[To Stewart Mitchell (1892–1957), American poet and at this time editor of The Dial, in which RF did not, in fact, place any of the poems collected in his next two books. ALS. Boston Athenaeum.]

Franconia N.H.

July 18 1920

Dear Mr Mitchell:

May I in turn ask you if you would wait for your poems till somewhat later than the date you name? I have promised others who were ahead of you everything I publish this year. I could let you have a group in time for your January or February number—and only too glad of the chance to appear solidly in The Dial.

With thanks that you should think of me, I am

Sincerely yours

Robert Frost

Will you kindly let me know?

[To Harriet Monroe (1860–1936), American poet, critic, and founding editor, in 1912, of Poetry: A Magazine of Verse. RF refers, in the opening paragraph, to "An Empty Threat," which remained unpublished until he collected it in NH. ALS. Chicago.]

Franconia N.H.

July 21 1920

Dear Miss Monroe:

This is The Threat I threatened you with a week ago. My idea in announcing it was to gain a little more time for any last touch or two I might see to give it and yet so commit myself to sending it that I couldn't keep it indefinitely and run the chance of spoiling it with too many last touches.[152] If you dont like the way it sticks out in various directions like a fretful hedgehog well enough not to bury it under a jarring heap of other peoples poetry please ask

---

of Los Angeles. The letters were differently worded but the import was the same. Mr. Rinehart was sick of Western civilization and proposed to found a colony of kindred souls in one of the South Sea Islands." Among these souls were to have been Clarence Darrow and several other people RF mentions. See RF's July 23, 1920, letter to Untermeyer.

152. See RF's March 18, 1920, letter to Lesley Frost, in which the text of the poem is discussed.

to exchange it for anything to eat wear ride or read in any of our departments. We are old friends and ought to be able to stand a little abuse from each other.

Is it fair to ask which of my two followers represented in your last issue is the better poet.[153] If you'll tell me, I'll tell you. Has a boy by the name of Walter Hendricks of Chicago ever used my name to introduce his poetry to you?[154]

Sincerely yours
Robert Frost

[*To Louis Untermeyer. ALS. LoC.*]

Franconia N.H.
July 23 1920

Dear Louis, My Quality Friend:

I have had to decline this[155] on the ground that I want to stay in the world a while longer to see what is going to happen; hadn't seen any finality in the war; must hang around till I see some in politics. Also on the ground that I prefer to contract my skin diseases from white people as being more likely to be white diseases.[156] My latest information from the South Seas is that this man's island is to be open island for pearls next year; in which case it will be full of divers and entertainment dives such as movies, con games, and shoot-

---

153. The July issue of *Poetry* printed poems by Raymond Holden and Edward Merrill Root.

154. Hendricks had become a family friend when RF taught him at Amherst (class of 1917). So trusted was he that, in March 1919, with RF still in Amherst, Elinor asked him to look after Carol, Marjorie, and Irma during her brief absence from the Franconia farm. When RF reached Franconia on March 19, Irma reported that Hendricks had made improper sexual advances to her, which occasioned considerable awkwardness, as Hendricks remained in or near Franconia through mid-May 1919. RF did not confront Hendricks about the matter, but he did quietly cut his ties to the young man. Over the years, as Irma's mental health deteriorated, it became clear that she suffered from paranoid fantasies, often of sexual predation, and RF concluded that Hendricks had been wrongly accused. The two men were reconciled thereafter. For further details, see *LRF-1, 656*. See also RF to Lesley Frost, September 9, 1920.

155. H. G. Rinehart's invitation to join the aforementioned colony in the South Pacific.

156. That is, diseases to which he had already been exposed, as opposed to tropical ones to which he had not. See also Rinehart's invitation (illustration on page 78): "It seems to me, Mr. Frost, that the white race is in a strange state—a mode of life quite foreign to that possible for the human species and live [*sic*]. . . . I divorced myself from the white race in 1912, and, after living with primitives about seven years, returning a year ago, I can better measure all by experience. O God, the years wasted living in Whiteland!"

the-chutes. It would be literary (almost) to run away from such things here to run into them there . . . [157] I told him you would go probably as you were retiring from the jewelry business: and if he couldnt get you he could try Edith Thomas who seems about to retire from poetry and even life itself from sheer satisfaction with the great good work she has been doing the last ten years. If you accept and go make it a condition that President Wheeler sha'n't go and spill the vanilla beans.[158]

Gee I wish I was done with life so I could go where I please. But if I could go I shouldn't light out for anybody's cast-off islands in the Pacific. Rockwell Kent knew a trick worth two of that for press agency stuff. I should bar Chas. Edward Russell if it were my funeral. Who is this Luke North that so untrue to his name Looked South?[159] . . . Neither do I understand how the intellectual keeps going unless it is by panning intellectuality like The Liberator. Catch on to the New radicalism and vote for Harding.

Sinceriously
Robbered Frossed

To be read with a foot rule.[160]

---

157. All ellipses as in the original.

158. The American poet Edith Matilda Thomas (1854–1925) was uncommonly prolific. Edward Jewitt Wheeler, then president of the Poetry Society of America, also edited *Current Opinion*.

159. These are references to the text of Rinehart's invitation to join his proposed colony. "One urge that caused me to go to the Islands was to find a home for the late 'Luke North' that he might do his work. Mr. [Clarence] Darrow, his life long friend, thought of going, too, but his Los Angeles trial in 1912 spoiled their coming and placed 'Luke' in the Single-Tax movement. Mr. Darrow had some Tahitian dreams for a long while after. I have just written to Mr. Chas Edw. Russell. He has been there and likes it. I have a letter from Prof. Bayard Boyesen, late of Columbia. He is interested." "Luke North" was the pseudonym of an associate of Darrow's, James H. Griffes (1868–1919), who had died the previous year. Griffes supplied a preface for Darrow's *Plea of Clarence Darrow in His Own Defense to the Jury That Exonerated Him of the Charge of Bribery at Los Angeles—1912* (Los Angeles: Golden Press, 1912) and subsequently threw himself into the "single-tax" movement in California, which had been started by Henry George during the years when RF as a boy lived in San Francisco. Rockwell Kent (1882–1971) was the painter, illustrator, and transcendentalist epigone of Emerson and Thoreau. Charles Edward Russell (1860–1941) was an American politician and journalist. He was one of the founders, in 1909, of the National Association for the Advancement of Colored People.

160. RF wrote the letter diagonally across the page of Rinehart's typed invitation (see next page); hence the suggestion that Untermeyer use a ruler to read it.

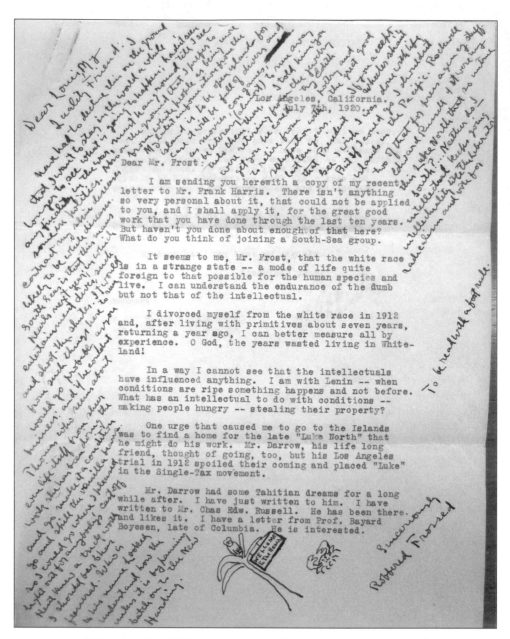

Los Angeles, California.
July 7th, 1920.

Dear Mr. Frost:

I am sending you herewith a copy of my recent
letter to Mr. Frank Harris. There isn't anything
so very personal about it, that could not be applied
to you, and I shall apply it, for the great good
work that you have done through the last ten years.
But haven't you done about enough of that here?
What do you think of joining a South-Sea group.

It seems to me, Mr. Frost, that the white race
is in a strange state -- a mode of life quite
foreign to that possible for the human species and
live. I can understand the endurance of the dumb
but not that of the intellectual.

I divorced myself from the white race in 1912
and, after living with primitives about seven years,
returning a year ago, I can better measure all by
experience. O God, the years wasted living in Whiteland!

In a way I cannot see that the intellectuals
have influenced anything. I am with Lenin -- when
conditions are ripe something happens and not before.
What has an intellectual to do with conditions --
making people hungry -- stealing their property?

One urge that caused me to go to the Islands
was to find a home for the late "Luke North" that
he might do his work. Mr. Darrow, his life long
friend, thought of going, too, but his Los Angeles
trial in 1912 spoiled their coming and placed "Luke"
in the Single-Tax movement.

Mr. Darrow had some Tahitian dreams for a long
while after. I have just written to him. I have
written to Mr. Chas Edw. Russell. He has been there.
and likes it. I have a letter from Prof. Bayard
Boyesen, late of Columbia. He is interested.

Written to Louis Untermeyer on July 23, 1920, Frost's note and
illustrations frame a letter from H. G. Rinehart inviting the poet
to join a colony in the South Pacific.

Courtesy of the Library of Congress.

[To George Browne (1857–1931), American educator. After graduating from Harvard with honors in classics (1878), he founded the Browne and Nichols School in Cambridge, Massachusetts, with his former classmate Edgar H. Nichols. ALS. Plymouth.]

Franconia

July 28 1920

Dear Browne:

Still here and likely to be here for some weeks yet—though you never can tell. The only thing working against it is Elinor, who is at this moment ranging the world to find the next place to move to. To-day she may be in Arlington, Vermont tomorrow in Milford, New Hampshire. Such enterprise for this time of year! May it not have to be its own only reward. Any other prayer would seem heartless.

Gee, I don't believe I could get you off a poem on barn raising without stimulant right off the reel like that. The best I might hope to do would be one on this barn raising without stimulant in time for the next. That's as timely as I am. I'm always started for the station by one train in time to catch the next one: which works all right except when there is no next one.

But I should like to see your friend Morgan[161] if we can arrange it any way. It's so long since I taught school or college that I almost forget the views I used to hold on pedagogy. However I know I did hold some that I make no doubt would reappear if called for in action. Probably I could trust Mr Morgan to rearouse them in me, to judge by what you say of him.

We have thoughts of taking a ride down to see you some day this summer. Maybe you'll see us yet if you keep your eyes peeled.

The poems in the Harpers (of which I never had a copy for myself) were Fragmentary Blue, Good bye and Keep Cold, Place for a Third and For Once Then Something.[162] I have just returned them the proof of another set of four, Wild Grapes, Fire and Ice, The Valley's Singing Day and The Need of Being

---

161. Arthur Ernest Morgan (1878–1975), American engineer and educator, president of Antioch College from 1920 to 1936. He had known Browne for some years, and had an interest in the Browne and Nichols School, where RF sometimes lectured. Under Morgan's administration, Antioch initiated its experiment in community governance, work-study programs, and abjuring conventional grades for narrative evaluations. Morgan's essay "Education: The Mastery of the Arts of Life" had appeared in the *Atlantic Monthly* in March 1918.

162. Specifically, in the July number of *Harper's;* the second set of poems RF refers to in this letter ("Wild Grapes," etc.) appeared in *Harper's* in December 1920.

Versed in Country Things. I don't know how many of these you've seen. Wild Grapes and Place for a Third are long ones. Funny, the way I've been discovered or caught writing poetry three separate times by the English. Three times is their charm. Lets hope they may have found me not to lose this time.[163]

Dig your trench and if I can possibly write a poem on barn raising without stimulant you shall have it.

Our best to you all.

Always yours
Robert Frost

[To Lincoln MacVeagh (1890–1972), soldier, diplomat, businessman, and publisher. Along the margin of the manuscript MacVeagh has penciled in a note: "About my going up to see Mr. Frost when H. Holt & Co. learned that Mr. Harcourt was trying his hardest to take him away." ALS. Jones.]

Franconia N.H.
July 29 1920

Dear MacVeagh:

Don't mind me, but come when it falls in with your other plans. Only let me know of course, so I won't be away up in the clouds or somewhere. Mrs Frost is still away home-hunting, but should be back tomorrow or next day. I want her here when you are here to take care of us if for no other reason. I'll show you some of the new verse when you come.

I should think that was a good page you sent as an example. We'll talk about it further.[164]

I'm glad to accede to the kind of request I enclose. I want before all else to be read by the school children I have spent so much time with.[165]

Sincerely yours
Robert Frost

---

163. Likely a reference to Theodore Maynard's recent article in the *New York Tribune* (June 27); Maynard (1890–1956) was an English poet and critic, though living in America. See RF's July 17, 1920, letter to Sidney Cox and also his September 4, 1920, letter to William Stanley Braithewaite (and the notes to both).

164. Perhaps a sample for the second edition of *MI,* to be published in 1921. RF had been dissatisfied with the poor-quality paper used in the 1916 edition, a product of wartime rationing.

165. We have been unable to identify the particulars of the request.

[To Wilbur L. Cross. ALS. Yale.]

Franconia N.H.

August 20 1920

Dear Mr Cross:

Here are the poems I want you to have, about as I want you to have them, and I trust not too late for you to read them where they will have the best chance with you. Omit one of the two longer, A Star in a Stone Boat or Two Look at Two, the second if you will be ruled by me. Of course you are free to omit all are in fact bound to unless they please you rather more than common.

With best wishes for yourself and the magazine I'm

Sincerely yours

Robert Frost

[To Edward Merrill Root (1895–1973), American poet and educator. ALS. ACL.]

Franconia N.H.

August 21 1920

My dear Root:

If you have on hand any of the kind of thing you think I would like, you would make no particular mistake in sending it to Mr Louis Untermeyer 310 West 100 St New York City just about now. Tell him I told you to send it. In recent letters to me he has talked himself into a frame of mind highly favorable to your work. My only caution is that you sha'n't show yourself too political in the poems you give him nor influenced much if at all by my bad example. All you fellows who ever came near me at Amherst have to be especially careful to keep off my premises.

Don't send him "Fire."[166] I want to keep that up my sleeve for an emergency.

Not too many at once—and none unless you are ready. Louis will keep, the more that he is expecting nothing at this moment. There is no haste in these things.

Sincerely yours

Robert Frost

---

166. Root collected a poem titled "Fire" in his 1927 volume *Lost Eden and Other Poems* (New York: Unicorn Press).

[*To Wilbur L. Cross. ALS. Yale.*]

Franconia N.H.

August 31 1920

Dear Mr Cross:

Your good opinion is more to me than much money. You know that. Still I must get as much money from you as you will spare to encourage American poetry in the person of me. So I am going to understand you to offer me one hundred dollars for the group of four. You do, dont you? That is considerably less than half as much a line as I am getting from people whose money is worth, we'll say, about half as much as yours. But let not this be anything between us. Pay me what you will or must. Only treat me like a friend and fellow countryman.

"Two Look at Two" does stand outside the group.

I'm betting that the same people who ask you how heavy the star was will ask you how practical Pegasus the horse was and how palpable the soul.[167] You'll just have to tell them yourself or refer them to me.

Always yours sincerely

Robert Frost

[*To Henry Reynolds Johnson, owner of Johnson's Bookstore in Springfield, Massachusetts. ALS. BU.*]

Franconia N.H.

August 31 1920

Dear Mr Johnson:

I have the book all right and will return it to you tomorrow or next day when I can get to the office to register it. I am sorry to have caused you anxiety by not acknowleging [*sic*] it sooner, though really this is soon for me. I am very glad to have seen the book and only wish Mrs Frost and I could run down to thank you for it and return it by hand, but the season forbids my venturing into the region of ragweed. I have to keep to my mountain fastnesses in August and September.

With best wishes to you and Mrs Johnson I am

Sincerely yours

Robert Frost

---

167. RF alludes to certain verbal details in "A Star in a Stone-Boat," which appeared, with "The Onset" and "Misgiving," in the *Yale Review* in January 1921.

[To William Stanley Braithwaite (1878–1962), American poet, literary critic, and anthologist. He was literary editor of the Boston Evening Transcript. *ALS. Middlebury.]*

Franconia N.H.

September 4 1920

My dear Braithwaite:

Of course I shall be glad to have you take the two poems for your book—so far as I am concerned.[168] I have no doubt The Yale Review and Harpers will be too, but will you make it right with them in form? I wish you would make the title of the one "To E. T." read "To Edward Thomas"—so, and no note of explanation about his battles and books.

It's a long time since I saw you or last heard what you were up to. I suppose you have been busy hailing English poets as fast as they come ashore. Still try to see an occasional American poet if you can in honesty—let me beseech you. That is to say, don't Medize any more than you have to to keep up with the times.[169] I say no harm and I mean no harm, as the song says in an anthology of yours I was looking over the other night.[170]

----

168. *The Anthology of Magazine Verse for 1920* (Boston: Small, Maynard) reprinted "Place for a Third" from *Harper's* and "To E.T." from the *Yale Review*.

169. In a subtle rebuke of literary Anglophilia, RF refers to Thucydides' criticism of the Plataeans for claiming they were the only Boeotians who did not "Medize." The Greeks referred to the Persian forces collectively as Medes, so to "Medize" was to submit to a foreign king. See chapter 10 of *The History of the Peloponnesian War*.

170. W. S. Braithwaite, ed., *The Book of Elizabethan Verse* (Boston: Small, Maynard, 1906). RF quotes a line from an anonymous song included in the book under the title "The Gift":

Fain would I have a pretty thing
  To give unto my Lady:
I name no thing, nor I mean no thing,
  But as pretty a thing as may be.

  . . . .

O Lady, what a luck is this,
  That my good willing misseth
To find what pretty thing it is
  That my Good Lady wisheth!
    Thus fain would I have had this pretty thing
      To give unto my Lady;
    I said no harm, nor I meant no harm,
      But as pretty a thing as may be. (312)

I'm sure I liked what Lola Ridge wrote about me better than what Maynard wrote, though Maynard was far from unsatisfactory.[171] The Nation for Dec 6 1919 had one of the most understanding things ever written about me. I wonder if you saw it.[172]

　　With best wishes for whatever you have in hand, I'm

　　　　　　　　　　　　　　　　Sincerely yours

　　　　　　　　　　　　　　　　Robert Frost

[*To George Browne. ALS. Plymouth.*]

　　　　　　　　　　　　　　　　Franconia N.H.

　　　　　　　　　　　　　　　　September 6 1920

Dear Browne:

　　You gave me to understand that if I looked hard enough for you at Littleton on the 24th of last month I should find you where the excitement over agriculture ran highest. All morning I looked till about two in the afternoon, but

---

171. On Ridge's essay see RF to Ridge, July 17, 1920. In his "Snow the Predominant Note in Frost's Poetry" (*New York Tribune,* Sunday, June 27, 1920), Theodore Maynard sounded a note that anticipated the remarks Lionel Trilling made—about the "terrifying" implications of RF's best poetry—at RF's eighty-fifth birthday dinner in 1959. Maynard wrote: "I have felt the winter present on almost every page of his books. Now, snow may mean either beauty or gayety or terror. It means every one of these things to Robert Frost—especially terror. With the soft gentleness of snow fear falls flake by flake in many of his piteous tales. The agony is increased imperceptibly to the point of heartbreak." He continued, "As a teller of stories of mood or impulse, this poet has no rival. And his masterstroke is that by which [he] achieves his subjective result by directly objective means. He is neither a realist nor a romanticist. But he has learned something from both and uses a sly trick (which is his own) of making his definite particularity refer to the universal." Maynard concludes, in lines that would have pleased RF (who often thought his humor either was missed altogether or was underrated): "There is much that I could say and could wish to say about [the poems], or about the whole body of his work. But the limitations of space forbid. The special quality of his humor with which I have not been able to deal at length makes me covet him as a neighbor. As I know that I shall never possess him as such, I will get as much compensation as possible by keeping his poems within arm's reach on my bookcase." Maynard reprinted the essay in his *Our Best Poets* (New York: Henry Holt, 1922).

172. George R. Elliott's "The Neighborliness of Robert Frost." See RF to Elliott, March 8, 1920.

in vain. You were not in the procession on horseback you were not at Remick Park demonstrating with a mechanical milker. No one that I buttonholed could give me any word of you. "What does he look like," a police man asked. "Brown, a salubrious browne, at this time of year when he is in the farmer phase" I answered. "Brown and interested—interested in everything human. By that last chiefly would you know him from another one." "Who is it wants him, his wife," said the policeman. "No, not his wife. His wife wants nothing, now that she has the vote and can use it to help elect Harding. I want him." "What for?" "To tell him something I have just thought of concerning metrics." "Why cant you tell it to me?" "Because it would take more attention than you can give standing here in the thick of the traffic on Main St between the Post Office and the Bank." The more I tried to withdraw from the conversation I had involved myself in the more suspicious he became that I had started something I must have some bad reason for not wanting to go on with. "See here, mister," he said, "either this is something you can tell me or you can tell it to the seargent [*sic*] at the desk." At this moment a seven-passenger touring car conveniently knocked me down and the policeman dragged me to the police station. The seargent [*sic*] asked to know what the charge was. "I have arrested him," said the policeman "for still-keeping." (The policeman struck me as German in idiom and point of view.[173]) "Still-keeping? Do you mean keeping a still? Has he made a statement? Have you smelled his breath?" "It smells of onion. I don't mean keeping a still but keeping still about a matter of apparent importance." "What matter?" "Ask him. I don't like to say it." "Metrics," said I. "Out with it while I keep hands off ye," says the seargent. So I went into my well known theories at length just as fully as I spread them out before a hundred contemporary clubs winter before last when I was fresh and confiding. In the end I demanded a jury trial. Then and not till then was anything done about the leg the touring car had snapped in two by running against it the wrong way with the hub of the front wheel.

You can see I had a day of it and so did the children who were witnesses to all this and will tell you if I lie. Of course it came to nothing, as all my looking for you came to nothing. But why should we forever ask that everything should come to something? Why, cant we just enjoy ourselves as we go 'long? Go 'long yourself, GB.

R.F.

---

173. Another joke having to do with German American attitudes toward Prohibition. See also the notes to RF's March 18, 1920, letter to Lesley Frost.

[To Louis Untermeyer. ALS. LoC.]

Franconia N.H.

September 18 1920

Dear Louis:

Still here more than anywhere else, though I now practically own a farm (all but paying for it) in South Shaftsbury Vermont and only one half of my family remains with me, one third of it being at Arlington Vermont in the Manse[174] and one sixth in New York campaigning, not for Cox, not for Harding (whom I should like to see elected if only I was surer he was anti-international) but for Melcher of the National Association of Book Publishers.[175]

As for you, you are campaigning as always for the honest word in poetry. Poor old Clinton Scollard and Louis Ledoux when you take your knife in hand to make excision![176] It is hard for me not to go over to the criminal's side in the day of retribution. I can run with the hounds till the hare is overtaken, but I die with the hare when he dies. But never mind me. Have at the buggers. Pond is in the bankruptcy courts and what bade fair to become the Disgustan Age of American Poetry from the influx of British Verse may yet turn out the Augustan.[177]

----

174. The "Brick House," a place in Arlington owned by the Canfield family, to which RF's friend the author Dorothy Canfield Fisher (1879–1958) belonged. Located on Main Street, it is now known as the Arlington Community House.

175. Frederic Melcher (1879–1963) was an American publisher, editor, and bookseller. James Cox, the nominee of the Democratic Party in the presidential campaign of 1920, lost to Warren G. Harding, who campaigned under the slogan "Return to Normalcy," by which he meant a pre–World War I America disentangled from European conflicts.

176. Clinton Scollard (1860–1932), American poet, professor of English at Hamilton College, and the husband of Jessie B. Rittenhouse; Louis V. Ledoux (1880–1948), a poet, literary critic, and scholar of Japanese art. Untermeyer included poems by Scollard in his *Modern American Poetry* (1919), but cut them when he issued a revised, expanded edition in 1921. Untermeyer did not anthologize Ledoux, though Rittenhouse had included Ledoux's "Mater Doloross" in her *Second Book of Modern Verse* (New York: Houghton Mifflin Company, 1919).

177. James Burton Pond Jr., head of the Pond Lyceum Bureau. The firm did eventually become bankrupt, though not until 1933.

Look at your Misc.[178] Isnt she a beauty for cover and topography [sic].[179] You needn't tell me you hadn't a hand in her make up. From Brace unhelped nothing like that ever. And I think five or six of your poets do themselves justice in it—five if you omit me. Harcourt is right in being proud of it. But make him send me two or three more copies of it. He only sent me two and I've had those taken away from me by force before I had time to inscribe them. What we want is sales but not to poor devils like me. I say sell to the rich till they are as poor as we are. That's the kind of a socialist me and I trust The New Republic are at this writing. I deny that there is anything Bolshevist in my position. Let the New Republic clear its own skirts.

I set Merrill Root on you.[180] Now see what you can do with him. See that he has a copy of Prof. Grenville's Manufacture of Verse to begin with.[181]

How about a movement to steer all the free versifiers to a country as free in name as Liberia.

I have various poems coming in different places, one of them a lyric written twenty years ago. I wonder if you can spot the old lyric. The editor of The———didn't.[182] I'd bother you to read some stuff in MS, but I dont want to ravish you of your vacation freshness so soon.

Did you happen to notice the Songo River when you were sailing on it—how it ought to lend itself to song and poetry? Longfellow took a stab at it before

---

178 *Miscellany of American Poetry.* See RF's July 17, 1920, letter to Untermeyer (and notes).

179. A pun. The book and type were designed by Quinn and Boden Company, Rahway, New Jersey. The cover features the title in gold print on a dark blue board. The original dust jacket carried the following note: "Ninety-four new and hitherto unpublished poems by Conrad Aiken, John Gould Fletcher, Robert Frost, Vachel Lindsay, Amy Lowell, James Oppenheim, E. A. Robinson, Carl Sandburg, Sara Teasdale, Jean Untermeyer, Louis Untermeyer. Each poet has been his own editor; each has selected and arranged his own contributions. None of the poems has appeared in book form; only seven have appeared in print." For a list of RF's contributions, see the notes to his April 28, 1920, letter to Untermeyer, where the book is first discussed.

180. See RF to Root, August 21, 1920.

181. See *RFLU,* 118, where Untermeyer explains: "A fictitious book which I had outlined in a prospectus, and then reviewed. It made straight-faced fun of the Lush and Rhetorical Sonnet, the Mouth-filling and Mystical Ode," and so on.

182. The poem is "Misgiving," published in the *Yale Review* (under the editorship of Wilbur Cross) in January 1921. For more on its age, see RF to Untermeyer, November 12, 1920, and January 19, 1921; and also RF to Cox, March 1, 1921.

fountain pens were invented.[183] Isn't it about due for a stab from someone else in the light of what we now know about everything?

Sinceriously
Robertus

[To Lesley Frost. The letter is not fully dated, but internal evidence indicates 1920. ALS. UVA.]

Franconia N.H.
September 19 [1920]

Dear Lesley:

The stone house it is. And Mama has gone along with Margery to the brick house at Arlington to lie in wait for it there.[184] Now if only our things were all packed and on the way. It looks as if I might be settled down to write again by Christmas. But never mind, we've got what we thought we wanted. There's a lot of fun ahead touching it up to our exact ideas. From now on we write ourselves as of South Shaftsbury, Vermont.

Your job sounds funny but not impossible if you can work yourself up to the sort of thing for a short go. Don't take it too seriously or too unseriously. You [can] be worse employed than urging people to buy a book.[185] I spent a good deal of my time as a teacher urging the same thing. I used to say that all our work in literature and composition fails if it doesn't put libraries large or small into houses.

Tell Melcher and Joseph I ran onto the rolling library at Manchester Vt and had a good talk with Miss Frank who seemed to have been getting experience as well as selling books. I was only a little surprised to learn that she had

---

183. Longfellow's "Songo River," composed in September 1875, appears in "Birds of Passage: Flight the Fourth," a suite of poems. Longfellow wrote five such suites. The Songo River connects Lake Sebago to Long Lake, in Cumberland County, Maine.

184. The Frosts had arranged to purchase the Stone House in South Shaftsbury, but until they were able to take possession, Elinor and Marjorie would live in Arlington so Marjorie could attend school in North Bennington. Carol and Irma remained with RF in Franconia.

185. As Arnold Grade notes, Lesley had taken a job as a writer and publicist for the National Association of Book Publishers, headed by Frederic Melcher (*FL*, 95). Joseph Anthony, mentioned several times in other letters, was her immediate superior; he had previously been employed by Harper and Brothers.

done better in Barré, Vermont, a rabble town, than at Bretton Woods the swell resort. Next time the library should be routed through medium-sized ordinary places when schools are in session. If the right people were interested it could draw up like a lunch cart and do business in front of the schools I should think.[186]

We have been getting a dose of Raymond.[187] I can't for the life of me make out what he takes us for, talking the way he has been of having business in New York and making Mama give him your address down there. All this before everybody. I can't believe he means to insult us. But he's a bad case of damn fool I have even less use for than I thought I had. From things he has said to me, he plainly thinks he needs tragic experience at he doesn't care whose expense before he can go on with his poetry. I see him in Greenwich Village before long cut loose from his family. It takes these Red Cross and Social Service meddlers to make a mess of themselves. I think he's fame-struck. Being with us and our reputation has put him beside himself. He'll be better when we are well out of the way.

You probably won't have much time to do the article about Gamaliel Bradford's A Prophet of Joy—not if you are going to have to do several articles a week on books in general.[188] Maybe a little later when you are in France.

Hope you have some luck about the flat or apartment for Irma and Mama.

I wonder if some of your business friends wouldn't know how you could buy your French money. I think it possible that you might buy it as we set out to of the American Express. You might ask at some large Express office.

Good luck with the propaganding and have a good time with it while it lasts.

---

186. RF refers to the Book Caravan, an outreach by The Bookshop for Boys and Girls (run by the Boston's Women's Educational and Industrial Union). Manchester and Barré were on its route. Mary Frank, who oversaw the Caravan, published an account of it in the *Bookman* ("Caravanning with Books," February 1921), but doesn't mention RF. Barbara Bader notes that, to founder Bertha Mahony's regret, "the Caravan had to stop at many 'fine summer places'—seashore and mountain resorts—to provide dollars-and-cents returns to the sponsoring publishers. What was the value of taking books to people who took books for granted? So she was gratified, even exhilarated, to report that sales in the industrial town of Barré, Vermont, equaled those in posh Northeast Harbor." See Bader, *"Treasure Island* by the Roadside," *The Horn Book Magazine* (January/February 1999).

187. Raymond Holden.

188. Bradford's *A Prophet of Joy,* published by Houghton Mifflin in 1920, was a collection of dramatic narratives written in rhymed octaves.

Carol and I had a great ride home over the best roads ever. The car pulled like a demon.

> Affectionately
>
> Papa

[To Lesley Frost. ALS. UVA.]

> Franconia N.H.
>
> September 23 [1920]

Dear Lesley:

The doctor says I am sick with jaundice and not able to be writing and moving. But able or not there are one or two things I must write to you.

Raymond tells me they have had two letters from you, one to Grace and one to him personally since you went away.[189] This is as many as we have had from your busy self. I can't think you are going on to take your fun out of playing with this sort of fire. I dont think you can be enough aware of yourself. Raymond has given everybody to understand that he is making business in New York an excuse for going down to see you this week. He is taking the Sunday night train down. I simply tell you so that you will have time to decide what to do. My way would be to get rid of him as I got rid of Walter Hendricks, so that not a word was said out about what was the matter.[190] Be away, be otherwise engaged, be anything you please to show your self-possession. He is no sort of person for youthful folly to trifle with. He's been talking all the bold bad stuff of the books he derives his poetry from—talking it right and left. I simply tell you and leave the rest to your common sense.

Look out for Joe too if it is as you seem to suggest in your letter.[191] Damn such people. You say we'll use him and drop him. We'll use him very little longer. You must get away without any ruction. We can't have scenes in our lives. But damn him from now out. I'm all on your side, only be careful, no youthful folly on your part. I'm on Harcourt's side too in the matter of the book, if the thing is as you say.

---

189. Grace Ansley Holden (1893–1989), Raymond Holden's wife; the marriage would soon end in divorce.

190. For details about the incident referred to here, see the notes to RF's July 21, 1920, letter to Harriet Monroe (see also *LRF-1, 656*).

191. Joseph Anthony.

The five hundred dollars is enclosed in this letter. I dont know about your cashing it and carrying it about in money. I wouldnt dare to carry as much myself and I have safer pockets than you. Best not cash it till on your way to buy the French money. I wonder if after all the American Express money orders would be what you want. Why not ask Melcher to help and advise you, mentioning me to him. I should feel pretty safe in his friendship.

Tell me more about Smythe's proposal.[192] It sounds amusing but not very feasable [sic].

Cheer up about the Stone House. Oh I almost forgot that I have told Mama about the DuChene's offer of their apartment for twenty five a month.[193] She may refuse it.

Affectionately

Papa

[To Lesley Frost. Text derived from Arnold Grade's The Family Letters of Robert and Elinor Frost (101). The manuscript of the letter (perhaps once held at UVA) has gone missing since Grade prepared the volume. Date derived from internal evidence.]

[Franconia, NH]

[late September 1920]

Dear Lesley:

Damn a father like Catherine's.[194] Not a word to you after letting her work all summer at you to drag you into her scheme.

---

192. William Ellsworth Smythe (1861–1922) was a journalist and writer and the founder of the Little Landers Movement, which aimed to settle small suburban lots with people who would farm their own properties, live off the land, and sell or trade the surplus for needed income. After World War I, he was an active supporter of the Rural Homes Bill intended to resettle returning soldiers in agriculturally engineered rural communities. When RF wrote this letter, Smythe was living in New York and working up an argument for such a plan that would be published as City Homes on Country Lanes (New York: Macmillan, 1921).

193. The offer of the Du Chênes' New York apartment concerned Irma Frost's intention to enroll at the Art Students League of New York. Aroldo du-Chêne de Véré (1883–1961), an Italian-born sculptor (often called simply Aroldo Du Chêne), had done the bust of RF that was reproduced as a frontispiece to the 1919 edition of MI. He and his wife, Eiley, had recently moved to New York.

194. As Arnold Grade points out (FL, 100n), Lesley's friend Catherine McElroy had intended to join Lesley on a trip to Europe until her father at the last minute denied permission. The trip was then canceled.

Don't worry about them though. We'll get you to Paris somehow.

Let me know if you got the 500 dollar check I sent.

We leave here Wednesday or Thursday. Address me at Arlington next.

Mrs Fobes letter is enclosed with her check.[195]

Affectionately

Papa

[*The following letter was published on October 6, 1920, in the Bryn Mawr* College News *(vol. 7, no. 2): 1. The* Christian Science Monitor *reprinted it on October 8, 1920. It had been addressed to an officer (name unknown) in the Reeling and Writhing Club at Bryn Mawr. The letter is transcribed here from the* College News; *the manuscript no longer survives.*]

[Franconia, NH]

[late September 1920]

We shall have to get a little more American literature directly out of the colleges or know the reason why. I see no better way to do it than by laying on our younger students the obligation to produce something besides exercises to be blue-penciled for details by teachers. The colleges haven't dared to expect absolute literature of mere students. Yet when you stop to consider, you find that before they were past the age of being students, nearly all the real writers that ever wrote had done something definite of the kind they were to be known for all the rest of their lives. Probably the colleges haven't expected enough of young writers.

But perhaps it is the country's fault. A young country is too easily satisfied with a mechanical proficiency in the arts that can at best never be better than amateurish. The country may not expect enough. And then again I am not sure the country is to blame. I don't know that either the country or the colleges could expect enough of young artists. The young artists have to expect it of themselves, by some miracle, for it to be enough.

---

195. Edith Hazard Fobes of Franconia, wife of J. Warner Fobes. The Fobeses had been Frost family friends since 1915; RF would speak at a memorial service for J. Warner on December 1, 1920 (see *CPRF*, 82–83).

[To Lesley Frost. Date derived from internal evidence. ALS. UVA.]

Arlington [VT]
Wednesday
[October 6, 1920]

Dear Lesley

Will you find time to go to the League and make sure that Irma's place is reserved for her in Bridgemans class.[196] Say she has paid her fee but has been delayed in getting to New York by sickness. I assume there will be no difficulty. You need wire only if she is refused admission to the class.

You should tend to this at once because Irma will come on the Saturday train (2.54 P.M. standard time—same one you took) unless warned not to. It looks now as if neither Mama nor I could get away to go with her. You will have to meet her at the train and take her to the DuChenes house. Why don't you move down there on Saturday yourself earlier in the day so as to make sure of the key and admission?

You may have to live with Irma a few days alone before Mama or I come down. Please take the way with her that will keep the peace. Remember that her strictness is part of her nature. Don't try to make her over. Some of it she will outgrow, but not all of it even by the time she is eighty. It has its beauty if you know how to look at it. When you find it a little agressive, [sic] you can disregard it.

This is in great haste to catch the mail.

Good luck with your articles.

Affectionately
Papa

Keep the five hundred dollar check in a safe place till we decide what to do with it. Also Mis Fobes' checks.

---

196. Founded in 1875, the Art Students League is located on West Fifty-Seventh Street in New York City. George Brant Bridgman (1865–1943), a Canadian American painter and writer, taught anatomy and figure drawing there.

*[To John W. Haines (1875–1966), English solicitor and amateur botanist. On letterhead
from "The Brick House." Portions of RF's correspondence with Haines are available
only in the form of photostats of the original documents. For details see LRF-1, 200,
n.21. ALS-photostat. DCL.]*

[Arlington, VT]

October 10 1920

My dear Jack:

I have been leaving Franconia, New Hampshire (a German English combination of names) to go and live in South Shaftsbury Vermont (an English
French combination). Our notions for making the change are not poetical,
however, but agricultural. We ask a better place to farm and especially grow
apples. Franconia winter-killed apple trees and some years even in July and
August frosted gardens. The beautiful White Mountains were too near for
warmth. A hundred miles further south and out of the higher peaks as we
shall be, we think we ought to be safer.

You will gather from the address that we are still in a state of transition.
We shall be here in Arlington while our furniture is on the way in the train
which in your language is called "goods," but in the language of ourselves
"freight."

Arlington, Shaftsbury, Rupert, Sunderland, Manchester, Dorset, Rutland,
the towns and counties are named after courtiers of Charles Second. It looks
as if some gunpowder plot had blown them up at a ball and scattered them
over our map.[197] I might wish they rang a little more Puritanly to my ear. But
as you know I make a point of not being too fastidious and forgetting about
the main issue.

---

197. Henry Bennet, 1st Earl of Arlington (1618–1685), who after the Restoration of the
Stuart Monarchy in 1660, was made Keeper of the Privy Purse; Anthony Ashley Cooper,
1st Earl of Shaftesbury (1621–1683), one of the principal architects of the Restoration;
Prince Rupert of the Rhine (1619–1682) fought with legendary dash for the Royalists
during the English Civil War and, after the Restoration, returned to England, where he
was appointed to Charles II's privy council; Henry Spencer, 1st Earl of Sunderland (1620–
1643), died fighting for the Royalists; Robert Montagu, 3rd Earl of Manchester (1634–1683),
served in the Cavalier Parliament (1661–1679); Charles Sackville, 6th Earl of Dorset (1638–
1706), was both a courtier and a poet; John Manners, 8th Earl of Rutland (1604–1679), was
named Lord Lieutenant of Leicestershire after the Restoration. The Gunpowder Plot of
1605 was a conspiracy to assassinate James I, with the aim of installing his daughter Elizabeth (1596–1662) on the throne as a puppet queen ruling in the Catholic interest.

How could you withhold all these years the encouraging things you had written about me?[198] From having the war so much on your mind I sup-pose—and from modesty. Never mind, they are interposed now just right to lift me out of the blues I have had so many of lately.

Well, the war is over. I don't know that I have said that to you yet. (We'll nei-ther of us ever say it to Edward Thomas.) But there are two or three more wars close at hand. There's a good prospect of wars from now on to the end. And the charm of that is that if we are going to have war all the time, it excuses us from thinking and talking of it quite as much as peace all the time excused us from talking about peace. Let's agree never to come nearer the subject of poli-tics national or international than I have come in the first portion of this letter.

Of course, justify anything you like in England. I'm obliged to John Freeman[199] for his interest. He can't be too strong in his prejudice against me for having been held to have inflamed Edward a little in his poetry. I wish he and I could meet and be friends. To have poems printed in England again will be like, a little like, sitting down of an evening with you in Gloucester.

Affectionately
Robert

[*To Louis Untermeyer. On letterhead from "The Brick House." ALS. LoC.*]

[Arlington, VT]
October 11 1920

Dear Louis:

I've been sick, joking aside. The trouble seems to be that I wasn't taken up carefully enough in Franconia nor replanted soon enough in South Shaftsbury. It has been a bad job of transplanting. I lost a lot of roots (the tap root entirely) and the roots I have left are pretty well impaired by too long exposure to the air out of the ground. You're a poet yourself and a finely constituted [*sic*]; so

---

198. While the "encouraging things" Haines had written have not been specifically identified, Haines's papers at the Gloucester Archives in Gloucester, England, include typescripts of appreciative lectures he gave about RF's poetry between 1918 and 1921.

199. John Frederick Freeman (1880–1929), literary critic, poet, and a friend of Edward Thomas's. A note written in Haines's hand, after the close of the letter, reads: "He [RF] met John Freeman when next in England [1928]. J.F. was once angry with me for saying RF had influenced him but he changed his mind."

you dont have to be told how it is with poets. The time of year too has been against me, let them say what they will in rural journalism. Even in the case of evergrins I find that the fall is not a favorable time for transplanting. And I'm not an evergrin. It has gone hard with me. You must excuse me if I dont find strength to fill pages with admiration for your New Adam. I was curiously prescient about him, wasnt I?[200] No "moth's kiss first" about him is there?[201] He ploughs and that's why he reads straight through as a book like a novel. The book has one name and one nature. The effect of it all's so vivid that it makes me want to ask personal questions; but I don't ask them, mind you. Sometime I will tell you the three worst poems in the book when I have had more time to look for them. Someone else who admired the book as much as I, said the only fault he had to find with it was too much "breasts"—not too many, but too much. However I wouldn't pick out any one poem marred by the breast motive. It is one of our books of poetry.[202]

-----

200. Untermeyer's new volume of verse, *The New Adam*, had lately been published by Harcourt, Brace and Howe. As for RF's "prescience," see his July 17, 1920, letter to Untermeyer.

201. See stanza 1 of Robert Browning's "In a Gondola":

The moth's kiss, first!
Kiss me as if you made me believe
You were not sure, this eve,
How my face, your flower, had pursed
Its petals up; so, here and there
You brush it, till I grow aware
Who wants me, and wide ope I burst.

202. *The New Adam* has in it no fewer than fourteen "breasts." As RF's remarks suggest, the book was written with a definite program. Untermeyer explains in his preface, "A Note on the Poetry of Love": "Almost the first thing that strikes one after reading a quantity of Eighteenth and Nineteenth Century English Poetry is the preponderance of love-poetry. It seems to have been not only the major theme of every minor poet; it was practically the only theme of even the acknowledged leaders. Sentimental love, ideal love, platonic love, lyric and libidinous love, love elegant and deluxe—the variety seems all encompassing at first glance. And then, beneath the apparent diversity of design, one is disturbed by a singular monotony. . . . Women had ceased to be human to [poets] and had become somehow both subnormal and super-terrestrial. . . . This combination of worship and bewilderment is faithfully reflected in the inability of most modern love-lyricists to write actually about love" (xiii). Having diagnosed the problem, Untermeyer redresses it in a sequence of love poems that in contemporary parlance might be called

I really don't know what's the matter with me unless its what I say. I can lift anything anyone else can lift, I was wishing only last night Levinski [sic] would leave Carpentier to me, and yet I seem barely able to be around.[203]

Still I'm yours consciously
Robert Frost

[To Lesley Frost. ALS. UVA.]

Arlington Vt
October 14 1920

Dear Lesley:

Mama is just home and she says you say nobody answers your questions; nobody appreciates your long letters: you might as well make them short notes just assuring us you aren't sick. That's a good one. I don't know about the questions but the long letters are in great demand: we want all we can get of them as full of news as they can hold. Mama brought some news with her, as that a menagery [sic] had broken loose in the DuChene's and was running all round over Irma in the dark like bad dreams.[204] But she was painfully short of intel-

---

"confessional." In saying that Untermeyer's Adam "ploughs," RF includes the sexual sense of the word, current since the late seventeenth century. Consider the lines that open the book:

Her body is that glorious gate
Opening on fresh and surging skies,
The door of flesh that holds a late
And larger Paradise.

Through this I plunge with hungry haste
Down the old garden, stock and root.

As for confessional motives in love poetry associated with Untermeyer (and with his wife, to whom *The New Adam* is dedicated), see the notes to RF's December 2, 1927, letter to Sandburg.

203. Georges Carpentier (1894–1975), a popular French boxer; and "Battling" Levinsky, born Barney Lebrowitz (1891–1949), a light heavyweight. They were scheduled to fight the next day, October 12.

204. See the close of RF's September 23, 1920, letter to Lesley.

ligence on some important heads. She couldn't tell, for instance, what the two articles were about that you were writing for the Sun and Times respectively.

She said you had rounded out your job with the Book Campaign with colors flying. To have staid as long as the business you were in lasted makes an auspicious beginning in life. Now for almost anything else you please, I should think. What a wide free choice you seem to have. I am not the least tempted to plan for you. My satisfaction is all in letting you plan for yourself since you are so able to. Only I could tell you if you asked me what to do to your co-öccupants of the DuChene apartment to set them back temporarily if not to get rid of them entirely. You can get in a kerosene can a gallon of gasoline (price 36 cents) and pour, literally pour, it into every crack and corner of the woodwork of the beds or cots and soak the canvass of them all along where it is nailed to the wood. Dont wet the mattresses: they are as uninhabited as the moon. You must do the deed very early in the day when no light or fire is lit in the room or going to be for a good many hours—that is till the gasoline has had time to evaporate and get out the windows. You can leave the windows open for the day. I say this only for your own comfort for the time being, not to save the apartment for Irma. The apartment will have to be given up. It will never do for Irma to go on with it. You may have to buy a cheap kerosene can. It is the best thing to buy the gasoline in and to put the stuff on with. Dont spare it. Make the wood bubble. Go over the beds twice perhaps. Then open the windows and get out.

This is the kind of letter I should hate to mail at the Franconia post office for fear Salome would open it for her amusement and keep it as a memorial of our private affairs.[205] Two or more letters that Carol and I sent from there to other members of the family never reached their destinations. We are sure of two. I wonder if you got all we wrote to you toward the last of it. I mustnt suspect the Franconia post office too much. I hear that letters are being lost everywhere in transmission.

One of your questions you complain of my not answering was whether I advised your reviewing Louis' Misc.[206] The idea has its attractions especially for the chance it would give you to be funny about your obligations to me

---

205. Salome Evelyn Colby (1904–1982). After graduating from Dow Academy in Franconia, she attended the University of New Hampshire. She later took a teaching position in Littleton, New Hampshire. Apparently while at Dow she also worked in the local post office.

206. Untermeyer, *Miscellany* (1920).

that would forbid your dealing with me one way or the other lest you should seem too grateful or not grateful enough. You could go on at a great rate with an ironical sideswipe at people who review their wives and intimate friends. But it would never do. I don't mean that part so much as the rest of it. You'd be in danger of converting too many friends and half friends into enemies. It would be going out of the way to seek trouble. Unless of course you found you had one good characterizing apiece for everybody in the book that was neither favorable nor unfavorable and could be delivered for its intrinsic interest and not seem evasive and non-committal. That would be a good kind of review: eleven ideas on art or life suggested by the eleven poets in the book. You could look the book over and see what it had for you. Eleven minus me. You could [not] carry on about me, especially if the review was to be signed.

All this reviewing is by the way for you of course, so you may as well put stiff while you are at it and find out what sort of thing it is. Why cant you do some of it from the Stone House in South Shaftsbury if you come home and dont go to France? You could run down for fifteen dollars a round trip once a month or so, making two or three days of it there if business called for it.

I think I must wish as much as you do you could go to France. I hate not to have you after all that has been said. How would it be to go for a shorter time than you intended—say three months—just to escape the reproach of having fizzled? You couldnt find someone to go with you? I haven't mentioned it to anyone—I've just thought of it—but wouldn't it be fine for you to take Margery, for some one to stick to on the voyage and go round with in Paris. Maybe this isnt feasable [sic]. It might cost too much for the family purse. I'll see what Mama says. I wish we all could go. I'm half scared to have you go alone. Mama speaks of the possibility of typhus over there this winter. And I can tell from a lot of things the French are out of love with [us] as are also all the rest of the world. All the more reason there should be no League of Nations. Vote for Debs if you want to, but don't vote for Cox.[207] And by the way how are you going to vote when you have no residence anywhere unless it is in Franconia? Or had you been long enough in New York to establish a residence for registration? I never heard how long it takes in New York.

Mama amused me with the vagaries of the She-Untermeyer. Louis socks us to her in the privacy of the hours when the house is empty of society. She's

---

207. James M. Cox, Democratic candidate for president in 1920; Eugene V. Debs was the Socialist Party candidate.

bent on punishing someone for my sins of inappreciation.[208] I'm sorry to have wounded her corpulency, but gee I have to allow myself the luxury of an occasional critical frankness. If she's a poet, so's my late uncle. What's the use! She has the merit of compression. Her poems would pass for tolerable daily themes in college. The ideas are about as much as you would expect in such work. The length is suitable. That may be saying a good deal for her. I can add to it that she's never nonsensical or strained or over precious and literary as Carl Sandburg in most respects greatly her superior, sometimes is. (Read the dedication of his Smoke and Steel for the kind of thing: "Listener to new yellow roses." Awful stuff. It vitiates many a good poem in his book.)[209] And still she amounts to too little. She hasn't brains enough to think with. Requiescat ex labore![210]

I was glad Cleaveland [sic] won (after seven such well piched [sic] games on both sides) and I wasnt too sorry Levinski [sic] lost, considering the interesting savage but intelligent man fighting with his tongue out and striking with the strength of ten because his conscience was so clear about the war, he lost to. I wish Carpentier were ours so we could be quite happy in wishing him to lick Dempsey.[211]

---

208. Jean Starr Untermeyer had hoped that RF would blurb one of her books (whether her 1918 volume *Growing Pains* or her 1921 volume *Dreams Out of Darkness* is not clear).

209. Sandburg dedicated *Smoke and Steel* (New York: Harcourt, Brace and Howe, 1920) as follows: "To Col. Edward J. Steichen, painter of nocturnes and faces, camera engraver of glints and moments, listener to blue evening winds and new yellow roses, dreamer and finder, rider of great mornings in gardens, valleys, battles." The photographer Edward Steichen (1879–1973) commanded the Photographic Division of Aerial Photography in the American Expeditionary Force during World War I; he retired as a lieutenant colonel in 1918. Sandburg had married his sister, Lillian Steichen, in 1907. Steichen and Sandburg would eventually collaborate on several important projects, including, in 1955, the *Family of Man* exhibition at the Museum of Modern Art in New York.

210. Modeled on "requiescat in pace" (R.I.P.), the tag (unique to RF) means something like "May she rest from the labor [of trying to think]," or "May I rest after the labor [of trying to read / think about her]"; or, with "requiescat in pace" behind it, "Her work will be the death of me." (We thank Mark Scott for the suggestion.) The last lines of "During Darkness," the last poem Jean Starr Untermeyer contributed to Untermeyer's *Miscellany* (1920) may also bear on the joke: "Take me under thy wing, / O death."

211. In the 1920 World Series, the Cleveland Indians beat the Brooklyn Dodgers five games to two. Levinsky had lost the October 12, 1920 bout with Georges Carpentier. Carpentier had been an aviator during World War I and had been awarded two of the

I think of another thing you asked about: a book of Hollister's.[212] It had gone into a box before you spoke. Do you think he is in a hurry for it? Something about the appreciation of music wasn't it. I'll trust him to appreciate music a while longer without the help of a book—just as I'll trust him to go the whole length in music without the help of Amherst College. I hope he'll take care of his health enough for practical purposes.

Carol lives on his car and its idiosyncrasies. He stops and goes as it stops and goes. Last night it came to a standstill in South Shaftsbury just when it was time to come home after having picked apples all day. He cheerfully had it towed to the garage where he put in four or five hours with the garage man over it before they found out that the trouble was with the make and break lever in the magneto. He didnt care. He was intending to walk home ten miles after ten oclock [*sic*] at night: but I forbade that by telephone. He likes it as well out of order as in order. He wallows in the dirty oils of it, ruining shirt on shirt.

I'd like a week down there to spend entirely in the Metropolitan Museum where Mama tells me she has been with Irma. I never had enough of such places.

Affectionately

Papa

[*To John Bartlett (1892–1941), American journalist and former student of RF's at Pinkerton Academy. The letter is substantially damaged, with multiple tears and missing text. Brackets enclose speculative readings. ALS. UVA.*]

Arlington Vermont

October 16 1920

Dear John:

Word reaches us in a round-about way that you two and your offspring are beautiful. But that is not the same thing as the assurance directly from you.

---

highest French military honors, the Croix de Guerre and the Médaille Militaire—hence, perhaps, RF wising he "were ours." On July 2, 1921, Carpentier challenged Jack Dempsey for the world heavyweight title and lost.

212. Carroll Hollister (1901–1983) left Amherst before his class graduated in 1922 and enjoyed a long and successful career as a concert pianist.

This is written to ask for your news—how you are and how you are working. I really must tell you again that I am anxious to see some of your literature. I wouldn't say so if I didn't [mean it.] Of course if I were as anxious [as a] detective bureau to find out who blew up J. Pierpont Morgan and Co[213] I could subscribe to all the magazines going and read and read them till I found your signature or came on internal evidence that marked something as unmistakably yours. You know you might say something that would give you away to me if to nobody else. As it is I confess I don't subscribe to a single magazine agricultural religious political or neither. I'm too lazy to go hunting for you at large. I've waited patiently for some years for a glimpse of you in print and now in all friendliness and for the last time but ten I demand it. You don't happen to work for Farm and Fireside do you? The editor, George Martin, has started sending me that on the [understanding] that I will let him [have] some [poetry] for it if I ever write any [more.][214]

I sort of broke loose [TEXT MISSING] months ago in [TEXT MISSING] And I'm sending [TEXT MISSING] I rather appear. But the main thing [TEXT MISSING] [is] that we have given [up on Franconia] without moving to Colorado.[215] For two summers running we had frosts on our gardens there in July and August and we decided not to give the place another chance. It was too much like murder in the state. It was final. We couldn't think of going west or any further west than the western boundary of New England because I have to be where I can earn a little money by lecturing at colleges especially now that I have chucked Amherst. I served my time at Amherst (four years) the same as at Pinkerton [in order] to show that as the father of a family I [would] do what I had to and then turned to something I liked to do better. And now I or Carol and I or we'll say Carol is going to plant some apple trees at South Shaftsbury and dig in and grow up with them. Don't fear for us. The good God will take care of them that don't put on any airs.

There, now say something in reply.

Affectionately
R.F.

---

213. On September 16, 1920, a bomb exploded in front of the J. P. Morgan Bank at 23 Wall Street, killing 38 people and injuring 143. The perpetrators were not discovered.

214. *Farm and Fireside,* at that time edited by George Martin, published "The Grindstone" in June 1921 and "On a Tree Fallen across the Road" in October 1921.

215. In 1917 the Bartletts had moved to Colorado in an attempt to relieve John's asthma and his wife Margaret's tuberculosis.

[*To George R. Elliott. ALS. ACL.*]

Arlington Vermont
October 23 1920

Dear Elliott:

I depose that I have moved a good part of the way to a stone cottage on a hill at South Shaftsbury in southern Vermont on the New York side near the historic town of Bennington[216] where if I have any money left after repairing the roof in the spring I mean to plant a new Garden of Eden with a thousand apple trees of some unforbidden variety.

That the health of my family is so-so and I am sorry to hear that you can't quite say the same of yours. Mrs Elliott's ailment is something I know little about. Our friend Dorothy Canfield Fisher has had it for some time and so far as I can see seems to be stimulated by it in mind and body.[217] Is it something that comes to nervous high-strung people to make them more nervous and high-strung?—and needn't be serious if it is looked after. You must make Mrs Elliott let up on her interests all she will.

That I am writing my Puritan Poem[218] so to speak and expect to finish it by—and by. Meanwhile look out for my set Snow Dust, The Onset, A Star in a Stone Boat, and Misgiving in The Yale Review, my set Fire and Ice, Wild Grapes, The Valley's Singing Day and The Need of Being Versed in Country Things in Harpers and other sets elsewhere as fast as I can supply the demand.[219]

That I am writing a drama than which—but I spare you.

---

216. Best known for the Battle of Bennington (August 16, 1777), a decisive rebel victory against British and Hessian forces.

217. Elliott's wife had been diagnosed with goiter. RF and his wife had recently visited Dorothy Canfield Fisher at her home in Vermont; Fisher helped them find the Stone House, in South Shaftsbury, mentioned here.

218. The "Puritan Poem" referred to here was published as "The Return of the Pilgrims" in *The Pilgrim Spirit: A Pageant in Celebration of the Landing of the Pilgrims at Plymouth, Massachusetts, on December 21, 1620* (Boston: Marshall Jones, 1921), written and produced by George P. Baker. RF never collected the poem and almost never spoke of it, but its fourth stanza was printed in *WRB* under the title "Immigrants."

219. The *Yale Review* published the group of poems mentioned here in January 1921; *Harper's* published the others in December 1920.

That I dislike the poetic style of Mr. Harding and that I shall vote for Jimmie Cox if I can persuade myself I dislike his poetic style any less.[220] If I complain of this pair as too much for me on such short notice, you wont think it is from a habit of finding fault with what is set before me. I saw the greatness of Cleaveland [*sic*] Roosevelt and Wilson in time to vote for them. And Wilson was a great man. The incalculable hypocracy[221] in all this talk against him for having tried courageously to be a complete leader. Blame him for having failed to be a complete leader but not for having tried to be one. I think he missed being one by just as much as he missed being a complete thinker. The man who could say "nothing permanent is ever achieved by force" was of the class a little too busy to think things out. Of course nothing permanent is ever achieved by anything, though I sometimes half feel as if the end of Carthage was pretty permanently achieved by the Romans. (You won't tell me you see anything so very Punic recrudescent in the world at the moment of writing.) (Or is it with Carthage as with the dinosaur? Force has wiped out the dinosaur, so that he is what is known as extinct. But not so his influence on our courses in paleontology: his soul or rather his bones go marching on.) There is a difficulty here that I make my excuse for turning from politics as a bad job anyway to say a word about your translation to England. There will be a friend or two I want you to see over there for love's sake if not for art's. Chiefest of these will be Jack Haines of Gloucester. I should think you might like to see something of Walter de la Mare too. I could give you a letter to Masefield.[222] But I only know him by letter and have no special entrée to him that you would not have yourself. You don't know how I wish I were going to see some of those fellows over there. Friendship stirs in me again now that the war is over and off my mind. It is like the spring of the year.

You are going to get a lot of writing done, when you are in England I'm sure. You're not going to spend all your free time looking for signatures of Shakespeare to refute Looney with.[223]

---

220. But see also RF's advice to Lesley in the October 14, 1920, letter: "Vote for Debs if you want to, but don't vote for Cox."

221. For another use of this variant spelling of "hypocrisy" see the second of RF's two letters to Lesley Frost dated to mid-March 1920.

222. RF had met the poets Walter de la Mare and John Masefield while living in England (1912–1915).

223. A reference to J. Thomas Looney, author of *Shakespeare Identified in Edward de Vere, the Seventh Earl of Oxford* (New York: Frederick A. Stokes Company, 1920).

I should have got it in when boasting of the family health that I had had a jaundice in the summer that answered in every particular to the diagnosis of jaundice except that it failed to turn me yellow. The doctor was flattering enough to say it would have turned me yellow if there had been any yellow in me to bring to the surface. Little the doctors really know us in our true moral inwardness. If they did they would not make such wild misses in prescribing for us. But seriousness aside I have been too sick or tired or discouraged or something most of the time to stir far from home this summer. I didn't get to Maine again after I saw you last. What awaits me in Augusta takes the strength out of me at the bare thought of going there.[224]

But I must see you soon.

> Always yours
> Robert Frost

Be sure to let me know if you come to New York. I shall make you come home past our place here and stop over a night or so with us. Just what are you planning between now and when you sail?

[To Ridgely Torrence (1874–1950), American poet and poetry editor for the New Republic *from 1920 to 1933. ALS. Princeton.]*

> Arlington Vermont
> October 26 1920

Dear Ridgely:

You'll begin to think I don't see the beauty of having a friend on the editorial staff of The New Republic. But I do and I mean to show it by sending you some poems I have on hand just as soon as I can find time and peace of mind to write them all over[225] I'm moving now (from Franconia, New Hampshire to South Shaftsbury Vermont), but the day must come when I shall be less moving than I have been, and then I promise you.

---

224. RF's sister Jeanie was at this time confined to the Maine Insane Asylum in Augusta, Maine.

225. The *New Republic* printed "A Brook in the City" on March 9, 1921, "Blue-Butterfly Day" on March 16, and "The Census-Taker" and "A Hillside Thaw" on April 6; all were later collected in *NH*.

You're not going to be where I can run across you in my first descent on the settlements this week.[226] I must see you, though, when I am down in December if we are going to continue to be anything more to each other than respecters of each other's poetry.

> Faithfully yours
> Robert Frost

[To Louis Untermeyer (who supplies the dating). ALS. LoC.]

> [South Shaftsbury, VT]
> [November 10, 1920]

Dear Louis:

I guess you'd better send any letters for me to Bennington Vermont, R.F.D. No. 1 and leave the rest to the good God we talked all round the other night without liking to name him—such is our modesty in the spirit as compared with our immodesty in the flesh.

And oh but I was sorry we couldn't go with you to Mecca (since we are on the subject of religion and flesh).[227] You might have spoken sooner I should think. As it was we didnt see how we could give up the idea of going to see the strike of the chorus and the leading lady and the riot of the audience at the Lexington which we had bought tickets for. It was a beauty. We sat a restive hour after starting time and at nine oclock [*sic*] a solitary man in citizen's clothes came before the curtain to ask us to bear with him five minutes longer: the trunk had been lost but was now found that contained what some lady was going to wear if she wore anything. At ten o'clock the same solitary figure a good deal aged with care reappeared in answer to a fierce and vindictive curtain call to say that it was all off: he had squared the chorus who had started the trouble only to end up in a run-in with the leading lady. He didn't know her name, but we could look it up on the program and remember her in our prayers as responsible for our misspent evening. When he denied his own leading lady in such words, someone behind or in the curtain gave an impetuous treble shriek of Oh!—you beast!, and the curtain was agitated and a great wave ran its length. He had the infuriated audience all on its feet in front

---

226. A reading RF was to give at Bryn Mawr on October 30.

227. In *RFLU* (119), Untermeyer identifies the reference as to an event held at the Mecca Temple in New York.

of him asking for its money back. He told them not to-night. He couldn't give them their money back because there was none in the box office, but if they would come to Allen and Fabiani's the next day some thing would be done for them. Irma went to recover our eight dollars but all she saw was a fight between two women; she saw the color of no money. He only said what he said to save his life by getting us to go home. He had no money anywhere, poor man. Which just shows you you don't know enough to appreciate how well off you are yourself.[228]

I doubt if we missed much by not hearing anybody sing, though judging from the way she shrieked the leading lady was a soprano—I wont say a good one because I don't know enough to know. We liked the riot and the place full of police. All that was wanting to round off my time in New York was a few bullets flying somewhere. I have to remember we saw a woman stoned in Van Dam St three nights after [the] election—not because she was a Magdalen [sic] but because she was a Democrat. All the little Italians were after her for Fiume and D'Annunzio. She fought with them and stood them off facing the stones. She was middle aged. New York, New York![229]

I'm enclosing a poem or two for old times sake.[230]

Yourn

R.F.

---

228. On November 6 the *New York Times* published an account of the incident at the Lexington Opera House (which opened in 1914) under the headline "Chorus Wants Pay; Opera Ends in Riot." The chorus insisted on payment in advance, as did also the soprano Ada Paggi. After several hours' delay a stage manager stepped out in front of the curtain to cancel the show, only to be met with jeers. Police were called in to quell the ensuing chaos. Once that was accomplished, an announcement was made to the effect that ticket holders could obtain a refund the next day at Allen and Fabiana, 101 West Forty-First Street.

229. On September 12, 1919, Italian forces commanded by the nationalist—and poet—Gabriele D'Annunzio (1863–1938) seized the city of Fiume (present-day Rijeka, Croatia). A year later, on September 8, 1920, D'Annunzio proclaimed Fiume the seat of the Italian Regency of Carnaro, which was never recognized. The Wilson administration and the Democratic Party had consistently favored a postwar settlement whereby Fiume would fall under Yugoslav rather than Italian rule. Two days after RF wrote to Untermeyer the Treaty of Rapallo was signed, establishing the Free State of Fiume and bringing D'Annunzio's power to an end. The New York press kept up a lively interest in the poet-warrior's exploits.

230. RF enclosed drafts of "Misgiving," "Dust of Snow," and "The Onset," all later collected in *NH*. The wording of the manuscripts differs from the published texts in only two instances, both in "Misgiving": line 9 has "the summoning blast" for "his summoning blast," and line 12 has "That leaves them no further" for "That drops them no further."

[To Louis Untermeyer. ALS. LoC.]

> South Shaftsbury
> Vermont
> November 12 1920

Dear Louis

I somewhat autocratically bade you address me when next you wrote at Bennington this state. You will do well not to do as you were told. Address me where you know I am viz at South Shaftsbury and I will explain later.

I am not going to let the fact that my typewriter was left behind me prevent my sending you a poem or three as per my promise given in the draughty subway high above the roar of the passing cars. Only one is a candied date for a place in your improved Anthropology of Latter-day Poetry for Male and Female Colleges[231]—the Onset; and I don't overurge that. It's a mistake to be too sure of the final rating of your latest written and your latest out. I really can't seem to entertain much doubt of A Tuft of Flowers The Death of the Hired Man, Mending Wall, Birches, Good Bye and Keep Cold The Runaway and Fragmentary Blue. I'd like to think The Onset belongs in that select company. But then so would I like to think everything I ever wrote belonged. I'm a frail mortal.

One or two corrections in your Robert Frost. You say you want the dates right. Lets be truthful about the farming: it didn't earn me a living. Make it "a few years teaching at Derry and Plymouth New Hampshire," and "place" not "farm" in Gloucestershire. You are welcome to any old golden opinions of me you like so long as you are particular about my facts.

Don't mind the one offending word in "Misgiving."[232] It is a good poem I wrote years and years and years ago and am now just publishing in The Yale Review. Dust of Snow has no traps for the unwary chronologists. It is simply a little poem done rather recently by me about as I am.

This is the last about me myself for a long time let's hope. So try to reorganize.

> Farewell.
> R.F.

---

231. The second edition of Untermeyer's *Modern American Poetry* (New York: Harcourt, Brace and Howe, 1921). The "one or two corrections in your Robert Frost" mentioned later in the letter concern a typescript draft of a biographical sketch Untermeyer prepared for the volume. All the changes that RF requested here were made.

232. The archaic word "fain" in line 7. The poem appeared in the *Yale Review* for January 1921; as for "unwary chronologists," see RF to Cox, March 1, 1921.

[*To George R. Elliott. ALS. ACL.*]

South Shaftsbury Vermont
November 16 1920

Dear Elliott:

It's you, you friend, who have been telling them they want to see something of me at Toronto. Don't think I don't appreciate the chance you gave me with yourself in the first place and have since given me with so many others. Where would I be if it weren't for you and the like of you?

I'm just going to tell you a matter that may amuse you. You know I left Amherst all so irresponsible. You must have wondered how I could go and come as I pleased on nothing but poetry and yet seem to be taken care of as if I hadn't defied fate. I've wondered myself. The latest interposition in my favor when I had ceased to deserve further clemency is an appointment as Consulting Editor of Henry Holt and Co.[233] I owe this under Heaven to Lincoln MacVeagh a younger member of the firm. The pay will be small but large for a poet and the work between you and me will be nothing but seeing MacVeagh once in a while in friendship as I would see you (if you would only come over here.) (Please let me know when you can come.)

I wrote you a considerable letter of late which I have strange misgivings about. I once by some crossing of the mental wires addressed a letter to you as Carl Young.[234] I hope I didn't do that in this case because it was too long a letter to lose. Not that it contained anything very important except assurances of my good will that I might not be able to formulate as well again and then again I might. I said something in it about the friend or two I want you to meet for me in England. I said something about having neither heart nor stomach for any of the candidates you had to offer for the Presidency. That was before the mob let out its roar against the life of one poor old broken man.[235] What

---

233. RF began work as a consulting editor for Henry Holt and Company on November 1 at a salary of $100 a month. He reviewed manuscripts and offered advice regarding Holt's list.

234. RF refers here to two earlier letters to Elliot, one mistakenly addressed to him as "Mr Young" (March 18, 1920), the other dated October 23, 1920. Karl Young (1879–1943) was a medievalist and professor of English at the University of Wisconsin–Madison.

235. On November 2 Harding defeated Cox by one of the largest margins in American history; hence RF's reference to the "mob's" repudiation of Wilson, who had led the Democrats (Cox's party) for nearly a decade.

a roar it was. They say Wilson tries to jest about it. No times are any less brutal than any other times.

> Always yours
> Robert Frost

[*To Lincoln MacVeagh. MacVeagh, then head of the trade department at Henry Holt and Company, penciled in a note on the letter: "After my 1st visit to Mr. Frost in hopes he would stay with H. Holt and Co." ALS. Jones.*]

> South Shaftsbury Vermont
> November 16 1920

Dear MacVeagh:

Not so much what you did as the way you did it convinces me that I have been right all along in looking for a business relationship into which friendship could enter. I like to see the opposite of cynicism in me rewarded. Of course thanks no end. And thanks to Bristol, too, if you'll convey them.[236] Now we're away for a fresh start and nobody's on our conscience. What's to prevent our achieving something?

Once you asked me for a fair copy of The Onset. I should think it might come in appropriately now.

We're at South Shaftsbury at last. Part of the roof is off for repairs, the furnace is not yet under us and winter is closing in. But we're here. Will you have the address made right on the books so that letters will reach me directly?

The proofs of Mountain Interval have come in. I guess I won't bother with them. Let's go ahead with the printing. I hope DuChene liked the idea of our using a picture of the head.[237]

I shall see you somewhere around December 9th when I'm down for my next at Bryn Mawr.

> Always yours faithfully
> Robert Frost

---

236. Herbert Bristol was president of Henry Holt and Company.

237. Proofs for the second edition of *MI* (published in April 1921). A photograph of Aroldo Du Chêne's bust of RF served as the frontispiece for the book.

[*To George Herbert Palmer (1842–1933), American scholar, translator, and professor of philosophy at Harvard. ALS. Wellesley.*]

> South Shaftsbury
> Vermont
> November 17 1920

Dear Mr Palmer:

You will have to admit I am rather wonderful in the way I have gone and come for twenty-five years on nothing but poetry and yet have always been taken care of somehow. As one who has suffered a friend's anxiety when I have gone away from things, you are entitled to derive all the comfort you can, I think, from the news when I have come back to them. This letter is to tell you that I am again all right as you would reckon all right. I am regularly attached to the house of Henry Holt and Company as a sort of consulting editor with nothing much to do. My duties were made ridiculously light for me at Amherst. They are made lighter with the same considerations in the new office. You may not be too glad I am to be paid for doing next to nothing: you may not think a sinecure good for me even at my age. At least you won't be sorry I am settled down again in an almost nameable occupation. Don't miss the point, though, that it is the reward of my simplicity in staking all on poetry as often as it becomes an out-and-out choice between poetry and anything else in the world. Some folly undeniably makes friends for itself that though they may lose patience with it can never quite stand by and let it come to grief. I suppose that is the secret of it. One ought not to presume on such folly and such friends too often, ought one?

We are going to live over here on this side of Vermont for a while where I can be easily reached from New York for consultation in my new capacity (this with an air of importance). If I am no nearer you and Boston, neither am I any further off and the trains are more convenient. I was deeply smitten with a consciousness of my own recreancy the other day when I came across in Philadelphia a picture of the very house with all the beautiful panelling I sighed over in Boxford last June.[238] What I have taken is no such house as that. We have a cottage with red gables above white limestone walls, dating well

---

238. RF refers to the Holyoke-French House, in Boxford, Essex County, Massachusetts. Built in 1704 and renovated in 1760, the house is now on the register of United States Historical Places. RF was in the Philadelphia area to give a reading at Bryn Mawr on October 30.

back to the Revolution. Some of the faced stones in it must have made a load singly for two oxen. There is no imported elegance, nothing that could not be worked out on the spot with a saw and a plane—those two tools. But the place has charms. I wish you could see it some time.

It gives me pleasure to think of you as busy and well.

Always yours
Robert Frost

[*To Henry Seidel Canby (1878–1961), editor, critic, and professor of English at Yale. Canby edited the* Literary Review *section of the* New York Evening Post *from 1920 to 1924. ALS. Yale.*]

South Shaftsbury Vt
November 25 1920

My dear Canby

My foot kicks out normally when I am struck below the patella: I don't think I am too tolerant; but I couldn't find it in my heart to push Pound under in the Atlantic if he should try to come ashore here. I should let him land and decide what to do with him afterward. And while I was deciding (if the decision were left to me) I should be perfectly willing you should support him out of the treasury of The Evening Post. Only I should advise you to pay him his salary with a ten foot pole so as not to get identified with him in anybody's mind. And if you were intending to exploit him a little to get some of your money back you could run him like a moving picture reel in a fire-proof compartment where when he really got going you could shut him in and keep him from spreading to the rest of the theater.

But what you want me to say is whether as I see it, he shows in this letter as good from his own point of view.[239] Mind you I like his letters. I'm always

---

239. See "A Letter from Ezra Pound," *Literary Review, New York Evening Post,* December 4, 1920. It reads, in part: "I think you will make a frightful (not necessarily commercially fatal, but frightful from an intellectual standpoint) mistake if you don't realise at once how utterly gone to pot England is, vie intellectual et littéraire, at this moment, after the five years of war and two of muddle. The manner in which any vital idea, any idea which really hits anything, is excluded from the whole press is amazing. . . . Hence the system of bribed knaves and carefully selected boobies (these latter often pleasant and university trained) who are put in command of the press." Pound then enjoins Canby to "consider also the Georgians and (far fetched) the poetry that brought down the [Herbert Henry]

glad in a low down way when someone else is willing to make an ass of himself to amuse me. It saves me the trouble of going crazy to amuse myself. But grant him all he asks: grant that he is suffering from such an interesting, such an exquisite, malady of the soul as hyperaesthesia. So is George Santayana. And see the difference. I dont believe Pound knows what he is suffering from. He simply knows there is something the matter; and he finds momentary rest from self-examination in supposing he has found what it is in the latest disease he has read about in the quack advertisements.

His real trouble is short circuiting. He thinks he thinks, and he may think more than he does anything else related to the arts, but his thoughts round-off too shortly, without going out and back through enough wire. He thinks for example that America could lead Europe by following Europe more closely than in the past. How could he state that and not clear it up for himself? He thinks his friend Tom Elliot's [sic] writing acceptably for The Times is not the same thing as De la Mares doing it. Yes, because Tom Elliot can honestly mean one thing to The Times' audience and another to himself and Pound and Lewis [240] But as I say I am grateful to anyone who will get himself up in such style to go on the streets. You'll never get me to discourage him. Let's have him over (at your expense) if only to affront the professors of grammar and syntax.

Frankly I'm disappointed (I fear I seem so) to find Pound so nearly where I left him when I last saw him before the war, except that he has lightened himself of two or three heroes. He has got rid of Yeats (because Yeats visited Wordsworth's grave, Yeats says) and Conrad (in Hueffer's quarrel).[241] Otherwise he

---

Asquith Government [in 1916]: 'Il [sic] cherchent des sentiments pour les accomoder [sic] a leur vocabulaire' ["they hunt for sentiments to fit their vocabulary"]. Symptom: a 'horror of exact statement' in politics and in the official poetry of the Asquith period." RF had of course been associated with the Georgian poets while in England (under the Asquith government). "What I get from your Literary Review," Pound later informs Canby, "is the sense that it is younger than the Times Literary Supplement; and I don't see why you should keep on the scum and left-over slush of a past English decade, or import into the U.S.A. merely the current cheapjack stuff."

240. T. S. Eliot regularly wrote for the *Times Literary Supplement*, as did Walter de la Mare. The English novelist and painter Wyndham Lewis (1882–1957) had been an associate of Pound's since the mid-teens, as a fellow "vorticist" and as a contributing editor to the short-lived magazine *Blast* (1914).

241. Ford Madox Ford (Hueffer), collaborated with Joseph Conrad on writing three novels, *The Inheritors* (1901), *Romance* (1903), and *The Nature of a Crime* (published in 1924, though written much earlier). Ford and Conrad later fell out over financial arrangements;

goes and comes on the same limited set of names—Flint, Aldington, Hueffer, Lewis and Brzeska.[242] They make a small world—a small Europe even—a small England. I wouldn't have America shirk the contemplation of small-ness. Science is as microscopic as it is telescopic. It may be intended art should be. Smallness may be of strictness. Good Puritans know what that means. I should want to be fair to Pound but for what he says about De la Mare. He knows he's dirty there. But for that I should try harder to think it was consci-entious strictness with him and not just meanness narrowing him away to nothing.

Having taken the letter, I had to say something about it in sending it back.

Always yours honestly

RF

[*To Leo Taylor, an editorial assistant for Henry Holt and Company, but otherwise un-identified. ALS. Princeton.*]

South Shaftsbury Vt

November 26 1920

Dear Mr Taylor:

I am sorry if my not returning the proofs has caused you inconvenience. I decided that as long as they were to go back after all I would run my eye over them—and was rewarded by finding a number of places where the spacing of the earlier edition could be improved on.[243] Such mistakes as I found were all in the earlier editions I suspect.

Very truly yours

Robert Frost

Ford also later complained that his contributions to the novels had not been adequately recognized.

242. The poet F. S. Flint (1885–1960); Richard Aldington (1892–1962), English poet and husband of H. D. (Hilda Doolittle); and the French-born sculptor Henri Gaudier-Brzeska (1891–1915), who, like Lewis, fell in with Pound and the vorticists.

243. The first edition of *MI* appeared in 1916; the second (1921) is under discussion here.

[To Julia Patton (1873–1953), a member of the faculty at Russell Sage College, which at the time was in its fifth year of operation. ALS. BU.]

South Shaftsbury Vt.

November 28 1920

My dear Miss Patton:

Your young nephew and I spoke the same language and when we talked we got at a good many things together. He told me all about your relation to the school you are in. I think it is something like my relation to such public as will listen to me. I take 'em practical and give them just the least lift by metaphor into poetry. If they are in a chronic state of poetry or aestheticism or literariness, they are spoiled for my purposes: I can do nothing for them. (They are welcome to do anything they can for themselves.) No metaphor can start fair except in practical people, or perhaps I should put it, except in what is practical in people, for I suppose there is something practical in almost everybody, however bookish and closed to experience. I could go on to show that the very refinement of culture presupposes a good share of the nature left practical: but I must save something to say to your practical girls when I have to face them.

It is hard to treat a letter like this of yours as business. But I am a poet with a living to earn, and the name of your school suggests means to pay the poor piper. I might be afraid of charging you too much; I am more afraid of not charging the shades of the Russel [sic] Sages enough.[244] The best way out of this quandary is to leave the price to you. Would the seventh or eighth of December be right for you?

You will tell me where Carl[245] is and what he is thinking about this year when I see you.

Sincerely yours

Robert Frost

My new address is
South Shaftsbury Vt.

---

244. Russell Sage (1816–1906) was a financier, railroad magnate, associate of Jay Gould, and a United States congressman from New York (1853–1857). Upon his death, his wife, Olivia Slocum Sage, inherited his fortune and devoted it to philanthropy, founding, among many other enterprises, Russell Sage College in Troy, New York, in 1916.

245. Presumably Patton's "young nephew." See also RF to Patton, December 12, 1924.

[To Louis Untermeyer. ALS. LoC.]

So Shaftsbury Vermont

December 5 1920

Dear Louis:

This is nothing except to apprize you that small watch of Switzerland (Tavannes) is running along very lovable and current on schedule time with new spring main introduced—if anything is to be said rather beforehand than retarde. So that it not failing I shall ought to catch train for New York by the forelock on Friday and Saturday and may easily see you a few momentoes.[246] I hope for you.

Sincere wishes

Robert Frost

No sign up for Mr D'Hell's novel work.[247] Where is it you suppose?

[To Ridgely Torrence. The letter is undated and without heading, but seems to be associated with RF's visit to New York on the weekend of December 11–12, 1920. ALS. Princeton.]

[South Shaftsbury, VT]

[December 8, 1920]

Dear Ridgley [*sic*]:

If you don't look out there will be a meeting of the Author-versus-editor's Association of North America at your house in Waverly Place some day or night next week to make final arrangements for our Less poetry for more money campaign of next year.[248] Meanwhile a Merry Christmas!

Very truly yours

R. Frost

---

246. Untermeyer explains in a note to *RFLU:* "The Tavannes timekeeper [which Untermeyer had given RF] came accompanied by a polyglot advertisement—which prompted Robert's broken-English reply to my inquiry as to its performance" (123).

247. Floyd Dell's novel *Moon-Calf* (New York: Alfred Knopf, 1921).

248. Harriet Moody owned the apartment on Waverly Place; the 1920 census lists Torrence as renting it.

[*To Lincoln MacVeagh. ALS. Princeton.*]

South Shaftsbury
December 15 1920

Dear MacVeagh:

I meant fully to see you again before lighting out on Monday; but the time got away from me. I had my talk with George Martin and then had to look sharp to make my train.[249] I particularly wanted to say a word to you about Dresbach (if that's his name).[250] Let's go slow on him. I should hate to be the cause of your missing a good book when it was right in front of you. Suppose there is somewhat too much of it to be good. Can't we consider cutting it down to its true self? That's what we should be here for. A lot of young writers only come to something by a reduction they make themselves or others make for them.

I wish we could happen to find a good clear case of poet next year. The field has staid about as it was in 1914.

I learned that there's a good night train leaving the Grand Central at 12.25 and setting you down here at 9 in the morning. You must try it before long, but not till we get at least a kitchen sink up for you to wash your hands of the railroad in.

Always yours
Robert Frost

[*To Roland Holt (1867–1931), son of Henry Holt and the vice president of Henry Holt and Company from 1903 to 1924. He was also a theater critic. RF was in the audience when* A Way Out *was performed at the Northampton Academy of Music on February 24, 1919. ALS. Jones.*]

South Shaftsbury Vt.
December 16 1920

Dear Mr Holt:

Of course I know how to be grateful for anything you may do or have done for my dramatic career which is just starting. I want "A Way Out" acted all it can be. Good of you to urge it on people.

---

249. Martin edited *Farm and Fireside;* see RF's October 16, 1920, letter to Bartlett.

250. Glenn Ward Dresbach (1889–1968), an American poet. Henry Holt and Company published his *In Colors of the West* in 1922.

The play is not just as I would print it if we ever bring it to book. The single time I saw it acted, I was inclined to think the killing unnecessary—at any rate on the stage. Asa might better have been dragged out fighting with feeble desperation. The final mystery would be all the greater.

I wonder if the Provincetown Players would try it. It is all important that it should be done by two players well matched in height and type. You could explain the change I propose in the ending.

I'm sure to do more plays and playlets—since you are good enough to ask. Just watch me, but not too intently.[251]

> Sincerely yours
> Robert Frost

[*To Ridgely Torrence. Date derived from internal evidence and from details provided by Lawrance Thompson in YT (159). ALS. Princeton.*]

> South Shaftsbury Vt
> [mid-December 1920]

Dear Ridgley [*sic*]:

Amy Lowell seems to think she has been asked to write your lead-off article; and let's let it go at that. She is sure to do it well. I'll try to have you a poem—a good one—better than any gone before. What an evening you gave me out of heart.[252]

> Ever yours
> Robert Frost

---

251. RF is replying to a letter of inquiry Holt had sent on December 10 in which he asked whether RF would like him to recommend the play to the Provincetown Players, and also whether RF intended to write more "playlets." Drafts of only two unpublished plays (aside from the published "masques") survive in finished form (see *CPPP*, 576–625).

252. Lawrance Thompson reports that RF spent the evening with Torrence in New York City on December 10, where he also met with the poet and dramatist Percy MacKaye, who would soon be instrumental in securing RF's fellowship at the University of Michigan; see RF to MacKaye, January 1, 1921 (and subsequent letters).

[*To Harriet Monroe. ALS. Chicago.*]

South Shaftsbury Vermont
December 17 1920

Dear Miss Monroe:

I fully intended you should have a few more poems to go with that Article,[253] so to call it; and you shall have if you can wait for me. People nearer than you (as New York is nearer than Chicago) and only less respected have got all I had on hand away from me. I am cleaned out for the moment. But I am having some more at a great rate.

And while you are waiting for me, don't you think I ought to have the Article back to rename and perhaps in places retouch? I'm never done with a poem till it's in print and then I try to feel done with it forever.

Thanks for the tip on English reviewing. Once Richard Aldington wrote about my books in all friendliness.[254] It seems to me he should ask them of me directly if he wants to have anything more to do with them. Suppose he were forgetting them on purpose, how should I look reminding him of them? I leave it to your judgement.

Always yours faithfully
Robert Frost

Please notice my new address.

---

253. "The Witch of Coös," published in *Poetry* in January 1922.

254. Aldington reviewed RF's *NB* in the *Egoist* in 1914; he was a regular contributor of reviews and columns to *Poetry,* including reports about literary goings-on in London.

[To Wilfred Davison (1887–1929), American scholar, educator, and the first dean of the Bread Loaf School of English (1921–1929) at Middlebury College. The text is derived from SL, 261. It is not clear why, in compiling that volume, Lawrance Thompson omitted some portion of the letter, as he appears to have done after the ellipsis. The misspelling of Davison's name is as given in SL. At the time Thompson prepared SL he listed the letter, in the form of a typed copy, as collected in the private archive of Reginald Cook. We have been unable to locate either the manuscript of this letter or the copy.]

South Shaftsbury Vt
December 19 1920

Dear Mr Davidson [*sic*]:

I have been a good deal interested in your new Summer School from afar off.[255] I have been wondering if what is behind it may not be what has been troubling me lately, namely, the suspicion that we aren't getting enough American literature out of our colleges to pay for the hard teaching that goes into them.[256] After getting a little American literature out of myself the one thing I have cared about in life is getting a lot out of our school system. I did what in me lay to incite to literature at Amherst. This school year I shall spend two weeks at each of two colleges talking in seminars on the same principles I talked on there. School days are the creative days and college and even high school undergraduates must be about making something before the evil days come when they will have to admit to themselves their minds are more critical than creative.[257] I might fit into your summer plan with a course on the Responsibilities of Teachers of Composition—to their country to help make what is sure to be the greatest nation in wealth the greatest in art also. I should particularly like to encounter the teachers who refuse to expect of human nature more than a correct business letter. I should have to cram what I did into two or at most three weeks. [. . .]

Sincerely yours,
Robert Frost

---

255. Soon to become the Bread Loaf School of English at Middlebury.

256. See RF's late September–early October letter to the Bryn Mawr "Reeling and Writhing Club."

257. An echo of Ecclesiastes 12:1: "Remember now thy Creator in the days of thy youth, while the evil days come not, nor the years draw nigh, when thou shalt say, I have no pleasure in them."

[To Otto Manthey-Zorn. ALS. ACL.]

South Shaftsbury Vt
December 21 1920

Dear Otto:

It was too late to do anything about your letter before you would be likely to be sailing for home on Dana St.[258] So I saved myself to welcome you. Here is a good place to be after what you must have seen over there. What a letter it was! You were born to be honest. You had the experience of living for a while in a country really prostrated by war. That I take it was about all your adventure came to. The future hasn't started out of the ground yet. But it was worth all the pains to find it out. I wish I could have an evening with you soon to hear in detail what this person and that person said about it when he was least trying to tell about it. We'll be settled soon so that we can entertain a friend. Will you come up? Its only a few miles further than you would come to Williams to see a game of football.

Greetings from all of us to all of you.[259]

Ever yours
Robert Frost

[To George Whicher. ALS. ACL.]

South Shaftsbury Vt
December 21 1920

Mr dear George:

A thought for you for Christmas.

And if you hear it told against me that I have become a literary adviser to Henry Holt & Co, please remember in extenuation that I may have done it to post myself where I could help a friend should he ever come to market with a novel made out of Stephen Burroughs.[260]

Always yours
Robert Frost

---

258. In central Amherst, not far from the college.

259. Ethel Manthey-Zorn, Otto's wife, and their son Richard.

260. RF wrote a preface to a 1924 reissue of Stephen Burroughs's *The Memoirs of the Notorious Stephen Burroughs of New Hampshire* (New York: Dial Press).

[To Carl Van Doren. ALS. Princeton.]

South Shaftsbury Vermont

December 27 1920

Dear Mr Van Doren:

I should like to do that and I thank the Department and particularly you for the chance.[261] I thank you too for the "real poet." Stick to it at least till I am dead and out of the way if you want to keep me good-natured.*

You said a good deal about small town life in America in reviewing Main Street lately: but not as much as I've been thinking I would get out of you in private talk. What I want to ask you will keep a while. I'm afraid you hold with Lewis and some others that a little European harm would do America good. You like to dream that small town life over there is perhaps more aesthetic than with us.[262] After the way I heard you give us credit for folk songs, I'm disposed to treat you as an authority on these states. I set up to know something about them. But you know more, I suspect. Nevertheless—

I haven't forgotten that I'm to be allowed to print a poem in The Nation when I have one with a person in it. As time was not of the essence of the agreement, I dont suppose I have to ask for an extension of time.[263]

Always yours friendly

Robert Frost

*and unspoiled: I can't be kept from spoiling after I am dead.

---

261. RF is responding to an invitation to read at Columbia on May 31, 1921, as Phi Beta Kappa poet.

262. In his unsigned review of Sinclair Lewis's *Main Street* (1920), published in the November 10, 1921, issue of *The Nation,* Van Doren had written: "His thesis is the standardization of the innumerable Main Streets of our small towns, the savorless flatness of that life, the complete substitution of the mechanical for the vital, the tawdry spiritual poverty of a people that 'has lost the power of play as well as the power of impersonal thought,' and the menacing extension, like a creeping paralysis, of this form of existence, so that the Minnesota Swedes exchange 'their spiced puddings and red jackets for fried pork-chops and congealed white blouses,' and trade 'the ancient Christmas hymns of the fjords for "She's My Jazzland Cutie."' He has a stern enough sense of the danger of what Alice Meynell once called 'decivilization' and of the incredible arrogance of the actors in that process."

263. "The Pauper Witch of Grafton" appeared in *The Nation* on April 13, 1921. See RF to Van Doren, April 22, 1921.

[To Wilfred Davison. ALS. Middlebury.]

South Shaftsbury Vt

December 27 1920

Dear Mr. Davison:

We are agreed on everything but the money.[264] I suppose you offer what you can. But I really couldn't give of my time and strength at that rate— particularly of my strength, which I find I have more and more to consider. It would be stretching a point to offer to come for a week and give five lectures for $150 and my expenses. I am sorry if that seems too much, for I wanted the chance to show my belief in what you have undertaken in literature and teaching.

With all good wishes for it, I am,

Sincerely yours

Robert Frost

[To Louis Untermeyer. ALS. LoC.]

South Shaftsbury Vermont

December 28 1920

Dear Louis:

Seriously now I am sick with disgust. My shrill New England whang! Am I shrill in speech thought or style? Does shrill or twang (twang is probably meant) describe me or anything I have done? I cant help suffering from such words. But is it for me to defend myself from them? I had about forgotten the existence of the poetry society of america when you and another friend came in on me with the news that I had been elected a something in it.[265] Of course it was without my knowledge and consent. You won't believe this. But Elinor will tell you I seldom get the society's printed letters and absolutely never open what I get. That is what I call exemplary. I am willing to speak defensively to you—but to not many others in this world. I'm capable of some humility with a friend. But ordinarily I'm a sufferingly proud devil. Maybe you'll tell me how

---

264. See RF to Davison, December 19, 1920.

265. RF was elected president in absentia at a meeting of the New England Poetry Club (not of the Poetry Society of America, as RF suggests) held on February 24, 1919. See *LRF-1*, 663–665.

I'll best score in the long run on the poetry society, by never mentioning it even to itself from this day forth or by noticing it so far as to ask it to resign me from the high office it has honored me with. And speaking of their honoring me with anything, that flock of pro-English sparrows, shall I honor them with a row?[266]

But oh, dear me there's better things to think of than our troubles. Our shrillness and our water pipes that aint in all vanish in the thought of the picture you two sent us. We never had this sort of thing to make a house with before till Chapin gave us the portrait of Elinor.[267] The faint landscape is lovely.

The rug Elinor sent Jean has a story you mustn't attempt to imagine and do in verse yourself because I shall do it for you someday and call it Under Foot. The truth is more tragic than anything you can imagine. But I don't want to frighten you so you won't like to have it around.

I'll see that you have photographs of the bust, front and left cheek.[268]

The only other news besides what you tell me (and by the way was Melvin right in ascribing the offensive words shrill and whang to Theodore Maynard?[269]) is the news that I have just had a cat named after me in Wash-

---

266. The context for the joke is rich. In America, the English sparrow (*Passer domesticus*) is an invasive species. In 1920 the bird was notorious for driving from urban and suburban areas such indigenous American songbirds as the tree swallow, bluebird, and house wren. English sparrows were first released in New York and Boston in the 1850s in an effort to control cutworms. The population explosion was exacerbated when Eugene Schieffelin, of the American Acclimatization Society, built birdhouses for the sparrows in Central Park. In 1859, William Cullen Bryant penned a poem titled the "The Old-World Sparrow," celebrating the advent of the English bird and its ability to control pests. However, the English sparrow, a seed eater, has little effect on insect populations. Once American ornithologists recognized that, and saw that English sparrows were decimating native bird populations, they mounted a campaign to extirpate them. Sentimentalists fought back. The so-called "Sparrow Wars" that ensued heated up in the 1870s and continued into the twentieth century. In 1912 the U.S. Department of Agriculture issued a pamphlet, *The English Sparrow as a Pest* (Farmers' Bulletin 493, by Ned Dearborn). At about the same time, Joseph H. Dodson and Company was aggressively marketing its patented "Dodson Sparrow Trap." Its advertisements called for a return of "native song birds" to "our gardens."

267. The artist James Chapin.

268. The Aroldo Du Chêne bust of RF, a photograph of which served as the frontispiece to the second edition of *MI*.

269. Nowhere in Maynard's "Snow the Predominant Note in Robert Frost's Poetry" is mention made of RF's "shrill New England whang," etc. Instead, the article praises him astutely. See RF to Braithwaite, September 4, 1920 (and the notes thereto). "Melvin" is

ington D.C. in the household of a friend of the outgoing administration (so I
can't see how it can lead to political preferment.) I shall have to go ahead with
my original plan to set my cap for Harding to alienate him from Edgar
Saltus.[270] You stick to what you stick to in spite of what it is and I stick to what
I stick to because of what it is. I am the more flattering. Yours because of every
thing

Robert Frost

[*To John Livingston Lowes (1867–1945), American scholar and literary critic, best known
now as author of* The Road to Xanadu: A Study in the Ways of the Imagination
(1927). Lowes was on the faculty at Harvard from 1918 to 1939. ALS. Harvard.]

South Shaftsbury Vermont

December 28 1920

Dear Mr Lowes:

On December 2nd I had it from you by telephone that you wanted to get
out of the bad business I had got you into; on December 9th (I'm particular
about the dates) I had it from Stork by telephone that he was sure you wanted
to stand by him: he had heard from you within two or three days, or more
recently than I had.[271] I knew he lied and I ached to call him a liar (though it
burnt out the fuses) and offer him any kind of satisfaction he demanded anywhere outside the limits of the city of brotherly love. But I had you and Miss
Bates to consider. You have just had one row and don't want a second; she as
a lady has probably never had any and doesn't want a first.

---

unidentified, although RF may be referring to Untermeyer's cousin and partner in the
jewelry business, Melville Untermeyer.

270. Edgar Evertson Saltus (1855–1921), American novelist and philosopher. As Untermeyer points out in *RFLU*, Oscar Wilde observed that in Saltus's novels, "Passion struggles with grammar on every page" (125). He adds that Saltus was a favorite of President
Warren Harding.

271. Charles Wharton Stork (1881–1971), American playwright, poet, novelist, editor of
Contemporary Verse (1917 to 1925), and professor of English at the University of Pennsylvania. RF had agreed, with Lowes and Katherine Lee Bates, an English professor at
Wellesley College and author of "America the Beautiful" (1893), to judge a poetry contest
Stork arranged, the prize money for which was to be donated by the businessman and
poet James Brookes More (1884–1960). See also RF to Lowes, February 10, 1921 (and the
notes thereto), and *LRF-1*, 716, for a November 19, 1919, letter from RF to Stork.

I see but few ways out of it for us as it stands. We could beg off on the grounds of sickness—not just sickness of the job, which we have tried and which hasn't worked—but such sickness as men die of. For plausability [*sic*] we could have our doctors certify us as suffering all three from different forms of insanity, as paranoia melancholia and mania. I choose mania and mean to manifest it in uncontrollable impulses to tear and trample poetry that ought never to have been admitted to print.

Or, seriously, we could take refuge in our original plan. We could say that after deliberation we found ourselves unable to do any better for him than we had agreed to do in the first place, name him ten poets we liked well or well enough (we could try to be cordial) or indifferently well. From these he would be perfectly free for all of us to pick if he must under the law his one or two to give the money to.

I will say for Stork that I never met such a sinister politician since I was a politician myself in the Bosship of Buckley in the worst days of San Francisco.[272]

Pardon so much letter, and accept my best wishes for as happy a new year as the circumstances will admit of.

> Sincerely yours
> Robert Frost

[*To Harriet Moody. ALS. Chicago.*]

> South Shaftsbury Vermont
> December 28 1920

Dear Mrs Moody:

If some things seem providential, what have you to say to the way we managed to miss each other in New York? Blaspheme not, you say, and I won't. But it is as permissible I hope to see design in things when they go wrong as when they go right.

I had fully meant to get round to Henry Holt's office before I caught my train for Vermont. If I had got round and heard that Padraic Collum [*sic*] had

---

272. Owing to his father's politicking in San Francisco, RF had in his youth met the infamous saloonkeeper and Democratic Party boss Christopher Augustine "Blind Boss" Buckley (1845–1922).

been looking for me of course I wouldn't be here now:[273] I would have been staying on in New York to talk over with you our apples not of discord but of harmony.[274] I had never a suspicion that you would be where I could see you. I had tried twice to get the Torrences by telephone on the off chance that they might be back from Ohio. Not having much hope, I gave up too easily. And now look at how blank the months stretch ahead of us before we can possibly meet.

True, I shall be in New York again toward the 20th of February if that is anything to you. I shall see the Torrences then, they willing.[275]

I have half a mind to accept the invitation of the Press Club in Des Moines to read to it late in January for the chance it would give me to look in on you in passing through Chicago.[276]

You want to talk about farms and I do for all I have invested in a farm and old stone (Paleolithic) house of some charm here just out of Bennington. To you alone I will confess I am still looking for a home. I may settle down and like this place. My present agony may be homesickness for the home I've left behind me rather than for the home that never was on land or sea. Something unusual is the matter with me so that I can do nothing but write poems plays and novels. I'm never so serious as when I'm in earnest. There must have been a reason for our missing each other so dramatically and it may have been to keep me from saying anything against this farm which I may live to be sorry for. I never saw a solitary fault in anything I owned before. Such is my loyalty. And I shall not begin at this late day. Things I have disowned are another matter.

---

273. Padraic Colum (1881–1972), Irish poet, novelist, playwright. Colum and his wife, Mary Gunning Maguire, lived in New York at the time.

274. An allusion to the Greek goddess Eris, whose name means "strife" and who is said to have been responsible for the Trojan War. At the wedding of Peleus and Thetis, to which she had not been invited, she tossed a golden apple into the party bearing the inscription "For the most beautiful one." Three goddesses disputed the prize. Paris of Troy was told to choose the winner. He chose Aphrodite, after she promised him the love of Helen, reputedly the most beautiful woman in the world.

275. RF and his wife were in New York from February 16 to February 24, 1921; they stayed with Harriet Moody at her apartment at 107 Waverly Place. Ridgely Torrence and his wife Olivia, often to be found at Waverly Place, in fact spent the winter of 1920–1921 in Oxford, Ohio, where Torrence was teaching at Miami University.

276. See RF to Moody, February 4, 1921; he never made the trip to Iowa.

In witness that I haven't disowned you or your household permit me to sign myself

Yours respectfully

Robert Frost

[To George Browne. ALS. Plymouth.]

South Shaftsbury Vermont

December 28 1920

Dear Browne:

Do you see what I have written above. You do, do you? And you want to know where in New England that hole is. Well west of the Connecticut O Praeceptor.[277] And it is not a hole, for it is in on a high hill beautiful for situation. But what did we want to go away off to the very verge and ragged edge of New England for? Perhaps so we could come as near getting out of New England as possible without saying we were out of it. No for no such reason. For no reason at all to be frank. We were captivated by a stone cottage a hundred and fifty years old—carried away like a lot of sillies. Stone charms ought to endure. We probably won't have cause to repent our infatuation in any change of the aspect of the object of our passion. A good many of the stones in our outer walls would have made singly a load for a yoke of oxen. But I refuse to defend our action. Here we are and here we mean to stay till we sell out and go somewhere else to settle down for good. This is not final. I can say that already. I talk like W. L. George looking cooly about for his fourth wife at his wedding (mind you, not funeral) with the third.[278] Preposition didnt come right.

No I'll tell you why we came away off here. It was to be where you could have a better excuse for not coming to see us than you had when you were in Plymouth and we in Franconia only twenty five miles away. As long as you weren't coming, we thought we'd supply you with sufficient reason for not coming.

---

277. Browne was the head (preceptor) of the Browne and Nichols School in Cambridge, Massachusetts. As for "that hole": RF puns on "bury" and "shaft."

278. Walter Lionel George (1882–1926), a French-born English novelist; he was thrice married, twice widowed.

But why be bitter? The League of Nations is scotched, all's well with the world.[279]

A sculptor[280] busted me so to speak this summer and there's a picture of the bust going round. If you happen to see it, don't think I am gone to join Julius Caesar and the rest of the Museumites. I am simply getting ready to last to be a precious stone when etc.

Remember me to everyone and particularly Mrs Browne (see what she did by voting!) and Jack in his fastnesses.[281]

Hoping the crime wave[282] so much talked of hasnt struck you personally I'm

Yours possibly more than ever
Robert Frost

[To Percy MacKaye (1875–1956), American poet and dramatist. When this letter was written he was poet in residence at Miami University, in Oxford, Ohio. ALS. DCL.]

South Shaftsbury Vermont
January 17 1921

My dear Percy:

Your letter finds me in a good frame of mind to listen to any proposal to rescue me from the public lecture platform for a living. I have had to interrupt one of my best spells of writing to go out talking this winter. I'm just home now from one lecture trip and about to go out on another; and I'm rather

---

279. Republican senators Henry Cabot Lodge and William Borah led domestic opposition to the Treaty of Versailles and successfully blocked the United States' entry into the League of Nations in 1919.

280. Aroldo Du Chêne.

281. John "Jack" Gallishaw, husband of Browne's daughter Eleanor. Browne's wife, Emily, was a suffragette; the Nineteenth Amendment, granting women the right to vote, had been ratified in August 1920, just in time for the fall election.

282. RF refers to the spike in crime occasioned by Prohibition. By late 1920 the matter had already been much debated, for example, in a December 11 editorial, "America's High Tide of Crime," in the Literary Digest of the New York Post: "That a 'wave of crime' is sweeping America with a deluge of murders, burglaries, robberies, and every kind of violence and lawlessness seems proved to some by the headlines reporting crime upon crime that greet us in every morning's paper."

sad about it.[283] Not that I don't always do more than enough writing to keep from being pitied as the father of a family in spite of everything. But I shouldnt mind doing still more, and if Dr Burton[284] would like to make provision for me while I did still more, I could only be grateful to him. I wonder if he realizes it might take from $2500 to $3000 in addition to the house you speak of to free me entirely from lecturing and one or two more worries I should be more productive without. I shouldn't want to ask too much of a person who had come so far out of his way to honor me with his interest in my welfare; but I give you it about as we have figured it out in family conference. We are a family of six, you know, still all dependent on me, though Lesley looks as if she might not remain so much longer, now that she is started with her own writing.

So much in appreciation of your plan as it touches me personally. A word as to its general import. Such things as you unfold are not supposed to be devised by Americans for American artists. If it were only for what the plan must mean for the country I should be grateful to you and Dr Hughes[285] and Dr Burton. Someone must benefit by it whether I can or not. The arts seem to have to depend on favor more or less. In the old days it was the favor of kings and courts; in our day I was beginning to be afraid it would have to be on woman's clubs. Far better your solution, that it should be on the colleges, if the colleges could be brought to see their responsibility in the matter. We are sure to be great in the world for power and wealth. Our government will see to that with appropriations and tariffs. But someone who has time will have to take thought that we shall be remembered five thousand years from now for more than success in war and trade. Someone will have to feel that it would be the ultimate shame if we were to pass like Carthage (great in war and trade) and leave no trace in the spirit.

---

283. On December 9, 1920, RF had given the first of three seminars on writing at Bryn Mawr; the second and third would follow on February 17 and March 10, 1921. On February 20, 1921, RF read at the Brooklyn Academy of Music, on February 23 at the Cosmopolitan Club in New York, and on March 9 at the Freneau Club in Princeton. In late March he spent a week as poet in residence at Queen's University, Kingston, Ontario.

284. Marion LeRoy Burton (1874–1925), then president of the University of Michigan, where RF would assume a one-year $5,000 fellowship in the fall of 1921.

285. Raymond M. Hughes (1873–1958), president of Miami University in Oxford, Ohio, from 1911 to 1927.

Don't you think so my dear Percy? I wish I could see you to hear and say more. But anon!

Our best to you all away out there in Ohio.

> Always yours
> Robert Frost

[To Louis Untermeyer. ALS. LoC.]

> South Shaftsbury Vt
> January 19 1921

Dear Louis:

Will you lend me exactly $150 for approximately three months? I believe you will, you generous soul; so I would be safe in thanking you in advance, if I were never going to write you another letter. But I am going to write you at least one more letter to enclose you a still better poem than I ever wrote before (naturally since I only wrote it last night, and our friend Wilbur Cross says I improve with every stroke, that is, I grow surer without growing duller—see my recent poem Misgiving written fifteen years ago and now accepted by an editor for the first time) and I will keep the profuseness of my thanks till then (not fifteen years ago or the first time: you'll have to figure this out as best you can. I'm wanted on the telephone.)[286]

> Yours more than ever
> Robert Frost

Notice the access of friendship[287]

---

286. On the poem "Misgiving," see also RF to Untermeyer, September 18, 1920, and November 12, 1920; and RF to Sidney Cox, March 1, 1921.

287. This phrase appears on the blank facing page of the letter, with a pointing finger drawn to highlight the valediction "Yours more than ever."

[To Harriet Moody. ALS. Chicago.]

South Shaftsbury Vermont
January 20 1921

Dear Harriet Moody:

Elinor and I are to be in New York on and about the twentieth (20th) of next month (February). We want to see you for the fun of a good talk before we do or don't decide to take this step into Michigan. Whichever we decide we'll be right. That's why we find it impossible to treat anything as momentous. If you oppose the step too much we shall think you have some reason for not wanting us as near you and Chicago as the step would bring us. Maybe you think there are enough poets within the first postal zone from Chicago. We shall listen to you with respect and encouraging smiles.

One thing as a mere woman of no practical experience[288] you may need to be told: our going to Michigan would not prevent our planting all outdoors with pines and apples. We could plant them in New England or in Michigan just the same.

Say (a little abruptly) you haven't seen this beautiful house that captivated us in passing last year. It is the easiest thing in the world for you to visit us here on your way to or from New York. We are on the main line from New York through Albany to Montreal and not more than two hours from Albany. If you can't be in New York in February when we are, will you agree to come here and see how you like this for the apple enterprise? This is important, though I will not have it momentous or even serious. We'll have to act soon.

Thank Theodore Maynard. I should be more pleased with your good opinion if you hadn't told me that time that I might be the best poet in America, but the best in America couldn't hope to come up to the worst in England. Have a little national pride. Dont you know it's provincial to look up to England? So is it to brag about America. What isn't provincial then will be the question before the house at the next meeting.

Always yours
Robert Frost

---

288. Said in playful irony: Moody founded and ran a highly successful catering business. See RF to Moody, June 26, 1920, and the notes thereto.

[*To John W. Haines. Transcribed from a typescript copy of the original letter, presumably made by Haines. TL-C. Gloucester.*]

South Shaftsbury,

Vermont, U.S.A.

January 20. 1921.

Dear Jack,

Yes, I saw what you wrote about Edward. You and I cared for him in a different way from the rest of them. We didn't have to wait till he was dead to find out how much we loved him. Others pitied him for his misfortunes and he accepted their pity. I don't know what he looked for from me in his black days when I first met him. All he ever got was admiration for the poet in him before he had written a line of poetry. It is hard to speak of him as I want to yet. You speak of him to my liking as far as you go, and I'm sure that is far enough for the present. I wonder what De la Mare will say in his preface to the poems.[289] Elinor and I once made it a little uncomfortable for De la Mare because he wouldn't come right out in hearty acknowledgment of what Edward Thomas had done for him by timely and untimely praise. I suppose De la Mare had really forgotten. Such we are as we swell up and grow great. I mentioned Edward to Dunsany when I saw him last year, and his memory was not so faulty.[290] Instantly he said, "Did you know him? He saw me first and in the very first review he wrote of me he said everything that has been said by everybody else since." That came unforced.

I remember once hazarding the guess that Edward hadn't been proved wrong so very many times in his first judgment of new poets that came up for judgment. Edward and I were pushing our bicycles up a hill side by side. My "not so very many times" stopped him short to think. He wasn't angry. He was disturbed. What did I know? Did I know of any. He should have said not any. No want of strength and decision there. Two or three times I stopped him short like that with the way I put something. He was great fun. I've often wondered when I began to disappoint such a critical and fastidious person. I

289. Walter de la Mare supplied a foreword to Thomas's *Collected Poems* (London: Selwyn and Blount, 1920). The American edition of the book followed in 1921, published in New York by Thomas Seltzer.

290. Edward John Moreton Drax Plunkett, 18th Baron of Dunsany (1878–1957), a prolific Irish writer who published under the name Lord Dunsany. He had embarked on a lecture tour of the United States in 1919–1920.

remember once thinking I had shocked him irreparably with a terrible parody of one who I believe I have sworn shall be nameless.[291] It was an attempt to be as tragic about the middle classes as the nameless one had been about the lower classes. Edward looked as if he couldn't believe his ears—or wouldn't. I felt that I had gone too far. But no. Later he made me palm it off on Locke Ellis for the actual work of the nameless one.[292] Locke Ellis took it as seriously and denounced so particularly the kind of mind that could conceive anything so repulsive that I never had the courage to un-deceive him as to the authorship.

I think Edward blamed most my laziness. He would have liked me better if I had walked farther with him. He wanted me to want to walk in Wales. And then I turned out a bad letter writer after I came home. That's the worst. I should have written him twice as many letters as I did write. But so should I have written you twice as many as I have. You have to assume that I think of you a thousand times for every once I write to you.

Some day soon we shall see each other and that will be better than many letters. I'm really a person who doesn't want anything in the world but my family and a few friends. And I don't want the friends all dead or in England. I demand sight of them. I could get importunate about it if I let myself.

I may succeed in getting an emissary to you this year, maybe more than one. The first will be on his way soon. His name is G. R. Elliott. He is a professor of English Literature at one of the colleges and a critic of parts. I've seen a good deal of him and come to care for him. He works too hard. This is his

291. Wilfrid Gibson, with whom RF had a falling-out in 1914. See RF to Haines, April 2, 1915 (*LRF-1*, 274): "And you mustn't tell me a single thing about Gibson if you dont want to detract from the pleasure of your letters from fifty percent up. I shall have to be made aware of his existance [*sic*] upon earth now and then anyway. But do you not remind me of him unnecessarily. Come to think it all over I cant help looking on him as the worst snob I met in England and I cant help blaming the snob he is for the most unpleasant memory I carried away from England; I mean my humiliating fight with the game-keeper" (alluded to later in the present letter). An April 7, 1915, letter from Haines survives at DCL; his postscript explains the reference to Gibson: "Your letter of April 2nd arrived five minutes ago just as I am posting this. I nearly tore it up on account of the reference to Gibson but have decided to risk it!" After reading RF's April 2 letter, Haines went back over the one here quoted and, for RF's delectation, stamped in purple ink the word "Hyppocrit" above the reference to Gibson.

292. Vivian Locke Ellis (1878–1950), English poet and dramatist. He and his wife, Clare, were friends of Thomas, who sometimes stayed with them at their house in East Grinstead.

year off for self-improvement. He may think Gloucester is a terrible journey from London and more than he can afford. Some of these professors have hard sledding. But I shall have him drop you a line when he gets over there and will you just ask him down to see you and the Cathedral and perhaps Ryton and a game-keeper? You'll like him and then he's from me to you.

Let's see what else. You spoke of a letter from J. C. Squire to me. I've seen none. I wish you had opened it. It might naturally have contained a small check which you would have been instructed to keep. Time I did something about the debt I owe you. I always pay everything in the end; which proves I am not a real poet, but it can't be helped. But check or no check I should like to have heard from Squire. I wonder if he wouldn't write again and tell me what he said. You can tell him that I was pleased to be in print in England again.[293] That she-publisher of mine over there keeps me in exile. I'll tell you about her in another letter and how it stands between us. We have her on the nip we're told by my publisher's lawyers here and by Heinemann's lawyer in England.[294] The worst she can do is bring a losing suit for spits when someone publishes my next book in England.

Tell me if you think of it whether you can see or have seen the four poems I had in Harpers for December and the four in The Yale Review for January. The poems were Fire and Ice, <u>The Valley's Singing Day, Wild Grapes,</u> The Need of Being Versed in Country Things, Snow Dust, <u>The Onset,</u> The Star in a Stone Boat, and Misgiving. I don't know whether you've seen the ones I've underlined.[295] They are among my best. I don't want you to miss them.

---

293. Sir John Collings Squire (1884–1958), British poet and critic, literary editor of the *New Statesman* and the *London Mercury*. The check would likely have been in payment for "The Runaway" and "A Favor" ("Snow Dust"), published in the *Mercury* in December 1920, marking the first time RF had poems in a British periodical since leaving England in 1915. RF collected both poems in *NH*. The "she-publisher" mentioned subsequently was Mrs. M. L. Nutt, head (since the death of her husband Alfred T. Nutt in 1910) of David Nutt, the London firm that issued RF's first two books. By virtue of her 1912 contract with RF she had attempted to lay presumptive claim to all rights to publish RF in England.

294. Henry Holt and Company did in fact secure RF from any further claims made by David Nutt (the firm soon went into receivership). See subsequent letters to Haines and Maurice Firuski concerning the disposition of unsold copies of the London editions of *ABW* and *NB*. The London firm of Heinemann would publish RF's *Selected Poems* in England in 1923.

295. In January 1921 the *Yale Review* printed "Snow Dust," "The Onset," "Star in a Stone-Boat," and "Misgiving." The rest of the poems here named appeared in *Harper's* in December 1920.

It was fine and startling to see the picture of Robin so tall.[296] It won't be long before he is playing on a team of hockey champions and writing poetry and botanizing and some things besides that his father never thought of doing. Why don't he come over here and be anything he pleases but a President? He can't be that unless he decides to be born in this country.

> Affectionately,
> Robert Frost.

[*To Louise Townsend Nicholl (1890–1981), who worked for the* New York Evening Post. *ALS. Harvard.*]

> South Shaftsbury Vermont
> January 21 1921

Dear Miss Nicholl

If there's one thing we hate as poets, it's seeming busy or in demand. Isn't that so. It's not because I'm either that I haven't sent you a poem for The Measure (Why did you put the "The" on!—to keep the critics from putting Good on?); its because I'm slow. I am slow. I'm measured. But I shall yet send you a poem, perhaps in this very letter if I decide you would listen to one I happen to have on the subject of measure.[297] Its an awfully old fashioned thing, so old that no one will ever notice the difference if I keep it till it is a little older. But we'll see when I come to seal the letter how I feel about it. There will be something else some time anyway. I swear to you. So don't mind if you don't find it enclosed. It would be foolish to mind at any rate till you wrote and made sure it hadn't been enclosed and hadn't been abstracted from the letter by some poetry fiend in transit.

The very best luck with the first number of The Measure. I shall look forward to seeing how you bring a little freshness into the poetry magazine field.

---

296. Son of Jack and Dorothy Haines.

297. Nicholl served on the editorial board of *The Measure: A Journal of Poetry* from 1921 to 1925. Its first issue, published in March 1921, printed RF's "The Aim Was Song." He would later place "In a Disused Graveyard," "The Kitchen Chimney," and "Gathering Leaves" in the magazine. The text of "The Aim Was Song" explains RF's remarks (see *CPPP*, 207).

Thank Maxwell Anderson for his card.[298] I shall be as good (or bad) as my word.

Sincerely yours

Robert Frost

[To DuBose Heyward (1885–1940), American novelist, playwright, and poet. In 1919, Heyward and Hervey Allen had founded the Poetry Society of South Carolina. ALS. S.C. Hist.]

South Shaftsbury Vt

January 22 1921

Dear Mr Hayward [*sic*]:

I did have your poem from Mallery and liked it a great deal.[299] That's the great thing, a poem. Poetry Societies are a more doubtful good. Plato wouldn't have any poets in his Republic; I wonder what he would have said to poetry societies. It doesnt follow of course that he would have barred them. I should like to come south to see you all personally and especially you who really mean to do something. But if I come I'm afraid it will have to be next year. I don't see a minute of time for a long journey this winter or spring. Some day write and tell me what you are producing. I might like to see a poem or two if you have something as good as The Mountain Woman.[300]

Sincerely yours

Robert Frost

---

298. Maxwell Anderson (1888–1959), American playwright, poet, and journalist, founded *The Measure*.

299. The go-between is Otto Tod Mallery (1881–1956), a Philadelphia-based economist and public works administrator. Mallery had been an editor of the *Forge*, a short-lived literary journal that had carried RF's poem "Locked Out" (first published in *MI*) in February 1917.

300. "The Mountain Woman" had appeared in the July 1920 issue of *Poetry*.

[*To Ridgely Torrence. ALS. Princeton.*]

South Shaftsbury Vt
January 23 1921

My dear Ridgely:

It is true I am a scout for Henry Holt.[301] How did you penetrate my disguise?

Now what I am particularly out for is left handers with something besides speed on the ball. Now I can't use spitters, the new rule having put them out of business.[302] I can get all the right handers I want out of the college English courses; and straight rather too slow ball artists a little wild on purpose to scare the batter out of the Poetry Society. Get me some good left-handers like yourself and Robinson[303] and I dont care how undeveloped they are: I have a market for them. I will pay you in poems of the realm for every one you bring along. Now heard of a return-ball pitcher in Honolulu. Now this is the rare case of a person with a gift for throwing a ball so that it returns in a circle square triangle or other figure without touching anything (not even the bat of the batter up) to the hand that threw it. Now this obviates the need of a catcher just as some kinds of street car obviate the need of a conductor to collect fares and some kinds of poetry obviate the need of a reader. I will give you one epic currency for such a find. Now I am on my way to Honolulu at this moment to look at this bird and if his wing is as per write-up, one wing is all he needs: we can use him. Now there is said to be such a thing as a man on the Nauscopee River[304] who can make one ball look like three at a time coming through the air, two of them of course visionary. Now I should want this visionary if I believed in him. Now I am in a position to make it right with you if you can put me next to anything.

---

301. RF began work as a consultant for Henry Holt and Company in November 1920.

302. Following the conclusion of the 1920 season, the American League banned spitballs.

303. E. A. Robinson, to whom Torrence had been close for nearly twenty years. The two men lived in the Judson Hotel off Washington Square Park from 1906 to 1909; "left-handed": the implication may be that Torrence, and most certainly Robinson, touched on themes both sinister and dark.

304. A river in Labrador, Canada, variously spelled Nauscopee, Naskopie, Nascanpee, and Naskaupi. It flows into Lake Melville.

I am enclosing four poems, but you must reject two of them and may reject three or four.[305]

I did try to raise you in Waverly Place.[306] I was disappointed not to find you; it seems such a long time since we talked.

What kind of small town is it out there with two poets and four colleges in it? I wish I could look in on you there, but I can't.[307]

I know you wont try too hard to like these poems. That would be not to give them a fair chance.

Our best to you both.

Always yours
Robert Frost

[*To Louis Untermeyer, as dictated to RF's daughter Lesley. The body of the letter is in her hand, although, as Untermeyer indicates, RF has signed it "in a purposely shaky hand" (RFLU, 126). LoC.*]

South Shaftsbury
Vermont
Jan 27, 1921

Dear Louis—

Robert Frost is coming he says, with the accent on the says: but he says it by telegram which isn't very binding, especially on a sick person, if he should manage to be sick. He has started to be sick now. The only question is, shall he continue to be sick till Feb 23rd, or shall he get well, enjoy a period of good health, then get sick again in time to make his excuses. Let us pray for light on this subject. I write this by the hand of another, or rather I dictate it from a bed of pain.

---

305. RF did publish four poems, presumably the ones mentioned here, in the *New Republic* in the spring of 1921: "A Brook in the City" (March 9), "Blue-Butterfly Day" (March 16), and "The Census-Taker" and "A Hillside Thaw" (April 6).

306. Harriet Moody's residence in New York City.

307. At the time Torrence was in Oxford, Ohio, at Miami University, his alma mater. The Western College for Women, which merged with Miami University in 1928, was also located in the town. (It isn't clear what other colleges RF may have in mind.) The second poet is Percy MacKaye.

There is something I particularly want to ask you. What are the first names of Smith, the editor of "The Century," and Mitchell, the editor of "The Dial," respectively?[308] I've got some excuses I want to make to them, too.

You can't honestly say that the Transcript Nigger[309] treated you any worse than the post Canby treated me and some other Americans in an article called "Ham and Eggs" Saturday.[310] What are we going to do about such things?

More when I'm better.

Yours,

Robbed Frossed

308. T. R. Smith (later editor in chief of Boni and Liveright) was managing editor of *Century Magazine* from 1920 to 1921; Stewart Mitchell was editor of *The Dial*.

309. William Stanley Braithwaite, literary editor of the *Boston Evening Transcript*. In *RFLU*, Untermeyer bowdlerized the noxious epithet, printing instead "Braithwaite."

310. Henry Seidel Canby's "Ham and Eggs" appeared in the *Literary Review* of the *New York Evening Post* on January 22, 1921. He reprinted it under the title "The Older Generation" in *Definitions: Essays in Contemporary Criticism* (New York: Harcourt, Brace, 1922): "The older generation is in a difficult situation, because, apparently, no one knows precisely who and what it is. The younger generation, of course, is made up of every one who dislikes Tennyson, believes in realism, reads De Gourmont, and was not responsible for the war. That is perfectly definite. . . . As for the older generation, what actually is it, and who in reality are they? The general impression seems to be that they are the Victorians, they are Howells and his contemporaries, they are the men and women who created the family magazine, invented morality, revived Puritanism, and tried to impose evolution on a society that preferred devolution by international combat. But these men are all dead, or have ceased writing. They are not our older generation. . . . The true older generation, of which one seldom hears in current criticism except in terms of abuse, remains to be discovered, and we herewith announce its personnel, so that the next time the youthful writer excoriates it in the abstract all may know just whom he means. Among the older generation in American literature are H. L. Mencken and Mrs. Edith Wharton, Booth Tarkington and Stuart P. Sherman, Miss Amy Lowell and Mr. Frank Moore Colby, Robert Frost and Edwin Arlington Robinson, Vachel Lindsay and Carl Sandburg, Mrs. Gerould and Professor William Lyon Phelps, Edgar Lee Masters, Joseph Hergesheimer, and most of the more radical editors of New York. Here is this group of desiccated Victorians, upholders of the ethics of Mr. Pickwick, and the artistic theories of Bulwer-Lytton. Here are the bogies of outworn conservatism, numbered like a football team. Mark their names, and know from now on that most of the books that you have supposed were solid in artistry and mature in thought, though perhaps novel in tone or in method, were written by the older generation" (167–168).

[To Hamlin Garland (1860–1940), novelist, short story writer, essayist, reformer, and philanthropist. A memorial service was held in the New York Public Library on March 1, 1921, to honor William Dean Howells, who had died on May 11, 1920. RF had received a letter from Howells not long after he returned to America in 1915, praising NB and inviting him to meet Howells in his offices in New York, which RF did. Howells devoted part of one of his Easy Chair columns in Harper's *(September 1915) to RF. In the event, illness prevented RF from attending the memorial service. ALS. Southern California.]*

South Shaftsbury

February 4 1921

Dear Mr Garland:

Sick man as I am (I am just up from a week in bed) I am tempted to accept your invitation for the chance it would give me, the only one I may ever have, to discharge in downright prose the great debt I owe Howells.

Howells himself sent me The Mother and the Father[311] after he saw my North of Boston. It is beautiful blank verse, just what I should have known from his prose he would write. My obligation to him however is not for the particular things he did in verse form, but for the perennial poetry of all his writing in all forms. I learned from him a long time ago that the loveliest theme of poetry was the voices of people.[312] No one ever had a more observing

---

311. Howells's *The Mother and the Father: Dramatic Passages* (New York: Harper and Brothers, 1909).

312. RF may (as Mark Scott has suggested) refer particularly to Howells's short story "The Magic of a Voice"—collected in *A Pair of Patient Lovers* (New York: Harper and Brothers, 1901)—in which the main character listens to voices through the wall in his hotel room: "A laugh came from the next room. It was not muffled, as before, but frank and clear. It was woman's laughter, and Langbourne easily inferred girlhood as well as womanhood from it. His neighbors must have come by the late train, and they had probably begun to talk as soon as they got into their room. . . . [The voices] rose clearly distinguishable from each other. They were never so distinct that he could make out what was said; but each voice unmistakably conveyed character. Friendship between girls is never equal; they may equally love each other, but one must worship and one must suffer worship. Langbourne read the differing temperaments necessary to this relation in the differing voices. That which bore mastery was a low, thick murmur, coming from deep in the throat, and flowing out in a steady stream of indescribable coaxing and drolling. The owner of that voice had imagination and humor which could charm with absolute control her companion's lighter nature." Compare RF's often-quoted remarks in a July 4, 1913, letter to John Bartlett: "I alone of English writers have consciously set myself to make music out of what I may call the sound of sense. Now it is possible to have sense without the sound of sense (as in much prose that is supposed to pass muster but

ear or clearer imagination for the tones of those voices. No one ever brought them more freshly to book. He recorded them equally with actions, indeed as if they were actions (and I think they are).

I wonder if you think as I do it is a time for consolidating our resources a little against outside influences on our literature and particularly against those among us who would like nothing better than to help us lose our identity. I dont mean the consolidation so much in society as in thought. It should be more of a question with us than it is what as Americans we have to go on with and go on from. There can be nothing invidious to new comers, emigrant Russians Italians and the like, in singling out for notice or even praise any trait or quality as specially American. Many of them must have it as much as the older stock. It is by what they have of it that they are drawn to what we have of it. We are just one more rough abstraction on some principle we needn't go into here from the mass that other abstractions have been made from before and others still will go on to be made from. Principles are always harder to talk about than men. Our best way to define to ourselves what we are is in terms of men. We are eight or ten men already and one of them is Howells.

The question is do you think I ought to make an engagement I may not be able to keep. I should be all right by March 1st. But suppose I weren't.

We must see more of each other for what we hold in common.

Always yours
Robert Frost

·

[*To Harriet Moody. ALS. Chicago.*]

South Shaftsbury Vt.
February 4 1921

My dear Harriet Moody:

Did you mean that if you could be in New York for a few days on each side of February 23rd you could have Elinor and me at the apartment in Waverly Place. We should like that. We could come right there from Philadelphia where

---

makes very dull reading) and the sound of sense without sense (as in Alice in Wonderland which makes anything but dull reading). *The best place to get the abstract sound of sense is from voices behind a door that cuts off the words*" (LRF-1, 122; emphasis added). For more on Howells and RF, see Mark Scott, "*North of Boston* and Frost's 'Great Debt' to William Dean Howells," *Robert Frost Review* 23–24 (2015): 34–53.

I shall have been teaching them a lesson in art morals and agriculture on the 18th.[313] Suppose we got there a little ahead of you; could we get in and wait a day or two for you? Is there anybody there? I take it, not, from what I hear from Ridgely. Could you send us a key now or tell us where to find a key?

I went to bed sick just after receiving the telegram from you and Ridgely. It would have made anybody sick to see the way the names of those poems you called for had got improved upon. And since I was going to be sick I decided to be very sick. I am just up around again today and feeling as cross as a last year's bird's nest. I had to give up the Iowa trip. Perhaps later, but I don't know.

You haven't actually forbidden me to go to Michigan I notice.

> Always yours
> Robert Frost

[*To Louis Untermeyer, who in RFLU mistakenly assigns the letter to 1920. RF did not move into the Stone House in South Shaftsbury, Vermont, until October 1920, and other letters place him in Franconia on February 8, 1920. Year derived from internal evidence. ALS. LoC.*]

> Sow Shaftsbury Vete[314]
> February 8 [1921]

Dear Louis:

I crawled out (I was going to say out of going to The Cosmopolitan[315])—I crawled out in the sun to-day and failing to cast any shadow, asked to be carried back to bed again. I guess it is the carving knife for mine: and I wouldn't care nearly so much if there was any advertisement in it. There is a Masters Mountain and right beside it a Frost Hollow hereabouts.[316] What can be done to bring low the mountain and cast up the hollow? You say.

> Yours
> R.

---

313. RF lectured at Bryn Mawr on February 18.

314. A joke playing off pronunciation: "Sow" for "South," "Vete" for "V-T" ("veet" / "vee-tee"), etc.

315. On February 23, RF would speak at the Cosmopolitan Club, at Fortieth Street and Lexington Avenue in New York.

316. Edgar Lee Masters (1868–1950) was often spoken of in connection with RF at the time; it rankled RF.

[To John Livingston Lowes. ALS. Harvard.]

South Shaftsbury Vt

February 10 1921

Dear Mr Lowes:

Here goes arbitrarily, then, in accordance with the enclosed letter of one of the best people who ever wrote good poetry. I have been sick in bed for a week or so with a complication of chagrin at not having proved equal to Stork and some sort of neuralgia.[317] I offer this not as an excuse for not having got this whole bad business over with long ago, but as a reason for getting it over anyhow here and now. Since all we have to do is take our decision and bid our will avouch it,[318] why stand shivering naked on the bank in air colder than the water we are going to plunge into? You ought to see how like the descent of a headsman's ax I can hand down an opinion on poetry submitted to Henry Holt for publication.[319] I'm a little ashamed before you and Miss Bates of having made such hard work of this case.[320] Before the world, not. At least after all the time I have taken the world won't accuse us of having piled the sin of hasty judgement on the folly of assuming to judge poetry at all in this way.

I'm not in favor of the proposal to spend any more of Mr More's money on Charles Wharton Stork (who tells us he supposes he comes as near being an aristocrat as you can get in a democracy.)[321] If we aren't to be allowed to dis-

---

317. For more on the occasion of this letter and Charles Wharton Stork, see RF to Lowes, December 28, 1920, and the notes thereto.

318. *Macbeth* 3.1: "and though I could / With barefaced power sweep [Banquo] from my sight / And bid my will avouch it, yet I must not. . . ."

319. Another reference to RF's work as a paid consultant to his publisher.

320. Katharine Lee Bates (of Wellesley), who, with Lowes (professor of English at Harvard) and RF, served as a judge for the poetry contest; for the results of the contest see RF to Charles Wharton Stork, March 4, 1921.

321. RF sounds an up-from-bootstraps, democratic note. James Brookes More (1859–1942) was a poet and self-made businessman from Arkansas whose varied enterprises included publishing, speculation in stocks, and ownership of an import business, an insurance firm, and real estate. See Mary D. Hudgins, "James Brookes More: Poet and Businessman," *Arkansas Historical Quarterly* 22, no. 1 (Spring 1963): 55–60. Unlike More, Stork was hardly a self-made man. Indeed, as RF implies, Stork was a proud descendant of Thomas Wharton (died 1719), who was the patriarch of an eminent Quaker family of merchants and politicians in Philadelphia that was already established by the 1680s. See Anne Hollingsworth Wharton, *Genealogy of the Wharton family of Philadelphia, 1664 to 1880* (Philadelphia: Collins, 1880).

tribute what he has already given, by all means lets let it all into two though they burst of it. I take six out of the fifteen you named me and ask you and Miss Bates to reduce the six by telephone to two for the first and second prizes. If you like to be nice in the matter you might finally send the two to me to decide which is which. (My, this is a lark!) I have listed my six about in the order of my interest in them.

1 Stephen Benét
2 Maxwell Anderson
3 Hilda Conkling
4 David Morton
5 Amanda Hall
6 Louise Driscoll

I wish Dorothea Prall and Sara Teasdale might be considered a little. You know Masefield is barred.[322]

Always yours sincerely
Robert Frost

---

322. Of the poets mentioned, only Stephen Vincent Benét (1898–1943), John Masefield (1878–1967); barred from the contest because he was British), and Sara Teasdale are now well remembered. For Maxwell Anderson, see the notes to RF's letter to Nicholl, January 21, 1921. Hilda Conkling (1910–1986), a child prodigy, composed poems between the ages of four and ten that her mother—Grace Hazard Conkling (1878–1958)—copied out. Frederick Stokes and Company brought out her *Poems by a Little Girl*, with a preface by Amy Lowell, in 1920. Conkling published no poetry beyond the age of fourteen. David Morton (1886–1957), a Kentucky-born journalist, editor, anthologist, and poet, graduated from Vanderbilt, taught high school in New Jersey, and joined the faculty at Amherst in 1924; his first book, *Ships in Harbor*, appeared in 1921. Amanda Benjamin Hall (1890–1948) scattered poems in a number of magazines during the 1910s and also was author of several novels; George Doran and Company published her first book of poetry, *The Dancer in the Shrine and Other Poems*, in 1923. Louise Driscoll (1875–1957) published *The Garden of the West* in 1922 (Macmillan). Dorothea Prall married the Polish-born American lawyer Max Radin in 1922. She translated a number of works, including poetry, from Polish into English.

[*To Harriet Moody. RF was due to lecture at Bryn Mawr on February 17. ALS. Chicago.*]

South Shaftsbury Vt
February 13 1921

Dear Harriet Moody:

We are off for Philadelphia on the 16th. Business over there on the 18th. We shall stop two days to say hello right and left and then come up to the apartment in Waverly Place Monday morning. Ridgely has keyed us for getting in.[323] I dont believe you are one little bit in earnest about being there to cook us Birds of Paradise. You're not a very serious-minded person anyway. I wish I knew where to find Padraic Collum [*sic*]. I'd like to talk you over with him.

Anyway you can't say I havent let you know.

Reservedly
Robert Frost

[*To Charlotte Rudyard Hallowell (1882–1972), writer and editor. Hallowell worked for* the New Republic; *her husband, Robert, was its business manager. ALS. BU.*]

South Shaftsbury Vt.
February 13 1921

My dear Charlotte Rudyard:

I've been meaning to write just the minute I got my mind made up what to write. From the first something in your letters and telegrams sounded as if there was a situation I must not fail to take in before I ventured to speak. I come of a cautious breed. I suspect your object in asking me to read at the Cosmopolitan Club was to try me and see if I wouldn't prove man enough to refuse.[324] My object in not refusing was to punish you for needing to try me. You should have believed in me too much for that. Ordinarily an invitation to read to a club of women is an honor and calls for thanks. I don't just see myself thanking you however for having put me in a position where you lose a hero and I lose one too.

---

323. Ridgely Torrence. "Birds of Paradise" (later): Moody ran a catering business.
324. RF would speak at the Cosmopolitan Club on February 23.

Till yesterday I had seen your hand alone in the business. The letter that came then disclosed what looks like a conspiracy of several of you to get me down to New York for some reason. Can it be for the sake of American literature to divert me for the moment from writing a kind of poetry you don't approve of, or is it to scotch me (but I am Scotch already. Louis isn't. You should scotch him) with stage fright so I wont write anything to worry my rivals perhaps ever again? I'm sure I can thank you all for your concern for American literature or my rivals—if you get my tone.

But seriously I have been seriously sick—a likely subject for the knife. I thought Louis must have told you. I have had to forget letters and engagements all I could. And I have to confess there is something in this engagement that particularly perplexes me. I don't understand what all this is between the Untermeyers and you about how I shall be fed. If it is anything you think I can understand will you write to me about it, addressing your letter in care of Judge Robert von Moschzisker 2101 DeLancey Place Philadelphia? I shall appeal from confusion to the Supreme Court of the Imperial State of Penna.[325]

Let's see, the last time we met we both said something clever about Amy Lowell. I know you did and I think I did. And look at Amy where she is now. And then on the other hand look at the Kaiser where he is.[326]

With real thanks for your well-meant attempts to drag me out of my obscurity I am

Always sincerely yours
Robert Frost

[To Ridgely Torrence, then teaching at Miami University, Oxford, OH. ALS. Princeton.]

South Shaftsbury Vt
February 13 1921

Dear Ridgely:

Im not keeping away from Oxford for the purpose of avoiding you you understand. Neither are you keeping away from New York for the purpose of

---

325. RF was in Philadelphia for a reading at Bryn Mawr on February 17; he stayed with Pennsylvania Supreme Court Justice Robert von Moschzisker (1870–1939), a friend since 1915.

326. Lowell underwent major surgery in 1920. Wilhelm II, having abdicated in 1918, was charged in 1920 with war crimes, for which the Netherlands refused extradition.

avoiding me, I understand. We really would like to see each other and it's time we did. We'll miss you beside the open grates in Waverly Place.

I forgot to ask you how you thought of publishing those poems.[327] I don't care and have no ideas on the subject beyond a suspicion that the best foot forward would be the one I call The Census-Taker. Whether you printed them singly or in group [*sic*] I thought in the night last night that would be the one to lead off with. Or am I wrong?

Aint teaching just like stealing candy from children?

Yours always

Robert Frost

[*To Halley Phillips Gilchrist (1876–1944), secretary to the Poetry Society of Southern Vermont. ALS. Middlebury.*]

South Shaftsbury Vt

February 13 1921

My dear Mrs Gilchrist:

Dont ask me where any of my friends are, or enemies either, at this time of year. It's as much as ever I know where I am myself. I can tell you for what it's worth my method for arriving at my own whereabouts. I do it by a process of exclusion. I make a list of all the places where I'm not, and then if there are any left I reason I must be in one of those. If there are none left, the method breaks down. I give myself up to the authorities for lost.

You come pretty near being right in your guess that I think poetry societies a rather roundabout way of producing American poetry. I can't find however that Plato who was opposed to poets was opposed to poetry societies. So just to be sociable, neighborly, off-hand, reckless and obliging (and I should have said inconsistent) I am going to let you make me an honorary member of your Poetry Society. I can think mainly of the honor (which I know how to appreciate) and cheer myself up with little pleasantries about the membership. Will you personally accept me on these terms? I shall be on hand at one of the meetings of the Society as soon as possible to thank you all for wanting me. I'm afraid it can't be on the 21st. Elinor and I are off for a week or more in New York and Philadelphia on the 17th. Be sure to let me know when there's another meeting.

---

327. For the poems referred to here, shortly to be published in the *New Republic,* see RF's earlier letters to Torrence of October 26, 1920, and December 17, 1920, and the notes thereto.

We <u>are</u> sorry you have been so sick at your house. Maybe it was out of sympathy that we were sick at about the same time too.

Our best to you and Mr Gilchrist.[328]

> Always yours sincerely
> Robert Frost

[To Louis Untermeyer. ALS. LoC.]

> South Shafts. Vt
> February 14 1921

Dear Louis:

I have since decided I meant the knife of the critics. Enclosed please look till you find one Valentine.*

> R.F.

*I gave out in the middle of cutting it out for you. Have Dick finish it.[329]

[To Sidney Cox. ALS. DCL.]

> South Shaftsbury Vermont
> March 1 1921

Dear Sidney:

Tell those young poets they did well: I liked their poems and especially the poem about the fish. You know how to take them to put them on their feet. Praise them in the absolute or not at all.

Did you see how your old friend Misgiving had turned up unaltered by time in The Yale Review for January? Mr Cross thinks it shows a marked improvement on what I was doing in 1915.[330]

---

328. Clarence Dyer Gilchrist (1874–1926). The couple lived in Arlington, some ten miles north of South Shaftsbury.

329. Untermeyer's son, Richard. In *RFLU* Untermeyer offers the following explanation: "The 'Valentine' turned out to be the corner of a high-school composition book. Robert had cut the design so that what was left of it was a lamp, a scroll, a wreath of laurel, a capitalized heading, HIGH COMPOSITION, and the legend, Literature is an Avenue to Glory."

330. In a July 10, 1913, letter to Cox, RF had enclosed "Misgiving" (then titled "A Misgiving"). See *LRF-1*, 126–127. Wilbur Cross edited the *Yale Review*.

Would you be interested in taking in hand an old rhetoric by William Vaughn Moody and bringing it up to date? Mrs. Moody was asking.[331] I doubt if you would. But don't hesitate to contradict me if you see money or advantage in the job.

I dont write letters lest my pen become hateful to me. I take it out in wishing I could see you. What do you say to seeing if you could find me a few engagements at say $125 a piece out there next year? I only speak since you suggested the idea. I get all I need for a living from eastern clubs and colleges.[332] Don't have me on your conscience for one moment. It just crossed my mind I might be tempted to bring Elinor out to see you both and the baby.[333]

Our best to you both—and the baby.

> Affectionately
> Robert Frost

[*To Charles Wharton Stork (1881–1971), American poet. See RF's February 10, 1921, letter to Lowes for more on the contest here discussed. ALS. SLU.*]

> South Shaftsbury Vt
> March 4 1921

Mr. Charles Wharton Stork
Editor of Contemporary Verse
Philadelphia, Penna.
Dear Sir:

Here then, since you must be ready to listen to it without further delay, is the decision of your judges in the contest for the three prizes so generously offered through your magazine by Mr Brookes More: that the first shall go to Miss Sara Teasdale, the second to Mr David Morton, the third to Mr. Stephen Benét.

> Respectfully yours
> Robert Frost

---

331. Harriet Moody, William Vaughan Moody's widow. William Evans, in his *Robert Frost and Sidney Cox: Forty Years of Friendship* (Hanover, NH: University Press of New England, 1981), suggests that the book in question may have been *A History of English Literature* (New York: Charles Scribner's Sons), which Moody coauthored with Robert Lovett in 1902.

332. Cox then taught at the University of Montana in Missoula.

333. Alice Cox (née Alice Macy Ray) gave birth to the couple's first child, Arthur, in May 1920. The Frosts had not yet met him. The visit to Missoula never occurred.

[To Loring Holmes Dodd (1879–1968), professor of English and art at Clark University, in Worcester, Massachusetts. ALS. BU.]

South Shaftsbury Vt

March 30 1921

My dear Professor Dodd:

    I don't particularly like the sound of having to say I am not to be lured from home any more by less than one hundred dollars and my expenses: but I took the resolution not to be a year or so ago and as I find it lets me see the world about as much as is good for my writing it has to stand and I have to be frank about it. You will understand that I am sorry if it keeps me from visiting Clark University.

Sincerely yours

Robert Frost

[To Elizabeth Farson (1851–1935), a principal in the Chicago public school system. The poem in question is "A Star in a Stone-Boat," published in the Yale Review *in January 1921. ALS. ACL.]*

South Shaftsbury Vt

March 30 1921

My dear Miss Farson:

    Thank you for Mr Crane's expert opinion on my poem in The Yale Review.[334] Evidently he will soon find out if he hasnt found out by this time all about my meteoric wings and tail. He would seem an interesting sort of man to cultivate. I wish I might have time for him sometime when south as far as Washington. But I am a good deal busier than you would think I could be considering. Once I was a teacher as you are and full of my work night and day. I am not much more my own master now. The demands on me, if I met half of them, would keep me entirely away from poetry. I am not speaking of them to complain. But isn't life funny.

Sincerely yours

Robert Frost

---

334. "Mr. Crane" is likely Walter R. Crane, a former dean and professor of mining and metallurgy at Pennsylvania State University, who in 1921 was working for the U.S. Bureau of Mines in Washington, D.C. See also RF's June 7, 1921, letter to Cross.

[To Henry Tunis Meigs (1855–1932), proprietor of The Maples farm in Romney, Indiana. ALS. Yale.]

South Shaftsbury Vt

March 31 1921

Dear Mr Meigs:

I must write you a few words if only to let you know where I am living farming (a little) and making poetry now-a-days. You see the address.

It was encouraging to hear from you in the old strain. I shall have to have another book for you soon since you seem to demand it. I wonder if you have seen what I have been printing in the magazines lately. I had a set of four in The Yale Review for January 1921 another of four in Harpers Monthly for December 1920 and another of four in Harpers for June or July 1920.[335] I feel pretty sure you would like some of them if you knew where you could lay hands on them easily. I shouldn't buy them. They will keep till they appear in book form. I'll copy a couple to tide you over till then.

I hope you'll always keep watch of me to see that I do no worse in poetry than I can: and I hope you'll write me now and then (in as legible a hand as possible)[336] and someday I promise you I will drop off a passing train to see you and we'll have a good talk. I often speak of you and oftener think of you. I've been glad of your support. It was you put it into my head to try some of my poetry on the readers of Farm and Fireside.[337] If I as farmer wrote the poems and you as farmer liked them, why shouldn't others as farmers like them too?

Always your friend

Robert Frost

---

335. "A Star in a Stone-Boat," "The Onset," and "Misgiving" appeared in the *Yale Review* in January 1921. "Wild Grapes," "Fire and Ice," "The Valley's Singing Day," and "The Need of Being Versed in Country Things" appeared in *Harper's* in December 1920. "Place For a Third," "Fragmentary Blue," "Good-by and Keep Cold," and "For Once, Then, Something" appeared in *Harper's* in July 1920.

336. Meigs penciled in a note here: "Mr. F had once before said I find your writing very hard to read."

337. *Farm and Fireside* published "The Grindstone" in June 1921, and "On a Tree Fallen across the Road" in October 1921.

[To Gilbert Campbell Scoggin (1881–1947), American scholar, translator, and professor of classical languages. Scoggin was on the staff of the Encyclopaedia Britannica from 1920 to 1922. ALS. Harvard.]

South Shaftsbury Vt
April 2 1921

Dear Mr Scoggin:

I am glad to give you any information I can.

I was born in San Francisco, Cal., March 26 1875;[338] educated at Dartmouth College and Harvard University; married to Elinor White, 1895. I have four children.

My father was of oldest English Colonial stock; my mother emigrated from Scotland.

I have been a mill hand at Lawrence Mass., a farmer at Derry N.H. I was a teacher of English at Pinkerton Academy from 1906 to 1911, a professor of English at Amherst College from 1916 to 1920. From 1912 to 1915 I was in England.

My books have been

A Boys Will, David Nutt, London 1913
North of Boston   "   "   1914
A Boys Will Henry Holt New York 1915
North of Boston   "   "   "
Mountain Interval "   "   1916

A Boys Will and North of Boston include work denied publication for twenty and ten years respectively.

There will be more than you can use here, but no great harm in that.

Sincerely yours
Robert Frost

[To C. F. D. Belden (1870–1931), chief librarian at the Boston Public Library. ALS. BU.]

South Shaftsbury Vt
April 8 1921

My dear Mr Belden:

I'm yours for June 23rd, if you will say that my reading may be anything up to ninety percent of my ten-minute performance. I stop talking when the frogs

---

338. Lawrance Thompson, RF's biographer, discovered some two decades later that RF's correct birth year is 1874.

start in the spring and don't usually recover speech for more than a minute at a time till I lift up my heart in thanks giving at Thanksgiving. Of course I'm honored to be asked to speak read or do anything else, but let me read mainly and I am yours, as I have said, for June 23rd,

Gratefully yours
Robert Frost

[*To Halley Phillips Gilchrist. ALS. Middlebury.*]

South Shaftsbury Vt
April 9 1921

Dear Mrs Gilchrist:

Strange that I shouldn't have thought of that way of looking at Poetry Societies with all the time I have on my hands for thinking. I suppose I must have judged them all by the mother of them all at New York.[339] You won't say that has a solitary member except yourself who doesn't write poetry—and come there to promote his own. (I am unjust: don't mind me.)

We wish you could have the lunch you speak of on Monday or at latest on Tuesday. We are off either Tuesday night or Wednesday morning for a Wednesday evening engagement at Syracuse.[340] Thanks for the invitation, but make it possible for us to accept, wont you?

Our best to you all.

Sincerely yours
Robert Frost

It will be fine to have you back again.

---

339. The Poetry Society of America, headquartered in New York City, was founded in 1910 by a small group of poets, professors, and editors, including Jessie Belle Rittenhouse and Witter Bynner.

340. RF gave a reading in Syracuse on April 15, and on April 25 attended a meeting of the Poetry Society of Southern Vermont, at which the poet Vachel Lindsay performed.

[To George R. Elliott. ALS. ACL.]

South Shaftsbury Vt
April 11 1921

My dear Elliott:

You should have had these letters long ago. But I have been sick busy or inspired all the time lately. You won't mind if you get the letters in the end.[341] You might not mind if you didn't get them at all. I am not sending them very much for you but mostly for myself. I long to touch hands through a friend going fresh from my presence with friends I have not seen since before the war. I am most selfish of all in wanting you to talk for me with J. W. Haines Esq Hucclecote, Gloucester. I have written directly to him about you and he will have been waiting to hear from you long before you get this. Please write to him when you can. You will make him happiest by talking of the poetry of Edward Thomas, next most happy by talking of mine.

I have spent a day and a night with your Paul E. Moore and seen your Canada since last I wrote.[342]

Won't you and your family be having the beautiful spring! Let me envy you a good deal. My best wishes to you all.

Always your devoted friend
Robert Frost

[To Harold Monro (1879–1932), British poet, publisher, editor, and bookseller. ALS. Trinity.]

South Shaftsbury Vt
April 11, 1921

My dear Monro:

You missed my emissary of a year ago.[343] The bearer of this is Mr G. R. Elliott my second. Unlike the first he is no publisher but he is the next thing to

341. Letters of introduction (including the letter immediately following this one, to Harold Monro).

342. On March 9, RF spoke at Princeton, where he was the guest of Paul Elmer More. After appearing at Bryn Mawr on the tenth, he traveled north to spend a week at Queen's University, Kingston, Ontario.

343. Lincoln MacVeagh, RF's editor at Henry Holt and Company, had traveled to England in 1920. See RF to Monro, January 1, 1920 (*LRF-1*, 721).

it, a critic and professor of literature, and I fancy would appreciate hearing what is new with you in poetry and if it would bear publication on this side, so much the better: he would enjoy passing the word along to me who would know how to act in the matter. (I speak with the assurance of one in a position for the moment to advise though not, alas, to command publication. For the moment I am a small part of the house of Henry Holt.)

But business aside, I want Mr Elliott to meet you. He's a great friend of mine. I shall see you myself sometime. Meanwhile greetings now and then through a chosen friend.

I wish Flint would think to write to me.[344]

> Always yours sincerely
> Robert Frost

[*To Julia Patton. ALS. BU.*]

> South Shaftsbury Vt.
> April 11 1921

Dear Miss Patten [*sic*]:

What will you think of my long silence? Everything, I am afraid, but the truth, which is that I have been away lecturing in one place and another chiefly in Canada where my mail didn't follow me. I suppose it is too late for me to come to you now. I could run down on the 29th or 30th.

I am sorry. This is my awful way of doing business.[345] The wonder is that I get any to do. It must be because friends gradually find out I mean no harm.

> Sincerely yours
> Robert Frost

---

344. The poet Frank S. Flint, whom RF had befriended in England in 1913.

345. See Rudyard Kipling, "The Pharaoh and the Sergeant," which had appeared during the summer of 1897 in three different periodicals—*The Graphic* in July, the *New York Tribune* in August, and *McClure's Magazine* in September:

> *(There were years that no one talked of; there were times of horrid doubt—*
> *There was faith and hope and whacking and despair—*
> *While the Sergeant gave the Cautions and he combed old Pharaoh out,—*
> *And England didn't seem to know nor care.*
> *That is England's awful way o' doing business—*
> *She would serve her God (or Gordon) just the same—*
> *For she thinks her Empire still is the Strand and Holborn Hill,*
> *And she didn't think of Sergeant Whatisname.)*

[*To Louis Untermeyer. ALS. LoC.*]

South Shaftsbury Vt
April 15 1921

My dear Louis:

My list to date has been The Brimming Cup, Miss Lulu Bett, The Moon Calf, Poor White, The Dark Mother, Main Street and for comparison The American (Henry James) and The Rise of Silas Lapham.[346] That's more novels for me in six months than I had read before in six years. I guess you and Dorothy Fisher must have set me to looking for something. Have I found it? The first half of Moon Calf is half a great book. The last half, the sinful half, didnt go down and it was a surprise that it didn't. I should have expected Floyd to be as convincing in his sins as in anything. I think he must have erred in relying too implicitly for his effect on a bare statement of what he had done. He wouldnt have thought anything good was good enough to deliver so unvarnished. He was caught thinking that anything bad was bad enough as it was in nature. He miscalculates our shockability. He doesnt even seem plausible. He sounds hypothetical.

I dont think you did Sherwood Anderson's girl justice in an otherwise first rate review of a first rate book.[347] She wasnt experimenting, poor thing. She was randoming as Alisande hath it.[348] If she had been experimenting she would have had the courage to go on as of right and wouldn't have let her father drive

---

346. Novels by, respectively, Dorothy Canfield Fisher, Zona Gale, Floyd Dell, Sherwood Anderson, Waldo Frank, and Sinclair Lewis. *The Rise of Silas Lapham* is by William Dean Howells.

347. In fact, Untermeyer admired *Poor White* (New York: B. W. Huebsch, 1920) immensely and "blurbed" it: "This novel, epic in scale, tremendous in implications, marks the emergence of Anderson as a great force in our native literature."

348. See Mark Twain's *A Connecticut Yankee in King Arthur's Court* (which RF occasionally taught): "The truth is, Alisande, these archaics are a little *too* simple; the vocabulary is too limited, and so, by consequence, descriptions suffer in the matter of variety; they run too much to level Saharas of fact, and not enough to picturesque detail; this throws about them a certain air of the monotonous; in fact the fights are all alike: a couple of people come together with great random—random is a good word, and so is exegesis, for that matter, and so is holocaust, and defalcation, and usufruct and a hundred others, but land! a body ought to discriminate—they come together with great random, and a spear is brast, and one party brake his shield and the other one goes down, horse and man, over his horse-tail and brake his neck, and then the next candidate comes randoming in" (New York: Charles L. Webster, 1891), 180.

her into marriage. The whole book's all right. You're not looking for a wrapper slogan to put on it; so I can say boldly to you it is the greatest novel since The Scarlet Letter, Little Women, and Ivanhoe.

Honestly now I'll bet you have kidded yourself into thinking the Foreword to Main St an ironic delicacy. Out here in the country we think the illusion to Cannibal invading Cartrage to enthrown the Corner Grocer on the Sugar Barrel is the Sage Cheese.[349] For Gods sake dont you set up next as an authority on what ought to be done to protect small towns from the ravages of sympathetic measles. Sink Lewis told an interviewer I know that America would be all right in twenty thousand years. But there wont be any American [*sic*] in twenty thousand years. The most fervid patriots are satisfied to sing it: they only expect the flage [*sic*] to "wave a thousand years."[350] Small towns do buy books; so what in Hell are the writers kicking about? Count me as in favor of reforming a whole lot of things downward. I keep hearing of Lewis round wanting to better small town people. I'm for bettering or battering them back where they belong. Too many of them get to college.

Did I tell you what scared me out of Monson the evening I arrived there to take possession of the farm by the Quarry?[351] It was a bevy of twenty college boys skylarking and swatting each other over the heads with copies of The

---

349. The malapropisms are deliberate ("illusion," "Cannibal," "Cartrage," etc.). RF assumes the mask of the sort of uncultured hick Lewis might disdain. The "foreword" RF refers to reads, in part: "Main Street is the climax of civilization. That this Ford car might stand in front of the Bon Ton Store, Hannibal invaded Rome and Erasmus wrote in Oxford cloisters. What Ole Jenson the grocer says to Ezra Stowbody the banker is the new law for London, Prague, and the unprofitable isles of the sea; whatsoever Ezra does not know and sanction, that thing is heresy, worthless for knowing and wicked to consider. Our railway station is the final aspiration of architecture" (New York: Harcourt, Brace and Howe, 1920).

350. See Henry Clay Work's "Song of a Thousand Years," composed during the Civil War:

Lift up your eyes, desponding freemen!
Fling to the winds your needless fears!
He who unfurled your beauteous banner,
Says it shall wave a thousand years!

351. A reference to RF's house-hunting forays in New England during the summer of 1920. He passed through the village of Monson, Massachusetts (population 4,828 in 1920), but did not buy a farm there. Monson Academy, the institution to which RF refers, was established in 1804.

New Republic in front of the village drug store.[352] It was too early for them to be summer colonists and I had it in the deed of the farm that there were to be no summer colonists in Monson anyway. Says I to myself, says I, and lights out for Boxford Mass, Rochester N. H., Brunswick, Waterford, Norway, Harrison and Skowhegan Maine. The only hotel in Monson has bedroom doors that though they may be locked can be seen over and under and I should say crawled over and under from the halls. Those were engaging so I engaged one door with room, looked at myself credulously in the mirror and then went out on the street to look for excitement till my family should arrive on the load of furniture that was coming to me. 'Twas graduation at the Academy; every one was shuffling reverently in white and black to some exercise that I as an outsider couldn't be expected to know the importance of. I didn't want to be an outsider. I was just on the point of mounting the Soldiers Monument and applying in a loud voice to the community at large to be taken in as soon as possible and treated as an insider when I ran bang into my bevy of twenty college boys all obviously out of tune with the village and not the least in the mood of its pitiful little function. They probably thought they were laughing at each other but what they were really laughing at was the notion of their ever having taken the Academy Graduation as an end and aim. At their colleges they had commencements, and there were even things beyond commencements: Rhodes Scholarships if you won them might take you to Oxford where you might hope to acquire a contempt beyond any contempt for small things you could show now. They knew now that there was nothing here that they would not some day be able to scorn. I fled them as I had fled their like thirty years before at Dartmouth. I never could bear the sickening sunsuvbijches belief that they were getting anywhere when they were getting toward their degrees or had got anywhere when they had got them. That's not it exactly; it was more their belief that they were leaving anybody behind who was not getting toward their degrees. I preferred to drop out of their company and be looked on as left behind. Of course all I had to do not to be left behind was to have one solitary idea that I could call my own in four years. That would be one more than they would have.

To Hell with these memories: I went free from the Little Collegers like Sinclair Lewis ages ago.

---

352. The joke is complicated by the fact that, as Untermeyer knew, RF had published four poems in the *New Republic* in March and April of 1921.

But the best writing of all is Coming Aphrodite.[353] Now I'm envious. We have had no such short story. You must agree with me. Every stroke of it to the very last. I wept for the sheer perfection—and I'm the fellow who won't allow artists to take artists for their subject. Conrad Aiken's Punch didn't get down to anything or rise to anything. I read it and that's saying a good deal for me. But it put it to you too much a la Browning.[354] The old inflection went against me. I'll tell you a funny thing: I had a leap of the mind (such as they call a hunch I suppose) just as I started to read that the two unaccountable loves for such a monstrosity were going to prove extreme refinements of lust, perversions of sophistication. They proved nothing special. The real Immortal Liar was Munchausen.[355] I only remember him away from women. Had he exaggerated amours? He should have a few.

You've been to Chicago while I've been to Canada. I read 'em most of your School Anthology up there.[356] It seemed to do them good. The people liked the poems and I liked the people. Carl had been before me and made the way easy with his slow smile and his banjo on his knee.[357] Lets try to get Lee Keedick[358] to put us on his circuit in a dual turn I have yet to think up—give me a minute to think, as Charlotte said. The only thing you play on is words

---

353. "Coming, Aphrodite!" appeared in Willa Cather's 1920 volume of short stories, *Youth and the Bright Medusa* (New York: Alfred Knopf).

354. The full title of Aiken's new book of poems was *Punch: The Immortal Liar* (New York: Alfred Knopf, 1921). Untermeyer later reviewed it favorably in the August 1921 *Bookman*. The first line of the first poem in the book, "Two Old Men who Remembered Punch," opens in a Browningesque way: "Do I remember Punch?—Listen—I'll tell you. . . ."

355. Baron Von Munchausen is a fictional character, created by Rudolph Eric Raspe, who appears in *The Surprising Adventures of Baron Munchausen* (Philadelphia: Henry T. Coates, 1869). The character is loosely based on Hieronymus Karl Friedrich Freiherr von Münchhausen (1720–1797), a German nobleman renowned for his tales celebrating his exploits.

356. In March, RF spent a week as poet in residence at Queen's University in Kingston, Ontario. He refers here to Untermeyer's textbook *Modern American Poetry* (New York: Harcourt, Brace and Howe, 1919); see also RF's July 23, 1921, letter to Untermeyer, in which he refers to the second edition of the book, which appeared in 1921.

357. Carl Sandburg often mingled music with readings of his poetry. The Frontenac Club Inn, in Kingston, has a room named in his honor. Among the club's founders were members of the faculty at Queen's University.

358. An influential literary agent in New York, head of the Lee Keedick Lecture and Musical Bureau.

and the piano. I excel on the penny whistle. Nothing to any of that. I have it! You know we talked of a Collusive Stunt after Brooklyn.* What do you say to working it up?—for next season—my nest is feathered for this.

Which puts me in mind I must send you a check when I know you're home again. Be patient with Dick and Jean.

Sufficiently for one letter

Robert Frost

*You from the platform I from the audience at one stand, vice versa at the next.[359]

[*To Carl Van Doren. ALS. DCL.*]

South Shaftsbury Vt

April 22 1921

Dear Mr Van Doren:

Thanks for the money and thanks for the French appreciation. I hadnt seen the article in Mercure de France.[360] I suppose everybody assumes we all subscribe to clipping agencies and that's why nobody bothers to tell us what's being said about us in print. Sometimes the loss is serious. It was some time

---

359. On February 20, 1921, RF gave a reading at the Brooklyn Academy of Music. In *RFLU,* Untermeyer provides an explanatory note: "A reading at the Brooklyn Academy of Music had been followed by a discussion which I had led. Afterward we joked about 'teaming up' for a series of collaborations on and off the platform" (130).

360. An essay by Jean Catel, "La Poésie américaine d'aujourd'hui," *Mercure de France,* March 15, 1920, 600–627. Catel writes: "Les trois livres de Robert Frost donnent parfois l'impression que l'Est des Etats-Unis est peuplé de fantômes" ("At times, the three books Frost has written give one the impression that the eastern part of the United States is peopled with phantoms") (614). Harriet Monroe had published a short notice of the article, "Discovered in Paris," in *Poetry* 16, no. 3 (June 1920): 148–151. In the spring of 1922, a number of American newspapers ran an article quoting Catel that first appeared in the *New York Times Book Review:* "Here at the University of Montpelier we are going to study Frost as a poet, together with recognized writers such as Shakespeare, Milton, Thackeray, etc. I hope Frost may know that there are a certain number of people here greatly interested in American poetry." The article (which was syndicated) then added: "The Sorbonne, too, announces that Robert Frost's works are now a requirement in the English teachers' course here" ("Books and Authors," *New York Times Book Review and Magazine,* April 30, 1922, 21).

before I heard of what G. R. Elliott said for me in The Nation and then only by chance.[361] I'm not usually where I can see the magazines and I can't afford to buy many of them. You might take this as a hint that I shouldn't mind seeing a copy of The Nation with my witch in it.[362]

I shall hope to see you when I am at Columbia late in May with a Phi Beta Kappa poem.[363]

Sincerely yours
Robert Frost

[To Maxwell Aley (1889–1953). Formerly at Henry Holt and Company, Aley in 1921 was the managing editor of Century Magazine. He and his wife, Ruth, had hosted RF's eldest daughter, Lesley, at their home on West Twenty-Fourth Street. ALS. DCL.]

South Shaftsbury Vt
May 7 1921

Dear Aley:

I can't remember your home address (my boast is that I can't remember anybody's); so I am sending this check for Lesley at The Century office. She will probably need the check to get back with.

I've been thinking of your plan for poetry next year. Why don't you restrict yourself to ten Giants and then give an equal space with what you give them to two entirely new poets of your own finding? I should like to talk with you

---

361. George R. Elliott had come to RF's notice when he published "Neighborliness of Robert Frost." See RF to Elliott, March 8, 1920.

362. "The Pauper Witch of Grafton" appeared in *The Nation* on April 13, 1921.

363. RF read as Phi Beta Kappa Poet at Columbia University on May 31, 1921. He apparently delivered an early version of what would later become "Build Soil," which he would also give as Phi Beta Kappa Poet at Columbia on May 24, 1932. None of RF's biographers has mentioned the 1921 appearance at Columbia, evidence of which has only come to light with the preparation of this edition. We must now date "Build Soil," at least in part, to as early as winter–spring 1921. The reference in the opening lines of the 1932 text of the poem is now clear (emphasis added):

Why Tityrus! But you've forgotten me.
I'm Meliboeus the potato man,
The one you had the talk with, you remember,
Here on this very campus years ago.

A number of people in the audience in 1932 had likely been there also in 1921.

about this. You know you are under obligations to do something for your country and the human race. Let your motto this year be find a poet.

Sorry I couldn't have lingered with you longer.

With best wishes to you and Mrs Aley and thanks for your goodness to Lesley I'm

Sincerely yours
Robert Frost

[To Marion Elza Dodd (1883–1961), proprietor of the Hampshire Bookshop, Northampton, Massachusetts, home to Smith College (hence an "enterprise for a lot of college girls to look on at"). ALS. ACL.]

South Shaftsbury Vt
May 16 1921

My dear Miss Dodd:

You are one of the few bookshops in the world where books are sold in something like the spirit they were written in. You are a splendid exibition [sic] of enterprise for a lot of college girls to look on at. I should think some of these, who hadn't just seen what to do with and for themselves after gradua- tion, might be inspired by your example to try to do in other small towns what you have done in Northampton. They couldnt do better with and for them- selves for that matter for the small towns, or for publishers and authors. I know publishers and authors who would like to encourage them.

Sincerely yours
Robert Frost

[To Wilbur L. Cross (editor of the Yale Review). ALS. Yale.]

South Shaftsbury Vt
May 21 1921

Dear Mr Cross:

I haven't actually on hand the best thing I ever wrote, but I have the second best and the seventh best (to be exact) and I believe I'll send them along to see if you can tell which is which. You have spoken of a long one. Both are rather long but far from my longest. I seem to myself to have had fairly good luck since I came to South Shaftsbury to live.

You say such pleasant things in your letters. You are a good editor.

Sincerely yours
Robert Frost

You see my new address?

"Maple" might be called a name romance. Paul is the Paul of the "heap big" lumber yarns.[364]

[To George Browne. Date derived from internal evidence. On May 31, RF read before the Phi Beta Kappa Society at Columbia University. ALS. Plymouth.]

South Shaftsbury Vt
[early June 1921]

Dear Browne:

I wish I could see you before you go to California. It's terrible for Jack and Elinor.[365] I say it because I know. I must write to Jack. I wish I could see him too. Be sure you send me his full address.

I'm just home from a not very successful reading to the Phi Beta Kappa at Columbia. I'm making in some haste a copy of a poem or two for you. There's a third I wish you could have too but the original manuscript seems no where to be found an unusual thing with my manuscripts. The Grindstone poem may amuse your kind of boys a little.[366] It goes home more to the kind who have had to grind for a living.

This is all in haste to catch you in time for your exercises. I wouldn't be left out of them after having been in so many years in succession.

With the best wishes

Always yours
R.F.

---

364. The *Yale Review* published "Maple" in October 1921; "Paul's Wife" appeared in *Century Magazine* in November.

365. Browne's daughter Eleanor (whose name RF misspells) and her husband John "Jack" Gallishaw. It is not clear what misfortune they suffered, although given RF's sympathetic remark it was likely the death of a child. The 1920 census records two sons under the age of two in the Gallishaw family, neither of whom survived to be registered in the 1930 census (by which time four younger children, aged three to eight, had been born to the Gallishaws). The Frosts had themselves lost two children.

366. In June 1921, "The Grindstone" appeared in *Farm and Fireside*. An RF poem had featured in previous commencement exercises at Browne's school.

[To Everett Glass (1891–1966), formerly a student of RF's at Amherst, later an actor
and playwright. He appeared in Invasion of the Body Snatchers (1956), among many
other films. ALS. BU.]

South Shaftsbury Vt

June 7 1921

Dear Everett:

Now if your hot cakes are still hot!

I should have written sooner if it wasnt for fear of not acting in character.
You know how particular we have to be now-a-days when everybody is so
woefully unthinking in the preservation of his artificiality.

Don't tell me you are all sold out: I am too late.

Send me something awfully good and make my reputation with the Holts
as poet-detector.[367]

My children all went down the valley to see Amherst trim Williams and
saw her.[368] I was somewhere else cutting a Fy Beater Caper.[369]

Always yours as formerly

Robert Frost

[To John W. Haines. ALS-photostat. DCL.]

South Shaftsbury

Vermont U.S.A.

June 7 1921

My dear Jack

Your letter has just come with the encouraging news. Wouldnt it be
restful not to have that woman hanging over me any more? I hate to
have to rejoice in anyones downfall (you know how unvindictive I am)
but I must say in the Madams case I'm afraid I don't care where she
falls—she may fall even on me—so she doesn't hang over me a moment

---

367. Glass's first work, The Tumbler, after an Old Legend: A Play in Two Scenes, was not
published until April 1926 (in the journal Poet Lore 37, no. 4: 516–536).

368. The rivalry between Williams and Amherst dates to the first intercollegiate baseball game ever played, on July 1, 1859. During the 1921 season, Amherst defeated Williams twice.

369. The "Phi Beta Kappa" poem given at Columbia.

longer.[370] It's a great wonder I havent been made nervous. Once she is out of the way and we are free of the menace of suits she might bring against us I shall have hope of finding a new and decenter publisher to take me up in England.

My copy of the contract between us is in the safe at Henry Holt's in New York. I will see that you have it immediately. I shall send it in another letter (registered) in a day or two. Here I can tell you something about it. It was made late in 1912 and called for four books from this hand and royalties and an accounting once a year from the lady. I gave two books A Boys Will and North of Boston and in return got nothing, neither royalty nor accounting. I asked now and then for at least an accounting. French shrugs and "Oh poetry, you know, can't be expected to make money." When I said it wasn't royalties I was asking for but merely an accounting, I got the last letter from her I believe I ever had. In it she told me Americans were all dollar chasers. Sometime in 1915 I called on her in form under legal advice for the performance of her part of the contract and receiving no reply, denounced the contract in form and have since acted as if it didnt exist. All this under legal advice. Both the Holts' lawyers and Heineman's [sic] said I was under no further obligation to her and Heineman was willing to publish everything I had written if I would share with him the expense of the farewell suit she would probably bring against us for spite. We were in the middle of these matters when Heineman died.[371]

Of course the writing she holds against me can be worth very little. But by all means let us get it if we can. I could see that Heineman rather shrank from the idea of a row for all his reputation as a fighter. Yet on the other hand he lost his temper when he heard that one of the Holts without consulting him had approached Mrs Nutt to see what she would take for a contract she had broken quite traverse.[372]

---

370. The French-born publisher of RF's first two books in England (and widow of the firm's founder, Alfred Nutt). The company, David Nutt, was in receivership. Haines would be instrumental in helping RF secure, through the Cambridge (Massachusetts) bookseller and collector Maurice Firuski, unsold copies of the London editions of *ABW* and *NB*.

371. Heinemann published RF's *Selected Poems* in London in 1923; the founder of the press, William Heinemann, had died on October 5, 1920.

372. See *As You Like It* 3.4, where Celia says of Orlando "O, that's a brave man! He writes brave verses, speaks brave words, swears brave oaths, and breaks them bravely, quite traverse, athwart the heart of his lover; as a puisne tilter, that spurs his horse but on one side, breaks his staff like a noble goose."

I have been away from home doing funny things to earn my living. I wish you could see me sometime talking on a platform. No I don't either because you would just add so much to the terror I still suffer from after five years of fitful appearance in public. I dont orate. I talk. I had to do it once in Philadelphia from the same rostrum with the one who shall be nameless.[373] You would have been amused at my covert malice. I did well for me. My last feat recently was to read what is called a Phi Beta Kappa poem at Columbia University in New York. I had a lot of fun writing the poem (an eclogue on Leisure for Poets from the text Deus nobis haec otia fecit) and no fun at all reading it.[374] I lost my terror in a cold rage at a lot of people who came in late after I had started reading. But the rage didnt seem to help matters much. Some time I must send you a copy of my ecologue for your private gaiety. It begins

> Tityrus someone's been saying that leisure is bad for poets
> Saying it mind you to possible patrons of poets
> Where it may well do mischief

I know it will amuse you to follow my argument and study out what's the matter with my hexameters (my first and at forty-six). And I have a fairy story named Paul's Wife for you when I shall find someone to make me a copy of it. A fairy story is another departure for me you will say, but wait till you hear the kind of fairy story.

Do you want me to send you a copy of the new Mountain Interval with a picture of a picture of me?[375]

Affectionately

Robert Frost

I'm glad if you and my Canadian friend got on together.[376]

---

373. Wilfrid Gibson. See RF to Haines, January 20, 1921.

374. For the Columbia event, see RF to Carl Van Doren, April 22, 1921. RF quotes line 6 of Virgil's first *Eclogue*, which reads, in English: "God has granted us this leisure."

375. The photograph of Aroldo Du Chêne's bust of RF.

376. George R. Elliott.

[To Wilbur L. Cross. ALS. Yale.]

South Shaftsbury Vt

June 7 1921

Dear Mr Cross:

Do you think I would have asked you to tell me which was my second best and which my seventh if I had known myself? I set up to be one of the thirty poets in America who can separate their bad poems from their good before they print them, but even I do not pretend to see much difference between one good one and another. Those two are fairly good aren't they?[377]

Do you know I cant see any reason why you shouldn't use some of that letter about my Star in a Stone-boat. Neither the person that sent it nor the person that wrote it is anyone to me.[378] I don't see why we poets and things should have to submit tamely to such condescension from scientific nobodies. I understand that American scientists and statesmen always make a point of not remembering the name of any American writer.

Time we took arms against such conditions.

You keep whichever poem you will for present use. I shall have something else for you by next year.

Always yours sincerely

Robert Frost

[To Harriet Moody. RF refers, in opening the letter, to the second edition of MI, issued in April 1921. ALS. Chicago.]

S. Shaftsbury Vt

June 7 1921

Dear Harriet:

Did you receive a copy of Mountain Interval from me? Or did it get lost on the way? Or didn't I send it?

------

377. "Maple" and "Paul's Wife"; see RF to Cross, May 21, 1921.

378. On the "letter" RF mentions in connection with "A Star in a Stone Boat," see RF to Elizabeth Farson, March 30, 1921. Farson had forwarded to RF some remarks on the poem by, it would appear, Walter R. Crane, who in 1921 was working for the U.S. Bureau of Mines in Washington, D.C. Cross did not use the letter.

This is just for once in a way to be writing when I am not on the defensive and have nothing to explain.

With the best wishes in the world I'm

Always yours sincerely
Robert Frost

When are you coming to see our apple farm?

[To John Van Alstyne Weaver (1893–1938), who held editorial positions at the Chicago Daily News *and the* Brooklyn Daily Eagle *before moving to Los Angeles in the mid-1920s to write for the screen. He published several books of vernacular poetry in the early 1920s, beginning with* In American *(New York: Knopf, 1921). ALS. BU.]*

South Shaftsbury Vt
June 7 1921

Dear Mr Weaver:

That's a good book in an accent I hope you may never lose and dont see why you should lose if you practice it more or less in speech as well as in writing. I think our art and nature have to meet each other about half way in these things. Keep the accent anyway whatever you do and whatever kind of people you act yourself out in. I should stick to the kind of people too if I could: I shouldnt drop them at any rate till I found something in myself I couldn't say through them. I should use every ingenuity too in trying to compass the best that was in me in their language and turns of idiom. High thinking never lost anything by being phrased in the vernacular. Cf. Ralph Waldo.[379]

---

379. RF has in mind Emerson's "Monadnoc," a poem he often quoted:

I can spare the college-bell,
And the learned lecture, well;
Spare the clergy and libraries,
Institutes and dictionaries,
For the hardy English root
Thrives here, unvalued, underfoot.
Rude poets of the tavern hearth,
Squandering your unquoted mirth,
Which keeps the ground, and never soars,
While Jake retorts, and Reuben roars . . .

But you have to remember that what I call their language is a spirit you have to catch for yourself and create a language of your own in. It is poetry to a certain extent to appreciate and appropriate folk things like "a jane," "to vamp" and "live wire" but it is not the highest poetry till you have learned from such examples "to make" in the same folk vein on your own account. The first person who said "a jane" like the first person who said "a nymph" was the real poet or at any rate the poet of the first instance.

Forgive all this. You couldnt have brought it on yourself even by asking unless I had believed you had written a book. Come on and have some fun doing it racier and better than any of us. Let's see something happen.

Always yours friendly
Robert Frost

I've been gadding a good deal lately, or I should have written you sooner. Hope we can see each other some time.

[To Sidney Cox. Date derived from postmark. ALS. DCL.]

South Shaftsbury Vt
[June 8, 1921]

Dear Sidney

I have a good looking book I should send you if I knew you were still there.[380]
Ever thine

R.F.

You havent written for so long.

[To John W. Haines. ALS-photostat. DCL.]

South Shaftsbury Vt
June 8 1921

My dear Jack:

I am enclosing several documents that should explain themselves better than I can explain them.

About my original copy of the agreement: I thought it was that that the Holts had. I probably have it somewhere here or in Franconia. I'm terrible

---

380. The second edition of *MI.*

about such things. I shall be on the look for it [*sic*]. You have all you need to go ahead with, though, havent you?

I shall write a real letter when it hasn't to travel in the same envelope with all this messiness.

Have at her as you value me.[381]

> Always thine in any event
> Robert Frost

[To C. F. D. Belden. ALS. BU.]

> South Shaftsbury Vt
> June 12 1921

Dear Mr Belden:

Thanks for your thoughtfulness. As you say, the time draws near.

I should be grateful if you would engage a room for me. I think perhaps it ought to be for the nights of the 22nd and 23rd.[382] I doubt the wisdom of my trying to make the rather round-about journey from here on the day of my reading.

> Sincerely yours
> Robert Frost

[To Percy MacKaye. The letter is a typed transcript, on MacKaye's Miami University stationery, of a telegram sent by RF. The reference is to University of Michigan president Marion LeRoy Burton's offer to RF of a $5,000 one-year fellowship. See RF to Burton, July 7, 1921. TG (copy). Miami, Ohio.]

TELEGRAM to Percy MacKaye,

> Oxford, Ohio,
> 25 June, 1921.

On consideration, gladly accept President Burton's offer.

> Robert Frost.

---

381. See RF to Haines, June 7, 1921.

382. On June 23, RF read at the Boston Public Library during the American Library Association's Swampscott (Massachusetts) Conference (June 20–27, 1921). Belden was on the local steering committee. For an account of the gathering, see *Bulletin of the American Library Association* 15 (January–November 1921): 55.

*[To Grace Hazard Conkling (1878–1958), a poet and professor of English at Smith. ALS.
UVA.]*

South Shaftsbury Vt
June 28 1921

My dear Mrs Conkling:

I should like to scatter a dozen or two of your circulars over the country if
I don't have to promise results to obtain them of you. And you needn't thank
me. I'll be doing it for myself and the cause as much as for you.[383]

Don't ask me too confidingly about what you ought to expect of publishers.
I dont feel that I am very much on the inside with that gentry. You wouldn't
look to me as an authority on them if you knew the story of my mix-up with
David Nutt in England. I might be a better and a truer poet if I were a business
man too. But I'm not a business man too. All I can tell you about royalties is
that fifteen percent seems good to me. It is what I get on everything, common
editions and preferred. I'm glad Hilda is going to have the honor of a special
edition.[384] You ought to be touched by this mark of her publisher's good
friendship.

I am grateful that you should have thought to link Edward Thomas' name
with mine in one of your lectures. You will be careful, I know, not to say anything to exalt either of us at the expense of the other. There's a story going
round that might lead you to exaggerate our debt to each other. Anything we
may be thought to have in common we had before we met. When Hodgson
introduced us at a coffee house in London in 1913 I had written two and a half
of my three books, he had written all but two or three of his thirty.[385] The
most our congeniality could do was confirm us both in what we were. There
was never a moment's thought about who may have been influencing whom.
The least rivalry of that kind would have taken something from our friendship. We were greater friends than almost any two ever were practicing the

---

383. See Conkling's *Imagination and Children's Reading*, a twenty-three-page booklet
issued in 1921 by the Hampshire Bookshop, in Northampton, Massachusetts, which had
been founded by RF's friend Marion Elza Dodd.

384. Conkling's daughter Hilda had published *Poems by a Little Girl* (New York: Frederick A. Stokes Company, 1920), with a preface by Amy Lowell. Her first book was followed by *Shoes of the Wind* (1922) and *Silverhorn* (1924), both also published by Frederick A.
Stokes Company. For more on her, see the notes to RF's February 10, 1921, letter to
Lowes.

385. The poet Ralph Hodgson (1871–1962).

same art. I dont mean that we did nothing for each other. As I have said we encouraged each other in our adventurous ways. Beyond that anything we did was very practical. He gave me standing as a poet—he more than anyone else, though of course I have to thank Abercrombie, Hueffer, Pound and some others for help too.[386] I dragged him out from under the heap of his own work in prose he was buried alive under. He was throwing to his big perfunctory histories of Marlborough and the like written to order such poetry as would make him a name if he were but given credit for it.[387] I made him see that he owed it to himself and the poetry to have it out by itself in poetic form where it must suffer itself to be admired. It took me some time. I bantered, teased and bullied all the summer we were together at Leddington and Ryton. All he had to do was put his poetry in a form that declared itself. The theme must be the same, the accent exactly the same. He saw it and he was tempted. It was plain that he had wanted to be a poet all the years he had been writing about poets not worth his little finger. But he was afeared (though a soldier). His timidity was funny and fascinating. I had about given him up, he had turned his thoughts to enlistment and I mine to sailing for home when he wrote his first poem. The decision he made in going into the army helped him make the other decision to be a poet in form. And a very fine poet. And a poet all in his own right. The accent is absolutely his own. You can hear it everywhere in his prose, where if he had left it, however, it would have been lost.

You won't quote me in any of this please. It is much too personal. I simply wanted you to know before you went ahead. The point is that what we had in common we had from before we were born. Make as much of that as you will but dont tell anyone we gave each other anything but a boost.

With our best wishes to you and the children. We shall look forward to seeing you at Middlebury.[388]

Sincerely yours
Robert Frost

---

386. Lascelles Abercrombie, Ford Madox [Hueffer] Ford, and Ezra Pound had favorably reviewed RF's first two books.

387. Thomas's *The Life of the Duke of Marlborough* was published in London by Chapman and Hall in 1915.

388. Both RF and Conkling were on the faculty of the Bread Loaf School of English in 1921.

[*To Carl Van Doren. ALS. Princeton.*]

South Shaftsbury Vt
June 28 1921

Dear Mr Van Doren:

I never saw any of the copies of The Nation to thank you for the way you treated my poem till day before yesterday when I saw both parcels of them at once.[389] They had been hung up at another Shaftsbury as often along the river banks at low water is the wood pulp they are made of. I dont know what started them along again unless it was rain and a rise in the river or a rise in some postmaster to more than his duty.

I hope you haven't lived to be sorry for the way you treated my poem. Treat some more that way sometime will you?

Another thing that for reasons I havent thanked you for is a compliment you paid me in your last letter. I wasn't bibliographer enough to know the extent of it and so thank you for it to measure. I'm not much further along as a bibliographer, but I have decided to take it simply and unsuspiciously as a great compliment and thank you for it greatly.

Why did you avoid me and my Phi Betta [*sic*] Kappa poem?[390] Did you avoid me on account of the poem or the poem on account of me?

Shall I see you when I am down for my talk on Poetic Displacement?[391]

Sincerely yours
Robert Frost

---

389. RF refers to "The Pauper Witch of Grafton," published in *The Nation* on April 13, 1921, and to the note there on contributors, which described him as follows: "Robert Frost, one of the most distinguished of American poets, is the author of three volumes of verse which distil into a few short poems all the substance which for forty years has gone into the local color short stories of New England."

390. See RF to Van Doren, April 22, 1921.

391. RF gave a talk at Columbia on July 12, as a part of the university's 1921 summer session. For RF's remarks on the event, see his July 17, 1921, letter to Holden ("I offended again . . .").

[*To John Erskine (1879–1951), professor of English at Columbia from 1909 to 1937. ALS. Columbia.*]

South Shaftsbury Vt

July 7 1921

My dear Erskine:

You are not to think I have forgotten my engagements of the night you so sympathetically waked my poor dead Phi Beta Kappa poem with me. I was to tell you when I felt like it what I made of your Metaneira.[392] All I can say is I hope I may have a chance in the way of business to tell a publisher sometime what I make of such another. You knew the play of blank verse wouldn't be thrown away on me. I have an idea it was the blank verse you were principally interested in hearing what I would say to. Of course it's lovely. You never fail to get something out of the relation of sentence to line. And the theme is lovely too, of the too maternal mother who from want of faith in the natural misses for her child the gift of the spiritual.

But why to objectify the idea and put it far enough away from yourself must you put it away off in antiquity and say it in heroes and gods. Why must you every time, I mean. All right for this poem; but why not next time say it in modern people. It is like diffidence, shyness, this remoteness in time and space. Get over it and you can break in on the age with your strength and insight. I'll bet I'm right.

Sincerely yours

Robert Frost

[*To Harold Goddard Rugg (1883–1957), a librarian at Dartmouth. ALS. DCL.*]

South Shaftsbury VT

July 7 1921

Dear Mr Rugg:

Thanks for the glimpse of Dartmouth poetry.[393] If I had not been so mercenary I should have met some of your promising young poets. You know

---

392. "The Sons of Metaneira" was first collected in Erskine's 1917 volume, *The Shadowed Hour* (New York: Lyric Publishing Company).

393. RF alludes to one of a number of anthologies that reprinted poetry originally published in Dartmouth's undergraduate newspapers. In 1925 he would himself supply

how naturally it comes about that the most unworldly are made worldly in self-defense against the world.

However I didn't start this letter to purge my soul with confession, but to ask a favor of you that granted will make your welcome warmer (and it will be warm anyway) when you come this way later.

My son will look in on you in a week or so on his travels about Vermont and New Hampshire hunting for rocks and minerals. He will have with him a young geologist from Hamilton College. Could I ask you to get them the advice of some geological person about interesting places up along? They are Walter Stone and Carol Frost.[394]

Always yours sincerely

Robert Frost

[To Louis Untermeyer. The manuscript of this letter is not among those Untermeyer deposited at the Library of Congress, nor have we been able to locate it. We rely on Untermeyer's transcription (RFLU, 130–131). However, there is reason to suspect that his dating may be wrong. We have found no evidence that Untermeyer visited RF in late June or early July 1921; in fact, RF was in New York City himself on or about July 10 (see RF to Raymond Holden, July 17, 1921).]

South Shaftsbury Vt

July 7 1921

Dear Louis:

No one put it into my head: I thought of it myself: there's that much good in me still, though[395] that's all there is. I mean there's that much thought

---

the preface to one such volume, *The Arts Anthology: Dartmouth Verse* (Portland, ME: Mosher Press). See *CPRF*, 95–96.

394. The geologist Ralph Walter Stone (1876–1964), after finishing his undergraduate degree at Hamilton, studied with Nathaniel Shaler at Harvard in 1900, only one year after RF had audited Shaler's course in historical geology. In 1901 Stone joined the U.S. Geological Survey, doing fieldwork in Montana, Alaska, Wyoming, North Carolina, and a number of other states. He was named a fellow in the Geological Society of America in 1912.

395. On Untermeyer's typescript for *RFLU* (held at LoC) the word is first given as "though." A terminal "t" was added at a later date, and in the left margin the word "thought" appears, with a mark indicating that the text was to be amended. And indeed *RFLU* (our copy-text) retains "thought." The reading, however, almost certainly should be "though," which is what we give here.

for other people. The rest of me is swallowed up in thoughts of myself. All the time you were here I read and read to you from my own works. You were partly to blame. You let me, to try me to see how far I would go in my self-assertion. You were stringing me, so to speak. You gave me all the line you had on the reel. And I took it. But there's this redeeming consideration. It did occur to me of my own motion though not until too late that you also may have had works to read from and were only diffidently waiting to be asked like the decent person you are. I'll be damned. It shows how far we can get along in our egotism without noticing it. I'm a goner—or almost a goner. The terrible example of others I could name I haven't profited by any more than I have by the terrible example of people I have seen die.

> *To prayer, to prayer I go—I think I go—*
> *I go to prayer*
> *Along a solemn corridor of woe*
> *And down a stair*
> *In every step of which I am abased;*
> *A cowl I wear,*
> *I wear a halter-rope about the waist,*
> *I bear a candle-end put out with haste.*
> *I go to prayer.*[396]

I shouldn't wonder if my last end would be religious; I weary so of cutting back the asparagus bed of my faults. I wonder what it is about prayer. I have half a mind to try it. I'm going to try to be good, if it isn't too late. Let the columnists mock as they will.

Yours
RF

---

396. This is the first version of a poem RF would return to, and revise, in two subsequent letters to Untermeyer: of September 26, 1921 (in this volume) and January 15, 1942 (see *RFLU*, 331.) The poem was not published in RF's lifetime.

[To Marion LeRoy Burton (1874–1925), president of the University of Michigan, on the occasion of RF's appointment to a fellowship there. ALS. UM.]

South Shaftsbury Vt

July 7 1921

My dear President Burton:

You had my telegram accepting your offer. It remains for me to thank you for having chosen me to be a representative of creative literature in this way at Michigan University. We'll waive the question of whether you might not better have chosen someone else for the honor. I should have thanked you almost as much if you had. The important thing is that you should have chosen anyone. I dont know why I am so gratified unless it is because I am somewhat surprised when men of your executive authority (yours and Mr Osborn's[397]) see it as a part of their duty to the state to encourage the arts; and I don't know why I am surprised unless it is because I base my expectation on what I have observed of our Presidents at Washington. We have had ten or a dozen in the White House in the last fifty years, all good men and all good executives, but only one of the lot of such sight or insight.[398] And we don't think that a large enough proportion for safety, do we?

I can see that the appointment may contemplate the benefit of education a little as well as of poetry and one poet. You would like it to say something to the world for keeping the creative and erudite together in education where they belong. And you would like it to make its demand on the young student. He must be about some achievement in the arts or sciences while yet he is at his most creative period and the college interposes to keep the world off his shoulders. The greatest nonsense of our time has been the solution of the school problem by forsaking knowledge for thought. From learning to thinking—it sounds like a progress. But it is illusory. Thought is good but knowledge is at least no worse and thought is no substitute for knowledge. Knowledge is certainly more material to the imagination than thought. The point is that neither knowledge nor thought is an end and neither is nearer an end than the other. The end they both serve, perhaps equally, is

---

397. Chase S. Osborn made his fortune in the newspaper business in Sault Ste. Marie before entering Michigan politics, ultimately becoming governor of the state (1911–1913). He served on the University of Michigan's Board of Regents.

398. Likely Theodore Roosevelt, who in 1905 secured for E. A. Robinson, then in difficult straits, a position at the New York Customs Office.

deeds in such accepted and nameable forms as the sonnet, the story, the vase, the portrait, the landscape, the hat, the scythe, the gun, the food, the breed, the house, the home, the factory, the election, the government. We must always be about definite deeds to be growing.

This is a long letter, but you will forgive it to my wish to show my appreciation of what you and Mr Osborn have done.

Sincerely yours
Robert Frost

[*To Thomas E. Rankin (1872–1953), professor of English at the University of Michigan. The following letter was found tipped into a book inscribed by RF in 1916. The reference to his "heart" already being with Rankin "out there" in Ann Arbor, however, suggests that the letter dates from July 1921, when RF accepted a position at the university. Apparently Rankin had asked RF to write a brief article introducing the English poet Alfred Noyes (who was to speak at Michigan). Noyes was on the faculty at Princeton from 1914 to 1923. ALS. Alger.*]

[South Shaftsbury, VT]
[July 1921]

Dear Mr Rankin:

I am sorry not to be able to give Alfred Noyes the welcome he deserves from the State of Michigan; but, as you may have noticed, I keep my pen pretty much out of prose and entirely out of contemporary criticism. Someone else will be found to do him justice I am sure. No English poet is more generally admired in the United States. He is a tuneful poet.

[Our] hearts are already with you all out there.[399] Mrs Frost joins me in best wishes to you and Mrs Rankin.

Sincerely yours
Robert Frost

---

399. RF apparently makes a slip of the pen in his last sentence, where the manuscript reads: "Are hearts are already with you . . ."

[To Percy MacKaye. ALS. DCL.]

South Shaftsbury Vt
July 16 1921

My dear Percy:

I got a letter off to President Burton as my first duty and then ran for the train to various places. I thought perhaps I might find time to write you my thanks on my travels; but I didn't. I seemed not to be alone for writing at all.

Well your great plan has its start. You have landed me. Who comes next?

I have to thank people in this order or exactly the reverse according to how you look at it: You President Hughes[400] President Burton and Mr Osborn. Of Mr Osborn I can only say, An American statesman and so considerate of the poor poet!

I haven't known exactly what the great plan was and it turns out somewhat different from what I should have expected. But it is all right. I am glad to lend myself to it in almost any shape. It seems the idea is fellowships of just one year in a place. When I said I could accept $3500 a year for myself and family I thought I might be going west for two or perhaps three years. The expense of moving would be distributed over two or three salaries. That amount wouldnt really have done for one year. President Burton saw that without my having to speak and made it $5000. You can see how a short time in a place will cost much more accordingly. They have rented me a house already for $1250. The house is furnished but they ask me to buy dishes and carpets, or bring these with me which I doubt if I can do. The house is very large; there'll be no hope of running it without one servant. So the money goes. But never mind it's their money in a sense and they want me to live in a style worthy of their own high idea of me. We've made up our minds to be in their hands for a good time and damn the economies. It will be a year-long picnic and we are free-minded enough as a family to break off our several affairs and take them up as seriously as ever again after the picnic is over. We're all in for it—all but one who will have to be left behind for school.[401] There'll be music and dancing and college yelling. We all like such things. A year of them will do our digestion good and a year out of our selfish pursuits will never be missed in the long run.

People have asked me what I wanted said about my honor in the papers. The question is what you want said to further your plan. Write me a descrip-

400. Raymond M. Hughes.
401. Irma Frost.

tion of it—my particular honor—that will help will you? I could use it right away in one quarter and another.

Very special: Lesley asks to know how she can get into communication with Arvia at Brattleboro.[402]

Our best wishes to you all

Affectionately

Robert Frost

Where is what you promised me of your recent work?

[To Raymond Holden (1894–1972), American poet, novelist, essayist, and editor. ALS. DCL.]

Sou' Shaftsbury Vermont

July 17 1921

Dear Raymond

In New York last week it came to my knowledge that Madam Nutt's receivers on representation of hers had made a claim to all the royalties I have ever had from Henry Holt and Co. It is at most a joke or a formality, I think I can say. We are perfectly safe. The law has been covered. Still for fear there should be an attempt made on me for what could be scared out of me I should like it better if the property you bought of me last year stood properly in your name.[403] It would put us all in an awkward position to have them attach it. So please have Mr Parker make out the deed for me to sign.[404] That's what I sent you the old deed for. (You got it all right, I think you said.)

I am beginning to sniff the air suspiciously on the point of taking flight from these weedy regions. It can't be long before you hear me come crashing through the woods in your direction. Don't shoot till you're sure who it is anyway.

I offended again in New York on Tuesday.[405] I haven't given a good talk in public this year I can safely say. I don't know what's the matter is [sic] unless

---

402. Arvia MacKaye (1902–1989), Percy MacKaye's daughter, a poet and the founder of the Rudolph Steiner Educational and Farming Association in Ghent, New York.

403. In 1920 Holden purchased the remainder of RF's property in Franconia, having purchased half of it already in 1919. See *YT,* 136–145.

404. Perhaps Wilbur T. Parker, a partner in W. T. Parker and Sons, a merchant enterprise in Franconia.

405. In a lecture on contemporary American poetry at Columbia University; see RF to Carl Van Doren, June 28, 1921, and the notes thereto.

it's indifference. I must brace up and try to care a little or else quit the platform for the desk.

Our best to you and Grace and the Du Chênes[406] and may the Lord keep you till we see you again.

> Ever yours
> Robert Frost

Receipted tax bill enclosed

[To Charles Lowell Young (1865–1937), American scholar and teacher. ALS. Wellesley.]

> Franconia N.H.
> July 21 1921

Dear Young:

You want castigation badly, but you won't get it from me. I abandon you to the discipline of your enemies.

I left Amherst as an example to you; and what good has it done? I will ask you just once more, Where is your book? [407]

I can't go walking with you and you wouldn't want me to go when I am at the writing so well. Lets get something done before the evil days.[408]

The trouble with some of us is that we substituted philosophy for religion at a certain point in our life and it spoiled us or damn near spoiled us for action. Ist [*sic*] not so?

More in anger than in sorrow

> Your judge
> Robert Frost

Will you condescend to look in The Harpers for July for signs of me? [409]

---

406. Aroldo Du Chêne and his wife, Eiley Hamilton Du Chêne; Grace was Holden's wife.

407. Young would not publish a book until 1941, when his *Emerson's Montaigne* (New York: Macmillan) appeared.

408. Ecclesiastes 12:1: "Remember now thy Creator in the days of thy youth, while the evil days come not, nor the years draw nigh, when thou shalt say, I have no pleasure in them . . ." This was a favorite of RF's at the time; see his letter to Wilfred Davison, December 19, 1920.

409. In July 1921, *Harper's* published "Place for a Third," "Fragmentary Blue," "For Once, Then, Something," and "Good-bye and Keep Cold," all subsequently collected in *NH*.

[To Louis Untermeyer. ALS. LoC.]

South Shaftsbury Vt
July 23 1921

Dear Louis:

It will be a hard book to displace from the schools.[410] It's a good one, and I say it who am as particular about the books I am praised in as I am about those I am condemned in. There's an income in that there book or I'm much mistaken. I don't want to get your hopes up too much, but I can't help telling you that a man named Fry has made more than a million dollars out of Frys Geographies.[411] If you do make a fortune, I speak now for a percentage. The percentage of benzoate of soda in jam would be all I should ask.[412] All right, it's an agreement. If anyone else asks you for a share in the profits you tell them they had theirs in flattery—let them read the book—especially Edgar Lee M.[413]

By the way I see that Mugsy [sic] McGraw has taken on to his pitching staff a product of my special course in writing at Amherst. His name is Zink and he will tell you that it was I and no one else who taught him style and control.

---

410. The second edition of Untermeyer's *Modern American Poetry*.

411. G. Cecil Fry published *A Text-Book of Geography* (London: Clive) in 1917; he wrote many other volumes like it.

412. About 0.1 percent. In the early years of the twentieth century, the canning industry lobbied government regulators for permission to use sodium benzoate as a preservative, which was contrary to the proscriptions of the Pure Food and Drug Act of 1906. By 1908, controversy over the chemical's safety reached the Roosevelt White House and its Department of Agriculture, which established a board that ultimately deemed sodium benzoate safe, pleasing the food industry but sparking public protest. Dr. Harvey Washington Wiley (1844–1930), chief chemist at the Department of Agriculture and a staunch advocate of the Pure Food and Drug Act, resigned in 1912, having concluded that the Roosevelt and Taft administrations, and James Wilson, secretary of agriculture, had together made its proper enforcement impossible.

413. Edgar Lee Masters, whom Untermeyer had praised highly in the 1921 edition of *Modern American Poetry:* "Frost and Masters were the bright particular planets of 1915, although the star of the latter has waned while the light of the former has grown in magnitude. Yet Masters's most famous book [*Spoon River Anthology*, 1915] will rank as one of the landmarks of American literature. In it, he has synthesized the small towns of the mid-West with a background that is unmistakably local and implications that are universal" (xxxiii).

He owes me everything but his degree.[414] And then people will question if any thing comes of teaching English!

You were right about lea[r]ning.

> Fait'fully
> Robert Frost

[*To Dorothy Dunbar Bromley (1896–1986), a journalist by training, who worked in the publicity department at Henry Holt and Company from 1921 to 1924; her husband, Stanley Bromley, also worked for the firm. This letter concerns a brochure or flyer that the publisher was preparing, perhaps an early version of* Robert Frost: The Man and His Work, *issued in 1923. ALS. UVA.*]

> South Shaftsbury Vt
> July 23 1921

My dear Mrs Bromley:

Just a few little things in your generous article I would have different. I think you'll find them sufficiently indicated in the manuscript.

I wish instead of what you say at the end you might bring in something about my very special interest in the problem of teaching English. Sometimes like others I give it up in despair. But I always come back hopeful to it and the places where it is being studied if not yet worked out. I have just been to lecture at the Middlebury Summer School of English on the prospects of what I may call the studio method in teaching English.[415] The experienced older painter allows inexperienced younger painters to set up their easels alongside of his for what they can get out of his example, stimulation, and shop-talk. So the experienced writer might receive inexperienced, but promising, or at any rate ambitious, writers into companionship. He might at intervals, that is, and their gain be no loss to him.

If you use my words in this, please change all "I's" to "he's." I dread being quoted too much, I suppose because I dread responsibility for anything but my poetry.

---

414. John Joseph "Muggsy" McGraw (1873–1934), a major-league baseball player and manager of the New York Giants. Walter Noble Zink (1898–1964), Amherst class of 1921, pitched for the Giants during his one-year career in the majors (his ERA was 2.25).

415. RF gave the lecture on July 17; it was his first appearance at the Bread Loaf School of English.

Robert Frost at the Bread Loaf School of English
in the summer of 1921.

Courtesy of Middlebury College Special Collections and Archives,
Middlebury, Vermont.

I hope I am not making you too much trouble. You are very good to do all this.

Sincerely yours
Robert Frost

I shan't go to Michigan for some time yet.

[To Ralph Farman Pratt (1878–1961) of Warner, New Hampshire, a painter and an il-lustrator of children's books. His principal paintings include Echo Lake *(a small lake near Franconia),* Franconia Notch, Mt. Washington from Intervale, Mt. Lafay-ette, *and* Moosilauke in October—*all sites with which RF was intimately ac-quainted. ALS. BU.]*

South Shaftsbury Vt
July 23 1921

Dear Mr Pratt:

Evidently we have liked the same things in New Hampshire. In thanking you for your letter, let me hope that if you are ever in the little village under Lafayette again you wont fail to look me up.[416] Best wishes from my art to yours

Always yours friendly
Robert Frost

[To Louis Untermeyer. ALS. LoC.]

South Shaftsbury Vt
August 8 1921

Dear Louis:

It can hardly be denied that I am going in October to Ann Arbor to become an idle-fellow of the University of Michigan for one year. If you know of any evidence to the contrary for Heaven's sake turn it in before it is too late. It looks as if I had been bought and paid for by an ex-governor of the state of Michigan named Osborn.[417] Tell me it isn't true.

---

416. Franconia.

417. See the notes to RF's July 7 letter to Marion LeRoy Burton.

That small poem of Jean's in the Virginian hay-stack![418] I can't lose it. Forty like it and time be damned. Nay twenty. Nay ten. Excuse my neighing.

There's an important story about art the refrain of which is Has the cow calved yet. I wish you would look it up in Grimm or Andersen.[419] Let me know when you have found it and I will interpret it to you. I am reminded of it by the fact that here I have been waiting since July 28th and our cow hasn't calved yet so far as we can determine by a microscopic examination of her pasture.

I have recently seen reason to believe that as a nation we are being kept out of our greatness in literature by what I may call the columnar attitude of mind, whether we write columns or only read them. Our habit is to be smart and guarded.[420] I am sailing on or about July 1st 1922. What is there to hold me here?

I dont know what your Dick has done this summer, but our Carol has found us a diamond (though but tourmaline) or so he reports from up along. Some time we'll make a party and christen it. You be thinking of a good name.

Last night I read the Gospel according to John and I confess I dont know what to think. Whicher has a theory that going to college is the modern equivalent of retiring into the desert.[421] Something suggestive I like in the word desert. You remember that beautiful line of Wilkie Collins in The Woman in White:

"Her son was drowned at Oxford at the age of eighteen."[422]

---

418. RF refers to *The Double Dealer*, a journal established in New Orleans in 1921. The front matter to the inaugural issue prominently featured the Virginia writer James Branch Cabell. Jean Starr Untermeyer's poem "Gothic" appeared in it, as did Louis Untermeyer's "Menagerie." Neither is listed in the table of contents. See also RF's August 20, 1921, letter to Untermeyer.

419. RF appears to have in mind a Danish folk tale that he likely encountered in Andrew Lang's *The Pink Fairy Book*, first published in 1897. The tale is "I Know What I Know." We thank Mark Scott for the suggestion.

420. Untermeyer explains: "Robert had met and liked Franklin P. Adams who, as F.P.A., conducted a newspaper column of casual prose and verse called 'Always in Good Humor' and, subsequently, 'The Conning Tower,' but he did not like 'the columnar attitude of mind.' He resented the quick disposals, the sophisticated town gossip," etc. (*RFLU*, 134).

421. George Whicher.

422. In Volume 3 of *The Woman in White* (London: Sampson Low, Son, 1860): "As events turned out, Mr. Philip Fairlie died leaving an only daughter, the Laura of this story, and the estate, in consequence, went, in course of law, to the second brother, Frederick, a single man. The third brother, Arthur, had died many years before the decease of

Eighteen is just about the age at which most of them get drowned at Harvard and Yale.

Carol wires that he camped out near a Latvian over against Grafton Sunday. I wonder if this is a Latvian that Lenine would be looking for.[423] I understand Lenine expects to find himself long enough armed presently to reach out and punish his enemies everywhere in all countries. I could easily scare myself thinking so sinisterly.

Tell this to our edgarly masters.[424] The Baptist minister and his wife have one hoighty-toighty daughter and none other child and she is freshest of all flesh on earth and in her their one deloight (apologies to Yea Robinson).[425] She's been fooling around with various and sundry, particularly with one Ross who is nineteen to her seventeen and to have it over with the minister caught Ross dragged him before his wife and made him marry his daughter. Now what as a sophisticated New Yorker and friend of Broun Hackett and Mencken would you suppose the town would make for a story out of a situation like this?[426] Small towns aint so very original in your scheme that they are likely to think of more than one thing of marriages enforced. The small town this time decided that it must be the mother being sick was afraid she might die,

---

Philip, leaving a son and a daughter. The son, at the age of eighteen, was drowned at Oxford" (238).

423. "Lenine" was a commonly used spelling at the time; David Muzzey employs it in an article RF had read in the spring of 1920; see RF to Lesley Frost, March 18, 1920. In the late 1910s, Bolshevik-backed forces sought unsuccessfully to gain control over Latvia. Lenin's saber rattling was much discussed in the American press in early 1921.

424. Meaning that the anecdote to follow, not being salacious, would not have found a place in Edgar Lee Masters's *Spoon River Anthology* (1915).

425. E. A. Robinson. RF appears to have these lines from Robinson's "Hillcrest" in mind:

Who sees enough in his duress
May go as far as dreams have gone;
Who sees a little may do less
Than many who are blind have done;

Who sees unchastened here the soul
Triumphant has no other sight
Than has a child who sees the whole
World radiant with his own delight.

426. Francis Hackett (1883–1962) edited the *New Republic* from 1914 to 1922; Heywood Campbell Broun Jr. (1888–1939), an eminent journalist based in New York City, founded the American Newspaper Guild. H. L. Mencken (1880–1956) was the great satirist of the American "booboisie."

and before she went wanted to see her daughter in off the range. And so it seems to have turned out—a maternal folly, nothing worse to the foulest imagination. No eight seven six or five months baby need be looked for. The next thing the mother did after safely placing her daughter was to exact an almost public promise from the minister that he would never marry again and then, instead of turning her face to the wall to die, start[ed] to get well with the doctor's permission (since her case was hopeless anyway) on Kickapoo Swamp Root Bitters.[427] What I write to commend is the freedom of the village mind that could see all this as it was unhindered by age long preconceptions.

Monroe[428] says the buckwheat has been behaving very badly with the bees. It will be sweet for a few hours in the morning and then for the rest of the day unyielding. It has put the hives all out of temper. Ordinarily Monroe does what he likes with the bees, shakes them off the combs, sweeps them into heaps, and carries them in his bare hand without being stung. They stung him twenty five times when he walked between the hives where he had a perfect right to be. They came looking for him away on the porch of his house to sting him right before me. The buckwheat had just the same effect on them that that kind of woman has on a man. And that's no tale from Maeterlink [*sic*].[429] I was so careless as to say to Whicher that Yeats was one of the few poets we could read right through entire. It's not true. We can't afford to grant him more than his due. He's disposed to crowd the rest of us as it is. I looked to see. Even where all is contrived to look so choice and so chosen there are whole pages that are nothing. We're all human. There's not enough of any of us to make a whole good book.

I have planted or have caused to be planted a Boh tree in India to sit out the rest of the dance under when I shall have done with vanities: and this without knowing what a Boh tree is. It may shed rain, but will it shed lightening?[430] Do I want it to? I go, incredible as it may seem to you. But before I go I want to see you to ask you several things. You have a wisdom that is of another race that I would fain draw on. Not now. Sometime. When I shall be moved

---

427. Dr. Kilmer's Swamp Root Bitters was a patent medicine of the kind often hawked at so-called Kickapoo shows—named for the Kickapoo Indian Medicine Company, which patented fraudulent medicines—common in the late nineteenth century.

428. Charles A. Monroe, postal clerk and beekeeper, was a friend and neighbor of the Frosts in South Shaftsbury. Untermeyer met him on his first visit to RF at the Stone House.

429. See Maurice Maeterlinck, *La Vie des abeilles* [The Life of the Bees] (Paris: Bibliotheque Charpentier, 1901).

430. The Buddha is said to have attained enlightenment seated beneath a Boh, or Bodhi, tree.

to speak of it again. It is of the kind of tears I have wept lately. I have never heard of them. Let's throw away just about nine tenths of what we have been and all that's columnar.

> Ever yours
> Robert Frost.

[To Louis Untermeyer. ALS. LoC.]

> Franconia N.H. (till September 15th
> only)
> August 20 1921

Dear Louis:

There was nothing the least invidious in my omission to mention your poem when I was mentioning Jean's. I didn't see that you had a poem in all that.[431] Why didn't you tell me on the fly leaf? Now that I know you had one, I shall have to look it up when I get back to the book.

You understand that we are only going to Michigan and only for eight months. You're not losing us even for a while. You can come out there if you will condescend, and we can come back here. Let us not consider ourselves separated. I may get neighborly with Henry Ford and get a chance to bring a new car for sale over the road from Detroit to New York now and then. It would save him freight and me passenger rates.

But I mustn't be columnar about it. How damaged we are by our newspapers.

I don't see how I am to get to New York and you and Aley and the ladies of the Cosmopolitan Club before I go.[432] I was smothered with hay fever this year. I shall have to linger in Franconia till the last moment. Listen: it wouldn't be an awful sacrifice for a good healthy person like you to run up to see me here. Fine night trains at this time of year both ways. Aw say, do it. I'd like to look at these mts once more through your eyes before I leave them more or less forever. Honestly! You want to look out or I may feel hurt.

> Ever yours
> Robert Frost

---

431. See the notes to RF's August 8, 1921, letter to Untermeyer.

432. RF had addressed the Cosmopolitan Club on February 23, 1921. Maxwell Aley was editor of *Century Magazine* (see RF's May 7, 1921, letter to him).

[To Halley Phillips Gilchrist. ALS. Middlebury.]

Franconia N.H.

August 20 1921

My dear Mrs Gilchrist:

A word or two in haste to forward you the cards for Mrs Bayard.[433] I shall write to Alfred Harcourt and Roland Holt to be expecting her.[434] I've been neglectful. I'm sorry.

It will be fine to meet the Poetry Society[435] before I go to Michigan. You make it any day between the 20th and 28th of September.

Our best to you all not forgetting Mrs Conkling and Hilda and her sister[436]

Sincerely yours

Robert Frost

[To Wilbur L. Cross. Date derived from internal evidence. ALS. Yale.]

[Franconia, NH]

[early September 1921]

Dear Mr Cross:

Thus I keep on writing the changes in myself into this poem while it is within my power.[437] This last change is most important. Please don't let the printers fail to observe it.

Yours faithfully

Robert Frost

---

433. Unidentified, though likely Florence Bayard (1894–1972) of Windham, Vermont; she was married to the Vermont landscape artist Clifford Adams Bayard.

434. Alfred Harcourt left Henry Holt and Company in 1919 to found Harcourt, Brace, and Howe. Roland Holt was vice president of Holt from 1903 to 1924.

435. The Poetry Society of Southern Vermont, of which Gilchrist was secretary.

436. Grace Hazard Conkling and her daughters Elsa and Hilda (the child-prodigy poet).

437. Circumstances suggest that the poem is "Maple," published in the *Yale Review* in October 1921. RF tinkered with its text considerably after its publication, as he prepared it for inclusion in *NH*, where it differs in more than fifteen respects from the text in the *Yale Review*. He may also have fussed over the poem before delivering it to Cross and the printers at the *Yale Review*. In any case, RF typically published groups of several short poems in that journal, not single poems, which further associates this letter with "Maple."

[*To Van Wyck Brooks (1886–1963), American literary critic, historian, essayist, and poet who at the time edited* The Freeman, *for which he may have asked Frost to write an essay. ALS. DCL.*]

Franconia N.H.

September 4 1921

My dear Mr Brooks:

I'm no such Puritan as to enjoy resisting temptation. It is hard for me to refuse you: but I must. Ask me anything but prose yet awhile. I used to say prose after thirty; then in the thirties, prose after forty. Still distrusting myself at forty odd, I now say after fifty. Out of what we dont know and so can't be hurt by, poetry: out of knowledge, prose. Wait till I get wisdom; wait till I sell out and move to "the place of understanding" by which Solomon (or was it David?) must have meant Chicago—the Middle West anyway.[438]

Sincerely yours

Robert Frost

[*To Louis Untermeyer. ALS. LoC.*]

Franconia N.H.

September 5 1921

Dear Louis:

You've got my hopes up and you've got to come or I shall be disappointed forever. On the Friday night train. I must have another good talk with you before I go west in the military sense of the words.[439] What am I doing this for? It's got all round that I am giving up New England and you.

Well I haven't.

R.

---

438. An arch reference to RF's pending move to Ann Arbor. Apparently, RF mistakes the biblical text. The phrase occurs in Job 28:12: "But where shall wisdom be found? and where is the place of understanding?"

439. "To go west" in the "military sense of the words" meant to die.

[To Charles Lowell Young. ALS. Wellesley.]

> Franconia N.H. (till September 11th
> only)
> September 6 1921

Dear Young:

Spaking[440] of your deserts (humble deserts), I wonder if you could figure out among them to be asked to take the sleeper from Boston next Sunday at 7.30 P.M., join me at Littleton in the morning, Monday, and go on to Groveton or Colebrook with me for a few days walk-around above the line of perpetual ragweed? The plan has to be pretty rigid both as to time and place. But let me beseech you to be simple and fall in with it. We could walk across from Colebrook to Willoughby Lake on roads untravelled by automobiles. Wire me you'll do it like a man.[441]

> Yours provisionally
> Robert Frost

[To Sidney Cox. ALS. DCL.]

> Franconia NH.
> September 8 1921

Dear Sidney:

And I want very much to talk with you. I dont see why the engagement with Michigan University should keep me tied up at Ann Arbor all the long year. But I suppose I ought not to be gone more than a week or ten days at a time and that not more than two or three times. You must have me out there for one of these. Let me tell you how I should like you to arrange it. Perhaps you could crowd enough into a week so that I could come clear off with $500 above expenses. You might have to run a day or two over the week. My demand lately has been $100 for one "lecture" or seventy-five a piece for two

---

440. Irish dialect, as often rendered in nineteenth-century books.

441. On several occasions RF went hiking with Young. The walk proposed here transpired between September 12 and September 17; the two men hiked from Upton, Maine, through Erroll and Dixville Notch to Colebrook, all in New Hampshire, and on to Willoughby, Vermont, by way of Canaan and Norton. See also RF to Sidney Cox, September 21, 1921.

or more in the same place. All would depend on how far apart your places were and how much time had to be wasted in travel. I'm vague about your distances. Whatever else you plan for you must be sure to leave me a good day or two outright to loaf round with you. That's more important than the $500 and expenses. Suppose you only get me $300 and expenses. I shan't weep. Better keep the rates up though. Don't you think so?

Remember you promised I was going to see two babies instead of just one. If I had time or Lesley I could make you a copy of Paul's Wife. But Lesley is in South Shaftsbury and I'm hurrying to get back there to get ready for Michigan. You'll have to wait till it appears in The Century in November. And then there's Maple! The next Yale Review will have Maple.[442] I havent written much this summer. Having to come off up here has broken me up.

I want to hear about your literary plans. Have they had any check that you should sign yourself stupidly. Or is it just that you are resolved to be stupid for fear of being tempted to be as smart as a column writer in this columnar age? I am with you there. Lets be as stupid as is necessary to be good.

Our best to you both.

Affectionately

R.F.

[To John W. Haines. ALS-photostat. DCL.]

Franconia N.H. (till next week
only)
September 11 1921

My dear Jack:

You won't say I haven't done pretty well for me with letters lately and soon you'll have to admit I have sent you a good many friends. This time I am asking you to receive my friend and great dependence Lincoln MacVeagh, the head of the literary department of my publishers here Henry Holt and Co. MacVeagh has become quite personal to me and I should want you two to meet anyway when you were within distance to strike hands. But over and above the wish to communicate you to each other is the hope that if you could sit down together for a good talk you could perhaps solve my problem in

---

442. *Century Magazine* published "Paul's Wife" in November 1921. "Maple," to which RF refers in the next sentence, did indeed appear in the *Yale Review* in October 1921.

England. I mean you could perhaps formulate terms to make me presentable to a new English publisher. I am prepared to feel greatly relieved to be free from Madam Nutt—if I am free and everybody can be made to accept me as free. Your letters have encouraged me to hope they can.

So that you'll know where to pick it up with MacVeagh, I should say he was one of our prominent young soldiers in the war, his people have long been prominent in our government at Washington,[443] and his interest in poetry is far from limited to mine or getting mine or anyone else's published.

With best wishes and all.

Always yours
Robert Frost

[*To Sidney Cox. ALS. DCL.*]

South Shaftsbury Vt
September 21 1921

Dear Sidney:

I'm just back from a long walk too, but one through tamer wilderness than yours. I did the three notches, the Willoughby Lake, the Franconia and the Dixville. One of my toes went wrong but I came through all right on the other nine.

I dont believe I understand very well what's wanted of me out there. I should think I might undertake to give one lecture and one class room talk for $125, if that is your idea. One hundred of it would be my regular fee for a public lecture, twenty five for expenses. That would account for all the money and I would throw the class room talk in for good measure. Or are you asking me to think of it in some other way. You say nothing about expenses. Perhaps it would be better for simplicity to offer me up in one lecture and one class room talk for the $125 flat and never mind expenses.

I should like very much to go in for an all-round-the-place series of talks recitals, songs dances and sitting-up exercises for my money after the manner

---

443. Lincoln MacVeagh's grandfather, Wayne MacVeagh, served as attorney general under President Garfield, and his great-uncle Franklin MacVeagh was secretary of the treasury under William Howard Taft. His father, Charles, would later serve as Calvin Coolidge's ambassador to Japan.

of Vachel.[444] But you dont want to take it all out of me in one winter. Save a little of me from these people if you can for a specimen.

If I seem a little greedier than I used to the English invader is to blame. I shall be asking the $125 less for the money as I keep saying than for the honor of getting at least half as much as you will pay second rate Englishmen. Not to wobble and look weak and silly suppose we put it that way with finality $125 flat for a lecture and a talk, $150 flat for two lectures, $175 flat for two lectures and a talk. I'm largely in your hands. Save me and my pride all you can but make me do my duty.

Aint we business-like? Oh and about the time. I should say any time after the first of January. January or February should be a good month.

Affectionately

Robert Frost

[To Dorothy Dunbar Bromley. The references herein are to work RF did for Henry Holt and Company as a consulting editor. ALS. UVA.]

South Shaftsbury Vt

September 21 1921

My dear Mrs Bromley:

I'm just in from a long walk across Vermont New Hampshire and part of Maine. This is a peripatetic revival for me. I used to walk immoderately. I dont know what set me off again unless it was some contagion. Please tell Holliday it is something I am inclined to blame him for.[445] He is the only person I could have got it from.

But this more [sic] than I meant to say on the subject of walking. I introduced it to excuse myself for various delinquencies. I should have written you sooner if I had any where to rest my elbow. About Hilda Aldington's essays: Mr Untermeyer seems interested in them.[446] Will you mail them to him at 310 West 100 St? I want to do what I can for them. I like them less than the

---

444. Vachel Lindsay often gave highly theatrical performances of his poetry.

445. Robert Cortes Holliday (1880–1947), author of *Walking-Stick Papers* (New York: George Doran, 1918), a collection of essays about walking.

446. The American poet H. D. (Hilda Doolittle, 1886–1961), at the time married to the English poet Richard Aldington (1892–1962). We have been unable to identify the manuscript in question. Much of H. D.'s prose was first published posthumously. See also RF to Untermeyer, October 12, 1921.

poems—considerably less. But in some ways they remind me of the poems. I respect them anyway as by the same author as the poems.

I shall return the Helen Hoyt poems with my disapproval to-morrow.[447]

I have heard of your article about me. It hasn't come my way. It was called fine.[448] Thank you very much.

We are off for Michigan next week.

Sincerely yours
Robert Frost

[*To Louis Untermeyer. ALS. LoC.*]

South Shaftsbury Vt
September 26 1921

Dear Louis:

Re the poem of yours in the Virginian Free-for-All brought up to us on appeal we wish to say it is a good thing. Decision of the lower court (viz E. A. Robinson) sustained.[449]

Do a whole lot of poems like that far from the question of love and labor. Leave the evils that can be remedied or even palliated. You are of age now to face essential Hell. Cease from the optimism as much that makes good as that sees good. Come with me into the place of tombs and outer darkness. When I say three begin gnashing your teeth.

I'm in earnest. Just as the only great art is inesthetic so the only morality is completely ascetic. I have been bad and a bad artist. I will retire soon to the place you wot of. Not now but soon. That is my last, my ultimate vileness, that I cannot make up my mind to go now where I must go sooner or later. I am frail.

---

447. RF's acquaintance with Helen Hoyt dates from February 1914, when she worked in the editorial offices of *Poetry* magazine; it was Hoyt who sent RF a check for £9 for "The Code—Heroics" (better known simply as "The Code"), printed in *Poetry* in February 1914 and subsequently collected in *NB*. Hoyt's February 5, 1914, postcard to RF, enclosed in an envelope bearing the logo of *Poetry* magazine, is held now at DCL.

448. See RF's July 23, 1921, letter to Bromley; the article in question (though we have been unable precisely to identify it) issued from the publicity department at Henry Holt and Company, in which Bromley worked.

449. See RF to Untermeyer, August 8, 1921.

To prayer, to prayer I go
(I think I go) I go to prayer—
Along a granite corridor of woe
And down a stair
In every step of which I am abased.
A rope I wear.
I wear a halter rope about the waist.
I bear a candle end put out with haste.
I go to prayer.[450]

Well this was waiting for me to get on at this corner. Today was on the calendars a thousand million years before they were printed. I seem to smile.

Yours yet awhile
R.F.

I hoped you might like James Chapin's defeated-looking microcephalus giant at the bottom of the picture.[451] This you understand is not particularly Paul but man with all the strength he needs and more strength than he has brains to know how to use. I have figured that out of my symbolics. But who said anything about an ogre or superman slumping heartbroken or overcome with raw food in front of his cave in the Arthur Davies' landscape.[452] The writer proposes and the illustrator disposes. The picture strikes me as arty. I congratulate you on your taste.

[To Dorothy Dunbar Bromley. ALS. Princeton.]

South Shaftsbury Vt (again)
September 26 1921

My dear Mrs Bromley:

I am returning herewith the manuscript of Helen Hoyt's poems. Will you do me the favor of copying in type if necessary my formal opinion of it as follows:

---

450. For an earlier version of this poem see RF to Untermeyer, July 7, 1921.

451. Chapin had done an illustration for RF's poem "Paul's Wife," soon to be published in *Century Magazine* (November 1921).

452. Arthur Bowen Davies (1863–1928), avant-garde American artist and a principal organizer of the celebrated Armory Show, in 1913.

I should be for encouraging such a promising young poet as Miss Hoyt, but not to the extent of publishing this whole heap of everything and anything at once. It is not that she writes in varying moods: she writes like different people. Her personality is nowhere near being focussed. The fun of the nonsense verse (Vegetable Fantasies and Rhymes about Hamp) is rather flat and pointless. There are scrapings from the minor magazines that seem to come to something; and probably a few more besides. It is the same story as with the other young poets I have had to pass on this year: enough for a slim cheap volume as an experiment for the writer and the public; but not enough for the pretentiousness of a regular full priced book.[453]

Mr Roland Holt writes that he has sent me two other manuscripts. I am on the look out for them.

Next week for Ann Arbor

> With best wishes
> Sincerely yours
> Robert Frost

[To Everett Glass. ALS. BU.]

> South Shaftsbury Vt
> September 26 1921

Dear Everett

I had hoped to see you and have a chance to soften to you with looks and tones the little unpleasantry I am constrained to put down in bleak black and white. I have liked all your poems measurably and some of them very well (as Agard[454] perhaps not too presumptuously ventures to remind me) but the book as a whole not well enough to force it into print against the indifference

---

453. Henry Holt and Company never published Helen Hoyt, although Harcourt Brace eventually did. Untermeyer also collected her "Vegetable Fantasies" in his 1935 anthology of children's verse, *Rainbow in the Sky* (also from Harcourt, Brace and Company).

454. Walter Raymond Agard, a classmate (class of 1917) of Glass's when both men studied with RF at Amherst. Agard later made a career for himself as a classicist. In 1939 he wrote an article titled "Robert Frost: A Sketch" for *Touchstone,* an undergraduate literary magazine at Amherst (for details, see *YT,* 553–554).

of others and let my will avouch it.[455] I should have had more than indifference to bear down in one case: I should have had the prejudice of a person who vows he will print no more war poetry by any poet not killed in action. He may seem incredible to you, but there he is and deaf to all such reasoning as that you are no more to blame for not having been killed in action than some others are for not being crazy enough to rate as poets.[456]

Will you forgive me my hard words? I'm terribly afraid you won't. And unless I were sure of your continued friendship I should have no right to go on and advise you, as I was going to, on the folly of bothering the head at all over the distinction between the obvious and the unobvious. Take care that you dont mean by the unobvious the far-fetched fine-spun wire-drawn and hair-split. The subtlest thing as the bark-and-lichen mimicing [sic] nest of the hummingbird, should be obvious when pointed out.[457] The one it is pointed out to should be stricken with self-reproach at not having seen it for himself. But as I say I have no right to pursue the subject under the circumstances.

I'm going to be sorry if you won't let me count myself your friend

As ever

Robert Frost

[To Roland Holt. ALS. Princeton.]

South Shaftsbury Vt

September 27 1921

Dear Mr Holt:

I make haste to say, By all means Babette Deutch [sic] unless you mind too much the slight flavor of the modernest [sic] and subvertionist in her book.[458]

---

455. *Macbeth* 3.1: "and though I could / With barefaced power sweep [Banquo] from my sight / And bid my will avouch it, yet I must not . . ." This was another favorite; see for example RF to John Livingston Lowes, February 10, 1921.

456. Glass enlisted in the U.S. Army on June 5, 1918, several months after the United States entered World War I.

457. The nest of the ruby-throated hummingbird (*Archilochus colubris*) is tiny and well camouflaged with an outer layer of lichen.

458. Babette Deutsch (1895–1982), American poet, translator (from the Russian), and novelist. Roland Holt had sent a typescript of her poem "Portraits and Pageants" on September 20. The firm did eventually add her to its list, publishing *Take Them, Stranger* in 1944.

She can write. She has more poetic idea than all the poets in manuscript I have read this year put together. She's a perceptible person.

While I'm about it a word about Piper.[459] He's a piper if he's anything. At least he's easy and unstraining. But he just doesn't impress me with anything he says. I cant seem to feel who's at me and where. I believe the matter is that this is too near the level of journalism. Sometimes it even smacks of the editorial page. I know it isn't half bad for what it is. Dont ask me to like it, though. Please don't print it.

With best wishes

Sincerely yours
Robert Frost

Piper in another package

R.F.

<hr>

459. Edwin Ford Piper (1871–1939), whose first book, *Barbed Wire and Other Poems,* was published in Chicago by the Midland Press in 1917. Roland Holt had sent RF a copy of the book, together with additional poems in manuscript, on September 21. Macmillan issued Piper's *Barbed Wire and Wayfarers* in 1924.

2

"The Guessed of Michigan"
September 1921–May 1923

Wait till I get wisdom; wait till I sell out and move to "the place of understanding" by which Solomon (or was it David?) must have meant Chicago—the Middle West anyway.
            —Robert Frost to Van Wyck Brooks, September 4, 1921

[To Louis Untermeyer. Date provided by Untermeyer. ALS. LoC.]

1523 Washtenaw Ave.

Ann Arbor Mich.

[October 12, 1921]

Dear Louis:

Notice the address—in the middle of the second thousand. I may not write it on every letter any more than you do yours. Try not to lose me.

I agree with Mencken in much that he says of you.[1] How true it is that friendship has made you blind to all fault in me and Carl Sandburg. You must learn to see us as we are. No you mustn't either. Isn't Mencken the ablest rotter we have almost? He makes me think of nothing but flight.

Not that I'm so very much good myself. But thats just it. I dont want to feel obliged to remember my sins everyday in fairness to such non-fur-bearing skunks as Mencken and a few others I could name. Oh I know they are intel ligent and all that. That is to say they have heard of Freud. You dont need to tell me.

As for this place where I am, it is all right, but it lacks finality, as the Wandering Jew said.[2] I have several other places yet to visit before I find rest. That

---

1. Presumably a reference to something Mencken had written in a letter to Untermeyer.

2. The legend of the Wandering Jew, condemned to roam the earth until the Second Coming of Christ, dates back to the thirteenth century in Europe. The tale figures in scores of literary works. "It lacks finality," here, because the appointment at Michigan was for one year only (although in 1922 the university would in fact renew it).

it is a place on the map and not a state of the mind I shall some day come to for relief, I am persuaded from the number of times I have come Balboa-like on the truth and not been helped. Today, for example, I made the discovery for myself that it was a mistake to ask to be directed on the way by any one I overtook or was overtaken by. If I didn't want to be embarrassed by his offering to go with me and see me on my way, the best person to ask was some one I met. It is a great truth and I had happened upon it. For a moment it eased my malady. But it wasn't enough to last beyond my determining why it was true. The old grief is back. "I'm bound away."[3]

You escape H.D. in prose.[4] I see it as you see it more or less; and more clearly with your confirmation. I'm glad I had you see the manuscript. I'm anxious to do such a person no injustice I don't have to from our common heritage of strife. Will you send the manuscript to

Marianne Moore[5]
14 St Lukes Place
New York City

and remember me to Jean and the children.

Always yours
Robert Frost

[To Sidney Cox. ALS. DCL.]

1523 Washtenaw Ave
Ann Arbor Michigan
October 12 1921

Dear Sidney:

That looks like such a little money for such a lot of wear and tear knocking round in the cars that I have half a mind to call it all off but perhaps two engagements right close together. You dont want to see your grandfather's grey head brought down in sorrow to the grave for fifty dollars a lecture.[6]

---

3. A line from the well-known folk song "Shenandoah": "Away, I'm bound away / Cross the wide Missouri." RF would recur to the song and the line in his late poem "Away!" (*CPPP*, 426–427).

4. See RF to Bromley, September 12, 1921.

5. American poet, critic, and editor (1887–1972).

6. See Genesis 44:30–31, where Judah speaks: "Now therefore when I come to thy servant my father, and the lad be not with us; seeing that his life is bound up in the lad's life;

The distances out there are more than we figured on, either of us. I haven't any right to ask any of you to bear the expense of them and I can't afford to bear it myself. It is better for me to operate near home. Then I can ask for my expenses and have my hundred dollars a lecture clear. I think I havent had less than a hundred for anything for more than a year. No doubt asking that keeps me out of some barn-storming, but it is designed to. The price seems to be just prohibitive enough to be protective. It saves some of me for poetry.

But I want awfully to see you, and having gone as far I'm not going to draw out entirely. I offer to make the trip to Missoula for my expenses. I should give one lecture and meet a class or two. In addition I should like one more lecture close by for a flat $100. I don't absolutely insist on the second engagement but I should like [it] as a sweetener.[7]

If I had the long jump I had when a young crickct! My strength is retiring from the surface. You will understand.

Always yours

Robert Frost

[To Louis Untermeyer. Date supplied by Untermeyer, who adds this note: "I had sent Robert a gold-handled knife which I had manufactured, and, since the superstition had it that a knife cuts friendship unless a copper coin is given in exchange, I demanded the penny" (RFLU, 138). ALS. LoC.]

1523 Washtenaw Ave

Ann Arbor Mich

[circa October 15, 1921]

Dear Sir:

Please find enclosed one sent which you know what you can do with. And see here, as sure as you dun us again, you will lose our business.

Believe me, viz.

Robert Frost

It shall come to pass, when he seeth that the lad is not with us, that he will die: and thy servants shall bring down the gray hairs of thy servant our father with sorrow to the grave."

7. The previous year Cox had taken a position at the State University of Montana in Missoula (now the University of Montana), and was hoping to bring RF over for a lecture series. RF never made it to Missoula: Cox's efforts to secure funds from the university administration met with no success (RFSC, 124).

*[To Carl Sandburg (1878–1967), American poet. The letter is undated, but internal evi-
dence suggests November 1921. Sandburg came to Ann Arbor in April 1922 to participate in a series of poetry readings arranged by RF. ALS. Illinois.]*

1523 Washtenaw Ave

Ann Arbor Mich

[circa November 1921]

Dear Carl

I am glad you wrote me two letters at a time to recall me to my better
self. Two should turn the trick: one wouldnt have done it. I must never be
allowed to forget that though for the year I am the guest under God and
Coach Yost of this vast institution of various things, still a guessed is not all
I am.[8] They may think they have outguessed me. Appearances may be
against me. But all the time deep down in me in my dungeon keep I a poet
aint I? Thanks, thanks, to thee my worthy friend for the lesson thou hast
taught, as one of the poets we have superseded (I assume we have) has rather
too beautifully said.[9]

All right then. I'm a poet and my name is R Frost. You will bear me out in
that. And as such I am invited to see the movies with you on your beat before
long.

I have forty things I want to say to you and a couple of sonnets to deliver
orally that I once directed at your head because you went right by my house
in the train from Montreal without getting off to see us. They would have
been printed in the Unpartizan if that had[n't] happened to it which did happen
to it.[10]

I shall be in Chicago not later than Dec 7 and maybe before.

Always yours

Robert Frost

---

8. Fielding H. Yost (1871–1946) was a legendary head football coach at Michigan.

9. RF quotes the first two lines of the final stanza of Longfellow's "The Village
Blacksmith."

10. The *Unpartizan Review*, originally the *Unpopular Review*, was a literary, political
and general cultural monthly published by Henry Holt and Company beginning in January 1914. Publication ceased with the January–March 1921 issue.

[*To Harriet Monroe. The letter is undated, but Joseph Parisi and Stephen Young date it to early November 1921 in their* Dear Editor: A History of Poetry *in Letters (New York: W. W. Norton, 2002). Internal evidence confirms this date. ALS. Chicago.*]

> 1523 Washtenaw Ave
> Ann Arbor Michigan
> [circa November 1, 1921]

Dear Miss Monroe:

How'll you swap the poem you have for a long poem in blank verse called "A Witch of Coos (Circa 1921)"?[11] Coos is the next county above where you were in the White Mountains. If you were there in August, you could probably have found us there by looking for us; and we are the boys what could tell you of pleasant places where you could stay for less than $8 a day. Well if we didnt meet in Franconia, probably we shall before long in Chicago unless you avoid me. Van Wyck Brooks has been telling me the future lies with the East in art.[12] I don't know what he knows about it. But I thought I would look around Detroit and Chicago a little before I came to any conclusions for myself. Of course I am hopelessly eastern in my accent: I have half a mind to call my next book The Upper Right Hand Corner; but thats no reason why I shouldn't view the lanscape [*sic*] o'er more or less impartially for a while yet.[13] I'll let you know when I am ready to award the palm to any section.

Well what do you say about the long poem?

> Sincerely yours
> Robert Frost

---

11. Monroe published "The Witch of Coös" in the January 1922 issue of *Poetry*.

12. In "On Creating a Usable Past," first published in *The Dial* in April 1918, Van Wyck Brooks argued that American artists might learn from European writers who could "view the past through the spectacles of [their] own intellectual freedom." In that essay Brooks also chastised RF's acquaintance Vachel Lindsay, blaming Lindsay's shortcomings in part on his Midwest provincialism: "And there is Vachel Lindsay. If he runs to sound and color in excess and for their sake voids himself within, how much is that because the life of a Middle Western town sets upon those things an altogether scandalous premium?" (340).

13. See Isaac Watts's hymn "There Is a Land of Pure Delight" (1707):

Could we but climb where Moses stood,
And view the landscape o'er,
Not Jordan's stream, nor death's cold flood,
Should fright us from the shore.

Emily Dickinson borrows the same line in "Where bells no more affright the morn . . ." However, that poem wasn't published until 1945.

[To Harriet Moody. Date derived from internal evidence. ALS. Chicago.]

> 1523 Washtenaw Ave
> Ann Arbor Mich
> [circa November 15, 1921]

Dear Harriet:

Just the few words you permit me.

My first engagement down your way will be at Oshkosh (do you get that?) on December 7 (Wednesday); you are welcome to me on the 4th, but if I come that early you must try to get me at least one more engagement to fill the gap between the 4th and the 7th. Percy Boynton might be spoken to I should think.[14] Dont let me lie rusting two whole days. You know how I need action.

Mrs Sherry has engagements to fill my time from the 8th to the 11th.[15] I shall have to return for an engagement here on the 12th.[16] Live absurdly is my motto.

Incidentally I mean to give you a glimpse of Elinor. She only partly knows it as yet.

Surely it is a beautiful thing Faggi has made of your Noguchi. I have the picture of it in Noguchi's book.[17]

> Ever yours
> Robert Frost

---

14. Percy Boynton (1875–1946) had become professor of English at the University of Chicago in 1903 and remained there until retirement in 1941.

15. Laura Case Sherry (1876–1947), a good friend of Harriet Monroe's, was the founder of the Wisconsin Players, an avant-garde acting troupe in Milwaukee, Wisconsin. This acting company, along with the Wisconsin Dramatic Society (loosely affiliated with the University of Wisconsin) revolutionized modern drama by helping establish the "Little Theater" movement, a consortium of small theater companies that challenged the conventional productions of the Theatrical Syndicate in New York. Sherry had arranged for RF to speak in Oshkosh and Madison, Wisconsin on December 7 and 8, and at Northwestern University in Chicago on December 10.

16. RF spoke in Detroit on December 12.

17. In 1919, the Italian-born Chicago sculptor Alfeo Faggi (1885–1966) created a bronze head of the Japanese poet Yonejirō Noguchi (1875–1947), which was placed in the collections of the Art Institute in Chicago—whence, perhaps, *"your* Noguchi," although the poet was also a friend of Moody's. A photograph of Faggi's sculpture served as the frontispiece for *Selected Poems of Yone Noguchi* (Boston: Four Seas, 1921; London: Elkin Mathews, 1921), the book RF refers to here. The opening remarks in Noguchi's preface may have interested RF: "I often wonder at the difference between the words of English Poets and the daily speech of

If December 4th is too soon for the Jeux Floreaux perhaps you will want to wait till later.[18] I am booked for Milwaukee for the next Sunday.

[*To Louis Untermeyer. ALS. LoC.*]

> 1523 Washtenaw Ave
> Ann Arbor Michigan
> November 23 1921

Dear Louis:

I'm so near dead of I dont know what all here that it wouldn't pay me to write much to you unless I was pretty sure you weren't dead there. So this'll be just a line or two to find out. It would be descent of you to acknowledge the resent scent I cent you.[19] For God's sake give some sign of animation besides the poems by Leonie Adams you keep printing in the New Republic.[20]

To some I am known as the Guessed of this University because I came as a riddle and was so soon solved. The fact that I was so soon found out is uppermost in some minds. In other minds what I was found out to be is uppermost, namely a radiator of the poetic spirit. To them I am known as the Radiator. I differ from other radiators not only in what I have to radiate but

---

common people; and I think that it is not necessary to go to Milton or Dryden for the proof. The poetical words used by Tennyson, Browning, Francis Thompson, and even Yeats, are certainly different from those spoken in the London streets or an English village shadowed by a church spire or darkened by dense foliage. But, on the other hand, how similar are the words of Japanese poets and those of the common people!"

18. L'Académie des jeux floreaux (Academy of the Floral Games), founded at Toulouse in 1323 to perpetuate the lyric school of the troubadours, is the oldest literary society in the Western world. During the annual games (which still take place), the best verses are awarded prizes in the form of different flowers. The regular Sunday literary salons at Mrs. Moody's Chicago home had acquired the name Les Petit Jeux Floreaux. As it turned out, RF gave a reading and talk in Chicago on December 15, which was a Wednesday, so not at Moody's regular Sunday salon; however, he did visit her while he was in Chicago, apparently on the sixteenth.

19. See RF to Untermeyer, October 15, 1921.

20. "April Mortality," by Léonie Adams (1899–1988), appeared in the November 23, 1921, issue of the *New Republic*. Untermeyer explains in a note: "I had 'discovered' Léonie Adams while she was an undergraduate member of the class of 1922 at Barnard College and I was able to get her unprinted poems published in *The New Republic*" (*RFLU,* 139).

also in where I have to work. Other radiators have to heat a room. I am expected to do something else to all out of doors. I only tell you to clarify my own mind. If it has come to this here let us face it. If I could will my job to you as Roosevelt willed Taft the Presidency I sure would. I find I do my best work on a diet of soft coal or carbide and water.[21] My state ranges through anabolical katabolical[22] and diabolical. Temperature, subnormal; which for a radiator is serious. Amy would tell you I was never serious before.[23]

Keep remembering me to Jean and Dick. They at least will understand.

Radiantly
Robert Frost

Edgar Guessed[24] of Detroit and I the Guessed of the University were brought together in public on the field of the cloth of gold yesterday and I wish you could have seen how happy it made the onlookers and the committee of burghers who had arranged for our meeting.[25] Eddie said significantly he knew Sylvester Baxter.[26] I didn't know what to answer, so I didnt take my thumb out of my mouth, Eddie asked me to call Bill Benét off him. I sullenly refused to interfere. I confess I didn't make a very good appearance. I looked jealous to the representatives of the press. Oh and another thing, one of your Liberator poets attacked me personally in the lobby of the Stattler

---

21. In the 1890s, coal miners began using lamps fueled by calcium carbide and water (which in combination generate acetylene). Thomas Edison's invention of a battery-powered tungsten lamp in 1913 put the older model out of use.

22. "Constructive" and "destructive" metabolic processes, respectively.

23. In her February 20, 1915, review of NB in the *New Republic* Amy Lowell had written: "The thing which makes Mr. Frost's work remarkable is the fact that he has chosen to write it as verse. We have been flooded for twenty years with New England stories in prose. The finest and most discerning are the little masterpieces of Alice Brown. She too is a poet in her descriptions, she too has caught the desolation and 'dourness' of lonely New England farms, but unlike Mr. Frost she has a rare sense of humor, and that, too, is of New England, although no hint of it appears in 'North of Boston.' And just because of the lack of it, just because its place is taken by an irony, sardonic and grim, Mr. Frost's book reveals a disease which is eating into the vitals of our New England life, at least in its rural communities."

24. Edgar Guest (1881–1959), an English-born American poet of extraordinary popularity who was often dubbed "the People's Poet."

25. On Tuesday, November 22, RF was honored, along with Edgar Guest, at a private dinner in Detroit.

26. Sylvester Baxter (1850–1927) was a Boston-based newspaper writer, urban planner, and poet. It was at Baxter's home in Boston that RF and Untermeyer met in 1915.

Hotel[27] [*sic*] because I had flopped by coming to live on Washtenaw Avenue. He denounced me to a lot of people who afterward looked me up in Whos Who to find out why I was worth denouncing. Gee, some of your Liberator people must want to live on a grand street pretty badly to take my living on one so bitterly.

[*To Harriet Monroe. The letter is undated, but the reference to a long poem in proof suggests RF composed the letter in November or December of 1921, shortly before "The Witch of Coös" was published in* Poetry *in the January 1922 issue. ALS. Chicago.*]

[Ann Arbor, MI]
[late November–early
December 1921]

Dear Miss Monroe:

I am asking Miss Sherry if her plans for me at Northwestern and Milwaukee admit of my having a meal with you on the 9th. If not will you wait for me till the 16th. All my time between the 9th and 16th looks full of engagements either down your way or back here. I shall have to come to Detroit for a lecture on the 12th and return to Chicago for one on the 15th. From the 7th to the 15th is the busiest week of my life. I've jammed all I could into it on purpose, so as not to be too long missed from the Michigan Campus. I wish Mrs [*sic*] Sherry might say I was free for the 9th because I shall have Mrs Frost with me then but probably not on the 16th.

The proof is fine and clean.

Sincerely yours
Robert Frost

It will be fun to see another long one where I have had The Code and Snow.[28]

---

27. The Statler Hotel in Detroit, which opened in 1915; RF had given a talk there on October 25. "Liberator poet": likely the Detroit native Stirling Bowen (1895–1955), who frequently placed poems in *The Liberator*. See RF to MacVeagh, April 10, 1922, for more on Bowen. Founded by Max and Crystal Eastman in 1918, *The Liberator* emerged as the premier socialist magazine of its time, succeeding *The Masses*, which the federal government had shut down at the outbreak of World War I. Untermeyer served as a contributing editor for *The Liberator*.

28. "The Code" originally appeared in the February 1914 edition of *Poetry* under the title "The Code—Heroics." "Snow" appeared in *Poetry* in February 1916.

[*To Thomas Alexander Boyd (1898–1935), an American novelist and journalist. The letter is typewritten on University of Michigan letterhead. TLS. Vassar.*]

University of Michigan

Ann Arbor

December 3, 1921

Dear Mr. Boyd:

I should be very glad to have you publish Paul's Wife to the Northwest.[29] The favor would be all to me. Thank you for asking.

Sincerely yours

Robert Frost

[*To Benjamin De Mier Miller (1856–1934), a wealthy Washington, D.C., businessman, socialite, and devotee of modern poetry. The letter is dated, but not in RF's hand. ALS. DCL.*]

Ann Arbor Mich

[December 20, 1921]

Dear Mr Miller:

Of course I am pleased to have Edward Thomas' name connected with mine, as I think he would be.[30] One has to be careful to put it just the right way. I didnt show him how to write. All I did was show him himself in what he had already written. I made him see that much of his prose was poetry that only had to declare itself in form to win him a place where he belonged among the poets. Van Doren comes near enough to the facts of our relationship and he is absolutely perfect in his description of Thomas' kind of poetry.[31] J. C.

---

29. Boyd was a reporter for the *St. Paul Daily News,* for which he wrote a literary column, "In a Corner with a Bookworm." "Paul's Wife" had appeared in *Century Magazine* in November 1921, with illustrations by James Chapin, which doubtless brought it to Boyd's attention. The poem was subsequently reprinted in the *London Mercury* 6, no. 33 (July 1922). For reasons unknown, Boyd did not reprint the poem.

30. RF refers to Mark Van Doren's review of Edward Thomas's *Collected Poems,* published in *The Nation,* December 7, 1921, 668–669.

31. Van Doren wrote: "As much as Mr. Frost, [Thomas] preferred difficult, subtle themes, and with all the obstinacy of his American friend he labored to treat those themes plainly, compactly, accurately. He seems to have been intent upon making each sentence as it came—not merely each line, or each phrase, or each epithet— credible and clear. . . . He seldom has the force of Mr. Frost—that husky, hidden force which displays itself suddenly from unexpected corners, from between the printed

Squier[32] [*sic*] (editor of Mercury) said to me the other day he thought Thomas the best of recent British poets. I'm glad it has come to that.

The editor of The Yale Review had his choice between Maple and Paul's Wife. He preferred Maple: Farrar preferred Paul's Wife.[33] "All is well and wisely put."[34]

Encourage Miss Monroe all you can. She does a lot for the cause and she's a good writer. I saw her more or less when I was in Chicago last week. She's enlarging her anthology of New Poetry.[35]

Fine to hear from you. Best wishes for Christmas and New Year.

Always yours faithfully
Robert Frost

Ann Arbor Mich (till the middle of June and then no more forever)

---

lines. His rural dialogues do not advance so swiftly, or through such significant veils of the imagination. When he absorbs us trance-like in a scene he leaves less of us there than Mr. Frost knows how to leave; his spell is not so continuous. But he is scrupulous; he understates; his cadences are carefully broken, as most good modern cadences must be; he is patient and, as often as possible, perfect" (668).

32. John Collings Squire edited the *London Mercury* from 1919 to 1934.

33. "Maple" was published in the October 1921 issue of the *Yale Review* (edited by Wilbur Cross). John Chipman Farrar was the editor of *The Bookman* from 1918 to 1927 and, later, the guiding spirit of the Bread Loaf Writers' Conference. "Paul's Wife" was published in *Century Magazine* in November 1921. For more on Farrar and RF, see also RF's April, 30, 1923, letter to Cox and his May 2, 1923, letter to Untermeyer.

34. From Ralph Waldo Emerson's "Fable," in which a squirrel says to a mountain:

Talents differ; all is well and wisely put;
If I cannot carry forests on my back,
Neither can you crack a nut.

35. The enlarged edition of Harriet Monroe's *New Poetry: An Anthology* would be published in 1923 (New York: MacMillan).

[To Frank Eggleston Robbins (1884–1963), American scholar and academic adminis-trator. "[1924?]" is penciled in at the head of the letter, but this is a mistake: RF was in Amherst in December 1924, not in Ann Arbor. Also, President Marion LeRoy Burton, referred to here, fell ill late in 1924; he died of heart failure on February 18, 1925. RF was in Ann Arbor in December of 1921 and also in January 1922, when the event here arranged took place. ALS. UM.]

Ann Arbor

December 20th. [1921]

Dear Mr Robbins:

Please thank the President and say I shall be happy to be with him on Jan-uary 18th.

With best wishes for a Merry Christmas and Happy New year I am

Sincerely yours

Robert Frost

[To Sidney Cox. Date derived from postmark. ALS. DCL.]

[Ann Arbor, MI]

[December 22, 1921]

Dear Sidney

Isnt it terrible the way I dont write to you. You'll begin to think I am mad at having got myself into the engagement with you at Missoula. I'm not. It's too bad there isn't some easier way to see you, but as long as there isnt, I'm going to make the best of it. Don't fail to appreciate what I'm doing though. I'm lazy and I'm past forty. By rights you ought to be made to come to me. You're young and on a regular salary and the father of fewer children as yet than I am. But we won't debate the matter. I'm coming as per my telegram.

I'm particularly anxious to see you for a talk about what you are up to in the arts. Your being held in check so long gives me some hopes of you. You'll keep getting deeper and deeper all the time unless you find an outlet in foolish complaint. People like James Chapin run off in talk of their deserts [*sic*].[36] Probably there's nothing the matter with what you write. Never mind. If you cant improve it you can always intensify its quality. No doubt as it is it would do very well as it is. Wait patiently till it becomes irresistible.

------

36. American painter and illustrator (and a friend of RF's since 1917).

I've been a busy man since I came hither. I hardly know myself for the same old lazybones you saw last in Franconia (wasn't it?)—no it was in New York at James Chapins, the aforesaid.

It occurs to me Mrs Moody may not have meant a book on rhetoric though that was what she said. If it was a book on American literature, would you be interested in bringing that up to date?[37] Probably not. It would be more fun to write the whole book fresh if you were going to have anything to do with it.

Our love to you all to the last least baby.[38] Merry Christmas. Happy New Year

Affectionately

Robert Frost

[To George Whicher. Date derived from postmark. ALS. ACL.]

[Ann Arbor, MI]

[December 22, 1921]

Dear George:

Your magazine was received and its contents were carefully considered. I will say of your President's address[39] that it must have sounded almost too tragic to those who knew what had been going on behind the scenes. To have to stand up and try to carry it off like that just after having been asked for the second time in a year to resign! Reeves here has been telling me how it took a claque (quorum pars magna fuit[40]) to induce the cheering that

---

37. Likely *A History of English Literature*, coauthored by Harriet Moody's deceased husband, William Vaughn Moody, in 1902; see the notes to RF's March 1, 1921, letter to Cox.

38. Barbara A Cox, born on November 11, 1921.

39. The speech President Alexander Meiklejohn of Amherst gave on the occasion of the college's centennial, titled "What Does the College Hope to Be during the Next Hundred Years?" It was printed in the *Amherst Graduates' Quarterly* (vol. 10, no. 4 [August 1921]: 327–347), a copy of which Whicher had sent to RF.

40. See Virgil, *Aeneid* 2.1–7:

Conticuere omnes, intentique ora tenebant.
Inde toro pater Aeneas sic orsus ab alto:
Infandum, regina, iubes renovare dolorem,
Troianas ut opes et lamentabile regnum
eruerint Danai; quaeque ipse miserrima vidi,
et quorum pars magna fui

followed.[41] Criticism is almost disarmed, but not quite. One has still to say in the interest of truth that the speech for all its airy bravado, is bad thinking and nonsense. By all means put the Russian Dostoievsky [*sic*] on an equality with our American Poe (whether they are equal or not) in our American colleges. Lets be magnanimous. Lets be magnificent. Lets do anything to make our Russian Jews feel quite at home.[42] The more Quixotic the sweeter. But how shall we assert the equality of Dosty and Edgar Allen? By asseviration [*sic*] in praise courses? By reading them side by side, one in translation, the other in the original? I should be afraid that the one read in the original would have an unfair advantage. I see no way but to read both in the languages they wrote in and even then Poe would have the advantage with us until such time as we divided ourselves in school and out of school equally between the Russian and English languages. What's the use of worrying about the selfishness of it?—the poets of our own language can't help meaning more to us than the poets of any other. God's to blame if anyone is. But I've always been slow to tell God his business.

I met a pleasant fellow in Evanston Illinois the other night who spoke pleasantly of you from hearsay if not from personal knowledge. Lew Sarrett [*sic*].[43] What's this he was telling me about your connection with the Boston Herald?[44]

"All were hushed, and sate with steadfast countenance; thereon, high from his cushioned seat, lord Aeneas thus began: 'Dreadful, O Queen, is the woe thou bidst me recall, how the Grecians pitiably overthrew the wealth and lordship of Troy; and I myself saw these things in all their horror, and I bore great part in them,'" trans. J. W. Mackail (New York: Macmillan, 1908).

41. Jesse S. Reeves (1871–1942), professor of political science at Michigan from 1910 until his death; he graduated from Amherst in 1891.

42. Meiklejohn proclaimed: "We are an Anglo-Saxon college, and so in greater part we must remain. And yet we are American. We may not keep ourselves apart either from persons or from cultures not our own. We dare not shut our gates to fellow-citizens nor to their influence. So we must welcome boys of other stocks. And if they do not come, we must go out and bring them in. Our undergraduate life must represent the country which it serves; students must keep it free from any taint of caste or aristocracy. And teachers, too, must keep our teaching free, open to all the riches which our people have to bring. We shall not lose our Shakespeare by learning Dante's world; nor is one false to Poe because one follows Dostoievsky. Our mother England gave us much; and yet she has not all that men may have" (344).

43. RF befriended the poet Lew Sarett at a December 10 reading at Northwestern University in Evanston. See also RF's August 2, 1922, letter to Sarett.

44. So far as we can determine, Whicher had none.

We are having a nice time as guests of this University. We hope our little farmed-out pony isn't missing us too much in South Shaftsbury.

Dont let my fault-finding bother you. Amherst will be herself again some day. Only I want you to see that I am as well out of her classic shades or shadings (nuances) as she is. Sense is sense even in the realms of the celestial.

I saw a good volume of poetry lately that's at once new and old. John Clare wrote it a hundred years ago and much of it is just out now.[45]

Merry Christmas to all four of you.[46]

Ever yours
Robert Frost

[To Charles Lowell Young. ALS. Wellesley.]

Ann Arbor Michigan
December 22 1921

My dear Young:

Do you remember the time we walked across Maine New Hampshire and Vermont together along the Canadian border?[47] You must be safely home from that journey by now and perhaps somewhat recovered from your disappointment at not being asked to ride more frequently on it. I dont know what your estimate is, but I think we walked about three hundred miles in all. Speaking roughly we may as well call it five hundred in telling of our exploits to such ladies as Katherine Lee Bates.[48] Even doubling anything won't make ladies half realize it.

In falling asleep at night it will long give me pleasure to recall the following people we encountered on our expedition:

The man beyond Dixville Notch[49] who was so lonely (let his wife tell it) that he couldnt keep from shouting to people in passing automobiles.

---

45. *John Clare: Poems Chiefly from Manuscript*, edited by Edmund Blunden and Alan Porter, was published in London in 1920 (by Richard Cobden-Sanderson) and in New York in 1921 (by G. P. Putnam's Sons).

46. In addition to George, his wife Harriet Ruth Whicher and their sons Stephen and John (four years old and one year old, respectively).

47. The previous September. See RF to Young, September 6, 1921; for another account of the walk, see RF to Cox, September 21, 1921.

48. Bates was Young's colleague in the Department of English at Wellesley.

49. In Coös County, New Hampshire (as are Errol and Colebrook), the setting for RF's poem "The Witch of Coös."

The mother in Upton whose ambition for her son was that he should rise to be a chauffeur for "rich guys."

The sentimental lady at the top of the Dixville Notch who wanted to think the quartz up there was early snow.

The drummer I heard asking another drummer at Errol if the rivers back there in the mountains were salt.

The boy in the drug store who remembered the days of Harry Brown as Supt. of Schools in Colebrook.[50]

The Forest Ranger on the platform at Colebrook.

The fat drummer you saw laughing at me over his nail-paring in the lobby at Canaan.[51]

The Habitant[52] we pleased by knowing the French name for the apples he sold us off his little old trees.

The Emigration Inspector in the train from Nortons Mills.[53]

The Water Wizard in the car that picked us up.

Mrs Meyers

Mrs Mowry.

The more I think of it the more certain I am that sentimentalism is what we kept saying it was as we shuffled along under our packs.

Did you see Maple in The Yale Review for October, Paul's Wife in The Century for November?[54] You must keep up with me in poetry as well as you did in walking.

Be seasonably merry at my bidding!

> Ever yours
> Robert Frost

---

50. Harold "Harry" Brown was assistant to Henry Clinton Morrison, superintendent of schools in New Hampshire, when RF taught at Pinkerton Academy and Plymouth State Normal School (now Plymouth State University) from 1906 to 1912; for references and letters to him, see *LRF-1*, 84, 128, 178–179, 251.

51. In Essex County, Vermont, as is Norton's Mills (better known as Norton), subsequently mentioned.

52. French for "inhabitant," referring particularly to the French immigrants who settled in present-day Quebec and its environs. The term fell out of use in the early twentieth century.

53. Norton lies on the Vermont-Quebec border.

54. The two poems, correctly identified here as to date of first publication, would be collected in *NH*.

[*To Jay Broadus Hubbell (1885–1979), professor of English at Southern Methodist University and editor of the four-volume anthology* American Life in Literature *(1914–1936), published by Harper and Brothers for the United States Armed Forces Institute in its series of War Department Education Manuals. Date derived from postmark. ALS. Duke.*]

[Ann Arbor, MI]
[circa December 23, 1921]

Dear Professor Hubbell:

Of course have my two poems for your book.[55] I am only too glad of your help in reaching out for more and better readers.

I suppose you've noticed that some of our free verse writers should more properly be called mixed verse writers and not merely because they are all mixed up in their thinking, but because while they stick to the old meters they permit themselves to change meters from line to line in the same poem. We won't mind what they do, though, if only they'll rise to poetic heights in the metaphor.

I enjoyed Mr Parks what I saw of him.[56] I wish it had been more.

Sincerely yours
Robert Frost

I'm at Ann Arbor a guest of Michigan University for the year.

RF

[*To Percy MacKaye. ALS. DCL.*]

Ann Arbor Mich
December 30 1921

Dear Percy:

Good to see your handwriting in the middle of all this hand printing. But better than letters of any kind is talk. We'll talk it up on January 10th. I don't know what my train will be. I shall come to you at Oxford just as soon as I can after my address at Ohio State on the evening of the 9th.[57]

---

55. "Mending Wall" and "The Tuft of Flowers" were reprinted in Jay B. Hubbell and John O. Beaty, eds. *An Introduction to Poetry* (New York: Macmillan, 1922).

56. Unidentified.

57. Oxford, Ohio, home of Miami University, where MacKaye was poet in residence; it is approximately ninety miles from the Ohio State University campus, in Columbus.

Lesley wants to be remembered to Arvia.[58] She promises to write to her. Happy New Year to you all.

Sincerely yours

Robert Frost

They call you a Fellow do they? We've decided to call me a Guest.

[To Dorothy Dunbar Bromley. The letter is undated, but internal evidence suggests the winter of 1922. ALS. UVA.]

[Ann Arbor, MI]

[circa January 1922]

My dear Mrs Bromley:

I dont know very much bout [*sic*] this Mr Kelly [*sic*][59] myself. He is by way of being a composer I think. He would never be missed if he was left out entirely.[60]

Im writing chiefly to ask you to copy from Percy Mackay's [*sic*] letter onto the enclosed letter his daughters address at Brattleboro and then mail the letter to her from your office to save time.[61]

With thanks for the trouble you are always taking for me I am

Sincerely yours

Robert Frost

On January 11, RF also read in Cincinnati, before the Ohio Valley Poetry Society, where the Frosts were hosted by J. M. Withrow, a physican, and his wife.

58. Percy MacKaye's daughter Arvia MacKaye, a poet, sculptor, and illustrator, lived in Brattleboro, Vermont.

59. The American composer Edgar Stillman Kelley (1857–1944), who had in 1921 been awarded a fellowship similar to RF's at Western College for Women, in Oxford, Ohio. Previously Western Female Seminary, it was later integrated into Miami University. On October 23, 1921, the *Washington Herald* ran an unsigned article, "Endowed Talent," which describes RF's appointment at Michigan, MacKaye's at Miami, Kelley's at Western, and a fourth such appointment given the composer Arthur Farwell by the Pasadena Music and Art Association: "If Robert Frost, Percy MacKaye, Arthur Farwell and Edgar Stillman Kelley can prove that an artist's work rises to higher levels when he does not have to keep one eye on the wolf at the door and one eye on public favor, Eastern colleges and art associations will undoubtedly follow in the footsteps of these Western and Middle Western pioneers and give other composers and writers the same freedom."

60. Bromley, a publicist at Henry Holt and Company, was apparently preparing a press release or advertisement.

61. The enclosed letter was likely from Lesley Frost.

[*To Gamaliel Bradford (1863–1932), American biographer, literary critic, and poet. Dated from internal evidence. ALS. Harvard.*]

> 1523 Washtenaw Ave
> Ann Arbor Michigan
> [circa January 15, 1922]

My Dear Bradford:

Will you join us in our "Miscellaney" [*sic*] of poetry this year if I ask it? I should hate to see you stay out.[62]

I wish I were where I saw more of you, for I'm your friend in all your works

> Robert Frost

[*To George Whicher. Date derived from the postmark. ALS. ACL.*]

> [Ann Arbor, MI]
> [January 18, 1922]

Dear George:

I make such haste as I am capable of to confess my shame, because if I don't confess it to-day, tomorrow I may not have it to confess.

I was utterly self-concerned when I wrote:[63] I forgot everything else in my anxiety to justify myself for having landed away off out here in competition with Edgar Guest so far from Amherst. I was just crying out from a fresh reading of Prexy's speech that he was as much too much for me as he was on the last day I saw and wrestled with him.[64] He's too cruelly unsound. I wailed then, I can't, I can't. I wail now, I couldn't have, I couldn't have.

But I shouldn't have forgotten everything else, I admit. As you say, there was Tip and there was Sheddy and there was Harriet in her Roman beauty: and if I might add one to the list, there was the Frenchman. I liked him for that he had a definite program.[65]

---

62. See RF to Untermeyer, February 1, 1922; see also RF to Bradford, circa early April 1922, and July 31, 1922.

63. On December 22, 1921.

64. Prexy: Alexander Meiklejohn. "Prexy" was American campus slang for a college or university president. RF refers in the letter to events associated with the celebration, in June 1921, of Amherst's centennial.

65. On the page opposite Meiklejohn's speech in the *Amherst Graduates' Quarterly* was a photograph of participants in a pageant, among them Whicher's wife, Harriet, who, in the person of "Alma Mater," was dressed in a Roman toga and crowned with laurels

If I weather my present difficulties with Mrs Conkling, we'll talk more presently about the prospects at Middlebury.[66] She has made it awkward for both of us by asking me to write the preface to Hilda's next book. I've been telling her Hilda doesnt need the publicity; I may need it, but would rather try to get along without it.[67]

Always yours
Robert Frost

[*To George R. Elliott. According to Elliott, who annotated the manuscript, RF mistakenly wrote "1921" for the year. ALS. ACL.*]

Ann Arbor Michigan
January 21 [1922]

Dear Elliott:

You'll begin to think I have made you over to Jack Haines to be friends with you in my place.[68] From what he writes I judge that would suit him. I trust it wouldn't suit you entirely. I'd no more make a friend over to someone else than I would let anyone adopt one of my children while I was still alive. No one gets away from me who ever really belonged to me. So you see what you are in for. You may as well make the best of it—unless, of course, you have

---

(facing page 237). John Mason "Tip" Tyler was Professor Emeritus of Biology at Amherst. Immensely popular on campus in his day, he was the first to teach Darwin's *On the Origin of Species,* which he reconciled with Christianity. His *Man in the Light of Evolution* (New York: D. Appleton) appeared in 1908. For the college centennial Tyler delivered a speech, "One Hundred Years of Amherst" (217–231). Frederick J. E. "Sheddy" Woodbridge (1867–1940), then dean of the political science, philosophy, and pure sciences faculties at Columbia, gave an address, "Amherst in Education" (253–263). Woodbridge was a graduate of Amherst, class of 1889, and had occasionally taught there as a visiting professor. The "Frenchman" here commended is Julien Jacques Champenois, then U.S. director of the National Bureau of French Universities. His address was titled "The Problem of Education in France Today" (319–326).

66. RF had contacted Wilfred Davison, dean of the Bread Loaf School of English at Middlebury, to suggest that he bring in Grace Conkling, which he did for the 1921 session. RF gave his first reading at Bread Loaf in July 1921; Whicher would teach there in 1922.

67. See RF to Grace Conkling, December 29, 1921. For more on her daughter Hilda, see the notes to RF's February 10, 1921, letter to Lowes.

68. See RF to Elliott, April 11, 1921.

the heart to find pretext for quarreling with me for the letters I dont write: I suppose I might be insulted into letting you go free. You could try calling me names. You could call me lazy, and see what that would do. If I resent the epithet it is more for its triteness than its fitness. It is no particular home thrust. I'm not lazy: I'm just sensible. All the matter with me is that I would rather see a friend once than write him a million letters. Oh much rather. I can't put it too strongly.

This year I am too far away out here to hope to see you. But this is only one year.[69] Next year I shall be in New England again with a will, where we can touch hands across the mountains.[70] This year to sociability. To the right-thinking no time is ever lost: I don't grudge the time I seem to throw away on my fellow men in banquetting [sic] and carousing: you never know what will come of anything. "Out of the good of evil born."[71] Nevertheless I mean not always to flock in crowds—nor long at a time. I must be about my next book or two. I haven't estimated it very closely, but I should think I must have the material on hand for a couple.[72]

I think of you often—you and your family and I'm in a way

Yours too

Robert Frost

[To Louis Untermeyer. Date derived from postmark. ALS. LoC.]

[Ann Arbor, MI]

[January 23, 1922]

Dear Louis:

I think, by gracious, I've lit upon something in free verse. But its so much better than anything I have seen in manuscript that I can hardly be-

---

69. Actually, the University of Michigan renewed RF's fellowship for the 1922–1923 academic year; see RF to Burton, October 8, 1922. See also *YT*, 200–201.

70. Elliott was on the faculty at Bowdoin College, in Brunswick, Maine, on the other side of the Green Mountains and White Mountains from where RF lived in South Shaftsbury, Vermont.

71. See the closing lines of Emerson's "Uriel."

72. Beginning in late 1922, and then on through the spring and summer of 1923, RF put together what would be his fourth volume, *NH*, published in November 1923. On March 15, 1923, Henry Holt and Company also published RF's *Selected Poems* (Heinemann issued the book in London).

lieve my senses.[73] I wish you'd look at it and tell me if I'm not right. Its a story to read straight on. And it's no application of any philosophy of the moment. It's a scot free delineation almost from the word Go almost to the tape. I'm lost in wonder at the way it keeps the ground and never soars. The ending regarded as a good one couldnt be worse, regarded as a bad one couldnt be better. It enters my armor where I didn't suspect there was a hole. It's a real novel.

There are bad spots in it to get rid of. It would stand some cutting. The four lyrics would have to come out. But that would be all right: the author gives us leave to make alterations.

I'm going to send it to you by express. Get it back to me as suddenly as possible. If it is missed too long, I dont know what they'll think I'm up to. I've let it lie around unread too long as it is from scepticism about new poetry in general.

Mind you I'm talking about a novel.

Ever yours
Robert Frost

[To Louis Untermeyer. ALS. LoC.]

Ann Arbor Mich
January 30 1922

Dear Louis:

Hoping the enclosed specimen may find a place in your museum of malformations not too far from that far call you had to the South Seas[74] I am

Yours truly
Robert Frost;

but if for any reason that is impossible (you may not have valued the call enough to preserve it in alcuhaul—you may even have closed out your museum to retire into Westchester County) hoping on the other hand

---

73. In *RFLU*, Untermeyer writes of this manuscript: "Memory refuses to react; there is not the faintest tintinnabulation of the smallest bell in the back of my mind" (141).

74. See RF to Untermeyer, July 23, 1920.

that you will return the specimen to me intact I am for the second time in one letter

Yours truly

Robert Frost

P.S. If them young people can't pull off anything, I'm going to see what I can do. I most dambly want to see you out here.[75] I have a new plan for defeating the divine purpose that I want to unfold to you before I lose interest in it.

Hurry that manuscript back to me.[76] I feel like a man speculating with money he holds in trust.

R.F.

Remember me to your wife and children. I saw your wife in The Bookman the other day. I thought she was looking very unusual. You must take good care of her. She acts to me like a person who was just about to sing some more. I must say she sang a bookfull last time.[77] Take care of her and she will take care of you. Believe me she has your best interests at heart. I'm sure of it. There, there. I didn't mean to strike the domestic note. You're not to cry. How emotional a poet it is at all! We all know you are happily married. There's no call for a demonstration. It's not yourself as a husband but the institution of marriage you are anxious to make out a case for? I can well believe it, knowing you as I do know you and what you have come through and up out of. But never you worry about the institution of marriage or any other institution for that matter. I'll take care of what institutions there are. And that just uses up my paper.

---

75. Untermeyer lectured and read at the University of Michigan on April 20, 1922, as part of a series of lectures RF organized.

76. See the previous letter to Untermeyer.

77. Jean Starr Untermeyer's most recent book had been *Dreams Out of Darkness* (New York: B. W. Huebsch, 1921). Marguerite Wilkinson reviewed it favorably in *The Bookman* for December 1921. In the same issue, Jessie Belle Rittenhouse, in "Poems of the Month," reprinted "Lake Song," which Untermeyer had originally published in *Century Magazine* in September 1921.

[To Louis Untermeyer. Writing on University of Michigan letterhead, RF has added
a department title and the designation "Official." Enclosed with the letter is a
typed, initialed copy of a poem RF never published. Date derived from postmark.
ALS. LoC.]

Dept. of Minstrelsy   Official
UNIVERSITY OF MICHIGAN
ANN ARBOR
February 1, 1922

Dear Louis:

Tell me about the book for this year.[78] You know I wanted you to let Gamaliel Bradford in with a poem or two even though you may not like him
too much. How about Elinor Wylie?[79] She's an entity all right. I hope she
wasn't at the movies on Sunday night when the roof fell in. Sunday night at
the movies was bad enough; and I hear she has been defying Jove's lightning
in other ways. Is there any truth to the rumor? Or is she simply a high-school
ma'am down among the senators and representatives?

What do you say if we start me off with Fire and Ice?—you seem to like
that so well.[80] After that I don't know what to say. You haven't seen The
Gold Hesperidee and The Grindstone. I wish I could leave it to you to
choose between them. But I dont know what has become of The Grindstone. The last I saw of it was in Farm and Fireside last year.[81] I'm not sure
you wouldn't like it better than The Gold Hesperidee. George Martin might
be able to help you find it if you thought it worth while. Martin is the editor
of F. and F.

---

78. *American Poetry, 1922: A Miscellany* (New York: Harcourt, Brace, 1922), the successor
to Untermeyer's *A Miscellany of American Poetry, 1920* (New York: Harcourt, Brace and
Howe, 1920).

79. Neither poet made the cut. Wylie was a by-word for scandal, owing to her several
marriages and numerous affairs (hence "defying Jove's lightning"). Her then-husband,
Horace Wylie, was an eminent lawyer in Washington, D.C. Their strange courtship, ex-
tending from 1910 to 1916, ostracized them from Washington society. The two would divorce later in 1922. As for the rest: on Saturday, January 28, the roof of the Knickerbocker
Theatre, at Eighteenth Street and Columbia Road in Washington, collapsed under the
weight of snow from a blizzard, killing ninety-eight people.

80. RF contributed the following poems to the *Miscellany* (1922), in this order:
"Fire and Ice," "The Grindstone," "The Witch of Coös," "A Brook in the City," and
"Design."

81. In the June 1921 issue.

Let's see—what else is there? There's Paul's Wife and A Witch of Coös to take one of. Did you see the Witch as remedied up at the last end in Harriet Monroe's Mag?[82]

I'll send The Gold Hesperidee along for consideration. You'll want Design. The Nose Ring is for you, not particularly for anyone else. You wont want it in the book. Keep it till next year till I have a set like it.

Ever yours
R.F.

The Nose-Ring

Honor's a ring in the nose that people give,
But it makes my sensitive nose more sensitive.
It makes me wince when I use my nose for a plow;
Where once I thought all thorns were on branch and bough,
Every root in the ground is thorny now.
Henceforth it seems I am not to get my girth
By going below the surface of the earth.
But let me get down again to the roots of things
And I will dispense with my honor in rings.

R.F.[83]

---

82. "The Witch of Coös" appeared in the January issue of *Poetry* (edited by Monroe). "Paul's Wife" appeared in *Century Magazine* for November 1921. All poems named in this letter other than "Design" and "The Gold Hesperidee," which RF saved for *AFR*, were collected in *NH*.

83. In *RFLU*, Untermeyer adds a note: "Besides 'The Nose-Ring,' not to be found among his published poems, Robert enclosed a reprint of a 'poem' by one C. R. D. S. Oakford entitled 'The Indices of Thought' and credited as follows: 'From the novel, *Society the Real Criminal*.'

The thoughts of woman and of man,
Are always traced upon the hand:
Upon the face and in the eyes,
And o'er the feet and legs and thighs,
A million virile thoughts imbed
Within the hairs on a woman's head.
The babe imbibes a mother's thought,
When from her breast she takes a draught.
Thoughts planted in the brain's deep wells
Conceived in embryonic cells,

[To Harriet Monroe. The letter concerns the contents and permissions for Monroe's enlarged edition of The New Poetry: An Anthology of Twentieth Century Verse in English *(New York: Macmillan, 1923). Date derived from internal evidence. ALS. Chicago.]*

> 1523 Washtenaw Ave
> Ann Arbor Mich
> [early February 1922]

Dear Miss Monroe:

I wonder if this book[84] reads as sad to other people as it does to Elinor and me. We've marked our preferences in it in the table of contents. Aren't some of them perfect? Thanks for consulting us.

Let me know if you have any difficulty in getting permission from the Holts to use these poems or mine.[85] They have been hardening their hearts a little

---

> *Develop into minds sublime,*
> *That fill the corridors of time.*

Untermeyer had been contemplating editing an anthology to be called *The World's Worst Poetry*. RF offered these couplets as a contribution, inserting three letters to make the name read "Indecencies of Thought." See *RFLU*, 143–144. In 1920 Charles R. D. S. Oakford, then forty-three, lived in Oklahoma City, where he worked as a government inspector. In 1910, while residing in Garden City, Kansas, Oakford had run for lieutenant governor on the Socialist Party ticket. *The Catalogue of Copyright Entries* (Washington, DC: Library of Congress, 1917) includes the following notice: "Oakford (C.R.D.S.) Indices of Thought. © Mar. 8, 1917. Arts and science pub. co., Dexter, Kansas." We do not know how the poem came to RF's attention; possibly Oakford mailed it to him. As for the "novel" (apparently self-published): the *Arkansas City Daily Traveler* for Monday, June 3, 1912, reported Oakford's arrest for defacing public property. He had painted the words "Society the Real Criminal" on a billboard owned by the Star Clothing Company. In the summer of 1912, Oakford was arrested again, in Oxford, Kansas, for committing the same crime, this time painting his slogan on public sidewalks. The *Arkansas City Daily Traveler* for July 16, 1912, describes Oakford as a "socialist" and "author," whose book *Society the Real Criminal* he was in town to promote.

84. Edward Thomas's *Poems* (New York: Henry Holt, 1917). After conferring with the Frosts, Monroe chose six poems from this for her anthology (in order): "There's Nothing Like the Sun," "The Word," "Sowing," "Adelstrop," "The Manor Farm," and "Beauty."

85. That is, poems from Thomas's book, or from RF's books (Holt published both poets). Monroe chose the following poems from RF's *ABW, NB,* and *MI* (in order): "Mending Wall," "After Apple-Picking," "My November Guest," "Mowing," "Storm Fear," "Going for Water," "The Code," "A Hillside Thaw," "An Old Man's Winter Night," "Fire and Ice," "The Aim was Song," and "The Hill Wife."

against the anthologists. I myself have just refused permission to Henry Van Dyke (if that's the way to spell or dispell him).[86] But you're special. And its not that I am just willing to be in your book; I'm eager to be in it.

My time in Chicago will be for several days from the 22nd on. So if the Society of Midland Authors[87] is still of a mind to gather to see me eat—

Sincerely yours

Robert Frost

[To Albert H. Sanford (1866–1956), professor of history at the University of Wisconsin–La Crosse from its founding in 1909 until 1936. ALS. La Crosse.]

Ann Arbor Mich

February 6 1922

Dear Professor Sanford:

I am asked by Mrs Stevenson[88] to send you anything I have that might be of help in getting ready for my coming to La Crosse on the 15th. I have on hand no press notices of either my books or public performances. The enclosed picture is my all. You should be able to find out anything you need about me from Amy Lowell's Contemporary Poets and Louis Untermeyer's New Era in American Poetry.[89] And I will answer your questions by mail.

Sincerely yours

Robert Frost

---

86. Henry Van Dyke (1852–1933) was a poet, professor of English at Princeton, and U.S. ambassador to the Netherlands during World War I. RF likely refers here to Van Dyke's *Book of British and American Verse* (New York: Doubleday, 1923), in which none of RF's poems appear.

87. The Society of Midland Authors was founded on April 24, 1915, by Monroe, Clarence Darrow, Hamlin Garland, Edna Ferber, Vachel Lindsay, George Ade, Mary Hastings Bradley, Emerson Hough, Howard Vincent O'Brien, James Whitcomb Riley, and William Allen White. Its purpose was to foster "a closer association among the writers of the Middle West."

88. Presumably Lulu Belle Stevenson (1889–1985), whom the census reports as having completed a college degree and living in La Crosse while RF was there.

89. Lowell's *Tendencies in Modern American Poetry* (New York: Houghton Mifflin Company, 1921) and Untermeyer's *New Era in American Poetry* (New York: Henry Holt, 1919) included biographical and critical essays on RF, with generous selections of his poetry.

[*To Sidney Cox. Dated from postmark. ALS. DCL.*]

[Ann Arbor, MI]
[February 7, 1922]

Dear Sidney

I wonder if I hadn't better pay for the Flinders Petrie.[90] I haven't lost the books: they are safe in my library in Vermont; but of course I can't reach that far to lay my hands on them now.

Tell Don Stevens I shall be speaking at Chicago University on February 23rd in the evening and shall hope to shake hands with him on your account and his own.[91]

Glad to hear you are all well.

Best wishes.
Always yours
Robert Frost

[*To George Whicher. ALS. ACL.*]

Ann Arbor Feb 8 1922

Dear George:

It would give you some idea of what you would be in for at Bread Loaf, if I wrote out a few of the things I may have carelessly said up there last summer.[92] I came pretty near going the whole length. I told them they wanted for teacher a writer with writing of his own on hand who would be willing to live for a while on terms of equality almost with a few younger writers. Almost I say. I wouldnt have him go so far as to carry his manuscript to them as they would be free to bring theirs to him. But I would have him stick at

---

90. William Matthew Flinders Petrie (1853–1942) a renowned British archaeologist and author of many works of Egyptology. RF's "the books" suggests the first three volumes of *A History of Egypt* (London: Methuen, 1894–1905). Volumes 4 and 5 were the work of other scholars.

91. Likely Donald Kenneth Stevens, a member of the class of 1922 at the University of Montana, where Cox taught.

92. RF gave his first reading at the Bread Loaf School of English on July 17, 1921. For the beginnings of RF's association with the school, see RF to Davison, December 19, 1920. See also *YT,* 161–162, 171–172.

nothing short of that. He would assign them work no more than they would assign him work. He would expect to take as well as give in as fair exchange as possible if not ideas of form, then ideas and observations of life. He would stay mainly at the level of the material where he would show to not too much advantage. That is to say he would address himself mainly to the subject matter of the younger writer as in good polite conversation. He would refrain from fault-finding except in the large. He would turn from correcting grammar in red ink to matching experience in black ink, experience of life and experience of art. There's the whole back side of every sheet of manuscript for his response. The proof of the writing is in what it elicits from him. He may not need to write it out. He can talk it out before the fire. The writing he has nothing to say to fails with him. The trouble with it is that it hasn't enough to it. Let the next piece have more to it—of Heaven Earth Hell and the young author. The strength of the teacher's position lies in his waiting till he is come after. His society and audience are a privilege—and that is no pose. On the rare occasions when he goes after the pupils it will be to show them up not for what they aren't but for what they are. He will invade them to show them how much more they contain than they can write down; to show them their subject matter in where they came from and what in the last twenty years they have been doing.

I kept repeating No exercises. No writing for exercise. The writer's whole nature must be in every piece he sets his hand to, and his whole nature includes his belief in the real value the writing will have when finished. Suppose it is a good bit of family tradition. It must be done once for all. It must be an achievement. And so on. You know how I get going and you know I mean it.

I've been outlining a plan for the reorganization of an English department with the President at Miami lately.[93] We agreed that it needed three sets of teachers, first a number of policemen with badges and uniforms perhaps but anyway with authority to enter every department in college and mark for the English department separately any and all papers written by students; second, a number of writers creative and critical, and third, a number of lecturers in criticism. There should be absolutely no writing required by an English teacher. The English policemen should do all their

---

93. Raymond M. Hughes, president of Miami University, in Oxford, Ohio, from 1911 to 1927.

hounding in the first year or two and have it over with. The writers and lecturers would be accessible informally, but at stated times to such young-sters as were pursuing writing on their own account. They would give credit (I mean credits) on application and at discretion. Oh lord look where I've got, and it's 2 AM.

Always yours

Robert Frost

All this plan lacks is someone to carry it out. I wish I had nothing else to do.

[To Irving L. Dilliard (1904–2003), American journalist and historian. When this letter was written, Dilliard was an aspiring writer in high school. Date derived from post-mark. ALS. SIUE.]

[Ann Arbor, MI]

[February 12, 1922]

Dear Mr Dilliard:

I dont believe I know "how I got my start."[94] I suppose I just kept writing what I wanted to write and occassonally [sic] trying to publish it; but I was twenty years at it before I published much of it. Of course I had to earn my living as best I could by one thing and another. I got little out of college and less out [of] literary courses in college.

With best wishes

Sincerely yours

Robert Frost

---

94. In his foreword to *Advice to a Young Writer: Letters to Irving Dilliard* (Edwardsville: Friends of Lovejoy Library, Southern Illinois University at Edwardsville, 1996), Dilliard describes the letter that provided RF's impetus for writing: "My high school years were 1921–1923. I was thinking about a career in writing, perhaps on a newspaper, as my favorite subject was English and I liked my duties on the local weekly, the *Collinsville* (Illinois) *Herald*. I had heard of schools of Journalism but knew little about them. So I decided to get some advice. I began to write to the authors of the time and ask them what they thought would be the best training for a writing career." For a more detailed account, see *Irving Dilliard Letters*, an online archive hosted by Southern Illinois University at Edwardsville.

[To Harold Witter Bynner (1881–1968), American writer, poet, and scholar. Date derived from postmark. ALS. Harvard.]

[Ann Arbor, MI]
[February 20, 1922]

Dear Witter

You did beautifully while here in making yourself so easy to entertain (I suppose your year of practice in putting up with anything in China deserves some of the credit[95]); but now you are doing dead wrong in not returning me the manuscript of Down the River.[96] No doubt you are trying to show your indifference to what is little more than a human document. But stop your putting on superior airs. You haven't to put them on with me to make your position clear. It is understood between us that the human document as literature is pretty well down the scale. You won't suspect me of any inordinate weakness for it and I wont suspect you. Yet even so we must take care of Down the River. You'll grant that as a human document it has its points; and in places it is almost more than a human document. While it is out of my hands I am as uncomfortable as a trustee speculating with the best intentions in the world with other people's money. No one reports to me, and I dont like to ask how the plans to have you back here are going forward. I dont doubt everything is all right. We all count on seeing you again soon.[97]

With best wishes for a warm winter whereever [*sic*] you are believe me Mr President[98]

Yours always
Robert Frost

---

95. Bynner had visited RF at the University of Michigan, where he met informally with a group of students. Beginning with his first trip to China (and Japan and Korea) in 1917, Bynner had become a student and translator of Chinese poetry. RF refers here to the year of study Bynner had more recently undertaken in China, from June 1920 to April 1921.

96. *Down the River* is a collection of colloquial narrative poems by Roscoe W. Brink, organized roughly by season of the year and "documenting," among other things, the life of an American family. Henry Holt and Company published it in July 1922. RF, a paid consultant at Henry Holt, had sent the manuscript to Bynner to read.

97. RF was organizing a series of five spring lectures. As it happened, Bynner did not appear in the series, which would bring Padraic Colum (March 1), Carl Sandburg (April 5), Louis Untermeyer (April 20), Amy Lowell (May 10), and Vachel Lindsay (May 24) to the University of Michigan. See also RF to Lowell, February 22, 1922. The speaker series crops up in a number of subsequent letters.

98. Bynner was president of the Poetry Society of America from 1921 to 1923.

[To Harriet Moody. Year and place derived from internal evidence. ALS. Chicago.]

[Ann Arbor, MI]

Tuesday Feb 21 [1922]

Dear Harriet:

I'm bringing Lesley instead of Elinor. Don't forget. I wouldnt have you take Lesley for Elinor. She calls for entirely different treatment. That is to say, she can be treated worse, though I shouldn't say there weren't bounds beyond which bad treatment ought not to go even in her case, young and tough as she is and of small account to her father.

If it could be arranged I should like to leave her a little while with you in Chicago for the good you would do her. The poor kid is rather sick of this institution and that through no fault of hers.[99] She's had splendid marks and liked seventy five percent of her teachers. But my line of talk isnt calculated to make her like any institution. You know how I'm always at it against colleges, in a vain attempt to reconcile myself with them. The part of them which the youngsters are most free in or where they could be most free, their own so-called activities, they are the most slavish and conventional in. Self sacrifice there must always be in religion and out of religion and with small people it seems to take the form of sacrificing their initiative and independence. You needn't tell poor dear Martha, but its [*sic*] Alpha Phi that has done for Lesley's love of Ann Arbor.[100]

We had a midnight visit from that greatest of actors Walter Hampden and his wife.[101] Up and at the heights I always say after an hour with anyone like that. I mean The heights! Up and at 'em. But you wont understand because you have no ambition. You have got over that last infirmity of noble minds grown nobler.

---

99. After attending Wellesley for nearly a year in 1917, Lesley Frost attended Barnard and the University of Michigan. Despite receiving high marks, she was not suited to academic life and never completed an undergraduate degree.

100. Martha Foote Crow (1854–1924), assistant professor of English Literature at the University of Chicago, lived for a time in Moody's house. When she was a student at Syracuse University in 1872, Crow was among the seven founding members of the sorority Alpha Phi. Michigan's chapter was chartered in 1892.

101. The distinguished actor and theater manager Walter Hampden (1879–1955) was born Walter Hampden Dougherty in Brooklyn and was trained in England. He enjoyed brilliant successes as Hamlet (1918) and Cyrano (1923) on Broadway. In addition to having a fifty-year stage career, he was cast as a character actor in a number of Hollywood films. He married Mabel Moore in 1905.

If you think they would like me at the Parker School Friday morning for whatever it was they said they would pay, I'm at their service.[102]

We shall arrive at the 43rd St station at 2.50 P.M. Thursday Feb 23. So if you dont want to meet us you'll know where not to be. But in any case I shall remain

Faithfully yours

Robert Frost

[*To Amy Lowell (1874–1925). TLS. Harvard.*]

Ann Arbor

Feb. 22, 1922

Dear Miss Lowell:

Miss Uki Osawa asks me to intercede with you for the young people who have been trying to bring you here to talk and read.[103] These are children. They tell me they began by not offering you enough money. They had nothing to reason from except the hundred dollars they gave Jack Squire, their only

---

102. The Francis Parker School in Chicago was founded in 1902 by a Civil War veteran, Colonel Francis Wayland Parker (1837–1902), just before his death. Parker modeled his curriculum on German pedagogical methods that emphasized language and literacy and wide reading in a variety of subjects. John Dewey nicknamed him "the father of progressive education."

103. Lowell spoke in Ann Arbor on May 10, 1922. Yuki Osawa (1896–1988) was born in Seattle to Japanese immigrants. At Michigan she worked with RF, befriended her classmate Stella Brunt, and joined the Whimsies (to which Brunt also belonged, and which provided the impetus for the lecture series here spoken of). She was naturalized under her husband's name as Yuki Otsuki in Honolulu in 1936, but moved to Japan shortly before the Second World War. She wrote Frost from occupied Japan in April 1946, when she was working in the Diplomatic Section, GHQ, Yokohama. The character of the prose, and her style of address, may explain RF's interest in her at Michigan: "My greetings to you across all these years, sea miles, and splurges of destruction and counter-destruction. My husband, daughter June, and I have survived. Our son Ray was drafted into a cadets' school last year and died of pneumonia a month after he entered. . . . He was saved from killing but not for peace. You have not been too far from me. Constantly your lines come to my mind. Yes, when death comes others walk only as far as the corner. . . . I did not fare so badly during the war. Our home was not bombed or burned. I did have to submit to the too-insistent hospitality of the police for three weeks and again spent a night with the gendarmes. However, those are experiences which one could not pay to have" (letter at DCL). Otsuki later returned to the United States, where she worked for the State Department in Washington.

poet English or American so far this year and I guess for several years.[104] If a hundred isn't enough ask a little more, but come and read to them. They are your fervent admirers and went after you of their own motion. I know the money is nothing to you except as the measure of how much you are wanted. Let me assure you that in this case you will be thought no less of if you charge no more than to you may seem a merely nominal sum, say, a hundred and twenty five or a hundred and fifty dollars. Make it as low as you will for them. They are taking a good deal on themselves in bringing so many poets at once where so few have ever been before. I suppose they told you they are having Louis, Carl, Vachel, and Witter Bynner too. It will be a great stirring up of poetry here. I'm interested in having you come for the chance it will give me to take it out in talk for all the letters I may intend to write you in the next year or two. Anything to save letter writing.

I have been asked by Mrs. Markham to judge between you and your rivals in poetry for the year past, but I don't know.[105]

Good luck to all your enterprises.

Cordially yours
Robert Frost

[*To Louis Untermeyer. Date derived from postmark. ALS. LoC.*]

[Ann Arbor, MI]
[February 23, 1922]

Dear Louis:

You <u>will</u> come for what these children can offer you I hope. They should be encouraged and so should I. I've got up this carneval [*sic*] of you, Carl, Amy, Vachel, and Bynner without anybody's knowing I was behind it. I had to be very indirect. I've said nothing to you about it because I wasn't sure it would be a go. Come and bring Jean and we'll have our semi annual pow wow in spite of fate and distance.

Always thine
R.F.

---

104. John Collings Squire.

105. Anna Catherine (Murphy) Markham (1859–1938), the wife of the poet Edwin Markham, was an author in her own right and served as secretary to the Poetry Society of America.

[To Louis Untermeyer. Date derived from postmark. ALS. LoC.]

[Ann Arbor, MI]
[March 12, 1922]

Dear Louis:

I think I should be for the Heine poem if I had to choose.[106] It cuts deeper with me just as A Deserter of the Desert cuts deeper than The Gold Hesperidee with you. I can see why, but life is too short and crowded to go into reasons in art.

Uki Osawa Stella Brunt et al. must have assigned you a date by this time.[107] They tell me they have done the best they can for you.

Lets see—was there anything else? If not, lets say so and quit for the moment.

Ever yours
Robert Frost

Thanks for what you said about Down the River.[108]

[To Jay Broadus Hubbell. Date derived from postmark. ALS. Duke.]

[Ann Arbor, MI]
[March 12, 1922]

Dear Mr Hubbell:

If you knew how much poetry, bad, worse, and worst, I was reading this year as of obligation to the State of Michigan you wouldn't ask me to read any more however good for the State of Texas.[109] You can imagine what the

---

106. Untermeyer explains: "A translation I had thought of printing in the *Miscellany*" for 1922 (*RFLU*, 144). The collection did include his "Monolog from a Mattress," a dramatic poem spoken by Heine. RF had published "The Gold Hesperidee" in *Farm and Fireside* in September 1921, but "A Deserter of the Desert" remains elusive.

107. April 20 (when Untermeyer spoke and read at Michigan). Brunt later became the personal secretary—and later still, the adopted daughter, and then the second wife—of Chase Salmon Osborn (1860–1949), the businessman and former governor of Michigan (1911–1913) who underwrote RF's first fellowship at the University of Michigan.

108. See RF to Bynner, February 20, 1922.

109. Hubbell had founded a student literary club, The Makers, and had requested that RF serve as judge for its annual poetry contest. Hubbell edited *The Southwest Review,* for

publicity of my position here has let me in for. If what the young college poets bring me were all. Theirs [*sic*] is some of it almost good. I won't say that two or three of them won't amount to something. I'd be surer of them, though, if I saw some sign of their assuming responsibility for themselves. They are too clinging. Still, as I say, they are almost good. And I expect to live with them while I am here. It is the school-girls, housewives, farmers and clergymen (one with a philosophical epic) I have brought about my ears—these people have poisoned my life.[110] Don't think me so heartless as not to have done the best I could for them. I have done so much that in the opinion of my family I am entitled to be considered all in. No pity called for. I state but the fact that the occasion demands. I am physically tired of poetry—fair-to-middling poetry. One proof of how tired I am is the way I actually cry over great poetry (when I have time for any) for being great. Perhaps you know the state of mind or health or whatever it is: and will make allowances.

> Sincerely yours
> Robert Frost

---

which he had also possibly asked RF to be a referee. RF would visit Southern Methodist University in November 1922.

110. The clergyman with the philosophical epic is likely Chester B. Emerson (1883–1973), an eminent divine in southeast Michigan, a regular contributor to the book review section of *The Detroit Free Press,* and author of *The Quest and Other Poems* (apparently self-published in 1922, though the date is uncertain). RF joked about the matter with the Whimsies, one of whom, Frances Swain, gave the following account in *The Inlander,* an undergraduate magazine published at Michigan: "[RF] told an anecdote about a minister who had written him testifying to eternal respect and admiration, and would not Mr. Frost just please criticize the enclosed original epic frankly? The servant of God would be grateful beyond words if the great hero among mortals would condescend to give him the truth about this one great piece of literature. The epic, by the way, had for a title some abstraction. Mr Frost obliged, replying that in all probability the clergyman's sermons surpassed his poetic compositions. Shortly thereafter, current periodicals began featuring invectives against the adored and admired luminary, suffixed with the name of the minister. 'Well, finally,' Mr. Frost confided, 'I just sat down and wrote that chap a letter that simply finished him—just the littlest, meanest letter you ever read.' After a sufficient number of seconds had elapsed for us to have finished picturing the worst—'But of course I never sent the letter'" (*YT,* 580).

[To Louis Untermeyer. Date derived from postmark. ALS. LoC.]

[Ann Arbor, MI]
[March 20, 1922]

Dear Louis

Will you send me with such haste as you are capable of, you slow old thing, one copy of your latest Modern American Poetry inscribed For Lois E. Whitcomb[111] from Louis Untermeyer (if that is the way you still spell your name)?—also a couple of copies uninstribed [*sic*]? You can get them cheaper than I can if I don't get them from you for nothing. Put them down or charge them up to publicity. Anything you can do to please Miss Whitcomb will please G. D. Eaton (concerning whom consult The Smart Set for March) and anything that pleases Eaton will give you standing with what Farrar says is the best college newspaper litterary [*sic*] supplement in the United States—namely that of The Michigan Daily.[112] A lot has to be done here for all of us to offset such a book as a man named Rankin (concerning whom consult The Smart St [*sic*] for some other month) wrote about Dargan Marks Rice and the like to the almost total exclusion of you me and the like.[113] The children (bless

---

111. Lois Elizabeth Whitcomb, of Seattle, was then a student at Michigan.

112. We are uncertain as to where John Farrar is on record, but see G. D. Eaton, "The Higher Learning in America: The University of Michigan," *The Smart Set,* March 1922, 69–76. Eaton begins: "It is a source of regret to me that I cannot give a picture of the University of Michigan that was. It comes to me only in a fragmentary way, in scattered legends from the townfolk. I don't say that the university was then better or worse, but somehow I regret the passing of the time when men kicked freely over the traces; somehow or other I regret the passing of the days when Ann Arbor was filled with young, hedonic devils, when today's high-school marking system was unknown, when Hallowe'en found the wooden sidewalks burning in the roads." About the university newspaper, Eaton writes: "The publications of the university are interesting despite the vapidity enforced by a cautious, grandmotherly faculty. First and foremost is the Michigan Daily. I am forced to laugh at its flabby editorials—pitiful attempts to recall the old swashbuckling spirit which fled as college men became younger, more impressionable, more easily dominated by Puritan zealots, more easily guarded by pedantic Sir Hudson Lowes [who confined Napoleon Bonaparte in St. Helena], strait-laced and afraid of the state."

113. Thomas Ernest Rankin, professor of rhetoric at the University of Michigan and the author of *American Writers of the Present Day: 1890–1920* (Ann Arbor, MI: George Wahr, 1920). Of RF Rankin writes: "Robert Frost has some dramatic power; in all his narrative and lyric poetry it is a tendency to the dramatic which singles itself out from all other tendencies to power. But if Frost is in the future to be known as a poet of eminence it will be for what his work now gives promise that he will accomplish rather

their bobbed heads) are on our side and only need a little encouragement in the way of a book inscribed with your name (which after all is nothing) to give us the victory. We'll fix Rankin—or rather you will—or I will if you'll supply the books.

Let's see what else was there I had on my mind—

In a hurry

R.F.

[*To Gamaliel Bradford. Date derived from internal evidence. On University of Michigan letterhead. ALS. Harvard.*]

[Ann Arbor, MI]

[circa early April 1922]

Dear Bradford:

Haven't you any more like the little black one about light? I can advocate that.[114] Hurry.

Always yours friendly

Robert Frost

---

than for what has yet been produced" (108). Of Untermeyer only this is said: "Louis Untermeyer, a writer of verse and a critic of no mean standing, while disposed to praise the 'new poetry,' admits that some of it is but the seeking of effect by dislocated prosody and punctuation" (109). Josephine Peabody Marks, Olive Tilford Dargan, and Cale Young Rice and his wife, Alice Hegan Rice, all come in for favorable notice. In "The Land of the Free" (*The Smart Set,* March 1921), H. L. Mencken ridiculed Rankin's book, first for its prose style, then for its argument: "Imagine a young man or woman outfitted with such a notion of the literature of the country as one finds in the tome of Prof. Rankin! Think of raising chickens and milking cows for twenty years to pay for such an education! I am surely not one to laugh at the spectacle. To me it seems to be tragic" (142).

114. RF had solicited poems from Bradford in the hope that Untermeyer might include them in his *Miscellany* (1922). See RF to Untermeyer, February 1, 1922. See also RF to Bradford, circa January 15, 1922, and July 31, 1922. Bradford had published three books of poetry to date, *A Pageant of Life* (Boston: Richard Badger, 1904), *A Prophet of Joy* (Boston: Houghton Mifflin, 1920), and *Shadow Verses* (New Haven, CT: Yale University Press, 1920). We have been unable to identify the "little black [poem] about light."

[*To Louis Untermeyer. Date derived from postmark. ALS. LoC.*]

[Ann Arbor, MI]

[April 4, 1922]

Dear Louis:

You will just naturally spoil everything if you let those Detroit Library people take you away from us. You were to have been the piece of resistance, coming right in the middle of everybody, and we wanted you for three nights running. A number of groups want to entertain you (or vice versa).[115] Sandburg has done for himself by arranging to get out of town to go to Detroit about three hours after he gets here.[116] The Detroit Librarians have butted in on purpose. Detroit doesn't matter. I want you to do something to solidify poetry here, so that in a year or two after they have flirted with a musician and a sculptor, they will be sorry they didnt stick to poets and poetry. Our art can do more to entertain them than any other art but foot-ball.[117] So let's entertain them unforgetably [*sic*]. Help me. It's not for myself I'm thinking, for I am done with vanities, but of you or some other poor devil when in rotation they get round to poetry again and are looking for a poet to keep. You know the plan—I assume you do. They are going right through the arts and then through them again till someone or something cries out in pain or gives way.

Stand by me. It is a biological necessity.

Steadily yours

Robertus

---

115. Untermeyer explains: "Another group connected with the University [of Michigan] had promised the Detroit librarians that I would come over one of the evenings while I was in nearby Ann Arbor" (*RFLU*, 146). He was scheduled to read at the university on April 20.

116. Carl Sandburg read, and sang, his poetry at Michigan on April 5.

117. For more on football, see RF to Sandburg, November 1921 (page 206), and RF to Bromley, June 11, 1922. A debate among administrators at Michigan was then under way as to how best to manage the fellowship, if it was continued. When RF arrived on campus in September 1921, President Burton had spoken of the possibility of awarding the fellowship to a sculptor. On May 4, 1922, the *Detroit Free Press* cited an unnamed dean who observed "that a critic of distinction might, sometimes, be considered as a creative artist," and so be eligible to succeed RF (2). During the 1920s, such fellowships as RF held at Michigan were, in fact, awarded chiefly to writers.

[To Lincoln MacVeagh, who penciled in "1924 or later?" at the top of the first sheet. However, internal evidence clearly places the letter in April 1922. ALS. Jones.]

[Ann Arbor, MI]
[circa April 10, 1922]

Dear MacVeagh:

I guess I'll let you send the Bowen MS. to me. I see the force of what your other advisor says of it.[118] I'm not over sorry for having failed for Bowen. He has other friends more congenial who ought to find him a publisher. Only my wish to be more or less just has made me put up with his young impudence.

We've been having a dose of Carl Sandburg. He's another person I find it hard to do justice to. He was possibly four hours in town and he spent one of those washing his white hair and toughening his expression for his public performance. His mandolin pleased some people, his poetry a very few and his infantile talk none.[119] His affectations have almost buried him out of sight. He is probably the most artificial and studied ruffian the world has had. Lesley says his two long poems in The New Republic and The Dial are as ridiculous as his carriage and articulation. He has developed rapidly since I saw him two years ago.[120] I heard someone say he was the kind of writer who had everything to gain and nothing to lose by being translated into another language.

---

118. Stirling Bowen (1895–1955) was a Michigan-born poet, fiction writer, and journalist. He published poems in a number of magazines in the 1920s, but never a volume of verse. He did, however, publish a small book in 1922, *An Appeal to the Nation's Courage* (Detroit, MI: Allied Printing, 1922) protesting the ongoing imprisonment of the Industrial Workers of the World organizer John Pancner. Pancner served time in the Cook County Jail from 1917 to 1919 and in the Leavenworth Penitentiary from 1921 to 1922.

119. Sandburg spoke on the topic, "Is There a New Poetry?"—answering in the affirmative, and celebrating free verse (*YT,* 179). His performance included readings from his own poetry and renditions of several American folk songs, for which he brought out his guitar.

120. Sandburg's "The Windy City" filled three pages, at two columns per page, in the March 22, 1922, issue of the *New Republic.* His "Slabs of the Sunburnt West," another long poem, appeared in *The Dial,* also in March 1922. RF first met Sandburg in 1917. It is not clear which occasion is here alluded to—perhaps a reading Sandburg gave before the Poetry Society of Southern Vermont, where he performed in the early 1920s.

Soon home out of this. The children are all already back and at the farm-ing.[121] There shall they see no enemy but foul weather.

Hurry the Bowen MS. right along will you?

Ever yours

Robert Frost

[To Marjorie Scott (1899–1989), daughter of the poet Catherine Amy Dawson Scott (1865–1934), who founded P.E.N. in London in 1921. ALS. HRC.]

Ann Arbor, Michigan, USA.

April 10 1922

Dear Madam

Disinterested friendship! I seem altogether in sympathy with the aim of your society and am proud to be made an honorary member of it.[122]

Sincerely yours

Robert Frost

Miss Marjorie Scott

Hon. Sec. of the P. E. N. Club

125. Alexandra Road

London

[To Louis Untermeyer. Date derived from postmark. ALS. LoC.]

[Ann Arbor, MI]

[April 13, 1922]

Dear Louis:

All right if that's the case. I haven't pretended to run this business. Only I had heard complaints from everybody of how Carl Sandburg had broken his

---

121. At this point, Carol, Lesley, and Irma Frost had already returned from Ann Arbor to the Stone House in South Shaftsbury, where RF would join them after being awarded an honorary MA at the University of Michigan commencement ceremony on June 19.

122. PEN—an acronym for Poets, Essayists, and Novelists—is an international coalition of writers that seeks to use literature as a vehicle for promoting understanding among cultures and to preserve freedom of expression. John Galsworthy served as its first president.

promise to stay for an evening with the Whimsies[123] and run away to the Detroit Librarians. I didn't know the Whimsies had themselves to blame. It is
no great matter. You go to Detroit then for Friday night.

Will you stay for a dinner at Dean Bursley's Sunday night then?[124] Will you
wire if you can?

People look forward to hearing you.

Hastily

R.

[To Louis Untermeyer. Date derived from postmark. ALS. LoC.]

[Ann Arbor, MI]

[May 2, 1922]

Dear Louis:

People are still calling pitifully for you on the telephone and at the front
door, and will not be consoled when I tell them you have gone to 310 West 100
St New York City.[125] They long to speak to you nose to nose and not through
a medium such as the postal service. And can you blame them? You were
their man and you done them brown.

And now dear Louis I want to ax you something privileged behind closed
doors. Please don't give me that picture by Leon Makielski as being too expensive a gift, Elinor thinks, for your means when you are leaving business.
I am buying The Red Tree for one hundred dollars and Elinor says that is a
whole lot for the impulses of two men combined to have come to.[126] Stet.

And say I find I have lost Conrad Aiken's address. Have you it. I'm in mortal
worry lest he should go ahead with me in his anthology on the assumption
that silence gives consent.[127] Help me. Elinor will let you in this case, because

---

123. The undergraduate literary club at the University of Michigan with which RF
was closely associated (they helped organize the spring lecture series).

124. Joseph A. Bursley, professor of engineering, was dean of students at Michigan.

125. The Untermeyer residence.

126. Leon Alexander Makielski (1885–1974), an American impressionist painter, taught
at the University of Michigan from 1915 to 1928 in the College of Architecture and Design. RF did in fact buy the painting named here. Makielski also painted a portrait of RF,
now hanging in the University of Michigan library (see illustration on page 262).

127. Aiken's *Modern American Poets* (London: Martin Secker, 1922) reprints eight poems
by RF ("The Road Not Taken," "Home Burial," "The Wood-Pile," "The Fear," "Birches,"
"The Sound of Trees," "Hyla Brook," and "The Oven Bird").

it will cost you no more than a postage stamp which she says I needn't enclose. Ain't I bitter?

You heard about the auditorium at Mankato that caught fire of itself when I was on my way to set it on fire with my eloquence.[128] Well the seeds of fire[129] you scattered around here slept till you had been gone a week and then broke out in several places at once, notably on the roof of the ell of this D'ooge house we live in.[130] Nothing but the prompt action of Elinor in calling me, me in calling central and central in calling the firemen and the firemen in coming saved the D'ooge antiques and art photography. The inside of the ell roof was the most beautiful smoothe [sic] sheet of pure yellow flame when I looked out to see if Elinor was telling the truth. So you see what poetry kindled.

Another good story and absolutely true: A drug store advertised on a window the confection of ice cream encased in chocolate known as Frost-bite. The book store next door not to be out done advertised my books as Frost-Bark—Very Little Worse than His Bite.

Don't fail to send Conrad Aiken's address.

Keep me in right with Dick[131]—at least till I can reassure him of my comparative interest in him next July.

> Ever yours
> Robertus

---

128. On February 5, 1922, a fire destroyed the auditorium known as Old Main at Mankato State Teachers College in Mankato, Minnesota.

129. See RF's remarks on *The Odyssey* in "Education by Poetry" (1931): "There is a better metaphor in the same book. In the end Odysseus comes ashore and crawls up the beach to spend the night under a double olive tree, and it says, as in a lonely farmhouse where it is hard to get fire—I am not quoting exactly—where it is hard to start the fire again if it goes out, they cover the seeds of fire with ashes to preserve it for the night, so Odysseus covered himself with the leaves around him and went to sleep. There you have something that gives you character, something of Odysseus himself. 'Seeds of fire.' So Odysseus covered the seeds of fire in himself. You get the greatness of his nature" (*CPRF*, 108).

130. The house was owned by Mary Worcester D'Ooge, the widow of Martin Luther D'Ooge (1839–1915), a professor of Greek at Michigan from 1870 until his retirement in 1912.

131. Richard Untermeyer, Louis and Jean Starr Untermeyer's son.

[To Sidney Cox. Date derived from postmark. ALS. DCL.]

[Ann Arbor, MI]
[May 2, 1922]

Dear Sidney:

It seems as if I had been going it nearer the edge of my strength than I had ever been before. The trip to Montana proved to be altogether out of the question.[132] I had the finger I wired you about and now I have been having a wry neck.[133] That's better I suppose than a wry mouth. Well, June is coming I say with something of the same grimness I used to use in the old days at Derry and Plymouth.

Some day I'll sit down and write you a real letter again from the heart. The mood will come. As I feel now I could no more write at any length than I could go back on old friends.

It'll be more to both of us than many letters to meet and talk again. You must look in on us (you and Alice[134] of course) for a night and a day or so in the summer. Then we'll talk fast and friendly.

Ever yours
Robert Frost

[To Charlotte Endymion Porter (1857–1942), editor of the journals Poet Lore *and* Shakespeariana, *and of the works of Shakespeare, Robert Browning, and Elizabeth Barrett Browning. ALS. BU.]*

Ann Arbor Michigan or
South Shaftsbury Vermont[135]
May 15 1922

Dear Miss Porter:

If you had two good men who could look and act pretty much alike I should like to have you try my little play called A Way Out. I have no copy I can lay my hands on here; but you could find it all printed in an early number of The

---

132. See RF to Sidney Cox, October 12, 1921.

133. We have found no telegram to Cox detailing RF's ailments.

134. Cox's wife.

135. The envelope has survived; the postmark confirms that the letter was sent from Ann Arbor.

Seven Arts of hallowed memory.[136] Two or three of the dramatic poems with that one drama should make quite an evening.

It's lovely of you to have continued to think of my work all this time. The only fault I have to find with your letter is for the reproach implied in it that I haven't written more plays in all the time I have had to write them in since you put the poems on before.[137] What have I been doing I wonder. Probably considering.

I shall be only too glad to see you do anything original you can with North of Boston. And I shall try to be on hand for any performance you may give. Don't count on me to take part however. I weary of the platform.

With thanks and all the encouragement I know how to give your worthy impulses, I am

Sincerely yours

Robert Frost

[To Louis Untermeyer. Date derived from postmark. ALS. LoC.]

[Ann Arbor, MI]

[May 19, 1922]

Dear Louis:

No, Amy didn't displace you in our affections.[138] You still hold the top of both batting and fielding lists. Amy upset a lamp and a water pitcher and was in turn herself upset when I told her what you said about the lumber-yard on her shoulder.[139] She called the janitor fool and damn fool to his

---

136. The play appeared in *The Seven Arts* in February 1917. The magazine, which debuted in November 1916, ceased publication in October 1917 (after eleven issues).

137. "The Death of the Hired Man" and "Home Burial," which Porter and Helen Archibald Clarke—sponsored by the American Drama Society—staged as plays in Boston on November 27, 1915. RF also gave a reading at the event. See his earlier letters to Porter, *LRF-1*, 379, 390, 396–397. For additional remarks about *A Way Out* in the present volume, see RF to Penniman, March 17, 1920; RF to Holt, December 16, 1920; and RF to Gallishaw, early December 1922.

138. Amy Lowell spoke and read at Michigan on May 10; Untermeyer preceded her, on April 20. See *YT*, 181–182, for an account of her misadventures on the podium.

139. Untermeyer notes: "During a question-and-answer period, I had remarked that the controversial Amy Lowell carried not only a chip on her shoulder but a whole lumberyard" (*RFLU*, 148).

face—this was out back before she went on—and she called Conrad of the Whimsies "boy" in the sense of slave.[140] She and I were ten minutes before the whole audience disentangling the lengthener wire on her lamp. As a show she was more or less successful. After it was all over she described Straus [*sic*] to some ladies, among them Mrs Straus, as the fussy old professor who stood round and didnt help.[141] Straus says she must have meant me. She laid about her. And in that respect she disappointed nobody. She only failed to live up to the specifications when she stole away from a house full of guests and came to my house to smoke her cigar in private. Her speaking and reading went well considering the uproarious start she made with the lamp and water. I never heard such spontaneous shouts of laughter. Out in front she took it all well with plenty of talk offhand and so passed for a first class sport.

I tell you all this to give you an idea of what you were better than. You have survived the eliminations and must prepare to measure strength with Vachel in the final.[142]

Here are the proofs[143]—and by the way I happened to notice when I was reading from your Modern Am Poetry that you had left a line out of Mending Wall: "There where it is we do not need the wall." It just barely hurts the sense.[144]

Perhaps you had better send the picture to South Shaftsbury, though I confess I am almost too impatient to see it.[145]

Ever yours
Robert Frost

---

140. Lawrence H. Conrad (1898–1982), then a student at the University of Michigan.

141. Louis Abraham Strauss (1872–1938) chaired the Department of English at Michigan from 1920 until 1937, the year before his death; his wife was Elsa Riegelman Strauss.

142. Vachel Lindsay was the last poet to appear in the spring series, on May 24.

143. Proofs of poems for Untermeyer's *Miscellany* (1922), to which RF contributed five poems. See RF to Untermeyer, February 1, 1922.

144. The line was missing in Untermeyer's *Modern American Poetry* (New York: Harcourt, Brace, and Howe, 1919), and also in the expanded edition Untermeyer published in 1921, but was restored in later printings.

145. Presumably the painting, *The Red Tree,* spoken of in RF's May 2, 1922, letter to Untermeyer.

[*To Harriet Moody. ALS. Chicago.*]

Ann Arbor [MI]

May 26 1922

Dear Harriet:

If you dont come up to Ann Arbor in the automobile on June 2nd and take us back to Chicago with you on June 3rd (you must rest here one night), we shall know it is because you won't and we shall make the best of it. It will be a sure sign you didnt really want to come for us the other time and were only too glad to get out of coming without having to back out yourself. But never mind that. We shall blame you and yet forgive you.

It would be a mercy if you would come however and snatch us away from the life here for a few days now and perhaps talk plans for snatching us away from it for next year. A crisis is at hand in which if you would you could say words to help us to a decision. You can't say them I suppose or you would have said them any time these eight months I have been in your neighborhood. I'll bet I have the requisite recklessness to go ahead any way on my own account and either come back to Ann Arbor in spite of the soul or stay away from it in spite of the body. It will take about the same degree of recklessness either way.

You could wire if we had anything to expect of you in the way either of advice or a visit.

There's you down there clamoring again for a letter sosoon [*sic*]. Haven't you just had one letter not more than a year ago, if not from me then from my wife or daughter and a telegram not more than a month ago. And whats a letter anyway?[146] What can I say to you in letter that I couldnt say in talk and haven't said many times over. If I seem to you niggardly of words written or oral (and I admit I am never talkative with the talkative), it is because I am afraid of throwing you into confusion by speaking too much at a time or too often. I shouldnt mind so much throwing you into confusion if ⌊it⌋ didn't seem to give you the idea that I was confused myself. But let's not worry. We'll all come clear to each other at once if I ever put us all into the book Miss Springer wants me to write.[147]

---

146. In fact, the last letter RF wrote her was dated February 21, 1922.

147. Unidentified, though perhaps Mary Elizabeth Springer (1850–1937), former secretary of the New York chapter of the Daughters of the American Revolution, the author of historical novels concerning women of the American Revolution, and the translator, into Spanish, of Benjamin Farjeon's *Bread and Cheese and Kisses: A Christmas Story* (New York:

I'll tell you about the things you sent when I see you. I'm afraid I'm too long broad and thick for any of them. It makes me sorry when I consider out of what sentiment they were given.

> Affectionately
> Robert

Terrible pressure being put on me to bring me back to Ann Arbor.

[To Lincoln MacVeagh. Date derived from internal evidence. ALS. Princeton.]

> [Ann Arbor, MI]
> [circa June 1922]

Dear MacVeagh:

Please send me in a hurry some six more Mountain Intervals to throw to my pursuers while I am escaping.[148]

This is just part of the letter I sent yesterday about George Sterlings book.[149] The more I think of it the more I like the idea of your consulting Jessie Rittenhouse about her friend. Say I suggested her. She's a friend of mine too.

> Ever yours
> Robert Frost

[To a Miss O'Brien (unidentified). Date derived from cataloger's note. ALS. BU.]

> Ann Arbor Mich
> [June 11, 1922]

My dear Miss O'Brien:

You are thoughtful: you have found things to write about: and that is more than can be said for most people now twiddling rhyme. What you havent put your mind on is the making of metaphor. You seem to have over-

---

Harper and Brothers, 1873). Benjamin Farjeon was the father of Eleanor Farjeon, who was a friend of Edward and Helen Thomas's.

148. The second edition of *MI*, issued in April 1921.

149. The letter referred to has not survived. Jessie Rittenhouse collected a number of poems by George Sterling (1896–1926) in her *Little Book of Modern Verse* (Boston: Houghton Mifflin, 1913). Henry Holt and Company brought out Sterling's *Selected Poems* in 1923.

looked the fact that fresh metaphor is everything in poetry—almost everything.[150] You score nothing by simply bringing in metaphor already made and in general use. Take your Healing. You are content to say "turquoise" sky "smooth curve" "sick" soul "draught of Life" "miracle" "Mother Nature." That is as you are now. You must cultivate a taste and faculty for making brand new metaphors as good as these were in the day of them. The least little simile, comparison, resemblance that comes to you as all your own is worth pages of such writing. I wonder if you haven't a suspicion of it. I'm sure all you need is to give your attention to the matter. You have the brains and the impulse.

Sincerely yours
Robert Frost

[To Dorothy Dunbar Bromley. ALS. UVA.]

Ann Arbor Michigan
June 11 1922

Dear Mrs Bromley:

I wonder if you couldn't write a note to the editor of The N.Y. Times and tell him where he was wrong in his paragraphs on the editorial page of June 9th about me and my having been chosen poet Laureate of Vermont by the State Federation of Women's Clubs.[151] Tell him I have had a residence in Ver-

---

150. For more remarks on metaphor, see RF's talks "The Unmade Word: or, Fetching and Far-Fetching" (*CPPP*, 694–697) and, of course, "Education by Poetry" (*CPPP*, 717–728; *CPRF*, 102–111, 270–276).

151. The *New York Times* published a "Topics of the Times" editorial on June 9 making sport of RF's ascension to the laureateship of Vermont, pointing out (with reference to *Who's Who*) that the poet had been born in San Francisco, had attended Dartmouth and Harvard, had a residence in Franconia, and taught at Amherst College. The editorialist referred to the South Shaftsbury home as a "summer place," regarded any claim RF might make to the title "farmer" with skepticism, and then described *NB* as a book of "free verse." First to defend RF with a letter to the *Times,* titled "Mr. Frost of Vermont," and published on June 18, was Halley Phillips Gilchrist, a poet and member of the Vermont State League of Women's Clubs. She stated that RF had been eligible to vote in Vermont for two years, that the South Shaftsbury property was indeed a genuine residence, and added, in closing: "To quote unofficially from Mr. Frost: 'I know of no critic in America, England, France or Vermont who supposes me to have written any free verse.'"

mont for some time. His edition of Who's Who cannot be up to the minute. You might seize the occasion to get in a stroke for the idea of the fellowship in Creative Art.[152] He seems not to have heard either of the idea or of my connection with it. Put it that he might be interested to learn etc etc. Be nice to him. You might send him copies of the English Dept. letter and the editorial comparing me with Yost the Coach (no others).[153] Perhaps you know someone in The Times office you could hand this to. That seems a chance to use them. I doubt if I should circulate them very generally as yet. Bernice Stewart will use them in her paper.[154] You might think of someone else to stir up personally. I want to see the idea furthered seriously.

Do see that I get those Mountain Intervals in a hurry won't you? I need a number of them this week for parting gifts.[155]

Thanks and best wishes.

Sincerely yours

Robert Frost

---

152. Bromley's letter, "Robert Frost of Vermont and Michigan," appeared in the *New York Times* on July 3, 1922. After affirming (again) Vermont's claim on RF, she duly devoted a paragraph to "the idea of the fellowship in Creative Art," and then referred the editors of the *Times* to the letter and article RF mentions here (she had enclosed copies of both). See also *YT*, 202–203.

153. Fielding Harris Yost enjoyed a successful run as head football coach at the University of Michigan from 1901 until 1923, and then again in 1925 and 1926. At an alumni banquet in Louisville, Kentucky, held during the series of readings RF had arranged at Michigan in the spring, President Marion LeRoy Burton wondered aloud whether RF or Yost was the more popular figure on campus. The remarks were cited in an editorial in the *Michigan Daily* (April 21, 1922), which noted that, though Burton had spoken "in a spirit of fun," there was a good deal of truth in what he said: "The interest in literature and in any pursuit which deals with the arts" had become "widespread" at Michigan, the unsigned editorial said, largely due to "the stimulating influence of Robert Frost" (2). See also page 5, note 7.

154. Bernice Stewart published an article entitled "Reviewing Robert Frost's Year in Ann Arbor" in the *Detroit Free Press* on June 25, 1922. It was reprinted as "Michigan" in *Recognition of Robert Frost*, edited by Richard Thornton (New York: Henry Holt, 1937).

155. RF left Ann Arbor for South Shaftsbury after attending the June 19 commencement ceremony at Michigan, where he was awarded an honorary MA. He was as yet unaware that the University of Michigan would, over the course of the summer, secure funds to offer him a second year-long appointment as Fellow in Creative Arts, which he accepted; it began in October 1922.

[*To Minnie Strong Latham (1865–1945), mother of Harold Strong Latham, who at the time this letter was written was editor in chief of the Macmillan Company. ALS. Middlebury.*]

Ann Arbor Michigan

June 11 1922

Dear Mrs Latham:

I must take a moment to tell you that I am altogether unlikely to find time for the article you are after. I know what Mrs Wilkinson has in mind, and she could get it from me if anyone could.[156] For several years I have been threatening to do it, but I am afraid it will have to wait a few longer. I shant probably settle down to the serious business of theorizing about verse till I stop writing verse. Have Mrs Wilkinson excuse me—and thank her.

Sincerely yours

Robert Frost

[*To John Bartlett. The letter is undated, but RF's description of his situation at the University of Michigan suggests it was written in June 1922. ALS. UVA.*]

[Ann Arbor, MI]

[circa June 11, 1922]

Dear John

Ive been thinking about you lately and wondering what I could do to get a letter out of you. I suppose I could write a letter to you.

Im still at Ann Arbor, Mich but the climax of annual improvement is about reached and it wont be many days before we book for home. We are Elinor and I. The children long since went ahead of us to set the hens and watch the apples and pears set themselves. Home is now South Shaftsbury Vermont about seventy miles south of Middlebury. So if I do get a letter out of you let it be addressed to me there.

---

156. Latham was soliciting a contribution for Marguerite Wilkinson's *The Way of the Makers* (New York: Macmillan, 1925), a collection of observations by poets on the poetic process. Wilkinson had already printed a few of RF's remarks on form in her earlier volume, *New Voices: An Introduction to Contemporary Poetry* (New York: Macmillan, 1919). She reprinted them without amendment in *Way of the Makers*. See *CPRF*, 79, 260. See also RF's April 21, 1919, letter to Wilkinson (*LRF-1*, 674).

Lets see you lived once for a little while in Vermont and once for a little while just across from it at Claremont.[157] Where havent you and I lived for a little while? You've lived a pretty well settled life in Colorado—pretty well. I guess I lived the longest I ever lived under the same roof on the farm at Derry. I was seven years there. I think of you in many places. Remember the cold day when I put you over the hill on foot toward Littleton NH? I cant get over the strangeness of having been in so many places and yet remained one person. I have kept Raymond,[158] Derry and a hundred other New England towns alive in my memory not only by passing through them now and then but by thinking of buying a farm in one or another of them. I keep reading of them seriously in Strouts Farm Catalogue.[159] I no sooner get settled in South Shaftsbury than I am at it again for some reason looking for another likely farm that could be bought right. I believe I'll end by buying a number of five hundred dollar farms in all sorts of places and holding them chiefly for the lumber on them but partly for a change of residence when I get restless. I could fix the houses upon them and rent them to medium poor city people who couldnt own their own or didnt want to because it tied them to summer after summer in the same place. What's the matter with that idea? Copyrighted!

Lesley Carol Irma and Margery write that there's all that heart could wish going on on the farm we have. We have a small horse (Morgan) we bought for a saddle horse when very young. We brought it with us at too much expense from Franconia. It has eaten its head off several times over when we have had to board it out in our absence on various errands of mercy and education in the winters. We were just beginning to resent what it had cost us when lo and behold on converting it into a driving horse we find we have a trotter. You may here [*sic*] of Carol or me on the turf next.

Not that I'm losing my interest appreciably in writing as an art. I shall have another book before many years. I've scattered poems enough around in the magazines for two books if I can get up energy enough to gather them together again.

This has been a year to wonder at. I don't know what I havent done this year. I've had no assigned work as you may have heard. I've been supposed to

---

157. In New Hampshire, a few miles east of the Vermont border.

158. Bartlett was born in Raymond, New Hampshire, and lived there again with his own young family in 1915.

159. Issued by the Strout Farm Agency (150-P Nassau Street, New York, New York). The *Catalogue* carried listings of farms for sale across the United States.

have nothing to do but my writing and the University has been supposed to have nothing to do with me but take credit for my writing. In practice it has turned out humorously. I've been pretty busy dining out and talking informally on all occasions from club meetings to memorial services on the athletic field on Decoration Day. I have felt nonsensical at times. But it's the first year of an experiment. We want to find out if every college couldn't keep one artist or poet and the artist or poet and college be the better for the mutual obligation. There'll be less lionizing when the thing settles down and people get used to the idea. Miami University at Oxford Ohio has undertaken Percy MacKay [sic] and Michigan University has undertaken me. That is as far as the idea has got yet. I'm probably coming back next year on a slightly modified plan. I am to be free to be clear away from the place for nine months out of the twelve. I've decided I would have to to get very much done. I'll have a house here but it'll stand empty in memory of me most of the time.

Oh gee I wish I could see you as on the day I left you on the corner in Derry Village and you set off for Vancouver[160] or on the day when I saw you with Margaret sitting on the high bank above the baseball field the year after you graduated or on the night when you turned up at my reading at Exeter or as on the day when you got punched in the eye by one of Kemp's boys from Sanborn (was his name White or Doble or what was it?[161]) or as on the day when you got mad at me about Pamir[162] or something in class or as on the night when you put the candles out on Doc Faustus with your finger ends and generally acted so like the Devil.[163]

---

160. RF saw Bartlett off, with his new wife, Margaret, in Derry, New Hampshire, when the Bartletts left for Vancouver in late summer 1911.

161. Sanborn Seminary, in Kingston, New Hampshire. When RF taught at Pinkerton Academy, Zachariah Willis Kemp (1857–1943) was its headmaster. Duffy Doe, a member of the Sanborn football team, Pinkerton's rival, once punched Bartlett, the captain and quarterback of the Pinkerton team. In the next play, Bartlett—his eye bloodied and swollen—scored the winning touchdown. RF honored him with a ditty, which he wrote on the blackboard: "In the days of Captain John, / Sanford Sem had nothing on / Pinkerton, Pinker-ton." See *RFJB*, 21–22.

162. See RF's December 25, 1912, letter to Bartlett (*LRF-1*, 80). He likely has in mind the lines about the Pamir Mountains in Matthew Arnold's "Sohrab and Rustum," a poem RF assigned to Bartlett's class.

163. Bartlett played Mephistopheles in the production of Christopher Marlowe's *Doctor Faustus* RF staged at Pinkerton Academy on May 26, 1910. See *CPRF*, 75–76, for RF's own published account of the series of which this production was a part.

Robert Frost, poet, has been the guest of the University of Michigan during the past year. His presence here has not only been a source of immeasurable pleasure for the student body, but it has been, as well, an inspiration

to those interested in the field in which he is considered one of the foremost men of his day. His presence here was made possible by a fellowship endowed by Chase S. Osborne, ex-governor of Michigan.

Two Hundred Eighty-six

Robert Frost as Fellow in Creative Arts at the University of Michigan in 1922.

Image from the Michiganensian, *Bentley Historical Library, University of Michigan.*

There was talk of my ranging west last winter, but I backed out. I'd go if Elinor would go with me next winter. I doubt if she will.

Our love to you all.

Affectionately

Robert Frost

[To Wade Van Dore (1889–1989). This letter inaugurated a long friendship between Van Dore and RF, who over the next seven years would read Van Dore's poems in manuscript and offer advice, the outcome of which in part was the younger poet's first book, Far Lake (New York: Coward-McCann, 1930). ALS. BU.]

South Shaftsbury Vermont

June 24 1922

Dear Mr Van Dore:

First about Thoreau: I like him as well as you do.[164] In one book (Walden) he surpasses everything we have had in America. You have found this out for yourself without my having told you; I have found it out for myself without your having told me. Isn't it beautiful that there can be such concert without collusion? That's the kind of "getting together" I can endure.

I'm going to send part of your letter to a farmer in Franconia N.H. where I lived and owned a small property until last year. The farmer is a friend of mine and will listen sympathetically to what I shall say about you. I dont know just what your plan would be. Would it be to camp out for a while on his land and then find a few boards and nails to build a shack of for the winter?

Franconia is my favorite village in the mountains. But it has to be said against it for your purposes that it has no very large library of its own and none nearer of importance to draw on than the State Library at Concord seventy miles away. New England is strewn with libraries as you may have heard, but what little money they have is necessarily spent on books that you and I would have read or wouldn't care to read, that is to say very standard works and harmless insignificant stories for children. I tell you all this so that you may know.[165]

---

164. Late in life, Van Dore would write a short pamphlet in which he paid tribute to the writer after whose example he had partly fashioned his life: Walden as the American Bible: A Gospel of Ecology (Clearwater, FL: Walden Wave Press, 1971).

165. In a memoir published late in his life, Robert Frost and Wade Van Dore: The Life of the Hired Man (Dayton, OH: Wright State University Press, 1986), Van Dore explains: "In

I am sure my friend Mr Willis Herbert would be good to you.[166] You will never see such a view as that from his fields. It is a valley view from below the heights. There is no lake in the neighborhood. You have to be content with just Mountains—Lafayette, Cannon Kinsman Moosilauke and further off the tip of Washington.[167]

I hope I tell you what you want.

> Sincerely yours
> Robert Frost

[*To John Collings Squire (1884–1958), British poet and critic, literary editor of the* London Mercury. *Date derived from internal evidence. ALS. BU.*]

> South Shaftsbury
> Vermont
> U.S.A.
> [July 1922]

My dear Squier [*sic*]:

I was moved by your poem about the stockyards in my honor to go out and kill two roosters and "dress them off."[168] I always do something to

---

Dearborn, Michigan, I had had a ninth-grade education in an inferior school. At the age of fifteen I took what I wanted out of my desk and went home without saying anything to anybody. . . . I had left school like a sleepwalker, and not until four years later while working in the J.V. Sheehan Bookstore in Detroit did I wake up. Then, down in the bookstore basement, I pulled a copy of *Autumn* out from a set of Thoreau and read writing clearer and stronger than any I had read before. Two years later I came across *Mountain Interval* by Robert Frost, and I was so excited at learning of a living writer with many of Thoreau's qualities that I wrote him a letter in which I stated my desire to put up a shack in New England and live as the author of *Walden* had for a time" (1). Van Dore had as yet no experience of New England, but he had spent considerable time, inspired by Thoreau, camping out in the woods of Michigan's Upper Peninsula, just south of Lake Superior, and in the woods of Canada, just north of it.

166. Willis Herbert (mentioned earlier in the letter as "a farmer in Franconia N.H.") was the man from whom RF bought his place in Franconia in 1915. Later, in 1929, Van Dore would "camp out" and work on RF's Gully Farm in South Shaftsbury while the place was being renovated. He would do the same at farms RF subsequently purchased; hence Van Dore's description of himself ("the hired man").

167. All in the White Mountains range.

168. Squire had dedicated "The Stockyard," a long poem in free verse about a Chicago slaughterhouse, to RF; it appeared in the *London Mercury* in June 1922.

imbrue myself personally in blood when I am reminded of the killing we all live by so that there shall be no danger of my being innocent of a sin I generally hire others to commit for me. I always do it lamely to poultry instead of bear and catamount. Usually I do it to only one rooster. This time I plunged in deeper and did it to two roosters. Just a bit of private symbolics. I'm not trying to start a new American religion.

Thanks for my name at the head of your poem and at the tail of several of my own in Mercury.[169] Thanks also for the checks you have sent.

I have great hopes of being over among you to see my book out with Heinemann in the spring.[170]

My best to you and Freeman.[171]

Always yours
Robert Frost

[*To Louis Untermeyer. Date derived from postmark. ALS. LoC.*]

[South Shaftsbury, VT]
[July 8, 1922]

Dear Louis

I wrote you a letter a week ago which you paid no attention to because I never sent it. It was all about the way the distinguished Greek and Latin Professor's Widow (pronounced Dogie as in The Chisholm Trail[172]) accused me out of a clear sky of having stolen or otherwise nefariously made away with one of the five iron pisspots she would swear she had distributed to the five bedrooms of the house she rented to us in Ann Arbor.[173] She wouldn't claim it was an Etruscan vase. Neither was it Mycenaean or Knossian ware. Nevertheless it represented a loss of fifty cents and she proposed to make a stink about it if not in it. I haven't admitted that I could have stolen a thing I no longer have any use for since I stopped drinking. If I did anything with it,

---

169. The *London Mercury* published three of RF's poems in 1922: "The Need of Being Versed in Country Things" (February), "To. E.T." (March), and "Paul's Wife" (July).

170. The London firm of Heinemann would publish RF's *Selected Poems* in 1923. RF did not, however, return to England for the event; he would not visit that country again until 1928.

171. John Freeman.

172. The cattle trail connecting Texas ranches to railheads in Kansas.

173. Mary Worcester D'Ooge, widow of Martin Luther D'Ooge. See also RF to Untermeyer, May 2, 1922.

I probably took it out into society to make conversation and lost it. I remember trying hard to break it over Carl Sandburg's head for his new mysticism and madness prepense[174]—but in vain. I may have dented it ten cents worth. I have asked her to let the ton of coal we left her in the cellar go toward that.

I got too bitterly funny about the episode in my other letter. I decided that I didn't mind the bitch as much as I made myself appear. I'm served exactly right for having spent so much of my life tolerating the lower and middle classes. Ive been punished often enough in the past for pretending not to see what was wrong with the poor. This is the worst I ever got it for affecting to stand in with the comfortably off. Menken [*sic*] wins.[175] My democracy has been 99 per cent unrealization. I left the world when I was young for reasons I gradually came to forget. I returned to the world at thirty three (sharp) to see if I couldn't recover my reasons. I have recovered them all right, "and I am ready to depart" again.[176] I believe I will take example of Uriel and withdraw into a cloud—of whiskers.[177] You may find me pretty bushy when you come by later in the week. It will be for a sign.

I'll save my adventure with Hughes the Secretary of State to tell you on your visit.[178]

---

174. See Samuel T. Coleridge, *Biographia Literaria,* Vol. 2: "As little difficulty do we find in excluding from the honours of unaffected warmth and elevation the madness prepense of pseudopoesy, or the startling hysteric of weakness over-exerting itself, which bursts on the unprepared reader in sundry odes and apostrophes to abstract terms" (London: Rest Fenner, 1817), 88.

175. H. L. Mencken's contempt for "democracy" had for some time been a matter of public record, as in this passage in *Prejudices: Second Series* (New York: Alfred Knopf, 1920): "The American colonists, in revolt against a bad king, did not set up a good king; they set up a democracy, and so gave every honest man a chance to become a rogue on his own account" (28).

176. See Walter Savage Landor, "Dying Speech of an Old Philosopher": "I warm'd both hands before the fire of Life; / It sinks; and I am ready to depart."

177. See lines 35–38 of Emerson's "Uriel":

A sad self-knowledge, withering, fell
On the beauty of Uriel;
In heaven once eminent, the god
Withdrew, that hour, into his cloud . . .

178. Charles Evans Hughes (1862–1948) served as secretary of state (1921–1925) under Warren G. Harding. He gave the commencement address at Michigan in 1922.

Here's looking for you and Jean. Stay as long as the law allows when you come.

Pretty much as ever

R.F.

Fail to say much about this in reply. Everybody reads your brilliant letters here; and the girls haven't been let into my shame as yet. Wouldnt it jar you? This is what my year among the teachers comes to. It reads like a fable to express my prejudice against education.

[To Leon Alexander Makielski (1885–1974), an American painter who taught at the University of Michigan from 1915 to 1928 (in the College of Architecture and Design). RF sat for a portrait by him in 1923. ALS. Private.]

South Shaftsbury Vt

July 8 1922

Dear Makielski:

I wish that Red Tree could get here before the Untermeyers go by next week.[179] I'm beginning to want to see if it's as beautiful as my memory of it.

Well, I've just waked up from the deathly sleep that overcame me the minute I struck South Shaftsbury. I spent the morning between the shafts of a wheel-barrow. That's the vehicle for me. When it comes to a full stop I can always get into it and sit looking back over the way we have come. In some ways it reminds me of a carriage in some ways of a horse and in some ways of an automobile. Shall we say it combines the good qualities of all three? Last night I drove mine out at midnight to the height of land on our farm and then sat back into it to view the country o'er[180] in the moonlight. In some ways reminds me of an easy chair that accompanies me like a faithful dog. I guess I'll have to drop into verse to do justice to it. You know it was invented by Leonardo da Vinci, your artist.[181]

Don't you dare turn up here unless you have sent the Red Tree ahead of you.

---

179. RF purchased *The Red Tree* (1923), and it remains in the poet's family. See also RF to Untermeyer, May 2, 1922.

180. An echo (again) of Isaac Watts' hymn, "There is a land of pure delight . . ." (1707): "Could we but climb where Moses stood, / And view the landscape o'er . . ."

181. Although independent and rival claims to being first have merit, da Vinci's notebooks do contain an original wheelbarrow design. In 1914, Floyd Dell had published in

While at Michigan in 1922–1923, Frost was a frequent visitor to the studio
of his friend and fellow faculty member Leon Makielski, who convinced
him to sit for a portrait. "Frost laughed when I first asked him to pose,"
the artist later recalled. "'What for?' he demanded.
'For my rogues gallery,' I told him."

Robert Frost Collection, Special Collections, University of Michigan Library.

Here's looking for you en route.

Best wishes to you and your wife, the college graduate.[182] Dont forget to look in on Mrs Moody when you are in Chicago.[183]

Ever yours
Robert Frost

[To George Whicher. Date determined from internal evidence. A cataloger, or perhaps Whicher, penciled in "1920" for the year next to RF's notation of the month and day. But RF had not yet bought the house in South Shaftsbury in July 1920, and in 1921 he spent several weeks after July 17 in Franconia. Thus, the likeliest date is 1922. ALS. AC.]

Sou' Shafts July 26 [1922]

Dear George:

What should you say to coming Saturday for over Sunday? We shall expect you. I have been thinking and talking of you. It seems a long time for us since we compared progress.

I learn from friends down there that your President proposed himself as a candidate for the presidency of the University of Pennsylvania. Has his heart left Amherst?[184]

You'll Ford the Mohawk I suppose.[185] Fine to see you.

Always yours fait' fully
Robert Frost

The Masses an essay entitled "Mona Lisa and the Wheelbarrow," of which RF may have taken note.

182. Anna L. Schmitt (1899–1969) graduated from the University of Michigan in May 1921; she and Makielski married two months later.

183. Harriet Moody.

184. In 1923, the board of trustees at Amherst would dismiss President Alexander Meiklejohn. His tenure there had been the subject of controversy since 1921, and it is possible that he was considering a move to the University of Pennsylvania in 1922, although the chief operating officer of that university was the provost; the university did not appoint a "president" until 1930.

185. That is, drive his Ford automobile either across or partway up (depending upon which route he took) what had recently been dubbed "The Mohawk Trail," one of America's first deliberately "scenic" roadways. Built between 1912 and 1914, and running east to west, the Trail now follows portions of Massachusetts State Highway 2. The road lies between Amherst and South Shaftsbury.

[To Wilbur Rowell. ALS. UVA.]

South Shaftsbury Vermont
July 27 1922

Dear Mr Rowell:

I've been intending all year to tell you something about my sister. But for a guest of the University with no stated duties I was kept pretty busy at Michigan.

Jean is still where she was. We have been on the point of seeing if some provision couldn't be made for her in the country where she could have a more individual existance [*sic*] not herded in an institution. She has been greatly improved, though not so much so that she isnt to my mind still a problem. Her case has never been clearly diagnosed. Dr Tyson is certain it is not one of dementia praecox. But in spite of the fact that she enjoys longer and longer lucid intervals in which she talks and writes like anyone else, she hasn't a real grip on herself and just when it begins to look as if she could be counted on, goes all to pieces again. I should have very little faith in her trying it in the world again as a free agent. She would be almost sure to neglect herself in the old way and relapse into wretchedness. Understand that I say this not too positively. I might possibly be persuaded to give my vote for putting her on a farm and paying her bills. The worst of it is that would of course necessitate her being thrown with Louie Merriam, who always hovers in the offing.[186] They couldn't be kept apart.

I ought to say that early in the spring when it had been actually arranged for her to leave the hospital and I sent her some money to buy clothes to be in readiness, she had an attack so serious that she resigned herself of her own judgement to stay where she was and handed over my money to the State of Maine to go toward her board. It is all too much for me. Any suggestions you have time to make will be gratefully considered.

With thanks for your friendly interest in these matters, I am

Sincerely yours
Robert Frost

You'll notice that my address is no longer Franconia, N.H.

------

186. For more on Merriam, see RF to Rowell, March 31, 1920, and the notes thereto.

[To Dorothy Dunbar Bromley. ALS. UVA.]

South Shaftsbury Vt
July 28 1922

Dear Mrs Bromley:

I highly approve of your offering the books to schools at a reduced price. Of course I understand that my profits will be reduced along with yours. The great thing is to get read by the rising generation.

Will you remind Mr MacVeagh, if you think of it, that he was going to send me two copies each of all three of my books unbound for me to correct and revise and select from for Heinemann?[187]

It seems good to be back on the land again after my year among the educating and the educated.[188]

With thanks for your care of me, I am

Sincerely yours
Robert Frost

[To Gamaliel Bradford. ALS. Harvard.]

South Shaftsbury Vt
July 31 1922

Dear Bradford:

I had hoped to get down to Boston to see you before you could demand an accounting of me. Perhaps you wouldn't have been as hard on me if you could have had by word of mouth what you now insist on having by letter. My aversion to letter-writing this time is altogether cowardly.

With the best intention in the world (as I trust you know) I have simply done you a disservice by asking for your poems for Untermeyer's Miscellaney [*sic*]. I was assuming too much authority. I had no right to invite you in, and so you aren't in and I am sufficiently rebuked for an officious fool.[189]

---

187. MacVeagh was head of the trade department at Henry Holt and Company, and RF's editor; from the unbound sheets of *ABW*, *NB*, and *MI*, RF would prepare the text of his *Selected Poems*, to be issued in March 1923 (in London by Heinemann, in New York by Henry Holt).

188. RF had returned on June 24 from Ann Arbor.

189. See RF to Untermeyer, February 1, 1922.

You'll wonder on what grounds I so far mistook myself. Well, no one I ever heard of was consulted when I was invited in and no one I ever heard of passed on the poems I contributed. I never was consulted about the admission of anyone else or the acceptance of anyone else's poems. That seems something to go on.

I supposed I was complying with every form in telling Untermeyer I meant to ask you for poetry for the Miscellaney and getting his permission to go ahead. I thought that settled it. But not so. All he meant to grant me was permission to submit your poetry to the judgement of the other contributors as a sort of board of consent. Both you and I were only submitting your poetry for approval if we had but known it, and it has been rejected as not up to your mark.

I'm an unpardonable mess-maker. But forgive me for the admiration I bear your work. Really you <u>must</u> forgive me. I'm wretched.

I don't believe in the buck-passing way the Miscellaney is run and shall get out of it—if I may be considered in.

> Always yours ineffectually*
> Robert Frost

*I'm thinking of how my opinion of your novel was overruled in Holt's office. But wait. Give me another chance.

[*To Lew R. Sarett (1888–1954), American poet, educator, and naturalist. ALS. Northwestern.*]

> South Shaftsbury Vermont
> August 2 1922

Dear Sarett:

You almost persuade me—but not quite. Your mighty mountains weigh much with me and friendship weighs more, but it won't do: I am heart-bound where I am. These kids here need my sympathy in their first farming.

I fully meant to bring my wife to see you at Evanston before you got away.[190] The state of her health forbade. Then it was my wife; now it is my children. You see what a family man I am. I don't know that I need to be ashamed, the way things are going for the family just at present. Floyd Dell, that professional free soul and enemy of regular marriage, has been appearing tamely

---

190. Evanston, Illinois, where Sarett was on the faculty at Northwestern University.

in the picture supplement of The Sunday Times with his new-begotten baby in his arms and his wife at his elbow.[191] Domesticity has him. But doubtless he would say he has merely exchanged one wildness for some other that doesn't yet appear. "Let Sandburg be coming into your mind."[192] A man must maintain his wildness in some shape to maintain his self-respect. I keep mine by never answering till too late the letters I get from important people.

Didnt we have a great old talk? Don't taunt me with not knowing what I'm missing by refusing your invitation to another such in a more beautiful place, and don't imagine that for refusing it I am any less

Faithfully yours

Robert Frost

[To Charles Lowell Young. On the envelope RF writes "From R Frost Franconia N.H." Date derived from postmark. ALS. Wellesley.]

[Franconia, NH]

[August 9, 1922]

Dear Young

At your service. Command me. But be sure to arrange it with Miss Bates so I'll run into no conflicts.[193] As a poet I have to be particularly careful about being taken care of.

Of course you understand I am coming to Wellesley only because I swore I would never come there again after what you told me. We must have discipline.

We'll go right on from where we left off in Peru.[194]

Ever yours

Robert Frost

---

191. Floyd Dell (1887–1969) both lived and chronicled the bohemian lifestyle of Greenwich Village. In 1919 he married the feminist activist Berta-Marie Gage and they moved to Croton-on-Hudson. Their son, Anthony, was born in 1922.

192. In 1921 Sarett, as the "poet of the wilderness," shared the lecture platform with his friend Carl Sandburg as the "poet of the city." Sarett regularly spent months living in the wilderness of Montana, Wyoming, and northern Minnesota.

193. Katherine Lee Bates, Young's colleague at Wellesley and a Frost family friend. RF would speak at Wellesley on October 24.

194. Peru is a town in central Vermont, located in the midst of the Green Mountain National Park, and on the Long Trail, the oldest long-distance hiking trail in the United States. RF and Young occasionally hiked in Vermont, New Hampshire, and Maine.

[To Louis Untermeyer. RF's date is facetious; he wrote the letter on September 1, 1922. ALS. LoC.]

Wolcott Vermont nr Canada

January 1st [1922]

Dear Louis

I walked as per prophesy till I had no feet left to write regular verse with (hence this free verse) and that proved to be just one hundred and twenty-five miles largely on the trail. Here I am stranded here without Elinor's permission to go on or come home. I slept out on the ground alone last night and the night before and soaked both my feet in a running brook all day. That was my final mistake. My feet melted and disappeared down stream. Good-bye.

Graditudinously yours

R.F.

I should admit that the kids all did two hundred and twenty miles.[195] I let them leave me behind for a poor old father who could once out-walk out-run and out-talk them but can now no more.

[To Louis Untermeyer. Date supplied by Untermeyer. ALS. LoC.]

Saint Johnsbury Vermont

nr. New Hampshire

[circa September 2, 1922]

Dear Louis:

Here I am out at St Johnsbury that famous town for St Johnswort, having for my part achieved peace without victory.[196] The children made

---

195. On August 15, Robert, Lesley, Carol, and Marjorie Frost, accompanied by Lillian LaBatt and Edward Ames Richards, set out to complete the Long Trail. Owing to poorly broken-in boots and swollen feet, RF quit the hike after four days; he and Richards departed the trail near Middlebury, Vermont. The Frost children and Lillian LaBatt, to whom Carol had proposed en route, completed the trail on September 4.

196. St. John's wort (*Hypericum perforatum*) is a perennial herb often used to treat depression. Its common name derives from St. John's Day, June 24, the date around which the flowers are usually harvested. RF quotes President Woodrow Wilson's famous address to Congress on January 22, 1917, during which he reiterated his pacifism and argued for a "peace without victory."

a record for the two hundred and twenty miles of Vermont from Mass to Canada. I am content that it is all in the family though as for me personally the laurels wither on my brow as of course they were bound to sooner or later. I am beginning to slip: I may as well admit it gracefully and accept my dismissal to the minor and bush leagues where no doubt I have several years of useful service still before me as pinch hitter and slow coach.[197]

While I have walked in pain, you have been dancing. Such is life. I shouldn't want you to miss any pleasure or improvement on my account. I trust you go back to the city with your mind made up, and I wish you always peace with or without victory, as you like it, but at all events peace. (You needn't think this is my wish for everyone indiscriminately. I have many variations of the expression for various cases. The Irish, for example, I always wish victory without peace.[198])

Yours wilsoniannualy
R. F.

I have just learned of the death of Lord Northcliffe[199] in my absence in the woods—when my back was turned. I am naturally deeply moved. When the cats away the mice will play.

Also hooray for Tilden![200]

---

197. RF puns on "slowcoach," the British equivalent of "slowpoke."

198. The Irish Civil War had begun on June 28, 1922.

199. Alfred Charles William Harmsworth, 1st Viscount Northcliffe (1865–1922), the owner and publisher of the *Times* (London), the *Daily Mail*, and the *Daily Mirror*, was a staunch supporter of British involvement in World War I and was highly critical of Prime Minister Herbert Henry Asquith, whom he deemed incompetent. Northcliffe's zeal in reporting the Shell Crisis of 1915 led to David Lloyd George's appointment as minister of munitions, which in turn allowed him to succeed Asquith as prime minister in December 1916. Northcliffe died on August 14, 1922.

200. The American tennis player Bill Tilden (1893–1952) won the U.S. National Championship (now the U.S. Open) on September 16 by defeating his fellow American Bill Johnston in a five-set thriller, during which Tilden dropped the first two sets and then won the final three. At the time Tilden was considered the greatest men's player in the history of the sport.

[*To Charles Lowell Young. Date derived from internal evidence. ALS. Wellesley.*]

Wolcott Vermont[201]

[circa September 3, 1922]

Dear Young

I went back on the trail on one leg and added fifty more miles to my sixty five. But it was against nature. Here I am knocked out again with the same little toe. So you needn't feel the least bit my inferior in the legs or character.

Those children though! Too much cannot be said for their grim forging. They had done their two hundred in fifteen consecutive days when they left me for a pitiable. May their deeds be remembered.

The best that's left of me to you
and Mrs Young,
R.F.

[*To Loring Holmes Dodd. ALS. BU.*]

Lisbon N.H.[202]

September 15 1922

My dear Mr Dodd:

I have been away on the mountain trails completely out of communication for more than three weeks. My wife has just brought me your letter here and I make haste to give you your answer.

Of course I should be glad to read for you at Clark University. Do you think we could arrange for some date before I start on my western tour in November? What should you say to Friday October 20, or Friday October 27?[203]

---

201. In the northeastern part of the state.

202. RF and his wife were staying at the house they once owned in Franconia (not far from Lisbon), which they'd sold to Raymond Holden in 1919 and 1920.

203. Owing to the renewal of RF's appointment at Michigan (which came in October), the reading had to be rescheduled for January 5, 1923. See RF to Dodd, November 4, 1922. As for the "western tour": this began on November 8, when RF departed for New Orleans, Texas, and Missouri, and ended with his return to Ann Arbor on November 20.

I am off for another few days walk now, but I shall surely be back in South Shaftsbury Vermont (where I belong) by the end of next week. So that will be the place to address any letter.

Thanking you for your kindness I am

Sincerely yours

Robert Frost

[*To John W. Haines. ALS-photostat. DCL.*]

South Shaftsbury Vermont USA

September 20 1922

Dear Jack

I am bad as you imply or openly assert. I'm very bad—judged solely as a man of letters. But you have to remember I never set out to be a man of letters in either sense of the word. I shouldn't object to being a philosopher (peripatetic) or a poet of some kind or a friend in perpetuity. And I'm damned if I dont believe I have some claim to being called all three, especially the first after what I have just done on foot over the mountain trails of Vermont. I came back from Michigan University all puffed out with self-hate that would have curdled the ink in my pen if I had tried to write you at that time. There was nothing for it but to get away from myself. You know they say there is no such thing as leaving ourselves behind; and they are right if they mean by railroad by automobile by airplane or by horse. But if we will do it on foot at a walk not at a run—at a walk deliberately, not thinking as we go so much as entertaining fancies, it is another matter that few nowadays have heard anything about: the escape from self is complete. It has been so complete in my case that no one would know me who didn't before 1914.[204]

I did something like 200 miles most of them painful to the feet, but all beautiful to the eye and mind. I wish you had been with me. I wished that many times as I walked. Really it has reached a point with me where I must see you soon either by getting you over here or betaking myself over there. If I can lay hands on the money I think you may see Elinor and me make the trip this winter or spring.[205] I may as well make up my mind to go to you. You will

---

204. Not coincidentally, the year in which RF and Haines first met.

205. The Frosts would not visit England again until the summer of 1928.

never come to me. You are afraid of this wild country—its size, manners and lawlessness.

Down on a rock on my farm there is a fern growing called the Walking Fern which I have adopted as my emblem.[206] I wonder if you ever heard of it. It is a little thing that spans its way along by rooting at the tips. I should like to send you a specimen if I thought it would be allowed to go through the mails.

I'm going to send you in a few days all the money I can raise to buy in those poor old first editions of mine with David Nutt.[207] I may ask you to store some of the books some where until I think what exactly to do with them. Some of my friends think they might be worth something here.

My best love to you all

Robert Frost

---

206. *Asplenium rhizophyllum,* native to New England, the Appalachians, and parts of the Midwest. As RF indicates, the leaf tips can form new plants at some distance from the parent. RF did in fact send Haines a specimen (under separate cover).

207. *ABW* and *NB,* published by David Nutt during RF's time in England: RF had had difficulties re-securing copyright from the company, and obtaining unsold copies and unbound pages. See subsequent letters from RF to Maurice Firuski (December 22, 1922; January 30, April 2, April 11, May 14, and May 22, 1923). A detailed account of the transaction prepared by the collector and bibliographer Pat Alger allows for the following summary. David Nutt and Company declared bankruptcy in 1921, and its remaining inventory was awarded to the London firm of Simpkin, Marshall, and Company, Nutt's chief creditor. Part of that inventory included 710 sets of unbound sheets of *ABW* (a total of 1,000 sets had been printed in 1913, some 290 of which had been bound for sale and review copies). Records of the number of sheets of *NB* printed in 1914 have been destroyed, but, as Alger indicates, it is safe to assume a print run more or less equal to that for *ABW* (about 1,000). In 1921, 300 sets of sheets for *NB* went to Simpkin, Marshall (the book had sold much better than *ABW*). The firm then bound and sold a limited number of copies of each book and later sent a royalty check for them to RF, derived mostly from sales of freshly bound copies of *NB.* Haines intervened in September 1921, fearful that unbound and unsold sheets of both books might otherwise be pulped. He paid for and received from Simpkin, Marshall 80 bound copies and 616 sets of sheets of *ABW,* and 80 bound copies and 200 sets of sheets of *NB.* Firuski, of the Dunster House Bookshop in Boston, expressed interest in buying the books from Haines, on condition that they all be bound, which Haines accepted. Haines kept a few copies of each book for himself, and sold to Firuski 686 copies of *ABW* and 259 copies of *NB.* The bindings varied, one result of which was a lively market for collectors. We thank Pat Alger for generously preparing the account of which this note is a digest.

[*To Lincoln MacVeagh. Date derived from internal evidence. ALS. Jones.*]

[South Shaftsbury, VT]
[circa September 22, 1922]

Dear MacVeagh:

The enclosed clipping will tell you what almost became of me in August and September.[208] I don't feel that it does me personally quite justice. I did some hundred and twenty miles actually on the trail and pretty actually on one leg. In this damned newspaper account I am made to drop out and set off for Franconia on foot. Nothing is said of the privations I underwent after that. Nobody [knew] or asked what became of me. When I dropped in my tracks from a complication of gangrenous housemaids knee and old man's sore toe I was gone through for what money I had in my pockets that might be useful to the expedition and then left for no good. You'll notice nothing more is said of me. Yet as a matter of fact I survived to walk a hundred and fifty miles further all by myself and sleeping out on the ground all by myself to Franconia up a White Mountain or two and then around Willoughby Lake.

I am sorry to have to admit that the Green Mountain Expedition proper was a success without me. It reached home with just one cent left over in its pockets after having wound up by sleeping one night in the graveyard for want of enough to pay for a nights lodging in the hotel at Johnson.[209]

I'd about forgotten literature and colleges. Between you and me I haven't had a blessed word from Burton. Either he must still have hope of the money to bring me back or he must have entirely forgotten my existance [*sic*].[210] It

---

208. An article about the family hike up the Long Trail ("the Green Mountain expedition"), written by RF's daughter Lesley and published, unsigned, in the September 13, 1922, *Bennington Banner* under the title "Long Trail, 225 Miles, Yields to Youth and Vigor." See *YT,* 199, 583.

209. In Lamoille County, northern Vermont, along the northern leg of the Long Trail.

210. Marion LeRoy Burton, president of the University of Michigan, where RF had been Fellow in Creative Arts the previous year. Burton did in fact raise the funds to bring RF back for the 1922–1923 academic year. The renewal of the appointment was announced in the *Michigan Daily* on October 10, quoting Burton's public remarks: "The work which Robert Frost has accomplished is, according to the statements of many students, one of the best things they have experienced during the [1921–1922] college year." On July 23, 1922, the *New York Times* had carried, on its "Books and Authors" page, an item about the fellowship, reprinting a letter the Department of English addressed to Burton: "We are of one mind on the subject. At the outset many doubts were expressed by members of the Faculty as to the wisdom of an experiment so remote from the

would be a fine cap to a glorious year if he never wrote to me again. That would free me to write the Atlantic article as I should enjoy writing it.

Here's some more Dresbach waiting for me. I'll send it right along.[211]

Thanks for those surprising checks from permission to anthologists.

I'm hoping to see Evans up here for a visit.[212]

Im also hoping to get down to see you soon.

Lots of fruit we're rolling in.

And by the way this is sent to your home address so it wont fall into the hands of my good friend Mrs Bromley.[213] I like to be advertised but not for having had a little fun walking. You never know nowadays.

Ever yours

Robert Frost

---

conventional trend of educational theory and practice [as was the fellowship]. We venture to assert that these doubts have been completely dissipated, and that no one who has been in a position to observe the situation will deny the benefits accruing to the university are incalculably richer than could reasonably have been expected." The letter then ascribes much of the success to RF: "We do not refer merely to Mr. Frost's preeminence among living American poets, indisputable though it be. We have in mind rather those qualities of character and personality that have endeared him to all that have come within the range of his influence. The rugged intellectual honesty that informs his poetry furnishes the obvious clue to the man. Combining pure ideality of purpose with keen common sense, boldness and a delicacy of imagination with a stern appreciation of the realities of life, he represents Americanism at its best." The *Times* recurred to the matter on its "Books and Authors" page for September 17, 1922, this time quoting RF: "Well, for one thing, I've had a good time here. I like to sit around and talk. I've done a lot of it here and made a lot of friends. And, then, too—and this is my serious reason—I want to give the creative fellowship further trial. I would like to prove that such a fellowship can be a success, because if it works here it will work all over the country. I have a plan for combing all departments for people who are interested in writing, for forming these people into groups and having them meet at my house evenings or afternoons for two or three months each semester. It would be an informal gathering of people interested in literature. Then I would try to arrange my time so that I might be more free to do my own work. I cannot work unless I am utterly free. When I sit down to write I must see before me a few days of undisturbed concentration."

211. The poet Glenn Ward Dresbach, whom Henry Holt and Company published. The allusion here is likely to his 1922 volume, *In Colors of the West*.

212. Charles Seddon Evans (1883–1944) joined Heinemann (William Heinemann Publishers) in London in 1914 and by 1922 had become chairman and managing director of the firm. Heinemann brought out the British edition of RF's *Selected Poems* in 1923.

213. Dorothy Dunbar Bromley worked in the publicity department at Henry Holt and Company.

[To Lincoln MacVeagh. Date derived from internal evidence. ALS. Princeton.]

South Shaftsbury Vt
[early October 1922]

Dear MacVeagh:

I've had a hurry-up call to come to Ann Arbor in time to be at the President's reception on Wednesday.[214] So the thing is settled for this year. I had an idea it would be by hook or crook.

I shall be back East again right away for engagements at Rutland Wellesley and Boston I had got my self in for fear there mightnt be any Michigan money this year. I expect to be in New York early in November on my way South.[215]

Evans hasn't come out to see us. I had hoped to talk with him. I may manage to get to England for a minute this winter.

Always yours
Robert Frost

[To Marion L. Burton. TG. Bentley]

[Bennington, VT]
[October 8, 1922]

PRESIDENT M L BURTON

UNIVERSITY OF MICHIGAN ANN ARBOR MICH

ARRANGEMENTS MOST AGREEABLE AS YOU MUST KNOW[216] THANKS FOR OURSELVES AND WHATEVER WE MAY BE SUPPOSED TO REPRESENT HAPPY TO BE WITH YOU AT RECEPTION ON WEDNESDAY

ROBERT FROST

---

214. On October 11.

215. A tour on which RF was scheduled to give readings in New Orleans, Austin, Dallas, Fort Worth, San Antonio, Waco, and Columbia, Missouri.

216. Although he remained anonymous at the time of the bequest, Horace H. Rackham, whose fortune derived from investments in the Ford Motor Company, contributed the $5,000 needed to renew RF's appointment. In the spring, when a renewal of the fellowship was far from certain, RF had informally discussed its possible terms with Burton. He would be far freer than he had been the previous year from official duties. For details, see Robert M. Warner, *Frost-Bite & Frost-Bark*.

[To Sidney Cox. Date derived from postmark. ALS. DCL.]

[South Shaftsbury VT]
[October 9, 1922]

Dear Sidney

That was a nice letter you wrote—so full of invitations. It would be fine for Lesley to visit you sometime. I'll send her out. But about me. I've just had a resounding telegram from President Burton to summon me back to Ann Arbor. And I go. Such are the terms of my engagement with him this year that I dont believe I am free to get in with anyone else for money. Any time I take away from Ann Arbor I am rather expected to use for producing bel-letr.[217] Would it be looking too far ahead [to] talk of arranging with you for October or November of 1923? My suggestion would be that you and Mr Merriam might give me five hundred dollars and my board and lodging and my wife's board and lodging and find me in the neighborhood not more than five lectures at enough apiece to pay our travelling expenses.[218] Is that as clear as if a lawyer had drawn it up? It would be fun to sit round with your friends out there in the shadow of the Rockies and more fun in October than in November, but probably November would be better for a lot of reasons. We'd talk of a better world than this.

Did my vanishing seem abrupt? I was thrown into a whirl by seeing so many of my understudies at once Walter Hendricks of Amherst and Chicago, Wade Van Dore of Tolstoi and Gandhi and Raymond Holden of the New Republic and half a million dollars.[219] Once you

---

217. That is, belles-lettres.

218. Harold Guy Merriam (1883–1980) had chaired the English Department at the University of Montana since 1919. The trip never occurred.

219. Walter Hendricks had formed a friendship with RF at Amherst (from which he graduated in 1917), and had in 1921 taken up a position teaching English at the Armour Institute of Technology in Chicago. On difficulties occasioned in 1919 when Irma Frost accused him of sexual impropriety, see the notes to RF's July 21, 1920, letter to Harriet Monroe, and RF's September 9, 1920, letter to Lesley Frost (see also *LRF-1*, 656). Wade Van Dore, whose longstanding friendship with RF began in the summer of 1922, professed the simple outdoors life as advocated by Henry Thoreau (and, by extension, Leo Tolstoy and Mahatma Gandhi). Raymond Holden, an independently wealthy poet and journalist, had built a house on land sold to him by RF in Franconia in 1919 and 1920.

were as young as these and as much impressed by me. Alice saved your soul.[220]

> Faithfully yours
> Robert Frost

Thank Merriam for his interest

[To Harriet Monroe. The letter is undated, but a date in another hand is written at the top. ALS. Chicago.]

> [South Shaftsbury, VT]
> [circa October 9, 1922]

Dear Miss Monroe:

What I meant to send you was a telegram of congratulation on the best ten years of literature any magazine has had in America and the best boost poetry has ever had from a poet.[221] But everything was driven out of my head by someone's coming on Friday and snatching me away in a car for a lecture away up at the other end of the state. You got congratulations enough without mine. Still I am sorry I didnt get in my word edgewise.

> Faithfully yours
> Robert Frost

Back to Michigan tomorrow.

[To Loring Holmes Dodd. ALS. BU.]

> South Shaftsbury Vermont
> November 4 1922

Dear Mr Dodd:

Rather late and unexpectedly I have entered into an engagement with President Burton to return to Michigan University for another year. I am afraid this is in conflict with my engagement with you as it now stands. I really ought

---

220. Cox's wife.

221. *Poetry* had been launched in 1912. See also RF to Monroe, December 4, 1922.

to be at my post out there as much as possible before Christmas.[222] After Christmas I shall feel more at liberty. Should you be willing or able to readjust your schedule so as to have me at Clark sometime in January or February?[223] I am sorry to trouble you in this way, but the excuse, you must admit, is better than most excuses.

Sincerely yours
Robert Frost.

[*To Harriet Monroe. ALS. Chicago.*]

South Shaftsbury Vt
November 4 1922

Dear Miss Monroe:

I don't care what people think of my poetry so long as they award it prizes.[224] You couldn't have pleased me more if you had gone deliberately to work to please me. Some have friends, some have luck, and some have nothing but merit. We'll assume me to have whichever of these will reflect most credit on all concerned.

Yours more than ever
Robert Frost

And by the way I am authorized by Mr Evans for Heinemann to give you permission to use the poems you asked for.[225]

RF.

---

222. In fact, after attending a reception in Ann Arbor on October 11, RF returned to New England for a round of lectures (already scheduled when he got word of the reappointment) in Rutland, Vermont, Boston, and at Wellesley College, shortly after which (on November 8) he set off on a lecture tour that took him to New Orleans, Texas, and Missouri. He would not spend time on campus at the University of Michigan until February, when he remained in Ann Arbor for two and half months.

223. RF spoke at Clark University on January 5, 1923 and stayed for the night at Dodd's residence.

224. The "Witch of Coös," published in the January 1922 issue of *Poetry,* had won the magazine's annual Levinson Prize ($200).

225. Charles Evans of Heinemann, in London. The poems in question are likely those collected in the British edition of *Selected Poems,* published by Heinemann in 1923. Since Monroe's enlarged edition of *The New Poetry: An Anthology of Twentieth Century Verse in English* (Macmillan) was also scheduled for release in spring 1923, Monroe was most

[To Louis Untermeyer. Date derived from postmark. ALS. LoC.]

[South Shaftsbury, VT]
[November 5, 1922]

Dear Louis:

If you really want to find out who wrote A Critical Fable just follow my advice and proceed as follows with Miss Amy Lowell.[226] Tell her you had it quite independently of me from a man named Ira Sibil that it was Nathan Haskell Dole the well-known-in-Boston punster.[227] Say I seem to have heard the same thing from George Herbert Palmer the well-known-in-Boston widower of Alice Freeman Palmer.[228] Be perfectly open and above-board if you want to get an appreciable rise out of her. Don't be funny. Station someone with a red flag two or three hundred yards on each side up and down the road to warn off the traffic before you touch this off.

Gee some Boston this time.[229] And now a long jump from where John Stark licked the British in 1777 to where Andrew Jackson licked them in 1814.[230] After that Ann Arbor.

---

likely securing permissions to avoid copyright infringement. See also RF's letter to Monroe in early February 1922.

226. Lowell published A Critical Fable anonymously (Boston: Houghton Mifflin, 1922), in homage to her cousin James Russell Lowell's A Fable for Critics (New York: G. P. Putnam, 1848). The title page attributes the book to "A Poker of Fun, Witt D., O.S., A 1."

227. Nathan Haskell Dole (1852–1935), a Boston journalist and poet (with a taste for puns), descended from an illustrious New England family that included missionaries, abolitionists, painters, and clergymen.

228. George Herbert Palmer (1842–1933), a translator of The Odyssey, literary critic, and the Alford Professor of Natural Religion and Moral Philosophy at Harvard until his retirement in 1913. RF had met him while enrolled at Harvard (1897–1899), and befriended him in 1915. Palmer's wife, Alice Elvira Freeman (1855–1902), served as head of Wellesley College and dean of women at the University of Chicago; she was also a poet. In his contribution to Books We Like (Boston: Massachusetts Library Association, 1936), RF listed Palmer's prose translation of The Odyssey as "by all odds the best" (CPRF, 123).

229. RF had read before the New England Poetry Club in Boston on October 23 and at Wellesley, outside Boston, on October 24, and had visited Amy Lowell in Brookline on October 25.

230. RF was about to embark on a lecture tour that would take him first to New Orleans, where Major General Andrew Jackson (1767–1845) defeated the British in 1814 (the fighting began in December 24, 1814, and concluded on January 8, 1815). Under General John Stark (1728–1822), rebel forces soundly defeated the British and Hessians in the Battle of Bennington, near South Shaftsbury, on August 16, 1777.

The Round Up was all right if it went all right.[231] John Farrar told me people in stripping circles had liked pretty much everything in it but James Oppenheim's contribution and mine—and mine was all right as a short story. Another time I think I shall stay out. People have a right not to like me exactly as I dont like Carl very well for the moment. Your Roast is good.[232] Now go ahead and cook in some form or other everything in the Bible. You be serious for a while and I'll be your parodist. Ghost Toasties or Manna Rechauffé; Fermented Scapegoat's Milk.[233] Bless you in all you undertake and forgive us our irreverence toward you as we also forgive your irreverence toward us. The only difference is that ours is less witty than yours and so harder to forgive.

I am at present hard at work translating one language into another.

I wish I could see you on my way through New York for as I have often told you I had rather see you once than write to you an hundred thousand times—Biblical an.[234] You see how thinking of the Bible can corrupt the style.

Pathé News that ends this vaudville [*sic*] show: In Detroit I was bidden to a feast with Eddy Guest;[235] even so in Vermont I am bidden to a feast with Daniel Cady.[236] Haply you never heard of Daniel Cady. Stop your ears with wax or you will hear. Today I was away on the mountain building an habitation enforced or reinforced against the hunting season. I heard in Rutland Vt that the wife of the President of The Rutland Railroad regarded Dorothy Canfield as local talent and as such refused to be interested in her.[237] "Why she hasn't

---

231. That is, the making of Untermeyer's *Miscellany* (1922).

232. "Roast Leviathan," one of Untermeyer's five contributions to *Miscellany* (1922), draws on a number of passages in the Bible.

233. Culinary jokes regarding the Holy Ghost (as a breakfast cereal, on the model of Post Toasties); leftover, reheated ("rechauffé") manna from the Exodus; and kefir, fermented goat milk, likely with an admixture of directives issued in Exodus 23:19 ("Thou shalt not seethe a kid in his mother's milk") and in Leviticus 16:8–26 (concerning the proper handling of scapegoats).

234. The phrase "an hundred" occurs scores of times in the King James Bible.

235. See the notes to RF's November 23, 1921, letter to Untermeyer.

236. Daniel Leavens Cady (1861–1934) was born in West Windsor, Vermont, and educated at the University of Vermont. He practiced law in New York City until retiring, in 1912, to Burlington, Vermont, where he wrote and published several volumes of poetry.

237. On October 18 RF had read before the Rutland (Vermont) Women's Club. While there he appears to have met Maude Emery Smith (1868–1949), wife of Alfred Holland Smith (1863–1924), the president of the Rutland Railroad. Though a resident of New York City, Smith frequently met with other officials in Rutland, the location of the home office for the railroad.

a reputable publisher, has she?" was her question. Tell Harcourt that.[238] The years we waste!

> Believe me
> Robert Frost

Complain your damndest that I don't write often; the fact remains that yours is the only address in the world that I can write right off without looking it up.

[To Louis Untermeyer. Date derived from postmark. ALS. LoC.]

> [South Shaftsbury, VT]
> [November 8, 1922]

Dear Louis

I think in the book I am sending you Raymond Holden goes further than any of my boys to date; otherwise I wouldn't be sending it.[239] You know how suspicious I am of these boys.

> Ever yours
> R.F.

[To Lincoln MacVeagh. ALS. Jones.]

> 1432 Washtenaw Ave
> Ann Arbor Mich
> November 28 1922

Dear MacVeagh:

I saw before I had gone many miles on the Katy that I wasn't going to last to get to New York—or probably wasn't.[240] If I had been absolutely sure I could have telegraphed "Can't keep appointment. Expect to die November 25th. Sorry." But one doesnt like to make gloomy predictions about one's health. It

---

238. Harcourt, Brace had already published two books by Dorothy Canfield Fisher: *The Brimming Cup* (1921) and *Rough-Hewn* (1922).

239. Holden's first collection of poetry, *Granite and Alabaster* (New York: Macmillan, 1922).

240. The Missouri-Kansas-Texas Railroad was nicknamed "The Katy." Three weeks earlier RF had embarked on a lecture tour that took him through the South.

looks too cowardly. It furnishes the Christian Scientists with too much to go on. One just waits patiently in silence till ones worst fears are realized. Then one can talk or telegraph.

What I suppose I felt coming on was the dengué (pronounced dang you) fever from a mosquito bite I got on my first day at New Orleans (pronounced differently from the way I was accustomed to pronounce it). Or it may simply have been the influenza. I was fighting a bad sore throat when I got to Columbia[241]—fighting it without medicine you understand. And now here I am at Ann Arbor in bed with a temperature.

The point is that I dont see how I can get to New York for some days yet. Will the business await my convalescence?[242] I am anxious to do my part with Van Doren.[243] I of course appreciate his friendly interest—and yours—you have doubtless cooked this up between you. It is possible that I may be able to get East on the 9th of December if you see anything in a date like that.[244] I may drop a line of thanks to Van Doren.

I had many and various fortunes on the expedition. My best audiences were at New Orleans, Austin Waco and Temple. These were large and seemed to know what I was joking about. In Fort Worth I was attacked by a Confederate veteran in a front seat. Though named after Robert Lee I dealt with him like Ulysses Grant.[245] The Mexicans in San Antonio failed to attend my lecture. I saw not a single one in my audience and he was a full blooded Aztec. None of this particular nonsense is for Mrs Bromley—that good soul.[246]

You notice my new address.

> Always yours faithfully
> Robert Frost.

---

241. Columbia, Missouri.

242. The business doubtless included discussion of the publication, in March 1923, of his first *SP*. See RF to MacVeagh, December 8, 1922.

243. Carl Van Doren, literary editor for *The Nation* from 1919 to 1922, was preparing a lengthy essay on RF, which was published in *Century Magazine* as "The Soil of the Puritans: Robert Frost, Quintessence and Subsoil" in February 1923, 629–636. Van Doren had also requested from RF a poem for *Century Magazine;* the result was the publication there, in September 1923, of "The Star-Splitter," with an illustration by J. J. Lankes, which marked the beginning of their collaboration.

244. RF did not make it to New York until the week of January 6–13.

245. See *YT* (211) for an account of the old Confederate heckler.

246. Dorothy Dunbar Bromley, in her capacity as publicist at Henry Holt and Company.

[To Alonzo John "Jack" Gallishaw (1891–1968), a teacher who was also the son-in-law
of George Browne, a Frost family friend whose daughter, Eleanor, he had married.
Date derived from internal evidence. ALS. ACL.]

[Ann Arbor, MI]

[December 1922]

Dear Gallishaw:

There's no one I'd rather do this for than you. If I've been slow, it's not from indifference but downright sickness. I have been in bed with influenza. I'm really not up to the job now. But what I can do, that I hasten along. I promise to follow with a little more in a few days. How much more fun it would be to see you for a talk than to have to write to you.

More presently sure.

Our very best to you both. We're your friends forever for the nice things you said against California as compared with New Hampshire.[247]

Ever yours

Robert Frost

I was born on Washington St, San Francisco Cal on March 26 1875[248]

My father William Prescott Frost born at Kingston N.H. was the eighth in descent from Nicholas Frost who settled at Kittery Maine in 1636. My father was editor and managing editor of the San Francisco Bulletin and San Francisco Post from just after his graduation at Harvard in 1872 till his death in 1885. He managed the city campaign for the Democratic party in 1884 when Cleveland was elected President.

My mother Belle Moody was born in Edinborough [sic], Scotland.[249] Her father and brother were both sea captains and were both drowned at sea.[250]

---

247. Gallishaw, though born in Newfoundland, lived in Grafton County, New Hampshire, where he and his wife, Eleanor, had a home. Later, after a short stint in Florida, the couple moved to Pasadena, California.

248. As Lawrance Thompson, RF's biographer, later discovered, RF was born in 1874, not 1875.

249. Actually, in Alloa, a town on the River Forth about thirty miles northwest of Edinburgh. The proper spelling of the surname is "Moodie."

250. See RF to MacVeagh, July 28, 1928: "I had supposed my mother's only brother died childless when very young in shipwreck." The cousin, John Moodie, who lived in New Zealand, surprised RF with a visit in South Shaftsbury in the summer of 1928; thereafter a correspondence between them developed.

She came to Columbus Ohio at the age of 16 to live with an uncle.[251] She taught in the High School at Columbus before her marriage.[252]

In graduating from the High School at Lawrence Mass. after four solid years of Latin and Greek and not much else I shared first honors with the girl I afterward married, Elinor White. I had some Dartmouth and more Harvard.[253] I spent most of my two years at Harvard on Latin Greek and philosophy. I had Santayana, Royce and Munsterberg but missed James whom I admired most and have been most influenced by.[254]

I read my first book through at the age of 14. It was Scottish Chiefs.[255] I wrote my first poem at the age of 15. That is to say I began to read just one year before I began to write. My first poem was a ballad, a long narrative about the expulsion of the Spaniards from Tenochtitlan.[256] My second was a lyric about waves as I remembered them at the Cliff House (San Francisco), my third was a piece of blank verse about Julius Caesar.[257] They were all published in the Lawrence (Mass) High School Bulletin. (I mean to look the one about the waves up some time.) As I began so I have continued about equally divided in interest between lyric and narrative in blank verse. I sold my first poem (My Butterfly in a Boy's Will) to The New York Independent when I was 18.[258]

My published works are A Boy's Will (David Nutt, London 1913; Henry Holt, New York 1915) North of Boston (David Nutt London 1914, six months before

---

251. Thomas Moodie, who worked in a bank in Columbus.

252. And also in Lewistown, Pennsylvania, where she met RF's father in 1872.

253. RF spent only a few months at Dartmouth, in the fall of 1892. He entered Harvard in the fall of 1897 and left in 1899, owing to family responsibilities. By then he had a son, Elliott (1896–1900), and a daughter, Lesley (born on April 28, 1899).

254. While at Harvard, RF took courses in philosophy from George Santayana, Josiah Royce, and Hugo Münsterberg, and also with George Herbert Palmer, who later became a friend. RF had hoped to study with William James, whose *Will to Believe* and *Principles of Psychology* were touchstones for him, but James was on leave during the whole of RF's time at Harvard. Later, at Plymouth Normal School, in 1911–1912, RF assigned James's *Psychology: the Briefer Course* and *Talks to Teachers* to his students.

255. An historical novel by Jane Porter, published in 1810, celebrating William Wallace, the Scottish nationalist who defeated the English army at the Battle of Stirling in 1297, but who was himself subsequently defeated and executed.

256. "La Noche Triste," inspired by his reading William Prescott's *The Conquest of Mexico* (see CPPP, 485–488). The poem first appeared in the Lawrence, Massachusetts, High School *Bulletin* in April, 1890.

257. See "Song of the Wave" and "A Dream of Julius Caesar" (CPPP, 489–492).

258. The poem appeared in *The Independent,* a magazine with a national circulation, on November 8, 1894, under the title "My Butterfly: An Elegy."

the war; Henry Holt New York 1915) Mountain Interval (Henry Holt New York 1916)

My next book will probably be called New Hampshire. So it's just as well you didn't say anything disloyal to the old state.

I published a one-act play called A Way Out in The Seven Arts Magazine.[259] It should have been called The Changeling. It would help you to my philosophy of attachment as opposed to detachment if you could find it in the library.

I have published perhaps a half dozen sonnets such as Into My Own and the Vantage Point in A Boy's Will and Putting in the Seed and Range Finding (written years before the war and only published at last to please a friend[260] at the front) in Mountain Interval. I have written very little except in perfectly regular iambic. About half my verse is rhymed and half unrhymed. A girl in some graduate-school recently wrote to ask whom I considered the chief representatives of the free-verse movement and what was my part in it. I replied that this was the first I had heard of my having had any part in it.[261] The chief representatives of the free-verse movement I had been most influenced by were Shakespeare (in the later plays) Milton (in Samson Agonistes) John Donne and some others (not excluding Horace) in their satires. I didn't think she meant any harm, but I must say education plays queer pranks with the intellect.

[To Harriet Monroe. The letter is undated, but a date in another hand is written at the top. ALS. Chicago.]

1432 Washtenaw Ave
Ann Arbor Michigan
|circa December 4, 1922]

Dear Miss Monroe:

Here I am back in Ann Arbor for a few weeks and here waiting for me is your request to publish my good opinion of you.[262] Aren't you afraid that, if

---

259. *The Seven Arts* was a short-lived periodical, on whose editorial board RF had served. *A Way Out* was published in its February 1917 issue. On what RF thought of the play, see RF to Penniman, March 17, 1920, RF to Roland Holt, December 16, 1920, and RF to Porter, May 15, 1922.

260. Edward Thomas.

261. We have been unable to find the letter in question.

262. Monroe had requested permission to publish the encomium to *Poetry* taken from RF's October 9, 1922, letter to her. On the manuscript of the letter she placed within

you publish it right now, people will think one of two things, either I got the prize for the good opinion or you got the good opinion for the prize?[263] I hate to have them make such underground connections. But absolutely just as you please in the matter.

I hope to see you some time before long—as long is now that I am growing older and time flies for me so. The first thing I know after the Fourth of July it's Christmas and then it's Fourth of July again.

Best wishes.

Always yours faithfully
Robert Frost

[*To Frederic Gershom Melcher (1879–1963), American publisher, editor, and bookseller. ALS. UVA.*]

Ann Arbor Michigan
Dec 5 1922

Dear Melcher:

Aint I the unpardonable neglecter of my friends and opportunities? Do what you please to me, but don't punish me.

For many weeks I haven't answered your letter to me, but now to make it up to you I am answering both your letter to me and your letter to Lesley (which I find in our lockbox here waiting for her) at the same time.

You have the dates and publishers of my first editions exactly right. The Holt edition of A Boy's Will and North of Boston have no additional material and no changes in the text that I am aware of.

I hope to see you when I am in N.Y. just after Christmas if you are visible.[264]

Best wishes and many thanks.

Sincerely yours
Robert Frost

---

brackets "the best ten years of literature any magazine has had in America and the best boost poetry has ever had from a poet." She did, in fact, use the remark at the head of the title page to the April 1923 issue of *Poetry* (and several subsequent issues).

263. "The Witch of Coös," first published in the January 1922 issue of *Poetry,* won the magazine's annual Levinson Prize ($200).

264. RF was in New York January 6–13, 1923.

[To Lincoln MacVeagh. Dating derived from internal evidence. ALS. Jones.]

[Ann Arbor, MI]
[circa December 8, 1922]

Dear MacVeagh

Please, please if you love me can this selected poems thing.[265] Everybody is misunderstanding. The enclosed from Rob Littell is just a sample.[266] I want the field clear for my new books. It is going to break my heart to have this old dead horse talked about and reviewed as if it were my present bid for notice. I'll write more when I feel less upset. I'm sure its a mistake. Of course if you've already spent good money to have it printed I shan't know what to say except Fate and Luck.

But ever yours just the same
Robert Frost

Tell Mrs Bromley I'm still at Ann Arbor for a few weeks.[267]
I've been sick in bed for some time.[268]

"Jag" is as it should be[269]
R.F.

---

265. RF's *Selected Poems* was slated to appear in March 1923 in both London and New York. Initially he opposed its publication, wanting a new book to be, as he puts it in the present letter, his "bid for notice" in 1923. RF was, however, pleased at the result (see RF to MacVeagh, May 30, 1923). And he would also have a genuinely "new" book out in 1923: Henry Holt and Company issued *New Hampshire,* his first to win a Pulitzer Prize, in November of that year.

266. Robert Littell regularly reviewed books for the *New Republic,* often with a sharp tongue. The enclosure was separated from the letter; we have been unable to identify it.

267. Again, Dorothy Dunbar Bromley.

268. After his exhausting lecture tour through the South.

269. That is, in line 54 of "The Code" (which would be reprinted in *Selected Poems*): "With a big jag to empty in a bay . . ."

[To John W. Haines. ALS-photostat. DCL.]

Ann Arbor Michigan USA
December 14 1922

My dear Jack

First let me ask you if you got my emblematic Walking Fern and if it was rumpled beyond recognition.[270] I sent it fresh off a limestone boulder in a fence corner of our South Shaftsbury farm; which by the way we have left the children to keep going in our briefer absence this year; and it's there you may write me rather than here. That is home and ever shall be. I was drawn back here by various inducements, chief of them that I was not to be in residence necessarily much of the time. I'm free to go away by myself on any and all excuses. I seem to be writing quite a trickle for the moment wherever I stay or travel but probably to keep it up I shall have to retire to the mock-hermitage (with four children and a wife) at South Shaftsbury Vermont.

Next let me wish you all three a merry Christmas.[271] The thing I should like to say to you is Hell, holding you by the right hand and trying to knock your hat off with the other. Would that [be] too American a familiarity on such short acquaintance? Let's see we've only known each other eight years and a half. But that's nearly the period of my active life which began in about 1914 and has kept me jumping back and forward with no aim like a grasshopper ever since.[272]

I have found a bookseller in Cambridge, Mass named Maurice Firuski who thinks he can undertake to handle all the North of Bostons in stock over there and all The Boy's Wills too.[273] I should think it might be the best way for him to buy them all through you and leave me out of it entirely. If it wouldnt be too much trouble you could see to their shipment from England. He would know

---

270. See RF to Haines, September 20 1922. RF had sent Haines two stems of walking fern (*Asplenium rhizophyllum*) in an envelope postmarked September 27, 1922 (containing, it would appear, no letter).

271. Haines, his wife Dorothy, and their son Robin.

272. Compare "The Figure a Poem Makes," the preface to the *Collected Poems of Robert Frost* (New York: Henry Holt, 1939), in which RF describes the "wildness" necessary to poetry, but which modern poets have cultivated to an untoward degree of "aberrance," as "giving way to undirected associations and kicking ourselves from one chance suggestion to another in all directions as of a hot afternoon in the life of a grasshopper" (*CPRF*, 131).

273. Maurice Firuski (1894–1978), owner of the Dunster House Bookshop in Cambridge.

how to get them through the customs office in America much better than I. I should just have a row with someone who I thought looked as if he thought I looked like a liar. I'll have Firuski (a Pole) make the certified check to you, and if the opportunity isnt still open all you have to do is send the check back. I'm sure there ought to be some sort of market for all that first edition dump.[274] Anyway Firuski is a good fellow and he is anxious to try to find one.

Merry Christmas! Happy New Year! Everything!

Always yours
Robert Frost

[*To Albert Beebe White (1871–1952), professor of history at the University of Minnesota. White spent the 1921–1922 academic year at the University of Michigan as a temporary replacement for Edward Raymond Turner (1881–1929). ALS. DCL.*]

Ann Arbor Michigan
December 14 1922

My dear Mr White:

Explanations from J. W. Beach through a common acquaintance have convinced me that I did him a grave injustice in my talk to you about him last year.[275] It all grew out of something he himself said at the time of his second marriage when I had been through a great deal with him and was out of sorts and ready to turn his own words against him.[276] I now see that he was as far as possible from meaning what I had all these years taken him to mean. This is merely a hasty note to undo at once any harm I may have done him in your estimation. Sometime when we meet I will tell you more and go more fully into regrets.

---

274. See RF to Haines, September 20, 1922.

275. Presumably in the fall of 1921.

276. J. W. Beach (1880–1957), an American poet and scholar, had been teaching English at the University of Minnesota since 1907. Beach struck up a friendship with RF in 1915, but the friendship was placed under strain by the circumstances of Beach's second marriage, to Dagmar Doneghy, on April 24, 1918, in which RF played an important but contentious role. RF took pleasure in Beach's "sinful" personality, but as a subject for anecdote this appears to have misfired, damaging Beach's chances for promotion at the University of Minnesota. Relations between the two were later patched up satisfactorily. For more on the incident see *LRF-1*, 610–611 and, in this volume, RF to Louis Untermeyer, February 11, 1926. The account in *YT* (216–18, 589–590) is hostile to RF and inaccurate on several details.

Last summer we were tied at home by having lost (or given up) the use of our car and so didn't get over the mountains to call on you. We shall hope to make it next year.

With best wishes to you and your wife,[277] I am,

Sincerely yours

Robert Frost

[*To Maurice Firuski (1894–1978). ALS. Jones.*]

[South Shaftsbury, VT]

[December 22, 1922]

Dear Firuski

It will be great fun—what we contemplate.[278] But don't you let Aiken and Kreymborg rush me off my feet. Staid bodies move slowly if they move at all. I write some thing every few minutes of course, but it takes me such a devil of a time to find out whether it is any good or not. I almost ought to publish it tentatively first and get a public opinion on it.

And here are the documents relative to our other business.[279] You'll see that they are not quite as I remembered them. That won't matter. You have only [to] adjust the price to the quantity. There are fewer of the better book and more of the other.[280]

The man to write to (and make your check to) is John W. Haines Midhurst Hucclecote Gloucester England. JOHN W. HAINES, MIDHURST, HUCCLECOTE GLOUCESTER. Pardon print, but English place names are so incredible that unless you see them in print you cant always believe your eyes. Remember me to Clement (thank him for his contribution to my good time in Rutland) and to MacVeagh and McLane.[281]

Always yours faithfully

Robert Frost

---

277. Mabel White.

278. A periodical, to be called *New Leaves* and published by Firuski's Dunster House Press, with poems by Alfred Kreymborg and Conrad Aiken, among others. The plans ultimately came to nothing. See RF to Firuski, April 2, May 14, and May 22, 1923. See also RF to Aiken, May 12, 1923.

279. The acquisition of unsold copies of *ABW* and *NB*.

280. The "better book": *NB*.

281. Percival W. Clement (1847–1927), born in Rutland, Vermont (where he once served as mayor), was governor of the state from 1919 to 1921. Lincoln MacVeagh, RF's

[*To Louis Untermeyer. Month and day derived from postmark. ALS. LoC.*]

South Shaftsbury, Vt. 1922
[December 23]

Dear Louis:

Dont go to Europe till I tell you something. It's about poetry. It should always be Beautiful and Dimned.[282] I should advise you to attempt nothing further under the old rules. Let this be—the last thing we take up when we meet, which should be next week.[283]

Meanwhile a Merry Christmas to you and Jean Starr Untermeyer the poet and vocalist.[284]

I am as adamant—I have decided to occupy the Ruhral Districts for an indefinite period.

Yours for Christmas
R.F.

[*To George Whicher. ALS. ACL.*]

[South Shaftsbury, VT]
[circa December 31, 1922]

Dear George:

You did us all three proud in The Quarterly.[285] You have a touch that keeps praise from being the least bit uncomfortable. Thanks for the way you bring me in.

---

editor at Henry Holt and Company, was the scion of an eminent American political family. The poet James Latimer McLane Jr., was a friend of MacVeagh's, and a man of whose poetry Firuski had taken notice in an article for *The Harvard Crimson* in 1919.

282. F. Scott Fitzgerald had recently published his second novel, *The Beautiful and Damned* (New York: Scribner's, 1922).

283. RF and his wife spent a week in New York City (January 6–13).

284. While in Europe, Jean would make her singing debut in Vienna. "Ruhral": RF puns on the French/Belgian occupation of the Ruhr district of Germany (then in progress).

285. That is, RF, Whicher himself, and John Erskine, in Whicher's "Creative Writing in the Amherst Curriculum," *Amherst Graduates' Quarterly* 12, no. 45 (November 1922): 8–14. The essay is a history of the Advanced Composition elective, as taught first by Erskine, then by Robert Utter (about whom Whicher has very little to say), then by RF, and, after the latter left Amherst in 1920, by Whicher himself. The article begins: "Writing may be regarded as a fine art like painting or music, or as a universal utilitarian accomplishment like table manners. The colleges long continued to regard it in the latter sense

I've just been reading your praises in a letter from Davidson of Bread Loaf. If you can possibly go back there next summer before you go to Europe, I really think you must. Davidson speaks of what you both did for the idea of this thing.[286] The idea has surely a hard course to steer between Scylla and Charibdis. Pronounce Scylla as in the country and translate Charibdis into overserious, and you'll have what I mean. You're the pilot for it.

Speaking of Ostler,[287] I met in Missouri, at Missouri indeed, a great friend of his, a teacher in literature there who has been discovering in himself a gift for locating water under ground with a forked stick.[288] He seemed a perfectly honest and sincere case of something that's too much for me. I happen to have just read The Golden Bough.[289]

---

and to teach it by methods of analysis and drill eminently fitted to prevent students from considering it in any other light. Outside the curriculum, however, writing as a fine art flourished among a few devotees and found a vehicle in undergraduate magazines. It was as though an art school should drill its pupils in the useful art of house-painting with some attention to the copying of Old Masters, while allowing them to find recreation for their leisure hours in sketching for themselves." After speaking of his "good fortune to be a student in the course under Professor Erskine and to spend with Professor Frost many hours discussing the training of young writers," Whicher continues: "Robert Frost, during his professorship, would have taught imaginative writing whatever the subject of his courses and would have taught it moreover by original ways of his own devising. His first care in the writing course was to preserve freedom of action for his students, respecting perhaps too highly in some cases the impetus that carried them into it. He invited, provoked, teased, and shamed them into writing, but was chary of employing compulsion. 'There was nothing I hated so much when I was young,' he once remarked, 'as to be told or commanded to do something I was about to do anyway.' Yet patient as were his ways of shepherding his class along, no one could have demanded higher achievement from them. He used to say that he regarded the course as an escape from the rest of the college, meaning an escape from a nagging and unnatural intellectual discipline into a situation where they could allow the believing and desiring part of their natures to grow."

286. Wilfred Davison, head of the Bread Loaf School of English (whose name RF often misspells). See also RF to Whicher, February 8, 1922.

287. Possibly George Ostler, lexicographer (*The Little Oxford Dictionary of Current English*, Oxford: Clarendon Press, 1930) and editor of Oliver Goldsmith (*The Plays of Oliver Goldsmith, Together with The Vicar of Wakefield* [London: H. Frowde, 1928]).

288. RF lectured and gave a reading at the University of Missouri on November 18, 1922.

289. James George Frazer, *The Golden Bough: A Study in Comparative Religion*, published first in two volumes by Macmillan in 1890, and subtitled *A Study of Magic and Religion* in its second edition, in 1900. By 1915 the book had been expanded to include twelve volumes. RF is almost certainly joking, at least as to having "just read" the encyclopedic work. In-

As someone has said rather bitterly I am to be described not as Mr Frost formerly of Michigan but as Mr Frost formally of Michigan.[290] I expect to spend a lot of my time in South Shaftsbury this year writing little verses. I got started and my breaks [sic] are burned out. It was in the agreement that I should be where I pleased to write. In theory they see that I should be, in practice they are going to get cross unless I make it up to them for the lack of my smiling presence on the campus (my cane spats and bowler) by publishing a book of something this year and dedicating.[291] Its a situation that can't last forever.

We're all six at home for the moment—except that three of us down in New York for the moment. I forgot.

I dont suppose this rain is raining on just us. It is pretty certain from what we read in the Bible to be raining as hard on unjust you in Massa-however you spell it. I shall have to look that word up before I publish my next book in which I use it once or twice as a term of abuse.[292] It's years since I wrote the word anywhere but on an envelope abbreviated. If I had any one left to type write for me in my old age I would cause the poem it occurs in to be copied for you.

---

stead, he alludes (indirectly) to T. S. Eliot's *The Waste Land*, published even as RF wrote to Whicher (in December 1922) Eliot writes, in his notes to the book edition of the poem (New York: Boni and Liveright): "To another work of anthropology I am indebted in general, one which has influenced our generation profoundly; I mean *The Golden Bough*; I have used especially the two volumes *Attis Adonis Osiris*. Anyone who is acquainted with these works will immediately recognise in the poem certain references to vegetation ceremonies."

290. RF was then in the middle of his second one-year appointment as Fellow in Creative Arts at the University of Michigan. He had in fact spent relatively little time on campus. After attending a reception there on October 11, RF set off on a round of readings (mid-October through November) that took him as far north as Rutland, Vermont, and as far south as San Antonio. He would not devote time to duties at the University of Michigan until February 1923, after which he remained on campus through early April (during which period he brought in Dorothy Canfield Fisher, Hamlin Garland, and Louis Untermeyer as guest lecturers).

291. RF's 1923 volume, *NH*, is dedicated "to Vermont and Michigan."

292. The word "Massachusetts" appears five times in "New Hampshire," RF's long satirical poem.

Merry Christmas—I mean Happy New Year to all—and every other good wish.

> Always yours
> Robert Frost

[To Lincoln MacVeagh. Date derived from internal evidence. ALS. Jones.]

> [South Shaftsbury, VT]
> [January 1, 1923]

Dear MacVeagh:

The question was whether to go down this week and thank you for the really beautiful books or to stay at home and read them.[293] I decided to stay at home and read them aloud to Carol to console him for the absence of his sisters who are in New York at the theatres.

But I'm coming to New York next week early. Will you say which evening will suit you best for having me, Sunday the 7th or Monday the 8th. And can you produce Van Doren for either?[294]

I've had a great time off here away from Ann. She doesnt mean to be, but she's a jealous paymaster or rather mistress. She wants to see something of me in person or in print (dedicated to her I suspect—the horrid thought!) for her five thousand.[295] I don't deserve any sympathy for my entanglement.

Happy New Year to you and everybody at Holt's and at home but particularly at home.

> Always yours faithfully,
> Robert Frost

I lecture in Worcester on Friday.[296]

---

293. The books were a Christmas gift from his publisher.
294. Carl Van Doren. See RF to MacVeagh, November 28, 1922.
295. RF would return to Ann Arbor five weeks hence.
296. At Clark University, as the guest of Loring Holmes Dodd.

[To A. J. Armstrong (1873–1954), professor of English at Baylor University. The text is transcribed from a version of the letter published by Lois Smith Douglas in Through Heaven's Back Door: A Biography of A. Joseph Armstrong *(Waco, TX: Baylor University Press, 1951). We have been unable to locate the manuscript.[297]]*

[South Shaftsbury, VT]

[circa mid-January, 1923]

. . . You surely gave me The Great Adventure down there towards Mexico, and I have only myself to blame if it was too fast and furious for my faculties to take in. . . . You are the master manager, and I was ready to say so with my latest breath, which is what I was about down to when I wound up in Missouri. . . . You are the friend indeed of wandering poets (I have no doubt, of poets fixed in their places). Browning is your presiding genius.[298] Under him it is your life to think for poets and to provide for them. I am sure I understand so much from having been in Texas if I understand nothing else. Sometime on another visit more at leisure "I shall desire more love and knowledge of you."[299]

---

297. Douglas quotes brief passages from two additional letters, the manuscripts of which we have also been unable to locate (they are not among Armstrong's papers). In the first, RF replies to a proposal that he undertake an extended lecture tour in Texas (of the kind, though not of the extent, Armstrong arranged for him in November 1922). It was likely written from Ann Arbor late in 1921: ". . . You scare me. I could never think of being away from home anything like 'the greatest part of the year.' Poor Vachel [Lindsay] has thus far failed to get married, so one place is as unhomelike as another to him. I can boast of no such artistic detachment." The second concerns another proposal to lecture in Texas, and likely dates to spring 1923: ". . . Let's not deceive ourselves. I may not write poetry as well as I ought to, but at least I write it better than I read it and talk about it. My future lies more and more at home. . . . Make Vachel keep the circuit open till I come round. I may be starved into it you know. Don't be impatient with me. If I'm a better poet than lecturer, I'm a better fellow than either. I like to think of you as a friend . ."

298. In 1918, Armstrong, a devoted reader and collector of Robert and Elizabeth Barrett Browning, donated his small collection of materials to Baylor University and thereafter contributed to and guided the growth of the collection. The Armstrong Browning Library of Baylor University now houses the world's largest collection of books, manuscripts, and memorabilia related to the lives and works of the Brownings.

299. Shakespeare, *As You Like It* 1.2, Le Beau to Orlando.

Robert Frost in 1923 at the home of A. J. Armstrong in Waco, Texas.
Photograph by Farmer. Courtesy of D. G. Sheehy.

[To Harriet Moody. Penciled in (in another hand) at the top right of the manuscript is "[1923?]." Internal evidence allows for a more precise dating. ALS. Chicago.]

[South Shaftsbury, VT]
[circa January 17, 1923]

Dear Harriet:

I'm heart-broken for you. You two had stayed brother and sister all these years against the world.[300] Your hold was a match for everything but death. You know better than I what to say to death. I'm willing you should say it.

We've all been down with grippe and now Irma has run into pneumonia.[301] I have hopes that she isnt going to be too sick. You can imagine the state Elinor is in.

I had one of my great times with Ridgley [*sic*] last week.[302] I always keep seeing a light as I talk with him and of course losing it as quickly: the thing is the seeing it. He's some consolation. Nevertheless I am ready to say when you are that pretty nearly everything is vanity.*

Affectionately
Robert

*Some time I propose to make you a short list of the things that aren't.

[To Lincoln MacVeagh. The text is transcribed from SL (287–288), which lists the manuscript as being in the archives at the Jones Library, Amherst. However, no record exists of its having been held there, and we have been unable to locate it elsewhere.]

[South Shaftsbury, VT]
[circa January 18, 1923]

Dear MacVeagh:

One after another we went to bed with grippe when we got home until finally Irma went down with pneumonia. It was terrible. We should have all died with her if she had died. But luckily she proved a mild case and is now

---

300. Moody's brother Frederick Tilden, eleven years her junior, had died on January 10.

301. RF suffered a bout of influenza that kept him at home in South Shaftsbury from January 14 to 30; the disease, as the letter indicates, struck most of the family.

302. When RF and his wife, Elinor, were in New York City, and stayed at Moody's residence on Waverly Place (where Ridgely Torrence also often stayed).

pronounced out of danger. Yesterday Carol froze an ear and a toe sawing with a cross-cut out in a zero wind. Irma has just given us such a scare however that nothing else will seem very terrible for some time to come.

Except with you folks and with Ridgley [*sic*] Torrence I don't believe I had a very good time in New York. I was trying too hard to do my duty, a thing that never pays.

I'd like to make you a list of the people I met and rather detested. It would be too long. A change of subject is called for. . . . [303]

Thanks for your kindness. You are the only hold (or should I say holt?) the Holts have on me I sometimes think.[304]

My thanks to Mrs MacVeagh too.[305]

Ever yours

Robert Frost

[*To Gamaliel Bradford. ALS. Harvard.*]

South Shaftsbury Vt

January 18 1923

Dear Bradford:

I've just been reading your Aaron Burr.[306] He's a beauty. On with the job. Dont spare to be a little wicked yourself over these wicked people. Not that I would have you make the judicious grieve, but you can afford to make the judicious guess. Tease us.

The echo of your voice reading has hardly died away in my ears.[307]

Ever yours

Robert Frost

---

303. The ellipsis is in *SL* (where it indicates that Lawrance Thompson has omitted several sentences).

304. MacVeagh left the firm in late 1923. The next four to five years saw RF increasingly dissatisfied with his publisher, a situation rectified by a renegotiation of his contract in 1928.

305. Margaret Charlton Lewis MacVeagh, known to friends as Bunny.

306. In the December 1922 issue of *Harper's*. Bradford subsequently reprinted it in his *Damaged Souls* (New York: Houghton Mifflin, 1923).

307. The two men likely met during RF's October 23–25 (1922) stay in and around Boston.

[To John Erskine. ALS. Columbia.]

South Shaftsbury Vermont
January 18 1923

Dear Erskine

I fully meant to see you when I was in New York unless you refused to let me; but it was grippe that refused to let me and sent me home to South Shaftsbury (Vermont) before my time. The worst of it is that I cant get back to you for the 25th. Your inaugural I suppose it is to be, and I should be happy to grace it in any way short of an eclogue.[308] I do not grudge you to the Poetry Society of America so long as it leaves you faithful to that more select Society of Us Three which I take it to be no less in being for Vachel's never having been notified of his election to membership in it.[309] Go forward and be the President of the Poetry Society of America without a qualm. You are sure to do it good.[310] I shall have to extend you my blessing from Ann Arbor where I am due at this moment and am only kept from being by serious illness in the family.[311] I should be speaking there today to all the assembled Presidents of the Colleges of Michigan. On the 25th I shall be speaking to the Michigan Alumni of Detroit. So you see I have my importance. It will sometime get so that engagements with me will have to be made years in advance.

Never believe much that I say. The fact is that I am receding and shall end pretty soon with being the farmer I started out with being. I lectured a hundred times last year, but it was the peak. I am now launched on a career of

---

308. Erskine had been elected president of the Poetry Society of America the previous year. "Eclogue" is a joke at RF's own expense about what appears to have been an unsuccessful rendering of an early version of "Build Soil," explicitly structured in Virgilian eclogue form, during a Phi Beta Kappa address at Columbia University on May 31, 1921. On this event see RF to Carl Van Doren, April 22, 1921, and RF to Erskine, July 7, 1921.

309. Vachel Lindsay. He and RF had first met, under the auspices of Harriet Monroe, in Chicago in 1917.

310. RF was active in the Poetry Society, but on occasion equivocal about it. See LRF-1, 397 (where he complains to Untermeyer about "enemies" on the "roster of the Poetry Society of America"), and 443–444.

311. Suffered by Irma Frost. But the sickest member of the Frost family, at this time, was RF himself, who had come down with influenza in November 1922 and suffered a relapse on returning to South Shaftsbury on January 14.

excusing myself from lectures. I did fourteen in fourteen days in November.[312] It was enough to make me see through it all.

I never quite give up the idea of a farm down in your corner of Connecticut. I may come browsing round there before all's said.

Such news reaches me from the great world as that common sense is now considered plebean [sic] and any sense at all only less so: the aristocrat will spurn both this season; an American poet living in England has made an Anthology of the Best Lines in Poetry. He has run the lines loosely together in a sort of narrative and copyrighted them so that anyone using them again will have to enclose them in double quotation marks thus: " 'I say no harm and I mean no harm.' "[313]

Best wishes for a prosperous administration.

Always yours faithfully
Robert Frost

312. On RF's tour of the southern states: see RF to Lincoln MacVeagh, November 28, 1922, and subsequent letters to others in December.

313. In referring to T. S. Eliot's allusive and "anthological" *The Waste Land,* published in December 1922 by Horace Liveright, RF quotes (doubly) an anonymous song included in W. S. Braithwaite's *Book of Elizabethan Verse* as "The Gift" (see note 170, page 83): "Thus fain would I have had this pretty thing / To give unto my Lady; / I said no harm, nor I meant no harm, / But as pretty a thing as may be." That the song is un-attributable—and from the Elizabethan period—may enhance the joke, given how many poems, songs, and plays dating to the sixteenth and seventeenth centuries Eliot borrows from and echoes. In a July 9, 1922 letter, written months before the poem appeared, Ezra Pound called *The Waste Land* "the justification of the 'movement,' of our modern experiment, since 1900"—a movement of which RF had been considered a signal part when he published *NB* in 1914. Pound reviewed *NB* in terms he otherwise reserved (at the time) for James Joyce's *Dubliners* and for D. H. Lawrence. No more. The following letter to Burton Rascoe—in which the refrain here used recurs four times—is but the first in a series of documents registering RF's difficult (and often vexed) relation to the emergent "high modernism." As for RF's "modernism," Randall Jarrell sought to set the record straight in *Poetry & the Age* (New York: Knopf, 1953), as did Lionel Trilling in a speech delivered at RF's 85th birthday dinner in 1959 (see *LY,* 266–269). Richard Poirier has given the matter more sustained attention than anyone, in his *Robert Frost: the Work of Knowing* (New York: Oxford University Press, 1977), "Modernism and its Difficulties" (in *The Renewal of Literature: Emersonian Reflections* [New York: Random House, 1988]), and *Poetry and Pragmatism* (Cambridge, MA: Harvard University Press, 1992).

[To Louis Untermeyer. Date derived from postmark. Enclosed was RF's undated, typed, and signed letter to Burton Rascoe taking umbrage at an article Rascoe had published in the New York Tribune. *That letter follows this one. ALS. LoC.]*

[South Shaftsbury, VT]

[January 20, 1923]

Dear Louis:

Elinor thinks perhaps I ought not to send a letter like this. You judge for us. If you dont think I'll live to be sorry just put it into another envelope and send it along to Burton.

I came home with grippe. Everybody has had it in the house and Irma has had pneumonia—yes. But its all right now.

I ought to let one at Burton. If you'd like the fun of seeing me punch him I'll come down and punch.

Ever thine

R.

[To Burton Rascoe (1892–1957), American journalist, editor, and literary critic. See the headnote to the previous letter. TLS. LoC.]

[South Shaftsbury, VT]

[January 20, 1923]

You little Rascol[314]:

Save yourself trouble by presenting my side of the argument for me, would you? (My attention has just been called to what you have been doing in the Tribune.) Interview me without letting me know I was being interviewed, would you?[315]

---

314. RF intentionally overlays an "l" over the *e* in Rascoe's name.

315. The "interview" RF mentions refers to Burton Rascoe's publication of a conversation the two engaged in during a cocktail party hosted by Lawton Mackall in early January. Published in the *New York Tribune* on January 14, 1923, Rascoe's "Bookman's Day-book" column characterized RF as follows: "Robert Frost in voice and demeanor reminds me much of Sherwood Anderson. He has the same deliberate and ingenuous way of speaking; he is earnest, earthy, humorous, without put-on, very real, likable, genuine. I admire him very much as a person. I regret that I find almost nothing to interest me in his poems. They are deft, they are competent, they are of the soil; but they are not distinctive." Rascoe then summarized RF's opinion of his modern contemporaries:

I saw you resented not having anything to say for yourself the other day, but it never entered my head that you would run right off and take it out on me in print.

I don't believe you did the right thing in using my merest casual talk to make an article of. I shall have to institute inquiries among my newspaper friends to find out. If you did the right thing, well and good; I shall have no more to say. But if you didn't, I shall have a lot to say.

I'm sure you made a platitudinous mess of my talk—and not just wilfully to be smart. I saw the blood was ringing in your ears and you weren't likely to hear me straight if you heard me at all. I don't blame you for that. You were excited at meeting me for the first time.

You seem to think I talked about obscurity, when, to be exact, I didn't once use the word. I never use it. My mistake with the likes of you was not using it to exclude it. It always helps a schoolboy, I find from old experience, if, in telling him what it is I want him to apprehend, I tell him also what it isn't.

The thing I wanted you to apprehend was obscuration as Sir Thomas Browne hath it.[316] Let me try again with you, proceeding this time by example, as is probably safest.

"Frost and I left the party together and went to Grand Central Station, where we talked for half an hour about Ezra Pound, T. S. Eliot, Conrad Aiken, and Amy Lowell. . . . Frost has little sympathy with Eliot's work, but then he wouldn't naturally; his own aesthetic problem is radically different from that of Eliot's. . . . 'I don't like obscurity in poetry,' he told me. 'I don't think a thing has to be obvious before it is said, but it ought to be obvious when it is said. I like to read Eliot because it is fun seeing the way he does things, but I am always glad it is his way and not mine.'"

316. RF appears to be recalling not a remark by Browne but an observation made about him and Sir Kenelm Digby in Samuel Johnson's "Life of Browne" (which also discusses the "obscurity" of Browne's prose style). We thank Mark Scott for the suggestion. Digby was a courtier, diplomat, and author of, among other things, a commentary on Browne's *Religio Medici* that dwelt, with disapproval, on its heterodoxy. Johnson's "Life of Browne" was often reprinted in editions of Browne's writings—for example, in the first volume of the *Works of Thomas Browne,* prepared by Simon Wilkin (1790–1862) and issued numerous times in the late nineteenth and early twentieth centuries. Johnson says of the controversy between Digby and Browne (Browne had answered Digby in the deferential manner peculiar to the day, and was himself then answered in kind): "Of these [Digby's] animadversions, when they were yet not all printed, either officiousness or malice informed Dr. Browne; who wrote to Sir Kenelm, with much softness and ceremony, declaring the unworthiness of his work to engage such notice, the intended privacy of the composition, and the corruptions of the impression [i.e., the unauthorized first edition of *Religio Medici,* upon which Digby had based his 'animad-

Suppose I say: Of all the newspaper men I ever met, you most merely resemble a reporter I once talked with casually on the street just after I had paid ten dollars in court for having punched a mutual friend.[317] I talked to him exactly as I talked to you, without the least suspicion that I was being interviewed. He must have taken sides with the mutual friend, for he ran right off to his office and published everything I had said as nearly as he chose to reproduce it.

There you have what I call obscuration. "I say no harm and I mean no harm," as the poet hath it; but the stupider you are the more meaning you will see where none is intended. The really intelligent will refuse to listen to such old-wives' indirection.

Or again, suppose I say: Just because you have won to a position where you can get even with people, is no reason why you shouldn't perform face forward like a skunk, now is it? I only ask for information.

There you have what I call obscuration. "I say no harm and I mean no harm," but the stupider you are the more meaning you will see where none is intended. The really intelligent will refuse to listen to such old-wives' indirection.[318]

Or to "lay off" you personally for the moment, suppose I say: I learn that someone is bringing out an Anthology of the Best Lines of Modern Poetry. He proposes to run the lines more or less loosely together in a narrative and make them so much his own that anyone using them again will have to enclose them in double quotes, thus:

"'What sayest thou, old barrelful of lies?'"[319]

---

versions']; and received an answer equally genteel and respectful, containing high commendations of the piece, pompous professions of reverence, meek acknowledgments of inability, and anxious apologies for the hastiness of his remarks. The reciprocal civility of authors is one of the most risible scenes in the farce of life. Who would not have thought, that these two luminaries of their age had ceased to endeavour to grow bright by the obscuration of each other?" If RF recalled the context in which *obscuration* is here used, it fits the case: the letter to Rascoe makes a farce of "the reciprocal civility of authors."

317. Lawrance Thompson gives an account of the incident in *EY*, 254–256.

318. Louis Untermeyer cut this paragraph when he printed the letter in *RFLU*.

319. From Chaucer's "The Wife of Bath's Prologue" in *Canterbury Tales*: "And to my fadres folk and his allyes / Thus seistow, olde barrel-ful of lyes" (301–302).

" 'Not worth a breakfast in the cheapest country under the cope.' "[320]

" 'Shall I go on, or have I said enough?' "[321]

These three lines are from Chaucer, Shakespeare, and Milton respectively. Please verify.

There you have what I call obscuration. "I say no harm and I mean no harm," but the stupider you are the more meaning you will see where none is intended. The really intelligent will refuse to listen to such old-wives' indirection.

Or suppose I say: Good sense is plebeian, but scarcely more plebeian than any sense at all. Both will be spurned in aristocratic circles this summer.

There you have what I call obscuration. "I say no harm and I mean no harm," but the stupider you are the more meaning you will see where none is intended. The really intelligent will refuse to listen to such old-wives' indirection.

I thought you made very poor play with what I said about the obvious. The greatly obvious is that which I see the minute it is pointed out and only wonder I didn't see before it was pointed out. But there is a minor kind of obviousness I find very engaging. You illustrate it when, after what passed between us, you hasten to say you like me but don't like my books. You will illustrate it again if, after reading this, you come out and say you like neither me nor my books, or you like my books but not me. Disregard that last: I mustn't be too subtle for you. But aren't you a trifle too obvious here for your own purpose? I am told on every hand that you want to be clever. Obviousness of this kind is almost the antithesis of cleverness. You should have defended your hero's work on one Sunday, and saved your attack on mine for another. You take all the sting out of your criticism by being so obvious in the sense of easy to see through. It won't do me the good you sincerely hoped it would.

---

320. From Shakespeare's *Pericles* 4.6: "How's this? We must take another course with you. If your peevish chastity, which is not worth a breakfast in the cheapest country under the cope, shall undo a whole household, let me be gelded like a spaniel. Come your ways."

321. From Milton's *Comus* (where The Lady addresses Comus):

Shall I go on?
Or have I said enough? To him that dares
Arm his profane tongue with contemptuous words
Against the sun-clad power of Chastity,
Fain would I something say, yet to what end? (lines 779–783)

You are probably right in thinking that much literature has been written to make fun of the reader. This my letter may have been. Do you remember what Webster said or implied about the farmer who hanged himself in a year of plenty because he was denied transportation for his grain?[322]—or what Nemphrekepta [*sic*] said to Anubis?[323]

When my reports are in on your conduct, I may be down to see you again.

I shall be tempted to print this letter some time, I am afraid. I hate to waste it on one reader. Should you decide to print it take no liberties with it. Be sure you print it whole.

Ever yours,

Robert Frost

P. S. Six years to derange less than six hundred lines of mixed verse, you say?[324]

P. S. Nothing human is beneath my notice.[325]

P. S. Why dont you kids do something for Marianne Moore.[326] <u>There</u> is something real of its kind.

P. S.[327]

---

322. See John Webster, *The Duchess of Malfi* (4.2). In listing the madmen her brothers sent to torment the Duchess, her servant names "A farmer, too, an excellent knave in grain, / Mad 'cause he was hindered transportation"—of his grain, as RF indicates. More particularly, he went mad—such is the implication, as Leah Marcus points out in the 2009 Arden edition (London: A and C Black) of the play—owing to "a 1613 proclamation forbidding export in time of scarcity" (272). RF may also echo the Porter in *Macbeth*, 2.3: "Here's a farmer, that hang'd / himself on the expectation of plenty."

323. Anubis is the son of Osiris and Nephthys (whose name RF mistakes). According to one version of the myth, Nephthys got Osiris drunk so as to ensure that *he* would seduce *her*; other versions have Nephthys disguising herself as Isis in order to seduce Osiris. In any case, what Nephthys (to take up RF's joke) "said" would have involved either obfuscation (if we imagine her addressing her son, Anubis); or it would have been calculated to "make fun" of or deceive Osiris (as RF says *Rascoe* believes much literature is written to do).

324. If Rascoe *had* reported that Eliot spent six years writing *The Waste Land,* he was wrong.

325. RF's echoes a line from *Heauton Timorumenos,* by the Roman playwright Terence (circa 185–159 BCE): "*Homo sum, humani nihil a me alienum puto*" ("I am human, and nothing human is alien to me").

326. Marianne Moore's first collection of verse, *Poems,* was published by the Egoist Press in 1921. This is the only postscript not typed but written in.

327. Blank. The joke being, apparently, that this last "P.S." really is *post* script.

[*To Charles Wilbert "Bill" Snow (1884–1977), American poet, educator, and politi-cian. ALS. Wesleyan.*]

South Shaftsbury Vermont

January 21 1923

Dear Mr Snow:

I'm indebted to you for your good opinion of my work and sometime I must try to repay you by going to Middletown to see you;[328] but I'm afraid it can't be this year. I've been kept away from Michigan too much as it is, by engagements I made before I decided to go back to Michigan this year and by sickness in my family.

Keep a warm place for me in your heart and some day you shall entertain me. I shall be on the look out for your book. May it have good luck.[329]

Thanks for having thought of me in the same course with Carl and Vachel.[330]

Sincerely yours

Robert Frost

[*To E. Merrill Root. Date derived from postmark. ALS. ACL.*]

[South Shaftsbury, VT]

[January 22, 1923]

My dear Root:

You were one of my favorite pupils and I shan't be able to forget you even though for reasons of your own you might want me to. We won't go into those reasons except to say, you mustn't let them count too much with you. If you dont want to write and publish poetry you are not to be embarrassed on my account. Take your time about the poetry that I am sure is in you. Keep it to yourself entirely unwritten for all me. You rank as a fellow poet with me in any case.

---

328. Snow was a member of the faculty at Wesleyan, in Middletown, Connecticut. In November–December 1926, RF spent two weeks in residency at Wesleyan; he would read there on a number of occasions subsequently. See his November 23, 1926, letter to Snow.

329. *Maine Coast*, Snow's first volume of poetry, was published by Harcourt, Brace and Company in 1923.

330. Carl Sandburg and Vachel Lindsay; Sandburg was a friend of Snow's and had read at Wesleyan.

And I shall be glad to come and read to your college in Richmond Indiana if you can have me on March 5th or 6th. I could talk a little on New Poetry in addition to reading. Could you pay $100 and my expenses from Chicago?[331]

> With best wishes.
> Sincerely yours
> Robert Frost.

Ann Arbor Mich

1432 Washtenaw Ave is one of my addresses.

[To Louis Untermeyer. Date derived from postmark. ALS. LoC.]

> [South Shaftsbury, VT]
> [January 23, 1923]

Dear Louis:

You and Jean think such wrath ill becomes me. I'm over it now anyway. We wont send the letter to Burton the rat.[332] My grounds for wanting to let him have both fists in succession in the middle of the face are chiefly that he stated me so much worse than I know how to state myself. That is the greatest outrage of small town or big town—misquotation. It flourishes worst it seems among these smart cosmopolites. But never mind.

We did have fun with Under the Tree.[333] Lesley had seen and liked it in MS in Chicago at Mrs Moody's.[334] Highly poetical and entrancingly gauche.

I'm glad you could say for the ambitious Raymond what you did.[335]

> Ever yours
> R.

---

331. A lecture was arranged for March 4, but illness prevented RF from delivering it. See RF to Root, February 26, 1923.

332. See the headnote to RF's January 20, 1923, letter to Untermeyer.

333. *Under the Tree* (New York: B. W. Huebsch, 1922) is a collection of poems by Elizabeth Madox Roberts (1881–1941) that was composed largely during her undergraduate years at the University of Chicago.

334. Harriet Moody.

335. Untermeyer's positive review of Raymond Holden's *Granite and Alabaster* (New York: Macmillan, 1922) appeared in the *New Republic* on January 24, 1923.

[To Dorothy Canfield Fisher (1879–1958), American author, educator, and social activist. Date derived from internal evidence. ALS. Vermont.]

[South Shaftsbury, VT]

[January 28, 1923]

Dear Dorothy:

Wouldn't it be fine if you could come out and John with you.[336] It would be as if we had appointed a meeting place about equally distant from Arlington and South Shaftsbury where it would be no harder for one party to come than the other in this terrible weather.[337]

The Michigan children who put me up to asking you will be delighted.[338] They had some poets last year and for sober relief thought they would have some novelists this. You're as far as I've got for them to date. I broached the subject to Ham Garland[339] last week but oh dear he and his Fink [*sic*] school[340] daughter have combined into a troop, the Garland Family Trapeze and Lightning Change Artists. The daughter actually appears beside her father first as his mother then as his wife and then as his daughter.[341] Could anything be more repulsive to our prejudices against line breeding?[342] The Michigan children can have him but only if they insist.

---

336. Fisher spoke at the University of Michigan in mid-March 1923. "John" is John Redwood Fisher (1883–1959), whom she had married in 1907. It would appear that he did come to Michigan with Dorothy: see RF to John Redwood Fisher, late February, 1923.

337. Arlington (where the Fishers lived) and South Shaftsbury are some ten miles apart.

338. The Whimsies, the undergraduate literary club that adopted RF during his time in Ann Arbor.

339. Hamlin Garland, who spoke at the University of Michigan on May 3, 1923 (*YT*, 591).

340. The Finch School, attended by both of Garland's daughters, was an expensive liberal arts preparatory school located on Manhattan's Upper East Side. It later became Finch College, which closed in 1976.

341. Garland's lecture program in 1922–1923 was titled "Memories of the Middle Border," and drew upon his two autobiographical volumes, *A Son of the Middle Border* (New York: Macmillan, 1917) and *A Daughter of the Middle Border* (New York: Macmillan, 1921); the latter was awarded a Pulitzer Prize in 1922. During the performances Garland's elder daughter, Mary Isabel Garland (1903–1988), would appear in period clothing playing the parts, successively, of her grandmother, Isabelle McLintock, and her mother, Zulime Mauna Taft. See Isabel Garland Lord, *A Summer to Be: A Memoir by the Daughter of Hamlin Garland,* ed. Keith Newlin (Lincoln: University of Nebraska Press, 2010), 21–22.

342. "Line breeding": a term used in poultry farming and animal husbandry for selective breeding, and sometimes for inbreeding.

I've heard that Willa Cather is either out of the country or about to leave it. I wish we could get her. Do you know about her?[343]

I've mislaid your letter and have only a general impression of the dates you proposed in it. Can the question of dates be left open till I go back to Ann on Tuesday?

And now we are right up to the edge of the ticklish question of pay. Novelists I'm afraid are coming higher than poets because their time need never be thrown away. We got Class A poets last year @ $150 flat. All things considered (your Canfield cousins,[344] the glory and us) are you going to let us have you for a couple of hundred?

Sincerely yours
Robert Frost

[To Maurice Firuski. Date derived from postmark. ALS. Jones.]

[South Shaftsbury, VT]
[January 30, 1923]

My dear Firuski:

There has been some misunderstanding about the books.[345] It seems Haines has bought all the books and had them shipped to him at Gloucester. He writes that he is giving them away to the worthy. They are his to do what he likes with; I can't find any fault with that. But I think he will let me have some of them for you when I explain matters more fully to him. Will you please leave the business to me? I should have been disposed to tend to it wholly myself if I had realized that the books had been taken over from Simpkins and Marshall.[346] They are not necessarily for sale now, and we may easily give offense by assuming that they are. Still—I can't really be made to believe there are enough worthy in England to absorb the whole

343. Willa Cather would sail to France in early April 1923. She had been planning to leave some time before but was prevented from doing so by a bout of influenza. Canfield Fisher, as RF knew, was one of Cather's closest confidantes.

344. Unidentified. Canfield Fisher's father, James Hulme Canfield (1847–1909), practiced law in Michigan in the early 1870s.

345. For details, see the notes to RF's September 20, 1922, letter to Haines. See also RF to Firuski, December 22, 1922, and RF to Haines, December 14, 1922. See also later letters to Firuski, during the spring of 1923.

346. Simpkin, Marshall, and Company, the London publisher.

thousand—not at any rate of the very worthy or even the worthy enough. Let me see what I can find out.

Sincerely yours

Robert Frost

Lincoln MacVeagh writes of having been browsing with you.[347] You found him appreciative, I'm sure.

Off tomorrow for Ann Arbor Michigan sure.[348]

[To Louis Untermeyer. Date derived from postmark. At the top of the first page RF has written "Back to Ann," indicating that he had returned to the University of Michigan for the spring semester. Enclosed is an annotated copy of the Monthly Bulletin *of the* Michigan Authors' Association.[349] *ALS. LoC.]*

Back to Ann.

[February 5, 1923]

Dear Louis

It might be a good idea to call the explanatory poems Notes. I'm pretty sure to call the book New Hampshire. The Notes will be The Witch of Coos, The Census-taker, Paul's Wife, Wild Grapes, The Grindstone, The Ax-helve, The Star-splitter, Maple, The Witch of Grafton (praps), The Gold Hesperidee (praps) and anything else I can think of or may write before summer.[350]

---

347. In Firuski's Dunster House Bookshop, in Cambridge.

348. RF returned to Ann Arbor on February 1.

349. RF commented on or emphasized a number of statements in the *Bulletin* (which was written in a hokey, informal style), a few of which are of note. He provides the underscoring and exclamation point here: "Edgar A. Guest's new book of poems 'All That Matters' has had an unexpectedly large sale. Eddy is improving every day.!" Here, too, the underscoring is RF's: "Every member of this Authors' Association should spend at least five hours a day in creative literary work. Are you doing this? . . . Send in your membership application today. Do not wait. Only the weakling hesitates." Finally, beneath the Michigan Authors' Association announcement that he had won a prize from *Poetry* magazine, RF appends a handwritten note: "Became a member by default, i.e. because he didn't appear in time and refuse to become a member. He says no notice was formally served on him of the danger impending."

350. The structure of *NH* may, in part, have been meant to send up the (at times mock) scholarship built into the book edition of T. S. Eliot's *The Waste Land*. Appended to that poem are copious endnotes drawn up by Eliot (at least initially) to bring it to a length suitable for separate publication (the notes do not appear in the text published in *The*

I'll go further and say that I may even bring out a volume of lyrics at the same time and refer to it in New Hampshire as The Star in the Stone-boat. I'm in a larking mood. I'll do almost anything for the sake of contraption.

I'm fearfully glad you've come to an understanding with MacVeagh.[351] I think you two could learn to like each other in a way.

If it isnt too much like fishing, please tell fools like Maynard in your essay on me in what sense of the word many of my poems are praise.[352] He says I never praise anything. Dont seem to contradict him or anyone else, but just point out how my undersaying and litotes is just as high praise in effect as someone's else oversaying hyperbole and superlative. Gee I hate to be so misunderstood.

I'm back out here as you may judge from the fact that last night I entertained a couple of young non-smokers till ten, went out calling till after midnight and read through a novel in MS by Lawrence Conrad between then and six this morning.[353] That takes rank with my fourteen lectures in fourteen days and three hundred lines of blank verse between ten at night and noon the next day.[354] I'm on a tear. Let who will be clever.

Let's see when was your date to come again? I'm wanting to see you. People all speak friendly of you and Jean.

Dial). Whatever the case, *NH* is divided into three parts: the title poem; a section titled "Notes," with fourteen poems, most of them long; and a section titled "Grace Notes," which includes thirty shorter lyrics. Footnotes to the title poem link it to poems and to specific lines in poems elsewhere in the book, often in illuminating ways.

351. Lincoln MacVeagh, RF's editor at Henry Holt and Company. Untermeyer, after publishing a number of volumes with Holt, began to work instead with Harcourt, Brace and Howe after Alfred Harcourt left Holt to establish his new publishing house in 1919.

352. Theodore Maynard writes, in *Our Best Poets: English and American* (Henry Holt, 1922): "Robert Frost's poverty of glamour is . . . to my mind a defect. Allied to it is his feeble capacity for praise. There is about him an absence of exultation and exaltation—the two principal marks of the major poet" (173). Maynard had published an earlier version of his essay on RF in the *New York Tribune* (June 27, 1920). See RF to Braithwaite, September 4, 1920, and RF to Untermeyer, December 28, 1920.

353. Lawrence H. Conrad was a University of Michigan student in whom RF took a special interest. His proletarian novel, *Temper,* was published by Dodd, Mead Publishing Company in 1924. He later published a number of articles on Michigan labor history and books of advice for writers.

354. The lecture series dates to October and November 1922. RF often said that "New Hampshire" was drafted at a single go (according to Lawrance Thompson, on or about July 15, 1922).

I want to send you a copy of The Star-splitter.[355] You don't care for The Gold Hesperidee.[356] There's something the matter with the last of it. And you think it doesn't cut very deep.

I wonder how the Raymond Holden book is coming on.

Do you notice how little light Boston throws on the sky at night. She hasnt had a heavyweight champion since John L. Sullivan. Let's think of all we can to say against her on Vachels [*sic*] account.[357]

Ever yours

Robert

Had a letter from Merrill Root yesterday.[358]

[To Carl Van Doren, editor of Century Magazine, *1922–1925. ALS. Princeton.]*

Ann Arbor Michigan

February 9 1923

Dear Van Doren:

I anticipated from the way you put your finger on Mowing when we talked that it was going to be all right so far at least as concerned the part of my work that was a "plant" or thing placed where it was for most to overlook but for a few to discover.[359] You told me the things I knew about myself all right. But you did better than that: you told me some things I didn't know. One in particular I want to thank you for without feeling constrained to tell you what it was.

---

355. RF sent "The Star-Splitter" to Untermeyer under separate cover on February 12, 1923. Noting some variations from the published version, Untermeyer printed it in *RFLU* (159–161). "The Star-Splitter," illustrated with woodcuts by J. J. Lankes, first appeared in the September 1923 edition of *Century Magazine*. RF's student Earle W. Newton would later publish the poem in a special letterpress edition in 1935.

356. First published in *Farm and Fireside* in September 1921, though not collected until 1936 in RF's sixth book, *AFR*.

357. Vachel Lindsay's "John L. Sullivan, the Strong Boy of Boston," dedicated to Untermeyer and RF, appeared in the *New Republic* on June 16, 1919.

358. For more on Root, see RF to Untermeyer, July 12 and September 18, 1920.

359. "Mowing" is discussed in Van Doren's essay "The Soil of the Puritans," where it is held to epitomize how RF "reaches his magic through the door of actuality." See *Century Magazine*, February 1923, 629–636.

I flatter myself that we go rather well together in an article like that. I mean your method is appropriate to what you have to deal with or what you have to deal with is appropriate to your method. We neither of us go into superlatives or even comparatives. It is our sufficient praise of a thing that we should linger over it at all to describe it. This, we say, is as it is in the first analysis; and a first faint color, an irredescence [sic], shimmers in the white light that smote us. We are stayers to the first analysis and perhaps second. God forbid that we should stay till the last, when the impression like a food taken too many meals in succession breaks up into its ingredients and falls to pieces in the mouth.

I'm so grateful for what you have done for me that I have a mind to ask if you aren't ready now to do something more—buy my Star-splitter (one hundred lines or so about the farmer who having failed at farming, burned his house down for the fire insurance and bought a telescope with what it came to) and if you like it give it the honorable position in your magazine you spoke of. But perhaps you had rather wait awhile.

Thanks again.

Always yours
Robert Frost

[To Thomas Moult (1893–1974), English journalist and poet. From 1922 to 1943 he edited a series of anthologies of the best British and American poems of the year. ALS. NYU.]

Ann Arbor Michigan USA.
February 9 1923

Dear Mr Moult:

I see every reason for being glad to have you use my Witch of Coos in your Anthology and thank you for having noticed it.[360]

Your letter has been a long time on its way to me. I want you to know that I am answering it at once.

Sincerely yours
Robert Frost

---

360. Moult reprinted the poem in his *The Best Poems of 1922* (London: Jonathan Cape, 1923).

[To Louis Untermeyer. Date derived from postmark. Only significant variations from the text of the poem as it appeared in NH are noted. ALS. LoC.]

[Ann Arbor, MI]
[February 12, 1923]

The Star-splitter

"You know Orion always comes up sideways.
Throwing a leg up over our fence of mountains,
And, rising on his hands, he looks in on me
Busy outdoors by lantern light with something
I should have done by daylight and in fact[361]
After the ground has frozen I should have done
Before it froze, and a wind throws[362] *a handful*
Of waste leaves at my smoky lantern chimney
To make fun of my way of doing things,
Or else fun of Orion's having caught me.
Has a man, I should like to ask, no rights
These forces are obliged to pay respect to?"[363]
So Bradford Kimball[364] *mingled reckless talk**
Of heavenly stars and huggermugger farming
Till having failed at huggermugger farming,
He burned his house down for the fire-insurance
And spent the proceeds on a telescope

---

361. "indeed" for "in fact" in *NH*.

362. "gust flings" for "wind throws" in *NH*.

363. Perhaps an echo of a poem in Stephen Crane's *War Is Kind* (New York: Frederick A. Stokes, 1899):

A man said to the universe:
"Sir, I exist!"
"However," replied the universe,
"The fact has not created in me
A sense of obligation."

364. The protagonist's name would be Brad McLaughlin in the published version (see note at the bottom of the poem as sent to Untermeyer).

To satisfy a lifelong curiosity
About our place among the infinities.[365]

"What do you want with one of those blamed things,"
I asked him well beforehand. "Don't you get one!"

"Don't call it blamed; there isn't anything
More blameless in the sense of being less
A weapon in our human fight," he said.
"I'll have one if I sell my farm to buy it."
There where he moved the rocks to plow the ground
And plowed between the rocks he couldnt move,
Few farms changed hands. So rather than spend years
Trying to sell his farm and then perhaps[366] not selling,
He burned the house down for the fire-insurance
And bought a telescope with what it came to.

He had been heard to say a number of times,
"The best thing that we're put here for's to see.
The strongest thing that's given us to see with's
A telescope. Some one in every town
Seems to me owes it to the town to keep one.
In Littleton it may as well be me."
After such loose talk it was no surprise[367]
When he came stumbling in the frozen ruts
One night and shouting "Help my home's on fire!"
Some threw their windows up, and one at one said
"Let them that set the fire put out the fire."
One at another, "Them or else their sons
Or sons' sons to the seventh generation."[368]

---

365. Richard Anthony Proctor's *Our Place among Infinities* (New York: D. Appleton, 1876) was one of RF's most treasured books as a teenager.

366. "perhaps" omitted in *NH*.

367. The next six lines are omitted in *NH*, replaced by the single line "When he did what he did and burned his house down."

368. See Numbers 14:18: "The Lord is longsuffering, and of great mercy, forgiving iniquity and transgression, and by no means clearing the guilty, visiting the iniquity of the fathers upon the children unto the third and fourth generation."

Mean laughter was exchanged between the windows[369]
To let him know we weren't the least imposed on
And he could wait: we'd see to him to-morrow.

But the first thing next morning we reflected
If one by one we counted people out
For the least sin, it wouldn't take us long
To get so we had no one left to live with.
For to be social is to be forgiving.
It wouldn't do to be to [sic] ~~hard on Brad~~[370]
Our thief, the one who does our stealing from us
We don't cut off from coming to church suppers
But what we miss we go to him and ask for.
He always gives it back that is if still
Uneaten unused up[371] *or undisposed of.*
It wouldn't do to be too hard on Brad
About his telescope. Beyond the age
Of being given one's gift for Christmas
He had to take the best way he knew how
To find himself in one. Well, all we said was,
He took a strange thing to be roguish over.

Some sympathy was wasted on the house
A good old-timer dating back along.
But a house isnt sentient. The house
Didnt feel anything. And if it did
Why not regard it as a sacrifice
An old-fashioned sacrifice by fire,
Instead of a new fashioned one at auction.[372]

One may be a good man though a bad farmer.[373]
Out of a house and so out of a farm
At one stroke (of a match) Brad joined the railroad

---

369. In place of "was exchanged between the windows," *NH* has "went about the town that day."

370. This line was not restored.

371. In *NH*, "unworn out" replaced "unused up."

372. See Genesis 8:20: "And Noah builded an altar unto the Lord; and took of every clean beast, and of every clean fowl, and offered burnt offerings on the altar."

373. Line omitted in *NH*.

As under ticket agent for a living[374]
Where his job when he wasnt selling tickets
Was setting out up track and down, not plants
As on a farm, but planets, evening stars
That varied in their hue from red to green[375]
According to the safety or unsafety.

He got a glass lens[376] *for six hundred dollars.*
His new job gave him leisure for star-gazing.
Often he bid me come and have a look
Up the ~~black~~ *brass barrel, velvet black inside,*
At a star quaking in the other end.
I recollect a night of broken clouds
And underfoot snow melted down to ice
And melting further in the wind to mud.[377]
We spread our two legs as we spread its three,
Pointed our thoughts the way we pointed it
And standing at our leisure till the day broke
Said some of the best things we ever said.[378]
That telescope was christened the Star-splitter
Because it didn't do a thing but split
A star in two or three the way you split
A globule of quicksilver in your hand
With one stroke of the finger, s~~pit, spat, spot!!~~*[379]
It's a star splitter if there ever was one

---

374. In *NH* this and the preceding line are replaced by:

At one stroke (of a match), Brad had to turn
To earn a living on the Concord railroad,
As under-ticket agent at a station.

375. RF refers to astronomical scintillation, caused by the refraction of light through the atmosphere so that stars appear to twinkle and change color.

376. "glass lens" becomes "good glass" in *NH*.

377. In *NH* a line is added here: "Bradford and I had at the telescope".

378. In *NH* RF added a note: "Cf. p21, 'A Star in a Stone-Boat;' and p. 73, 'I Will Sing You One-O.'"

379. The canceled "spit, spat, spot!" becomes "in the middle" in *NH*. See "Saliva," in *The Encyclopedia of Superstitions, Folklore, and the Occult Sciences of the World* (Chicago: J. H. Yewdale and Sons, 1903): "Boys out bird-nesting in Salem, Mass., years ago, would spit in the palm of one hand and then strike the saliva a quick blow with the forefinger, saying,

And ought to do some good if splitting stars
'Sa thing to be compared to splitting wood.

But after all, as Brad himself would say,[380]
Do we know any better where we are
And how it stands between the night tonight
And a man with a smoky lantern chimney,
How different from the way it ever stood?
I mean do we know for all our looking?[381]

*Subject to change without notice. Probably the name will be Brad McLaughlin.

Robert Frost

   The Witch of Grafton was published in The Nation a year or so ago.[382] I havent a copy of it on earth.

[To E. Merrill Root. TG. ACL.]

[Ann Arbor, MI]
[February 26, 1923]

E. MERRILL ROOT

HAVE BEEN SERIOUSLY ILL BETTER POSTPONE LECTURE WAIT FOR LETTER[383]

ROBERT FROST

'Spit, spat, spot, / Tell me where the bird's nest is'" (312). RF, of course, spent much of his boyhood after 1885 in eastern Massachusetts. The meaning of the asterisk is not clear.

   380. In *NH* this line is replaced by "We've looked and looked, but after all where are we?"

   381. The final line is omitted from *NH*.

   382. "The Pauper Witch of Grafton" appeared in *The Nation*, April 13, 1921.

   383. The lecture had been slated for March 4 at Earlham College in Richmond, Indiana, where Root then taught. See also RF to Root, March 23, 1923.

[*To John Redwood Fisher (1883–1959), Vermont educator, the husband of Dorothy Canfield Fisher. Date derived from internal evidence. ALS. Vermont.*]

[Ann Arbor, MI]

[late February 1923]

Dear John:

I'm glad you are coming along,[384] though I haven't decided what to do about it yet. I wish I could get a court uncovered for us to show each other up on to these hunkses the professors.[385] I meant "off" not "up." We'll have to leave a good deal to the inspiration of the moment. We can always talk and walk. We can go and look at President Burton who just missed the Senatorial toga by less than a mile lately.[386] Such we are and unto such do we have entree through the Muses. But more nonsense anon when you arrive.

I sent Dorothy a subject for her talk because she asked for one. I wish she'd choose her own and <u>wire</u> me at once a good catchy title for it for the Sunday papers.

Carol has a new incubator and a new 35-dollar rooster and I'm ordering two or three hundred apple trees to stick peas with.[387] What's your brag?

Don't be scared by my talk of entertainment. If I do entertain you it will be so's you'll never know it.

Ever yours

Robert Frost

---

384. Fisher accompanied his wife to Ann Arbor, where she delivered a lecture (arranged by RF) in mid-March 1923.

385. RF evidently enjoyed pitting himself in tennis against Fisher, *sportif* and almost a decade RF's junior. See RF to Dorothy Canfield Fisher, circa August 30, 1926.

386. Marion LeRoy Burton had been one of a number of Michigan worthies canvassed to replace Truman Handy Newberry (1864–1945), who in November 1922 had been forced to resign from the U.S. Senate on suspicion of electoral corruption. Newberry's successor, James J. Couzens (1872–1936), was announced on November 29, 1922.

387. Prunings from apple trees are a common source of pea sticks (plant supports). On the $35 rooster, see *YT*, 185–186, and 581.

[To Witter Bynner. Date derived from postmark. ALS. Harvard.]

[Ann Arbor, MI]
[February 27, 1923]

Dear Bynner:

I dont know exactly where you are, and having let you get lost, I don't deserve to find you. All the same I am going to hope to find you with this. Somebody with a capital S will perhaps help me.[388]

Are you, for the admiration you know we bear your work, coming to see us again this year? You remember your promise to my wife and me personally as well as to the youngsters in the University.[389] You would lecture and read of course but the main thing is that you would give me a chance to express a friendship that just because I dont or wont write letters you may have been lead [sic] to suspect me of not feeling.

The time would be the middle of April.

Ever yours
Robert Frost

I wish you would telegraph, collect, whether or not you'll think of it and what it will cost the Whimsies to bring you.[390]

[To Witter Bynner. Date derived from internal evidence. ALS. Harvard.]

[Ann Arbor, MI]
[March 1923]

Dear Witter:

I begin to think there is really such a thing as badness and my not having written you a word all this year is it. Your telegram is terrible in the way it brings in your relief at having heard from me at last. I'm a tender-hearted person: it agitates me as much to give relief as to give pain. To have given both in the same case is almost too much for me.

---

388. The letter was addressed to Bynner first at "Sunmount, Santa Fe," and then, with "Sunmount" crossed out, to "College St., Santa Fe."

389. In early February 1922, Bynner had visited the Frosts and met with students in Ann Arbor. See RF to Bynner, February 20, 1922. He did not return in 1923 for a reading.

390. RF often interceded to help the Whimsies meet their budget.

I can't take your answer as final. You have now an additional reason for coming to see us, namely, to show forgiveness. You say you have a bad throat, the same thing I have been in bed with four times for a total of six weeks this winter. I got it first down among the Ku Klux in Texas and barely got back alive.[391] But we'll be out of these woods by April.[392] At least I hope so. I hope you are better already. Your having no fever is an advantage. You can name your own time for coming. Only make it this year when I can share you with the young Ann Arboreals. Another year I shall be in Vermont.[393]

> Please.
> Always yours
> R.F.

[To Harold Goddard Rugg. Date derived from internal evidence. ALS. DCL.]

> [Ann Arbor, MI]
> [March 1923]

My dear Rugg:

Will you tell me where on the enclosed you want my name. I don't find any natural place—unless it is at the end of "Going for Water."

I wonder if you know Miss Monroe is just getting out a new edition of her anthology about fifty percent larger than the old one.[394] I thought you might like to wait for that.

---

391. RF had given five readings in Texas in autumn 1922, during an election season that would put Klausmen in the majority in the state legislature.

392. With perhaps a pun on the city's name. The Frosts left Ann Arbor for South Shaftsbury in early April (only to return a month later to wind up their affairs).

393. Though he was unaware at this date that an offer would be made, in June RF accepted a position at Amherst College (again) for the 1923–1924 academic year.

394. "Going for Water" appeared first in *ABW*, but the reference here is to its placement in Harriet Monroe's *The New Poetry: An Anthology* (New York: Macmillan, 1917), which also reprinted "Mending Wall," "After Apple-Picking," "My November Guest," "Mowing," "Storm Fear," and "The Code" (the last with the subtitle, "Heroics," it originally bore when Monroe printed it in *Poetry* in February 1914). In April 1923, Monroe issued an enlarged second edition of book, *The New Poetry: An Anthology of Twentieth-Century Verse in English* (New York: Macmillan). At more than six hundred pages, the 1923 volume would be twice the size of the original, not 50 percent larger, as RF suggests.

Yes, I shall be back in Vermont by the middle of June. I'm only here for the year you know.[395]

I expected you to look in on us last summer. We chased each other in circles. I was at Hanover when you werent there and at Willoughby when you weren't there and probably you were at South Shaftsbury when I wasn't there.[396] Hope to see you another summer.

Always yours friendly
Robert Frost

[*To Ridgely Torrence. Dated from internal evidence. ALS. Princeton.*]

Ann Arbor Mich
March [1923]

Dear Ridgley [*sic*]:

Would you care for this one? It would have to be printed in late April or early May—to be in season.[397]

The way you treated Stopping by Woods on a Snowy Etc made a lot of people think they liked it.[398]

With wishes to see you for another talk.

Ever yours
Robert Frost

---

395. RF's second appointment at the University of Michigan (1922–1923) was for one year, like his first (1921–1922). After his year back at Amherst (1923–1924), he would work at Michigan again, under different terms, and for the last time, during the 1925–1926 academic year.

396. During August 1922, with Carol, Lesley, Marjorie, and Marjorie's friend Lillian LaBatt (later Carol's wife), RF departed South Shaftsbury to hike the Long Trail in Vermont, taking him up near Lake Willoughby. After this he and his wife, Elinor, went via Littleton, New Hampshire, to Franconia (some ninety miles north of Hanover), where he spent September. Rugg often went to Lake Willoughby to search for ferns. He was an avid botanist, as was RF.

397. "Our Singing Strength," first published in the *New Republic* on May 2, 1923, and subsequently in *NH*. The poem's first line reads, "It snowed in spring on earth so dry and warm."

398. The poem appeared in the *New Republic* on March 7, 1923. Most poems printed in the *New Republic* at the time were simply laid into a column of prose. But "Stopping by Woods on a Snowy Evening" was set apart, with "Moon Rider" by William Rose Benét (a horse-and-snow poem of a different color), in a section headed "Two Winter Poems" that occupied the better part of a page.

[*To Louis Untermeyer. TG. LoC.*]

ANN ARBOR MICH

1923 MAR 15

LOUIS UNTERMEYER

HOTEL PFISTER[399]

MILWAUKEE WIS

COME ON DONT STAND TALKING ABOUT IT FRIDAY NINE THIRTY

ROBERT FROST.

[*To Lincoln MacVeagh. Date derived from internal evidence. ALS. Jones.*]

[Ann Arbor, MI]
[March 16, 1923]

Dear MacVeagh:

I should think your letter made it all right. Aint I the bother? I don't really suppose it matters a damn what people mistake the book for. A book's a book.[400]

My purpose holds (thus far) to have New Hampshire with Notes (and perhaps Grace Notes) this fall. How soon will you want to begin to announce it and when will you have to have the manuscript?

Mrs Bromley asks me timidly if I would mind naming my ten favorite books.[401] They are [the] first ten books of the Bible especially Leviticus and Numbers. But you mustn't tell her so for fear of shocking the lady in her. Or is she like the fellow I heard of who told a girl she couldn't shock him; she might disgust him?

An end of this Ann Arboreal life soon.[402]

---

399. The Pfister Hotel in Milwaukee, Wisconsin, built in 1893 by Guido and Charles Pfister, was one of the first fully electrified hotels in the nation.

400. *The Selected Poems of Robert Frost*, published simultaneously in New York and London on March 15, 1923. RF had initially entertained doubts as to whether it was the right time to issue a selection of his poetry. See RF to MacVeagh, circa December 8, 1922.

401. Dorothy Dunbar Bromley. See also note 72, page 503.

402. RF returned to South Shaftsbury on April 11, and then again, after one more visit to Ann Arbor, in June.

Busy times on the farm at home from what we hear.
Best wishes.

Ever yours

Robert Frost

Ridgley [*sic*] Torrence did the hansome [*sic*] thing by the little poem.[403]
Louis U. is looking in on us for over Saturday.

We had a great talk with Walker. I wish he had stayed longer. Remember
me to him.[404]

*[To Alfred Harcourt (1881–1954), publisher and a cofounder of Harcourt, Brace and
Howe. The text is transcribed from YT (224–225). Lawrance Thompson states (YT,
591) that he was granted access to it, presumably in the early to mid-1960s, through the
offices of Charles Allan Madison, an executive at Henry Holt and Company from 1924–
1962. No additional record of this letter exists, and no correspondence to or from RF is
currently believed to be in the Houghton Mifflin Harcourt archives.]*

[Ann Arbor, MI]

[March 23, 1923]

[. . .] Your Louis Untermeyer (and mine) has just been here generously
talking about everybody's poetry but his own and it would be no more than
poetic justice if I bought some of his own and distributed it where it would
do the most good among the Ann Arboreals.[405] So if you will please, have sent
me six copies of Roast Leviathan and the bill.[406]

I might have ordered these of your business department, but I wanted the
chance to say hello to you personally and tell the farmer in you that I am this
year setting out four hundred apple trees against my old age and am otherwise disporting myself on the land.[407]

---

403. See RF's previous letter to Torrence (March 1923). In a note penciled in the
margin, MacVeagh adds: "[RF read 'Stopping by Woods'] to me in MS in my apartment
on Waverly Place."

404. Stanley W. Walker, whom MacVeagh identifies in a marginal note as "a salesman at
Holt." In fact, Walker was head of sales.

405. RF invited Louis Untermeyer to deliver a second lecture at the University of
Michigan in March 1923 (the first had been in April 1922).

406. Untermeyer's latest collection, *Roast Leviathan,* had been published by Harcourt,
Brace and Company in January 1923.

407. Harcourt had been born on a fruit farm in Lloyd, New York, that had been
bought by his grandfather Jacob Elting in 1839. On RF's plans for an apple orchard in

Also I ought to say a word about Dorothy Canfield another of your first-string putters of it across.[408] She recently made a speech here that will stand as a record for lovely till she herself surpasses it.[409] She ought to be made to write it down and a whole book full like it. There is something she gives in such a talk that she has never yet been able to get into a book. It was an unpretentious wonder. [. . .]

[To E. Merrill Root. Date derived from postmark. ALS. ACL.]

[Ann Arbor, MI]
[March 23, 1923]

Dear Root

I'm still wobbling from my late influenza.[410] Both my wife and I think I ought to put off further lecturing as long as I can. What should you say to waiting for me till next fall or early winter?[411] I know of others out this way who will probably want me then and take you all together I should think I might make up a respectable little tour in your neighborhood. I'm awfully sorry about now. But I've had a low-down bad winter and you must forgive me. Tell me you do.

Always yours
Robert Frost

South Shaftsbury (and the scaling up of his ambitions in that line), see RF to John Redwood Fisher, late February 1923.

408. Dorothy Canfield Fisher was, like Untermeyer, on the Harcourt, Brace and Company list. *Rough-Hewn* had been published in 1922 and *Raw Material* would appear in 1923.

409. On the arrangement of this visit to Ann Arbor, see RF to Dorothy Canfield Fisher, January 28, 1923. For the lecture, see RF to Elliott, October 15, 1924.

410. RF suffered a serious bout of influenza in December 1922 that kept him confined to bed for weeks; several relapses followed in the coming months.

411. Root taught at Earlham College in Richmond, Indiana, and had asked RF to lecture there. RF gave readings at the University of Michigan on May 29 and May 31, though not at Earlham; his acceptance of a new post at Amherst in the fall of 1923 kept him away from the Midwest until March 1924.

[To Wilbur L. Cross (editor of the Yale Review*). Dated from internal evidence. "Apr 1923" is written in at the top right, likely by Cross. This suggests that the letter was written prior to April 11 because on that day RF returned to South Shaftsbury (see his second postscript). ALS. Yale.]*

[Ann Arbor, MI]

[circa April 2, 1923]

Dear Mr Cross:

These are instead of me. I should like to drop in on you myself. But fate keeps me rattling around in the interior this year.

Be good to the poems. At least they are two things: they are regular verse and they are by a hand practiced in regular verse. Some of the stuff you have had was in free verse, which is bad, and some of it was in regular verse by a hand practiced in free verse which is worse. It's a funny world, as Edward Thomas and I got so we would say almost simultaneously once in so often. But these and other matters may be left for when we meet.

I shall have a long poem for you one of these days. The only long poem I have now is for no magazine: it is for my book which shall be called New Hampshire. I may be tempted to show it to you when I'm sure of it, but not for publication. It's a lark of mine.[412]

Thanks for your kind letter and best wishes to you.

Sincerely yours

Robert Frost.

PS If you like the poems and decide to keep any of them, I hope it may be for your June number.

Order
Nature's First Green
To Earthward
I Will Sing You One-O.[413]

PS I shall find the Review at South Shaftsbury Vermont when I go home next week. Thanks for that.

---

412. The title poem of the new book. See RF to John Erskine, circa December 1, 1923, where "New Hampshire" is described as "a lark . . . with a leg band."

413. All of these poems were published in the *Yale Review* in October 1923 ("Nature's First Green" under its familiar title, "Nothing Gold Can Stay").

[*To Maurice Firuski. ALS. Jones.*]

Ann Arbor Mich

April 2 1923

Dear Firuski

Don't blame me entirely for all the bother you are having over these books.[414] And if the bother is too much for your nerves just say so and end it. Haines now asks me to say definitely from you what you are giving us for the books over and above the price of the sheets the binding and importation. Suppose we agree on some price apiece for A Boys Will and North of Boston separately. I was so far out of my estimate of the number left that the agreement we arrived at means nothing now.

I'll have to have a little talk with Conrad, the sinner. Stick to the original five says he.[415] The original five were Conrad Aiken J. G. Fletcher E. A. Robinson and R. Frost—those four and no more. It puts a new face on the business when they become Conrad Aiken, Wallace Stevens, Alfred Kreymborg, J. G. Fletcher, and R. Frost, just as it does on the other business when the disparity between A Boys Will and North of Boston grows so over night.[416] But Conrad is a good boy. I must tell him what terribly nice things Louis has to my knowledge been saying about him lately. It is necessary to have a heart even on the Supreme Bench.

I've just heard of an artist in the art dept. here who has been warned not to try to sell any of his own pictures in the state on account of the general objection among manufacturers and business houses to having to compete in the open market with prison labor.[417] Dont tell any one till I get back to Vermont.

Ever yours

Robert Frost

---

414. Unsold copies of the David Nutt (London) first editions of *ABW* and *NB*. For details, see the notes to RF's September 20, 1922, letter to Haines.

415. Again, for *New Leaves*, a periodical that, in the end, came to nothing. See other letters to Firuski dating to winter and spring 1923.

416. See RF to Firuski, December 22, 1922: contrary to RF's hopes, copies and unbound sheets of *ABW* outnumbered considerably those of *NB*.

417. It is unclear whether the joke actually refers to anyone at Michigan, though RF did know some of the faculty in the Department of Architecture and Design through his friendships with Leon Makielski (1885–1974) and Jean Paul Slusser (1886–1981), both of whom taught in the program. See RF to Slusser, September 19, 1927, and RF to Makielski, July 8, 1922.

[To Sylvester Baxter (1850–1927), a Boston-based newspaper writer and urban planner who also wrote and published poetry. Transcribed from the New England Quarterly *36, no. 2 (June 1963): 241–249, where the letter is quoted, apparently in full, by R. C. Townsend in an essay entitled "In Defense of Form: A Letter from Robert Frost to Sylvester Baxter, 1923." Townsend noted at the time that the letter was in the possession of the family of Owen D. Young. Our efforts to locate the letter have been unsuccessful. Townsend does not date the letter beyond saying it was written about a month after "Stopping by Woods" appeared in the* New Republic *(on March 7, 1923).]*

[Ann Arbor, MI]

[circa April 7, 1923]

Dear Sylvester:

I'm surprised at you that you should be the one of all my poetical friends to miss the reason for the repetend in Stopping by Woods. There should be two reasons one of meaning and one of form. You get the first and fail of the second. What the repetend does internally you come very near: what it does externally is save me from a third line promising another stanza. If the third line had been dead in all the other stanzas your judgement would be correct. A dead line in the last stanza alone would have been a flaw. I considered for a moment four of a kind in the last stanza but that would have made five including the third in the stanza before it. I considered for a moment winding up with a three line stanza. The repetend was the only logical way to end such a poem. I am afraid you have hurt your nice sense of form by writing too much free verse lately. Why don't you do your outcast Christmas tree in tight tight regular verse?—And let me see it.[418]

Bill Benét's is a terrible example of really first rate poetical words and lines that come to nothing in the aggregate. In detail he is a little like De la Mare (in this particular poem). But with De la Mare the whole poem is always the thing. He is never just a texture.

---

418. Baxter published only one volume of poetry, *The Unseen House* (Boston: The Four Seas, 1917). No poem to do with a Christmas tree appears in it; presumably RF is referring to a poem sent to him in manuscript. In his preface to *The Unseen House*, Baxter defends "free verse," the principles of which he regards as poorly understood. The poems in the volume range from several in more or less conventional form (with regular stanzas and rhyme), to free verse proper, to prose poetry.

Winnifred Wells' [*sic*] poem is good.[419]

You and Connick will be welcome. I was reminded of Connick by some beautiful windows of his I saw in Columbia Missouri early in the winter. Can you give me his address? I'd like to write him a line.[420]

Take my word for it you wont often look on as flawless a piece of work as Stopping by Woods. It seems to me you show little faith not to believe that I could have wound up the poem in any way I thought best. But I forgive you.

Ever yours

Robert Frost

I stood the Texax [sic] trip and twelve lectures rotten and have been sick as a result of it all winter. I've had flu on flu. Hope you are flourishing.

---

419. William Rose Benét's "Moon Rider" and Winifred Welles's "Cloth-of-Gold" appeared in the March 7 issue of *The New Republic* that printed "Stopping by Woods."

420. The "Texax" trip, as RF calls it in his postscript, took him to a number of cities in the South in November 1922. An additional engagement in Missouri followed before RF returned to Ann Arbor, as the reference to the windows he saw in Columbia, Missouri (where he read on November 18), indicates. Charles Jay Connick was an artist whose work in stained glass RF admired. As it happens, Connick later produced a stained-glass medallion based on a theme in "Stopping by Woods."

A manuscript draft of "Stopping by Woods on a Snowy Evening" reveals
the fond exaggeration in Frost's later recollections of its composition: "It
was written in a few minutes without any strain."[421]

Courtesy of The Jones Library, Inc., Amherst, Massachusetts.

---

421. Our transcription of the document follows. Cancelled words and phrases are
given in brackets:

[The steaming horses think it queer]
[To]

[To Maurice Firuski. Date derived from postmark. ALS. Jones.]

South Shaftsbury Vermont

[April 11, 1923]

Dear Firuski

All that is needed to prevent misunderstanding is an explicit offer of so much a copy for North of Boston and A Boy's Will over and above price of sheets, binding, packing, shipping and customs dues. Make it to Haines and me jointly. I want him to know exactly what there is to divide and then leave it to him to say where I come in. We have to be all the more careful with friends. The two hundred you sent me I still hold as a check awaiting a final arrangement.[422] Lets finish it up and start the books across.

Always yours

Robert Frost

The [horse] little [mare?]* horse [would] [begins to] must think it queer
[We] To stop without a farmhouse near
Between [a forest and a lake] the woods and frozen lake
The darkest evening of the year

[He] She gives her {his}** harness bells a shake
To ask if there is some mistake
The only other sounds the sweep
Of easy wind and [fall of] downy flake.

The woods are lovely dark and deep
But I have promises to keep
[That bid me give the reins a shake]
[That bid me on. And there are miles]
And miles to go before I sleep
And miles to go before I sleep

---

* William Logan has (very tentatively) suggested that "mare" is here struck out (a suggestion the abandoned "she" and "her" may support).

** "his" was added in a later draft/fair copy (as must have been what became the first stanza).

422. For discussion of the check and payment in question, see also RF to Haines, December 14, 1922, and RF to Firuski, December 22, 1922, and April 2, 1923. For details about the entire transaction, see the notes to RF's September 20, 1922, letter to Haines.

[*To Lincoln MacVeagh. ALS. Alger.*]

South Shaftsbury Vt
April 11 1923

Dear MacVeagh:

No contract have I seen.[423] Are you sure you sent one? I'll sign anything you send.

Home again with the kids.[424]

I suppose I am now expected to go ahead with New Hampshire.

Always yours
Robert Frost

You were going to send me a few of the Selected Poems. Is there another copy of the first to be had for Baylor College in Texas?[425]

[*To Eunice Tietjens (1884–1944), American poet, novelist, journalist, and editor. In 1913, she became associate editor at* Poetry. *The letter is undated, but internal evidence suggests the spring of 1923. ALS. Newberry.*]

[South Shaftsbury, VT]
[circa April 15, 1923]

My dear Eunice Tietjens:

I have had to give you this as I remember it. I cant lay hands on a copy of it high or low in the time you allow me.[426] As I say I wrote it in about 1895 when I was twenty. The Youth's Companion printed it once. There are two others earlier in A Boy's Will which you are welcome to, should you prefer them,

---

423. Presumably for *NH*.

424. RF had just returned to South Shaftsbury from Ann Arbor, where he had been since February 1.

425. On November 16, 1922, RF gave a reading at Baylor University, in Waco, Texas, at the invitation of A. J. Armstrong. That visit gave rise to the request.

426. This fact may date and place the letter to RF's time in South Shaftsbury in the spring of 1923, from April 11 to May 15, during the first few weeks of which he was confined to the house by a serious bout of influenza. Had he been in Ann Arbor he might readily enough have obtained (either himself or through a student or colleague) a copy of *The Youth's Companion,* the item in question, from the university's library.

Now Close the Windows (1893) and My Butterfly (1892).[427] Deal with me as you see fit.[428]

With best wishes for your term in office, I'm

> Sincerely yours
> Robert Frost

My regards to Miss Strobel.[429]

[*To Wilbur L. Cross (editor of the* Yale Review). *Date derived from internal evidence. ALS. Yale.*]

> [South Shaftsbury, VT]
> [circa April 20, 1923]

Dear Mr Cross

In asking you to print my poems in the June Review I suspect I was like you when you said the novel was getting thinner and thinner:[430] I had no reasons at the time of writing. I doubt if I would be as good as you at thinking

---

427. "My Butterfly" was actually composed in 1893–1894.

428. The August 1923 issue of *Poetry*, devoted to "the poetry of youth," was divided into two sections, youthful poetry by established poets and poems by youthful poets. Tietjens, acting as editor, wrote a prose work titled "Apologia" that contrasted the situation of poets in America before and after the "dramatic revival" coincident with the founding of *Poetry* in 1912. She had solicited poems from established poets such as Lindsay, RF, Masters, Teasdale, Lowell, and Robinson. Tietjens chose RF's "The Flower Boat," which had first appeared in *The Youth's Companion* on May 20, 1909 (fourteen years, RF reports, after it was written). RF later collected it in his 1928 volume, *WRB*, adding the note "Very early."

429. A poet, fiction writer, and critic, Marion Strobel (1895–1967) was an associate editor of *Poetry* between 1920 and 1925.

430. See the conclusion to Cross's *Development of the English Novel*. First published in 1899 (New York: Macmillan), the book was frequently reissued and became a standard work in the field. Cross writes: "What is to happen in the first quarter of the twentieth century, it would be most hazardous to prophesy. Besides tearing down and building anew the internal structure of the novel, the contemporary novelists would seem also to have modified permanently its outer form. Hardy has cut the three-volume novel down to one volume. The short-story has found its own beautiful art; but it can never hope to become a universal type, for it gives scant room. Kipling, who has experimented all the way from three to three hundred pages, is bringing into fashion a novel of from twenty-five to fifty pages. . . . To the novel of the future, Kipling, who is gathering to himself present-day tendencies, may be pointing the way" (293–294).

up reasons after the fact; so I won't try. We'll have the poems in in the fall just ahead of the book they'll be in: and thanks for letting them in at all.[431]

You shall see New Hampshire before long—I mean the poetic counterfeit of New Hampshire. For the moment I'm too busy roughing out the new to be polishing off the old.

That was a good magazine, every article of it.

Sincerely yours
Robert Frost

[To Richard Wedge Morin (1902–1988), then a student at Dartmouth (class of 1924). He was editor of the Dartmouth Bema, *an arts magazine that ran in the mid-1920s. ALS. DCL.]*

South Shaftsbury Vt
April 28 1923

Dear Mr Morin:

Do you mean serious poetry? You know I have no prose to print, serious or unserious.[432]

Sincerely yours
Robert Frost

[To Sidney Cox. Date derived from postmark. ALS. DCL.]

[South Shaftsbury, VT]
[April 30, 1923]

Dear Sidney:

I'm just returning to an interest in life after my fifth fluenza in one winter. What's come over me? Some one suggests that it may be I write too much poetry about snow and ice. [433] I am pretty much inclined to harp on those strings.

---

431. See RF to Cross, circa April 2, 1923.

432. RF subsequently sent Morin "The Birthplace," which he published in the *Dartmouth Bema* for June 1923. See RF to Morin, May 12, 1923.

433. RF refers again to Theodore Maynard's depiction of his "frostiness" in *Our Best Poets: English and American.* See RF to Untermeyer, February 5, 1923.

It's so long since I said what I would do with you next fall that I shall have to ask you to refresh my memory of it.[434] I don't see why I shouldn't give a reading or two to the outside world. Had I said anything to lead you to suppose that I wouldn't? But tell me exactly what the plan was as to dates duration and money.

I've been fairly absent from Ann Arbor this year and not half the sensation in the Michigan papers I was last year. I don't know what I think of the berth now that I'm about to rub my eyes and climb out of it. The sleeping in it was only so-so.

Your old friend spoke to the author's taste when he said what he said about Stopping by Woods. The more I think of it the surer I am of that there poem.

A woman stopped at our door here in South Shaftsbury last week who went to school to you and me in Plymouth.[435] I cant say her name as it then was for the life of me. But I remembered her well. Her father was a house painter in Plymouth and a great fox hunter on Sundays.

An article in the Bookman accuses me, Im told, of having few intimate friends.[436] All the better for the few. Dont you say so. As one of the few you are in a position to judge. Over how much territory would I have to spread myself to escape the charge of being a cold Yankee?[437]

Ever yours

Robert Frost

434. See RF to Cox, October 9, 1922.

435. Helen Fonta Lougee. Her father, Frank W. Lougee, was a house painter who owned a paint shop in Plymouth when the Frosts lived there. She had studied with both RF and Cox, who met in Plymouth in 1911. RF was then teaching at the Plymouth Normal School; Cox, at Plymouth High School (*RFSC*, 4).

436. See John Farrar, "The Literary Spotlight XIX: Robert Frost," *The Bookman*, May 1923: 304–307. RF seems at this date not to have read the offending article, although he soon would do so (see RF to Untermeyer, May 2, 1923). When he saw it, he was all the more chagrined to discover counted amongst his few "close friends" "the blunt souled Wilfrid Wilson Gibson," with whom he had had a serious falling-out in 1914 (for details see *LRF-1*, 274–275; see also *EY*, 467–468).

437. In the *Bookman* piece Farrar writes that RF "spent most of his life where thermometers remain near and often below zero for three months of each year."

[To Marion Elza Dodd, proprietor of the Hampshire Bookshop in Northampton, Massachusetts. ALS. ACL.]

South Shaftsbury Vermont
April 30 1923

Dear Miss Dodd:

I have a reason for wanting to ask a great favor of you. And the reason is that within a couple of years the family of us and particularly two of my daughters mean to open a book store somewhere in New York State (possibly at Albany which is near us here) on somewhat the same lines as yours if not nearly as large.[438] Anyone might have predicted from my enthusiasm for what you were doing (equal in importance to the work of the department of English in Smith College) that any day I might be tempted to go and do likewise[439] or if I couldn't do it myself, get someone else to do it for me. It is the kind of thing I delight to look on at if I can't actually take part in it. You're not to infer from this, however, that our store will be my idea and enterprise and somebody's else hard work. As a matter of fact it is almost entirely the idea of the two daughters I speak of and will have to be their hard work.

Now for the favor which you may have seen coming. I wanted to ask if before they entered on this considerable undertaking, you wouldn't give one of them, Lesley, the elder, a job in your store for six months or a year to learn book selling under you.[440] You have met Lesley, but may have forgotten her. She is twenty-three, inured to all sorts of college society and at once bookish and a girl of action. She wouldn't expect more than enough to pay for her board and lodging and, if you were doubtful about having enough for her to do to earn that much would of course take less. The apprenticeship and not the pay is the object. You'd never find her in the way.

With best wishes, I'm

Sincerely yours
Robert Frost

---

438. Lesley and her sister Marjorie would launch their shop, The Open Book, at 124 South Street, Pittsfield, Massachusetts, in June 1924. RF dropped by to help them prepare on May 29.

439. See the conclusion of the parable of the Good Samaritan (Luke 10:37).

440. Dodd offered Lesley the job; see RF to Dodd, May 15, 1923.

3

A New Regime at Amherst

May 1923–September 1925

I shall have to stay here in New England for one place wherever else I may manage to be in September. That's clear now. And the reason is that from an unnatural curiosity about education and its problems I've just been getting myself freshly involved in the affairs of Amherst College. I couldn't stand by and let it be said of the poor thing that it was no longer a place for rebels. How would you like it said of you that you were no longer a place for rebels?

—Robert Frost to Lew Sarett, August 1923

[To Louis Untermeyer. Date derived from postmark. ALS. LoC.]

[South Shaftsbury, VT]
[circa May 2, 1923]

Dear Louis

Stop brittling if you dont want to be called brittle-minded.

And gee didnt it make me feel lonesome when my friends were counted by Farrar and found to come to just two, you and Gibson. Figures cant lie; but sleeping lions can if you let them; and I wish Farrar had let them.[1] As long as I went unrealizing I was happy. But I suppose the day of reckoning had to come: and it was all day with <u>me</u> though I dont believe it can have taken Farrar all day just to count two unless it was a door-to-door canvas he made and it was a long way between the two doors. I cried myself to sleep that night. Just two friends, one of those about to leave me to go to England and the other in England already.

But candidly I <u>am</u> going to feel rather unsupported with you out of the country. There's something to what Johnny says. He has spoken a half truth. He is mistaken about Gibson. But he is right about you. Subtract you and what have I left? The worst of it is I have no faith in its being a merely temporary subtraction. It will be just like you to get drowned both going and coming. It's the good swimmers that always get drowned at sea, they say, whether because they are apt to be careless about falling

---

1. For details, see the notes to RF's April 30, 1923, letter to Cox.

overboard or because when the ship goes down they feel some delicacy about piling into the life boats. There seems to be something in swimming as in tennis that is incompatible with bad manners. Your wife wont thank me for this my raven's crockery[2] on the eve of your putting out to sea—moaning of the bar as Tenneson [*sic*] would call it.[3] But if it is hard for her, think how hard it must be for me. I refuse to spare myself. Why should I spare her? We want the truth—the truth about friendship no less than about marriage.

When are you going?

That's good of Jean to stand by my little poem before all the world. Stopping by Woods on a Snowy Etc is my best bid for remembrance. Jeans another friend; Farrar never thought of her.[4]

Surely I'll have time to write you again. I must write you a nice letter for Abercrombie.[5]

Ever yours
Robert Frost.

---

2. *RFLU* has "croakery," but the manuscript is clear.

3. See Tennyson, "Crossing the Bar": "And may there be no moaning of the bar / When I put out to sea."

4. Jean Starr Untermeyer, Louis's wife. *The Bookman* featured a "Poems of the Month" column, which she supplied for the June 1923 issue of the journal. There, she singles out RF's "Stopping by Woods on a Snowy Evening" for special notice: "'There is so much of awe and beauty implicit in the great major themes—life, death, love, grief—that centuries of usage and the most minor of minor poets cannot quite annihilate their magic. On the other hand, it takes mastery both technical and, for want of a more definitive phrase, let us say spiritual, to be able to take the trivial, the commonplace, the evanescent moment and invest it with poignance and significance. In the following poem Robert Frost performs just this feat of genius. His theme is of the slightest texture—it is hardly a theme at all—just a picture of a man, halting on his homeward ride at twilight to look at darkening woods. And yet with no effort of description, the whole color and feel of dusk is here, and the knell of loneliness that comes and goes only to return again"—whereupon she quoted the poem in full (447).

5. See RF to Lascelles Abercrombie, June 9, 1923.

[To Maurice Frink (1895–1972), American journalist, historian, author, and educator. ALS. Private.]

South Shaftsbury Vt

May 12 1923

Dear Mr Frink:

Will you send your copy of North of Boston to me at Ann Arbor Michigan (1432 Washtenaw Ave) sometime during the next two weeks?[6] That's the best place to catch me. I shall be happy to put my name in the book for you. Thank you for caring enough to ask me.

Sincerely yours

Robert Frost

[To Richard W. Morin. ALS. DCL.]

South Shaftsbury Vt

May 12 1923

Dear Mr Morin

I thought you might like this in writing for someone perhaps to tuck away in one of my books after you get through with it. You could give it to my friend Harold Rugg if no one else wants it.[7] My regards go with it.

Thank you for thinking of me to ask me for a poem. I hope I'm giving you what you will like a little.[8]

Sincerely yours

Robert Frost

---

6. Upon receipt of the book (the American, and third, edition of *NB*), RF copied out a passage from "Birches" above his signature and the inscription "For Maurice Frink." (The passage extends from "So was I once myself a swinger of birches" to "I'd like to go by climbing a birch tree." Frink pasted the present letter into the copy opposite the inscription.)

7. Harold Goddard Rugg, a librarian at Dartmouth.

8. RF enclosed a manuscript, signed version of "The Birthplace," later included in *WRB*, from the text of which it differs as follows: "My father built beside a spring" became (in *WRB*) "My father built, enclosed a spring" (line 3); "Reduced the growth of earth to grass," became "Subdued the growth of earth to grass" (line 4). "The Birthplace" was first published in the June 1923 issue of the *Dartmouth Bema*.

[To George Whicher. Internal evidence dates the letter to the second week of May 1923. ALS. ACL.]

[South Shaftsbury, VT]
[circa May 12, 1923]

Dear George:

You have a right to look sanctimoniously down along your nose when in the same breath you wish me out of Michigan and into Bread Loaf. I am afraid you are a sinner and a wag. Nevertheless I'll tell you what I will do if you'll pretend hard enough I'm needed: I'll come up for two lectures on two successive days. Will you tell Davidson [*sic*]⁹ you have got me to promise that, damn your eyes? You and I won't talk of money. Tell Davidson he must satisfy me there, damn <u>his</u> eyes. I only ask one thing of you and that is that you will absolutely protect me from cameras and such like adulation. Just give it out at announcement-time that I don't want anybody to pay any attention to me at all except when I am lecturing and then I want everybody to pay attention to me and to hurrah for me like Hell.¹⁰ I really wouldnt consent to come if I didn't think you could save me from a repetition of what I went through last time.¹¹

I did boast to the Van Dorens of my excesses, didnt I? Those two make quite a family of boys.¹²

---

9 Wilfred Davison, dean of the Bread Loaf School of English.

10. RF read and lectured at Bread Loaf in July 1923, having skipped its 1922 session.

11. In his unpublished "Notes on Conversations with Robert Frost" (held now at UVA), Thompson reports, in an entry dated June 24, 1946: "It seems that Davidson [*sic*] came down to Amherst to get Frost interested in the Bread Loaf idea. And on his way up to Franconia that first year [1921], with Mrs. Frost and the children, he had stopped at Bread Loaf to read and talk. But the adulation and the failure to include the family in the cordiality of the welcome dampened their spirit, and Frost probably would not have come back if Davidson hadn't pleaded. So it began, and they soon laid claim to him, although he had congenital doubts as to the value of such a conference for writers."

12. Carl and Mark Van Doren. The former published a generous and lengthy essay on RF, "The Soil of the Puritans," based in part on conversations with him.

Chicken pox? Where did you get it? We've been having grippe and pneumonia.[13] I trust you didnt nearly die. None of us did—not even the pneumoniac—Irma.

I think b'jink I'll go back to M'ich on Tuesday.[14]

> Be good.
> Ever yours
> Robert Frost

[To Maurice Firuski, owner of the Dunster House Bookshop in Cambridge, Massachusetts. Date derived from postmark. ALS. Jones.]

> [South Shaftsbury, VT]
> [May 14, 1923]

Dear Mr Firuski:

I suppose I had better be left out of the first number of New Leaves. I can't keep everybody waiting till I come to an understanding with Conrad. I just want him to let me let Louis U. in if he wont let him in himself. I happen to have been seeing [some] lovely things Louis U. has been writing about Conrad lately: and I'm grateful if Conrad isn't.[15]

I've become so rediculously [*sic*] de trop in this deal about my books that I sometimes wonder how I ever imagined I was a party to it.[16] It seems like I dream that the books were ever offered to me by Simpkins and Marshall through Jack Haines.[17] However it's not the least matter. You and Haines settle it between you. The main thing is that Haines should be satisfied. It will

---

13. On RF's health problems throughout winter 1922 and spring 1923, see RF to Root, March 23, 1923 (and notes thereto).

14. RF returned to Ann Arbor on Tuesday, May 15. He gave readings at the University of Michigan on May 29 and 31.

15. *New Leaves*, the proposed but now imperilled periodical to be published by Firuski's Dunster House Press. See RF to Aiken, May 12, 1923. See also RF to Firuski, May 22, 1923, and the notes thereto, for the unhappy resolution of the affair and for Conrad Aiken's refusal to be party to an enterprise involving Untermeyer.

16. The unbound sheets and printed copies of David Nutt's editions of RF's first two books, *ABW* and *NB*, which Firuski and Haines were negotiating to dispose of safely, lest they be pulped; the scheme was successful. See *YT*, 587. The books wound up in Firuski's shop. For details, see the notes to RF's September 20, 1922, letter to Haines.

17. The London publishing house, Simpkin, Marshall.

clarify the situation if I simply get out entirely and return you your check for two hundred dollars.

After one more look in at Ann Arbor I shall be free to go where I please again. You may see me before long.

Sincerely yours
Robert Frost

[To Marion Elza Dodd. ALS. ACL.]

Ann Arbor Mich
May 15 1923

Dear Miss Dodd:

I'm grateful to you for your generosity and so is Lesley. We feel as if the important first step had been taken toward our bookstore.[18] Lesley will write you at once to make an appointment with you for some time within a couple of weeks, if that will be soon enough. Of course she must have the experience of the stock-taking in June. She has been out here with her mother to wind up our affair with Michigan University. I've just rejoined them here after one of my more or less literary jaunts in the wild. I picked up your letter in passing through South Shaftsbury Vt where part of the family sticks uncompromisingly to farming.[19]

Don't I make my movements sound as complicated as those of a moon that revolves round an earth that revolves round a sun that revolves round God as yet alone knows what? I should hate to have to figure on a chart my path through the void. Void is perhaps too severe a word.

I must see the big new store myself.[20] I like these community centers best that ask no subsidies or endowments, no favors from anyone except the ordinary ones of enlightened business.

With best wishes and thanks

Sincerely yours
Robert Frost

---

18. See RF to Dodd, April 30, 1923. Under discussion is the store, The Open Book, that Lesley would open with her sister Marjorie in Pittsfield, Massachusetts, in 1924.

19. RF's son Carol, at the Stone House in South Shaftsbury. When Carol married Lillian Labatt in November 1923, RF gave the property to the couple.

20. Dodd was proprietor of the Hampshire Bookshop—something of a Northampton institution.

[To George Whicher. Internal evidence suggests a date in mid-May, 1923. ALS. ACL.]

[Ann Arbor, MI]

[circa May 15, 1923]

Dear George:

I shall have to take back what I said in my last letter.[21] I wrote it without consulting Elinor's wishes enough. I had promised her in a way she had understood me to promise that there should be no more lecturing after April 1st this year. This was in my interest, in the interest of my writing. You know my slovenly way of spreading myself round in loose talk that get's [sic] neither me nor anybody else anywhere. She's right: it's time I shut up long enough to get my last poems written. At any rate right or wrong she is entitled to a voice in the matter. I'm going to do as she says for a while and see how I like it. It lets me out of having to think of money for the family as much as I was feeling I had to. It has that strong recommendation. And it is so heroic on her part that I should think it must silence criticism on yours and mine. Gee does anybody suppose I would lecture as badly as I do if I could find anybody to take the responsibility for my staying off the platform entirely?

You can show this to Davidson [sic] if necessary to save you from embarrassment.[22]

Forgive me my selfishness and believe me as much as a selfish person can be another's

Yours ever

Robert Frost

[To Maurice Firuski. ALS. Jones.]

Ann Arbor Mich

May 22 1923

Dear Mr Firuski:

I think your offer is handsome, and I am sure Jack Haines will think it so too. You will be doing as much for two of us as you originally undertook to do for only one. You become the chief looser [sic]—the only looser—by the

---

21. See RF to Whicher, May 12, 1923, and June 9, 1923.
22. Wilfred Davison.

confusion we've been thrown into trying to do business from three corners at once.

I've just had the nicest kind of a letter from Conrad in which he protests his willingness to get out and let Louis Untermeyer come in.[23] But of course it is awful nonsense. Conrad is one of the very best of us and he knows I rate him so. I'd get out before I'd let him out.

Let's let the thing die down for the moment. After we have seen each other and had a few personal talks things may look different.

I appreciate your generosity about the book and let it never be said I don't.

Sincerely yours

Robert Frost

The family all liked your "large number of a scarce book."[24]

---

23. The poet Conrad Aiken. In his *Conrad Aiken: Poet of White Horse Vale* (Athens: University of Georgia Press, 1988), Edward Butscher explains: "A more distressing situation involved Robert Frost. With Firuski's assent, Aiken and [John Gould] Fletcher had decided to launch a poetry magazine, New Leaves, to be published by Dunster House, and they approached Frost and [E.A.] Robinson for their cooperation in planning the venture. . . . Frost informed Firuski that he would not participate unless Untermeyer was also asked to join, a proposition that Aiken angrily rejected   In May 1923, [Aiken] wrote to Firuski from Winchelsea: 'I have just written Frost that I won't stand in the way, and that, if he will only come in provided that Louis does also, I will peacefully go out. I officially notify you to that effect, and beg you to act accordingly, and keep my stuff out if you hear from Frost or the others that Louis is to be "in."' . . . Aiken was no doubt convinced that he was proceeding on the most ethical of principles, but his action suggested a personal hostility toward Untermeyer and growing antipathy toward literary politics of any stripe, since, as Frost pointed out in a May 12 reply to his ultimatum, the founding group had at his request already been enlarged to take in [Alfred] Kreymborg, [William Carlos] Williams, and [Wallace] Stevens. Moreover, as he must have known his friend would, Firuski abandoned the entire scheme when confronted by Aiken's absence. Aiken placed the blame on Frost in a June 20 letter to [Robert] Linscott: 'New Leaves is dead: beheaded, as Emily [Dickinson] somewhere puts it, by the blond assassin, Frost'" (391). See also RF to Aiken, May 12, 1923, and RF to Firuski, May 14, 1923.

24. Presumably Firuski's characterization of the copies of *ABW* he had just acquired through Jack Haines. Far more copies of it than of *NB* had remained unsold.

[*To Lincoln MacVeagh. Date derived from internal evidence. RF was away from home (i.e., South Shaftsbury) in late May to give two readings in Ann Arbor (May 29 and 31). ALS. Jones.*]

[Ann Arbor, MI]
[May 30, 1923]

Dear MacVeagh:

You made me a beautiful book to look at.[25] I may wonder as much as I like about the trouble you take for me: all I can see to do about it is thank you once in so often.

Apparently you have fixed it with the best people so that my worst fears are unlikely to be realized. Only Menken [*sic*] of the lot contrives to sound a trifle sinister.[26]

Come up when I get home and we'll concockt [*sic*] New Hampshire.

I'll write you a poem inside of this.[27]

Always yours
Robert Frost

[*To Lascelles Abercrombie (1881–1938), British poet. This letter, in an envelope marked "For Lascelles Abercrombie England Introducing Louis Untermeyer," was enclosed in the letter to Untermeyer that follows. ALS. LoC.*]

South Shaftsbury Vermont
U.S.A.
June 9 1923

Dear Lascelles

The first I ever heard of Louis Untermeyer was from you; the first thing I ever read of his was in your shadowy library at the Gallows Ryton (of terribly mixed memory); you introduced him to me when you knew more about him

---

25. RF's *Selected Poems* appeared in March 1923 in both London and New York. RF had originally opposed its publication, wanting *NH* to be his "bid for notice" in 1923 (see *YT*, 219; see also RF to MacVeagh, circa December 1, 1922). Later that same year RF would, with MacVeagh, "concokt" *NH*. It appeared in November and won RF his first Pulitzer Prize.

26. Reference unclear; we have found no remarks by Mencken about the matter.

27. "In a Disused Graveyard," published in the August 1923 number of *The Measure* and then collected in *NH*.

than I; I introduce him back to you now that I know more about him than you know.

He is one of our best poets, especially in his first book Challenge[28] and in his latest Roast Leviathan which you would be sure to like. He is our best critic and so naturally a great admirer of your work. It was only the other day that he brought me your Ham and Eggs.[29] He is my great friend and so not unnaturally a great admirer of my work. In politics he is still somewhat the reckless idealist in spite of all time and his wife,[30] who is a sound thinker as well as a most charming lady, have been able to do to make him see reason. He puns, often successfully.

Most of this I tell you so that you will be good to him for his own sake (and his wife's). I can hardly ask you to be good to him for my sake without risk of presuming too much on how you may be supposed to feel toward me after all these years of neither seeing each other nor writing to each other. I trust you are still a little my friend as I am

Much yours
Robert Frost

[To Louis Untermeyer. Date derived from postmark. Untermeyer was then in Paris. ALS. LoC.]

[South Shaftsbury, VT]
[circa June 9, 1923]

Dear Louis

Now look unless you tell me where you are over there I shall be driven to trying to reach you through the diplomatic service.

I'm home from Michigan but I havent parted with the book to MacVeagh yet.[31] Something's come over me.

Dont present the letter to Abercrombie unless you absolutely like it.

File your itenerary [sic].

R.

---

28. Louis Untermeyer's third collection of poems, *Challenge* (New York: Century, 1914).

29. Abercrombie's dramatic poem "Ham and Eggs" appeared in *The Chapbook: A Monthly Miscellany* in February 1923.

30. Jean Starr Untermeyer.

31. *NH.*

[To George Whicher. ALS. ACL.]

[South Shaftsbury, VT]
[circa June 9, 1923]

Dear George

I am empowered to say that if you dont think it too ridiculous for me to change again I can undertake to come to Bread Loaf for one day's lecturing and you may so inform Davison.[32] Elinor came down off her high mountain when she heard about how nice you had been. And you <u>were</u> nice. We were both affected by your magnanimity. A little run up to see you will never be felt in any vital spot.

The thing I liked best in all your Saxonian was the encounter with a fawn. Line after line of that was all right. My second choice was the second poem by Burgess which seemed to me rather an imitation of Robinson than of Browning.[33]

I expect to be seeing Merrill Root within a few days. What memories the name calls up.[34]

Good luck.

Ever yours
Robert Frost

––––––––––

32. For previous uncertainty over RF's appearance at Bread Loaf in July 1923 see also RF to Whicher, May 12, 1923, and May 15, 1923.

33. *The Saxonian* was a literary magazine founded by the English Club at Middlebury College (Bread Loaf is affiliated with Middlebury). The first poem RF mentions, from the 1922 *Saxonian*, is "A Chance Encounter," by Annie E. Harris, which in certain respects resembles RF's own "Two Look at Two" (*CPPP*, 211–212). The poem tells of a walk in May in which the poet and a friend wind up at a small pool of water:

And as we looked the peaceful trees were shaken
By something roughly pushing them apart;
What was it! man, or beast, or fabled monster!

A fawn it was! who coming there for water
Saw strange reflections looking out at him,
And raised his head before a drop was tasted
To see the same forms standing on the rim.

Was it an age, or only just a minute
That we stood still, dumb animals all three . . . (118–119)

The second poem, by D. L. Burgess, is titled "Parody on R. Browning" (105).

34. Memories, that is, of RF's first year on the faculty at Amherst College in 1917, when he met Root and first worked with Whicher.

[To Sidney Cox. Date derived from postmark. ALS. DCL.]

I'm at South Shaftsbury Vt

[June 18, 1923]

Dear Sidney:

I begin to think you are having trouble about finding all the money you wanted for me.[35] Don't concern yourself too deeply. Remember what I always used to tell you about taking life as the leaves grow on the tree. I dont have to tell you that perhaps now that your wife Alice looks after you so understandingly and well.

If you can't have me out one way why not propose another cheaper if not quite as good. Of course Im perfectly willing to be farmed out in the town to read a time or two. Maybe two weeks would be all you could afford of me—and enough of me. Let's not be afraid of each other. The worst we can do is give each other offense.

The one thing I am unalterable about in the stipulations is that I shant be exposed to anything as deadly as the spotted-fever-tick.[36]

Ever thine

RF.

Does this help you?

[To Lincoln MacVeagh. Date derived from internal evidence. ALS. Jones.]

[South Shaftsbury, VT]

[circa June 22, 1923]

Dear MacVeagh

I've decided to be good and stop writing any more into the New Hamp shire poem. You shall have the manuscript in a week or so now.

Please tell Falcone in so many words how profoundly he has interested me in myself.[37]

I'd like to see you for a talk and a game of ball sometime pretty soon.

---

35. Paid appearances in Montana for the tour RF and Cox had been mooting since 1921. See RF to Sidney Cox, March 1, 1921; September 8, 1921; September 21, 1921; October 12, 1921; May 2, 1922; October 9, 1922. The trip never took place.

36. *Dermacentor andersoni,* also known as the Rocky Mountain wood tick, is the vector of a number of diseases, the most deadly of which is Rocky Mountain spotted fever.

37. We've been unable to identify Falcone.

I had a good evening with your Mr Henry Holt at his place between the mountains and the lake when I was in Burlington for my degree.[38]

They've asked me by telegraph to come me back to Amherst.[39] What do you know about that? Dont tell the Bristols.[40] Don't tell anybody. Its going to be embarrassing to stay out of the row or to go into it.[41]

Our water system failed us—somewhat mysteriously. There was plenty of water at the spring. The pipes were all new and as they should be. The plumbers were baffled. So it fell to me to see what I could do. First I tasted a drop of the water from the pipes with my head cocked on one side. Then I scratched my head. Then I went directly to a definite place in the system and laying my finger on [a] particular spot said There—if you open the pipes with a Stilson[42] there you will find a frog as dead as—Genevera in the water works of Seville.[43] They opened the pipes and it was as I said. But instead of de-

---

38. The University of Vermont awarded RF an honorary LHD (Doctor of Humane Letters) on June 18. On hearing that RF was to be in Burlington for the ceremony, Henry Holt (1840–1926), the founder of Henry Holt and Company, and by this point retired, hosted him at Fairholt, a summer house he had built in Burlington in the late 1890s. (Frederick Law Olmsted surveyed the land and laid out plans for the mansion.)

39. President George Olds, who succeeded Alexander Meiklejohn as president of Amherst, had just offered RF a new position at the college similar to the one he had held at Michigan, to begin in September.

40. That is, the family of Herbert Bristol, then president of Henry Holt and Company.

41. RF refers to the controversies surrounding Meiklejohn's resignation from Amherst, an event that made the New York papers. See *YT*, 228, 591–592. The most prominent notice of the event in the press was an article by Walter Lippmann, "The Fall of President Meiklejohn," *New York World*, June 24, 1923, editorial section, page 1. Meiklejohn had served as President of Amherst College since 1912. In an act steeped in controversy, he was dismissed by the Board of Trustees for a number of reasons, including his refusal to take due part in capital campaigns; disputes over his management of an increasingly divided faculty; disputes concerning his politics, and his ideas as to what constituted a "liberal" education; and queasiness, on the part of the trustees, about his frequent salary overdrafts and (as many saw it) lavish lifestyle. See Adam R. Nelson, *Education and Democracy: The Meaning of Alexander Meiklejohn, 1872–1964* (Madison: University of Wisconsin Press, 2001), 100–115. In his parting address to the college (Commencement Day 1923), Meiklejohn—to the delight of the assembled students—likened his overseers to the Pharisees (and himself implicitly to Christ).

42. A type of wrench.

43. A reference to the celebrated waterworks built by Juanelo Turriano (1500–1585) at Toledo. RF's allusion is obscure, but the waterworks figure in "The Illustrious Scullery Maid" ("La Ilustre Fregona"), a short story by Cervantes, who was born in Seville.

lighting to honor me for the one thing I can do well viz diagnose a difin-gulty[44] with a mechanism, the most anyone could find to say to me was Let it be a lesson to you to keep such a strainer at the spring as will henceforth ex-clude frogs from the system. So our days pass in pastoral tranquility. So also may yours.

As ever

R.F.

[To Morris Palmer Tilley (1876–1947), professor of English at the University of Mich-igan. ALS. UM.]

South Shaftsbury Vt July 20 1923

Dear Tilley:

I wonder how the Amherst cataclysm seemed from where you sit serene. I wonder how it would have seemed if I had said nothing to prepare you for it. I suppose you would have been entirely taken in by the papers you young in-nocent. The trustees mercifully let Meiklejohn have it in the papers any way he pleased to help him get another job. You noticed how carefully his spokesmen kept to the word liberal and avoided the word radical.[45] The in-sincerity of that lay in the fact that before he had to go to the public with his case Meiklejohn had rather gloried in the name of radical. The whole pub-licity was over artful. When you get right down to it and inside of it there was practically no principle at all involved in his dismissal whether of radi-calism or liberalism. He went because he divided his house against itself.[46] And I'll tell you how he did it. He took sides with the consciously, the obvi-ously clever on his faculty as against the merely sound and able. He sicked [*sic*] the ornamental on to amuse themselves at the expense of the useful. The useful turned and rent him. He perished with the ornamental and <u>obviously</u>

Ginevra, the Spanish and Italian spelling of Guinevere, is also mentioned in "The Illus-trious Scullery Maid" (as is the city of Seville, several times, though the action transpires chiefly in Toledo).

44. Spelled to mimic the dialect of the plumbers; the reading is clear in the manuscript.

45. That is, to avoid drawing unwanted attention at a time when "radical" was the term most often bestowed on persons prosecuted or fired for ideological reasons, whether by the federal government or by state governments, during World War I, the Red Scare, and throughout the 1920s.

46. See Mark 3:25.

clever. The intolerance and illiberalism was all his in the first place. His staider faculty would have tolerated him if he would have tolerated them; but he wouldn't. He gave them notice almost in so many words that he would shoot them down as fast as he could find real teachers to fill their places. The fact that some of them were full professors and so bulletproof was nothing. If he couldnt kill them he could at least wish they were dead. He was too high minded for any modus vivendi. This isnt radicalism: it isn't liberalism: it is damned illiberalism and lack of tact. It is downright inability to make a Table Round, let alone hold it together, once it is made.[47]

The news of this letter must consist largely in the announcement that I shall probably go back to Amherst for a while out of indignation at such a hypocritical perversion of the facts. I shan't be expected to teach much. You'll laugh. But such I am. I can't stay out of what interests me. I'm not very detachable.

I might go and tell you one or two more contributory causes for Meiklejohn's downfall. He had gradually lost the friendship of the trustees by spending about three or four thousand a year of their private money besides the salary he had from them officially. For half of his administration he had nine thousand a year, his rent, fuel and light: the last half he had twelve thousand five hundred, his rent, fuel, and light.[48] He ran just as much behind on twelve thousand five hundred as on nine thousand. He must have lived at the rate of seventeen or eighteen thousand a year laterly [*sic*]. The trustees didn't pretend to judge him for living beyond his means. He may have been all the more a genius for that he squandered money. Their turning against him was no expression of opinion either way on the time-honored question of whether or not a genius should have to pay his way in the world. They were simply tired of paying it for him out of their own pockets. Very likely they would have been willing to let anyone else support him if anyone else could have

---

47. An echo of Tennyson's *Idylls of the King*, which RF read closely, and often quoted. Here he likely calls to mind the following lines from the section of the poem titled "The Holy Grail":

And when King Arthur made
His Table Round, and all men's hearts became
Clean for a season, surely he had thought
That now the Holy Grail would come again;
But sin broke out.

48. Worth $173,834 in 2016 dollars.

been found to. He made them tired. Dwight Morrow from having been one of his best friends, became one of his most indifferent.[49]

Such is life.

Best wishes to all.

> Ever yours
> Robert Frost

[To Lincoln MacVeagh. ALS. Jones.]

> South Shaftsbury Vt
> July 22 1923

Dear MacVeagh:

A lot of my poems seem to have got sick of waiting round so many years to get into a book and gone off somewhere. I can't find them on the home grounds. All I can see to do is to try whistling for them and after that advertising.

Lesley's been away or I should have had everything retyped uniform. I'd like it awfully well if you could have a copy of the whole book typed down there for me and charged. Miss Flagg[50] did New Hampshire so well and friendlily. (You dont know what I know: she's a poet herself: she just sent me a very good thing about Lilacs: tell her I said so: I must write and thank her.)

We draw to an end of this long waiting. You've been patienter with me than I've been with myself.

I've bitten off the Amherst chew. Tomorrow I'm going to look up Hocking to see if he wont help us part of the year in philosophy.[51] I may start right for

---

49. Dwight Whitney Morrow (1873–1931)—a lawyer, businessman, partner at J. P. Morgan, and diplomat—was a graduate of Amherst (class of 1895, of which Calvin Coolidge was also a member). He served on the Amherst Board of Trustees when Meiklejohn was asked to resign. For more on the matter, see RF to Untermeyer, August 12, 1924.

50. MacVeagh's secretary, as he indicates in a note on the manuscript; she typed the title poem for the new book.

51. Ernest Hocking, professor of philosophy at Harvard. When Meiklejohn was forced out, a number of faculty members loyal to him also resigned in protest. RF sought to stop the gap. His friendship with Hocking and his wife, Agnes, dates to April 1915, when the two met in Cambridge and Hocking gave him a copy of his *The Meaning of God in Human Experience: A Philosophic Study of Religion* (New Haven, CT: Yale University Press, 1912). "What ministers to me most perhaps is your doctrine of freedom in necessity," RF

England after Abercrombie in aesthetics.[52] Dont worry about me. There's a divinity that shapes our extremities.[53]

Theres fun in the book and there's some beauty.[54] We'll say that now beforehand and we wont be scared out of it by anything that happens.

Send me the copy of N.H. you have—will you?[55] I can use it to show a little.

> Ever yours
> Robert Frost

[To William Ernest Hocking (1873–1966). ALS. Harvard.]

> South Shaftsbury Vt
> July 28 1923

Dear Hocking:

That proved to be President Olds trying to reach me from New York by telephone and none of my family in extremis. He wanted me to be sure and make you understand that, in asking what I asked, I spoke for him and the trustees as well as for myself. He had been disturbed by the way I had rushed right off on my own account to get you. I trust I left neither him nor the trustees out of my appeal. They want you at Amherst to help start over (I'm afraid we may have to go back a little way to start over) for the same reasons that I want you for, your name and what it will say and

---

wrote Hocking on April 3, 1915, having read the book. "I have poetry for that too [in 'Mowing']: 'The fact is the sweetest dream that labor knows.' The fact is not one thing and the dream another to be kept separate. We have learned to dream in the fact. Labor has taught us so to dream. The line is charged with pragmatism. I must read deeper for your understanding of reason" (*LRF-1*, 277).

52. Lascelles Abercrombie, with whose family the Frosts lived during their last months in England (1914–1915). Abercrombie had recently published *An Essay Towards a Theory of Art* (London: Martin Secker, 1922).

53. *Hamlet* 5.2: "There's a divinity that shapes our ends, / Rough-hew them how we will."

54. That is, in *NH*, then being readied for publication in November. The book contains some of RF's best lyrics, but is also unusual in its organization: footnotes to the satirical title poem refer to poems elsewhere in the volume—a structural feature that (as has been noted), some regard as a sendup of the (often mock-scholarly) notes Eliot appended to *The Waste Land*.

55. The poem, not the typescript of the book; RF read it for the first time at Bread Loaf.

your wisdom. The only difference between me and the trustees is that I probably feel more deeply than they in the matter: I probably take my anti-intellectualism more seriously than they. Your promising to give just one little right course of lectures would be like coming to my personal rescue.

I shall think I would have done better to write you that in the first place instead of trying to say it, if all my talk at large in Greensboro comes to nothing; I shall think I spoiled everything by having too good a time and talking too much. So are causes lost.

Ever yours

Robert Frost

[To Lincoln MacVeagh. Date derived from the postmark. Postcard, signed. Jones.]

[South Shaftsbury, VT]

[July 28, 1923]

Dear MacVeagh

Never mind typing any more of the book. The proofs will do well enough. Coming right along with An Empty Threat and other poems.[56]

Have just seen some more of Lankes. Do wish we could have three for the book –a frontispiece for each section.[57]

Ever yours

Robert Frost

---

56. "An Empty Threat" appeared in *NH*, the book under discussion here.

57. Julius John Lankes (1884–1960), a distinguished artist, illustrator, and author, would provide woodcuts for several of RF's books. He did four for *NH*: one opposite the title page; one each for the sections subtitled "Notes," and "Grace Notes"; and a fourth, which was placed at the end of the volume. For a detailed discussion of the relationship between RF and Lankes, see Welford Taylor, *Robert Frost and J. J. Lankes: Riders on Pegasus* (Hanover, NH: Dartmouth College Library, 1996).

[To Helen Flora McAfee (1884–1856), assistant and later managing editor at the Yale Review, *where she was a colleague of Wilbur Cross. ALS. Yale.]*

South Shaftsbury Vt

July 28 1923

Dear Miss McAfee:

My betters have sometimes taken the liberty of rhyming singular and plural. I dont believe I mind it for once in a way and I hope you dont. Thank you for noticing.[58]

Will you please tell me where I am to address Mr Cross at this time of year? I have a poem I promised to show him.

Sincerely yours

Robert Frost

[To Harold Monro. ALS. Trinity.]

South Shaftsbury Vermont U.S.A.

July 28 1923

Dear Monro:

Never shall it be said of me that I earned my living by taking money from a good little magazine in distress.[59] I return your check herewith.

Show your appreciation of one poem by asking for another when you want it.

I surely must get over some time between wars and refresh your memory of me if not my memory of you. Mine of you hardly needs refreshing. I can see you pretty much as you were the night the Poetry Bookshop opened and I began my public career as a poet by speaking to the first poet I had ever met.[60] From that everything else for me has followed. Naturally I have a sentiment that keeps me from forgetting.

Ever yours

Robert Frost

---

58. The rhyme to which McAfee likely refers is "constellations / Speculation" in "I Will Sing You One-O," due to be published in the October issue of the *Yale Review*.

59. RF refers to Monro's *The Chapbook,* which had printed "Stopping by Woods on a Snowy Evening" in its April 1923 issue.

60. F. S. Flint, whom RF met at the opening of the Poetry Bookshop in London on January 8, 1913. See *LRF-1,* 89.

[*To Lincoln MacVeagh. Date derived from internal evidence. ALS. Jones.*]

[South Shaftsbury, VT]
[circa August 10, 1923]

Dear MacVeagh:

What was I thinking of that I didn't write your name in over The Star in a Stone-boat? I'll have to authorize you to write it in for me.[61]

I'm asked to send the MS of New Hampshire. I thought you had it. All I seem to have is the copy Miss Smith made for me.[62] Im sending you that.

I think I had better see the page proofs don't you? I've added so much—notes and a whole poem and your name.[63]

I had the lovely time with you all down there in the woods—down front in the woods instead of up back in the woods. You ought to call your place the Clearing.[64] May Bunny remember me a while and may your well never go dry.

Ever yours
Robert Frost

[*To Wilbur L. Cross (editor of the* Yale Review). *ALS. Yale.*]

South Shaftsbury Vt August 17 1923

Dear Mr Cross:

Alas and alack as de la Mare's fish said in the pan.[65] Alas one of the poems you wanted is just about to be published in The Century and alack the other has already been published in The New Republic.[66] But I am the gainer in confidence by your having wanted them. I accept it as a peace offering.

You strike just the right dubious note in congratulating me about going back to Amherst. I ought to have been poet enough to stay away. But I was

---

61. "A Star in a Stone Boat" appeared first, with no dedication, in *The Yale Review* in January 1921. In *NH* the poem bore, after its title, the dedication "For Lincoln MacVeagh."

62. Unidentified.

63. RF's early September letter to MacVeagh acknowledges receipt of the proofs. See also RF to MacVeagh, September 10, 1923.

64. Presumably the MacVeagh family summer estate in Dublin, New Hampshire, named Knollwood. Bunny is MacVeagh's wife, Margaret Charlton Lewis MacVeagh; the two married in 1917.

65. Walter de la Mare, "Alas, Alack!," in *Peacock Pie: A Book of Rhymes* (London: Constable, 1913).

66. "The Star-Splitter" and "Our Singing Strength," respectively.

too much of a philosopher to resist the temptation to go back and help show the world the difference between the right kind of liberal college and the wrong kind. You were on my trail at Ann Arbor. You say you talked me over with the Lloyds and others there.[67] I know what you said: that I concerned myself too much for my own good with what was going on round me. I never could keep out of things. But I can get out of them. That's my saving virtue. I <u>will</u> bite the hook if it is baited with an idea, but I never bit one yet that I couldn't wriggle off before it was too too late.

I was never for detachment, social, moral, or physical. I like consequences, and I like them objective no less than subjective. They are depth as I understand it. Life's not just touch and go. You may remember I am not good at short calls. I like to settle down to something. I went to enquire into a young philosopher yesterday. I meant to spend the afternoon over him. If the afternoon had been all, I should have come home as wise as I went. But fortunately I missed my train and the evening was added to the afternoon and just before midnight and my next train he all came out: he was a Ph.D. of Harvard 1921 who believed in suicide as the only noble death and in no God.[68] He said he classified in the census as a monist, but you could count on there being no moaning of the bar when he embarked.[69] Now if I hadn't formed the habit of staying round after everything was supposed to be over, you can see what I would have missed. And by the way what a detached or detachable young man you [sic] made himself seem.

Aren't the Lloyds right ones.

Mind you I dont insist on the "Doctor."[70]

> Yours faithfully
>
> Robert Frost

---

67. Alfred Henry Lloyd (1864–1927), professor of philosophy and dean of the graduate school at the University of Michigan, and his wife, Margaret E. Lloyd, née Crocker.

68. This young philosopher remains unidentified. At George Olds's behest, RF had been seeking candidates to fill vacancies in the Philosophy Department at Amherst (see *YT*, 249–250). RF gives a similar account of the young man in an August 24, 1923, letter to Charles Lowell Young.

69. See Tennyson's "Crossing the Bar": "And may there be no moaning of the bar / When I put out to sea." RF quotes the same line from the poem in his letter to Louis Untermeyer, circa May 2, 1923.

70. A reference to RF's award of an honorary LHD (Doctor of Humane Letters) from the University of Vermont on June 18, 1923.

You can see from the way I started large that I didn't expect to find so much to say to you.[71] There's more still—but I spare you.

[*To Julius John Lankes (1884–1960), American artist and woodcut illustrator. The letter, which initiates a lifelong friendship with Lankes, is undated, but internal evidence indicates RF wrote it in late August 1923. ALS. HRC.*]

South Shaftsbury Vermont
[circa August 20, 1923]

Dear Mr Lankes

Just as most friendship is feigning, so is most liking a mere tacit understanding between A and B that A shall like B's work as much and as long as B likes A's. In our case I see good circumstantial evidence that there was no such sordid bargain. I liked your work before I knew you liked mine; you apparently liked mine somewhat before you knew I liked yours. Such a coincidence of taste can never be forgotten It ought to settle it between us.

I'm hoping Lincoln MacVeagh will arrange with you to do the three frontispieces for the three parts of my new book, New Hampshire.[72] I mean I'm hoping you'll want to do it. I know he wants you to. I should tell you I've already seen some of your things used as illustration for my Mountain Interval in the library of a man in Worcester.[73]

About these pictures you've heaped on me. Woodcuts are a form of art I'm the absolute victim of and yours are such beautiful examples of it. I shall treat them as they deserve, particularly the back side of a village in snow and the warm Indian Summer and the Deserted House, and The Apple Tree.[74] And

---

71. The postscript is written vertically along the left-hand edge of the first sheet of the letter (which averages six to seven words per line as opposed to nine to ten words on the last sheet—hence RF's comment about having "started large").

72. RF became acquainted with Lankes when he noticed Lankes' woodcut *Winter* in the January 1922 edition of the *The Liberator*. Charmed by the woodcut's visual resonance with his own poetry, RF chose Lankes to illustrate his poem "The Star-Splitter" when it appeared in the September 1923 issue of *Century Magazine*.

73. RF first became aware of Lankes' interest in his poems at the Worcester, MA, home of Clark University professor Loring Holmes Dodd, who had arranged for RF to read there in January 1923. Dodd had acquired several Lankes prints, and, noting an affinity with RF's poems, had inserted the prints into his personal copies of *NB* and *MI*.

74. Among the prints Lankes gave RF are *Winter*, *Indian Summer*, *Deserted House*, and *Apple Tree and Grindstone*.

The *Century Magazine* publication in September 1923 of
"The Star-Splitter" with five woodblock decorations was the
first collaboration between Frost and J. J. Lankes.

"The Star-Splitter Title Page" (1923) by J. J. Lankes. Courtesy of the Estate of J. J. Lankes.

so I might go on. Im not alone in this: my whole family thanks you for the pictures.

I have the invitation I wanted to look in on you and some day before long I shall look.

> Sincerely yours
> Robert Frost

[*To Gamaliel Bradford. ALS. Harvard.*]

> South Shaftsbury Vermont
> August 24 1923

My dear Bradford:

I've just been quoting your Tom Paine and the distinction you make between his liberalism and that of Thomas Jefferson, the one resting on the minor certainties, the other on the larger uncertainties.[75] I'm all for the second wherever it shows itself (and I suppose there have been better examples of it than Thomas Jefferson). It's the recognition of the littleness of our knowledge in comparison with our ignorance that makes us gentle and considering. You are in the secret. Wish to be a rebel sometimes as I sometimes wish to be a mathematician or a landscape gardener. But don't expect me to let you be anything but what you are. Your melancholy, if not a cure for woes, is at least good relief. I once spent an hour on a park bench with a queer doctor and that

---

75. RF refers to Bradford's new collection of biographical essays, *Damaged Souls* (Boston and New York: Houghton Mifflin, 1923). Bradford writes: "You sometimes meet a shrewd, thoughtful, uneducated mechanic who in half an hour will afflict you with reasons, old as the world, but perfectly new and perfectly convincing to him, reasons that smother you like a heap of feathers, as light and as suffocating. Such was Thomas Paine. He had no faintest conception of the huge, involving, shadowing night of ignorance which descends upon the mind that knows something of past and present and honestly and profoundly begins to think. Perhaps he was better off without such conception. The sense of one's own ignorance does little positive good in the world, shatters no idols, rights no wrongs. But it has some pale and negative merits, such as tolerance, patience, humility. It would have done Paine good, if he could have remembered the saying of the great Jefferson, whom he admired, and who was something of a rebel himself: 'Error is the stuff of which the web of life is woven and he who lives longest and wisest is only able to weave out the more of it.' And ignorance has also the merit of tranquility, I have 'reposed my head on that pillow of ignorance which a benevolent Creator has made so soft for us, knowing how much we should be forced to use it,' says Jefferson again" (68–69).

was all I could get him to claim for his medicines (simples), that they would give good relief, and often <u>good</u> relief.[76] Only reformers, he said, ever effected cures. That wonder happened in Manchester, New Hampshire, if you know where I mean.

Tom Paine is your second best paper though I doubt if you make him out a really damaged soul. He gets into your classification by courtesy or discourtesy. I'm not quite sure of John Brown's title.[77] Otherwise the assortment is perfect.[78] I love Aaron Burr and P. T. Barnum in the same boat. Burr's was what O'Shaughnessy calls an "exquisite malady of the soul"; Barnum's a deformity for the sideshow.[79]

> Always the friend of all you do
> Robert Frost

[*To Charles Lowell Young. ALS. Wellesley.*]

> South Shaftsbury Vermont
> August 24 1923

Dear Young:

Meeting people who have developed separately is as much fun as anything. I inspected a young Harvard Ph.D. and found him of the opinions that there was no God and that we all ought to commit suicide.[80] I dont mean that he developed those particular opinions separately from everybody (he probably picked them up in some course in the history of philosophy); only that he de-

---

76. In 1912, RF wrote a poem, "Good Relief," which closes:

I heard a doctor of the Kickapoo
By torch light from a cart-tail once declare:
The most that any root or herb can do
In suffering is give you good relief. (CPPP, 523)

The Kickapoo Indian Medicine Company was once the most successful promoter of "medicine shows" in America.

77. That is, his title, or claim, to the designation "damaged soul."

78. In addition to Burr, Paine, Barnum, and Brown, Bradford included portraits of Benedict Arnold, John Randolph, and Benjamin Franklin Butler.

79. See the opening lines of "The Disease of the Soul," by Arthur O'Shaughnessy (1844–1881): "O exquisite malady of the Soul, / How hast thou marred me!"

80. For more on this unidentified philosopher, see RF to Wilbur Cross, August 17, 1923. Ultimately, RF gave up scouting and himself agreed to teach a course in philosophy.

veloped them separately from me; and so burst on me with them more or less as a surprise. I asked him at once if one followed from the other on the ground that it wasn't polite for his creature to exist when God the Creator didnt exist, just as it wouldn't be the thing to remain seated when a lady was standing. His face lighted with intelligence for a moment at the unexpected reinforcement. Such is the infant mind. You may have heard that I am going back to live with it at Amherst. Will you come that far from Wellesley to see me some time?

I'm tempted to send you some of my new book New Hampshire.[81] Its full name is New Hampshire a Poem with Notes and Grace Notes. It will be in three parts, the main poem on New Hampshire, my narrative and dramatic poems connected with passages in this by asterisk and my lyrics not connected at all. The poem on New Hampshire was a spree. I wrote the four hundred lines of it practically all between ten one night and ten the next morning.[82]

I think of you often and wish you had the upper hand of that bevy of school-ma'ams. I dont trust that many of them at one time.

Yours affectionately
Robert Frost

[To Lew Sarett. The letter is undated, but RF's account of returning to Amherst and the reference to Sarett's poem suggest late August 1923 (early in September RF went up to Maine to see his sister Jeanie, and to camp). ALS. Northwestern.]

South Shaftsbury Vt
[late August 1923]

Dear Sarett:

Your beautiful poem in The Atlantic only serves to remind me unpleasantly of how badly the world and I treat our poets.[83] I haven't kept my appointment

---

81. See RF to MacVeagh, September 10, 1923, in which a request is made for extra sheets of proofs to give to a few people as gifts.

82. As Lawrance Thompson reports, on or about July 15, 1922, and in South Shafts-bury (the same night RF wrote "Stopping by Woods on a Snowy Evening").

83. The September 1923 issue of *The Atlantic* printed Sarett's "To a Wild Goose over Decoys," the text of which seems to account for RF's remarks (it was the only poem by Sarett in the magazine that year):

O lonely trumpeter, coasting down the sky,
Like a winter leaf blown from the bur-oak tree

with you have I? But I am trying to learn from my juniors and meliors[84] not to blame myself for my faults. I do what is in me to do and leave it to Him most concerned to reconcile it with the general order.—No I don't either. Pay no attention to me when I talk that way. I'm an unmerciful self-judge and I hereby condemn myself to all but death for breaking my promise to appear to you with all my family in August in the State of Idaho.[85] I had hoped that I might redeem myself and get to you in early September. But no I can't unless by the miracle of being in two places two thousand miles apart at the same time; for I shall have to stay here in New England for one place wherever else I may manage to be in September. That's clear now. And the reason is that from an unnatural curiosity about education and its problems I've just been getting myself freshly involved in the affairs of Amherst College. I couldn't stand by and let it be said of the poor thing that it was no longer a place for rebels.[86] How would you like it said of you that you were no longer a place for rebels? You'll understand and just defer our next meeting

---

By whipping winds, and flapping silverly
Against the sun,—I know your lonely cry.

I know the worn wild heart that bends your flight
And circles you above this beckoning lake,
Eager of neck, to find the honking drake
Who speaks of reedy refuge for the night.

I know the sudden rapture that you fling
In answer to our friendly gander's call—
Halloo! Beware decoys!—or you will fall
With a silver bullet whistling in your wing!

Beat on your weary flight across the blue!
Beware, O traveller, of our gabbling geese!
Beware this weedy counterfeit of peace!—
Oh, I was once a passing bird like you.

When Sarett published his *Collected Poems* in 1941, he placed this one first.

84. *"Melior"* is Latin for "better."

85. Sarett was an accomplished naturalist, and when not teaching at Northwestern University, where he was professor of speech, he traveled widely in the American West. He worked from time to time as a park ranger.

86. That is, after the dismissal of President Alexander Meiklejohn and the resignations of a number of younger faculty members in protest.

till a little later. Some time you'll either bring me to those mountains or bring those mountains to me.

Forgive me and remember me to your wife.[87]

> Ever yours
> Robert Frost

[*To Lincoln MacVeagh. ALS Jones.*]

> [Marr's Camp, Indian Pond, ME]
> [early September 1923]

Dear MacVeagh:

My revised address is Marr's Camp Indian Pond Tarratine P.O. Maine.[88] Some mail has gone back from the other address. But the proof came all right.[89] And here it is. It begins to look fairly clean. I depend on you to give it a good going over and I believe I should like to see it once more when it is folded in pages and the line and page numbers are in place—unless you are sure I don't need to. Between us, I wish we could have this book freer from errors than the other three.

I wonder if somewhere in the book there ought not to be something about as follows: Many of these poems have previously appeared in Poetry, The New Republic, The Measure, The Yale Review, Farm and Fireside, The Bookman, The Century, The Atlantic, Mercury, Harpers, and The Chapbook to all of which the author acknowledges his obligation.[90]

Another small matter: I am asked to put in a good word with you for a Miss Bogan who may call at your office looking for work.[91] All I can say for her of

---

87. Margaret Husted Sarett.

88. RF visited his sister, Jeanie, at the Maine Insane Asylum, in Augusta, in September 1923. While on the trip, he camped on Indian Pond.

89. The proofs for *NH*.

90. No such note appears in the book.

91. The poet Louise Bogan (1897–1970), who had just returned to New York after a three-year stint in Vienna, and whose first book, *Body of This Death: Poems,* would soon be published (New York: R. M. McBride, 1923). She did not, it appears, ever work at Henry Holt and Company. Bogan subsequently married (and later divorced) RF's acquaintance Raymond Holden, and served as poetry editor of *The New Yorker* for forty years.

personal knowledge is that she certainly has written some good verse for The New Republic. I am told that she would be a good gate keeper in your doors or almost anything else except stenographer.

Ever yours
Robert Frost

Gee, I've come off without Louis' address.[92] Have you it handy?

[To Lincoln MacVeagh. Dating derived from internal evidence. ALS. Jones.]

Marr's Camp
Indian Pond
Terratine P.O.
Maine
[September 10, 1923]

Dear MacVeagh

This is all the paper there is in the Maine woods.[93] Excuse it.

I wish you <u>would</u> be the one to propose the book to Evans.[94] Then if he doesn't want it, it will be easier for both most concerned.

You were quite right about those mistakes still lingering in the text I had been over so carefully. I do miss them. On my second time over I found almost as many mistakes as on my first time over. Let our object be to have this book cleanest of all.

What do you suppose? Or don't you suppose anything. It is safest not to suppose anything in this case; because I have to report having found the philosopher I was on the hunt for in myself.[95] On my way home from our talks together[96] I said Why not? And the next day being called on the telephone from Amherst to say what courses I would announce for this year in English, I proposed to give one in philosophy on Judgements in History, Literature, and Religion—how they are made and how they stand, and I was taken on

---

92. Louis Untermeyer was in Europe at the time.

93. RF composed the letter on lined legal paper of a kind he almost never used for letters.

94. Charles Evans, of Heinemann, RF's London publisher.

95. See RF to Hocking, July 28, 1923, and RF to Young, August 24, 1923.

96. Presumably at Knollwood, the MacVeagh family estate in Dublin, New Hampshire.

by the department like odds of a thousand to one.[97] Well the debacle has begun. [Here] begins what probably won't end till you see me in the pulpit.

This doesn't alter my plan to give some class a lot of reading just off the main line of English literature.[98] I shall want the lists of books you were going to get me and want them badly when I get home out of this toward the middle of next week. Send them to South Shaftsbury (whether few or many) if you will. I'd say send the proofs there too unless you mail them by Friday or Saturday of this week.

I wonder if it mightnt be a good idea for me to show three or four people copies of the book in proof as a compliment. Could I have a couple of copies? I'd be discrete with them.

Ever yours

Robert Frost

[*To Louis Untermeyer. Date derived from postmark. Although the envelope is postmarked in Boston, internal evidence indicates RF wrote the letter from Maine. ALS. LoC.*]

[Marr's Camp, Indian Pond, ME]

[September 13, 1923]

Dear Louis

This is to prepare you on the only paper available in the Maine woods (away down north of Bridgton) for a letter I contemplate writing you.[99] I don't want to come on you all at once after so long a silence with the accumulations of that silence.

I'm going to give the first course I ever gave in philosophy next year on Judgements (or less technically Verdicts) in History, Literature and

---

97. In the Amherst catalog for 1923–1924, the course description in the outline of the curriculum in philosophy reads: "Judgments in history, religion and the Arts. A study, by the case method, of how such judgments are arrived at and evaluated." The course was offered as an elective for juniors, with RF having the say as to who, among those who elected it, would be allowed to enroll in the weekly class, which met on Monday at 8 P.M. in the library.

98. Lawrance Thompson reports that RF assigned to the literature class in question Melville's *Typee*, Thoreau's *Walden*, Emerson's *Representative Men*, George Borrow's *Lavengro: The Scholar, the Gypsy, the Priest*, autobiographies by Edward Gibbon and Benvenuto Cellini, and the poetry of Christina Rossetti (*YT*, 252–253).

99. As is the preceding letter to MacVeagh, this is on lined legal paper.

Religion—how they are made and how they stand. As you see I am on my way into the church. What did I tole[100] you, Doctor, if you went away and left me with nothing to lean on but God? It is too late to do anything about it now (at any rate by mail). You may as well accept it. But I do wish you could come home and mitigate a little the complications that are sure to ensue. That will be the burden of my letter when I write it. I shall go on to wish you were where I could invite you in on this job at least once in the year. You could be of great assistance in a course run as this will be by the case method or as I like to put it the illustration-first method.

And I'll tell you all about my next book in the letter when I write it. Already some of my staider friends have stuck at the levity of the title and of the forced use of notes.[101] They say it doesnt seem like me but (with a sigh) after all they had felt that I was changing. O gee.

And I'll mention Europe in my letter too. Sure I will! I'll congratulate you on having found it wanting. I'll just lay in and do this matter of your not deserting us justice.

I'll write the letter next week.[102] Meanwhile my love to you all.

> Ever yours
> Robert Frost

Theres a wild duck quacking foreninst[103] me in rapids of the river—six wild ducks! Lots of wild life here and some tame.

[To Lincoln MacVeagh. The text given here is derived from SL, 295. Lawrance Thompson lists the letter as being at the Jones Library in Amherst, Massachusetts, but no record exists of it having been held there. For reasons unknown, Thompson appears to have omitted the opening portions of the letter.]

> South Shaftsbury [VT]
> [circa September 20 1923]

Dear MacVeagh:

[. . .] The rather terrible discovery has been made that the Amherstians who have read "New Hampshire" are sure I mean Alexander Meiklejohn now

---

100. A common usage in nineteenth-century dialect writing.
101. The full title of the book being *New Hampshire: a Poem with Notes and Grace Notes*.
102. If RF wrote such a letter, it hasn't survived. He next wrote Untermeyer in November (enclosing a copy of *NH*).
103. Anglo-Irish dialect for "in front of" or "opposite."

of New York by my "New York Alec" and my whole poem as a controversy to the Amherst controversy.[104] I was thunderstruck. Of course the Alec will have to go much as I hate to sacrifice the rhyme.[105]

The Lankes pictures are well enough.[106] They haven't the distinction of some of those he gave me however. He's worked in too great haste and not done himself quite justice. I like the grindstone one best, the first in the book probably next best.[107]

Fifty tried to get into my seminar in Fill.[108] As a first exercise in it I sent them out with lanterns to find the originals in life of the half dozen philosophies we talk and write. Queer doings at Amherst. Plainly our philosophies are but descriptions of a few attitudes toward life already long since taken in living.[109]

Tell Bunny[110] I said so.

Ever yours
Robert Frost

---

104. That is, the recent resignation of Meiklejohn as president of Amherst College. Following this, Meiklejohn announced plans to form a new, experimental liberal arts college, possibly in New York.

105. Nonetheless, the "New York alec" was retained in the poem, conversing with the poet "about the new school of the pseudo-phallic."

106. J. J. Lankes' woodcuts in *NH*.

107. The frontispiece, which depicts a small farm house in a New England vale, with a mountain rising beyond.

108. The course RF offered at Amherst for the 1923–1924 academic year in philosophy.

109. A contention made many times by William James, as here, in *Pragmatism* (New York: Longmans Green, 1907): "The history of philosophy is to a great extent that of a certain clash of human temperaments. Undignified as such a treatment may seem to some of my colleagues, I shall have to take account of this clash and explain a good many of the divergencies of philosophers by it. Of whatever temperament a professional philosopher is, he tries when philosophizing to sink the fact of his temperament. Temperament is no conventionally recognized reason, so he urges impersonal reasons only for his conclusions. Yet his temperament really gives him a stronger bias than any of his more strictly objective premises. . . . Wanting a universe that suits it, he believes in any representation of the universe that does suit it. . . . Yet in the forum he can make no claim, on the bare ground of his temperament, to superior discernment or authority. There arises thus a certain insincerity in our philosophic discussions: the potentest of all our premises is never mentioned" (5–6).

110. MacVeagh's wife.

[*To Frederick Pohl (1889–1991), an American author who wrote on a range of subjects, most notably prehistoric contacts between Native Americans and Northern Europeans. ALS. BU.*]

South Shaftsbury Vt
Sept 29 1923

Dear Mr Pohl:

I am sorry, but I am able to add nothing to your strange story either one way or the other, unless it is something to say that on the occasion in question at Middlebury no one was further from my thoughts than my old friend Preston Shirley.[111] It would have been another matter at Dartmouth. I have never been there without thinking of him and our intimate days together in Wentworth Hall in the fall of 1892—thirty years ago.[112]

I could see that Mrs Shirley was greatly affected (as was I) by the surprise of suddenly finding out so much more than we had anticipated about each other.[113] I wonder if her imagination may not have worked backward in the excitement of the moment and made her think she was seeing and had even seen things which she wasnt and hadn't. The suggestion of the situation was of course very strong.

Will you give my kindest regards to Mrs Shirley when you see her again.

Sincerely yours
Robert Frost

---

111. RF lectured at Bread Loaf (in Middelbury) in July 1923.

112. Preston Shirley (1875–1905) had been RF's closest friend during his brief time at Dartmouth in 1892 (see *LRF-1*, 284). In a comment on a typed copy of this letter dated October 24, 1966 (ACL), and in partial explanation of the mysterious event it describes, Pohl notes: "It seems to me that Mrs Shirley, who I do not remember, had expressed some belief in a spiritualistic appearance of Preston Shirley, or maybe an imagined telepathic communication about him from the poet, and she wondered whether Robert Frost at Middlebury had been specially thinking of Preston Shirley."

113. Either Mrs. Barron Shirley, wife of Preston Shirley's brother, or Carolyn Shirley Leonard, Preston Shirley's sister. See William A. Sutton, *Newdick's Season of Frost: An Interrupted Biography of Robert Frost* (Albany: State University of New York Press, 1976), 344–345.

[*To Lincoln MacVeagh. Date derived from internal evidence. ALS. Jones.*]

[Amherst, MA]

[October 18, 1923]

Dear MacVeagh:

All sorts of complications have brought me out here again before I intended to come.[114] I'm soft you know and at people's mercy. I obey unspoken commands.

The book will have to be delayed a week or so while I finish this job up. For the moment I'm eating nothing at home but milk.

It was not so bad about Lesley as we feared. At any rate she was not a plain case of any thing in particular that could be operated on. There seems to be some obscure poisoning as from the teeth or tonsils yet not from either. She'll just have to be watched.

I read to all who would come last night and shall read again Thursday.[115] I'm fighting my way out.

Ever yours

Robert Frost

I've lost Louis' foreign address. Can you supply it?[116]

[*To Louis Untermeyer. The manuscript is missing from the Untermeyer papers on deposit at the Library of Congress, and we have been unable to locate it. We rely instead on Untermeyer's dating and transcription in RFLU.*]

Amherst, Mass. U.S.A.

November 1923

For Louis Untermeyer—this figment of his creative criticism.[117] He thought it into existence by publishing a review of it before it was written.

Robert Frost

---

114. RF had given a reading and lecture at Pilgrim Hall in Boston on October 14, but returned to Amherst for a reading on Wednesday, October 17, given under the auspices of the Christian Association.

115. RF returned to Boston for a joint reading with Amy Lowell at Steinert Hall on Thursday, October 25, arranged by the New England Poetry Club.

116. Louis Untermeyer was still in Europe.

117. A copy of RF's fourth book, *NH*. In speaking of it as a "figment of [Untermeyer's] creative criticism," RF refers to the considerable attention and space given him and his

[*To Thomas Moult. ALS. BU.*]

Amherst Mass U.S.A.

November 6 1923

Dear Mr Moult:

I can't lose, on the contrary I am sure to gain by having you include The Star-splitter and Stopping by Woods on a Snowy Evening. Have them both and welcome.[118]

Will you make a note of my address so that in another such emergency or in the event of your ever coming this way on a visit you will know just where to find me? I shall hope to see you some day if only to pay the thanks I owe you for your kindness to me in The Bookman.[119]

Sincerely yours

Robert Frost

---

poetry—since RF had published his last book, *MI,* in 1916—in Untermeyer's *The New Era in American Poetry* (New York: Henry Holt, 1919), *A Miscellany of American Poetry* (New York: Harcourt, Brace, and Howe, 1920), *Modern American Poetry* (New York: Harcourt, Brace and Howe, 1919; revised and enlarged, New York: Harcourt, Brace, 1922), and in *American Poetry: A Miscellany* (New York: Harcourt, Brace, 1922). The latter two books printed eight poems that went into *NH.* See Alan T. Gaylord, "The Imaginary State of 'New Hampshire," in Greg Kuzma, ed., *Gone into If Not Explained: Essays on Poems by Robert Frost* (Crete, NE: Best Cellar Press, 1976), 10. We thank Mark Scott for the suggestion.

118. Moult reprinted the poems in his *The Best Poems of 1923* (London: Jonathan Cape, 1924). Both are in *NH.*

119. At the time, two unrelated periodicals called *The Bookman* existed, one in London, the other in New York. Moult wrote for the London *Bookman* in the 1920s, but he had published no essays on RF in it. Possibly RF misremembers Moult as editor of, or somehow involved with, *The Bookman Anthology of Verse, 1922* (New York: George H. Doran, 1922). John Farrar edited the volume, which included a poem by Moult, and in its preface had this to say about RF: "There are many striking omissions [in the book]. I should like to have been able to include something by Robert Frost, whose ability to portray mountain character is one of the finest gifts of American men of letters, and whose farmhouse in the Vermont hills proves a quiet oasis to many city-weary travelers as it did to me in the midst of a blinding winter snowstorm." RF had also just published "A Fountain, a Bottle, a Donkey's Ear, and Some Books" in the *The Bookman* (New York) 58, no. 2 (October 1923): 121–124.

[To Dorothy Dunbar Bromley. The letter is undated, but the context suggests RF refers to NH, published in November 1923. ALS. UVA.]

[Amherst, MA]

[circa November 15, 1923]

Dear Mrs Bromley:

Please tell me another time where you want my signature and whether you want any more than my signature. I'm afraid I have done these wrong.[120]

R. F.

[To Lincoln MacVeagh. ALS. Jones.]

Amherst November 19 1923

Dear Lincoln—

(if it isnt too late to change my name for you). The only move you would have to seek my approval of before you made it would be getting out and leaving me alone with the heirs of Henry Holt.[121] I'll bet that is what you are contemplating: but if I thought at all seriously, I would come right down to New York to talk you out of it. I have had half a mind to come down to New York anyway on general principles. It's not so easy, however, to get away. There seem to be all sorts of demands on me not down in the con tract.[122] I'm very tired and even nervous with it all. Imagine having to give hours every day to boys who aren't satisfied to have you acknowledge and notice their disagreement with you: they insist on your being disturbed by it. I had one in here all yesterday afternoon who simply went wild, <u>cried</u> wept[123] and tore his hair because I stolidly refused to be annoyed by his opinions in art. He called me unfeeling. It's the old story of my frostiness. It makes people weep.

---

120. *NH* was the first of RF's books to be issued in both a regular trade edition and a limited, signed edition (he speaks of the latter here). Henceforth all of his books would be so issued.

121. MacVeagh did in fact leave Henry Holt and Company to found the Dial Press in 1924.

122. RF's contract with Amherst.

123. In the manuscript, "cried" is underlined, with "wept" written in above it; neither is struck out.

Carol's marriage was only a little of a surprise.[124] He and Lillian had been engaged for some time.[125] They were such children that I didn't want to commit them to each other by taking much notice of the affair or saying much about it. I doubt if I thought it would survive Lillian's first year at college. But it turned out in a way to show that I was no judge of the intensity of children. Lillian's first year at college it was that didn't survive. She quit, homesick, and Carol went right to her mother and got her. It was all done in a week. I may be frosty, but I rather like to look on at such things. And I like children to be terribly in love. They are a nice pair. Lillian is an uncommonly pretty little girl. She is pretty, quiet and unpractical. She has been a great friend of the girls in the family for some years. All she has done is transfer herself from the girls to the boy. We'll see how completely she deserts the girls.

How much better I like the falling in love than the falling out of love. If it wasnt for the real danger of falling out sooner or later I should like the falling in entirely. My pain of the day today is the news that my friend Chase Osborne of Michigan after forty years of apparently happy married life has just fallen out of love with his wife and she with him.[126] They've been everywhere and into everything together, in the best kind of companionship, a stalwart pair of adventurers and explorers. It is too bad to see them give up beaten by the wear and tear. Something hates us and likes to spoil our fair beginnings. Let me not croak too hoarsely, though I am sick with a cold in the throat.

I confess I am a little disappointed with Bliss Carman's choice.[127] I think I will enclose a letter for you to forward him in the matter: and see what good that will do.[128] I don't know how he will take my interferance [sic]. I have liked

---

124. Carol Frost, twenty-one, married Lillian Labatt in East Arlington, Vermont, on November 3, 1923.

125. Lillian Labatt joined Lesley, Carol, Marjorie, and RF on their hike up Vermont's Long Trail in August 1922. While on the hike, Carol and Lillian fell in love, and by the time the hike was completed, in early September, Carol announced his intention to marry her.

126. Chase Salmon Osborn (1860–1949), businessman, governor of Michigan (1911–1913), and underwriter of RF's first fellowship at the University of Michigan (1921–1922), had married Lillian G. Jones in 1881. The two would soon divorce.

127. See RF to Bromley, January 1924. William Bliss Carman (1861–1929) was a Canadian poet, critic, and anthologist.

128. The location of the letter to Carman (if it survived) is unknown.

Henry Holt's 1923 promotional pamphlet, *Robert Frost: The Man and His Work*, features a photograph of Frost by DeWitt Ward on the front cover and a J. J. Lankes' woodcut on the back.

Courtesy of the Robert Frost Collection of Pat Alger.

his poetry in the day of it. But I have never told him so or come to close acquaintance with him. Will you address the letter?

Ever yours
Robert Frost

I'll come down if necessary to dissuade you from anything rash.

*[To Dorothy Dunbar Bromley. Internal evidence dates the letter to late November
1923. ALS. UVA.]*

[Amherst, MA]
[late November 1923]

Dear Mrs Bromley:

And will you let me have six more of the <u>Selected</u> Poems?[129]

I am sending New Hampshire to all the enclosed list as requested by Mr
Walker.[130]

May I ask one favor more of you? Will you see to it that I have a copy of
John Erskine's article when it comes out?[131] Of course I must thank him specially. I'd like to thank anyone else who does any signed article you happen
to see and like. Don't bother too much.

Well this flurry is about over. We have published a book of verse. May it
not prove a worst-seller. The Frosts need money to furnish their new home
in Amherst with antiques.

Always yours sincerely
Robert Frost

---

129. Published in March 1923.

130. Stanley W. Walker was the sales manager at Henry Holt and Company. *NH* had
been published on November 15.

131. John Erskine's "Present Tendencies in American Literature" appeared in the *New
York Times Book Review* on December 23, 1923. In it Erskine deplored the deficiencies of
contemporary literature, but he reserved high praise for RF: "Mr. Frost has succeeded
more than any one [sic] else in appropriating to himself a peculiar subject matter, and he
is valiant in defense of the manner in which he writes his stories. I always feel the poems
deserve a less casual and less conversational treatment, and knowing as we all do the passion for his subject and his art which animates Mr. Frost, I still expect him to do master-
work in a great style" (3).

I don't know if Mrs Frost has told you: we need a photograph or two by Ward. The profile is kindest to me.[132] Could you get us that?

[*To Frederick Melcher. ALS. UVA.*]

Amherst Mass November 24 1923

Dear Melcher:

Whatever I come to Montclair to do it will be in exchange for your coming here once to talk to my class. That is to say you will speak for the same price I speak for. As long as no money will change hands we may as well be exorbitant and establish high records for ourselves. Suppose we make it Chesterton and Tagore's figure—one thousand dollars.[133] We can decide later whether we will publish it. I'm in doubt whether it mightnt do us more harm than good. It would do something for our dignity to climb into the thousand-dollar class; but on the other hand it might merely make us look greedy.

Do I understand that you want me to keep Friday Jan 11 instead of Sunday Jan 13 for you?[134] You can have either if you speak now.

I really hope you like the book as much as you are helping it.[135] The main thing is that the right people shall like it. I don't want it to be thrown away on such as you.

Always yours
Robert Frost

---

132. DeWitt Ward's photograph of RF appeared on the front cover of a brochure, *Robert Frost: The Man and His Work* (New York: Henry Holt, 1923), issued by the publicity department at Henry Holt and Company. See illustration on page 375.

133. It is doubtful that G. K. Chesterton or Rabindranath Tagore garnered $1,000 speaking fees in 1923.

134. RF has crossed out "Feb" in both dates and written "Jan" above them. However, in his next letter to Lincoln MacVeagh, RF speaks of going to Montclair, where Melcher lived, to speak on February 11.

135. *NH.*

[To Wilfred Davison. The text given here is derived from SL, 298. There, Thompson listed the letter, in the form of a typed copy, as being in the hands of Reginald Cook. We have been unable to locate either the letter or the copy.]

[Amherst, MA]

[circa December 1, 1923]

Dear Mr Davison:

I don't suppose you would want to come down here for a serious talk with me? I've been thinking I'd like to see either you or Mr Collins.[136] You've done something with Bread Loaf to make it different from the ordinary American school in more than location, but, as I look at it, not nearly enough.[137] You're missing a lot of your opportunities up there to make a school that shall be at once harder and easier than anything else we have. I'd be interested to tell you more about it if you should come down for a visit overnight;[138] and I'd be interested in coming up for longer than my stay of last summer or the summer before, might even stay a week, if you would excite me with something rather more advanced in educational experiment.

By all means have Powell if a good ordinary academic is all you want.[139] That's all he is. He won't set your buildings on fire and he won't start anything you never heard of before. Safety first! But you mustn't expect me to have time for adventures in safety. Just because you are in the woods and mountains is no distinction to talk of. You've got to get into something deeper than woods and mountains. It's to be in the councils of the bold that I have been tempted back to Amherst.

I don't mean to shake you all up. I desist.

Sincerely yours

Robert Frost

---

136. Edward Day Collins (1849–1940), the provost at Middlebury College.

137. Bread Loaf School of English, at Middlebury, of which Davison was dean.

138. Davison visited RF at his home on Dana Street in Amherst on December 22, 1923. See YT (259–262) for Davison's account of the event. He writes: "Regarding Bread Loaf, Mr. Frost's idea was that we should have there a Pastoral Academy, where freedom should abound. He would have no formal restraint, but he would be free to send students home at any time when they failed to take advantage of their opportunities. He would have very few formal lectures and recitations. For these he would substitute conferences and discussions . . ." (260). On Bread Loaf, see also RF to Whicher, February 8, 1922.

139. Chilton Latham Powell, professor of English at Amherst.

[*To George Roy Elliott, as identified by the Amherst College Library cataloger, who also notes—in a hand unlike Elliott's—that the letter accompanied a gift of RF's NH, which had been published some two weeks earlier. Date derived from internal evidence. ALS. ACL.*]

[Amherst, MA]
[circa December 1, 1923]

A mere Christmas present not for review in public or private. Since the time when you deplored "A Star in a Stone-boat" and of the three other poems with it in The Yale Review found only half of one (Dust of Snow) to commend, we have gone separate ways in art.[140] I want you to know, however, that I still think of you as a personal friend.[141] Thank you for the beautiful and impressive anthology you sent.[142]

Best wishes to you and your family.
Robert Frost

[*To John Erskine. Dated from internal evidence. ALS. Columbia.*]

[Amherst, MA]
[circa December 1, 1923]

Dear Erskine:

I'm often crossed with just such doubts myself. Why will I perform such tricks on the honest old blank verse with my eyes open? It must be because I'm tempted beyond my strength. It is my way of wickedly sinning. The more I resolve not to do it the more inevitably I seem to do it when my blood is up.

---

140. In a note, Elliot singles out the reference to his having "deplored" "A Star in a Stone-Boat," saying, "I doubt this. I don't recall it." The poems mentioned here all appeared in the *Yale Review* in January 1921.

141. The tiff alluded to is likely a joke (see RF to Elliott, February 10, 1924). "Dust of Snow" is one of the shorter poems RF ever wrote, consisting of one sentence in two stanzas of four- or five-syllable lines; commending "only half" of it would be quite a jest. RF and Elliott remained lifelong friends. It was at RF's urging that Elliott joined the faculty at Amherst in 1925. At the memorial service for Elinor Frost held on April 22, 1938, Elliott served as an honorary pallbearer (her body had been cremated). RF addressed one of his last letters to Elliott and his wife, Alma.

142. George Roy Elliott and Norman Foerster, *English Poetry of the Nineteenth Century: A Connected Representation of Poetic Art and Thought from 1798 to 1914* (New York: Macmillan, 1923).

I suppose I'm a self-shocker. I used to get all the excitement I craved out of making lines like this:

Oň thĕ whīte wāll prĕsēntĕd tŏ thĕ r̄oad.

I think you can probably find lines as extravagant as that in almost anybody's blank verse. It's but the next step beyond – vv – v – vvv – which is to be found everywhere and which is responsible for Charlie Cobb's theory of tettrameters [*sic*].[143] The hanker of my sophisticated ear is always luring me further. I admit that

On the síde it presénted to the róad[144]

is out of bounds.

We won't insist too much on the title poem.[145] You and I know enough to know a lark when we see one with a leg band. It all comes down to a few lyrics, when all's said, and a few such things in blank verse as Birches, The Mountain, The Census-taker, An Old Mans Winter Night, and probably, in spite of its faults to the ear, The Death of the Hired Man.[146]

So very much about me for once to show you that what you think of me isnt much worse than what I think of myself.

I'm grateful for what you wrote

Ever yours

Robert Frost

---

143. Charles W. Cobb (1875–1949), an economist and mathematician at Amherst, co-creator of the Cobb-Douglas production function. His theory of tetrameters is set out in "A Type of Four-Stress Verse in Shakespeare," *New Shakespeareana*, January 1911; "A Scientific Basis for Metrics," *Modern Language Notes*, May 1913; and "A Further Study of the Heroic Tetrameter," *Modern Philology* 14, no. 9 (January 1917).

144. From "Maple" in *NH*. Cobb's theory was that certain lines commonly classified as pentameter in fact contain only four stresses. What Cobb called "heroic tetrameter" was a ten-syllable line of four feet the second of which extended over four syllables (the other feet containing two), with only the second syllable stressed: a "– v v – vv v – v –" pattern, in RF's notation, where "–" signifies a stressed and "v" an unstressed syllable. In common with Gerard Manley Hopkins, albeit almost certainly not influenced by him, Cobb implicitly denies there can be such a thing as a pyrrhic foot in English. The point RF has picked up from Cobb is the frequency in blank verse of lines containing clusters of three unstressed beats, although his model scansion is not the same as Cobb's.

145. "New Hampshire," the longest poem RF had published to date, and one written in a deliberately plain, conversational idiom.

146. The first and fourth poems named are in *MI,* the second and fifth in *NB,* the third in *NH*.

[To Mary C. Goodwillie (1870–1949), Baltimore social luminary, organizer, among other worthy causes, of the Baltimore Poetry Society, and president of the Friends of the Johns Hopkins University Library. ALS. Hopkins.]

Amherst Mass

December 3 1923

Dear Miss Goodwillie

Let me answer your first question of several by saying I remember you so well that I recognized your hand-writing on your envelope. And I had just been thinking you were one of those I must try with my new book to see if they still preferred the least English poetry to any American poetry. I must send you a copy of New Hampshire[147] with our names written in it if you will let me.

Let me answer your second question by saying the Von Moschziskers are among the best imaginable.[148]

Your third by saying that I should like to read again for you.[149] Could you have me on February 21, 22, or 23 and do you think I could earn one hundred dollars and my expenses?[150]

Your tenth (unless I am mistaken in my count) by saying that I think I can bring Mrs Frost with me. She is more foot-loose than she once was now that Lesley is selling books, Marjorie is selling books,[151] Irma is at the Art League[152] and Carroll [sic] is married and farming.[153] Lesley and Marjorie

---

147. Published on November 15, 1923.

148. Robert von Moschzisker (1870–1939) and his wife, Anne, née Vogdes Macbeth (1881–1954). Von Moschzisker had been appointed chief justice of the Pennsylvania Supreme Court in 1921; he would serve until 1930. RF met him in 1915.

149. RF first spoke at Goodwillie's invitation on January 28, 1917, giving a talk at her home in the afternoon and then an evening talk before the Contemporary Club in Baltimore. See *LRF-1*, 506.

150. RF gave a reading at Johns Hopkins University on February 23, 1924.

151. Both had been given an internship to learn the business by Marion Elza Dodd, proprietor of the Hampshire Bookshop in Northampton, Massachusetts. See RF to Dodd, April 30 and May 15, 1923.

152. Irma Frost had been studying, intermittently, at the Art Students League of New York since the fall of 1920.

153. Carol had married Lillian Labatt on November 3. RF gave the new couple his place in South Shaftsbury to farm.

expect to have a bookstore of their own presently when the place shall have been pitched on.[154]

　With best wishes.

Sincerely yours
Robert Frost

[To Lincoln MacVeagh. Date derived from internal evidence. ALS. Jones.]

[Amherst, MA]
[circa December 15, 1923]

Dear Lincoln

　I forgot all about the enclosed agreement. Sorry.[155]

　I'll bet Stephen Burroughs' Memoirs would be much read again.[156] I'll borrow the copy in our library here and fetch it down along when I come for my lecture at Montclair on February 11.[157] You'll say it's fun even though you may not be able to use it. I don't know where there's as good an American book lying buried.

　I'm busier autographing than I ever was before.[158] Some people seem to like the book whether for its being already cut and ready to open anywhere or for its pictures or its type and binding or its lyrics.[159]

------

154. Originally envisaged as being in New York State (see RF to Marion Dodd, April 30, 1923), the place eventually "pitched on" was Pittsfield, Massachusetts, where The Open Book was launched in the spring of 1924.

155. Presumably an agreement associated with MacVeagh's new operation: he had left Henry Holt and Company late in 1923 and founded the Dial Press. It was not affiliated with the magazine *The Dial,* although the offices of both enterprises were in the same building, 461 Park Avenue South. On the manuscript of the letter, MacVeagh has penciled in several explanatory annotations, But he assiduously erased the one over this sentence at some point (it may have concerned his hope that RF would leave Henry Holt and join him at Dial).

156. *The Memoirs of the Notorious Stephen Burroughs* (Albany, New York: B. D. Packard, 1811). MacVeagh had asked RF whether he ought to reissue the book on Dial Press's first list, in 1924. He did, and RF wrote a preface for it (see *CPPP,* 705–708 and *CPRF,* 85–87, 263–264).

157. On a visit to Frederick Melcher, the editor of *Publishers Weekly,* who had a house in Montclair, New Jersey.

158. Autographing copies of the signed, limited edition of *NH,* the first of RF's books to be issued simultaneously in both trade and limited editions.

159. J. J. Lankes provided four woodcuts for the book, which was bound in green board covers, with the title and author's name printed in gold on the spine and on a small

Wish I could see you. I'm impatient to hear the particulars.[160] But you wont come up and I can't come down till I get rested from psychoanalizing [*sic*] the cases of Meiklejaundice.[161] I've got to get into condition to finish a line or two in a long poem (rather long) I mean to give The Dial.[162]

I swear to tell you in a day or two whether I have succeeded in overcoming the prejudice I contracted against Cain from a casual glance at its evolution-istic preface.[163] Oh dear oh dear.

Ever yours
Robert Frost

---

gold plate laid into the front cover toward the top and to the right. Apparently the inspi-ration for the design was the first line in "Nothing Gold Can Stay": "Nature's first green is gold. . . ."

160. Of MacVeagh's plans for his new press.

161. RF's way of describing the business of undoing what he took to be the damage President Alexander Meiklejohn had done to Amherst and its students before he was forced to resign by the board of trustees in the summer of 1923.

162. RF never published a poem in *The Dial*.

163. The reference is to the typescript, then titled "The Death of Cain," of a long poem by Chard Powers Smith (1894–1977). The book was not published under that title, but appeared instead, in 1936, as *A Prelude to Man* (New York: Peter Pauper Press) in a limited edition of 375 copies, to which Maxwell Anderson, Stephen Vincent Benét, Bennett Cerf, Eleanor Roosevelt, and other worthies subscribed. Smith dedicated the poem to E. A. Robinson in a letter written to him on July 7, 1934, and had it printed in the front of the book (Robinson did not live to see it in print: he died in 1935): "This poem, as you know, was begun in 1923 and, being only recently finished and finally revised, repre sents my most ambitious effort. As an expression of personal affection, and in recogni-tion of your position as our leading contemporary poet, I ask that you permit me to dedicate it to you." Beneath this dedication, Smith had Robinson's response—a letter dated July 8, 1934—printed, although in it Robinson speaks a bit warily of *The Prelude to Man* as "altogether unusual" and "generally successful." A reviewer for *Scribner's Maga-zine* called the book "an epic of evolution." In a letter to Smith dated August 26, 1935, Robinson Jeffers spoke of the poem, which he had not yet read, as tackling "a splendid difficult De-rerum-natura kind of subject," adding: "I am sure you have managed it well, if [E. A.] Robinson liked it." See James Karman, ed., *The Collected Letters of Robinson Jeffers, with Selected Letters of Una Jeffers: Volume 2, 1931–1939* (Stanford, CA: Stanford University Press, 2011).

[*To Morris Tilley, professor of English at the University of Michigan. Date derived from internal evidence. ALS. UM.*]

[Amherst, MA]

[circa December 15, 1923]

Dear Tilley

I sent you Bursley and Burton each a copy of New Hampshire by express more than a week ago.[164] I let myself be lead [*sic*] to suppose express might be better than post at this season. A letter from Mrs Bursley says nothing about having received a book. So it begins to look as if I had made a mistake.

Of course I shall be happy to read again for a University audience.[165] We'll fix up a date in the neighborhood of April 1st unless that comes wrong for you. Elinor will tell you about my calendar. I wonder if you would ask the Whimsies what their plans would be. They have been asking about mine. Can theirs be reconciled with yours? You know I would rather have two audiences in Sara Caswell Angel [*sic*] than one twice the size in Hill.[166]

There's a matter that's just come up in my mind to trouble me. You must wonder at my coming to Amherst after what I said to you about coming back to Michigan. But if you stop to consider you will see no great inconsistency. Michigan on year-to-year contract and no prospect of settling down and making myself at home was out of the question. I may not have made myself clear enough on that point when you felt me out on our walk that day. I was too homeless for my age out there and too dissatisfied with the way Burton conceived of the fellowship. If someone had asked me to give one seminar a week out there as long as I wanted to stay for 5000 a year I

---

164. Marion LeRoy Burton was president of the university; Joseph A. Bursley, professor of engineering, was dean of students.

165. RF spent March 30 through April 3, 1924, in Ann Arbor, during which time he served as poet in residence, staying with Bursley and his wife, attending programs in his honor, and giving a public reading.

166. The Whimsies was a student literary society, several of whose members RF befriended when he taught at Michigan during the 1921–1923 school years. Angell Hall and Hill Auditorium are both on the campus at Michigan (the second much larger than the first). Angell Hall was named for Sarah Caswell Angell (1831–1903), wife of James Burrill Angell, who served as president of the university for thirty-eight years, from 1871 to 1909.

should have taken him up.[167] I liked the folks. I made more and closer friends than I ever did before.

Merry Christmas to you all.

Ever yours
Robert Frost

Hope you will like the book.

[*To Witter Bynner. ALS. Harvard.*]

Amherst Mass
December 21, 1923

Dear Witter Bynner

If I knew your shining number, street, and village I should be sending you for Christmas, with affectionate greetings, the following two books: my New Hampshire and my Selected Poems.[168]

One of the two books you have just caused to be sent me without inscription or autograph (and it serves me jolly well right) is a reminder that I am not the first one to sprinkle the name of New Hampshire all over a poem. But yours is a lovely mounting thing of song while mine frankly goes on foot or feet.[169] I don't know what you will say to mine. You had best perhaps say

---

167. Michigan offered RF just such an appointment in the fall of 1924. He accepted it only to resign and return to Amherst the following year. The return to Amherst was all but necessitated by the illnesses and related difficulties that beset his children, who lived in or near South Shaftsbury, Vermont, and Pittsfield, Massachusetts. RF continued to support all but one of them.

168. RF addressed the envelope, which survives, to Bynner care of Alfred A. Knopf, Bynner's publisher, with a note: "Please hasten forward." Someone at Knopf added the correct address: Box 1061, Santa Fe, New Mexico.

169. Bynner had sent RF a copy of his volume of poetry, *The New World* (New York: M. Kennerley, 1915), in which New Hampshire figures in such enraptured lines as these (utterly different from RF's informal, conversational, though not pedestrian, "New Hampshire"):

A little hill among New Hampshire hills
Touches more stars than any height I know.
For there the whole earth—like a single being—fills
And expands with heaven.
It is the hill where Celia used to go
To watch Monadnock and the miles that met

nothing to it, but pass it by and hasten on to where I am lyrical, and there is no embarrassment for either of us.[170] We are all agreed about lyric anyway. You yourself are at your very best in your lyrics. I have seen The New World before, but from this rereading have realized more than ever your special quality among us and the place so much your own it gives you. You are one of the half dozen poets who aren't lost in the general poetic society or in each other.

Ever yours
Robert Frost

[*To Herbert Dickinson Ward (1861–1932), American journalist and author. ALS. ACL.*]

[Amherst, MA]
Dec 27 1923.

Dear Mr Ward:

I knew your father and both your aunts so well (they were the first friends of my poetry) that I could almost feel as if I had always known you too.[171] I am greatly pained at what has overtaken Miss Susan. I had just been thinking I

In slow-ascending slopes of peace.
 She said: "When I am here, I find release
From every petty debt I owe,
The goods I bring with me increase,
The ills are riven
And blown away. And there remains a single debt
Toward all the world for me,
A single duty and one destiny."
 "There shall be many births of God
In this humanity,"
She said, "and many crucifixions on the hills,
Before we learn that where Christ trod
We all shall tread; and as he died to give
Himself to us, we too shall die—and live."

From 1906 to 1915, Bynner had lived in Cornish, New Hampshire, home to the Cornish Art Colony (which arose in about 1885, after a number of artists followed Augustus St. Gaudens to his retreat there).

170. Almost all the lyric poems in *NH* are gathered in its third section, titled "Grace Notes."

171. William Hayes Ward and Susan Hayes Ward were the editor and poetry editor, respectively, of *The Independent* (New York) when RF started placing poems there in the mid-1890s. Hetta Ward was their sister.

must get to South Berwick again while she was still of this world. And now I am too late.[172] I don't suppose she would know me if she saw me or would get any pleasure out of a letter. We had a grand talk about poetry together the last time I went to South Berwick. I didn't notice that her faculties were failing then. She gave me the only material I was ever able to make a poem to order out of—some childhood memory of her own. You could find it if you looked in my latest book under the title Wild Grapes.[173] I wish I had published the fact that it was written by request of Susan Hayes Ward as a companion-piece of another poem of mine called Birches. She said Birches was for boys and she wanted me to do another like it on nearly the same subject for girls. For all we so seldom saw each other we were great friends. My wife and I both cared for her more than I can tell you.

You ask me to your class reunion at a time when I am at my worst for practical purposes. I am nursing a throat that has been bothering me for more than a month. I don't believe it will do for me to go out speaking in a spoke-laden[174] after-dinner atmosphere—not if I am intending to get into shape for next term's work. I have had to ask Duffy [sic] to excuse me from an engagement to speak for him at Courtland [sic] NY.[175]

I shall be delighted to look you up in Brookline. Thank you for the invitation.

Amherst smiles serenely.[176]

Always yours faithfully
Robert Frost

---

172. Susan Hayes Ward died several weeks later.

173. Details of the origin of this poem are given in CPRF, 194–95.

174. The reading in the manuscript is clear: RF is possibly punning on the sense of "spoke" as "impediment," or "opinion," sixteenth- and seventeenth-century usages.

175. The Cortland Normal School, established by the New York State Legislature in 1868, now the State University of New York College at Cortland. "Duffy" is likely Hugh M. Duffey, born in 1841, previously a member of the local board of the Cortland Normal School, or his son, Hugh Duffey Jr., born in 1884.

176. Herbert Ward was an alumnus.

[*To Charles Lowell Young. Date derived from postmark. ALS. Wellesley.*]

[Amherst, MA]
[December 29, 1923]

Dear Young:

I ought to be shot or called names for denaturing my Christmas present to you.[177] But you should beware of a man who is in the act of getting out a book. He is like an army going into battle. He is almost as dangerous to his friends as to his enemies. You have found that out now.

But lets make up.

I wish you would publish a book. I honestly do for <u>my</u> sake.[178]

Ever yours
Robert Frost

[*To Dorothy Dunbar Bromley. ALS. UVA.*]

Amherst
Dec 30 1923

Dear Miss Bromley

Smith's book is remarkable for imagery and idea, if not for cadence.[179] Why dont you indulge Stephen Benet if he very much wants to see it published? It wont quite do for me. The terrible evolutionary preface is against it and so is the length of the second poem. I suppose it is the second poem that is most prejudicial. It is not only too long, but it is carried too near the level of shouting like platform oratory, albeit the platforms it is delivered from seem to be boulders and peaks. The really good idea in it depends too much for expression on the word Fear—forever with a capital F. But the book shows power and generosity. Out of such wealth there is sure to be some interesting development. Out of quantity comes quality and from nowhere else in my opinion.

---

177. No record survives of what RF means here by "denaturing" his present to Young, almost certainly a copy of *NH*, although the reference likely is to an inscription of some kind. See RF to Young, August 24, 1923, for a discussion of *NH* as RF was preparing the book for the press.

178. It would be nearly two decades before Young brought out a book, his 1941 study, *Emerson's Montaigne.*

179. Again, a reference to "The Death of Cain" (see the postscript), by Chard Powers Smith. See the notes to RF's December 15, 1923, letter to MacVeagh.

Smith should be worth keeping track of and even holding onto. I like his mind so well I wish I liked his book better.

I shall have to have ten more of my books to cast on the waters.[180]

Thank you for Mrs Harriman's book.[181] More than one of us will be sure to enjoy it.

Nice of Maynard to write this way.[182]

With best wishes for a Happy New Year.

Sincerely yours

Robert Frost

The Death of Cain goes by mail today.

[*To J. J. Lankes. ALS. HRC.*]

Amherst

December 31 1923

My dear Lankes:

Though your pictures began pouring in so many months ago, they didnt really become mine by my reckoning till they were framed and on the wall. That was near enough Christmas to make them all Christmas presents along with the book plate which came last. They make our dining room as they made my Christmas. There are several of them I can't get over. No one ever dug a better thing out of wood than that benighted back side of a village in snow or than that unearthly-lighted empty house.[183] I'm proud of

---

180. *NH* (and—given the plural—perhaps also *SP*). As for "casting" them "on the waters," see Ecclesiastes 11:1.

181. Florence Jaffray "Daisy" Harriman (1870–1967) was an American socialite, suffragist, social reformer, organizer, and, later, diplomat. Henry Holt and Company published her memoir, *From Pinafores to Politics*, in 1923.

182. The reference to Maynard is unclear, but perhaps it is to Theodore Maynard, *Our Best: English and American Poets* (New York: Henry Holt, 1922), or to a note concerning it forwarded by Bromley to RF. The book reprinted Maynard's laudatory essay on RF, "Snow the Predominant Note in Frost's Poetry," originally published in the *New York Tribune*, June 27, 1920. See RF to Braithwaite, September 4, 1920, and the notes thereto.

183. Among Lankes' gifts, RF singles out woodcuts entitled *Winter* and *Deserted House*, and a bookplate that featured the Stone House (in South Shaftsbury) along a rutted dirt road.

having thought of you for the book. People have all spoken of your part in it. We wont attempt to divide the honors, however, separating yours from mine. We'll hold them in common like true communists of the Golden Age, who talked no economics neither any sociology. Sometime soon we must have a little black and white book together of verse and picture in equal measure.[184] But first I wish you would beat about New Hampshire and Vermont a summer. You speak of hay fever. Where do you run to from that? I probably know more about refuges from poisonous pollens than anyone they haven't killed. We must talk them over when I see you as I hope to late in March on my way to Ann Arbor on business.[185] You arent expecting to come to New York are you? Because if you are I wish you would come round by way of Springfield and stay with us a night or two. It wouldn't be much out of your way.

> Ever Yours
> Robert Frost

[*To Mabel B. Lovell, née Mabel B. Brackett (1870–1942), of Cranford, New Jersey. It is undated, but "1924" is penciled in at the top of the first sheet, likely by Lovell. Lovell, herself a poet, was involved with Women's Clubs in New Jersey, and placed a poem in the anthology* A Book of Verses by New Jersey Clubwomen *(Newark: New Jersey Federation of Women's Clubs, 1929). ALS. BU.*]

[1924]

My dear Miss Lovell

Your question asks too much because it doesnt allow me enough. I don't believe I can keep my list down to ten.[186] I could be more comfortable in a list of fifteen. This is partly because they are alive. I could judge them more closely if they were dead. Let these be my choice for the moment:

---

184. The project never got off the ground. See RF to Lankes, July 6, 1925.

185. In March RF would travel to Ann Arbor for a short residency, and also to meet with the University of Michigan's president, Marion LeRoy Burton, who had been authorized by the board of regents to offer RF a position as a Fellow in Letters at a salary of $5,000 a year.

186. Penciled in are check marks beside the following poets in RF's list of his American contemporaries (again, presumably by Lovell, who had asked for a "top ten"): Lindsay, Robinson, Sandburg, Lowell, Aiken, Bynner, Teasdale, Masters, Benét (from whose name RF omits the accent), and Markham.

Vachel Lindsay

E. A. Robinson

Carl Sandburg

Amy Lowell

Conrad Aiken

Louis Untermeyer

John Gould Fletcher

Witter Bynner

Sara Teasdall [*sic*]

Alfred Kreymborg

Edna St Vincent Millay

Elinor Wylie

Edgar Lee Masters

William Rose Benet

Bliss Carman

Edwin Markham

Give me an inch and I takes [*sic*] an ell. My fifteen stretches into sixteen. The last two perhaps only ought to count as one because, though they are just as good as anybody else and are both still living, they seem to have wound up their writing. Attach no significance to the order; the sixteen are somewhere near equal in my estimation. If you restricted me to five, they would probably be the first five.

Sincerely yours

Robert Frost

[To Dorothy Dunbar Bromley. Dated from internal evidence. ALS. UVA.]

[Amherst, MA]

[circa January 1924]

Dear Mrs Bromley

All I meant was that shorn of its preface and somewhat reduced as to its second part the Cain book would be pretty surely worth publishing. It may possibly be worth publishing even as it is. The stuff of it is poetical: I can see that. I'm struck with the anthropological idea of the first part and the psychological idea of the second part. But I'm not quite won. Why won't Stephen Benet take the whole responsibility for it if he likes it so much?[187] I'm honestly not satisfied with it; the man I see behind it in the author is so much better than the book.

Will you let the Oxford Press know at once that Bliss Carman has our permission to use such poems of mine as he likes.[188] He has been good enough to listen to me about some of them; the choice of the rest I cheerfully leave to him.

I am enclosing a letter to the Manchester Union lady that may help her with her article.[189] I should think she might like to bring the Derry house into her story. Derry is almost a suburb of Manchester—only ten miles out by trolley.

That's a live book of Edgar Singers.[190] I read almost through it at one go. I must tell the boys about it.

Sincerely yours

Robert Frost

[*To George H. Sargent (1867–1931), American bibliographer, book collector, and journalist. For some years he wrote a column, "The Bibliographer," for the* Boston Evening Transcript, *about rare books. Sargent had a summer place called the Elm Farm, in Warner, New Hampshire. Date derived from postmark. ALS. UFL.*]

[Amherst, MA]

[January 9, 1924]

Dear Mr Sargent:

Your letter stirs me to fellow feeling. Apparently we have had like aspirations, and we have met with somewhat the same disappointments. Farming seemed the ideal occupation to combine with poetry, if you couldnt have poetry alone, as of course you couldn't. So I ran away to the land instead of

---

187. Stephen Vincent Benét had recommended "Cain."

188. Bliss Carman selected several of RF's poems for his *Oxford Book of American Verse* (New York: Oxford University Press, 1927). See also RF to MacVeagh, November 19, 1923 (page 374).

189. The article, entitled "Robert Frost Sings Lyrics of State," appeared in the *Manchester Union Leader* on January 28, 1924, in the "About Books and Those Who Create Them Section" of the paper. No author is listed, but the initials "A. M. S." appear after all notices in the section. The editors thank Rebecca Stockbridge of the New Hampshire State Library for her help with this annotation.

190. Henry Holt and Company published Edgar A. Singer's *Modern Thinkers and Present Problems* in 1923.

running away to sea. It was a reckless plunge. All I knew of farming I had acquired by working out on farms in spring and summer vacations. I had learned to plant most seeds take care of hay and keep hens laying. (I had always bred hens since childhood in San Francisco.) But I had never learned horses or cows. I couldnt milk a cow. We came out better than was to be expected on these premises. We lived as farmers six or seven years poorly of course and with some help from outside and going a little deeper into debt every year.[191] I remember being troubled in conscience about declaring myself a farmer to the census-taker. I decided that I was a genuine farmer though a bad one. But if I was wretched I was happy. Farming wasnt just an expense. It was part of a living. And it was an idyl; it was woods and fields and a chance to have it out with myself in solitude. I went to the farm in Derry N.H. dubious in health and afraid of the world.[192] The farm reconstituted me.[193] By my reckoning it was a success and so was I as I have never been before or since. I like a few people to know the truth of the matter. I dont want credit for feats of farming I never performed.

In England we raised some vegetables and kept some hens.

I should like to hear the rest of the story of how I kept the peace between the rival poets. Maybe it was by being amused at Pound's challenge to Abercrombie.[194]

---

191. The Frosts lived on a farm in Derry, New Hampshire, from 1900 to 1909. RF took a teaching post at nearby Pinkerton Academy in 1906, bringing to a close the family's six-year attempt to live by farming alone. As for "help from outside": the Derry farm was purchased for RF by his paternal grandfather, William Prescott Frost Sr., who also willed to RF a $500 annuity to continue for ten years after his death—he died in 1901—at which point it would rise to $800 and RF would be given sole ownership of the farm. RF sold the Derry farm in November 1911, after accepting a position at the Plymouth Normal School, in Plymouth, New Hampshire. See RF's poem "On the Sale of My Farm" (*CPPP*, 519).

192. RF suffered from pulmonary complaints (among other things), a matter of some concern to the family, given that his father had died of tuberculosis.

193. Compare this account of the Derry years to the one given in *LRF-1:* "I kept farm, so to speak for nearly ten years, but less as a farmer than as a fugitive from the world that seemed to me to 'disallow' me. It was all instinctive, but I can see now that I went away to save myself and fix myself before I measured my strength against all creation. I was never really out of the world for good and all. I liked people even when I believed I detested them" (265).

194. The reference is to a tale about which Sargent had apparently queried RF. Ezra Pound detested the yearly *Georgian* anthologies, edited by Edward Marsh beginning in 1912, in which the poetry of Lascelles Abercrombie, a Frost family friend, was a fixture.

Sometime I shall hope to meet you, either by your coming over the mountains to me or my coming over the mountains to you.[195]

Sincerely yours

Robert Frost

Amherst for the winter

[To Robert Hillyer (1895–1961). The letter is undated, but a note in another hand appears in the top-right corner of the letter; internal evidence confirms it. ALS. UVA.]

[South Shaftsbury, VT]

[January 25, 1924]

Dear Hillyer:

You must think I'm lazy or very busy or just stuffy and hard to please. I don't know what I am in these days. I don't have to be anything nameable with you do I?

Thanks for wanting the Census-taker.[196] You made no mistake with me in singling it out from my others. It's one I have had complacent moments over.

If I say nothing of your poems it is because I havent got round to sending Braithwaite my check for them yet.[197] Im sure from the book you gave me

---

In an October 12, 1915, letter to Harriet Monroe, Pound called Abercrombie a "literary hencoop" (D. D. Paige, ed., *Selected Letters of Ezra Pound: 1907–1941* [New York: New Directions, 1971], 64). Forrest Reid recalled that Pound once challenged Abercrombie to a duel "for advising young poets to abandon realism and study Wordsworth." Abercrombie suggested that the two poets use as weapons unsold copies of their own books. See Humphrey Carpenter, *A Serious Character: The Life of Ezra Pound* (New York: Dell, 1988), 178–179.

195. The White Mountains. They rise between Warner, New Hampshire, where Sargent had his farm, and Franconia and Sugar Hill, New Hampshire, where the Frosts typically summered to get above the hay-fever line, and where they had lived from 1915 to 1920.

196. "The Census-Taker," first published in the *New Republic* on April 6, 1921, and later collected in *NH*.

197. We have been unable to identify the poems. RF may refer to Hillyer's *The Coming Forth by Day: An Anthology of Poems from the Egyptian Book of the Dead, Together with an Essay on the Egyptian Religion*, published in Boston by B. J. Brimmer (1923), a firm founded by William Stanley Braithwaite, with whom RF had been acquainted since 1915. RF later wrote a whimsical letter-in-verse, "A Restoration," to Hillyer that drew on materials in *Coming Forth of Day*. See Edward Connery Lathem and Lawrance Thompson, eds., *Robert*

you are in the right road for you.[198] Now go the whole length of it. And I'll be watching.

Always yours friendly
Robert Frost

[To George R. Elliott. Elliott marked up the manuscript, underlining two sentences, for which he provides annotations, given in the footnotes here. The book under discussion is NH. ALS. ACL.*]*

Amherst Feb 10 1924

Dear Elliott

Of course you would know I was just teasing you.[199] I was fishing for just what I got. I know no one whose praise I like better than yours. If I can be as good as you make me out in some respects I am perfectly willing to be as bad as you make me out in other respects. I quite give up that line to you.[200] It is an unideal son of a bitch. I am incapable of the defense of it you put into my mouth. Nothing is ever sacred merely because it came to me that way.

These dulcet prose essays[201] you send are a proof if any is needed of how near together we have kept for all we haven't seen each other for two or three

---

Frost: Poetry and Prose (New York: Holt, Rinehart and Winston, 1972), 310 311; the letter-poem is also in *CPPP* (544–545).

198. Possibly a manuscript of Hillyer's *A Halt in the Garden* (London: Elkins, 1925). Hillyer was awarded a prize of $100 for the title poem by the *Stratford Monthly,* the magazine in which the poem first appeared.

199. See RF to Elliott, circa December 1, 1923.

200. Elliott here adds a note: "I cannot recall the verse I objected to. GRE."

201. Elliott here adds a second note: "probably including my essay on Arnold," a reference to his "The Arnoldian Lyric Melancholy," published in *PMLA* 38, no. 4 (December 1923): 929–932. It begins on a note RF would have seconded—he never regarded the sources of Arnold's, or of any good poet's, melancholy as chiefly "contemporary," that is, of their day only: "Matthew Arnold is in general so confidently clear as to the nature of his own poetry that the reader is apt to credit him when he insists upon the contemporary sources of its melancholy. But those contemporary sources will appear much dimmer when the second or third centenary of his birth (December 24, 1822) shall come round. The 'two worlds' that the poet wandered between will doubtless be rather nebular on the rear horizon, and the carefully wrought stanzas concerning them may seem the 'stretched metre of an antique song.' The cursory commemorating reader, when he reaches the poem on Growing Old, may toss the volume aside with the remark that 'this old fellow carefully architectured his gloom, but added here too obvious a gable'" (929).

years (it must be) now. Odd that we should both have been writing of the Arnoldian misgivings.[202] How anyone can see in the author of The Scholar Gypsy [*sic*] a rock on which to climb out of the water!

Compare RF in his 1935 "Letter to *The Amherst Student*": "You will often hear it said that the age of the world we live in is particularly bad. I am impatient of such talk. We have no way of knowing that this age is one of the worst in the world's history. Arnold claimed the honor for the age before this. Wordsworth claimed it for the last but one. And so on back through literature. I say they claimed the honor for their ages. They claimed it rather for themselves. It is immodest of a man to think of himself as going down before the worst forces ever mobilized by God" (*CPRF*, 114). As for the close relationship between RF and Elliott: the following year, 1925, at RF's urging, Elliott left the chair he had held for twelve years at Bowdoin and joined the Department of English at Amherst; a year later, in 1926, partly at Elliott's urging, Amherst brought RF back from the appointment he had accepted (again) at the University of Michigan.

202.   RF refers to a passage from the title poem to his 1923 volume, *NH*, which he had sent Elliott as a Christmas gift:

> *I know a man who took a double ax*
> *And went alone against a grove of trees;*
> *But his heart failing him, he dropped the ax*
> *And ran for shelter quoting Matthew Arnold:*
> *" 'Nature is cruel, man is sick of blood':*
> *There's been enough shed without shedding mine.*
> *Remember Birnam Wood! The wood's in flux!"*
> *He had a special terror of the flux*
> *That showed itself in dendrophobia.*
> *The only decent tree had been to mill*
> *And educated into boards, he said.*
> *He knew too well for any earthly use*
> *The line where man leaves off and nature starts.*
> *And never overstepped it save in dreams.*
> *He stood on the safe side of the line talking—*
> *Which is sheer Matthew Arnoldism,*
> *The cult of one who owned himself "a foiled*
> *Circuitous wanderer," and "took dejectedly*
> *His seat upon the intellectual throne"* . . . (*CPPP*, 161)

The last lines quoted are from Arnold's "The Scholar-Gipsy," which speaks of "this strange disease of modern life, / With its sick hurry, its divided aims, / Its heads o'ertax'd, its palsied hearts . . ." For a detailed discussion of Arnold as he figures in "New Hampshire," see Donald G. Sheehy, " 'Everybody's Sanity': Metaphor and Mental Health in Frost," in *Robert Frost in Context*, ed. Mark Richardson (New York: Cambridge University Press, 2014), 352–355.

I'm a good deal out of sorts with you for not having stopped on your way past here to or from Ann Arbor. But probably there was something in the conditions of your ticket that forbade.

My best to you. I must see you some time again before long.

Ever yours
Robert Frost

I'm out of luck that you didnt get my book to review.

[To Morris Tilley. Undated, but "[1924?]" has been penciled in at the top of the sheet, by a cataloguer or by Tilley. A more precise dating is afforded by the chronology Lawrance Thompson prepared while at work on his biography of the poet, and by another letter to Tilley, dated February 20. RF and his wife, Elinor, visited Ann Arbor briefly, from March 30 to April 3, 1924, during which stay RF did in fact give one public reading (see RF to Tilley, February 20, 1924). ALS. UM.]

[Amherst, MA]
[circa February 10, 1924]

Dear Tilley

No it wouldn't do. It would look too much as if I were trying to shout the Laureate down.[203] It is his inning this year. It becomes me to slip into and out of town with my hand bag like the merest traveling salesman. Our main object is to see you all again. You wouldnt suspect how warmly we are looking forward to that. Don't hire a hall for me.

Ever yours
Robert Frost

Sorry about the mumps.

---

203. RF had been invited to spend part of the spring as poet in residence at the University of Michigan, which he was reluctant to do. Robert Bridges, named British poet laureate in 1913, visited the United States in 1924. The trip was occasioned by an offer of the Fellowship in Creative Arts at the University of Michigan, which RF had been the first to hold (from 1921–1923). Bridges resided in Ann Arbor from early April to June 1924, when the university awarded him an honorary degree. Hence RF's wish to get in and out of town before Bridges arrived, so as not to appear to "shout the Laureate down."

[*To John W. Haines. ALS-photostat. DCL.*]

Amherst Mass U.S.A.

February 18 1924

Dear Jack:

Did you ever receive the copy of my new book I sent you in December? I think if you did you would have found something to say about it however embarrassed you may have been by the rather nonsensical prefatory poem in it. At least you would have said you liked the poems in it that you liked before they were in it. I can only conclude that it got lost; and I'm sorry, for I wanted it to remind you of us at Christmas. But it will be easy to send you another.

I'm teaching too hard this year. I suppose it is good for me in the eyes of the inscrutable.

Our love to you all.

Ever yours

Robert Frost

[*To Morris Tilley. ALS. UM.*]

Amherst Mass

February 20 1924

Dear Tilley:

I see no great need of my reading again so soon at Ann Arbor. Neither I nor the University will have changed enough to make me a novelty to it. Why do you bother to try to get me an audience? Let's just spend the time in friendly talk about who the five greatest moderns are. But if you are committed to getting me an audience, know that my time with you will extend from Sunday afternoon March 30 to early Thursday morning April 3, and you may act upon me accordingly.[204] It will be fun to see several of you again. I got to be a good deal more Ann Arboreal than I should suppose I could have

---

204. RF did travel to Ann Arbor as here specified, where he gave a reading at the university and attended events held in his honor.

at my age. A few people and streets and a lot of the outlying landscape are pretty well incorporated in me.

Ever yours

Robert Frost

Of course I must sit with the Whimsies an evening.[205]

[*To Ferris Greenslet (1875–1959), American writer and editor. Greenslet worked at Houghton Mifflin, publishers of the book RF discusses in this letter. Apparently Greenslet had sent it to him for comment. ALS. Harvard.*]

Amherst March 4 1924

My dear Greenslet:

Only last week I sat up all night with the Miller over a son,[206] and here I am called on by Miss Norton to sit up with him again over a daughter.[207] The product of his grinding may be flour; the bi-product is certainly difficult children. Miss Norton makes him a sympathetic figure. I could have taken the book at one reading on my interest in him, let alone the tune he lives to. It's a not unsophisticated measure. You must have known I would like the way Miss Norton throws and all but breaks the accents of speech across the accents of her meter. Where has she been getting her hand in for such virtuosity?[208] She reminds me a little of Christina Rossetti in Goblin Market.[209]

---

205. The undergraduate literary society The members RF knew best were Yuki Osawa, Stella Brunt, Dorothy Greenwald, and Halsey Davidson.

206. Poems and stories dealing with millers and their sons are legion. The likely candidate here is Walter de la Mare's "The Miller and His Son," in his collection *Songs of Childhood* (London: Longmans, Green, 1902; rev. ed., London: Longmans, Green, 1923).

207. Grace Fallow Norton (1876–1962), American poet. In July 1923 *Poetry* had devoted half an issue to her narrative poem "The Miller's Youngest Daughter: An Unfinished Story," subsequently reprinted in book form as *The Miller's Youngest Daughter* (Boston and New York: Houghton Mifflin, 1924), which RF refers to here.

208. Norton's first volume of poetry, *Little Gray Songs from St. Joseph's* (Boston and London: Houghton Mifflin), had appeared in 1912. *The Miller's Youngest Daughter* is written in stanzas of varying structure and length (the principle motive being quatrains, though these rhyme in differing ways).

209. Christina Rossetti (1830–1894), English poet, admired and often taught by RF. "Goblin Market" (1862) is her best-known poem. Norton's *Little Gray Songs* is derivative of Rossetti's religious verse.

She has this in common with Christina Rossetti that her imagery is rather of the ear than of the eye. She excels in imagining the inflections of speech.

Thanks for the book. We all liked it.

> Sincerely yours
> Robert Frost

[To John Gould Fletcher, who was at the time in England. ALS. Arkansas.]

> Amherst Mass USA.
> March 8 1924

Dear Fletcher:

Now if you will send along your manuscript I will see what can be done about it.[210] I think I have found you a publisher you may want to settle down with for life and be at rest. Of course I can promise nothing definitely. Let me not get your hopes up too high. He is not accepting your book through me unread. But all he has to do is like it half as well as your others, and I guess it will be a go. He is in a position to choose the poetry for a new firm. You may know his name, Donald Warner,[211] something of a poet himself and a greater friend of mine than anyone now left in the Holts. I failed with you there, for one reason, because the Holts were all upset in the literary department from the going of MacVeagh.[212] I dont think I shall fail this time. I make no bones of saying I am eager to pay you in a lump sum for the generous backing you have given me through thick and thin. I should hate to think I fell below the ordinary statesman in acknowledgement of my political debts. We profes-

---

210. The Fletcher manuscript that RF was unable to place with an American publisher may have been *Parables,* which was published in a limited edition by K. Paul, Trench, Trubner (London) in 1925. See also RF to Fletcher, May 24, 1924.

211. Perhaps a slip of the pen (or of memory). The likeliest candidate is Donald Brace (1881–1955), who joined Alfred Harcourt in 1919 when both left Henry Holt and Company to start a new firm, Harcourt, Brace and Howe. Brace had been particularly active in bringing poets to the firm, including Carl Sandburg and Claude McKay. The company seems to answer to the account RF here gives of it as a place a poet "may want to settle down with for life and be at rest."

212. Lincoln MacVeagh, with whom RF had worked closely, left Henry Holt and Company—to RF's chagrin—in December 1923 to found the Dial Press. In speaking of "failing with" Holt, RF alludes to his role as a paid consultant to the firm on acquisitions.

sional sensibilitists have to be on our guard against deadening. The professional feeler is too apt to get so he can't feel except professionally.

Ever yours
Robert Frost

[*To Louis Untermeyer. The letter is undated, but the postmarked envelope—addressed
to Untermeyer in Vienna, Austria—survives. ALS. LoC.*]

[Amherst, MA]
[circa March 10, 1924]

Dear old Louis:

Since last I saw you I have come to the conclusion that style in prose or
verse is that which indicates how the writer takes himself and what he is
saying.[213] Let the sound of Stevenson go through your mind empty and you
will realize that he never took himself other than as an amusement.[214] Do
the same with Swinburne[215] and you will see that he took himself as a
wonder. Many sensitive natures have plainly shown by their style that they
took themselves lightly in self-defense. They are the ironists. Some fair to
good writers have no style and so leave us ignorant of how they take themselves. But that is the one important thing to know: because on it depend our
likes and dislikes. A novelist seems to be the only kind of writer who can
make a name without a style: which is only one more reason for not both
ering with the novel. I am not satisfied to let it go at the aphorism that the
style is the man.[216] The man's ideas would be some element then of his style.
So would his deeds. But I would narrow the definition. His deeds are his
deeds; his ideas are his ideas. His style is the way he carries himself toward
his ideas and deeds. Mind you if he is down-spirited it will be all he can do to
have the ideas without the carriage. The style is out of his superfluity. It is

---

213. RF would later elaborate on many of the ideas in this letter in his "Introduction"
to E. A. Robinson's *King Jasper* (1935) (*CPRF*, 116–122; 282–288).

214. Robert Louis Stevenson (1850–1894), Scottish novelist, poet, and essay writer.

215. Algernon Charles Swinburne (1837–1909), English poet, playwright, novelist and
critic.

216. On August 25, 1783, Georges-Louis LeClerc, Comte de Buffon (1707–1788), delivered his *Discours sur le style* to the Académie française, wherein he exclaimed, "Writing
well consists of thinking, feeling and expressing well, of clarity and wit, soul and
taste. . . . The style is the man himself."

the mind skating circles round itself as it moves forward. Emerson had one of the noblest least egotistical of styles.[217] By comparison with it Thoreau's was conceited, Whitmans bumptious.[218] Carlyle's way of taking himself simply infuriates me.[219] Longfellow took himself with the gentlest twinkle. I don't suppose you know his miracle play in The Golden Legend, Birds of Killingworth, Simon Danz or Othere.[220]

I own any form of humor shows fear and inferiority. Irony is simply a kind of guardedness. So is a twinkle. It keeps the reader from criticism. Whittier when he shows any style at all is probably a greater person than Longfellow as he is lifted priestlike above consideration of the scornful.[221] Belief is better than anything else and it is best when rapt above paying its respects to anybody's doubts whatsoever. At bottom the world isn't a joke. We only joke about it to avoid an issue with some one; to let some one know that we know he's there with his questions: to disarm him by seeming to have heard and done justice to his side of the standing argument. Humor is the most engaging cowardice. With it myself I have been able to hold some of my enemy in play far out of gunshot.

There are people like John Gould Fletcher I would fain not have let in on myself; if I could have held them off all my life with smiles they could take as they pleased. But John G. pushed through my defenses. Let me tell you what happened. It was amusing. You might like to pass it along to Huebsh [sic]: you know him so well.[222] You could quote this part of my letter word for word. Three months ago John Gould Fletcher wrote me saying "I learn you have a book out. I wish you would use your influence with Henry Holt & Co. to

---

217. Ralph Waldo Emerson (1803–1182), American essayist and poet.

218. Henry David Thoreau (1817–1862), American author and naturalist, and Walt Whitman (1819–1892), American poet.

219. Thomas Carlyle (1795–1881), Scottish essayist and philosopher.

220. RF refers respectively to Henry Wadsworth Longfellow's "The Nativity: A Miracle Play" from *The Golden Legend* (1851), "The Poet's Tale: The Birds of Killingworth" (1863), "A Dutch Picture" (1878) (which RF refers to by its opening line: "Simon Danz has come home again, / From cruising about with his buccaneers"), and "The Discoverer of the North Cape" (1858) (which RF refers to by its opening line: "Othere, the old sea captain, / Who dwelt in Helgoland . . .").

221. John Greenleaf Whittier (1807–1892), American poet and abolitionist.

222. B. W. Huebsch (1876–1964) was the first firm in America to publish the works of James Joyce and D. H. Lawrence. He also published Sherwood Anderson's *Winesburg, Ohio* in 1919.

help me get a book out. I am sending them a manuscript." I spoke to Lincoln MacVeagh in the matter. He said he wouldn't publish John Gould Fletcher's book for two simple reasons: first because it wouldnt sell and second because he hated the kind of thing Fletcher wrote. I said I wouldn't ask him to publish it to get me a good review or save me from a bad one. Obviously he might have published Fletcher's book and charged it up to advertising mine. Maurice Firuski knew about this and made haste to tell me the minute it was out that I had got the bad review in The Freeman.[223] No doubt I deserved it on two counts that we needn't go into. But I can't excuse Fletcher his bad taste— worthy of Washington politics or New York business. Have I not written in New Hampshire that it's no wonder poets some times have to <u>seem</u> so much more businesslike than business men?[224] It is because they are so much less sensitive from having overused their sensibilities. Men who have to feel for a living would unavoidably become altogether unfeeling except professionally. And The Freeman's part in it interests me. It just shows how hard it is for an American publication, however lofty its pretensions, to keep from lending itself to blackmail and corruption. Probably The Freeman is having the most superior editorials on the state of affairs in Washington. There endeth all that might concern the editors and publisher of The Freeman.

We havent given up the idea of getting to France and England this summer. Amherst goes sadly, I'm afraid I have to admit. I'd like to look at it receding from the deck of an outward bound ship. The trouble seems to be the usual one in this world, to stop being crazy without falling stupid. But you know me, Al.[225] I'm always on the point of jumping overboard because the ship is

---

223. John Gould Fletcher's review of *NH*, which had appeared in *The Freeman* on February 27, 1924.

224. In the following lines:

> *Do you know,*
> *Considering the market, there are more*
> *Poems produced than any other thing?*
> *No wonder poets sometimes have to* seem
> *So much more business like than business men.*
> *Their wares are harder to get rid of.* (CPPP, 155)

225. Ring Lardner's *You Know Me Al* (New York: Charles Scribner's Sons, 1916) chronicles the adventures of a brash minor league baseball pitcher, Jack Keefe, through a series of letters he writes home to his friend Al. From 1922 to 1925, Lardner wrote a syndicated comic strip of the same title, based on the book.

unseaworthy. Take my advice and never jump unless the ship is actually sinking or on fire. All ships are relatively unseaworthy.

You did not err. The story in the Bookman was Lesley's.[226] But be more truthful than common. You never recognized it from any family resemblance. You had many clues to help you: The knowledge that Lesley was writing under an assumed name, the personal note on her devotion to stone-breaking in Vermont and the name Leslie. You mustn't tell her any more that she repeats her father. The charge is dangerous to her further development. She has been held back long enough by our discretion and her own. It's time she let out in prose and verse. The bookstore she has contemplated is going to be a mistake if she is driven to it by our coolness to her in her art. I haven't wanted to do anything to excite her to creation. Anyone of mine who writes prose or verse shall be a self-starter. But neither do I want to hold her from it too much or too long. I know you'll sympathise with me in this as much as in anything I have at heart.[227] I thought her story all poetry. I hadnt seen it before it was in print.

I wish I could see you and hear all about what you are getting done. And I hope Jean likes her voice better and better.[228] One reason for our wanting to get over is to see you both off your native heath. It would be fun meeting there where we never met before, maybe a foretaste of our meeting in heaven by accident at a soirée of Mrs. God's. Mrs. Olds the new Presidents wife gives lots of soirées and dinners—if that's all that's needed.[229]

Affectionately
Robert.

---

226. Lesley Frost's short story "Brought to Earth" was published under the nom de plume Leslie Field in *The Bookman* in February 1924.

227. Because Untermeyer also had a child (Richard).

228. Jean Starr Untermeyer had early in her marriage to Untermeyer envisioned a career as a professional singer.

229. Marion Elizabeth Leyland Olds, wife of George Daniel Olds, president of Amherst.

[*To Louis Untermeyer. Internal evidence suggests RF composed the letter on March 11, not March 12, as Untermeyer dates it in RFLU. ALS. LoC.*]

[Amherst, MA]

[circa March 11, 1924]

Dear Louis

I sent you a long enough letter without this yesterday. Amusing to see Robinson squirm just like any ordinary person in a tight place trying to keep in with his neighbors. It goes down with Laura E. Richards.[230] Funny motions life makes. We must try to be comparatively honest.

R. F.

---

230. RF enclosed two clippings from the Gardiner (Maine) *Journal*, both devoted to E. A. Robinson's sonnet "New England," which had occasioned controversy in his native town. The poem reads:

> *Born where the wind is always north-north-east*
> *And children learn to walk on frozen toes,*
> *Intolerance tells an envy of all those*
> *Who boil from birth with such a lyric yeast*
> *Of love that you will hear them at a feast*
> *Where demons would appeal for some repose,*
> *Still clamoring where the chalice overflows*
> *And crying wildest who have drunk the least.*

> *Passion is here a soilure of the wits,*
> *We're told, and Love a cross for them to bear;*
> *Joy shivers in the corner where she knits*
> *And Conscience always has the rocking-chair,*
> *Cheerful as when she tortured into fits*
> *The first cat that ever was killed by Care.*

"New England" was published in the British journal *The Outlook* in November 1923. The first clipping RF passed along—dated January 25, 1924—consisted of a letter and poem penned by Gardiner businessman D. H. Darling and printed under the headline: "NEW ENGLAND'S INDIGNATION—EDWIN ARLINGTON ROBINSON'S POEM CONDEMNED—DAVID DARLING LOYAL CRITIC." Darling considered the sonnet an insult to the region: "The British find rocks enough to heave at us without our help," he wrote. "I would prefer to remind the world of the rugged virtues that made New England what it is to an exposition of her faults—especially on the hearths of her [old English] ancestors"; he then supplied an eight-line poem extolling the region. The second clipping—a letter composed by Robinson's friend and mentor Laura E. Richards, published in the *Journal* on February 7, 1924—was headlined "EDWIN ARLINGTON ROBINSON'S 'NEW ENGLAND' EXPLAINED." Richards,

[To Robert Hillyer, who at the time was serving as president of the New England Poetry Club. The letter is undated, but internal evidence indicates that RF wrote it in March 1924. ALS. UVA.]

[Amherst, MA]
[circa March 12, 1924]
Mister President—

Dear Sir:

I have a volume of poetry in safe keeping for you.[231] I trust you want that. But don't tell me you want me to read in public for you. Not really. Why you wouldn't come yourself. You'd be off down in Pomfret establishing a country residence so that if anything goes wrong in education we cannot say you did it.[232] April would be too late to read poetry indoors anyway wouldnt it?

Ever yours
Robert Frost

---

a prominent Gardiner author, defended the poet: "I am sure that Mr. Darling will be as glad as I am to learn that there has been a misapprehension as to the intention of Mr. Robinson's fine sonnet on New England. Our poet (we firmly claim him as ours, though all the English-speaking world now acclaim him) writes to me, in reply to a letter of mine: 'As for the sonnet on New England, your letter makes me wonder if you didn't read it the wrong way. It was supposed to be aimed at those who patronize New England.'" Richards then offered Robinson's sonnet "The Sheaves"—never before published—as an example of his art at its best. Robinson himself responded to Darling in a letter to the *Journal* on February 14: "If Mr. Darling will be good enough to give my unfortunate sonnet one more reading, and if he will observe that Intolerance, used ironically, is the subject of the first sentence ('Intolerance born where the wind, etc.') he will see that the whole thing is a satirical attack, not upon New England, but upon the same patronizing pagans whom he flays with such vehemence in his own poem." For details, see Scott Donaldson, *Edwin Arlington Robinson: A Poet's Life* (New York: Columbia Universty Press, 2007), 386–388.

231. Likely *NH*.

232. At the time, Hillyer was living in Pomfret, Connecticut.

[To Lincoln MacVeagh. Undated, but MacVeagh penciled in "Postmarked Amherst May 5 1924" at the head of the letter. ALS. Jones.]

[Amherst, MA]

[May 5, 1924]

Dear Lincoln:

I have more than half a mind to write a page or two for the great book. How much should I have to hurry?[233]

You are safely back from the waste lands then.[234] Do you come staggering under the weight of a lot of new books to publish?

It looks as if I were coming down with Elinor to read a poem from some one of my four book[s] to the P.E.N. Club of which I am told I am an honorary member.[235] I must see you.

Remind Bunny of me once in so often.[236]

Ever yours

Robert Frost

I was up in South Shaftsbury helping Carol plan[237] trees last week. Cold but fine up there.

[To Dorothy Dunbar Bromley. ALS. UVA.]

Amherst May 24 1924

Dear Mrs Bromley

We must humor you. I'll try to get you a snapshot within the next few days.[238] Please tell the San Francisco bookseller from me that though

---

233. MacVeagh adds a note: "About introduction to 'Memoirs of Stephen Burroughs' published by Dial Press." See RF to MacVeagh, circa December 15, 1923.

234. Here, MacVeagh penciled in: "Europe." RF playfully refers to T. S. Eliot's *The Waste Land* (1922).

235. RF was with his wife in New York from May 13 to May 17 to receive an honorary membership in PEN (Poets, Essayists, Novelists), an organization founded in 1921. He also gave a reading while at the meeting.

236. MacVeagh's wife Margaret.

237. The manuscript reads "plan," which may or may not be a slip of the pen for "plant." Carol was laying out an orchard at the Stone House farm RF gave him and his wife, Lillian, as a wedding present in 1923.

238. Presumably for the publicity department at Henry Holt and Company.

> *I remember I remember*
> *The house where I was born*[239]

and could take him right to it, I couldn't for the life of me direct him to it with any accuracy. He's to consider that I haven't seen San Francisco since 1885. It is or was a house on a northwest corner of Washington St about three blocks east of Levenworth [*sic*] St. This sounds as mysterious as Poe's Gold Bug.[240]

I wrote the whole of New Hampshire between ten o'clock one night and ten the next morning and then in a daze topped it off with Stopping by Woods on a Snowy Evening.[241]

But let Edward Anthony do it. He can invent better stories about me than I can myself—and funnier. It's an amusing book he's written.[242]

You'll have more advertising material when I start reaping degrees in June. Watch me—or I may take some that dont belong to me.[243]

Sincerely yours
Robert Frost

---

239. From stanza 1 of "I Remember, I Remember," by the British poet Thomas Hood (1799–1845):

> *I remember, I remember,*
> *The house where I was born,*
> *The little window where the sun*
> *Came peeping in at morn;*
> *He never came a wink too soon,*
> *Nor brought too long a day,*
> *But now, I often wish the night*
> *Had borne my breath away!*

240. The plot of Edgar Allan Poe's short story "The Gold Bug" (1843) hinges on a map in the form of a cryptograph.

241. On or about July 15, 1922, at his home in South Shaftsbury, Vermont. Both poems are in *NH*.

242. Edward Anthony (1895–1971), who was briefly (1923–1924) associated with Henry Holt and Company, had in 1921 published a volume of light verse titled *Merry-Go-Roundelays* (New York: Century), an entire section of which is devoted to the follies of publishing houses, publishers, beleaguered manuscript readers, and book reviewing. Anthony subsequently had a long career in publicity, advertising, and publishing (in addition to writing). In 1924, Henry Holt issued his book of baseball stories, *Razzberry!*, to which, presumably, RF here refers. In 1928 Anthony was eastern press director for Herbert Hoover's presidential campaign.

243. Middlebury College honored RF with an LHD (Doctor of Humane Letters) degree in June 1924.

[*To John Gould Fletcher. ALS. Arkansas.*]

Amherst [MA]

May 24 1924

Dear Fletcher:

You <u>are</u> anxious. If the manuscript was registered I should think you must know by this time that I received it.[244] I received it all right and have thus far failed with it just once. I didn't want to have to report till I had given it one more trial. The one more trial will be with The Open Road Press, so-called, of which the enclosed circular will give you a full description.[245] I promise nothing from it. Understand that. I am not an agency and make myself answerable to no one as such. I am doing more for you now than I have done for anyone else for a long time. But you begged it of me. While you were doing me a disservice with my book[246] you were something more than willing to let me do you a service with yours. The first publisher I had in mind refused so much as to look at your book.[247] I don't count him one. And I don't regard his prejudice. He was more out of patience with me for wanting to help you than with you for having done what you could to hurt me. He rather laughed at your first letter in which you mingled hints of interest in my book with the flat request that I should find a publisher for yours. I refuse to be influenced by such considerations. If your book is any good I want to see it published. And even if it isnt any good I think it ought to be published on your own authority and belief in it. So really two publishers have rejected it—one without seeing it: the other in good set terms that I spare you. If nothing comes of The Open Road Press you shall have your manuscript back with the assurance that I have done the best I could for it.

Faithfully yours

Robert Frost

---

244. Fletcher was in England at the time. See also RF's March 8 and May 24, 1924, letters to him.

245. The Open Road Press was founded in 1924 by Schuyler B. Jackson. RF, Vachel Lindsay, Hervey Allen, and Padraic Colum served on its editorial board. A three-page prospectus for the press was printed in 1924.

246. Fletcher reviewed *NH* unfavorably in *The Freeman* (see RF to Untermeyer, March 10, 1924).

247. Lincoln MacVeagh.

[To Llewellyn Jones (1884–1961), a British-born editor and literary critic. From 1914 to 1932 he was the literary editor of the Chicago Evening Post. *ALS. Alger.]*

South Shaftsbury Vermont

June 9 1924

Dear Jones:

Ive been timber cruising lately and havent had my mail less than twice forwarded. Your article wasn't very specially delivered.[248] The fact is, I had heard of it and liked it before it reached me. But I like it still better now that I have seen it. You say me as I like to be said. Jimmy Chapin has just been here agreeing with me about what I owe you.[249] You are one of the few I count on for security. Why dont we see more of each other? Couldn't you come East crooked enough next time to touch at Amherst for a visit with us?

College has tired me a little, but farming heals all.

Ever yours

Robert Frost

[To John Gould Fletcher. ALS. Arkansas.]

South Shaftsbury Vermont U.S.A.

June 10 1924

Dear Fletcher:

First and last I must own I havent liked your way of coming at me with your manuscript. Your introductory letter was as much too adroit as your follow up letter was too rude. But you are one thing; your verse is another. I havent wanted to let your departures from the expected in conduct prejudice me in the least against your poetry. I think I estimate that at somewhere near its worth. And I have done the best I could for it, as some three or four pub-

---

248. Jones had published an essay on RF in the *American Review*, March–April 1924, 165–171. "Timber cruising" is a technique whereby the total amount of lumber on a given plot of land is estimated by extrapolation from a sample stand of trees.

249. The painter James Chapin, who had done a portrait of RF and illustrated the 1919 limited-edition reissue of *NB*.

lishers could testify. Their objections to the book were largely businesslike. You mustn't mind them. Incident closed.

Sincerely yours
Robert Frost

Manuscript returned by registered mail

[To Robert Hillyer. ALS. UVA.]

South Shaftsbury Vt
July 24 1924

Dear Hillyer:

If you think we'd better, of course yes. Only can't we make it November instead of October?[250] I fear I shan't be quite all back from the woods before the first of November. I restart life hard. But do with me as you like—I'm

Always your friend
Robert Frost

[To George R. Elliott. ALS. ACL.]

South Shaftsbury Vt
July 26 1924.

Dear Elliot [*sic*]:

Of course, yes. I could talk on Style (I have a new explanation of it) or on Vocal Imagination or on How to Have Ideas or even on The Humor of Longfellow.*[251] As you may have heard, I'm not very different on the platform from what I am in conference. I neither make a speech nor deliver a lecture. I only talk right on.[252]

---

250. Hillyer, then president of the New England Poetry Club, had asked RF to do a joint reading (see RF's March 12 letter to him). No record of such a reading exists.

251. In May 1925 RF would give a speech, "Vocal Imagination," at the Bowdoin Institute of Modern Literature. See also RF to Elliott, October 15, 1924. As for what RF was saying about "style" in 1924: see his March 10, 1924, letter to Untermeyer.

252. See Shakespeare, *Antony and Cleopatra* 3.2:

I am no orator, as Brutus is;
But, as you know me all, a plain blunt man,

One year more of little Amherst and then surcease of that particular sorrow.[253] I like to teach, but I don't like to teach more than once a week now. I'm become a spoiled child of fortune. I may be drawn back to Michigan or I may take to the woods.[254]

I'd like to see the weedy rocks again along your surfless shore—and you all.

Ever yours
Robert Frost

*I wish someone else would do this one and spare me the temptation. It should be done.

[To Otto Manthey-Zorn. ALS. ACL.]

South Shaftsbury Aug 6 1924

Dear Otto:

I was waiting to see if I wouldnt get over last year before I went down to start talking about next year. I've kept thinking when I got up in the morning that I was myself again, but by noon or two or three or four o'clock I found I wasn't. The last of the poison hadn't quite gone out. I had still some more sweating in the hay-field to do. You may wonder what it was in the teaching that left me so laid out. It was my sins. I blame nobody but myself. But after having blamed myself, I next excuse myself. I'm past my set teaching. I don't really want to teach very much any more. Least of all do I want the worry of a losing fight in education with a lot of people who are good enough as they are. I prefer to take defeat in life elsewhere as a poet now. It's natural I should have shifted my stand. This doesnt mean that I am deserting Georgie Olds off-hand.[255] I shall get through another year the best I can before resigning.

That love my friend; and that they know full well
That gave me public leave to speak of him:
For I have neither wit, nor words, nor worth,
Action, nor utterance, nor the power of speech,
To stir men's blood: I only speak right on. . . .

253. From Edgar Allan Poe, "The Raven": "vainly had I sought to borrow / From my books surcease of sorrow."
254. RF returned to the University of Michigan in 1925.
255. George Daniel Olds, acting president of Amherst.

But Erskine or Boynton, it is all one to me: I am out and wouldn't presume for a moment longer to concern myself with the future of Amherst College.[256] You'd better be careful about your next she-president however. Ill say so much.[257]

It won't make any real difference this time to you and me. We'll keep up seeing each other once in so often and if I ever settle anywhere into another idle fellowship as at Ann Arbor, I'll try to have them drag you there too.

The store[258] wags on and the farm wags on darn well all things considered. Did you ever see an unpractical person with as many irons in the fire as I have right now? I have really had too much to think of all year. I like it, but—let's not talk about it any more. Let's have a good time summering in the water or a rocky peak and come back in the fall with a heart prepared for both the Whichers, father and son.[259] I ought not to speak of any human being that way and Elinor would forbid me if I were audible. The Whicher's [*sic*] mean well, father and son. And so do you and I.

Ever yours,
Robert

[*To Louis Untermeyer. ALS. LoC.*]

South Shaftsbury Vermont USA
August 12 1924

Dear Louis:

I havent reported on Amherst yet. I found that the college does belong as charged to Mr Dwight Morrow of J. P. Morgan & Co—your bankers in Paris. But so does Smith College belong to Mrs Dwight Morrow. They might belong to worse. The Morrows are the kind of rich who take good care of their playthings. Morrow is certainly intelligent and so liberal, he tells me, as to

---

256. John Erskine (who once taught at Amherst), professor of English at Columbia University; Percy Boynton, professor of English at the University of Chicago.

257. The wife of the president, Marion Elizabeth Leyland Olds. See RF to Untermeyer, March 10, 1924 ("Mrs. Olds . . . gives lots of soirées and dinners—if that's all that's needed").

258. Lesley and Marjorie's bookstore, The Open Book, in Pittsfield, Massachusetts.

259. George Frisbie Whicher, professor of English at Amherst, and his father, George Meason Whicher (1860–1937), who was moving to Amherst upon his retirement from Hunter College (New York City).

have sat in until very recently anyway at the councils of the New Republic. Mrs Morrow is a member of the Poetry Society of America. Between them they have just put David Morton on the Amherst faculty, I am told over the telephone.[260] The question of David Morton was worrying President Olds when I came away. He could have wished him a poet he knew more about. I couldn't help him much because I didn't know much myself. The Morrows pressed for Morton as the winner of some sort of Poetry Society Prize. President Olds is not young. I have seen him worn out with running to New York all year for instructions and permissions.

The boys had been made uncommonly interesting to themselves by Meiklejohn.[261] They fancied themselves as thinkers. At Amherst you thought, while at other colleges you merely learned. (Wherefore if you love him, send your only son and child to Amherst.)[262] I found that by thinking they meant stocking up with radical ideas, by learning they meant stocking up with conservative ideas—a harmless distinction, bless their simple hearts. I really liked them. It got so I called them the young intelligences—without offense. We got on like a set of cog wheels in a clock. They had picked up the idea somewhere that the time was past for the teachers to teach the pupil. From now on it was the thing for the pupil to teach himself using, as he saw fit, the teacher as an instrument. [263] The understanding was that my

---

260. Dwight Whitney Morrow, a partner at J. P. Morgan and an alumnus of Amherst, served his alma mater as a lifetime trustee from 1916 to 1931. Morrow also served as an adviser to the Allied Maritime Transport Council, which was established during World War I to coordinate shipping among the allies. In February 1919, the AMTC merged into the Supreme Economic Council, which was instrumental in helping create the League of Nations. Elizabeth Reeve Morrow (1873–1955), née Cutter, was an alumna of Smith; she published poems in leading magazines and wrote several children's books. From 1920 to 1926 she served as the alumnae representative to the Smith board of trustees and would eventually serve as acting president of the college in 1939. David Morton's first book of poems, *Ships in the Harbor* (New York: G. P. Putnam, 1921) won the Golden Rose Award, sponsored by the New England Poetry Club. At the urging of the Morrows, the Amherst College board of trustees appointed him to a faculty position.

261. For more about Alexander Meiklejohn's forced resignation (and his controversial tenure) as president of Amherst, see RF to Tilley, July 30, 1923, and also the notes to RF's June 22, 1923, letter to MacVeagh.

262. See John 3:16. RF may refer (if only in jest) to Richard (Dick) Untermeyer, Louis and Jean Starr Untermeyer's son (then seventeen years old).

263. In 1924, Amherst established a policy that allowed juniors and seniors who were on the dean's list to cut an unlimited number of classes.

leg was always on the table for anyone to seize me by that thought he could swing me as an instrument to teach himself with. So we had an amusing year. I should have had my picture taken just as I sat there patiently waiting, waiting for the youth to take education into their own hands and start the new world. Sometimes I laughed and sometimes I cried a little internally. I gave one course in reading and one course in philosophy, but they both came to the same thing. I was determined to have it out with my youngers and betters as to what thinking really was. We reached an agreement that most of what they had regarded as thinking, their own and other people's, was nothing but voting—taking sides on an issue they had nothing to do with laying down. But not on that account did we despair. We went bravely to work to discover, not only if we couldnt have ideas, but if we hadnt had them, a few of them, at least, without knowing it. Many were ready to give up beaten and own themselves no thinkers in my sense of the word. They never set up to be original. They never pretended to put this and that together for themselves, never had a metaphor, never made an analogy. But they had I knew. So I put them on the operating table and proceeded to take ideas they didnt know they had out of them as a prestidigitator takes rabbits and pigeons you have declared yourself innocent of out of your pockets trouserslegs and even mouth. Only a few resented being thus shown up and caught with the goods on them.

I went up to Middlebury and put the finishing touch on myself and my teaching for the year.[264] I speak literally. I am sick to death almost with having gnothied so many people.[265] It seems to have come hardest on my liver or kidneys this time: whereas in the old days the straight teaching I did, wholly unpschycoanalytic [sic], only ruined my first and second stomachs, particularly the first that I ruminated with. I wasnt happy at Middlebury, the scene of my rather funny failure last year with New Hampshire (the poem not the book). The Whichers were there, the old man Poetry Societist, George and the wives, and I was aware that for some reason they were not helping me much. George is his father's son.[266] He's the petty sort of half friend. I found

---

264. A reference to the Bread Loaf School of English, where RF first read in 1921.

265. As Mark Scott has suggested, RF's Englishing of (and play on) the ancient Greek injunction "Know thyself," γνῶθι σαυτόν; usually transliterated *gnōthi seauton*.

266. Whicher's father, George Meason Whicher, was a poet and classicist; he was married to Lillian Hope Frisbie. George Jr., was married to Harriet Ruth Fox.

him out in several deceits and concealments I dont admire.[267] He catches the
germs of the people he's with. I left him a protective wash against Meiklejaundice when I came away. But he got the bug though in attenuated form, as
is like him.

Lets talk about something healthier. The farm goes rip-roaring as no farm
ever went with me. Carol has hired almost nothing done this year. He has
ploughed and done all the haying himself. Fun to look on at—I always so
dreamed of being a real farmer; and seeing him one is almost the same as
being one myself. My heart's in it with him. I have to strive not to put my
mind in and interfere with advice. Let him go it. We've given him the farm
outright as I may have told you. Lillian is an unspoiled little girl easy to interest in everything in the world.[268] She's hard at it preserving a jar of something for every one of the 365 days in the year.

Lesley's store is well started. She ought to have some of your books autographed. She'll have to wait for them, I suppose, till you get home. I believe
she is at the Williamstown Political Institute today with her truck (called the
Knapsack) full of appropriate books to sell.[269] She's almost too enterprising
for her health. If you see anything over there such as the little hand-carved
figures in wood that might add a touch to the shop, do buy it at my expense.
She must have atmosphere. You and Jean will like the place when you see it.
The address is The Open Book, 124 South St, Pittsfield, Mass.

Dont expect me in the Misc. this year if you don't want me to make me
nervous.[270] I'm jaded with the pulls on me that I cant answer to. I've made up
my mind that with a few people to abet me I won't do one single thing in verse
or out of it or with it till I God damn please for the rest of my natural life. The
same for prose. I'm not going to write any more letters of obligation. Im going
to wait till I want to say a particular thing in a particular letter to a particular
person if I wait till the Second Coming. What did I get into writing for if it

---

267. In *RFLU*, Untermeyer excised this and the previous sentence.

268. Lillian Labatt Frost, Carol's wife.

269. Lesley Frost named her truck the Knapsack, as she often used it to sell books on
the road. The Williamstown Institute of Politics was a forum for international political
debate founded in 1920.

270. A reference to a (more or less) biennial anthology edited by Untermeyer and published by Harcourt, Brace. The first anthology, issued in 1920, bore the title *A Miscellany
of American Poetry;* additional "miscellanies," varying slightly in title, appeared in 1922,
1925 (the book under discussion here), and in 1927. RF didn't, in fact, contribute a poem to
Miscellany (1925); see also RF to Untermeyer, August 31, 1925.

wasnt for fun? This is my first letter under the new ruling. You may be sure it is no letter of obligation.

Ever yours
Robert Frost

[To Frank Eggleston Robbins, at the time assistant to the president at the University of Michigan. ALS. Bentley.]

South Shaftsbury VT
August 25 1924

Dear Mr Robbins:

In the first place, Jesse Lynch Williams would mean more to the undergraduates than anyone else dramatic you have named.[271] He wouldn't be cold water on their prejudices. He is a practical playwright who has held himself in ideals well above the ruck of Broadway. The young intelligents couldn't make fun of him.

Moreover I should count on him to get the idea of the fellowship better than anyone else you have named. He is all alive to the America of the moment. He would meet you at least half way in any educational experiment.

He is a man comparatively young, full of his plans. You catch him right at a point in his development where you can broaden his experience (he has only been to Princeton) and add to his reputation, considerable as that already is. He would get as much out of Michigan as Michigan would get out of him. Which is as you want it to be.

You'd find him a good all-round participator. He would take all the interest you would let him in your various dramatics. He wouldn't have to be dragged into anything by the ears.

And he's good company—and so also is his wife, my wife bids me be sure to add.[272] You would all like them both.

---

271. The playwright Jesse Lynch Williams (1871–1929) was in fact offered the Fellowship in Creative Arts at Michigan; he held it for the 1925–1926 academic year. (Williams had been awarded the first ever Pulitzer Prize for Drama in 1918 for his play *Why Marry?* It opened on Broadway at the Astor Theatre on Christmas Day, 1917, and closed on April 19, 1918.) In 1924 the fellowship had been filled only partially, with a three-month residence by the British poet laureate, Robert Bridges (see RF's February 10, 1924, letter to Tilley).

272. Alice Laidlaw Williams (1872–1960), author of the cookbook *Sunday Suppers* (New York: Duffield, 1912).

But I'll tell you who could tell you <u>all</u> about him, and much more intimately than I can—Donald Stuart of Princeton.[273] I wish you would write to Stuart.

Williams is your man. I'm more and more convinced.

You are good people not to forget any least expense a friend may have been put to in your service. I appreciate your sending me that great big voucher to fill out. I shall frame it.

Best wishes.

Faithfully yours
Robert Frost

Address for the next few weeks
    The Open Book
    124 South St
    Pittsfield
    Mass

[To Dorothy Dunbar Bromley. ALS. UVA.]

South Shaftsbury Vt
August 26 1924

Dear Mrs Bromley:

You may well say I have disappeared without bubbles. I notice you don't ask where is that photograph I owe you.[274] R. Frost never forgets a promise, though he may sometimes fail to keep one. I have been having trouble with my friends; whom I have so persuaded of my modesty that they wont take my picture chopping wood, raking hay, mowing, hoeing, or shoeing a horse even when I command them to. They put me off with jibes about running for the presidency.[275] It's a shameful state of affairs.

---

273. Donald Clive Stuart (1881–1943), professor of dramatic literature at Princeton. Williams graduated from Princeton with the class of 1892, to which he dedicated his first book, *Princeton Stories* (New York: Charles Scribner's Sons, 1895).

274. See RF to Bromley, May 24, 1924.

275. As if against Calvin Coolidge (Republican), John Davis (Democrat), and Robert M. La Follette (Progressive, and born in a log cabin)—the field of presidential candidates in 1924.

We were interested in the review in The Times—if for no other reason, because it seemed to imply that you had found someone to take the book in England.

Thanks and best wishes,

Sincerely yours
Robert Frost

[To Otto Manthey-Zorn, on "Sugar Hill, New Hampshire" *letterhead. ALS. ACL.]*

[Sugar Hill, NH]
Sept 13 1924.

Dear Otto:

I have just written his Olds that owing to hay-fever I am not quite ready for the fray.[276] Till I am, will you do anything you can to help him hold my classes at bay? I should be back in Amherst next Monday night or at latest Tuesday day. And I only hope that when I am back you for one won't wish I had staid away.[277]

Yours for aye
R.

[To Frank Eggleston Robbins, on "Sugar Hill, New Hampshire" *letterhead. The Frosts were staying with their friend Edith Fobes, widow of J. Warner Fobes. ALS. Bentley.]*

[Sugar Hill, NH]
September 15 1924

Dear Mr Robbins:

I wired Jesse Lynch Williams as follows the minute you bade me go ahead: "After what you had written Walter Eaton, surprised to learn that you now hesitate about going to Michigan.[278] Authorized to offer you fel-

---

276. Again, George Daniel Olds, acting president of Amherst.

277. "Staid" for "stayed" was relatively common from the late seventeenth through the mid-nineteenth centuries.

278. The writer Walter Prichard Eaton (1878–1957), a Frost family friend.

lowship in form. Have agreed with Eaton from first that you are the one for it. If necessary will come down from the mountains to make you come through."

Enclosed is the answer I got; and I'm afraid it sounds sufficiently final.[279] I wonder what put Williams off the idea.[280] He had seemed full of it in his letters to Walter Eaton, even going so far as to give references like an applicant for a job. Discovering that he was only an alternative to Owen Davis may have offended him.[281] You never can tell with these proud geniuses.

Will you pass this along to President Burton and say how sorry I am to have failed? I operate at a certain disadvantage from away up here in the mountains.

Sincerely yours
Robert Frost

[*To Marion LeRoy Burton. TG. Bentley.*]

[Amherst, MA]
[October 11, 1924]

PLEASE WIRE IF YOU WOULD BE WILLING TO HAVE ME OFFER WALTER EATON A LITTLE MORE THAN FIVE THOUSAND[282]

ROBERT FROST

---

279. The enclosure was later separated from the letter.

280. In fact, Jesse Lynch Williams *did* ultimately accept the offer.

281. Owen Gould Davis (1874–1956) was, like Williams, a then-celebrated American dramatist. He had won the 1923 Pulitzer Prize for Drama for his play *Icebound*. It premiered at the Sam H. Harris Theatre in New York on February 10, 1923, and closed in June.

282. RF was paid $5,000 a year when he held the fellowship from 1921 to 1923.

[*To Marion LeRoy Burton. TG. Bentley.*]

[Amherst, MA]

[October 13, 1924]

CAN SEE MR OLDS[283] VERY MUCH WISHES OFFICIAL ANNOUNCEMENT COULD BE PUT
OFF TILL AFTER HIS INAUGURATION NOVEMBER FIFTEEN STOP MUST DO WHAT WE
CAN NOT TO MAKE IT HARD FOR HIM

ROBERT FROST

[*To George R. Elliott, professor of English at Bowdoin College. "Fall of 1924" is penciled in at the head of the first sheet, presumably by Elliott, who often annotated the
letters he received from RF. Reference to the Bowdoin/Amherst football game in the
postscript allows for a more precise dating. ALS. ACL.*]

[Amherst, MA]

[circa October 15, 1924]

Dear Elliott:

Glad to help you all I can—which isnt much. Robinson won't speak for
love or money. He stays off the platform on principle.[284] I doubt if you could
get O'Neill. He makes too much out of his plays for lecture fees to tempt
him. Still you might try him. He'd be worth meeting if not listening to. You

---

283. George Daniel Olds would soon be inaugurated as president of Amherst; he
wanted Burton to defer announcing the offer to RF of a lifetime appointment as Fellow
in Letters at Michigan until after he (Olds) was in office. Shortly after Olds's inauguration, RF resigned his position at Amherst to move, again, to Ann Arbor. He would resume
teaching at Amherst in January 1927.

284. The reclusive E.A. Robinson. Elliott had solicited RF's help in rounding up
speakers for the Bowdoin Institute of Modern Literature—convened in May 1925 to com-
memorate the centennial of the class of 1825, of which both Nathaniel Hawthorne and
Henry Wadsworth Longfellow were members. RF led the series off (see also his July 26,
1924, and June 25, 1925, letters to Elliott). Following him were Edna St. Vincent Millay,
Willa Cather, Carl Sandburg, Hatcher Hughes (American playwright), John Dos Passos,
Margaret Deland (American short-story writer), James Stephens (Irish poet and novelist),
the French literary scholar Edmond Estève (who lectured on Longfellow in French),
Christopher Morley (American poet and literary critic), and the critics Irving Babbitt and
Henry Seidel Canby.

know he spends some of his time in a blessed swound.[285] Don't bother with
Owen Davis: he's nothing. Some people look on him as a reformed sinner
because from having written plays as they were written twenty years ago
he has turned to writing them as they are written now. He simply chimes
in for success. Willa Cather is A No 1. You <u>must</u> have her, and you may tell
her I said so. Besides being a real figure in letters, she's both thinker and
speaker.[286] Miss Millay is a great audience-killer. Boys and girls equally fall
for her charm. She loses nothing of course with them by her reputation for
dainty promiscuity. She only trades on that to the extent of here and there
a whimsical hint. She is already a love-myth. I dont have to tell you how
much I admire her less flippant verse. She will succeed anywhere.[287] Morley
is good and you could get him if he got home from England in time.
Hergesheimer I know next to nothing about. I've heard he was coarse and
boastful. I shouldn't mind that too much if he were able.[288] I suppose you
know Dorothy Canfield is good on the platform. I wish she could give you
the talk she gave us at Ann Arbor on the subject matter of her Crazy Quilt
story.[289] And don't forget Amy.[290] She's a shining lecturer, whatever else you

---

285. A reference to Eugene O'Neill's infamous drinking, by way of a line from the
first stanza of Robert Louis Stevenson's poem "Heather Ale: A Galloway Legend":

From the bonny bells of heather
  They brewed a drink long-syne,
Was sweeter far than honey,
  Was stronger far than wine.
They brewed it and they drank it,
  And lay in a blessed swound
For days and days together
  In their dwellings underground.

286. RF had been an admirer of Cather since 1916. See *LRF-1*, 414. See also RF to
Bartlett, January 1, 1926 ("Cather is our great novelist now").

287. RF listed Millay as among the best sixteen (American) poets then writing (see RF
to Lovell, January 1924).

288. Joseph Hergesheimer (1880–1954), American novelist whose renown peaked in
the 1920s.

289. Dorothy Canfield Fisher published the short story "The Bedquilt" in 1906; it was
among her most popular. RF brought her to the University of Michigan to read in
March 1923. See RF to Fisher, January 28, 1923, and August 30, 1926.

290. Amy Lowell, whose biography of Keats would be published in 1925 by Houghton
Mifflin.

may or may not grant she is. I wonder what we are going to say to her life of Keats.—Yes and Percy Boynton is all right—more than all right. He's a first-rate lecturer.[291]

Good luck. Best wishes. (Wasn't I prompt this time?)

Ever yours

Robert Frost

I left Mrs Wharton out. I never heard of her lecturing.[292]

What do you mean by beating us this way in football? Did you beat us unconsciously?[293]

[To Marion LeRoy Burton. ALS. Bentley.]

Amherst Mass

October 19 1924

Dear Mr Burton:

The mistake was in your not being the one to invite Walter Eaton and Jesse Lynch Williams personally in the first place. You could have made them feel the honor more than any of the rest of us.

You know how I am: it is very hard for me to take my heart off any thing I have got it set on. While I am a little cross with Eaton for stopping to dispute at such a time about a few dollars here or there, still I can't get over wanting to see him in the Fellowship this year, if it is only for the friend it will make of him and the help he will be afterward in finding the young promisers in the dramatic line. He's really on the crest at this moment with

---

291. Percy Holmes Boynton (1875–1946), professor of English at the University of Illinois.

292. Edith Wharton.

293. On Saturday, October 11, 1924, Bowdoin College defeated Amherst 16–14. Coverage of the game in the *Bowdoin Orient* for October 15, 1924, likely explains RF's joke: "There is no doubt that Bowdoin was outplayed, for Amherst made 20 first downs to Bowdoin's 7, and completed 11 of 24 forward passes attempted for a total of 136 yards. Bowdoin tried 6 passes but completed only one. . . . Cronin's drop-kick from the 37 yard line scored a goal from the field after five minutes of play and proved to be the margin of Bowdoin's victory in the end" (*Bowdoin Orient* 56, no. 12: 1). RF had been a football enthusiast since his days cheering on John Bartlett—captain of the football team at Pinkerton Academy—in 1909.

such a book just out as his charming Actor's Heritage.[294] He's no small part of what the drama is doing in America. And you know I don't just say this to boost an intimate. When I first went after him this summer I scarcely knew him: you put him into my head. He would be surely right for us in every way.

Now I have this to propose. What he sticks at apparently is the fear of a big rent out there. He has heard from someone the worst of Ann Arbor rents. Do you suppose it would be possible for the University to find him a small house or flat for less money than he thinks? I will even go to this length: if you can find such a house or flat I will hire it for mine as from January 1st 1926[295] and let him have the use of it for nothing till the middle of June. I could keep it on then till I got something bought or built for permanence.[296] Dont say this sounds foolish. I ought to be willing to do more for the University considering how generous the University has been with me. In addition the University might promise him two or three hundred dollars worth of lectures. I had him almost in my grasp the other day. He really wants to go to Ann Arbor. It will be a mercy to him to overcome his hesitation. Just a tiny little house on a quiet street would be the final stroke. On a quiet street of course if I am to step into it when he goes out.

Set your mind at rest about Mr Olds.[297] I had told him that it might not be possible to keep the secret long. I think he sees now that there was nothing to make a secret of. He is my good friend. I didn't want him to feel that he was hurt in any way by our action. That is to say I wanted him to have time to be reconciled to my leaving him.

Sincerely yours
Robert Frost

---

294. *The Actor's Heritage: Scenes from the Theatre of Yesterday and the Day Before* (Boston: Atlantic Monthly Press, 1924).

295. Apparently a slip of the pen; the fellowship in question began in 1925 (it went to Williams, not Eaton). In 1924 the fellowship had been held for only part of the year, April to June, by Robert Bridges. Possibly Eaton hoped to make similar arrangements.

296. RF had accepted a lifetime appointment at Michigan. He and his wife, Elinor, moved back to Ann Arbor in September 1925.

297. See RF's October 13 telegram to Burton.

[To Walter Prichard Eaton. Date derived from internal evidence. ALS. UVA.]

[Amherst MA]
[late October 1924]

Dear Eaton:

The Ann Arboreals seem less bent on Williams than they were on you. We know what's good for them, however, and must see that they get it. Don't you want to write me a little note about Williams that I could show Burton? I mean one free from Barkis jokes.[298]

Ever yours
R. F.

[To Mary Elizabeth Cooley (1904–1978), at the time an undergraduate at the University of Michigan, and the daughter of Charles Horton Cooley (1864–1929), professor of sociology at the university, and his wife Elsie Jones Cooley (1864–1953). ALS. UM.]

Amherst November 10 1924

Dear Miss Cooley:

I shall surely never count it against you that you have scattered grains of my poetry to the uttermost parts of Wisconsin. I always say that the best criticism of a book is some story of something done with it; at any rate I'll thank no one particularly for any other kind of mine. Abstract appreciation is all too much alike. I think even lectures on literature should be narrative.

I shall soon be where I can see more of your poetry. You should still have a year to go after this, unless you are rushing through in three years. You mustnt graduate the minute we get there.

Sincerely yours
Robert Frost

---

298. Mr. Barkis, a character in Dickens's *David Copperfield,* humorously woos Clara Peggotty and convinces her to marry him.

[*To Morris Tilley. Dating derived from internal evidence. ALS. UM.*]

[Amherst, MA]
[circa November 10, 1924]

Dear Tilley:

It looks as if the Azazeels [*sic*] must have thought we got to be pretty good friends in my two years out there. I'm grateful to them for still wanting me after having had me round so long on trial as it were. My warmest thanks to all of them.[299]

Now I shall know what to call myself when asked. I have tried one name and another on myself to be in the fashion with the Vers Librists Vorticists Dadaists on every hand but nothing came anywhere near a fit unless it were Synecdochist and that only somewhere near. It was sufficiently like Schenectadist to connote electricity and the General Electric Company.[300] Where it came short was in mystification. I had given it up as not enough of a puzzle and was about reconciled to going without a nom de guerre when along you come and make me an Azazeel (correct me with a blue pencil if my spelling is at fault). That's what I can henceforth call myself without the fear of being too obvious. That will give me a mystery no one will pluck the heart out of or so I fondly flatter myself for the simple reason that I can't define it myself except by example.[301]

Well, old friend, we are going to be where we shall see a lot of each other again. I shall count on you more than on anyone else to help me find out how to make the most of what the University has given me. We must conspire to manage me with the wisdom of the serpent.[302]

It <u>would</u> be good if I could live just a step out of the way. I wonder if there is nothing just off Geddes up there on top of the hill.[303]

---

299. The Azazels, misspelled here, to which Tilley belonged, was an informal club founded in 1908 whose members were senior faculty at Michigan.

300. General Electric is based in Schenectady, New York.

301. See Hamlet's remark to Guildenstern (*Hamlet* 3.2): "You would play upon me; you would seem to know my stops; you would pluck out the heart of my mystery; you would sound me from my lowest note to the top of my compass; and there is much music, excellent voice, in this little organ, yet cannot you make it speak."

302. Matthew 10:16: "Be ye therefore wise as serpents, and harmless as doves."

303. The Frosts rented a house at 1223 Pontiac Road, north of the main campus. See also RF to Lurie, February 26, 1925.

We were terribly sorry to hear that President Burton was seriously ill. He overworks. I hope he will come through all right. We shall be anxious for news of him.[304]

Our best to you.

Ever yours

Robert Frost

[To Louis A. Strauss (1872–1938), professor of English at the University of Michigan. ALS. UM.]

Amherst Mass

November 10 1924

Dear Strauss:

Handsomely was the way to do this thing if it was going to be done, and handsomely you have all certainly done it. I am still dazed with the pleasure you have given me. I begin to wonder if I shall be able to wait till next year to take up my desk in your office. I may have to come out for a special desk-warming beforehand. My mind is already out there with you.

As you know, I have a weakness for ideas, particularly in education. The idea of the Fellowship rouses the very teacher in me. Moreover I am not averse to a great big gift once in a lifetime when it comes my way. And I rather like honors: But what exerts the main attraction in Ann Arbor is simply friends. You don't need to be told it, but I'm telling you just the same.

My best to you and your family[305]—and believe me

Ever yours

Robert Frost

---

304. Burton did not recover; after a brief rally, he died on February 18, 1925. RF delivered an address at a memorial service held on May 28, 1925, the text of which is reprinted in *CPRF,* 89–94.

305. Strauss's wife, Elsa, and their daughters Margaret and Elizabeth, who lived at 1601 Cambridge Road in Ann Arbor.

[*To Walter Ernest Tittle (1883–1966), American illustrator and portrait painter whose subjects included RF's contemporaries Willa Cather, G. K. Chesterton, Joseph Conrad, and Edward Hopper. We have found no record of a Frost portrait by Tittle. ALS. HRC.*]

Amherst Mass
November 10 1924

Dear Mr. Tittle

I seem no nearer getting to New York than when I heard from you a month ago. Might I take advantage of your offer to come here? Mrs Frost and I would be happy to have you stay with us. I know your work and, though a citizen of a free country, should be proud to become your subject.

Sincerely yours
Robert Frost

[*To Nina Moses Burton (1875–1966), wife of Marion LeRoy Burton. ALS. Berkeley.*]

Amherst
November 12 1924

Dear Mrs Burton:

Tell Mr Burton when you can how anxious we have been for him. He must get well and then take care of himself. We want him to preside over Michigan University for years and years. He must know our deep regard for him—both mine and Mrs Frost's. We have been saying poet never had better friend.

Most faithfully yours
Robert Frost

[To Norman Foerster (1887–1972), American literary scholar and a prominent figure in the New Humanist movement. At the time this letter was written, he was a professor of English at the University of North Carolina. ALS. Stanford.]

Amherst Mass

November 16 1924

Dear Mr Foerster:

Yes Elliott has talked about you and so has Hanford of Michigan.[306] But I know you through more than their talk. I know you through your own good writing.

And of course you are welcome to any of my poems you will carry to college readers.[307] It would not be my way to charge you a cent for them. I will do what I can to make my publishers ease up on you a little.

I can commend your choice of the poems. Only if I might offer a suggestion, I wish you might top off with one more lyric such as The Oven Bird, Reluctance or The Road Not Taken. Don't let me tempt you against your better judgement. I'm especially pleased that you didn't overlook The Mountain. I sometimes wonder how I wrote that poem. Now let us fix the dates. Mowing is the only uncertainty; but 1900 is about right for it. Mending Wall, 1913. The Mountain 1913. The Black Cottage 1905. The Death of the Hired Man 1905. Birches 1915.[308]

We must meet sometime.

Sincerely yours

Robert Frost

---

306. George Roy Elliott and James Holly Hanford. Hanford (1882–1969), a Milton scholar, taught at the University of North Carolina from 1914 to 1921, spent one year on the faculty at the University of Michigan, and then joined the faculty of Western Reserve. He would have known Foerster from their time together at North Carolina.

307. In his (Foerster's) *American Poetry and Prose: A Book of Readings, 1607–1916* (New York: Houghton Mifflin, 1925).

308. As he often did, RF dates "The Black Cottage" and "The Death of the Hired Man" to their inspiration at Derry rather than to their composition in England. An early version of "The Black Cottage" was written in Derry, but it bears only a tangential relation to the dramatic monologue printed in *NB*.

[To Frank Eggleston Robbins. ALS. Bentley.]

South Shaftsbury Vt
November 28 1924

Dear Mr Robbins:

I had been thinking of de la Mare for next year. For the good name of the Fellowship, I should hesitate to bestow it on two English men in succession.[309] But doubtless some of you have satisfied yourselves that persuading de la Mare to stay for the rest of this year would be easier than persuading him to come back for as much of next year. In that case I should hardly know what to say. Probably you had best take him when you can get him—if not next year, then this, and never mind the objections. There's no Englishman I'd rather see honored in America. He's a personal friend now, but I admired him before ever I knew him.[310]

I was glad to hear that Mr Burton was probably safely through. He has had too narrow an escape.

Thanks for your letter. Dont overvalue my advice.[311]

Sincerely yours
Robert Frost

[To Frederic Melcher. ALS. UVA.]

Amherst
December 10 1924

Dear Melcher:

The Harvard psychologists have been asking us writers if in our experience the act of creation doesn't just naturally articulate into a state followed by an idea followed by some work. Old Christopher Smart said that what

---

309. British poet Walter de la Mare, then on a lecture tour in America, did not, as it happens, take a fellowship at Michigan. The other Englishman alluded to is Robert Bridges, who held the Fellowship in Creative Arts from April to June in 1924.

310. For RF's remarks about de la Mare's poetry, see *LRF-1*, 227. Partly on RF's recommendation, Henry Holt and Company issued the American edition of his *The Listeners and Other Poems* in 1916.

311. See RF to Eggleston, August 25 and September 15, 1925.

God created had to be determined dared and done.[312] As long as we keep to triplets I dont much care. You take this letter. I determined to write it a year ago. So far so good. The next thing was to dare to write it, and I'll tell you it took a lot of courage after not having written it for so long. I didnt know how you might take it. But at last I have decided to be brave and here I am actually at it; and before you know it it will be done, for, believe me, it is going to be short. I am off letter writing except to the most favored people and even those are going to have to be satisfied with notes.

You may have noticed that you don't get much thanks or much pay for what you have done for me in the last few years. Well here is where you are going to get both. Eternal gratitude for always reading me aloud everywhere (it keeps coming round to me how much you help my cause) for the bookplates for Pittsfield and for the more genteel letters.[313] Moreover seventy-five dollars (enclosed) for stirring us up to a better bookstore in Amherst. We surely have the better bookstore and it would be my strength and my refuge in teaching literature if I were to continue here. Lowell is timid. The prospect rather scares him. But he has enterprise and resource: he is sure to make out.[314]

I'd rather see you once than write you a thousand letters. So when you are anywhere near us be sure to stop over with us for a night—at Amherst South Shaftsbury or Ann Arbor. There may be some chance to look in on you at New York during the winter.

You know I'm your friend.
Robert Frost

---

312. See the last lines of (English poet) Christopher Smart's "Song of David," which celebrates the incarnation: "And now the matchless deed's achieved, / Determined, Dared, and Done."

313. Melcher, a well-known editor and publisher, had helped Lesley and Marjorie Frost establish The Open Book in Pittsfield, Massachusetts.

314. James A. Lowell resigned his position as assistant librarian of the Converse Memorial Library at Amherst and purchased the Amherst Bookstore from Charles F. Dyer in August of 1924. The editors thank Cynthia Harbeson of the Jones Library in Amherst for her assistance with this annotation.

[To Mark Antony DeWolfe Howe (1864–1960), American author and editor. ALS. Harvard.]

Amherst December 12 1924

My dear Howe:

It shall be a letter this time if you will let me off with not much more than my "Yes gladly" of the telegram. Mrs Frost will come with me. We shall be coming from the farm at South Shaftsbury Vermont and it looks from such time tables as I command as if we could expect to reach Boston at about 3.30 P.M. on Saturday January 3rd. One hundred and fifty is my usual fee: but I do not always ask it of friends. Speaking as poet to poet, how much do you think the club would think fair?[315] Set it at that.

We'll be delighted to stay with you and Mrs Howe.[316] You are too kind in all this.

Ever yours
Robert Frost

[To Julia Patton, professor of English at Russell Sage College. A note, presumably in Patton's hand, appears to indicate that RF spoke at Russell Sage on April 13, 1925 (which indeed fell on a Monday). RF had read at the college before, in December 1920. ALS. BU.]

Amherst, December 12, 1924

Dear Miss Patton:

Russell Sage College would be one of my pleasantest memories, were it only for the heartfelt way you resented it when some rude honker made me jump for my life that rainy day I was there with you on the streets of Troy.

---

315. The arrangements are for a lecture-reading at the Saturday Club (founded in Boston in 1855 by Ralph Waldo Emerson, among others), of which Howe was an officer. As for "poet to poet": Howe had published two volumes of poetry, *Shadows* (Boston: Copeland and Day, 1897) and *Harmonies: A Book of Verse* (Boston: Houghton Mifflin, 1909).

316. Frances "Fannie" Huntington Quincy Howe (1870–1933), a writer of short stories and essays (though never under her own name), and a descendant of the distinguished Quincy family, which included President John Quincy Adams (1767–1848).

Do you really want me to come again? My regular fee has grown to be one hundred and fifty dollars, if that isnt too much to pronounce. You could divide the burden as you suggest, between the schools.[317] I shouldnt think it would necessarily be too hard to address both at once. I could manage the Monday afternoon all right.

How can you explain the goodness of these Michigan people to me?

I often speak of Carl.[318] I wish coming where you are might mean seeing him too.

Sincerely yours

Robert Frost

[*To Wilbur Rowell. ALS. UVA.*]

Amherst Mass

December 12 1924

Dear Mr Rowell:

I'm sure Jean wants me made her guardian now.[319] So if you <u>would</u> help me in the matter, I should be grateful. I don't see how we could claim a residence for her anywhere in particular. But, as you say, the estate is in Essex County and her share of it might well be paid from there.[320] You know best. We can take action at your convenience. I shall be ready when you are ready.

---

317. That is, between Russell Sage College and the Emma Willard School, a preparatory school for girls, both in Troy, New York. Eliza Kellas, head of the school, helped found Russell Sage College in 1916, together with the suffragist Margaret Olivia Slocum Sage, who named the new college for her husband, Russell Sage, a New York financier and politician. The school and the college had a uniquely close relationship thereafter.

318. Her nephew. See RF's November 28, 1920, letter to Patton.

319. RF's sister, Jeanie, was still in the Maine Insane Asylum, in Augusta, to which she'd been committed in April 1920.

320. After the death of his father in 1885, RF moved with his mother and sister to Lawrence, Massachusetts, the hometown of RF's paternal relatives and the then county seat of Northern Essex County (in 1999 the several geographical divisions of the county were dissolved). Jeanie was born there in June 1876, when RF and his mother, Isabelle Moodie Frost, came east on a visit from California.

Jean hoped for a long time that she was going to be able to try the world again. She has about given that up now. The most she can expect is to be made to feel at home where she is. She will be easier in her mind, I'm sure, when she is using her own money to pay her expenses.

It was kind of Mrs Rowell to ask me to Lawrence again. I shall enjoy being with you.[321]

> Sincerely yours
> Robert Frost

[To Robert Mark Wenley (1861–1929), head of the Department of Philosophy at the University of Michigan from 1896 until his death in 1929. ALS. Bentley.]

> Amherst December 12 1924

Dear Mr Wenley:

What I can do for Mr Carritt I will.[322] Anyone with "the latest information about aesthetics" ought to come in well for a change after all the shovelling archaeologists we have had to listen to lately. But don't count too much on my help. I'm beginning to let go here, as already somewhat more of my next college than of this.

Thanks for the kind word. We are glad to be taken back.

> Sincerely yours
> Robert Frost

---

321. RF spoke in Lawrence on March 31, 1925.

322. The British philosopher of aesthetics Edgar Frederick Carritt (1876–1964) taught in the Department of Philosophy at Michigan during the 1924–1925 academic year (he had previously been at Oxford), while Professor D. H. Parker was on leave. Apparently Wenley had asked RF to inquire as to the possibility that Carritt might find a place at Amherst (none was found for him). Carritt wrote a number of books, including *The Theory of Beauty* (New York: Macmillan, 1914).

[To Harriet Monroe. ALS. Chicago.]

Amherst Mass

December 19 1924

Dear Miss Monroe:

That is the question, Where am I? I now have three homes—homes, mind you, not just summer and hunting camps—three going on four, all bought and paid for out of poetry.[323] So that even when I may be said to be <u>at</u> home, I am nowhere in particular. Your letter reached me in one place, your article later in another. You may not have heard, but I am thinking of concentrating residence in Ann Arbor where you can put your finger on me.[324]

Your letter need not have been so worried about your article.[325] So long as you dont give me credit for Robinson's (or Tennesons [sic]) Enid you may regard relations between us as unstrained.[326] It is a good article and a

---

323. A bit misleading, except insofar as the point ("Where am I?") concerns the itinerant life the poet had led, and would continue to lead throughout the 1920s. RF bought his Franconia farm in 1915, largely with funds from royalties and lecture fees (see RF to Edward Thomas, August 15, 1916 [*LRF-1*, 474]). He then sold it in parcels in 1919 and 1920. He bought the Stone House in South Shaftsbury outright in 1920, and then gave it to his son, Carol, on the occasion of his marriage to Lillian Labatt in November 1923. In December 1924 RF had yet to purchase a third residence, though obviously he was contemplating one in Ann Arbor, even as he had in mind a fourth (for himself and his wife) near South Shaftsbury (which they would not purchase, as it happened, until late 1927; instead, in the interim, they rented a place in North Bennington). The house the Frosts rented in Ann Arbor from 1921 to 1923 was also secured through his poetry—that is, through his Fellowship in Creative Arts at Michigan.

324. In October the University of Michigan had offered RF a lifetime appointment as Fellow in Letters, to begin in autumn 1925. He would keep it for only a year. Persistent family obligations in South Shaftsbury and an offer of a similar appointment from Amherst would bring RF back east in 1926.

325. Monroe published a laudatory article titled "Robert Frost" in the December 1924 issue of *Poetry* (146–153).

326. Enid figures in the Arthurian legends. Lawrance Thompson reports a 1935 dinner party at which RF chided E.A. Robinson for having put his hand (as he did in several books) to the Arthurian lore so soon after Tennyson had done the same (*YT,* 418). When the present letter was written, Robinson had already devoted two books to the old tales, *Merlin: A Poem* (New York: Macmillan, 1917) and *Lancelot: a Poem* (New York: T. Seltzer,

real Christmas present if I may take it as such done up as it comes in red.[327] I had been hinting round to the family for something simple to wear in my hair when I am out with the Opera Club this winter toadying to various and sundry Continental pretenders; and here I get a whole crown.

Nay but seriously I am pleased with your article especially where it warns people against taking me too seriously.[328] My debt to you has piled up to some altitude above sea level since you first printed blank verse of mine in 1913.[329] We have grown to be old, if not yet quite first name, friends. May we never be less.

Merry Christmas to you and a great discovery or two in poetry for 1925. And you mustn't keep getting bowled over by cars. Better by Gourjeefs [*sic*] and Kings of the Black Isles than by cars.[330]

> Always yours faithfully
> Robert Frost

[*To Harold Rugg. ALS. DCL.*]

> Amherst Mass
> Dec 19 1924

Dear Rugg:

Of course for old Dartmouth if I can. But you must give me my own sweet time about it. I'm a slow person and only made slower by driving, as no doubt

---

1920). He would publish a third, *Modred,* in 1929 (New York and Princeton, NJ: Brick Row Bookshop).

327. The cover of the December issue was poinsettia red.

328. Monroe writes: "When it comes to personal confession—to autobiography, so to speak—Mr. Frost refuses to take himself seriously. He has to laugh—or rather, he has to smile in that whimsical observant side-long way of his" (151).

329. The year is incorrect. The first poem RF placed in *Poetry* (February 1914) was "The Code," which is indeed in blank verse (collected in *NB*). In *Poetry* it bore the subtitle "Heroics."

330. Presumably a reference to the mystic and guru George Ivanovich Gurdjieff (1866?–1949), who had begun lecturing in America in 1924. Among his influential literary acolytes were Alfred R. Orage, editor of the *New Age,* and the American writers Jean Toomer and Waldo Frank. The story "The Young King of the Black Isles" is told in book 9 of *The Arabian Nights: One Thousand and One Nights.*

my first teacher remarked in the first school I ever went to. I have had to insist on deliberate speed.[331]

   Merry Christmas to you and good skiing (so to spell it).[332]

Ever yours
Robert Frost

---

331. From Francis Thompson's "The Hound of Heaven" (1893):

From those strong Feet that followed, followed after.
  But with unhurrying chase,
  And unperturbèd pace,
Deliberate speed, majestic instancy,
  They beat—and a Voice beat
  More instant than the Feet—

RF first read "The Hound of Heaven" in a Boston bookshop in 1895 (*EY*, 196–198), and
he told the tale of its effect on him early and late in a 1953 talk. See Reginald Cook,
Robert Frost: A Living Voice (Amherst: University of Massachusetts Press, 1974), 38–39.
RF typically used Thompson's epithets "deliberate speed" and "majestic instancy"
without attribution. For example, Gorham Munson, in *Robert Frost: A Study in Sensibility and Common Sense* (New York: Doran, 1927), writes of a comment RF made about
George Santayana in 1926: "Santayana gave a course which [RF] recalls with pleasure
in the 'golden speech' and the 'deliberate speed, majestic instancy' of the exposition
of this brilliant thinker" (34). Of course, the phrase "deliberate speed" is well known
to Americans unacquainted with "The Hound of Heaven." According to the legal
scholar James Chen, "deliberate speed" appears in no fewer than seven Supreme
Court opinions written between 1911 and 1955: one by Oliver Wendell Holmes, five by
Felix Frankfurter (whom RF befriended in the 1930s), and the seventh by Chief Justice
Earl Warren in the case known as Brown II (1955). The latter opinion, in adopting the
"deliberate speed" formula, set no clear deadline for integrating Southern schools
(integration had been mandated in *Brown v. Board of Education of Topeka, Kansas* [1954],
which negated the "separate but equal" doctrine established in *Plessy v. Ferguson*
[1896]). For details, and a review of the literary origins of the phrase as used in the law,
see James Ming Chen, "Poetic Justice," *Cardozo Law Review* 28.2 (2006): 581–622. (Also
available online.) We thank Mark Scott and James Chen for assistance in drafting this
note.

332. Rugg was an avid winter sportsman, and often accompanied the Dartmouth
Outing Club on its expeditions.

[*To J. J. Lankes. ALS. HRC.*]

Amherst Mass

December 20 1924

Dear JJ:

You cant honestly say you have seen as many new poems by me this year as I have seen new pictures by you. We have to admit that you have treated me better than I have treated you. Well, you are younger than I and ought to treat me better. You have treated me something perfect. My house is one gallery of your black and white imagination. And I'm still as fresh as a visitor in it: I cant look at it without seeing it. It will be a long time before I can look at such a picture as your Winter without seeing it.[333]

We are leaving Amherst boys for Pittsfield books and South Shaftsbury cows.[334] I hope to experience benefit by one or other of the changes. That will be my Christmas present to myself if I get it.

I see Jennings once in a while.[335] Dont give that fellow too much chance to talk as if he told you how to make your pictures. The subnormal rich are a little too condescending. He started to tell me how to make my poetry the last time he was here. I spoke loud to him. Don't you speak loud to him. You did it once and once is enough. But keep him his distance. Let him buy all the pictures he will and babble his childish connoisseurship. But dont let him think he has any personal handle to you such as your ear or nose. I want you to get all the good you can out of him without any of the harm. He ought to spend some money on you. Besides what he earns in brushes, he has $5000 a year from his mother to play with.

---

333. Lankes' *Winter* first appeared in the January 1922 edition of the *The Liberator*.

334. RF alludes to The Open Book, his daughters' bookstore in Pittsfield, Massachusetts, and to Carol and Lillian's farm at the Stone House in South Shaftsbury, Vermont.

335. The Fuller Brush salesman and specialty art dealer Edward Phelps "Ned" Jennings (1895–1966) and his wife, Margie, had commissioned Lankes to design their Christmas card in 1924. Jennings also never paid for, nor returned, several prints Lankes had commissioned him to sell. Jennings had been instrumental in selling the American artist Edward Hopper's prints to the Metropolitan Museum of Art and the British Museum. Jennings's mother, Laura Jennings, née Park, who had married Bennington, Vermont, resident, Frederick Beach Jennings, was the daughter of the railroad and banking tycoon Trenor W. Park.

We still consider in the matter of the press.[336] Probably we had best not go into printing till the book and cow businesses are running themselves. Carol Lesley and Margery are working hammer and tongs.[337]

You are going to visit us next summer. And we'll be looking in on you now and then perhaps if we get to going back and forward between Vermont and Michigan.[338] Amn't[339] I the scattered resident? You takes your choice of where you'll think of me as living.

The best kind of Christmas to you and your family.

Ill write again some day not too distant but I'll think of you many times before I write.

> Always yours
> Robert Frost

Jennings means well. We mustnt be too hard on him.

[*To Sidney Cox. ALS. DCL.*]

> South Shaftsbury Vt Dec 31 1924

Dear Sidney

I'm not going to take much ink to tell you what I have to tell you. Something went wrong between you and Davison after I left that looks to me as if it had spoiled your chance for the moment of coming East.[340] I am inclined to think it was your success with your classes and with some of your fellow teachers. Your hit with Canby Farrar and Miss Holbrook excited a jealousy you took no pains to disarm by devoting some of the time every

---

336. See RF to Lankes, July 6, 1925.

337. "Odds, bobs, hammer and tongs" is Captain Hook's preferred expletive in J. M. Barrie's *Peter Pan*. The phrase derives from a refrain in one of Royal Navy officer and novelist Frederick Marryat's sea ballads. See *Snarleyyow, or The Dog Fiend* (1837): "Odds, bobs, hammer and tongs, long as I've been to sea, / I've fought 'gainst every odds—and I've gained the victory."

338. At the time Lankes lived in Gardenville, New York, which the Frosts would have passed en route to Ann Arbor.

339. RF's contraction for "Am not."

340. Cox taught in the summer of 1924 at Bread Loaf, where, evidently, he had a falling-out with Wilfred Davison, dean of the school. At the time, Cox was professor of English at the University of Montana.

day to self-deprecation.[341] There alone is where you have to take your share of the blame: you didn't sing puisne for life-insurance.[342] You could have kept Davison self-satisfied as easy as π or 3.141592. You absolutely had him the last I knew. But you considered him too slight a person to waste the wisdom of the serpent on and the consequence is he seems rather to have enjoyed being in a position not to help you get anywhere.[343] Why would you be so independent?

He tells me he expressed himself to the Vassar people as not particularly impressed, but they mustnt take his word for it: let them apply to Canby and Frost.[344] But after such a beginning they just naturally didnt apply to Canby and Frost, at least not to Frost. They turned to Miss Branch and she put the finishing touch on you.[345] It is too bad to have our fate hang by such threads, but such is fate or luck or whatever you call it. You are enough of a tactician to see that it would do no good for me to interpose in the very teeth of the Vassar ladies unwillingness to be advised by me. Least said, soonest forgotten. We dont want the check to amount to an incident. This chance lost, our cue is to get as ready as we can for the next.

I didnt ask Davison particularly what he and Miss Branch found the matter with you. I don't care what they found the matter with you. You dont—because you know as well as I what prompted their criticism. They couldnt name their real objection to you. So they murmured something about the sincerity and radicalism you valued yourself on: you werent half as radical as you thought you were and as for sincerity why make a catch word of it? You cant contend with such talk. You wouldn't want me to. You see you have pressed against them too hard; you have made them feel you

---

341. Henry Seidel Canby; John Farrar, editor and publisher, director of the Bread Loaf Writers' Conference 1926–1928; Miss Holbrook is likely Myra Coffin Holbrook, a graduate of Vassar and Wesleyan and an associate professor of English at Simmons College in Boston. The head of her department at Simmons, Robert Malcolm Gay, lectured at the Bread Loaf School of English from 1925 to 1927.

342. "Puisne": lower in rank, inferior (compare "puny"). To "sing puisne," as RF uses it here, means, roughly, to affect modesty, to flatter.

343. Matthew 10:16: "Be ye therefore wise as serpents, and harmless as doves."

344. Canby had approached the president of Vassar, Henry Noble MacCracken (1880–1970), as to the possibility of a position for Cox there. Nothing came of it, fueling suspicion that Davison had intervened to Cox's disadvantage (*RFSC,* 128).

345. Possibly Anna Hempstead Branch (1875–1932), a poet and the founder of the Poets' Guild of Christadora House.

too much. A good rule is, Go easy with your self-declarations and chal-
lenges, if you dont want common ordinarians to retaliate with a nasty little
Pshaw or shucks! Youve got too big a thing ahead for any flourishes in the
announcement.

I wish I could see you for a little talk. If Davison asks you back next
year, I am half inclined to advise your coming: that is if you could come
with colors flying. Of course I wouldnt have you do anything to humil-
iate yourself. Nor would I have you come if you thought the cards were
stacked against you. You know best whether you think the minds are too
small for you to have any chance with. Stay away from any certain defeat
of course.

Don't you let this business bother you. Teach, write. I dont say where you
are going to break into prominence first and it doesnt matter where. But it
will be in one or the other soon I'm sure. I wish it could be in the writing.
Keep growing and eliminating there. Put all you've got into one more great
think. You're bound to make it—indeed in my opinion you've already made
it. But you wont mind giving them good measure. Pile it on till they acknowledge the avalanche.

This isnt a Christmassive or New Yearly missive, but after all you arent suffering where you are. There'd be no special mockery in my wishing you a
Happy New Year. You can be happy a little longer where you are if you want
to be. So be.

I'm your friend
R.F.

Wouldn't it count with your people out there if you came East a second
time?

[To Leonidas W. Payne (1873–1945), professor of English at the University of Texas. ALS.
HRC.]

Amherst Mass
January 4 1925

Dear Mr Payne

You might well doubt the authenticity of any answer from me on time.
The great thing about this letter is that it is characteristically late. Let's
hope that it isn't too late to get me into your anthology with the seven

poems you ask for.[346] But that must be as may be. It cant be too late for proving me a true friend—true to form I mean. For that purpose the later the better.

But to be serious in a serious matter, please accept my apologies for silence. One thing that kept me from writing sooner was my desire to write more at length to you than to the generalty. I had been looking round for someone besides Armstrong at Waco to take it out on for the pleasure I had in Texas.[347] And your letter sort of gave me an opening and made me decide to lavish myself on you. But I had to get around to a real undertaking like that—I had to get around to it. To me six months are pretty much as one day. All I ask in this age of speed is to be allowed to go slow. An oxcart on a soft dirt road, cost what it will, is my idea of a self-indulgent old age. One of the charms of Texas was that the trains I rode on down there were all six hours (just as I am six months almost to a day) behind schedule. Some people wanted to spoil a good story by blaming the retardation on the late war.[348] Absolutely the only sleeper or waker I saw on time was the one you put me onto that night with a gift of fruit outward bound from Austin. It was lovely—I mean of both Texas and you.

And yet speed is a thing I can see the beauty of and intend to write a poem in free verse on if ever I am tempted to write anything in free verse. Let's see how do you write the stuff:

> *Oh thou that spinnest the wheel*
> *Give speed*
> *Give such speed*
> *That in going from point A*

---

346. Payne's *Later American Writers: Part Two of Selections from American Literature* (New York: Rand McNally, 1926) included "The Pasture," "Mowing," "Mending Wall," "The Code," "The Grindstone," "Nothing Gold Can Stay," and "Birches."

347. RF visited the state in November 1922 and gave a reading at the University of Texas at Austin, where Payne taught. The trip had been initiated by A. J. Armstrong, professor of English at Baylor University, in Waco, where RF also spoke.

348. The Railway Administration Act of 1918 had formalized Wilson's emergency nationalization of American railroads in December 1917, thereby creating the United States Railroad Administration. When railroads were reprivatized in 1920, the terms under which they were to be compensated for use and lost income were contested for years. The post–World War I rebuilding and improvement of American roads and highways was federally funded and swift; the restoration and modernization of railway lines was unsubsidized, uneven, and slow.

To point B
I may not have had time to forget A
Before I arrive at B
And there may result comparison
And metaphor
From the presence in the mind
Of two images at the same instant practically.

Or again:

Oh thou that spinnest the wheel,
Give heed!
Those long curves of the road to left and right
That I have hitherto experienced with the eye
And with the eye only,—
They are too long-drawn for me to feel swayed to
Till my rate of travel shall have risen to a mile a minute.
Swiften me
That I may feel them like a dancer
In the sinews of my back and neck.[349]

But I desist for want of knowing where to cut my lines unhocus-pocusly.

You are welcome to the seven poems, should you still want them. I will ask my publishers not to charge you for them, but if they do charge, please let me know the amount and I will at least get it greatly reduced. Remember me particularly to the Katy with which I feel I have much in common.[350]

> Sincerely yours
> Robert Frost

The person to address at Holt's is Henry Holt Jr.

---

349. Penciled in lightly here, apparently in RF's hand, is the note "end of free verse."

350. The Missouri-Kansas-Texas Railroad was popularly known as "The Katy." The main point of comparison is tardiness, but RF might also be noting that the company's Texas operations, begun in 1872, were roughly the same age as he.

[To Herluf Trolle-Steenstrup, author of When I Was a Boy in Denmark: A Chron-
icle of Happy Days *(Boston: Lothrup, Lee and Shepard, 1923). Steenstrup, born in Copenhagen in 1883, became a US citizen in 1921. ALS. BU.]*

Amherst Mass

January 8 1925

Dear Mr Trolle-Steenstrup:

Forgive me for having let your letter go unanswered so long, but it came
just after I had had to cut myself off from all correspondence for a while on
account of my health.

I shall be glad if I am not too late to give you the help you ask for. Some of
the poems in my books I care most for are The Death of The Hired Man,
The Mountain, The Black Cottage, and Mending Wall in "North of Boston";
Birches and The Road Not Taken in "Mountain Interval"; and The Runaway,
Stopping by Woods on a Snowy Evening and Paul's Wife in "New Hampshire." I should be pleased to present you with any of the three books you
havent in your possession.

Miss Amy Lowell has covered the story of my life in her Tendencies in
Modern American Poetry. So also has Louis Untermeyer in his Modern American Poetry.[351] Mr Untermeyer is a trifle more accurate of the two.

Thank you for the interest that prompted your letter.

Sincerely yours

Robert Frost

[To Charles Wharton Stork, American poet and the editor of Contemporary Verse.
ALS. Yale.]

Amherst January 14 1925

Dear Stork

How can you ask me such a thing when you know how I suffer on a mixed
program?[352] It is bad enough alone, but when I am to have an hour to myself

---

351. Lowell's *Tendencies in Modern American Poetry* (New York: Macmillan) appeared in
1917; pages 79–138 are devoted to RF. See *LRF-1* (580–581, 586–589) for RF's reaction to the
portrait there drawn of him. Untermeyer's *Modern American Poetry*, 2nd ed., revised and
enlarged (New York: Harcourt, Brace and Howe, 1921), provides a biographical sketch of
RF (174–177).

352. The annual banquet of the Poetry Society of America, held in New York.

on the platform I can at least rise with the confidence that I shan't mind, may even enjoy a little, the last half of it. After that noche triste[353] with Wilfred [sic] Gibson and the pȳano player at the Browning Club in Philadelphia years ago and the permanent injury it did to my heart, I resolved never to be caught that way again, and I believe I never have been.[354] You wouldn't want literally to sacrifice me in honor of your elevation to the throne.[355] My ingrediency will never be missed in the poetic salad of the meal. Come, be nice to me. Say I am excused. I'm glad I have as President a friend with whom I can be as perfectly frank in my cowardice. I'm sure it wouldn't help matters for me to be there merely as a silent accessory, or I might offer to sit beside you and hold the ravening eaters at bay. It would be foolish for me, though, to come clear down to New York just to sit inscrutable. I want to abet you what I can. I'm your backer in your office; but you wont mind my admitting I like you better as a poet than as an official. I always enjoy anything of yours I come across in the magazines.

> Ever yours
> Robert Frost

[To Charles Wharton Stork. TG. SLU.]

> Amherst Mass
> Jan 24 1925

CHARLES WHARTON STORK

LOGAN POST OFFICE

PHILADELPHIA PENN

YOU FORGET I MADE THIS SACRIFICE FOR POETRY SOCIETY ONCE BEFORE DONT THINK I SHOULD BE FORCED TO MAKE IT AGAIN YOU HURT MY FEELINGS BUT TO SHOW FORGIVENESS OFFER TO COME DOWN AND SIT BESIDE YOU CANNOT SPEAK

> ROBERT FROST

---

353. Spanish for "night of sorrow."

354. Having published his *Collected Poems* in 1917, Wilfrid Gibson embarked on a reading tour in the United States. The event recalled here must have been in that year, but we have been unable to find a record of it in newspapers. RF refers to the same event in a June 7, 1921, letter to Haines.

355. As president of the Poetry Society of America.

[To Frederick Melcher. ALS. UVA.]

Amherst Mass

January 26, 1925

Dear Melcher:

I won't say I dont like to be made of by the right sort of friends. I am going to let you give me that triumphal dinner on my fiftieth birthday if it is understood beforehand that I dont much deserve it and that I don't necessarily have to look or act exactly the age.[356] Let's see I'm supposed to be getting all this for certain poems. Should you mind telling me offhand which poems? Now wouldn't it be awful if you didnt know any of my poems to name them offhand? You'd be embarrassed.

Dont forget to ask the Untermeyers. Louis has [been] proposing a little frame-up to console me for my grey hairs. But I told him you were ahead of him in solicitude.

I must always be your good friend

Robert Frost

[To Bernice Lurie (1891–1982), wife of Harry Lawrence Lurie (1892–1973), who received his graduate degree in sociology at the University of Michigan in 1923, during RF's first appointments there (1921–1923). ALS. UNH.]

Amherst Mass

February 26 1925

Dear Mrs Lurie

We think that that small house would be just the thing to complete and save the poem—if poem our life is going to be out there. Your description of it is by implication an appreciation of me such as few have written. It's a coincidence that several times this year I have been wondering aloud if

---

356. RF wasn't "exactly" the age. He was already fifty, having been born, though he didn't yet know it, in 1874, not 1875. The dinner was held at the Hotel Brevoort in New York City on March 26. Carl Van Doren was master of ceremonies; guests included Dorothy Canfield Fisher, Wilbur Cross, Walter Prichard Eaton, the Untermeyers, Willa Cather, Elinor Wylie, and Elizabeth Shepley Sergeant. Sergeant would later publish a biography of RF, *The Trial by Existence* (New York: Henry Holt, 1960). RF's wife and their daughters Irma and Lesley also attended.

you wouldnt be the one to help us find something like us. The idea of over across the track has been a great temptation. And it's another coincidence that my friend and well-wisher the conservative kind Tilley suggested all on his own initiative that he didnt see why we shouldnt be allowed to lie more or less dormant in some such corner as away over there.[357] Now what I dont know is whether or how much if any he had been feeling out the general sentiment about how I am to be taken this time in Ann Arbor. I had perhaps best go a little cautiously. I wouldnt have them feel that like an out curve to a right-handed batter I am going away from them at the same time I am going toward them. But we do want the house Ford admired—we want it more than anything else we havent got.[358] Will you just give me two or three weeks to make sure that I can have it with a perfectly clear conscience? I know Burton would have been entirely on my side in living where I could live freeest.[359] Is two or three weeks too long to ask you to wait on what I consider no great uncertainty?

And meanwhile will you tell us about rent. I suppose the house is unfurnished. We were expecting to take furniture with us this time, as for a longer stay.

What wanderers we all are. Wherever we can get a little more excited over ourselves there we go on the shortest notice. I shall be sorry not to have you Luries for neighbors in Ann Arbor, but you're no doubt getting what you want in Chicago. You must enjoy writing me at leisure than when in the rush at Detroit. And doesnt he find Social Service more humanly various than teaching?[360] My best to him. Tell him that all the people that

---

357. See RF to Tilley, November 10, 1924, and March 17, 1925.

358. Robert M. Warner in *Frost-Bite & Frost-Bark*, says of the house at 1223 Pontiac Road: "It was a handsome nineteenth century cottage that well fitted [the Frosts'] needs and tastes; it was later purchased by Henry Ford and moved to Greenfield Village" (32).

359. Marion LeRoy Burton, who had arranged the appointment for RF, had died a week earlier, on February 18. "Freeest" is a spelling more or less obsolete since the eighteenth century.

360. Harry Lurie had just taken a post as superintendent of the Jewish Social Service Bureau in Chicago. He later served, in New York City, as executive director of the Bureau of Jewish Social Research (1930–1935) and of the Council of Jewish Federations and Welfare Funds (1935–1954).

didnt give him that Amherst fellowship are out of here and I trust duly punished, the Algerines.[361]

Sincerely yours

Robert Frost

*[To Edward Morgan Lewis (1872–1936), an American professional baseball player, edu-
cator, and academic administrator. ALS. BU.]*

Amherst February 28 1925

Dear Mr Lewis:

You mustn't ask me this year. I did it for you last year.[362] That was my
present to you and the State of Massachusetts. It might also be regarded as
my state income tax. I pay no other. My home is in Vermont. But this year I
have much too many lectures in the way of business to do any for pleasure.[363]
No, but seriously, I am too overwhelmed with demands on me. You'll have
to let me off with what I did last year, and forgive me.

I've been thinking I didn't see as much of you as I'd like to.

Best wishes; may you be made President soon and preside long.[364]

Always yours friendly

Robert Frost

---

361. The "Algerines": scoundrels, rogues, pirates. It is not clear which fellowship at
Amherst RF has in mind (the college offered a number of them).

362. On June 13, 1924, RF had spoken before the Massachusetts Federation of Women's
Clubs at the Massachusetts Agricultural College.

363. RF spoke in Philadelphia on March 5, at Franklin and Marshall College on
March 6, at Wilson College (Chambersburg, Pennsylvania) on March 9, and at the
Ogontz School (now Penn State Abington) on March 12. Four more readings followed in
March and May: in Lawrence, Massachusetts on March 31, Ann Arbor on May 1, Bowdoin
College on May 4, and Vassar on May 22.

364. Lewis had in fact been named president of the Massachusetts Agricultural College (now the University of Massachusetts Amherst) in 1924. He resigned in 1927 to assume the presidency of the University of New Hampshire, where he worked until his
death in 1936.

[To Wade Van Dore. Date derived from postmark. ALS. BU.]

[Amherst, MA]
[February 28, 1925]

Dear Van Dore:

Your writing pleases me for a vein of thinking in it that is all your own; but it is not punctuation you leave room for improvement in. Dont worry about punctuation.[365] You have still something to learn about managing your sentences so as to fit your verse form without distortion and loss of the point. We have all something still to learn there. It is the last place where we achieve perfection. You've come a good way bravely. Now you please me.

I'm glad you are so much of a real poet. Theres [*sic*] a weight to you that I look in vain for amoung [*sic*] the verse twiddlers in general. They have beauty for one thumb and truth for the other and they sit and twiddle them round and round each other.[366] You arent afraid to think hard and take life hard

Always your friend
Robert Frost

Let me keep track of you in these paths. I've been looking again and I find much of this really lovely and original—underivative:—I was sending it back but I believe unless you demand it I will keep it to show to a friend or two. Send me more as you get on, poet.

---

365. In a February 26 letter enclosing a poem, Van Dore had written: "Here's a poem I wish you would look at. If it does not please you, please return it without comment; if it does, I would appreciate any advice you could give concerning punctuation etc." RF wrote his reply on the sheet of paper Van Dore used to type the request, which now sits above the letter like a header.

366. As if unable to move beyond the last lines of John Keats's "Ode on a Grecian Urn":

"Beauty is truth, truth beauty,—that is all
   Ye know on earth, and all ye need to know."

[To Morris Tilley. ALS. UM.]

Amherst March 17 1925

Dear Tilley:

You first said the word over the Huron for us when we came to live with you again.[367] I wonder if anything may have happened to change your mind about the wisdom of our going over there for a home. Would it look as if we were running away entirely from the obligations of our fellowship? Of course we would be doing no such thing. But would it look as if we were? I ask because we have just heard of a small house on Pontiac Street we can have for seven hundred a year. From the description and pictures of it the Luries have sent it appears just the thing. Getting out of rent for seven hundred would leave us rich enough for an automobile and that with the telephone would keep us from being really very far off. Or so I should think. Elinor is writing the Bursleys for their judgement.[368] Perhaps you and Mrs Tilley wouldnt mind talking it over with them just as if it were your own affairs. We wont let it go any further till we have considered it inside our own little circle, will we? But there is need of dispatch. Let me hear from you in a day or two.

And I warn you that I am not always going to call you Tilley when we resume daily relations.

Ever yours
Robert Frost

---

367. The house the Frosts hoped to rent, and did in fact rent, was at 1223 Pontiac Road, north of the Huron River as it passes through Ann Arbor (more distant from the center of the campus than the family had been during RF's first appointment at Michigan [1921–1923], when they lived at 1523 Washtenaw Avenue). See RF to Tilley, November 10, 1924.

368. Joseph A. Bursley and his wife, Marjorie Knowlton Bursley. Bursley, a professor of mechanical engineering, served as the dean of students at the time. He had helped the Frosts find the place on Washtenaw Avenue in 1921.

[*To Clifton A. Towle (1876–1963), superintendent of schools in Exeter, Rockingham County, New Hampshire. Towle had invited RF to speak at the annual meeting and banquet of the New Hampshire Schoolmasters' Clubs, to be held in October 1925. Enclosed with the invitation was a copy of the program from the 1924 meeting (when Towle had been serving as president). ALS. BU.*]

Amherst Mass
March 18 1925

Dear Mr Towle:

What a pity your convention comes in October instead of in September. In October I shall be away out in Ann Arbor entering on my new fellowship at the University of Michigan. And I should so much like to meet the teachers of New Hampshire. Some other time perhaps you will ask me again. My going to Michigan does not mean that I am giving up New England. I shall be back and forward between the two places. You might well have hit on a date when it would be easy for me to be in the East. But this October happens to be the one month when I must positively be at my post out there.

An old-time New Hampshire teacher's compliments to the New Hampshire teachers of today.

Thank you for the thought that prompted your letter.

Sincerely yours
Robert Frost

[*To Bernice Lurie. ALS. UNH.*]

Amherst March 25 1925

Dear Mrs Lurie

Well we have duly made enquiry and we find that our best friends in Ann Arbor are not only willing but anxious to see us settled in just such an out-of-the-way place as your cottage over across the tracks and river. What will be good for me, they want me to have; and they are sure that will be good. So we hereby accept your offer, and will begin to pay you rent on the cottage from any date you say. I suppose we will move out there on or about the first of October to be at such opening affairs as the President's reception.[369]

---

369. When this letter was written, Alfred Henry Lloyd (1864–1927), professor of philosophy and the dean of the graduate school, was acting president of the University of Michigan. By the time RF arrived on campus in the fall, Clarence Cook Little (1888–1971) had been officially appointed to succeed Marion LeRoy Burton.

The plan of the house as you draw it looks to us pretty nearly just right for our purposes. The fireplace will be fine for my seminar and the heat you are going to carry upstairs will make it so I can use one of the upstairs rooms for a study (so to call it, though I may never do anything but play patience in it.[370]) I have just one suggestion and that is about the location of the bathroom. Sometime you might be willing to put it somewhere else, if some other place can be found for it. You know best whether it would go into the closet upstairs between the two rooms and so as to be reached from the front stairs. Another way that occurs to me would be to leave it where it is, but close the door, I mean build in the door, to it from the sitting room and make an entrance to it from the "very small room" beside it. That would put the very small room out of commission except as a sort of hall and clothes closet. We would of course pay for changing the bathroom.

We are simply pleased to death to have reached a happy decision like this and are eternally grateful to you folks for having come in with your proposal in just the nick of time. It looks as if we had very little more to think of before we migrated.

You neednt worry a minute about our being disappointed in the house. I am sure we see it all pretty much as it is and are not going to like it a bit less than our idea of it.

Best wishes to you both.

Sincerely yours
Robert Frost

[*To Clifton A. Towle. ALS. BU.*]

March 25 1925
Amherst Mass

Dear Mr Towle:

If you are sure you feel that way about having me at the Convention, of course I must try to be there. I recognize New Hampshire's special claim on me, her schools' more special. I missed being born in the State, but my father was born at Kingston, my children were born at Derry. Such as I am for a teacher, her schools made me.[371]

---

370. Patience is better known in the United States as Solitaire.

371. That is, Pinkerton Academy, in Derry, New Hampshire, where RF taught from 1906 to 1911, and the Plymouth Normal School, now Plymouth State University, where he

You have counted I suppose the cost. It will come to right around two hundred and twenty five dollars everything included. That is more than you will ever get me to say I am worth. I advise you to think twice before you undertake to pay it.[372]

Thanks for your kind letters.

Sincerely yours

Robert Frost

[To Crystine Yates (1904–1983) (later, Mrs. Aubrey F. Soyars), a high-school student in Dickson, Tennessee. RF wrote in response to a query about the meaning of the sigh in "The Road Not Taken." Larry L. Finger, a professor at Olivet College, to whom the letter had been given by Soyars, published it in American Literature in 1978.[373] Unable to locate the manuscript, we rely on his transcription.]

Amherst Mass

April 1925

Dear Miss Yates:

No wonder you were a little puzzled over the end of my Road Not Taken. It was my rather private jest at the expense of those who might *think* I would yet live to be sorry for the way I had taken in life. I suppose I was gently teasing them. I'm not really a very regretful person, but for your solicitousness on my behalf I'm

your friend always

Robert Frost

---

taught during the 1911–1912 school year. His work in the classroom at Pinkerton had drawn the attention of New Hampshire State Superintendent of Education Henry C. Morrison, who invited RF to speak at teachers' conventions. Ernest Silver, headmaster at Pinkerton from 1909 to 1911, brought RF with him to the Plymouth Normal School when he assumed the presidency. For more on RF's interest in and commitments to education in New Hampshire, see his letters to Silver and to Harry Alvin Brown, director of the New Hampshire Bureau of Education Research (LRF-1, 63, 70, 75, 84, 104, 127, 164, 178, 214, 236, 250, 252, 271, 615).

372. RF addressed the annual meeting of the New Hampshire Schoolmasters' Club on October 18, in Laconia, as part of a lecture-reading junket that took him also to Philadelphia, Baltimore (Johns Hopkins), and Chapel Hill (University of North Carolina).

373. See Larry L. Finger, "Frost's 'The Road Not Taken': A 1925 Letter Come to Light," *American Literature* 50, no. 3 (1978): 478–479.

[To Louis Untermeyer. Enclosed with this letter is a typescript, "Class Hymn," which RF wrote while a senior at Lawrence High School in Lawrence, Massachusetts. The poem was set to the music Beethoven composed for Friedrich Schiller's "Ode to Joy" (1785), the most famous musical motif in the Ninth Symphony. Date derived from postmark. ALS. LoC.]

[Amherst, MA]

[circa April 10, 1925]

Dear Louis

Wouldn't it jarr [*sic*] you to have this brought up against you by a whole chorus of former classmates thirty three and a third years or one third of a century after the fact? I went to Lawrence prepared at worst to have some of my old unpaid debts thrown in my face.[374] Here you have one of the first half dozen poems I ever wrote to a finish.[375] I have got to confess to someone. It gives me strange powers of speech.

Still yours

R.

Miss Elsie Sergeant wants to ask you about my weaknesses for a New Rep article. I showed her this myself.[376]

---

374. RF spoke in Lawrence, Massachusetts (where he went to high school), on March 31.

375. The poem appeared as follows in the Lawrence, Massachusetts, High School *Bulletin* in June 1892:

> CLASS HYMN—1892
>
> LAWRENCE HIGH SCHOOL
>
> WORDS BY ROBERT L. FROST
>
> MUSIC BY BEETHOVEN

> There is a nook among the alders
> Still sleeping to the cat-bird's "Hush";
>   Below, a long stone-bridge is bending
> Above a runnel's silent rush.

> A dreamer hither often wanders
> And gathers many a snow-white stone;
>   He weighs them, poised upon his fingers,
> Divining each one's silvery tone.

> He drops them! When the stream makes music,
> Fair visions with its vault-voice swell:
>   And so, for us, the future rises,
> As thought-stones stir our heart's "Farewell!" (CPPP, 498)

376. Elizabeth Shepley Sergeant's article, "Robert Frost, a Good Greek out of New England," appeared in the *New Republic*, September 30, 1925.

[To Morris Tilley. TG. Bentley.]

[Amherst, MA]
[April 21, 1925]

PLEASE WIRE AT ONCE MY EXPENSE IF SOMEONE HAS BEEN APPOINTED OR IS BEING
CONSIDERED FOR OTHER FELLOWSHIP IF SO WHO[377]

ROBERT FROST

[To Richard H. Thornton (1889–1977), American educator, editor, and publisher. Formerly a professor of English at the University of North Carolina, Thornton joined Henry Holt and Company in 1924 as head of the foreign-language department. ALS. DCL.]

Amherst April 23 1925

Dear Mr Thornton:

Should you be willing to reduce the price a little more on the poems Miss Winifred Johnston wants to buy for an anthology she is making for schools?[378] She admits that the price you ask is moderate, but says she is too poor to meet it. This once as a favor to me will you ease up a little. Suppose you make it thirty-five or forty for the five if it will make her any happier. On general principles I dont think you charge a bit too much. She just touched me into

---

377. The Fellowship in Creative Arts that first brought RF to the University of Michigan in 1921 was continued when he left it in 1923. Faculty and administrators at Michigan occasionally sought his advice as to who should be awarded the position; he nominated Willa Cather in 1924, and was disappointed when the committee in charge thought it unwise to give the fellowship to a woman; and he helped bring playwright Jesse Lynch Williams to the campus for the 1925–1926 academic year. Tilley replied to RF's telegram with a telegram of his own (the text of which he penciled in on the wire he received from RF): "No one being considered for other fellowship. If you have anyone in mind please let us know. Glad to have you thinking of this. Did you take the house?" "The house" is a reference to the house at 1223 Pontiac Road, which RF agreed to rent on March 25; see his letter of that date to Bernice Lurie. See also RF's June 24, 1925, telegram to Acting President Alfred H. Lloyd.

378. Winifred Johnston (1892–1985), a graduate of the Universities of Oklahoma and Chicago. In 1932 she would publish a verse anthology (coedited with Andrew Robert Ramey), *New Hesperides* (New York: T. Nelson and Sons).

putting in a word for her. I hate to bother you, and I wont bother you again for some time—I promise.

Sincerely yours

Robert Frost

[To Julia Patton. The letter is undated, but a pencil notation in another hand indicates "April, 1925/Troy, N.Y." ALS. Private.]

[Amherst, MA]

[circa April 30, 1925]

My dear Miss Patton:

Thanks for the pleasant time you gave me[379] and I wonder if the enclosed books would mean anything as remembrances from me to any [of] your girls or fellow teachers. I had intended to have them with me for distribution to my audience.

With best wishes to you and Miss Jenny.[380]

Sincerely yours

Robert Frost

[To Louis Untermeyer. Date supplied by Untermeyer. ALS. LoC.]

So Shaft [VT]

[June 20, 1925]

Dear Louis

It seems to me that's a very mature sentiment for an American of any age, that about your having gone back on everything but the world. It can never be said again that living in Europe a year and five twelfths with the Second Coming of Casanova did nothing for you.[381] There are very few things so small that the least of us can't profit by them.

---

379. See RF's December 12, 1924, letter to Patton arranging the lecture at Russell Sage College, which took place on April 24.

380. Patton shared a household in Troy, New York, with Florence G. Jennie and her mother, Susan W. Jennie. Florence also taught at Russell Sage College.

381. Possibly a reference to Rockwell Kent. Kent, an accomplished philanderer, lived in Arlington, VT, just up the road from South Shaftsubury. In 1925 he abandoned his wife

I suspect that what lies at the bottom of your schmertz [*sic*] is your own dereliction in not having gone to her Keats Eats just before Amy died. She got it on us rather by dying just at a moment when we could be made to feel that we had perhaps judged her too hardly.[382] Ever since childhood I have wanted my death to come in as effectively and affectingly. It helps alway [*sic*] anyway it comes in a career of art. Whatever bolt you have shot you have still, as long as you are alive, that one in reserve. But of course it always does the most good on a world that has been treating you too unkindly.

I didn't rise to verse but I did write a little compunctious prose to her ashes. And I did go before the assembled college to say in effect that really no one minded her outrageousness because it never thrust home; in life she didn't know where the feelings were to hurt them any more than in poetry she knew where they were to touch them. I refused to weaken abjectly.[383]

I dreamed that as I wandered by the way I was assured by you that I neednt worry anymore to run hither and thither currying favor with lectures and recitations: my mark was made as much as it was ever going to be made. I could go back like Cincinattus [*sic*] to my plough.[384] And you dont know what

---

Kathleen and spent the next two years in France. RF may also have known about Kent's illustration (twelve prints) of Giacomo Casanova's *Memoirs* (New York: Aventuros, 1925).

382. RF and Untermeyer both politely declined to attend a party at the Hotel Somerset in Boston hosted by Amy Lowell (1874–1925) in celebration of her fiftieth birthday and the release of her two-volume biography, *John Keats* (Boston: Houghton Mifflin, 1925). Lawrance Thompson speculates that RF declined Lowell's invitation because she was one of the few guests conspicuously absent from his own fiftieth birthday party, held at the Hotel Brevoort in New York on March 26, 1925. Having spent considerable energy writing her biography and distressed over negative reviews in England, Lowell died of a stroke two weeks later, on May 12, 1925.

383. RF's tribute, "The Poetry of Amy Lowell," appeared in the *Christian Science Monitor*, May 16, 1925 (it is reprinted in *CPRF*, 88). Heeding a request by George Daniel Olds, RF commemorated Amy Lowell before the Amherst College student body on May 14, 1925.

384. Lucius Quinctius Cincinnatus (519–430 BC), Roman aristocrat, farmer, and statesman. In 458 BC, the Senate named him *magister populi* to suppress an uprising south of Rome. According to Livy, when a group of senators approached Cincinnatus to solicit his help, they found him plowing a field. Cincinnatus accepted the title, assembled an army, and promptly defeated the Aequi at the Battle of Mons Algidus (458 BC). After concluding the peace, he resigned his position and resumed farming. Livy reports that the entire episode was over in fifteen days. Cincinnatus has long been held up as an emblem of civic virtue.

a relief it was. I wept with gratitude toward you. You mean to say, I cried,
I am free to putter my days out without ever writing any more if I dont want
to write? What's the use of trying to beat Two Look at Two, you answered.[385]
Will your frosty mantle to Wilbert Snow.[386] And with that you swung your
1917-model Something-Aperson [*sic*] car into the Bennington-Brattleboro-Keen
[*sic*] road for the Poetry Society at Peterboro [*sic*]. The souvenir pennons ban-
narets [*sic*] all over your car were flapping Robinson, Aline Kilmer, Abbie
Brown, etc.[387] And you had on one of these new fashioned tail lights that kept
winking Stop Stop Stop.

This dream could have been worked out more carefully to make it mean
more if I had turned it over in my mind longer before I wrote it out. It will do
well enough as it is for a Freudian diagnosis. It combines a good deal.

The first cousin of Waldo Frank and the third or fourth of Loeb the Darrow
ward charge came to me the other day with a tale of just having broken away
from his psychoanylist (sp.) after a scene in which he had handed the psychoanylist a letter and made him read it while he waited.[388] He said it was a very
bitter letter full of technical terms. I asked him what had the psychoanylist

385. "Two Look at Two" first appeared in *NH*.

386. Charles Wilbert Snow (1884–1977), American poet and professor of English at
Wesleyan. Untermeyer had once opined that Snow's poetry, which focused primarily
on village life along the Maine coast, was "obviously though perhaps unconsciously indebted to Robert Frost." See *RFLU*, 173.

387. The 1917 Apperson Silver was a V-8 speedster designed for the Apperson Motor
Company by Conrad T. Silver, owner of the Silver Motor Company in Manhattan, New
York. Traveling east on Vermont Route 9 and New Hampshire Route 102, a motorist
would drive through Bennington and Brattleboro, Vermont, and Keene, New Hampshire, before arriving at Peterborough, New Hampshire. As for the "Poetry Society": RF
refers to the MacDowell Artist Colony, founded in 1908 by an American composer, Edward MacDowell, and his wife, Marian. Along with Louis and Jean Starr Untermeyer,
who spent the summer of 1925 at the colony, were the poets Edwin Arlington Robinson
(1869–1935), Aline Murray Kilmer (1888–1941; the wife of the poet Joyce Kilmer), and the
children's author Abbie Farwell Brown (1891–1927). Brown's biography for young adults,
The Boyhood of Edward MacDowell (New York: Frederick A. Stokes, 1924), chronicled Mac-
Dowell's education in Europe.

388. Waldo Frank (1889–1967) was an American novelist and literary critic whose first
novel, *The Unwelcome Man* (Boston: Little, Brown, 1917), is a psychoanalytic look into the
life of Quincy Burt, who, dissatisfied with modern society, contemplates suicide. A critique of Victorian gentility and industrial sterility, the novel advocates a return to the
transcendental ideas of Emerson and Whitman. Clarence Darrow (1857–1938) was an

done, psychoanalyzed him? It seems he had done worse, he had introspectro-sized him. At least I said he had supplied you with the language to deal with him in. He had and I made him eat it. Have you been-ah-sick, I suggested. My mother is a subnormal society has-been and last month my brother com-mitted suicide.[389] Why did your brother commit that? Because he was tired of the varnish business that belongs to the family and was engaged to be mar-ried to an already married woman. Strange that that hadn't occurred to me. The boy is a perfectly unobjectionable last year's graduate except for a poem as I remember it about Gods [sic] face being painted on the sunset sky. God's face <u>painted!</u> This must be some of this God-the-Mother cult. Unless he meant the Virgin Mary.

Captain Mattison our postmaster and a man who has been to France wanted to know of me what they had gone into court out in Tennesee [sic] for, to settle it once and for all who we were descended from, monkeys or the Virgin Mary? Speaking of the Virgin Mary.[390]

And so I might sustain the theme indefinitely that you nor I nor nobody knows as much as he doesnt know.[391] And that isn't all: there is nothing anybody knows however absolutely that isn't more or less vitiated as a fact by what he doesnt know. But of this more in my next book which I cant

---

American attorney famous for defending Richard Loeb and Nathan Leopold, two teen-agers who murdered Loeb's second cousin, Bobby Franks, on May 21, 1924.

389. At the time, "subnormal" was a term of art in reform programs devoted to the diagnosis, classification, and placement of persons with intellectual abilities deemed de-fective. The reformers often helped standardize diagnoses and ameliorate the living con-ditions of the severely disabled, but many of the organizations to which they belonged were indebted to early-twentieth-century eugenicists' notions that civilization could be strengthened by segregating the disabled and preventing them from bearing children. The student RF mentions here is unidentified (and possibly fabricated, at least in part, for purposes of satire).

390. Irwin Mattison (1888–1934), who had served in the U.S. Army during World War I, was appointed postmaster of South Shaftsbury on October 20, 1922. In the spring and summer of 1925, Clarence Darrow defended John T. Scopes in the famous Scopes Monkey Trial. Scopes had been accused of violating the 1925 Butler Act, which made it unlawful for anyone to teach evolutionary theory in Tennessee public schools. The trial, broadcast by radio in much of the nation, pitted Darrow against William Jennings Bryan. Scopes was eventually found guilty, but the verdict was overturned on a legal technicality by the Tennessee Supreme Court.

391. RF added in the margin: "And so I will sustain the theme indefinitely."

make up my mind about, whether to throw it to Holt Harcourt MacVeagh or Knopf.[392]

I recently ran across a biological fact that interested me, as facts go. It establishes exclusiveness much lower down in the scale than you would expect to find it. Exclusiveness in love. Way way down.[393]

> Exclusively yours
> Robert Frost.

[*To Alfred H. Lloyd (1864–1927), then acting president of the University of Michigan. TG. Bentley.*]

> [Bennington, VT]
> [June 24, 1925]

SUGGEST WALTER EATON VANWICK [*SIC*] BROOKS LOUIS UNDERMEYER [*SIC*] ARTHUR[394] [*SIC*] CROWE RANSOME [*SIC*] OR MARK VANDOREN LAST TWO YOUNG WRITERS LESS KNOWN MIGHT TAKE FIVE THOUSAND AND FREE RENT TO BRING SOME HOUSE PROVED STUMBLING BLOCK LAST YEAR HAVE DISCUSSED THIS WITH EFFINGER AND STRAUSS[395]

> ROBERT FROST

---

392. RF would eventually renew his contract with Henry Holt and Company in 1928. The new contract increased his royalties from 15 percent to 20 percent (after five thousand copies of each book sold), provided for a $2,000 cash advance, and a stipend of $250 per month for five years. In November of that year, Holt published *WRB*.

393. RF may be poking fun at Louis Untermeyer's affection for the poet Virginia Moore (1903–1993), whom he had met at the MacDowell Colony that summer. In 1926, Untermeyer would divorce his wife, Jean Starr Untermeyer, and marry Moore.

394. Someone (possibly Lloyd) corrected "Arthur" to "John" in pencil.

395. John Robert Effinger, professor of French and dean of the College of Literature, Science and the Arts at Michigan; and Louis A. Strauss, professor of English. The writers here nominated for the Fellowship in Creative Arts are the theater and drama critic Walter Prichard Eaton, the literary critic, biographer, and historian Van Wyck Brooks, and of course RF's friend, Untermeyer. John Crowe Ransom (1888–1974) was thirty-seven at the time; his first two books had appeared in 1924. Mark Van Doren (1894–1972) was younger, and had so far published only one book of poetry, in 1924, and two books of literary criticism, in 1916 and 1920. In 1920 he had joined the faculty at Columbia University, where he would spend his entire teaching career. The fellowship for 1925–1926 ultimately went to the dramatist Jesse Lynch Williams.

[*To George R. Elliott. At the head of the letter Elliott penciled in "after the Institute [of Modern Literature] June 1925." He also added "about 25" between June and 1925 in the date where RF inscribed it. ALS. ACL.*]

South Shaftsbury June [circa 25] 1925

Dear Roy:

I'm sorry this had to happen, but we've been riding for it and I can't say it wasn't expected. Elinor had a serious nervous collapse early last week.[396] I saw it wasn't going to do to leave her and I should have wired regrets then, but she hated to be the cause of my failure to keep an engagement and kept me waiting on from day to day to see if she wouldn't be better.[397] I was actually on the point of setting out for Brunswick on Wednesday, but at the last moment my couraged [*sic*] failed me—she looked so sick. The amount of it is, my way of life lately has put too much strain on her. All this campaigning goes against her better nature and so also does some of this fancy teaching, my perpetual at-home charity clinic for incipient poesis, for instance.[398] Time we got back into the quiet from which we came. We've had our warning. I'll tell you more about it when I see you if you make it worth my while by forgiving me first.

Shall we proceed to the consideration of Longfellow?[399]

Ever yours

R.F.

I hope nobody thought there was anything the least bit temperamental in my staying away from a degree.

---

396 In fact, she had suffered another miscarriage (the last of several over the course of the marriage); see *YT*, 282–283, 617.

397. The engagement was to receive an honorary degree from Bowdoin College, where Elliott taught.

398. At both Michigan and Amherst, RF often convened the small seminars he taught at home.

399. On May 4, RF had delivered a talk, "Vocal Imagination," using extracts from Henry Wadsworth Longfellow's works as examples, at the Institute of Modern Literature convened by Bowdoin to celebrate the centennial of the class of 1825. See also RF to Elliott, October 15, 1924, and *An Institute of Modern Literature at Bowdoin College, Brunswick, Maine, from May 5 to May 16, 1925, in Commemoration of the Centennial Year of the Graduation of the Class of 1825* (Lewiston, ME: Lewiston Journal, 1926). The institute ran from May 4 through May 15.

I have just read what you wrote in The Virginia Quarterly. I must give you the poem you ask for somewhere between Snow and The Death of the Hired Man but longer than either. That shall be my thanks.[400]

[To Lincoln MacVeagh, who penciled in "Postmarked June 25" on the manuscript. ALS. Jones.]

South Shaftsbury Vt.

[June 25, 1925]

Dear Lincoln:

On the contrary I was thinking that Marianne Moore had been turning you against me. You undoubtedly sent me that little folder today to twit me on her having run into the second edition.[401] The handwriting on the envelope was your own personal. Be careful, or you'll make her a household word. Then where would she be?—at once rare and common? Like her for all of me. "All those that change old loves for new, pray gods they change for worse."[402] Speaking of worse, we drew off rather worsted from our

---

400. See Elliott's "An Undiscovered America in Frost's Poetry," *Virginia Quarterly Review* 1, no. 2 (July 1925): 205–215. RF has in mind the following passage: "Frost's humor . . . never quite bubbles; when it tends to do so it loses its own fine distinction. On the other hand, it never quite subsides. It is a ripe northern whiskey, far from entirely 'made in America,' rare and socially helpful at the present time. Casual callers would appreciate it better, I think, if Mr. Frost would now assign to it a more elaborate decanter than heretofore: I mean, a narrative poem like 'Snow' and 'The Death of the Hired Man' fused together and ten times longer" (207).

401. MacVeagh's Dial Press issued a second edition of Moore's *Observations* in 1925; the first edition had appeared in 1924.

402. See George Peele, *The Arraignment of Paris* (1584), where Oenone sings to Paris (1.5):

My love is fair, my love is gay,
As fresh as been the flowers in May,
And of my love my roundelay,
My merry, merry, merry roundelay
Concludes with Cupid's curse:
They that do change old love for new,
Pray gods they change for worse.

RF would have known the song more immediately from its placement under the title "Fair and Fair" in *The Oxford Book of English Verse*, ed. Arthur Quiller-Couch (New York: Oxford University Press, 1900).

year's teaching and lecturing, Elinor worse worsted than I. I would have given anything for a baseball game any time these three months.[403] But what's a fellow to do that combines so many occupations and arts? I'm too played out to travel anywhere right now. But can't you come up here for a few days? You'll find me annointing [*sic*] my wounds on a warm rock from which is a view of the young growing orchard you dug so many holes for two years ago.

I'm proud to have become at once a laree and a penatee to Bunny and I must come to see her before I go to Michigan, if you think I wont disillusion her.[404]

I mean it—come up.

> Always yours
> Robert Frost

[*To Wilbur Rowell. ALS. UVA.*]

> South Shaftsbury Vermont
> June 27 1925

Dear Mr Rowell:

To tell the truth, I never got up my courage to ask my friend W. R. Brown to go on my bond.[405] I wasnt sure, but I was afraid from the way you spoke that it might be asking a good deal of him. I am relieved by your suggestion that I buy a bond. I am not at home in these matters. I need to be told what to do.

It's good Jean wants me appointed her guardian.[406] She can be very sane in a letter—and in conversation too at times. Elinor and I went to see her a few

---

403. In March, April, and May, RF spoke several times in and around Philadelphia; in Washington, DC; in New York City; in Lawrence, Massachusetts; in Ann Arbor; at Bowdoin College; and at Vassar. In speaking of Elinor as "worst worsted," RF has in mind the illness that ended with a miscarriage earlier in June.

404. "Bunny" is MacVeagh's wife, Margaret. The Lares and the Penates were *di familiares*—household deities—in ancient Roman religion, which the classicist MacVeagh would have known. RF returned to Ann Arbor in September 1925 to take up his new post at the University of Michigan as Fellow in Letters (he would resign a year later).

405. Warren R. Brown (1873–1957) was an Amherst realtor and friend.

406. See RF to Rowell, December 12, 1924.

weeks ago and found her fairly well.[407] I was surprised at the personal interest Dr Tyson, the Superintendent, showed in her and the special account he was able to give of her case.[408] I am sure she has the best care and is at least as happy as I have seen her for years. That's not happy enough to smile much. I just mean she has her satisfactions from day to day almost like a normal person.

We are back in our stone house in the mountains and I suppose you are having week ends in your stone house. Remember me to Mrs Rowell. Tell her few things have happened to me in my not unromantic career like the triumph you gave me in Lawrence.[409]

> Always yours sincerely
> Robert Frost

[To Eunice Tietjens. ALS. Newberry.]

> South Shaftsbury Vermont*
> June 28 1925

Dear Mrs Head:[410]

Since getting your letter in Amherst I have been all the way to Ann Arbor and consulted my friends there among the Deans about Michigan as a university for unsilly girls.[411] I had my own idea before I went and I only

---

407. Elinor Frost's interpretation of her encounter with Jeanie was quite different. In a letter to Wilbur Rowell on September 3, 1925, she writes: "We were in Augusta the first week in May, and she [Jeanie] was not able to talk sensibly or coherently for five minutes. Dr. Tyson is a man of ability, culture, and great sympathy. He takes a special interest in Jean, and I think they have tried very hard to cure her, but he does not now expect that she will ever be able to live outside an institution" (*SL*, 317–318).

408. Forrest Clark Tyson, MD (1881–1953), was appointed superintendent of the Augusta State Hospital (of which the Maine Insane Asylum was a part) in January 1914.

409. When RF read there on March 31.

410. RF here addesses Tietjens by her second husband's name, not her professional name (which derives from her first marriage to Paul Tietjens, whom she divorced in 1914).

411. On May 1, 1925, RF gave an address in Ann Arbor at memorial services for President Marion LeRoy Burton, who had died on February 18. While there, he made inquiries on behalf of Tietjens' daughter Janet (1908–1990), who matriculated instead at the University of Wisconsin, where she graduated in 1931 with a degree in geology. See also RF to Tietjens, circa February 1, 1926.

got it confirmed. I am sure Janet would thrive socially and every way either in her own home bringing her family with her, or in one of the four girls' dormitories. Otherwise she wouldn't. Coeducational colleges are no places for girls who have to live around town in boarding houses. Their life is too much of a struggle. We all agreed on that. What Michigan needs more than resident poets is a few more girls' dormitories such as Helen Newberry and Martha Cook.[412]

Of course starting early like this and with a girl like Janet there will be no trouble about getting into a dormitory. I shall be glad to attend to this for her. She must be sure to come. Now that you have put it into my head, I dont see how our literary club out there can get along without her.[413]

Best wishes to you and Mr Head.[414]

Sincerely yours
Robert Frost

*Here for the moment, but off for the White Mountains later. Where are you to be when? We shall probably be settled for our longest stay of the summer at Sugar Hill after the first of August. We should be delighted to see you at either place.[415]

[*To Sidney Cox. ALS. DCL.*]

South Shaftsbury Vt
July 5 1925

Dear Sidney
If you see any of the aftereffects of physical labor in this letter you may know that it is from hand mowing—my brow is still wet with what Longfellow

---

412. The Helen Newberry Residence (built 1913) and the Martha Cook Building (1915) were all-female residence halls. They remain so today.

413. Likely a reference to the undergraduate literary society that had published, during RF's first stint at Michigan, the magazine *Whimsies*. In 1924 the magazine was renamed *The Inlander;* RF would publish "The Minor Bird" in its January 1926 issue (collected as "A Minor Bird" in *WRB*).

414. Cloyd Head, a playwright and theatrical director.

415. During August and September, RF, his wife, Elinor, and their daughter Irma stayed in the guest cottage on the Fobes place in Sugar Hill, which is adjacent to Franconia, New Hampshire.

called honest,[416] and this being Sunday I am just after having broken the Sabbath quite traverse like a puisne tilter.[417] Great to be home farming.

For you to say when you will come down and see us. When Davison was signing up his faculty our voyage to Europe looked far more probably [sic] than it does now though between you and me I can't say it was ever more than probable enough for an excuse to go to a ball game or stay away from a lecture. In other words we have <u>subsequently</u> decided not to go to Europe enough so's you'd notice it. Peace is more my style than Europe. Orestes like I pray for it or like Dante in the not-too-well-known-and-in-danger-of-being-forgotten poem on him by Parsons the American dentist.[418]

But we'll save me and my needs to talk over when you come and you and your needs too. I confess Davison threw a slight scare into me and right after seeing him I might have been inclined to think that what you needed was—well cautioning. I now know better.[419] I thought maybe you had been inordinately erring on the right side—as in farming for instance. I hold that all farming is erring on the right side. So don't be offended. But as I say I now doubt if you erred at all. On every hand right, left, before and behindhand reports are that you taught 'em dizzy. Sally Cleghorn was the latest. I heard her say unasked that a fellow named Cox with his breezy western energy was worth the price of admission to the rodeo.[420] I saw my chance to

---

416. See stanza two of Longfellow's "The Village Blacksmith" (1840):

His hair is crisp, and black, and long,
His face is like the tan;
His brow is wet with honest sweat,
He earns whate'er he can,
And looks the whole world in the face,
For he owes not any man.

417. See *As You Like It* 4.3, where Orlando "as a puisne tilter . . . spurs/his horse but on one side, breaks his staff like a/noble goose." Compare RF's use of "puisne" in his December 31, 1924, letter to Cox.

418. In Aeschylus' *The Eumenides*, Orestes, pursued by the Erinyes, prays to Athena; famously, the goddess is tardy in responding, although her intervention is effective when it eventually comes. RF also refers to Thomas William Parsons's "On a Bust of Dante" (1841): "The single boon for which he prayed/Was peace, that pilgrim's one request" (lines 31–32). This prayer is not granted. Parsons was, by trade, a dentist.

419. See RF to Cox, December 31, 1924.

420. Sarah Norcliffe Cleghorn (1876–1959), a poet and reformer who lived in Vermont for most of her adult life.

shock her by telling her you were from Bates. It shocked her like a bit of or bite off conservative dogma.[421] Her eyes went round and round like the Hermits boy who then doth crazy go.[422] She couldn't get used to that. Which just shows you.

While I am about it I may as well enquire if you ever found one crumb of the erotic in the four Gospels. You know Plato virtually says himself two thousand years before Freud that the love of the invisible, philosophy, is a sublimation of τα ερotικα, sex love the mans love not only of fair girls but also of fair boys.[423] The metaphor with him is always drawn from sex. Is it ever a single moment with Christ? Great play has been made with the ladies, not all of them sinless, he had around him. Is it anywhere hinted that his business with the most sinful of them was other than to bid them sin no more? Is the erotic note ever struck?—with or without charm? The great test would be the analogies of argument. They're never are they sensual or even sensuous. It's reached a point with me where I've got to have it out with myself whether I can think of Christ as but another manifestation of Dionysus, wine in his beard and the love leer in his eye. Is he even a little Pagan? Isn't he pretty nearly all Puritan for better or worse?

Always yours

Robert Frost

The real reason for our decision not to go to Europe was Elinor's health. I doubt sometimes if she ought to risk the sea-sickness. Maybe she'd stand it in a big swift boat.

---

421. Bates College in Lewiston, Maine, which Cox attended from 1907 to 1911. His grandfather, Benjamin Francis Hayes (1830–1906), was one of the founding faculty. Bates was founded by Free Will Baptists, although by the time of Cox's arrival it had become nonsectarian; Cleghorn was noted for her Christian Socialist views, which she strenuously advocated in her poetry, so it is presumably Cox's association with doctrinal severity that discommodes her.

422. A reference to Samuel Taylor Coleridge's *The Rime of the Ancient Mariner* (1798), part 7, where the Pilot's boy (not the Hermit's boy) goes mad.

423. This is the burden of Socrates' arguments in both *The Phaedrus* and *The Symposium*.

[To J. J. Lankes. The letter is undated, but internal evidence indicates RF composed it in early July 1925. ALS. HRC.]

[South Shaftsbury, VT]
[circa July 6, 1925]

Dear Lankes:

I dont call it very good news that you are going South to live.[424] Your letters lately sound as if there were something the matter—just when I had been getting up my hopes that you were really going to sell woodcuts and move out onto Easy Street where the chauffers [*sic*] sleep at the wheels of luxury by the curbing. Your distress is my distress. But let's not be too discouraged. If you get me too discouraged, I shall be wishing all my friends would get respectable jobs with Dayton Cash Register companies and leave the vicissitudes and privations of art to me alone who can stand them better for myself than for other people.[425] I wish I could promise to have some poems for the book we were going to do together. But wishing does no good. On the contrary, wishing in an emergency does actual harm. It locks me.[426] You'll have to take my friendship for what help there is in it for the present. I know one thing you are the best woodcutter in or out of the woods now cutting wood.

I'd like fearfully to see you and hear the whole story.

A large number of us here are sick or enervated or something—if you can get any comfort out of that by comparison.

Our young apple trees are doing well however. Fifteen years and we shall be able to live on them without publicity. Thats what I'm hanging on for.

Ever yours
R. F.

over

---

424. In July, Lankes moved from Gardenville, New York, to Hilton Village, Virginia, a rural enclave near Yorktown.

425. The National Cash Register Company was founded in Dayton, Ohio, by John Henry Patterson in 1884. NCR was one of the first modern American companies to offer benefits packages to employees.

426. RF's December 20, 1924, letter to Lankes suggests that the two had considered the possibility of starting a small press and of collaborating on a book. Here RF appears to demur a second time. See also RF to Lankes, December 31, 1923 ("Sometime soon we must have a little black and white book together of verse and picture in equal measure"). In any case, he and Lankes would work together on *WRB*.

Speaking of neighbors, Carol, who is young and frank, has made a good start with ours here. He has threatened Bronson to have the law on him for a dead horse that stinks toward us when the wind is SS.W., Lane to have the law on him for chickens he can keep at home, Potter to have the Law on him for a bull of low breeding that wants to miseginate [*sic*] with our registered Holstein Friesians. We are bounded on the north by Persey [*sic*].[427] He's the only one we aren't at a stand off with. Sounds vigorous?

[*To E. Merrill Root. Dated from postmark. ALS. ACL.*]

South Shaftsbury Vt[428]
[July 11, 1925]

Dear Root:

I'll hope hard to have had you a poem before your term of office expires. I'm the more likely to that nothing depends on it. Nothing does depend on it, does it? You'll be pleased if you get one, but you'll be just as exactly as all right if you dont.

I cant be certain about the poem but what I can be certain about is the testimonial. I can tell the Gugum Man Felshps Ltd that you are one of the three best young poetic prospects in the country any time you say.[429] Only you must instruct me how to address such an institution or body, as I haven't my Etiquette and Complete Letter by me on the farm.[430] I've been kept from the greatest enterprises in life from embarrassments no larger than this.

Good wishes.

Yours surely
Robert Frost

---

427. Census records and South Shaftsbury property deeds suggest that the most likely candidates for RF's neighbors in 1925 are Grant Bronson (1865–1926), John B. Lane (1886–1965), Lewis Van Nest Potter (1875–1951), and Edward Russell Percey (1874–1942). The editors thank Judy Stratton, town clerk of South Shaftsbury, for her help here.

428. On the manuscript, RF drew a pointing finger directed at the address.

429. The Guggenheim Fellowships were inaugurated in 1925. Root was never awarded one.

430. Likely, *Chesterfield's Art of Letter-Writing and Complete Rules of Etiquette* (New York: Dick and Fitzgerald, 1857).

[*To John W. Haines. ALS-photostat. DCL.*]

South Shaftsbury
Vermont USA.
July 21 1925

Dear Jack

Yesterday we were haying in America: we got in about two tons of Timothy not unmixed with clover.[431] We sold to people passing in their cars some five hundred stems of sweet peas at a cent apiece. Lesley called us up on the telephone from her bookstore in Pittsfield, Mass. forty miles below us in the same valley to say she was just back from a fairly successful business trip with her book caravan (a converted Ford truck) to the extremity of Cape Cod. Such might be said to be a day with us. It sounds sufficiently I hope as if we made our living as honest farmers, florists, and booksellers.

A night is not very different. Last night I was awakened by the cackling of a hen in a brood coop across the road and rising set out just as I was to see what was molesting her reign. It proved to be a skunk a quiet offensive little varmint of the New World that operates like a chemical fire extinguisher to subdue ardors. I should have had a gun with me, but I hadnt. I hadnt even a pogamogon.[432] All I had was a dog. There was no moon. On my way over I got involved barefooted with a spring-toothed harrow and fell heavily. It should have been a lesson to me but it wasn't: for I got involved with it again on my way back. We gave the skunk a good barking at. The skunk is a dignified soldier who will walk away from anybody but run away from nobody. We should have been able to do him some damage. If there had been more light there would have been another story. The dog and I got gassed. I had to throw away my night gown before I reentered the house. The dog wont smell like himself for a month especially when it rains. Our casualties were four chickens killed before the main body could be brought up.

So you see what it is like.

Why I dont buy a ticket and hoist sail for England when I long to see you as much as I do! We would have to take a walk in Leddington and Ryton if I came over. I should probably die of internal weeping. We could call on the

---

431. Timothy-grass (*Pheleum pratense*), introduced into North America in the early eighteenth century.

432. A bludgeon used by Native American peoples in the Great Lakes and Plains regions (more commonly spelled "poggamogan").

ladies, Mrs Badney across from the Gallows who knocked at our door one dark dark night with the news that the Germans had landed in Portsmouth and Ledbury was up—side—down[433] (this was her version of the foolish American Christmas ship bearing gifts to the Germans equally with the Belgians French and English);[434] and Mrs Farmer next to Little Iddens who was a tree-poisoner as I've heard.[435] She poisoned a whole apple orchard of her own husband's planting to keep it from coming into the possession of her brother when he ousted them from the farm they had rented of him. She had been punished by the courts. The law was against her, poor lady. I can still hear her making a tremendous noise with a rattle to scare the blackbirds from the cherry trees. She was doing her best to live down her crime. I can't tell you how homesick I am. For the moment I can't seem to content myself with the characters I am in the way of meeting here. A fellow said to me the other day he supposed the trial at Dayton Tennessee would settle it once for all whether we were descended from monkeys or the Virgin Mary.[436] At least he knew that the same people who doubted the Biblical account of creation found it hard to believe in the Immaculate Conception. All sorts of people get educated in this country. I am so deep in the educational problem that I dont write any oftener than I used to. I'm consulted on the way to handle a poem in school so as not to hurt it for the sensitive and natural. You have no idea of the authority I have become. I might do some good if good were a thing that could be done.

Our love to you all

Faithfully thine
Robert Frost

By and by I'll write you another.

---

433. "Mrs Badney" is Elizabeth Hyett; see RF to Lesley Frost, September 11, 1928.

434. The USS *Jason*, dubbed the "Santa Claus Ship," sailed on November 14, 1914, from New York to Plymouth laden with Christmas gifts to succor the deprived children of Europe, including, as RF complains here, German children.

435. A neighbor of the Frosts during their time at Little Iddens.

436. The trial of John Scopes, accused of violating a Tennessee state law forbidding the teaching of evolutionary theory in the state's schoolrooms, had begun on July 10, 1925. The "fellow" in question is Irwin Mattison, the South Shaftsbury postmaster (see RF to Untermeyer, circa June 20, 1925).

[To Josephine Ketcham Piercy (1895–1995), an instructor in the English Department at the University of Indiana. ALS. Indiana.]

South Shaftsbury Vt

July 26 1925

My dear Miss Piercy:

You mustnt ask me for such talk in the summer. It's what I earn my living by six months in the year as a regular attaché of three colleges now and lecturer at large with a good number more.[437] You must let me beg off. I want to play and loaf and sleep and be speechless. You will probably get enough answers out of us to such a letter for a good solid course without my help. It will be my loss to be left out of it. But I must accept the loss. I commend your idea. Thanks for thinking of <u>me.</u>

Best wishes.

Sincerely yours

Robert Frost

[To William Hughes Mearns (1875–1965), then head of the Lincoln School (part of Teachers College, Columbia University) and formerly a professor at the Philadelphia School of Pedagogy. He had sent RF a copy of his anthology of poetry Creative Youth: How a School Environment Set Free the Creative Spirit *(New York: Doubleday, 1925). ALS. BU.]*

South Shaftsbury Vermont

July 27 1925

Dear Mr Mearns:

I just think it's the height of teaching and I'm proud to see my name so inextricably mixed up with it.[438] Away with any doubt whether you had a

---

437. RF's principal obligations were to Amherst College, which he had just left, and to the University of Michigan, where he would again take up a post in September 1925. In addition he had a more or less regular "attachment" to the Bread Loaf School of English at Middlebury College.

438. RF is mentioned a number of times in *Creative Youth,* and Mearns's remarks about teaching have a Frostian cast. The same is true of the preface Otis W. Caldwell wrote for the volume: "We have drilled, memorized, analyzed, dissected, and philosophized upon and within the 'world's best literature.' At the end we have often found our pupils examinable regarding certain standard selections, but mechanically unsympathetic with them; and there was no burning fire within driving them toward en-

right to make so many young poets. You would deny that you made them poets. You simply let them become poets. You cut the air away before and poetry naturally rushed in behind. You made poetry the line of least resistance to them. I know something about it but you know more and have more energy for it. You say forty wise things of the first water in your preface both about reading and writing. That Tom-Prideaux-boy says I can come to see you some time when I am in New York next year; and I'm coming. You must tell me about him.[439]

　My thanks for the book

Sincerely yours
Robert Frost

---

deavors to shape their own reflections and buoyant visions into forms worthy of record in print. In literature, as in some other subjects, we have regarded pupils as learners, not prophetic doers, and have sought to instruct them, and have not tried to lead them to create. . . . We need to recognize that many, possibly most, pupils are essentially creative, but that our systems of education have forced adult standards and judgments until timidity regarding one's own writing has too often supplanted the naturally adventurous spirit of those who really wish, and very often slyly endeavor, to express themselves in verse and prose" (vii–viii).

　439. Mearns opens *Creative Youth* with a discussion of "Circus," a poem by Tom Prideaux (Prideaux had been one of Mearns's students at the Lincoln School): "When a portion of Tom Prideaux's 'Circus' was read before the New York Art Club at one of its annual Authors' Nights, William Rose Benét [a friend of RF's] shouldered through the audience to demand further particulars about the poet and to read for himself the description of the acrobats in glittering regalia careening at their dizzy heights 'like birds among the jungles of a dream.' Amid the clamor of voices all about us he read the concluding lines:

> *Then bowing when their lauded act is ended*
> 　*And tossing kisses, jaunty and so glib,*
> *I wonder if they really comprehended*
> 　*They've tickled Death along his bony rib!*

'That makes the small hairs rise on the back of my neck,' he said warmly; 'and I always know it's a good poem when the small hairs rise on the back of my neck!'" (1).

[To William Orton Tewson (1877–1947), journalist and literary critic. ALS. UVA.]

[Sugar Hill, NH]

[August 25, 1925]

Dear Mr Tewson:

For sheer usefulness in every modern encounter, I consider "So I have heard and do in part believe" the most beautiful single line of English verse.[440] It should be found early in the first act of Hamlet, Horatio speaking.

Your letter has just reached me. I am in the woods a fugitive from everything and all but cut off from mail

Sincerely yours

Robert Frost

On my own trail; August 25 1925[441]

[To Witter Bynner. ALS. Harvard.]

Sugar Hill N.H.

August 29 1925

Dear Witter:

If you knew how long and hard people had had to keep after me for anything they ever got out of me. My good nature will promise you a preface or poem that my indolence can't be expected to deliver in months and years perhaps. Why is this so I wonder. Am I good-natured because I am indolent or indolent because I am good-natured? You may think I assume the good nature too easily. But I really am good-natured and I really do want to write you a little preface if you can wait for it. You couldn't hold the book up, could you, till I could see what I could do? No one can say I ever failed to keep an appointment in person. In writing is not in person. I never in my life have kept an appointment in writing. I was to have written a poem for their hundred and fiftieth at Concord and Lexington but when the time came for

---

440. Presumably Tewson had asked RF what he considered the best line in English verse. In 1926, Tewson put an open question to writers in the *Literary Review* of the *New York Evening Post*: "Do you care what the critics say about you?" Many responded, but not RF (the responses are held now in the archives at the Library of Congress).

441. RF was then with his wife, Elinor, and their daughter Irma at the Fobes place, near Franconia.

it I just didnt turn up with it.[442] I dont claim that this weakness makes me amiable or even interesting. Please like me in spite of it.

This is Sugar Hill N.H. on a back road. But dont tell anybody. I am feigning to be in Canada a fugitive from injustice.

I have hardly more than cheeped in verse this summer.

Let me write the preface. But for God's sake don't hold me to a date with it, if you don't want to drive me distracted.[443]

We think of you often in changing rings from hand to hand.

Ridgeley's [sic] was a good book.[444]

> Ever yours
> Robert Frost

[To Louis Untermeyer. ALS. LoC.]

> Sugar Hill NH.
> Aug 31 1925

Dear Louis:

The best Aiken poem is probably Arachne, the best Benet the wily Fawn (not the linsey Jesse), the best H D the Recording Angel and Richard Aldington the best Eliot I or II or possibly III the best Fletcher To Hell with Whores (line 21) the best Kreymborg Neighbors the best Vachel Buffaloes, the best Amy her Communication to you or me (and by the way I hear there is a British-started story going round that I shortened her life by not liking her Keats. I think someone must have got me mixed up with you) the best Edna Saint I (the rest are pretty bad except for line 8 in V and stanza 2 in VII) the best Ransome [sic] as far as Ive got Thinking Drinking the best Robinson

---

442. The sesquicentennial anniversary of the Battles of Lexington and Concord (April 19, 1775) was widely observed in New England and in the country generally; commemorative stamps and coins were issued by the U.S. Postal Service and the U.S. Mint. It is not clear which organization RF was to have written a poem for, and in any case this may well be a joke. (Emerson had written his best-known poem, "The Concord Hymn," for the dedication of the obelisk commemorating the Battles of Lexington and Concord in 1836.)

443. RF never produced a preface for a book edited or written by Bynner. See also RF to Bynner, April 5, 1926.

444. Ridgely Torrence's second collection of poetry, *Hesperides* (New York: Macmillan), appeared in 1925.

Gardiner Maine the best Sandburg Star Monkey (because when we stopped some one in a car to ask him what he meant by crowding us into the ditch he promptly answered "Oh ho yah hi yi yippy lulu the meaning was five six seven five six seven"—just like that) the best Sara Teasdale On the South Downs and There Will be Stars the best Jean (and I trust you are being good to her) Bitter Bread and Midnight the best you Disenchantment and the Poetry Contest in Kansas the best me The Minor Bird and The Night Light.[445] All of which is to prove to you that though a poet I do read other people's poetry. Only I don't do it as poet but as teacher of literature in Amherst Michigan and such like places.

Honestly I hope you folks arent going to pull any thing boneheaded. It will be a poor advertisement of my philosophy if it won't keep my most intimate friends from getting unmarried. Think how any foolishness on your part is going to involve me and cut out the cheap talk. That is what I say unto you both.[446]

We are enjoying a descent of bears upon this region. If we survive it there should be much to tell. They are as thick as caterpillars in a pest year. If you never hear from me again you will know that I have probably been killed by a bear hunter for the bounty on bears which is large enough to be worth taking any risk for. $5. A baby bear was knocked on the head in our Tamarack. Six of

---

445. In surveying the assembled contents of *A Miscellany of American Poetry* (New York: Harcourt, Brace, 1925), RF refers to Conrad Aiken's "The Wedding"; William Rose Benét's "The Fawn in the Snow" and "Jesse James" ("linsey," Untermeyer notes, because like linsey-woolsey, the poem was coarse and reminded RF of Vachel Lindsay); Hilda Doolittle's "Let Zeus Record," which begins: "I say, I am quite done, / quite done with this; / you smile your calm / inveterate chill smile" (she was estranged from husband, Richard Aldington); T.S. Eliot's "Three Dream Songs" (later part of "The Hollow Men"); John Gould Fletcher's "Painted Women"; Alfred Kreymborg's "Neighbors" (part of a longer work titled "Seven Movements"); Vachel Lindsay's "The Flower-Fed Buffaloes"; Amy Lowell's "A Communication" (addressed to neither RF nor Untermeyer); Edna St. Vincent Millay's "From a Very Little Sphinx"; John Crowe Ransom's sonnet, "Thinking, Drinking"; E.A. Robinson's sonnet "New England"; Carl Sandburg's "Monkey of Stars" (the refrain of which RF parodies); Sara Teasdale's "On the South Downs" and "There Will be Stars"; Jean Starr Untermeyer's "Bitter Bread and Weak Wine" and "Midnight Vision"; Untermeyer's "Disenchantment" and "Song Tournament: New Style"; and RF's own "The Minor Bird" and "The Night Light." For reasons never explained, the *Miscellany,* when published just months later, contained no poems by RF.

446. In 1926, Untermeyer would divorce his first wife Jean Starr Untermeyer to marry the poet Virginia Moore.

the Fobes sheep have been eaten.[447] A mother and two cubs went up the road by our house the other evening tearing down the small cherry trees along the wall. You could see where one of the cubs had wiped his bottom on a large stone and left traces of a diet of chock cherries[448] and blueberries. I almost got one cornered in our pasture last night but he lifted the wire and went under the fence. It is terrible.

Ever yours

Robert Frost.

[*To Sharon Osborne Brown (1891–1965), literary critic, anthologist, and professor of English. ALS. BU.*]

Sugar Hill N.H.

September 10 1925

Dear Mr Brown:

Your list would be The Onset, The Fear, A Time to Talk, and, as an alternative to one of these, The Gum Gatherer. But you say it is not unalterable and you are open to suggestions from me. My list would not be very different: The Onset, The Fear, The Gum Gatherer (good so far) and one more, either The Mountain (my best as I see it), Birches or Stopping by Woods on a Snowy Evening. I have no wish to embarass [*sic*] you with too much of me. But if I am in at all, I like my group in an anthology to look fairly rounded. You know best if you have room for four of mine.[449]

You seem to be near us. If you were riding in the mountains before you went home it would be fine if you could drop in on me for a talk. I am at the Fobes Farm Sugar Hill N.H.

Sincerely yours

Robert Frost

---

447. RF was with Elinor and Irma at the cottage on the Fobes place.

448. A New England variant of "choke cherry" (*Prunus virginiana*).

449. Brown chose "The Mountain," "The Onset," "The Fear," and "Stopping by Woods on a Snowy Evening" for his book *Poetry of Our Times* (Chicago: Foresman, 1928).

[To David Morton, American poet and a member in the English Department at Amherst. Day of the month derived from the postmark. ALS. UVA.]

Sugar Hill [NH]

Sept [11] 1925

Welcome to Putting in the Seed.[450] See you sometime before long. Good of you to want the poem.

Teach 'em poetically.

R. F.

[To Sheridan Gibney (1903–1988), a member of the Amherst class of 1925. ALS. BU.]

Sugar Hill N.H.

September 13 1925

Dear Gibney:

No I don't shake my head at your way of work. On the contrary I nod it. No one can say I ever asked him to do as I do. Go forth and follow your own bent.[451]

If Conrad Aiken asks you to a tennis tea or something play easy; don't be overwhelming.[452]

Good luck.

Affectionately

Robert Frost

Give me your address now and then

---

450. "Putting in the Seed," a sonnet, first appeared in the magazine *Poetry and Drama* in December 1914 and was later collected in *MI*. It is not clear why Morton wanted a copy, but the previous year he had published his own book of sonnets, *Harvest* (New York: G. P. Putnam, 1924).

451. Gibney soon embarked on a successful career as a screenwriter and playwright, after a three-year stint (1926–1929) as a teacher at Hobart College (Geneva, New York). Late in his career he wrote scripts for *The Man from U.N.C.L.E.* and *The Six Million Dollar Man*.

452. The advice given here is obscure, but may concern Aiken's delicate state of mind. Aiken's father had murdered his mother before killing himself when Aiken was a boy, and Aiken was troubled as an adult by fears for his own sanity.

4

To Michigan Again (for a Lifetime in a Year)
October 1925–June 1926

*Well, old friend, we are going to be where we shall see a lot of each
other again. I shall count on you more than on anyone else to help
me find out how to make the most of what the University has given
me. We must conspire to manage me with the wisdom of the
serpent.*

—Robert Frost to Morris Tilley, November 10, 1924

Robert Frost stands outside his Pontiac Street residence in Ann Arbor in a
photograph taken by friend and art faculty member Jean Paul Slusser.

Robert Frost Collection, Special Collections, University of Michigan Library.

[To Wade Van Dore. Date derived from internal evidence. ALS. BU.]

1223 Pontiac St
Ann Arbor
[October 1925]

Dear Van Dore:

I didnt half see the poems you brought the other day.[1] Couldnt you bring them back (and some more with them) Wednesday afternoon?—or, if it suited you better, Friday afternoon? Suppose I expect you Wednesday unless you write and say Friday. The poem you copied into your letter was a poem I'm sure. The feeling of things goes deep with you

Always yours
Robert Frost

---

1. For an account of the visit, see *YT*, 286–287.

[To Charles Wharton Stork. Dated from internal evidence and from a cataloger's note,
"October 6, 1925," penciled in at the top right of the manuscript. ALS. Yale.]

1223 Pontiac Road
Ann Arbor Michigan
[October 6, 1925]

Dear Stork:

No one I'd rather have introduce me.[2] Kind of you to be willing.

I can get down to Philadelphia on the afternoon of the 26th and have that night with you. But I must get away right after noon of the 27th for Baltimore. I don't know how to find you. Shall I just call you on the telephone and ask for directions when I get to the Broad St Station or will you drop me a line of help before I start from here?[3] Maybe I shouldn't go clear to Broad St and maybe if you knew my train you would meet me. I should like to leave New York on the 2 o'clock P.M. if there is such a train. Don't take too much trouble to collect me. I shall turn up somehow. Pleasant to see you and your family again in your home as in the days that were.

Sincerely yours
Robert Frost

[To Edgar David Cass (1865–1939). A graduate of Dartmouth College (BS 1897), Cass
was a schoolteacher and principal in Manchester, New Hampshire, and president of
the New Hampshire Schoolmasters' Club in 1925, when RF addressed it on October 18.
ALS. BU.]

Ann Arbor Michigan
October 13 1925

Dear Mr Cass:

Of course I must accept your invitation to speak though I have no belief in myself at all as an after-dinner speaker. This in confirmation of my telegram, which I sent instead of a letter when I saw how long your letter had been back

---

2. At a reading delivered in Philadelphia on October 26, 1925. Stork was a Philadelphia native and had until 1916 taught English at the University of Pennsylvania.

3. Broad Street Station, in central Philadelphia.

and forward following me around.[4] Thank you for what I am sure was never intended to make me miserable.

Sincerely yours

Robert Frost

Second letter just received.

[To Lesley and Marjorie Frost. Dated from internal evidence. ALS. UVA.]

[Ann Arbor, MI]

[late October 1925]

Dear Kidds[5]:

Your printed matter received. In reply am giving you a large order for one copy of Canfield's Made to Order Stories which please send promptly as not to a member of your family.[6]

Advise one of your firm keep a scrapbook. Have some letters and stuff to give you good start. Enclosed find couple souvenirs of Harry Kemp author of Tramping on Life.[7] Others to match. Make no mistake: dont neglect important branch of your enterprise.

Yours (off to Chicago to speak a good word for Harriet Monroes Poetry) ly

R. F. D. Ph. D.

---

4. Before arriving in Ann Arbor in late September, RF had spent six weeks in Sugar Hill, New Hampshire, and in South Shaftsbury, Vermont. For other letters pertaining to the lecture, see RF to Towle, March 18 and 25, 1925.

5. An archaic spelling of the word for young goats found in Arthur Golding's 1567 translation of Ovid's *Metamorphoses* and in several translations of Virgil.

6. In *FL*, Arnold Grade indicates the printed matter was a brochure announcing the opening of The Open Book. On this basis he dates the composition of the letter to 1924. However, while the "printed matter" may indeed be a brochure advertising that event, the publication of Dorothy Canfield Fisher's *Made-to-Order Stories* (New York: Harcourt, Brace, 1925) suggests RF composed the letter in 1925.

7. Harry Hibbard Kemp (1883–1960) was an American poet and prose writer who spent a good deal of his youth tramping around the country by riding the rails. His *Tramping on Life: An Autobiographical Narrative* (New York: Boni and Liveright, 1922) became a bestseller.

[To Charles E. Bayly Jr. (1897–1954), an editor at Henry Holt and Company. Dated from internal evidence. ALS. Princeton.]

> 1223 Pontiac St
> Ann Arbor Mich
> [November 1925]

Dear Mr Bayly:

I should be glad to give you my opinion for what it is worth. I ought to know Hill's work, but don't seem to.[8] Tell me a little about him. It would help to know about how old he is and how long he has been at the verse.

I have been off in Grand Rapids and Chicago[9] or I should have answered you sooner.

> Sincerely yours
> Robert Frost

[To John Freeman (1880–1929), British literary critic and poet; he had solicited an essay from RF about his own work. Dated from internal evidence. In response to Freeman's request, RF encloses, on two separate pages, a handwritten summary of his aesthetic principles. ALS. HRC.]

> Ann Arbor Michigan U. S. A.
> November 5, 1925

Dear Freeman:

If I wrote myself up it would have to be in verse since I write no prose and am scared blue at any demand on me for prose. I suppose I could do it openly in verse with perfect propriety. Nearly every poet has paid himself tribute at least once in verse, of course always in the third person under some such title as "The Poet." He will say for instance:

---

8. Frank Ernest Hill (1888–1969), formerly literary editor of the *New York Sun,* in 1925 head of the editorial department at Longmans, Green. In 1927 he would publish, with Joseph Auslander, *The Winged Horse: The Story of Poetry and the Poets* (New York: Doubleday). He had been writing verse for fifteen years—as he explained in a December 14, 1928, letter to RF (held at Princeton)—but had published none in book form. Further correspondence on RF's side has not survived, but his judgment of Hill's poetry was likely unfavorable: Henry Holt published no books by Hill.

9. Giving lectures.

> *The poet in a golden clime was born,*
> *With golden stars above,*
> *Dowered with the hate of hate, the scorn of scorn,*
> *The love of love—*

meaning himself, Alfred.[10] We gather from this that Alfred was pleased to be able to say he was at once a matchless soul and a pretty good matcher; he gave 'em as good as they sent, not just tit for tat but tat for tat.[11] Or don't we?

I'm surprised to find all these things so long afterward still lodged in the heart of a friend. Jack Haines is one of the faithful. I simply must get over to see him next summer before he changes too much from the botanist who shyly scraped acquaintance with me over flowers in the highway near Leddington one day in 1914 and once let me stand on his shoulders to pull spleenwort[12] from a crevice in a cliff by matchlight in the evening.

I couldnt ask anyone to state me closer. In corroboration I might scratch on another sheet a few more things I remember saying in the days when my theorising was strong upon me.[13] My theory was out of my practice and was probably a provision of nature against criticism. I haven't felt the need of talking about it as much lately as I did once. I still hold to it.

What are these articles I hear Helen Thomas has been publishing about the early loves of Edward? Am I going to be kept from seeing them?[14]

You havent given me much time. Your letter overtook me only yesterday and here it is November 5th.

No, I only taught psychology once upon a time. Yes I am as you surmise all American-Anglo Saxon. But I am only half a Yankee. My father* was a

---

10. RF quotes from Alfred, Lord Tennyson's "The Poet," first published in 1830.

11. In British English "tat" (as used here) means rubbish. The joke is at Tennyson's expense: a good deal of what he wrote was second rate.

12. Spleenwort, a type of evergreen fern, is so named for the spleen-shaped sori (spore-bearing botanical structures) on the underside of the fronds.

13. In 1913 and 1914, RF wrote a number of letters from England, mostly to American friends, outlining his theory of "the sound of sense," "sentence sounds," and the "abstract vitality of our speech." Many are gathered in *CPPP* (664–686). See also the letters indexed in *LRF-1* under the heading, "Frost, Robert Lee; topical index: poetics," etc. (795).

14. Helen Thomas (1877–1967) records the intimacies of her early relationship with her husband, Edward Thomas, in her memoir *As It Was* (London: William Heinemann, 1926).

ninth-generation Yankee. My mother was born in Scotland, a pure Scot except, I am told, for a dash of French far back.

I was brought up on Melville. My daughters live in his home town Pittsfield Mass. Dont dare to set up to like him any better than I like him.[15]

I know whose shade I have to thank for your kindness to me. Well the world was a sad place before we found it so.[16]

You might inscribe a book to me some time.

Sincerely yours
Robert Frost

*Old Devonshire stock

The brute tones of our human throat that may once have been all our meaning. I suppose there is one for every feeling we shall ever feel, yes and for every thought we shall ever think. Such is the limitation of our thought.

The tones dealt in in poetry may be the broadest or again they may be the most delicate*

Vocal reality. . . . observation of the voice.

Even in lyric the main thing is that every sentence should be come at from a different dramatic slant.

Fool psychologists treat the five sense elements in poetry as of equal weight. One of them is nearly the whole thing. The tone-of-voice element is the unbroken flow on which the others are carried along like sticks and leaves and flowers.

These are scraps from a lecture I once came near reading. Here's another:

All I ask is iambic. I undertake to furnish the variety in the relation of my tones to it. The crossed swords are always the same. The sword dancer varies his position between them.

*Probably cited Magna est veritas and The Garden to show how my theory held at different levels one almost colloquial another in the grand manner.[17]

15. Macmillan published John Freeman's *Herman Melville* in 1926.

16. A reference to the death of Edward Thomas, with whom Freeman had also enjoyed a close friendship.

17. Coventry Patmore's "Magna est Veritas" and Andrew Marvell's "The Garden" (though it is possible that RF has in mind, instead of the latter, Henry Austin Dobson's "A Garden Song," which he knew from Arthur Quiller-Couch's *Oxford Book of English*

Sentences may have the greatest monotony to the eye in length and structure and yet the greatest variety to the ear in the tones of voice they carry. As
in Emerson.[18]

The imagination of the ear flags first as the spirit dies down in writing. The
"voices" fail you.

Some of the highlights, the most vivid imaginative passages in poetry are
of the eye, but more perhaps are [of] the ear.

The vocabulary may be what you please though I like it not too literary;
but the tones of voice must be caught fresh and fresh from life. Poetry is a
fresh look and a fresh listen.

The actor's gift is to execute the vocal image at the mouth. The writer's is
to implicate the vocal image in a sentence and fasten it printed to the page.

I ask no machine to tell me the length of a syllable. Its length with me is
entirely expressional. "Oh" may be as long as prolonged agony or as short as
slight surprise.

Some have proposed inventing a notation to make sure the tones intended. Some have tried to help themselves with marginal adjectives. But
the sentences are a notation for indicating tones of voice. A good sentence
does double duty: it conveys one meaning by word and syntax another by
the tone of voice it indicates. In irony the tone indicated contradicts the
words.

One might make a distinction between intoned poetry and intonational poetry. Of course they interpenetrate.

Verse (New York: Oxford University Press, 1900), and which he quotes in his notebooks
(*NBRF*, 667).

18. RF held to the view. See his 1959 essay "On Emerson": "I had a talk with John Erskine the first time I met him on this subject of sentences that may look tiresomely alike,
short and with short words, yet turn out as calling for all sorts of ways of being said aloud
or in the mind's ear, Horatio. I took Emerson's prose and verse as my illustration. Writing
is unboring to the extent that it is dramatic" (*CPRF*, 202). See also "The Last Refinement
of Subject Matter: Vocal Imagination" (*CPRF*, 136–139; 299–304).

[To Marion Edwards Park (1875–1960), president of Bryn Mawr from 1922 to 1942. ALS. Bryn Mawr.]

Ann Arbor Michigan
November 8 1925

My dear Miss Park:

I should be glad to lecture again at Bryn Mawr if you will wait for me till I go East in the middle of January for my two weeks with the boys at Amherst. How would January 14th or 15th be?[19]

I have no more pleasant recollections of a school and college than my five visits with the poets of Bryn Mawr.[20] There were several of those girls who couldn't very well expect not to be held to their promise. It is time I was inquiring after them with a portentous manner. I dont forget that their drawing me into their education was largely their own idea. It was the kind of thing I like to have happen.

Thank you for your kind letter.

Sincerely yours
Robert Frost

[To Franklin B. Folsom (1907–1995), then a student at the University of Colorado Boulder. Date derived from postmark. ALS. BU.]

[Ann Arbor, MI]
[November 10, 1925]

Dear Folsom:

It will have to be no more than a word. And that's more than most get out of me now-adays. But you write a more fetching letter than most.

You can say what you do about Davies without disparagement.[21] You characterize him closely enough. I like him for what you say he is. I like a good

---

19. On January 15, 1926, RF spoke on the topic "Beyond Prose and Reason: Metaphor" at Bryn Mawr. After speaking at Union College, in Schenectady, he read at Amherst, where he spent about two weeks, stopping by also to look in on Marjorie and Lesley Frost's bookshop in Pittsfield, Massachusetts.

20. Among the students RF had met during visits to the college in 1918 and 1920 was Kathleen Johnston (Bryn Mawr class of 1920), who as Mrs. Theodore Morrison would play a significant role in RF's later life, from 1938 until his death in 1963.

21. W. H. Davies (1871–1940), British poet. For more remarks on Davies's work, see *LRF-1*, 192–193, 227.

many kinds of poet from the author of Lycidas up down or out sideways.[22] I'll bet you do too. Lets keep that straight through all our criticism: the different ways of being an artist arent better or worse than each other: they remain, after all is said and done, simply different.

I knew Davies in England and found him exactly what I had expected from his poetry. His observation is that of a lost child: he easily sees wonders. I have no doubt he offers all he says about the butterfly on an unsweetened stone for scientific fact.[23] He wrote a small book of prose on Nature which might help if you could get hold of it. Theres a passage in it about a really truly gold bug that cant fly because of the metal he is made of.[24] It sounds to me like belief.

Good luck.

Sincerely yours
Robert Frost

Nothing to report since New Hampshire. Nothing coming for a year or two yet.[25]

---

22. John Milton wrote "Lycidas."

23. See Davies's poem "The Example":

Here's an example from
A Butterfly;
That on a rough, hard rock
Happy can lie;
Friendless and all alone
On this unsweetened stone. . . .

24. See W. H. Davies, *Nature* (London: B. T. Batsford, 1914): "One summer's day, when I was walking along the hedgerow, I saw a gold bug. I do not mean a fly that was yellow, or the colour of gold, but one that was really made in parts of that solid metal. When it tried to soar it came slowly to earth, because of its weight; and so it was quite plain that parts of its body were made of solid gold. I would have hardly thought this possible, had I not seen with my own eyes how its weight brought it down and made it incapable of a long flight" (26).

25. RF's next and fifth book, *WRB*, would appear in 1928.

[To Lesley Frost. Dated from internal evidence. ALS. Private.]

[Ann Arbor, MI]

[mid-November 1925]

Dear Lesley:

The proper study of the school boy is his professors, you tell Harold from me.[26] He knows as much already. He will only need to be reminded of it to be made ashamed. And knowledge of professors isn't enough: it is necessary to remain while in college not above using that knowledge. That is to say, in college you must play college. It is really a very much more human and a very much less intellectual game than some of us are prone to fear.

I wish I could transcribe for you the complaint of Gibbon is his Autobiography against the Oxford of his time. One of his tutors was so bad that he shields him with a blank for his name. His other was nothing. There was no oversight to keep him from any excess mental physical or moral. Before anybody knew it he had become a Roman Catholic and had to be expelled from Magdalen. Just think of the neglect that would let a boy of sixteen wander so far in the mind as to arrive at a belief in transubstantiation. Gibbon never forgave them. But I don't know. We owe the best parts of the Decline and Fall to Gibbon's education having gone wrong at that point. Couldn't we lay down the general rule that where education goes wrong just there it is most educative. But again I don't know. I'll never forget the day when a dozen of us were telling each other exactly as if we knew what was the proper training of a child in the way he should go and I was suddenly aware and by something in my manner made everybody else aware that we had Mrs Patterson in our midst whose highly educated son had just broken an uncommon family pride by jumping into the ocean from a liner and drowning himself to rectify the mistake of his second marriage. From sheer embarrassment before God I said for all of us What are we talking about all so self-assured?

Mama was saying she hoped no mistakes would be made in the education of such a cute little fellow as Prescott (We'd just been reading yours and Marj's letters).[27] Amen says I. You hear that, God? We are saying we hope no mistake

---

26. Likely Harold Newman, then a student at Amherst. For details about him, Edward Gibbons's autobiography, the Patterson suicide, and other matters touched on in this letter, see the introduction to the present volume, where the letter is discussed in detail (pages 5–14).

27. RF's grandson, William Prescott Frost (1924–1989), at the time thirteen months old.

will be made in the education of Prescott Frost South Shaftsbury Vermont U.S.A. on the Earth. A word to the All-wise should be sufficient. There's nothing we can do about it if you ignore the hint. We are not threatening to stop going to church. (We've pretty well stopped already.) We were just discharging any responsibility we might be supposed to have in holding you to what we admit is almost entirely your own business. No disrespect intended. We believe in you. Go in and win. At any rate do the best you can. We are with you at every opening we see in your fight against the Older God—I mean Chaos Chronos Column (Newspaper) Saturn Satan or whatsoever alias he turns up under.

"I saw where" a fellow of this university working for a doctors degree and disporting herself in public said some new music had no counterpart in modern times unless it were Debussys Submerged Cathedral and De la Mares poetry.[28] She found nothing but the Irish in us Americans for it to appeal to. One piece by a French man and all pieces by an English man. Such brain porridge. Cheap metaphor nowhere near a mark. Exibition [*sic*] of trained mind. I wonder how these scholars recognize each other when they meet. By what signs. Accuracy is a word they traffic in. I ask for the deadliest accuracy in a comparison. It must prick something. There are all sorts of ways of saying Hell! Say it with the mouth pulled open downward and somewhat to one side. You three girls[29] can practice till you get something satisfactorily tired and disgusted. I saw Lizette Reese in Baltimore. She had just been refusing to meet Edna Millais [*sic*] at the Kinsolvings.[30] She says she is about done with such Churchly toleration for prostitution and hard drinking as some people now a days go in for. She dared to say that right in Knopfs[31] office the other day before Heywood Broun and a lot of joyous hell birds and what do you suppose they did? They burst right out laughing at her. She said she thought they

---

28. The French composer Claude Debussy (1862–1918) published his piano prelude "The Sunken Cathedral" in 1910. RF refers also to English poet Walter de la Mare (1873–1956).

29. Lesley, Marjorie, and their friend, Mary Ellen Hager (in Pittsfield).

30. Lizette Woodworth Reese (1856–1935), an American poet, and a strong influence on Edna St. Vincent Millay—so there is some irony in Reese's disapproval, as reported by RF, of the younger poet's sexual morality. Reese lived in Baltimore, where RF had lectured in October. Wythe Leigh Kinsolving (1878–1964) was an American poet, Episcopal priest, and political journalist active in the Democratic Party.

31. Journalist and editor Heywood Broun (1888–1939) and publisher Alfred A. Knopf, New York literary figures well-known for refusing to cater to genteel tastes.

were making fun of her. She gave them her opinion of Jurgening since they would have it.[32] She'll be seventy in two years. She's not afraid of them. She's not the only Puritan by all I hear tell. Johnny Farrar has been getting right up and walking right out of the theatre in protest against something said or done in the play.[33] MacVeagh tells me.[34] He has been roasted at the stake or column for it by all his old friends. Of course you have to forgive some of them; they never heard of the cult of evil before. It is all so new to them. But you cant help being glad that some are sticking to the plain unmystical literal decencies. It leaves you free to tend to your farming. Dick Potter may go to jail for liberally attracting girls out hiking and telling them his name was Beagle.[35] But the thought of Lizette way down below Mason and Dixons line should reassure us. Something still stands fast.

R.

Check for book-debt enclosed.[36] No receipt asked for. See that I am crossed off wont you? Send us Mrs Elliots [sic] (of Northhampton [sic]) best book.[37]

Miss Urban once of Amherst High School has been asking for you kids.[38]

32. James Branch Cabell's *Jurgen: A Comedy of Justice* (New York: Robert M. McBride, 1919)—a romantic fantasy that satirized papal infallibility—was prosecuted on grounds of obscenity by the New York Society for the Suppression of Vice in 1920. In 1922, Cabell and the book's publisher, Robert M. McBride, won the case, arguing that the "obscene" passages in question were simply double-entendres and actually reinforced virtue.

33. John Chipman Farrar (1896–1974), editor, at the time, of *The Bookman*. Farrar also taught at Bread Loaf.

34. By 1925, Lincoln MacVeagh, who had been RF's editor at Henry Holt and Company, was serving as president of the Dial Press, which he had founded a year earlier.

35. Most likely Richard Potter (1902–1967), the son of RF's South Shaftsbury neighbor Lewis Van Nest Potter.

36. See RF to Lesley and Marjorie ("Dear Kidds"), late October 1925.

37. Ethel Augusta Cook Eliot (1891–1972) of Northampton, Massachusetts, was a well-known author of children's books.

38. Anna Augusta Urban (1896–1988); later Mrs. Carlon Weston Ray.

[*To Lesley Frost. Date derived from internal evidence. ALS. UVA.*]

[Ann Arbor, MI]

[early December 1925]

Dear Lesley:

You needn't be afraid of our failing to appreciate what you have done to Pittsfield. What you have done to Pittsfield you have done also unto us. It makes me feel younger.

But take care of yourself. You'll have to be casting about for more reliable help than your present partners if the business is going further. That's evident. Mary Ellen[39] hasnt the health and Marj of course cant be asked to have the devotion to a thing she isnt really committed to. Shes torn two or three different ways at her age and with her mind. The book store has got to be part time with her till she sees clearer.

I've seen a little of them in all three of the bookstores here, Slater's Grahams and Wahrs.[40] Slater seems to be stealing the business from the other two partly by enterprise and partly by book knowledge. He has improved the looks of his store a lot. He gets hold of the professors by giving them all 20% discount. They return the favor by keeping him ahead of their assignments for classes. I like him pretty well. Graham is a gentle charming person who speaks of the Four Horseman [*sic*] in the same bracket with The Education of Henry Adams as high brow and called someone's protegé his prodigy (but we all have terrible moments of word blindness like that sometimes). I just met Wahr himself for the first time in his downtown bookstore yesterday. Hes the character. He still supports the Whimsies magazine.[41] Now and then he prints a book. He says he has a whole lot of first editions of poetry in his cellar I might like to see. He bought the lump from an instructor who needed money. I'll tell you if I pick up anything for your shelf of firsts.

---

39. Mary Ellen Hager of Lancaster, Pennsylvania, the family friend who helped Lesley and Marjorie manage The Open Book.

40. Ann Arbor bookstore proprietors Myron E. Slater, who owned Slater's Book Shop, on State Street; Charles Graham, who owned two bookstores on either end of campus called Graham's (later bought out by Slater); and George Wahr, who owned two bookstores, on Main Street and State Street.

41. *Whimsies* had been a University of Michigan student literary magazine (and the name generally given to the group of students who produced it, several of whom RF had come to know well during his first stint at Michigan). In 1924 the name of the magazine was changed to *The Inlander* (though RF seems unaware of the fact).

I dont believe Vachel[42] wanted to see us as much as he wanted an engagement. He didnt come anyway and we dont know where he is. And I cant autograph his books for him. I autographed my own and sent them back.

People often speak of you where I wander. I seldom remember their names.
A Miss or Mrs Hinchman talked you and your doings up to us at Grand Rapids.[43] And right there in Ann Arbor who do you suppose called on the telephone for you and Marj but that Canadian Johnson (I think) that worked in
the Gen Electric?[44] I didnt ask him to the house. I didnt exactly know how he
stood with you folks.

Lawrence Conrad seems the best bet here.[45] Mary Cooley may do something and then again she may turn to active life.[46] She's not madly ambitious
in the arts. I shouldn't say there was much stirring. We dont know what to
think of the place this time.

Besides the books I have ordered I wish you could get me in a hurry three
of Weygandt's A Century of the English Novel (Century Co) and four of
Mearns' Creative Youth (Doubleday?).[47] I want them right off for Christmas
presents. Perhaps you could have them sent directly from the publishers to
me. The bill could go to you. Or would that mix things up?

Affectionately

Papa

---

42. Vachel Lindsay.

43. Unidentified.

44. Unidentified, although RF mentions the "Johnson boy" again in his letter to Lesley
of April 17, 1926.

45. Lawrence H. Conrad (1898–1982) was first an undergraduate, then a candidate for
an MA, and finally teacher of rhetoric (1923–1928) at the University of Michigan, where he
had formed a friendship with RF. His first novel, *Temper,* was published in 1924 (New
York: Dodd, Mead).

46. Mary Elizabeth Cooley received her BA in English from the University of Michigan in 1926 and an MS in geology from Michigan in 1927. She would later serve at Michigan as the coordinator for the Hopwood Awards, an annual scholarship for aspiring
creative writers.

47. Cornelius Weygandt, *A Century of the English Novel* (New York: Century, 1925) and
William Hughes Mearns, *Creative Youth: How a School Environment Set Free the Creative
Spirit* (New York: Doubleday, 1925). For remarks about the latter, see RF to Mearns,
July 27, 1925.

[*To Sidney Cox. Dated from postmark. ALS. DCL.*]

[Ann Arbor, MI]
[December 5, 1925]

Dear Sidney:

I just think it is too terrible.[48] There are absolutely no consoling thoughts about it—not of this world anyway. It is the worst form of balked desire. Let it die down if you want to. Talk will help it die down of course. Some people encourage talk for that reason. But dont let it die down if you dont want to. We have a right to keep any memory we please even to soul sickness. Repression is not forbidden in the Bible. I should use repression if it did me any good—I mean gave me any satisfaction. To Hell with the new ways of being good and the new reasons for being good. They are simply unresolved equations that look what they aren't.

Im sorry sorry

Affectionately yours
Robert Frost

[*To John Bartlett. The letter concerns the possibility that Carol Frost might travel to the Bartletts' home near Boulder, Colorado, to convalesce from a difficult respiratory ailment. ALS. UVA.*]

Ann Arbor Mich
Dec 11 1925

Dear John:

We wrote to Carol at about the same time we were writing to you. At about the same time you were answering, Carol apparently wasn't. Don't you get too ready to have him for Christmas company. He will be moved to act slowly if at all. He's a good boy and faithful to what he sets his hand to; which is the same as saying not unamiably obstinate. His heart is in his Vermont projects, the flower garden and the orchard. It will come hard for him to break off and start all over. He has something of my father in him that won't own up sick.[49]

---

48. Cox's two-year-old son, Robert, had died of chicken pox toward the end of November (*RFSC*, 124).

49. RF's father, William Prescott Frost Jr., died from a long-neglected lung ailment, believed to have been tuberculosis.

Its from no ideal of gameness either. He's just naturally self-disregardful. He rather dispises [*sic*] frail careful people. But never mind. He may listen to us in the long run. He may sooner than I expect. Anyway we had to make a beginning with him.

Well you have your children to suffer with. You know how it is. A broken leg from an automobile![50] It sounds like a narrow escape. I hope the leg was all.

More soon when I hear from Carol. This is just to thank you for your letter, you old friend.

Always yours
R.

[*To J. J. Lankes. Date derived from internal evidence. ALS. HRC.*]

[Ann Arbor, MI]
[circa December 12, 1925]

Dear J.J.

I take this way to ask you where you are so that I can ask you something else almost as important. I've lost you. For heaven's sake write your address plainly thus as I do mine 1223 Pontiac St Ann Arbor Mich. Welcome home wherever home is.[51]

R. F.

---

50. Bartlett's son, John Jr., had been struck by an automobile while he was crossing the street to catch a streetcar.

51. In July of 1925, Lankes had moved from Gardenville, New York, a suburb of Buffalo, to 130 Villa Road, Hilton Village, Virginia, a rural settlement close to Yorktown.

[*To Harold Roy Brennan (1896–1986), at this time an undergraduate student at Wesleyan who had written to RF about his relationship with Edward Thomas. Brennan included an abridged version of RF's response in an essay ("Poet of the Countryside: Edward Thomas,") published in the* Cardinal, *a recently founded Wesleyan literary magazine, in 1926.[52] ALS. Wesleyan.*]

Ann Arbor [MI]

December 16 1925

Dear Mr Brennan:

Edward Thomas had about lost patience with the minor poetry it was his business to review. It took me to tell him what his trouble was. He was suffering from a life of subordination to his inveriors [*sic*]. Right at that moment he was writing as good poetry as anybody alive but in prose form where it didnt declare itself and gain him recognition. I referred to paragraphs here and there in such a book as The Pursuit of Spring[53] and pointed them out. Let him write them in verse form in exactly the same cadence and he would see. Thats all there was to it. His poetry declared itself in verse form and in the year before he died he took his place where he belonged among the English poets.

Remember me to Mr Snow.[54]

Sincerely yours

Robert Frost

[*To Otto Manthey-Zorn. Date derived from postmark. ALS. ACL.*]

[Ann Arbor, MI]

[December 17, 1925]

Dear Otto:

The andirons are the same I am sitting in front of and the hour of night is about as bad as it used to be, but the fireplace is different, better, and the neigh-

---

52. William Evans has detailed the history of this letter in "Robert Frost: The Unpublished *Cardinal* Letter," *American Literature* 59, no. 1 (1987): 116–118.

53. Thomas had published *In Pursuit of Spring* (London and New York: T. Nelson) in 1914. It was a record of a bicycle journey from London to the Quantock Hills, a range west of Bridgwater in Somerset, England.

54. Charles Wilbert "Bill" Snow, a member of the English faculty at Wesleyan. The *Cardinal* had been founded under his auspices.

borhood is worse. We live over back of the gas works in the old Fifth Ward among our postmen, present and former, and whereas in Amherst it took all our resistance to keep out of Masonry, here it takes it all to keep out of a local society for changing the name of Jones St and encouraging lawns. Life is hard to keep out of anywhere.

It looks as if I had run into another exciting president to talk about.[55] He has got the regents to organize him a large scout system for looking over the pupilage in the state schools before admission to college: and he has roused up the Catholicity by announcing it several times over that birth control is as much a part of his university program as any other control, male or female. He is more in favor of babies after they are born than before they are born: I will even go further. I am more in favor of them six months after they are born than six minutes. This very day he has declared a holy war on rum in the fraternity houses: Five boys per house or two faculty members or one hired proctor will take the responsibility of drying the stuff up. The houses shall choose. And any fraternity that breaks the law will lose its charter. The whole state is simmering with excitement. He's a youngster with no interest in noble sentiments. What he wants is something earth-shaking to do. Some think he doesnt realize how troublesome trouble can be. To the boys his birth control may seem a little amusing. I heard one fellow say to another "Why you can find those things all over the parks and golf links and even streets of Ann Arbor." I guess they thought he couldnt teach them much there. What he is driving at is something national, I suppose. He is in with Havelock Ellis and Mrs Sanger.[56] Me, I think, think it had better be taken up at the next Disarmament Conference under the head of Pistols and other short arms.[57] Seriously procreation is a nation's most powerful weapon and the hardest one to forbid it the use of by international law and League of Nations. It is a subject for thoughtful prayer or prayerful thought. If I were the Ku Klux with its aims and ideas the chief secret I would impart to all its members to keep sa-

---

55. Clarence Cook Little (1888–1971), a geneticist, succeeded Marion LeRoy Burton (1874–1925) as president of the University of Michigan.

56. Henry Havelock Ellis (1859–1939), British psychologist, author of the six-volume *Studies in the Psychology of Sex* (1897–1928); Margaret Sanger (1879–1966), social reformer and founder, in 1921, of the American Birth Control League.

57. Article Eight of the League of Nations Covenant stated a commitment to "the reduction of national armaments to the lowest point consistent with national safety." The most recent attempt to put this into practice had been the Washington Naval Treaty in 1922.

cred would be that we were all going to have ten children apiece before the Jews and Catholics got wise. That would be the best march they could steal on the non-Nordics. I would bring on a pressure of white population that would actually suffer itself almost to bursting.

Elinor went to Pittsfield last night to see Marj who is in the hospital there with influenza or something. I may follow if she gives the word. It wouldnt be long anyway before we began to think of heading for Amherst. But I rather wanted to stay still where I was for a few weeks. Elinor may bring Marj out here if she is well enough to move. I'm weary of this scattered way of living. Either I mean to become an explorer and live homeless entirely or to settle down and raise chickens with a single post office address.

I hope Marj will be all right. She hasnt flourished lately. Her thinking is too much for her. She's getting everything at once instead of in courses as in college. College seems artificial in its way of subdividing wisdom and absurd too but at least it never hurt any one who took it obediently.

Dont have it too cold on Dang St.[58] Remember I prefer Sarsaparilla to Ginger Ale. Where shall we play tennis this winter? Oldsie made a great impression here.[59] He pleased everybody by enjoying himself so much. All your new faculty sound like stars. Be fun to see you.

Ever yours
Robert Frost

[To J. J. Lankes. Date derived from internal evidence. ALS. HRC.]

[Pittsfield, MA]
[late December 1925]

Dear J.J.

You get the letter back and thanks to no one this time but me. This Langwell [*sic*] has the right idea to make you rich and famous in one volume.[60] On

---

58. RF originally wrote "Dana St" and then modified it to "Dang."

59. George Daniel Olds, president of Amherst, had visited Ann Arbor to attend the November 2, 1925, inauguration of Clarence Cook Little as president of the University of Michigan.

60. Daniel Longwell (1899–1968), an editor at Doubleday, Page, had arranged for Lankes to provide the woodcut illustrations for an American edition of the Nobel laureate Selma Lagerlof's autobiography, *Marbacka* (New York: Doubleday, Page, 1926).

with the business before any stones grow under his feet. Something like that is what I've been calling down from heaven on your head. Now its struck.

We're East on trouble. We've been having sickness in the family for Christmas.[61] I'm not the kind to be cheerful when there is nothing to be cheerful about. Nor merry either. I'm sulking. Somethings got to be done about me to save me from living in so many places at one time and restore me to the land. I'm a farmer I tell you and was never meant for what I've got into. You talk as if you were badly off with the job printers you have to deal with. But look at me in my predicament.

I wish I could have seen you on your way back from Venice. I've used your Italian letter on college idiots with good results.[62]

> Ever yours
> Robert Frost

Next stopping place
Amherst Mass till Feb 3.[63]

[*To Marion Edwards Park. ALS. Bryn Mawr.*]

> Pittsfield Mass
> December 30 1925

My dear Miss Park:

I'm afraid the name of my lecture will have to be Beyond Prose and Reason.[64]

It was thoughtful of you to offer me the refusal of company for dinner. At Bryn Mawr I shall want the company. Allowance will be made for me, of course, if I look a little scared and absent.

> Sincerely yours
> Robert Frost

---

61. RF and Elinor had traveled from Ann Arbor, Michigan, where RF was Fellow in Letters, to Pittsfield, Massachusetts. At the beginning of December 1925, Marjorie Frost contracted pneumonia, from which it took her months to recover. She also exhibited symptoms of pericarditis.

62. In the summer of 1925, Lankes had traveled through Europe, spending much of his time in Bavaria and northern Italy.

63. RF spent two weeks in residency at Amherst in late January.

64. RF spoke at Bryn Mawr on January 15, 1926, on the topic "Beyond Prose and Reason: Metaphors."

[To Ridgely Torrence, whose most recent book of poems, Hesperides, *had been published by Macmillan in 1925. RF enclosed a signed fair copy of "The Passing Glimpse," as it was then titled, with the dedication "To Ridgely Torrence / On last looking into his 'Hesperides.' " RF retitled the poem "A Passing Glimpse" when he brought it, also bearing the dedication, into* WRB. *Dated from internal evidence. There is no salutation. ALS. Princeton.]*

[Pittsfield, MA]

[January 1926]

This isnt submitted for publication and you neednt think it is, you self-important old—friend.[65] I send it to your magazine because I dont know where you live and what's more I dont care. I just knew if I waited long enough I would happen to write something that would serve better than an obliged letter as acknowledgement of the book you were good enough to send me without e'er an inscription to me in it but with plenty of dedication to Harriet Moody. Doesn't she think shes blessed.[66]

R.L.F.

[To John Bartlett, on letterhead from The Open Book, *Lesley and Marjorie Frost's bookstore in Pittsfield, Massachusetts. The letter is undated, but internal evidence and corroboration from Margaret Bartlett Anderson confirm that RF composed it around New Year's Day, 1926. Anderson expurgated the name Carl Ladd, the entire second paragraph, and much of the third paragraph from her transcription in* RFJB. *ALS. UVA.]*

[Pittsfield, MA]

[circa January 1, 1926]

Dear John:

You and Margaret were my favorite kids at Pinkerton you know whether taken singly or as a pair. So it wont be anything on me particularly if you happen to come out right. I mean I wont be as sorry as Carl

---

65. Nonetheless, "The Passing Glimpse" was published in the *New Republic*, of which Torrence was poetry editor, on April 21, 1926.

66. RF is cramped for space at the end of the sentence and the final word is only partially legible. Torrence dedicated the book to Moody, in whose Waverly Place apartment the Torrences often stayed, as did RF.

Ladd for example.[67] Mind you though, I dont insist on success. Feel perfectly free to come out any way you please. Lose if you think it will get you in better with God. I shall still write you letters oftener than I do anyone else except my very own children.

I don't think Carl Ladd had deteriorated. He might have if there had been any room below him. You should have seen him as he sat smiling and selling life insurance on our piazza that sunny Sunday morning last summer. I wonder if he knew what was in my head. Remember how I let him sell me a book I didnt want in the old days? Well I'm damned if he didnt make the identical same appeal to my sympathies. Aw lemme have the satisfaction of being able to say I have you to my credit. Only this time the cards were stacked against him had he but known it. No life insurance company would have me as a risk. I'm very sure of that. What's more no one in the family wants me insured. My books are a fairish insurance anyway. He's too fatuous to take in a situation like mine. We'll forget him. Im glad he didn't score off you.

I can answer a few of your questions. I'm doing at Ann Arbor next to nothing now.[68] I shall have one seminar a week in writing of all kinds but hand next term. You wouldnt say I wrote much. I have done four small books in twenty eight years, one in seven. I think the rate increases a little. I cant be sure. I have got so I answer almost no letters. Do I lecture? I talk as much as I am able to. The platform takes it out of me. One year I hurt myself. Pullman training dining out and wagging a swallowtail[69] behind a lecturn [*sic*]. This year we are limiting me to less than last year. To give you some idea. I do them by rounds or flights. First round this year: State Teacher's Association Laconia N.H. public show Philadelphia, Johns Hopkins, Baltimore, State University College Hill North Carolina and so home with a cold to bed. I am just about to break loose again. I begin at Bryn Mawr come up to Schenectady and then go to Amherst for two weeks of one thing and another. Oh I forgot I did another set of three, one at Chicago and two at Grand Rapids. Later I go to Iowa State and Illinois State—and Detroit I believe. I try not to have more than three or four on a trip. This we still feel is more than is good for me. My

---

67. Carl M. Ladd (1891–1980) was a 1910 classmate of John Bartlett's and Margaret Abbott's at Pinkerton Academy. The 1920 federal census lists Ladd's occupation as a life insurance agent.

68. RF's appointment as Fellow in Letters required little to no regular teaching.

69. Slang for a tuxedo or a dress suit coat.

worst year was forty exposures. Some of the time I have needed the money but mostly I havent. I must have told you I have had tours planned that would have taken me through Colorado. But I didnt feel up to them. I'd like well enough some excuse to visit you. I guess I'll have to visit you without an excuse some time. That's what it will come to.

I am not sure of hanging on long at Ann Arbor though the position is supposed to be for life. It's too far from the children for the stretch of our heart strings. Carol probably wont be budged. And heres Lesley and Marjorie in the book business in Pittsfield. We've just come on to be with Marj for an operation for appendicitis. She's been having bronchial pneumonia. We dont like to be scattered all over the map as long as we dont have to be. Elinor stands being separated from the children worse than I do. What I want is a farm in New England once more.

One advantage of being here is it gives me a chance at all the brand new books without money and without price. I've just read Lord Grays [sic] Twenty-five Years[70] (corker) Charnwood's Gospel of St John[71] (worth a look into if you want to know the latest higher criticism) The Panchatantra[72] (the most ancient book of anecdotes, source of most now going) and Max Eastman's Since Lenin Died[73] (in hopes of getting the truth at last from our fiercest

---

70. Edward Grey, 1st Viscount Grey of Fallodon (1862–1933), was a British statesman who served as foreign secretary from 1905 to 1916 and Ambassador to the United States from 1919 to 1920; he was later leader of the Liberal Party in the House of Lords. Grey's two-volume memoir, *Twenty-Five Years, 1892–1916* was published by Frederick A. Stokes in 1925.

71. Godfrey Benson, 1st Baron Charnwood (1864–1945), was a British statesman and biographer. His *According to St. John* was published by Little, Brown in 1925.

72. *The Panchatantra*, trans. Arthur W. Ryder (Chicago: University of Chicago Press, 1925). The Panchatantra, dating from third century BC India, consists of a series of interconnected animal fables. In an undated entry in his notebooks, RF includes it in a list headed "Ten Books" (compare the whimsical list given in his March, 16, 1923, letter to MacVeagh): "Emerson's Poems / Panchatantra / Pascal's Pensées / O Shaugnessey / [Darwin's] Voyage of the Beagle / Poe entire / [Lewis Mumford's] Golden Day / [Sir Thomas Browne's] Pseudodoxia / [Jean-Jacques Rousseau's] Emile / Percy's Reliques [of Ancient English Poetry] / Leviticus" (*NBRF*, 265). RF often quoted British poet Arthur O'Shaughnessy's celebrated "Ode" in his public readings: "We are the music makers, / And we are the dreamers of dreams. . . ." But given the nature of this list of "ten books," he may refer to O'Shaughnessy's *Lays of France, Founded upon the Lays of Marie de France* (London: Chatto and Windus, 1871).

73. *Since Lenin Died* (New York: Boni and Liveright, 1925).

American Communist). Gee they're all good books. Any book I cant let alone is a good book. I go months years without reading a thing. Then I read 'em at the rate of three a day. Willa Cather is our great novelist now. Her Professor's House[74] is all right. I wonder what you say to such an able but sordid book as Sherwood Anderson's Dark Laughter.[75] Probably you wont find that last in your public library.

I'll try to write you a letter of ideas another time. This is all things. My lecture at Bryn Mawr will be on the subject For Poetry to Surpass Prose—if that tells you anything.[76]

Eighteen below here yesterday.

> Have a good year.
> Always yours
> R.F.

[To Wilfred Davison. Transcription derived from a typed copy of the letter with a note at the top of the page in an unidentified hand: "Undated (probably 1925) Postmarked Pittsfield, Massachusetts." Internal evidence suggests it was written on or about January 1, 1926. We have been unable to locate the original document. TL-C. Middlebury.]

> [Pittsfield, MA]
> [circa January 1, 1926]

Dear Mr. Davison:

You mustn't wish me anything this year but my whole summer free from teaching. I shall want a spell of breathless quiet after all this campaigning.[77] You don't hear of all my doings—naturally; but they are disgraceful for quantity (not to say quality), and even so they are less numerous than they might be if I weren't so firm in my refusals. I know how well off you are with Gay,

---

74. *The Professor's House,* Cather's seventh novel, was published by Knopf in 1925.

75. Anderson's sexually explicit novel, *Dark Laughter* (New York: Boni and Liveright, 1925), was his only bestseller.

76. RF delivered the Ann Elizabeth Sheble Memorial Lecture on January 15. The subject was metaphor.

77. RF had given seven readings in October and November, traveling from New Hampshire to Philadelphia to Baltimore to Chapel Hill to Chicago and Grand Rapids. He would soon embark on another such "campaign."

Farrar and Mrs. Wilkinson.[78] So I am not going to have you on my conscience the least bit. Go on and prosper.

I'll tell you what I am going to have on my conscience, though, and that is the case of Thomas Jacob. I've been meaning to ask you or Mr. Moody about the boy.[79] He surely baffles my understanding. Not a word of an answer did I get out of him to the kindest letter I ever extended myself to write.[80] I simply begged him to go home for his own sake and mine—if I was anything to him. Some day there may be no more nations and no more races and everywhere perhaps will be home (we'll grant it for the sake of argument), but until that time we may as well accept without resentment the ancient distinction between kin, neighbor, fellow citizen and fellow man and not expect to be treated in exactly the same way by all. Let my fellow man console himself with the thought that far though he is from the center of my regard, my fellow animal is farther. Beyond Saturn are Neptune and Uranus. There are things I would do to my fellow animal that I would hardly be guilty of doing except in extremity (close siege as in Deutcronomeny [sic] Chap—Verses—or Polar expeditions) to my fellow man.[81] Only a sentimentalist will turn them the

---

78. In 1926, for the first time, a short session devoted exclusively to creative writing was to be conducted immediately after the Bread Loaf School of English. John Farrar was in charge of the program. Marguerite Wilkinson and Robert M. Gay, of Simmons College, were returning faculty in the School of English, of which Davison was dean.

79. Paul Dwight Moody (1879–1947), president of Middlebury College from 1921 to 1942. Thomas Jacob (1897–1989)—or, by birth, Yahkub—was a native of India, where he attended Malabar Christian College in Calcutta. He immigrated to the United States in 1923 and completed a BS with High Honors in English at Middlebury in 1925 and an MA there the following year. He also contributed poems and book reviews to *The Saxonian*, a literary magazine at Middlebury. Jacob then attended Harvard, earning a Sacrae Theologiae Baccalaureus (Bachelor of Sacred Theology) in 1929. In 1946 he joined the faculty at Goddard College, in Plainfield, Vermont.

80. We have been unable to locate the letter.

81. See Deuteronomy 28:53: "And thou shalt eat the fruit of thine own body, the flesh of thy sons and of thy daughters, which the LORD thy God hath given thee, in the siege, and in the straitness, wherewith thine enemies shall distress thee." The reference to cannibalism among explorers concerns the 1845 British expedition led by Sir John Franklin in search of the Northwest Passage. None of the 129 members survived, and by the mid-1850s rumors of cannibalism had arisen from interviews with the Inuits of King William Island, who told of piles of human bones. Recent scientific analyses of the bones have confirmed the rumors. See Simon Mays and O. Beattie, "Evidence for End-Stage Cannibalism

other way about and prefer Michael Arlen to Ben Hecht or a lap dog to a baby.[82] Jacob has no right to out-and-out family favors from us. I don't see what he's thinking of.

Have a good year—1926

Sincerely yours

Robert Frost

We are on here with a sick daughter.[83]

[*To Sidney Cox. On letterhead from The Open Book. Dated from postmark. ALS. DCL.*]

[Pittsfield, MA]

[January 1, 1926]

Dear Sidney:

You are probably well out of it at BreadLoaf. I'm glad Davison let it go at parting as friends.[84] You and he might have confessed to antipathy before all was said and done. But you havent (have you?), and I'm relieved. I guess I'm not very good about judging who should be joined together. I'm sure I never would have submitted you to him for criticism if I had given it a moments thought. I'm too proud of your kind of teaching.

---

on Sir John Franklin's Last Expedition to the Arctic, 1845," *International Journal of Osteoarchaeology*, August 4, 2015. Available online.

82. Michael Arlen (1895–1956), born Dikran Kouyoumdjian to Armenian parents in Bulgaria. He immigrated to England, where he achieved notoriety with the publication of *The Green Hat* (London: W. Collins, 1924), a depiction of Jazz Age excess whose heroine, Iris Storm, was modeled on the Anglo-American heiress Nancy Cunard. Arlen assumed a public persona as outrageous as that of his fictional characters, dressing impeccably and driving a yellow Rolls Royce as he mingled in London's social and literary circles. He wrote with what Alec Waugh described (in an article published in *Harper's* in February 1955) as a vivid style—soon labeled Arlenesque—"with unusual inversions and inflections with a heightened exotic pitch." Ben Hecht (1894–1964), born in New York of Russian Jewish émigré parents, came to prominence as a foreign correspondent and columnist for the *Chicago Daily News*. His first novel, *Eric Dorn* (New York: Putnams and Sons, 1921), and first full-length drama, *The Egotist* (1922), established the direct, forcefully colloquial style—drawing on his apprenticeship as a reporter covering the underside of Chicago life—that would lead to his extraordinary success as a screenwriter.

83. Marjorie.

84. For more on Cox's difficulties at Bread Loaf, see RF's December 31, 1924, and July 5, 1925, letters to him.

You're a better teacher than I ever was or will be (now). But I'd like to put it to you while you are still young and developing your procedure if you dont think a lot of things could be found to do in class besides debate and disagree. Clash is all very well for coming lawyers politicians and theologians. But I should think there must be a whole realm or plane above that—all sight and insight, perception, intuition, rapture. Narrative is a fearfully safe place to spend your time.[85] Having ideas that are neither pro nor con is the happy thing. Get up there high enough and the differences that make controversy become only the two legs of a body the weight of which is on one in one period on the other in the next. Democracy monarchy; puritanism paganism; form content; conservatism radicalism; systole diastole; rustic urbane; literary colloquial; work play. I should think too much of myself to let any teacher fool me into taking sides on any one of those oppositions. May be I'm wrong. But I was always wrong then. Its not just old age with me. Im not like Maeldune weary of strife from having seen too much of it. (See Tenn)[86] I have wanted to find ways to transcend the strifemethod. I have found some. Mind you I'd fight a healthy amount. This is no pacifism. It is not as much anti-conflict as it is something beyond conflict—such as poetry and religion that is not just theological dialectic. I'll bet I could tell of spiritual realizations that for the moment at least would overawe the contentious. That's the sort of thing I mean. Every poem is one.[87] I know I have to guard against insisting on this too much. Blades must be tempered under the hammer. We are a political nation run on a two-party system: which means that we must conflict whether we

---

85. See RF to Mary Cooley, November 10, 1924: "Abstract appreciation is all too much alike. I think even lectures on literature should be narrative."

86. Alfred Tennyson's "The Voyage of Maeldune" (1880) ends with the hero "weary . . . of the travel, the trouble, the strife and the sin."

87. See Lawrance Thompson's report of a conversation he had with RF in 1940: "He said some nice things about the relationship between argument and statement in poetry. The reason why poetry fails when it becomes propaganda is because it has to do with denials of social values that are debatable. But poetry is at its best when it makes observations in the realm of spiritual values which are perceived in realms where there is no room for argument. The crowding of points of view occur in social relationships, but in the higher realm of spiritual perceptions the atmosphere is not crowded. We can all find room for agreement on the point of a pin! And thus the wisest poet works toward the realm of spiritual perceptions. 'We don't join together in singing an argument.' Songs are built around everlastingly perceived spiritual values which are true for us all—love and longing and sorrow and loneliness" (*CPRF*, 286).

disagree or not. School must be some sort of preparation for the life before us. Some of our courses must be in <u>row</u>ing. Dont let me oversay my position.

They say time itself is circular and the universe a self-winding clock. Well well just when it reaches the back country that the universe is a mechanism and what reason have we to suppose we are anything but mechanisms ourselves the latest science says it is all off about the universe it isnt a mechanism at all what ever we fools may be.[88] It will take fifty years for that to penetrate to the Clarence Darrowians and Daytonians.[89] The styles start in Paris and go in waves, ten years from crest to crest, to the

---

88. The referent of "they" in "they say" is unclear, perhaps deliberately so, but RF would appear to be talking about Enlightenment cosmologies that either avoided questions of the origins and ends of the universe, or denied them outright. Via William Paley's influential version of natural theology and the "uniformitarian" methodology urged by the geologist Charles Lyell, this tradition fed into Charles Darwin's representation of organisms as survival machines. Another possible referent is Friedrich Nietzsche's concept of eternal recurrence, but Nietzsche viewed "mechanical" philosophies with contempt. The second law of thermodynamics (one of the subjects RF discussed during his encounter with Niels Bohr at Amherst in 1923) had temporarily put paid to steady-state cosmologies: even if the universe were to continue unchanged forever it would require periodic replenishment of convertible energy. The function of gravity in the general theory of relativity also undermined steady-state models of cosmic evolution, although Einstein resisted the implication through the introduction of the cosmological constant. While it is too early for RF to be referring to the uncertainty principle in quantum mechanics, his interest in the latest developments in the physical sciences is well attested. Louis De Broglie's wave-particle duality had been announced in 1924 (*Recherches sur la théorie des quanta*, University of Paris, PhD thesis), and a later sentence in this letter—"The styles start in Paris and go in waves"—lends credence to RF's having heard of this work. Finally, "whatever we fools may be" is an echo of Puck's "What fools these mortals be" (*A Midsummer Night's Dream* 3.2).

89. Clarence Darrow (1857–1938), lawyer for the defense at the Scopes Trial in 1925 (see RF to Haines, July 21, 1925). Wilbert Snow reported RF as hostile to Darrow and generally sympathetic to William Jennings Bryan at the trial. Darrow, RF believed, "depended too much on rationality to solve the problem of human existence" (*YT*, 629–630), so, per RF, the anti-mechanical animus of "the latest science" will discomfort Darrow when it eventually reaches him. But the letter to Haines suggests that it is the creationists who are at fault, for their shocking and embarrassing ignorance of how the world actually works.

ends of the earth. Let us put in some of our time merely sawing wood like William II.[90]

Be good

Ever yours

Robert Frost

No I mustnt think of teaching this year. Perhaps another year if you stay on in Montana that long.

[*To Edward Lewis Davison (1898–1970), a Scottish-born poet who had immigrated to the United States in 1925. Dated from internal evidence. An annotation in pencil below the address reads "late May 1926," but this is surely wrong (RF was not in Pittsfield in late May; he was in Ann Arbor). This is the first of RF's letters to Davison, who had sent to RF letters of introduction. RF would bring Davison to Bread Loaf in the summer of 1926. ALS. DCL.*]

124 South St Pittsfield Mass

[circa January 7, 1926]

Dear Mr Davison:

I have been wanting to see you very much. My difficulty has been in deciding where it would be, here in Pittsfield Mass., now or soon, or at Ann Arbor Mich. later when I should get back there. My stays anywhere this year have been of such uncertain length. What should you say to coming to Pittsfield sometime in the last two weeks of January to lecture for my daughters?[91] It looks now as if I were to be settled in the neighborhood for at least three more weeks. You and I would manage a good talk or two together away from everybody else. Our friend Mrs Crane may have spoken to you in the matter.[92] The fee the girls pay their speakers is $100. I wish it could be more.

---

90. Kaiser Wilhelm II (1859–1941), the deposed German emperor, who had taken up wood chopping in his enforced retirement from public life.

91. At The Open Book. No record of Davison's having spoken there exists. RF spent the last two weeks of January in residency at Amherst before returning to Ann Arbor.

92. Josephine Boardman Crane (1873–1972), a Cleveland-born educator and philanthropist who had established the Berkshire School for Crippled Children in Pittsfield in 1916. For another reference to her, see RF to Lesley Frost, August 21, 1928.

I mean to find you in New York Wednesday if I can.[93]

We'll arrange something somewhere before you go home.

> Sincerely yours
>
> Robert Frost

[To Marion Parris Smith (1879–1964), professor of economics at Bryn Mawr. Dated from internal evidence. ALS. UVA.]

> The Open Book
>
> 124 South St
>
> Pittsfield Mass
>
> [January 11, 1926]

My dear Mrs Smith

I am writing this not to thank you for the rug but to get my excuses over and out of the way for not having thanked you sooner. Then I shall be free to devote myself entirely to thanking you in person when I see you—as I am expecting to this week.[94]

We had received and accepted the beautiful rug but had had hardly time to wipe our feet on it (let alone decide whether we would ever wipe our feet on it or not) when we were called away from our little old colonial house (really colonial—Henry Ford would have bought it for an antique if his architect had pronounced it sound enough to move to Dearborn[95]) in Michigan by the serious illness of one of our daughters here in Pittsfield.[96] We have made very bad work of our divided life so far this year. This attempt (bold at our age) to be about equally eastern and western may defeat itself like trying to

---

93. RF passed through New York City on Wednesday, January 13, en route to Philadelphia.

94. RF delivered the Ann Elizabeth Sheble Memorial Lecture at Bryn Mawr on January 15.

95. RF's words proved prophetic. In 1937, Henry Ford purchased RF's Ann Arbor home, a Greek Revival house built in the 1830s for the politician Thompson Sinclair, and moved it to Greenfield Village, an open-air museum Ford had founded near Dearborn, Michigan, that featured many famous houses built in the nineteenth century.

96. On Marjorie Frost's illness, see the notes to RF's late December letter to Lankes. Marjorie's health, and the psychological difficulties attendant upon it, were a major concern for RF and Elinor Frost over the coming years, and are frequently mentioned in the correspondence.

sit on more than thirteen to fifteen eggs at once. It may addle the eggs and give the hen a nervous breakdown. Life has never been a choice for me. I can honestly say I have seen but one thing presented to do at a time. Until now anyway. Wouldnt it be terrible if in old age life should turn on me and begin to present itself to me in alternatives and nothing but alternatives? That would be just like life which by definition is that which carefully prepares you for one thing and then confronts you with something else.

Best wishes and thanks.

> Sincerely yours
> Robert Frost

[*The recipient of this letter, Hubert N. Hart (1904–1986), published it in facsimile as part of an article titled "I Remember Robert Frost," which appeared first in* Confrontation *3 (Winter–Spring 1970), a journal associated with Long Island University, and was reprinted in* Amherst Alumni News *23, no. 2 (Fall 1970). Hart, a professor of English at C. W. Post College (now Long Island University) at the time the article appeared, had been a student of RF's at Amherst in 1924–1925. "The Amherst Catalogue,"* he recalls, *"said something romantic like: 'Advanced Creative Writing. Limited to ten students. Permission of the instructor required before registration.' The instructor was Robert Frost. Frost was fifty and the last thing anyone could say of him was that he was patient with students. Students were generally illiterate, stupid and wet behind the ears. I was one and twenty and easily awed." Hart stumbled upon RF having crullers and coffee in the student lounge and got permission to take the course. "The Olympian," as Hart calls him, offered this advice: " 'And listen, Hart, I'm going to teach you to write destructively.' With this he chuckled, quietly but delightedly. I was to learn that some words were taboo.* Creative *and* beauty *were among them. The only creative job was God's." ALS. ACL.*]

> Amherst Mass
> January 20 1926

Dear Hart

Maladjusted is such a common thing to be nowadays, I don't wonder you are tired of being it. The only two common things I seem able to stand being are alive and married. You are both of those. You know how both feel.

Actually married after four years as good as married sounds romantic in a way I like.

Im glad to hear you say you are thinking a hell of a lot. I'd count on you to think—think and agonize. Don't for my sake agonize too much. Some of the time you must smoke life like a cigarette and enjoy it like a weekend with a girl you can call your own. The deeper down you get with pleasure the deeper down you will get with pain—assuming that pain is what you want to fathom. The great thing to remember is that nothing need fluster you. You are of the kind to use anything you can survive. Sooner or later all will prove grist to you.

I'm not so much at Ann Arbor yet as you might suppose. We went out there and got settled in a little old house over across the tracks behind the gas works where the neighbors carry dinner pails and not books (Two of the friendliest of them are mail carriers and carry every kind of letter but belle).[97] We haven't lived there long however. Sickness in the family brought us home in December and we have been in Pittsfield ever since. You see where I am writing from now—having just arrived for a visit. You never can tell where I'll turn up: I can almost set up to be a seven-city man like Homer.[98]

Speaking of Homer did you see John Erskine's slightly amusing trivialization of him that all the professors consider such a live novel? Several shots at the novel lately have interested me, Porgy (most of all), Dark Laughter, The Professor's House and Drums.[99] But I dunnow.

Show 'em some teaching. You can.

Show me some writing.

> Always yours
> Robert Frost

Have you heard a single word from Yeh?[100]

---

97. The house was on the north side of Ann Arbor at 1123 Pontiac Road, well away from the main part of the University of Michigan campus.

98. See Thomas Heywood (circa 1670–1641), *The Hierarchy of the Blessed Angels* (London: Thomas Islip, 1635):

Seven cities warred for Homer, being dead,
Who, living, had no roof to shroud his head.

99. Erskine, *The Private Life of Helen of Troy* (Indianapolis: Bobbs-Merrill, 1925); DuBose Heyward, *Porgy* (New York: George H. Doran Company, 1925); Sherwood Anderson, *Dark Laughter* (New York: Boni and Liveright, 1925); Willa Cather, *The Professor's House* (New York: Alfred A. Knopf, 1925); and James Boyd, *Drums* (New York: Charles Scribner's Sons, 1925), a novel of the Revolutionary War.

100. George Kung-chao Yeh (1904–1981). Hart explains that Yeh had been "a Chinese student [at Amherst] whose poems in English, oddly flavored with Chinese imagery and idiom, impressed Frost. George Yeh became a distinguished Professor of English in China, Exchange Professor at Cambridge." Yeh later served (1958–1961) as ambassador of

[To Eunice Tietjens. ALS. Newberry.]

124 South St

Pittsfield Mass

[circa February 1, 1926]

Dear Eunice Tietjens:

Look how I let the time go by. I have been kept here at or around home all winter by the serious sickness of our Marjorie. But the minute I get back to Ann Arbor next week I will see what can be done for your Janet.[101] Marjorie was one of the reasons I wanted Janet to come to Michigan for. But it may as well be said first as last, nothing can be built on the future wereabouts [*sic*] of the Frosts. I may be teaching (so to call it[102]) at Michigan next year and then again without prejudice to anything anywhere, I may be farming in Vermont.[103] They are some of the best friends out there I have ever had and I hope they arent going to be less my friends if I find I have to live away from them. I only speak my misgivings. Nothing is certain yet.

I wish Marj and Janet could meet sometime. They must be about of an age[104]—and they have both been reared in intellectual as distinguished from academic interests.

Sorry we didnt see you last summer and sorry the play didnt hold the stage longer.[105]

Sincerely yours

Robert Frost

---

the Republic of China (Taiwan) to the United States. Amherst awarded him an honorary degree in 1959. Incidentally, Yeh was an associate of William Empson when the latter taught at Peking National University in the late 1930s. See William Empson, *The Strengths of Shakespeare's Shrew* (Sheffield: Sheffield Academic Press, 1996), 211.

101. Janet Tietjens (1908–1990) was the daughter or Eunice Hammond Tietjens and the composer Paul Tietjens. She matriculated at the University of Wisconsin (not Michigan), was active in literary clubs, and graduated in 1931 with a degree in geology. See also RF to Tietjens, June 28, 1925

102. The appointment RF then held at Michigan did not require him to give regular courses.

103. As it happened, RF accepted an offer to return to Amherst in the fall of 1926.

104. Marjorie was born on March 28, 1905.

105. Tietjens's *Arabesque,* a musical drama, had a Broadway run of less than three weeks (October 20–November 7, 1925).

[*To Louis Untermeyer. ALS. LoC.*]

Ann Arbor Mich
Feb 11 1926

Dear Louis

We have been East two whole months with a sick Marjorie and are now divided over her, Elinor having stayed on to take care of her and I having come to Ann Arbor to make some show of teaching a little for my year's pay. Im sad enough about Marj but I am more busted up than sad. All this sickness and scatteration of the family is our fault and not our misfortune or I wouldnt admit it. Its a result and a judgement on us. We ought to have gone back farming years ago or we ought to have stayed farming when we knew we were well off.

I put my own discombobulation first to lead up unnoticeably to yours. I've heard things about you that sound like suffering.[106] And I must see you. I'm no authority on trouble for all the success you ascribe to me in settling Joseph Warren Beach's troubles in the day of them.[107] I'm just your plain friend in favor of the unmelo dramatic [*sic*] status quo. Not for me to argue anything where I don't know. I just want to hear you talk.

But I dont want my seeing you here or hereafter to have to depend on any arrangements I can make with an agent. Please no agents between us. You assign a day or two to visiting me on your way back and fix it up now with your agent yourself. Tell him you want such and such a date left blank in honor of me. It will make him respect me and wonder who I am that can be taken

---

106. Untermeyer's marriage to Jean Starr Untermeyer was failing.

107. Joseph Warren Beach, professor of English at the University of Minnesota, married his second wife, Dagmar Doneghy, on April 22, 1918. According to RF, Beach, though in love with Doneghy (and apparently intimate with her), had been reluctant to embark on a second marriage. RF claimed to have challenged Beach to marry Doneghy and agreed to serve as best man if Beach followed through. Accepting the challenge, Beach and RF picked up Doneghy and drove until they found a spot where the couple could be alone. Returning to the car where RF waited, Beach announced the engagement. The three drove to Indiana, where the wedding took place two days later. Writing to Lesley Frost shortly thereafter, RF suggested that he had "personally conducted the elopement of Joseph Warren Beach that awful sinner with an assistant of his in the graduate school. . . . It was cruel of me to marry him off, but I had to do it" (*LRF-1*, 610). RF's jocular way of talking about the incident had repercussions for Beach; see RF to White, December 14, 1922.

time out for so regardless of expense. I will do my best to have got you a lecture here and you can pass him his rake-off. But I dont want to bind myself to anything as I stand with the community at this moment from having rather pleasantly over-stayed my leave (as tacitly understood.) And I don't want to lose you in the machinery of your profession. Rather would I you had remained a jeweler to the poor than that you should get so platform proud as to be undealable [*sic*] with except through the heartlessness of agency.

I aint foolin. The letters and forms of agents go entirely against my school of poetry. In many a college and town I have been told in so many words of the wonderful form that has to be filled out before you can meet the author of the latest life of Lincoln.[108] It flatters me to have a few great men entirely off hand with me. I like to think I have got where they are.

JW really seems to have been serious in that marriage. I made up my mind he should be as serious as lay in me to make him. He rather played it on me the day he used me for a chaperone to sit in his ford [*sic*] car for respectability while he stole off and fornicated in whatever takes the place of alders in Minnesota.[109] I could see he thought it was funny to be so romantic at my expense. So to be equally funny and romantic at his I went straight on from that moment and inside of two days had him sewed up in marriage for the rest of his life. I bought em the only champaign [*sic*] I ever blew any one to either epi or prothalamial.[110] I wanted to know who the laugh was on last. Really I'm glad now if it was on no one. But you mustnt play lascivious tricks on me for a literary man. I help hasten the consequences. One practical joke deserves another. Of course mine was the more serious of the two. I can be rather unthinking. One of my faults is a love of the excitement of putting a thing through—or a person. Propose me now some dates—please.[111]

> Ever yours,
> Robert Frost

---

108. Carl Sandburg's *Abraham Lincoln: The Prairie Years* (Harcourt, Brace) came out in 1926.

109. In *RFLU*, Untermeyer deleted the phrase "and fornicated."

110. Epithalamium and prothalamium: poems written (respectively) on the occasion of a marriage, or in anticipation of it.

111. Untermeyer did indeed visit RF in Ann Arbor in late spring 1926, though not to lecture. See RF's May 3, 1926, and May 3, 1927, letters to him (both of which mention the meeting, though to different ends).

[To Louis Untermeyer. The text of this letter is composed on a typed invitation to RF from the Reverend Samuel Drury (1878–1938), headmaster of St. Paul's Preparatory School in Concord, New Hampshire, asking RF to participate in a World War I memorial service dedicated to the forty-eight St. Paul's alumni who had died in the war. In 1926, the St. Paul's Alumni Association published St. Paul's School in the Great War: 1914–1918, *a compilation of biographical sketches commemorating those who had fallen in battle. Date supplied by Untermeyer. RF uses no salutation. ALS. LoC.]*

[Ann Arbor, MI]

[circa March 14, 1926]

A Drury for your Morton.[112] And mind you I never even heard of him before. I cant make out his name. Probably headmaster of the young aristocrats up there. I told him it was all very rush me off my feet and friendly but it arose from a misunderstanding. It was very likely my Phi Beta Kappa poem of 1916 come home to roost.[113] But that wasnt really a lapse into laureatism. It was no poem written for the occasion. Im a good fellow and all that but I cant be seduced by any such twisted flattery as this. Thicker says I. Thicker. I'd like to see my virtue really tried for once.

Louis Louis. Dont talk to me about forgiveness. I'm not Peter Rhadamanthus.[114] I've simply felt my natural sorrow that two such good friends of mine as you and Jean should be winding up your affair.[115] As I said before I wish I could see you for a day. It couldnt do you any harm. I wouldnt even try to ground you in my philosophy and religion. I'm long since past my confidence in meddling. All my meddling but once has been more or less in the comic spirit anyway.

Say something expansive to all the Coxes for me. Tell Sidney to teach 'em up.[116]

---

112. That is, like the poet and educator David Morton (appointed to the Amherst faculty in 1924), Samuel Drury was an author (occasionally noted in *The New York Times* and elsewhere). In 1926, Macmillan brought out his *Schoolmastering: Essays in Scholastic Engineering*. Untermeyer adds, in a note to the letter: "Drury was distinguished as an essayist and greatly admired by those who came in contact with him" (*RFLU*, 180).

113. On June 19, 1916, RF read "The Bonfire" as Phi Beta Kappa poet at Harvard University (many associated it with World War I at the time).

114. RF conflates St. Peter, to whom Christ gives the keys to the kingdom of heaven (Matthew 16:19) and Rhadamanthus, the son of Zeus and Europa, who according to classical mythology sits in judgment of the dead.

115. Untermeyer had sued for divorce.

116. Untermeyer embarked on a lecture tour that took him as far as Missoula, where the Cox family then lived (Sidney Cox was professor of English at the University of Mon-

Be good according to your lights.[117] (A man is as good as his lights I heard a butcher say.)

Ever yours

R. F.

[*To Harold Rugg. ALS. DCL.*]

Ann Arbor

March 19 1926

My dear Mr Rugg:

Until I emerge into a settled life I can call my own you have very little hope of any prose out of me. We may as well face the facts. I'm too pulled and hauled for any writing more than a bit of verse now and then. And you'll notice I have little of that for publication. It must be more than a year since I was seen in print anywhere. Sickness has had something to do with it. One of my daughters has been seriously sick all winter and I myself have been far from well. It makes me sorry to say these things. You must take me as you find me. Anyway I'm

your well wisher

Robert Frost

[*To Wade Van Dore. Date derived from postmark. ALS. BU.*]

[Ann Arbor, MI]

[March 23, 1926]

Dear Wade:

I wish I could be here when you come.[118] Tomorrow (Wednesday) I am off for Iowa and Illinois to be gone the rest of the week.[119] Can't you put off coming till Sunday after next. I've been thinking about you and I want to see you soon again.

---

tana). See also RF to Cox, April 8, 1926 ("Louis didn't put you up [to it] did he?").

117. See Matthew 5:16: "Let your light so shine before men, that they may see your good works, and glorify your father which is in heaven."

118. At the time, Van Dore lived close to Ann Arbor, at 4892 Edmonton Avenue in Detroit.

119. RF gave a reading at Iowa State University, in Iowa City, on March 25, and one at the University of Illinois Champaign-Urbana on March 29.

It is great if by anything I have done you have gained time. Only don't be betrayed into taking art easy. I know you wont be. So why am I advising? Spread out spread out and look into all the corners of your own mind and nature now—and into all the ends of literature to see what it is in its fullness. Look over fences into what you are not sure is any concern of yours even. I mean read all sorts of things with a writer's eye—since you are going to have time.

Better come a week from next Sunday.

Always yours
Robert Frost.

[To Lesley Frost. Date derived from internal evidence. ALS. UVA.]

[Ann Arbor, MI]
[circa March 23, 1926]

Dear Lesley:

I just want to say in answer to part of your letter to Mama that Dwight has made us all like him.[120] He put the finishing touches on me with the send-off he gave Marj when she came away. We can see with our own eyes that he is a graceous [sic] and splendid fellow. I can see that there are few things that he hasn't a head for. For the rest I am glad to see him as you see him. I take your word for it that he is really good—by which you mean, I suppose, that we could trust him to be good to you.*

Affectionately
R.

*It would have to be very good you understand.

When I get back from Iowa and Illinois I am going to play Seward to your Lincoln[121] and submit seriatim some proposals for the future conduct of your book store administration. Nothing I havent said before orally.

Gee I had the most scratching screeching row of females all over me in my class last night that ever befell me in pedagogy. The little she devils lit into

---

120. James Dwight Francis (1897–1988), whom Lesley would marry in 1928.

121. William H. Seward (1801–1872) served as secretary of state during Abraham Lincoln's administration. Although he had lost the Republican nomination for president to

me—as nearly as I could make out for nothing but to assert their equality to me. I'm drawing to the end of such adventures.

[To Harriet Moody. TG. Chicago.]

ANN ARBOR MICH

MCH 30—1926

MRS WM VAUGHN MOODY

2970 ELLIS AVE

CHICAGO ILL

CAUGHT THROAT TELLING LIES IN IOWA SO DIDNT STOP IN CHICAGO FOR FEAR OF BEING INVALIDED ON YOUR HANDS WRETCHEDLY SORRY NOT TO SEE YOU AGAIN HAD MUCH MORE TO SAY WELL WELL TALK FROM LATER AT CUMMINGTON[122] TELL JAMES [STEPHENS[123]] GET WELL[124] LOVE TO YOU HIM AND ALL.

ROBERT FROST

[To Witter Bynner. Date derived from postmark. ALS. Houghton.]

[Ann Arbor, MI]
[April 5, 1926]

Dear Witter

For my part, my daughter, the best poet in the family, has been dangerously ill for twelve weeks now, my wife is prostrated and my heart indisposed to prefaces.[125] Jesus Mary what a year you have chosen to get cornered and to

---

Lincoln in 1860, Seward nevertheless campaigned hard for him and remained one of his most loyal and trusted advisers.

122. Moody owned a house in Cummington, Massachusetts (the William Cullen Bryant Homestead), northwest of Amherst.

123. The surname is written in by hand on the telegram, presumably by Moody.

124. The Irish poet and novelist James Stephens (1882–1950) was then in Chicago, one among a number of stops on his American lecture tour. On February 13, 1925, Stephens spoke at Amherst, after which he stayed with the Frost family. Stephens's *The Crock of Gold* (New York: Macmillan, 1913) had long been a favorite of RF's.

125. RF and his wife so admired Marjorie's poetry that after her death from puerperal fever in 1934, they prepared a volume of her verse, printed in a fine edition by the Spiral Press and titled *Franconia* (1936). It is not clear what Bynner had asked RF to write a

corner in. In the last homecoming to roost, the exigencies of the irrespon
sible are more ruthless than the most military of law and order. But I forgive
you them even as I hope to be forgiven a murder I once did. The question is
what am I going to do for you. I'm damned if I see in my confusion. I havent
had a metaphor for months. This is the twilight of the mind—before God it
is. I'll go out to grass at a word in the wrong key. Aren't we in a terrible mess?

> Yours (and have mercy on me)
> Robert Frost

[*To Burrhus Frederic (B. F.) Skinner (1904–1990), who was just completing a BA in
literature at Hamilton College, and would soon go on to Harvard, where he received a
PhD in psychology in 1931. ALS-photostat held at Jones Library, original held at
Hamilton.*]

> Ann Arbor Michigan
> [April 7, 1926]

Dear Mr Skinner:[126]

My long delay with these stories has given you time to think of some things
about them for yourself, alternating between doubt and confidence. It has
probably done you good: so I won't apologise for it.

You know I save myself from perfunctory routine criticism of ordinary
college writing on purpose to see if I can't really help now and then someone
like you in earnest with the art. Two or three times a year I make a serious
attempt to get to the bottom of his work with someone like you. But it's all
the good it does. I always come a long way short of getting down into it as
far as the writer gets himself. Of course! You ask me if there is enough in the
stories to warrant your going on. I wish I knew the answer to that half as
well as you probably know it in your heart. Right at this moment you are
very likely setting your determination to go on, regardless of anything I say,
and provided only you can find within a reasonable time someone to buy

---

preface for—he published several books in 1926 and 1927. The likeliest candidate is the
1926 reissue of his 1917 book *Grenstone Poems: A Sequence* (New York: Alfred Knopf, 1926),
for which Edgar Lee Masters supplied a new preface.

126. For reasons unclear, the name has been scissored out of the photostat held at the
Jones Library.

and read you.[127] I'd never quarrel with that spirit. I've a sneaking sympathy with it.

My attempt to get to the bottom of a fellow writer's stuff this time put this into my head: All that makes a writer is the ability to write strongly and directly from some unaccountable and almost invincible personal prejudice like Stevenson's in favor of all being as happy as kings no matter if consumptive,[128] or Hardy's against God for the blunder of sex, or Sinclair Lewis's against small American towns or Shakespeare's mixed, at once against and in favor of life itself. I take it that everybody has the prejudice and spends some time feeling for it to speak and write from. But most people end as they begin by acting out the prejudices of other people.

There are real niceties of observation you've got here and you've done 'em to a shade. "The Laugh" has the largest value. That's the one you show most as caring in. You see I want you to care. I dont want you to be academic about it—a writer of exercises. Of course not too expressly, overtly care. You'll have to search yourself here. You know best whether you are haunted with any impatience about what other people see or dont see. That will be you if you are a you. I'm inclined to say you are. But you have the final say. I wish you'd tell me how you come out on thinking it over—if it isnt too much trouble—sometime.

I ought to say you have the touch of art. The work is clear run. You're worth twice anyone else I have seen in prose this year.

Always yours
Robert Frost

Belief belief. You've got to augment my belief in life or people mightily or cross it uglily. I'm awfully sure of this tonight.[129] April 7 1926.

---

127. Skinner's only major work of fiction is *Walden Two* (New York: Macmillan, 1948).

128. The Scottish novelist and essayist Robert Louis Stevenson (1850–1894) suffered from tuberculosis and moved often in search of a climate suitable to his health—to the Mediterranean coast of France, to the Adirondacks, and finally in travels across the Pacific and South Pacific to Samoa, where he died.

129. The suggestion as to the necessity of "augmenting" his belief in "life," and the insistence that he is "awfully sure" of that necessity "tonight," may reflect RF's anxieties about his daughter Marjorie's health, and about his wife's utter exhaustion (see RF to Bynner, April 5, 1926). Within three weeks of writing the present letter RF would accept an offer to return to Amherst, in no small part so that he could be nearer his children and spare Elinor the difficulty of shuttling between Michigan and Vermont whenever illness or misfortune struck them.

[To Sidney Cox. Dated from internal evidence. ALS. DCL.]

[Ann Arbor, MI]
[circa April 8, 1926]

Sidney Sidney

I'd laugh at you if you said the word. But at least you want the predicament you are in taken seriously.[130] I suppose I can laugh at what you say about my warning of last summer.[131] I've forgotten the warning. Would it if observed have kept you out of this mess with editors chancellors and viziers? Then you ought to have observed it to the letter.

You'd call this shining in a way I suppose. And I can tell you how you can shine more if you think it would help you any to become a national figure. By calling in Menken [*sic*] and Mark Van Doren in the case.[132] You could do it through me or on your own. I'd stir them up. Only I should want to be sure you were prepared to get out of teaching entirely and go onto the stage or into independent journalism. You'd have to <u>make</u> a place for yourself in those even. There wouldn't necessarily be one waiting for you in either of them.

This may decide you in favor of getting out of teaching into something where you wouldnt be forever having to mind your step. If its got so you find things daily that teaching keeps you from saying and doing it is a slavery: you ought to leave it. You can see the relief Stark Young and Stuart Sherman feel

---

130. Cox was caught up in a scandal involving the University of Montana literary magazine *The Frontier,* for which he was the faculty adviser. (See also RF to Untermeyer, May 3, 1926.) Copies of the magazine were distributed to Montana high schools as part of a campaign to encourage applications to the university, and two pieces it contained caused considerable offense, the phrase "son-of-a-bitch" receiving particular opprobrium. Cox was the person responsible for vetting the contents of the magazine and most of the public outcry was directed at him. The Montana State Board of Education reprimanded him and he was instructed to make a public apology, which he did (see *RFSC,* 126–27).

131. Regarding a contretemps Cox had with Wilfred Davison at Bread Loaf, see RF's July 5, 1925, letter to Cox.

132. H. L. Mencken had long been a great scourge of Comstockery, the New York Society for the Suppression of Vice and censorship (see his "Puritanism as a Literary Force," in *A Book of Prefaces* [New York: Alfred Knopf, 1917]). Mencken had also spoken with hostility of the professoriate during the Eaton case, to which RF refers later in this letter (for more on Eaton, see RF to Untermeyer, March 20, 1922). Mark van Doren (1894–1972), professor of English at Columbia, was literary editor of *The Nation,* a prominent champion of progressive causes.

in having escaped from professorship.[133] Some people belong in New York and it's no use their hiding it from themselves.

The boy (G.D Eaton) who was personifying frankness to the Michigan campus when I was here two years ago went your Frontier stuff several better.[134] He stirred up such a stink and managed his public rumpus so skillfully that Menken took his part and helped him on graduation to a columniatist [*sic*] job on The N.Y. Telegraph where I saw him holding forth a week or so ago on Jesus Crist's [*sic*] Old Man.[135] I dont know how much he has had to play up to Menken. But something has gone against his conscience in their relation I take it: because he has lately turned on Menken and bitten the breast at which he fed. Perhaps he wanted a change of diet from milk to blood. He has become almost the strongest expresser in NY. His owners however instead of showing pride in him have just decided to economise by discontinuing his department. He has performed very heroically. He is now writing heroically right and left for people to say they cant get along without his column. I've seen his circular letters in the pockets of some of the boys here.[136] In low politics this would be called working up a fake clientele. Its a hard world and doesnt get any easier.

I tell you all this to cheer you up the way my emergency nurse from Camp Devens cheered me when I had pneumonic flu with tales of the deaths she

---

133. Stark Young (1881–1963) had left Amherst in 1921 to devote himself to writing full-time. Stuart Sherman (1881–1926) had resigned his position as chairman of the English Department at the University of Illinois in 1924 to become the editor of the "Books" column at the *New York Herald Tribune*. He would die of a heart attack in the summer of 1926.

134. In 1922, Geoffrey Dell Eaton (1894–1930)—then a student at the University of Michigan   had called "most history professors" "senile, simple, and misguided asses" in the pages of the university's *The Michigan Daily*. President Marion LeRoy Burton ordered that Eaton be barred from contributing to all student publications. Eaton's punishment caused a national stir. *The St. Louis Star* (November 28, 1922) commented on Eaton's offending words: "Such a falsehood deserves rebuke. Comparatively few history professors are senile."

135. Eaton did write for the *New York Morning Telegraph*, including pieces irreverently supporting Mencken's irreverent editorial style at the *American Mercury*. See, for example, Eaton's "Change the American Mercury? Bosh! Its Genius Answer," *New York Morning Telegraph*, April 18, 1925. We have been unable to locate the article RF alludes to here.

136. That is, on campus.

had been in at there.[137] She took my hands and showed me how I could tell myself when I was going to die by the blackness that would come to my fingernails.

I'm not blaming you for not wanting to have to get along with the kind of man who wrote the Anaconda editorial.[138] But you'll have to get along with somebody of course you know even at Hanover. There may be some ideal office where the employees fall forward in orgasmic exhaustion from saying simply everything only to rise, resume, and fall forward again all day long, but I wouldnt know where to find it. There are bounds set in all company. I'm sorry—almost. I make it seem sad anyway by putting it so baldly.

Gee I wish you could get to Dartmouth and settle down. You're just as capable of being original in what you are bothered by as in other things. Everybody today goes in for being bothered because he cant say simply everything to ladies and in print. I choose to be bothered because if I am reminded of a book in conversation everyone thinks it must be a favorite with me or one I was just reading last night. No one makes any allowance for the power of likening to call up a remoteness. What will yours be? And let's change our favorite thing to be bothered by in the people and country every few months. But let's stick to our wives and children. Remember what Swedenborg used to say about the "sin of varieties."[139] And by the

---

137. Camp Devens (now Fort Devens), a military base west of Boston. RF had suffered a severe bout of influenza during the 1918–1919 pandemic.

138. The *Anaconda Standard* (Butte), which styled itself "Montana's Leading Newspaper," published an editorial on Sunday, April 4, 1926, pronouncing Cox "unfit to be the preceptor of youth." The editorial declared, "The good people of Montana will be amazed and disgusted when their attention is directed to the current number of 'The Frontier,' a quarterly publication issued under the seal of the University of Montana. . . . Filthy, suggestive, obscene and vulgar, the material published in this issue of the magazine, as representing literary thought and effort at the Montana institution, will bring a sense of shame and indignation to every honest person in the state. . . . The 'staff' of this magazine states that the board of editors, composed mostly of girls, is the class in creative writing, with Sidney Cox as instructor." The unsigned editorial winds up with a demand for instant action to "cleanse" the university of "such foul contamination" as *The Frontier*, and Cox, had introduced.

139. "Lust of varieties" was how Emmanuel Swedenborg characterized the motives for adultery in *Conjugial Love*, published in 1768. RF's mother, Isabelle Moodie Frost, had

way I see The Dial is going to mix us religion (Catholic) with its sensuality—an old familiar blend.[140]

Is there anything new? I mean in your situation now.

Louis didn't put you up to sanctioning the number did he?[141]

Nobody knows here but the President:[142] I'm not coming back next year.
Going to have another aberration back to the land.

You should have heard me standing off a club of scientists the other night
on the subject of evolution.[143] I'm not a good debater but they are so sure of
themselves in evolution that they havent taken the trouble to think out their
position. All I had to do was ask them questions for information. The last one
led up to was Did they think it was ever going to be any easier to be good. I
wouldnt call it an evolution unless there was hope of screwing virtue to the
sticking point so it would cost less effort and vigilance than now to maintain.[144] Amelioration was as much as they could make me see. The funny
thing was there [sic] surprise at my unscientificalness. They made more awful
breaks. Sometime I'll tell you about them. I believe I'll never forget them.
They just jumped off the edge. Me I didnt have to expose myself. I was just
out for information. Tell me, I'd say.

become a member of the Swedenborgian Church, inspired, RF later recalled, by her
reading of Emerson (*CPRF*, 200).

140. *The Dial*, since its move to New York in 1918, had become a major outlet for literary modernism, which is probably what RF means by its "sensuality." It is difficult to
trace a drift toward religion, let alone Catholicism, in the 1926 and 1927 volumes of the
magazine.

141. Louis Untermeyer. "The number": the issue of *The Frontier* that landed Cox in
trouble. Untermeyer had visited the Cox family during a trip west in the spring of 1926
(see RF to Untermeyer, March 14, 1926).

142. Clarence Cook Little, who had succeeded Marion LeRoy Burton (the man responsible for bringing RF to Ann Arbor) as president of the University of Michigan.

143. President Little was a geneticist whose ardent promotion of eugenicist policies
riled RF. After Little's appointment as president of Michigan, the number of scientists
elevated to administrative posts at the university increased considerably.

144. An ironic variant on Lady Macbeth's (*Macbeth* 1.7) "But screw your courage to the
sticking-place," uttered to fortify her husband in the scheme to murder Duncan.

We've had a long seige [*sic*] of sickness. Marj has been in bed sixteen weeks with several things and three times at the hospital—one for an operation.[145] Elinor is much worn.

But our best to you all.

> Ever yours
> Robert Frost

I'll throw another word into Lambuth.[146]

[To Lesley Frost. Dated from internal evidence. UL. UVA.]

> [Ann Arbor, MI]
> [circa April 30, 1926]

Dear Lesley:

All over with Michigan but the final disentanglements and reproaches. We are putting off the longest we can our declaration of intention. Effinger knew more than a month ago and Little was supposed to have known. Effinger had promised to tell him. I found yesterday that Effinger hadnt got his courage up. Very embarrassing for me who am already pretty far committed to Oldsie.[147] Like trying to change from one escalator to another going in the opposite direction. May cost me a good hard sit down not to say fall. One thing has led to another till such a point has been reached. Amherst friends merely set out to give me a round of four colleges (Amherst, Wesleyan, Bowdoin and Dartmouth) to earn a living from in eight weeks of the year. In the end Amherst has decided to keep me for Amherst. The thing is practically negotiated. Oldsie will stop over in passing through on Monday and clinch it. But do

---

145. In March 1926, while still convalescing from pneumonia and pericarditis, Marjorie Frost, diagnosed with chronic appendicitis in December 1925, underwent an appendectomy (*YT*, 618–619).

146. David Lambuth (1879–1948), professor of English and chairman of the English Department at Dartmouth from 1921 to 1925. Whatever RF said, it was not detrimental to Cox, because on April 30, 1926, it was announced that he was leaving the University of Montana to join the Dartmouth faculty (*RFSC*, 127).

147. John Robert Effinger (1869–1933), professor of French and dean of the College of Literature, Science, and the Arts. "Oldsie" is George Olds, president of Amherst since Alexander Meiklejohn resigned in 1923. He had persuaded RF to rejoin the faculty at Amherst; the appointment required that RF be present on campus ten weeks a year, during which he would offer an informal seminar.

nothing to spread the news. I wish we might keep out of the papers with it till June.[148]

Right in the middle of everything I get an offer of the Gummere Chair of English at Haverford College. There has been no one found for the place since Gummere died.[149]

It will be a relief to be back in New England and its getting so I cant go without a house and barn of my own a minute longer. It took this bad year to find out what was expected of us here. I wasnt just sure from my memory of talks with Burton how much I was going to be permitted absences.[150]

It has felt to me from hints and attitudes as if we were wanted for constant neighbors and companions. Every time I left town has been noted and re-marked on. Mrs Effinger who as yet isnt in on the resignation secret was asking the other day why we didnt summer here. Its a false position. They want us to act as if their charm had prevailed over New Englands. Thats going some and Ive gone as Bert Williams said.[151] Lets not exaggerate anything. We have liked a lot of people here and wish they would stay friends (but prob ably they wont when they find us out). I havent liked the kids as well this time. The young assertiveness prevailing everywhere east and west seems a little more crude and impolite out west. And I find I'm not fond of teaching girls in their new state of mind. They started out escorting me home from night classes and proposing canoe rides and when I blocked that turned on me in some sort of sex resentment and gave me one of the worst classes of wrangle and flat contradiction I ever had. The same little missies have sat mum at the Whimsies and never helped with an observation or a comparison in the five years I have done my best to entertain them; much less have they ever started any subject of their own. Suddenly out of some sex mischief they break loose and storm me not with subjects, observations and comparisons (such would be welcome) but with contradiction and abuse. I could compose these matters if I cared to. But I seem off such people. I'm willing to grant their equality if thats all they are fighting for. You'll remember that this isnt the

---

148. Olds made the announcement at an alumni dinner in Amherst on June 19.

149. Francis Barton Gummere (1855–1919), a specialist in Anglo-Saxon literature and folklore, was professor of English at Haverford College from 1887 until his death in 1919.

150. President Marion LeRoy Burton, who had in 1924 offered RF the lifetime appoint-ment he was about to resign.

151. RF alludes to the African American vaudeville actor Bert Williams's 1916 song, "I'm Gone before I Go."

first time I ever was off the common people. I'm a great whiffler in my love for the common people. I just naturally seem to shift from some to others and so on to none of them at times.

The new store sounds boss. I wish Marj could have been in on the excitement. She comes on terribly dragging. Mama probably told you the doctor called it a delayed convalescence. Poor comeback I suppose that means as with a person bad at repartee. Miss Murphys[152] exuberance when here yesterday about did for Marj temporarily. Then the Johnson boy held her at the telephone too long. (He spoke from Detroit).[153]

Speaking of Pittsfield friends of yours, I saw Gale Sonderguard [sic] in Miss Bonstelle's Detroit Stock Co do Jessey [sic] Lynch Williams Why Not.[154] I talked with her out back about you and Marj and Lula. I thought she did well though as a whole Williams wasnt very well satisfied with the presentation of his play. Irma and I saw both his plays Why Marry and Why Not.

Marj has been reading Lawrence Conrads novel Figures in the Town[155]— great in part she says preposterous in part. Theres a play here of the Osborn boy's to read; and I must read the poetry (by negroes) in the Opportunity Prize Contest.[156]

About this pass book and check. Very important to tend to it at once. Deposit the five hundred dollars right off and send the pass book right back to me so I wont be worried about it. Register it carefully. I have reasons for

---

152. Presumably Alice E. Murphy (1875–?), a teacher from Stratford, New Hampshire, and a friend of the Frost family.

153. "The Johnson boy" is a Frost family acquaintance who had once worked for General Electric (see RF's letter to Lesley in December 1925).

154. *Why Not?*, a play about divorce by Jesse Lynch Williams (1871–1929), debuted in 1922. His *Why Marry?* had opened in New York's Astor Theatre on December 25, 1917. Laura Justine "Jessie" Bonstelle (1870–1932) was an American actress, theater manager, and entrepreneur who established the Jessie Bonstelle Stock Company and Detroit Civic Theatre; from 1925 to 1927, Gale Sondergaard (1899–1985), an American actress, worked with her.

155. Lawrence H. Conrad, whose acquaintance RF had earlier struck at the University of Michigan. No bibliographic record exists for the title RF mentions.

156. American playwright and screenwriter Paul Osborn (1901–1988) was a graduate of the University of Michigan. RF may allude here to Osborn's first successful play, *Hotbed,* produced in 1928. RF had agreed to serve as a judge in the Opportunity Poetry Prize Contest, sponsored by *Opportunity: A Journal of Negro Life*, of which sociologist Charles Spurgeon Johnson (1893–1956) was editor.

wanting to pull everything out of the Ann Arbor Savings Bank suddenly enough to be noticed by them. Dont let the check lie a minute.

Tell us some more news. Sleep all you can.

Affectionately
[Unsigned]

[To Wilbert Snow. ALS. Wesleyan.]

Ann Arbor Michigan
May 1 1926

Dear Snow

Old devil me, not to write you sooner about the fun it was going to be at Wesleyan in your grand big foursquare colonial with you.[157] It's no excuse that I dont write letters to anyone. You arent just anyone and the circumstances arent just ordinary. It's more like an excuse that I havent had the peace of mind for writing letters or anything else this winter. We've had a long long sickness in the family. Marjorie our youngest and the best poet in the family had to go and give us a scare almost for her life. Good diagnostician as I am (I'm a better diagnostician than critic) I havent been able to tell what ailed her besides pneumonia pericarditis and apendicitis [*sic*], but it may partly have been finding out the world too fast among people a little too old for her. Theres strain isnt there in outside life-thinking that there never is in inside school-thinking.

I suppose you have been scattering poems all over the face of periodicality. I follow no magazines any more to see.

It seems I am about to receive a volume of poetry from Mitchell of Hartford with your compliments.[158] All set—or braced. Tell me about the poetess.

---

157. See RF to Snow, November 23, 1926. RF spent two weeks in a residency at Wesleyan from November 18 to December 12.

158. Edwin Valentine Mitchell (1890–1960) was a Hartford, Connecticut, bookseller, publisher, and author. It is impossible to determine beyond doubt the "poetess" in question, but it may be the English poet Muriel Stuart (1889–1967). Mitchell's list in 1926 included *New Poems and Old,* a collection by Stuart. Her radical treatment of issues of sexual politics would have reverberated with Snow's socialist politics, but her work had also been hailed by Hugh MacDiarmid and Thomas Hardy.

I am going farming again in New England. We've got to get settled nearer the farmer son.[159]

Not prepared to say yet when I am coming to you. All's up in the air. Best wishes to you and Mrs Snow.

> Always yours
> Robert Frost

[To Louis Untermeyer. The last page from the manuscript is missing from the Untermeyer papers at LoC. Beginning with the phrase "Other ratiocinations," we have relied upon Untermeyer's transcription in RFLU to complete the letter. Date derived from postmark. ALS. LoC.]

> [Ann Arbor, MI]
> [May 3, 1926]

Dear Louis

Progressive in love politics and religion, reactionary in education. You had to be reactionary in something to be human. I have given some minutes of my life to helping get the text book [*sic*] where it couldn't be told from a book for a gentleman's library. I've lived to see some pretty good specimens of the advanced text book, stripped to the bare text, freed entirely of "busy work" improvement-play and teachers machinery. I accept school just as I accept the sonnet form or any other social convention: only it seems to be in me to want to make the school as un-schoollike as possible. I should like the books carried away from it not to have any dreary ma'armish connotations that would destine them to the attic or the second hand dealer's dump. But let not God consider me. I know damn well the subtle ways he turns and passes and turns again.[160] All that can be said when my best friend and one of the best minds minding starts on the back track is the laugh is at my expense. Teaching will

---

159. Carol Frost at the Stone Cottage in South Shaftsbury. On or about the day this letter was written, May 1, President Olds of Amherst met with RF in Ann Arbor and officially offered him a third appointment, to begin in the 1926–1927 academic year (RF actually resumed teaching in January 1927).

160. See Emerson's "Brahma":

If the red slayer think he slays,
Or if the slain think he is slain,
They know not well the subtle ways
I keep, and pass, and turn again. . . .

be teaching after I have done my prettiest to translate it to an Elysian Academe. I don't pretend not to be a fool. Teaching is not really where I live anyway, come to think of it. So no wonder I am amused by the contretemps of your arriving at text books just when I was leaving them.[161] I conclude that things like that dont matter between us—nor does anything else in a friendship dating back to Baxters high perched house in Malden and the Blaney dinner party on Beacon Hill in May 1915.[162] Beseech you no trepidation before me. Go somewhere else to tremble if tremble you must about anything on earth. For all I know text books illustrated or unillustrated may be one of the best illustrations of my favorite truths that we keep coming back and back to. Ive written about em.[163]

It's a brilliant book, as I may say who have read everything in it but the list of teachers on your side. I don't know that I would have the least reservation about it if it could be contemptuously sold to teachers as an example of what everyone of them ought to be expected to do for himself but cant do, the poor fish.

Something in the first number of the unreactionary Masses made me notice your omission of Carmelite Jeffers. What is it about this bird? I keep hearing that the mightiest (Robinson and the Van Dorens) have fallen for him.[164]

---

161. Untermeyer had just published his *Yesterday and Today: A Comparative Anthology of Poetry* (New York: Harcourt, Brace, 1926)

162. RF met Untermeyer on May 4, 1915, at the home of Sylvester Baxter, 42 Murray Hill Road, Malden, Massachusetts. RF also dined with the socialite and patron of the arts Edith H. Blaney (1868–1930) and her husband, the artist Dwight Blaney (1865–1944), at 82 Mount Vernon Street, their home on Beacon Hill in Boston.

163. In "The Black Cottage" (collected in *NB*), where the parson-narrator says:

> As I sit here, and oftentimes, I wish
> I could be monarch of a desert land
> I could devote and dedicate forever
> To the truths we keep coming back and back to.
> So desert it would have to be, so walled
> By mountain ranges half in summer snow,
> No one would covet it or think it worth
> The pains of conquering to force change on.

164. Robinson Jeffers (1887–1962), American poet, lived in Carmel, California; in the early 1920s he began work on Tor House and Hawk Tower, his home overlooking the Pacific Ocean. Like Jeffers, Untermeyer—who had served as the literary editor of the socialist magazine *The Masses*—passionately argued against militarism. E. A. Robinson,

It is fine to be in a position to help the young comers like Laing and Schacht.[165]

The Discoverer is one of the best poems you ever discovered.[166]

You remember what I thought of Humbert Wolf [sic].[167]

No Elliot [sic], Gibson, Moody, Abercrombie. Oh well.[168]

But I wish you might have kept Ridgely in.[169]

You're not coming to lecture was a great blow to me. I counted on you to make it up to them for all I havent done this year. It has been awful. And next year, I expect it to be anywhere. [In brackets confidentially I have my port-folio packed light to light out. I said I was going farming, and I'll be as good as my word. Meet me by moonlight five weeks from tonight in Vermont. I have a rendezvous with life.][170] To a mob of Whimsies who clamored about our house I explained that if lecturing had been all, but it was the combina-tion of lecturing and being lectured that had kept you away. They mustn't blame you or me too much either. But seriously I needed you.

Other ratiocinations orally when we encounter. Gee I have just had an in-voice of wisdom I'll bet you would give anything to get the benefit of before

---

Carl Van Doren and Mark Van Doren praised Jeffers's *Tamar and Other Poems* (New York: Peter G. Boyle, 1924). Untermeyer did not include Jeffers in his anthology.

165. Untermeyer discovered the emerging poets Alexander Kinnan Laing (1903–1976) and Marshall Webster Schacht (1905–1956) in the pages of *Dartmouth Verse*. He included Laing's "Triolet" and Schacht's "The First Autumn" in *Yesterday and Today*

166. "The Discoverer" is a poem by Nathalia Clara Ruth Crane (1913–1998). A prodigy, she published her first book, *The Janitor's Boy and Other Poems* (New York: Thomas Seltzer, 1924), when she was only eleven years old.

167. British poet and civil servant Humbert Wolfe (1885–1940). RF's estimate of Wolfe was positive. According to Susan Bonner Walcutt, an undergraduate at the University of Michigan and member of RF's poetry seminar in the spring of 1926, RF read and com-mented favorably upon Wolfe's "The Grey Squirrel," "The Lamb," "Tulip," and "Iliad" (see *YT*, 620). Untermeyer included Wolfe's "The Lilac" and "Journey's End" in *Yesterday and Today*.

168. Heeding the request of the teachers who reviewed a draft of *Yesterday and Today*, Untermeyer omitted poems by T. S. Eliot (1888–1965), Wilfrid Gibson (1878–1962), Wil-liam Vaughn Moody (1869–1910), and Lascelles Abercrombie (1881–1938).

169. Ridgely Torrence.

170. "I have a rendezvous with life" is an allusion to the first line and title of a poem written by Alan Seeger (1888–1916) in the last year of his life, "I Have a Rendezvous with Death." Untermeyer included it in *Modern American Poetry* (New York: Harcourt, Brace and Howe, 1919). A young Countee Cullen (1903–1946) wrote a poem in response to Seeger: "I Have a Rendezvous with Life" (printed in *The Anthology of Newspaper Verse for 1920*, ed. Franklin Pierre Davis [Enid, Oklahoma, 1921]).

I have lost confidence in it on anybody else. I took it on a bad debt that has been owing ever since I was in the hen and pullet business in Derry.[171]

Tadpoles is always a good poem. And so is the One-hoss Shay. There's a laster and another laster. Happened to notice them.[172]

I came within an ace of going to near Philadelphia to live last month. What?[173]

There was a talk on philosophy that haired me up considerably here lately.

Carol is planting cultivated blueberries. Marj is very slow about getting up. Elinor takes her very much to heart.[174]

Affectionately

R.

Did Cox tell you the state-wide trouble he was in? I hope he gets to Dartmouth.[175]

[*To George R. Elliott. Date derived from postmark. Elliott himself penciled in "I urged Pres. Olds to bring R.F. back to Amherst" at the end of the letter. ALS. ACL.*]

[Ann Arbor, MI]

[May 10, 1926]

Dear Roy:

We've been converging on each other's neighborhood ever since you wrote the essay on my neighborliness in 1917, till at last it seems we are about to find ourselves on the same faculty in the same town.[176] One story is rounding out. From now on comes the sequel. Don't you go and spoil it by picking up and

---

171. While living on his farm in Derry, New Hampshire, RF had made a short-lived attempt at poultry farming (1900–1906).

172. RF refers to Untermeyer's "Boy and Tadpoles" and Oliver Wendell Holmes's "The Deacon's Masterpiece; or The Wonderful 'One-Hoss Shay,'" both of which Untermeyer included in *Yesterday and Today*.

173. See RF to Lesley Frost, April 30, 1926; he had been offered a professorship at Haverford College (outside Philadelphia).

174. RF's son, Carol, began cultivating blueberries on the farm in South Shaftsbury.

175. For Cox's recent troubles at the University of Montana, see RF to Cox, April 8, 1926. Following the incident Cox was hired by Dartmouth University, where he would have a long and distinguished teaching career.

176. Actually, in 1919. See George Roy Elliott, "The Neighborliness of Robert Frost," *The Nation*, December 6, 1919, 713–715. RF had recently accepted a new post at Amherst, where Elliott taught. Elliott had been instrumental in persuading President Olds to offer

coming to one of these big western universities you dont seem to think so badly of from all I can make out. Wouldn't it be a joke if our migrations should cross each other and you should come back west just as I came back east. Stay in Amherst. You are a large part of what I bargained for in returning.

The five thousand is a lot for ten weeks.[177] I'm satisfied with the amount. What I am after is detachment and long times alone rather than money. Nobody knows how much less money I have taken in late years than I could have. Enough is enough. So say I and all my family fortunately agree with me. For at least one or two of them less is enough than for me. There's where my real success lies, if [I] may be accused of having any, in being so uncursed in my family.

Think of the untold acres I can shade up in the forty weeks of every year I am going to have free for farming. Suppose I live like Landor till ninety.[178] That will give me one thousand six hundred weeks all to myself to put in at any thing I like. I hadnt thought of it before but by that calculation I have more freedom ahead of me than I have behind (and I have a good deal behind.) All in all it has been such a lucky and original life that I can't understand my ever being for a moment cross or difficult or dissatisfied or cast down. I come west on an impulse; I go back east on an impulse; and nobody says a word.[179] I am simply indulged in everything regardless of my deserts. Where is there a case parallel? And over and <u>above</u> everything I have had the fun of writing a few poems.

Margery begins to lift the load she was off our hearts.

Our love to you all.[180]

> Ever yours.
> Robert

the post to RF (even as RF had earlier persuaded Olds to bring Elliott from Bowdoin to Amherst in 1925).

177. RF's new professorship was endowed by the John Woodruff Simpson Foundation and required of him not regular courses but informal seminars of about ten weeks (offered once per year, January to March).

178. British poet Walter Savage Landor (1775–1864).

179. Not to be taken entirely at face value. Family troubles had made it all but impossible for RF to remain in Ann Arbor.

180. Elliott and his wife, Alma, had two children, Jane and Ann.

[*To E. Merrill Root. ALS. ACL.*]

Ann Arbor Michigan
May 10 1926.

Dear Merrill:

What you and I want is a good long talk together. I'd give as much as you to get to the bottom of your unsuccess.[181] I wonder if you have tried too many ways. I suppose this would be too far for you to come for an interview. We can't entertain friends in the house as we are fixed. We have had a lot of sickness lately and are not up to company. But I would give you any number of hours. I'd put you up at a hotel here or if it would be any more convenient for you—if you were coming east in July or after June 25th and were passing anywhere near us—at the little hotel at South Shaftsbury Vermont.[182] We could have a thorough afternoon and evening together over your work and problem. It beats me why with your brains (not to mention anything else) you cant do about what you please in poetry.

We leave here for the east on June 8th or 10th.[183]

South Shaftsbury is thirty five miles pretty straight in from Albany New York. Ever your friend

Robert Frost

[*To George Whicher. Date derived from postmark. ALS. ACL.*]

[Ann Arbor, MI]
[May 10, 1926]

Dear George:

It deserves remark in this connection that I have at last developed a one legged writing table the materials of which can be found in almost any wood

---

181. Possibly Root's failure to win a Guggenheim Fellowship, for which he had asked RF to supply a testimonial (see RF to Root, July 11, 1925). Root, a poet, was also having difficulty getting published.

182. The identity of this hotel is difficult to establish precisely. The likeliest candidate is the Hastings Hotel, which had been operating since the late 1860s (though it bore different names in the early twentieth century). We thank Carole Thompson and Tyler Resch for their help.

183. RF was in Brunswick, Maine, on June 14, to receive an honorary doctorate from Bowdoin College.

shed and assembled in a minute. The specifications call for one stick two and one half feet long, one piece of wallboard two by one, and two board nails. Once built it can be used in any seat on earth with or without arms. You see the gain. Strange chairs have no longer any terror for me. Formerly what often kept me from moving where I listed was the fear that I mightnt find a chair there that I could be felicitous in. The chair I could write in had to have just the right arms to support a shelf stolen from the closet and not interfere with my elbows. I actually took a Morris chair in a packing case to England to make sure of having just what I wanted. You hope I am properly ashamed of owning to such limitations? I am. But they are a thing of the past. This new invention saves me. At last I am free to wander as much as I would naturally. But dont be disgusted. Naturally may not be as much as you might think from what you know of me. I honestly mean to cleave to Amherst this time till long after the compulsory retiring age. Ninety is the mark I have been setting myself with Roy Elliot[184] [*sic*] —Landor's furthest north—ninety is the Pole isnt it?—where a lot of things are true about time and space that are true nowhere else. And so on off into my mysticism where you wouldnt care to follow me. It is an open covenant, then, openly arrived at (awful stuff to fob a nation off with) that ninety shall find me writing my last least lump of lyric at Amherst.

You, Roy, Otto, Powell, Morton and I! It sounds like a Table Round with no Modred hanging round.[185]

I'm going to permit myself the largest farm house on it that I can buy in south western V.T.[186] Something so big that if the crime wave went over it and the robbers came in the windows the different members of the family couldn't hear each other getting murdered.[187] Wide hall right through the middle. Four open fire places downstairs and four up. Running spring water in the kitchen sink. Tie-ups for twenty cows. Barn in the way of the view.

---

184. See RF to Elliott, May 10, 1926.

185. George Roy Elliott, Otto Manthey-Zorn, Chilton Lathem Powell, and David H. Morton, all on the faculty at Amherst at the time. Modred—more often spelled Mordred—figures in Arthurian legend as a traitor.

186. In 1929, RF settled on a 150-acre farm in South Shaftsbury known as the Gully Farm. It was about a mile distant from the Stone Cottage, the farm he had purchased in 1920 and given to his son, Carol, and his wife, Lillian, in 1923.

187. Much print was devoted to the "crime wave" of 1926 in the *New York Times* and other newspapers; it was often ascribed to the effects of Prohibition.

My Louis has a new high school anthology of modern poetry out with exactly two poems in it by his last wife and two by his next.[188] That looks more dispassionate than I'm afraid it is. Our John Erskine has become a great authority with the press on how such things are to be taken by friends and relatives.[189] Nevertheless I feel put in a hard position. Jean has as good as forbidden us to recieve [*sic*] Virginia. That hangs Louis up in Limbo. Our best to you both.[190]

Ever yours
Robert.

[To Otto Manthey-Zorn. Date derived from postmark. ALS. ACL.]

[Ann Arbor, MI]
[May 10, 1926]

Dear Otto

I thought I would have to bring you out here, but from the moment I left Amherst things began to shape toward your bringing me back there. Anyway we are going to get our heads together again. It doesn't matter where. Now we can go on with our plots against system and the system from where we left off.

I consider it all settled, though I can't say I have quite had my parting interview with Little.[191] I know well enough what I am to him. He would like me to stand steady as a symbol of the arts so he would be free to tend to administration and biology. I don't mean that entirely. He's a liberal soul and I'm sure wants everything to have its chance. I like him a lot in spite of his having for motto More mice and less men.[192] I heard him tell his wife he had

---

188. Louis Untermeyer's *Yesterday and Today: A Comparative Anthology* (for which see RF to Untermeyer, May 3, 1926). The book includes "End of Summer" and "Lullaby for a Manchild," by Jean Starr Untermeyer, whom Untermeyer married in 1907, and "Joan of Arc, 1926" and "The Good Ground," by Virginia Moore, whom he would marry in 1927.

189. John Erskine had taught at Amherst from 1903 to 1909.

190. Whicher's wife was Harriet Ruth Fox.

191. Clarence Cook Little, president of the University of Michigan.

192. See Robert Burns's "To a Mouse": "The best laid schemes of mice and men / Gang aft agley." Little's research focused on the breeding of new strains of mice for oncological interventions.

a thousand mice born in his laboratory last week. Thats going some in mice for the president of a society for human birth control.[193]

He warned me against being selfishly motivated in my present move. So I'm glad I can say I shall have less a year by a thousand and some income tax (salaries in state universities are untaxable) than he pays me. I may be selfish but I'm not greedy—anyway I try to preserve the appearance of not being greedy.

And another reason for not wanting to seem greedy was something our old Micky said in convocation, I am told, when he was here the other day.[194] We used to starve our poets to death but now we feed them to death says Micky. Some took that as a slap at this university for having spoiled me with a salary of six thousand a year. Pretty low from a man who probably hasnt had less than fifteen thousand a year on an average since he was forty. He cant really be worried about my being tamed by having enough to give my four children a very modest start in life. Fifteen and twenty thousand (part of it begged) havent tamed him. He has stayed just as wild in the belfry as ever. It must be he grudges poets their least little. And that while pretending to be the only friend to the arts our educational system has produced. We'll ask him how much he thinks wouldnt hurt me and cut it down to his figure. He started on fifteen hundred a year with me and then raised it to twenty five hundred. But I wonder if those were the days when he means we starved our poets to death. Its not a matter of food any way. Hes begging the question as usual. It's a matter of drink. The only way to make poets live is drink them to death. He knows that as well as anyone. Why doesnt he say so like a man and do some good in the world?

Ethel[195] says you are off to Europe for the summer. Will that hold strike or no strike?[196] It might be all the more interesting for your young political sci-

---

193. See RF to Manthey-Zorn, December 17, 1925.

194. Alexander Meiklejohn, forced to resign as president of Amherst College in 1923, had been responsible for RF's first appointment there. RF had been neither supportive of Meiklejohn's self-styled "radical" educational ethos nor displeased when the trustees deposed him. Controversies to do with Meiklejohn's salary and expense accounts contributed (in some small part) to his dismissal; see the notes to RF's June 22, 1923, letter to MacVeagh.

195. Manthey-Zorn's wife, née Bray.

196. The council of the British Trades Union Congress had called a general strike for May 4, in solidarity with locked-out coal miners who were protesting pay-cuts and the imposition of longer working hours. The strike was initially effective, but the strikers'

entists to be in on the deflation of empire now beginning to dramatize in England.[197] It will go by starts and stops of course. Before you can get there the first episode may be over and it may be a year or so before the second gets on. This would be at about the point of the invasion of the Teutons and Cimbri or perhaps it is a little further along at the battle say of the Teutoberg Forest. The day of the Goths is not quite yet. [198] But again there is something besides baseball to buy a paper for.

Oldsie was the same old good old Oldsie when he was with us.[199]

I want to see you before you are swallowed up in the end of Europe.

Ever yours

Robert

[*To Sidney Cox. ALS. DCL.*]

Ann Arbor May 17 1926

Dear Sidney

Im totally glad.[200] Not the least of its beauties is that it comes so exactly in the nick of time to leave your enemies wondering where you disappeared to. It couldnt be more fun.

And I couldn't wish you a better place to bring up in than Dartmouth if I tried. Dartmouth is one of my favorite colleges, though unfortunately I cant say I have its yell at my tongues end for this great occasion. And thats a large

---

morale was worn down by hardheaded government policy and the show of considerable resistance on the part of the middle classes. The strike ended in defeat for the strikers on May 13.

197. For at least part of the trip Manthey-Zorn escorted a group of Amherst students to an International Confederation of Students.

198. The Teutons and Cimbri invaded Italy in 103 BC, and were defeated at Acquae Sextiae and Vercellae in 101 BC. The battle of Teutoburg Forest saw three Roman legions defeated by a confederacy of Germanic tribes in 9 AD (an event often seen as decisive in the Roman failure to conquer and settle German lands east of the Rhine). The Visigoths sacked Rome in 410 AD.

199. George Daniel Olds, president of Amherst. He'd visited RF in Ann Arbor in early May.

200. About Cox's appointment to the faculty at Dartmouth following his recent difficulties and humiliations at Montana (see RF to Cox, April 8, 1926).

hearted lot you are going to find around you—all men and not one of them an old woman—not one of them cursed with fastidiosity.

You'll duff [sic] in and do us all credit with your teaching. You are one of the two or three best teachers going up. Lawrence Conrad here is another and Hughes Mearns author of Creative Youth seems to be another.[201]

Be good to Lambuth and Robinson them and their wives and to Brooks Henderson, him and his epic, and to young Morse (whose uncle was an old friend of mine) and especially to Donald Bartlett when he gets back from Europe next year or year after next. Like prim Harold Goddard Rugg in the library too for my sake. And old Lord who taught me Greek in 1892 and remains one of my pleasantest memories! The dean was a classmate of mine so be careful how you make him jealous. The head librarian Goodrich is one of the good minds. I wish you were going to see anything of my friend Dallas but he has gone to be bishop of the diocese at Concord N.H. There's a story about him I must tell you some day. I mustnt tax you with too many people to swallow whole for no reason but my command.[202]

---

201. Lawrence H. Conrad. William Hughes Mearns (1875–1965) was a pedagogue and poet and the author of *Creative Youth: How a School Environment Set Free the Creative Spirit* (Garden City, NY: Doubleday, Page, 1925). On the latter, see RF to Mearns, July 27, 1925.

202. Respectively, David Lambuth (1879–1948), professor of English at Dartmouth, Chair of the English Department, 1921–1925; Kenneth Robinson (1891–1961), professor of English; Walter Brooks Drayton Henderson (1887–1939), Jamaican-born poet, assistant professor of English, his epic being *The New Argonautica: An Heroic Poem in Eight Cantos of the Voyage among the Stars of the Immortal Spirits of Sir Walter Ralegh, Sir Francis Drake, Ponce de Leon and Nunez da Vaca* (New York: Macmillan, 1928); Stearns Morse (1893–1976), instructor of English, later Dean of Freshmen at Dartmouth, 1946–1956 (his uncle was Henry Moses Morse, a lawyer involved in RF's purchase of the Franconia farm in 1915 [*LRF-1*, 350]); Donald Bartlett (1902–1989), who was to join the faculty in 1927 and go on to become professor of biography and Japanese; Harold Goddard Rugg (1883–1957), assistant librarian and instructor of modern art, later to become professor of modern art (he taught the history of the book and of printing); George Dana Lord (1863–1945), professor of classical archaeology; Nathanial J. Goodrich (1880–1957); John Dallas (1880–1961), Episcopal Bishop of New Hampshire, 1926–1948. The dean of the college was Craven Laycock (1866–1940), Dartmouth class of 1896.

I like to have you like what I wrote about Amy Lowell.[203] I wonder if Louis is right about it being better taken in disconnection from her.[204] He may be. I leave it to you to decide. The two main ideas in it came to me quite apart from her. Still I thought maybe they applied. I never was a great reader of her work.

My best to you both.

Always yours in all
Robert Frost (vague about
puritanism)

[To Louis Untermeyer. Date supplied by Untermeyer. ALS. LoC.]

[Ann Arbor, MI]
[circa May 17, 1926]

Dear Louis:

Some of what you must have taken for ironies were the flattest simplicities.[205] I really insist on nothing in education. My own preference any day would be a book like your Singing World for a text book [*sic*].[206] (It happened to be lying where Marjorie had left it on the sofa when I sat down to read your letter.)[207] The beautiful bare text for me. Teachers who dont know what to do with it, let them perish and lose their jobs. I dont allow for the existance [*sic*] of teachers who depend on "teachers helps." But I dunnow! There are more people on earth than are provided for in my philosophy   latitudinarian though I try to be.[208] I am willing to let you judge for me. So I said and I meant

---

203. "The Poetry of Amy Lowell," published first in the *Christian Science Monitor*, May 16, 1925, and reprinted in an anthology Cox edited with Edward Freeman, *Prose Preferences* (New York: Harper and Brothers, 1926). See *CPRF*, 88, 264.

204. Louis Untermeyer.

205. See RF to Untermeyer, May 3.

206. The textbook RF prefers to Untermeyer's *Yesterday and Today* is *This Singing World: An Anthology of Modern Poetry for Young People* (New York: Harcourt, Brace and Howe, 1923).

207. Marjorie Frost had just traveled with her mother to Ann Arbor (from Pittsfield, Massachusetts) to recover her health.

208. See *Hamlet* 1.5: "There are more things in heaven and earth, Horatio / Than are dreamt of in your philosophy."

it. If there are teachers in quantity who need your help you must help them. Only do it as little as you can and withdrawingly so as to throw them finally on their own resources like the Phillipene [sic] Islands when they shall be fit for independence (You know our national promise.)[209]

Ill tell you what you could do to please me the next time. Where notes and suggestions for study (teachers helps) seem inevitable you could offer them by word of preface as the merest samples of what the teachers are expected to get up for themselves. Of course there is matter for remark in poems. Nobody denies that. But it must be solemnly laid on every body in this world to make his own observations and remarks. Thats what we mean by thinking and thats about all we mean. A teacher says to a pupil: "Watch me notice a few things in the next few months: lets see you notice a few things too." But the teachers observation must be genuinely his own. A little if it is his own, will induce more mental action in his pupils than a great deal supplied him by you—you old wholesaler.[210]

By the way "banter" struck me as one of the best words ever used to explain me.

We'll meet then soon.

Its shaping up apparently for me to earn my living by a couple of weeks at each of two or three colleges next year and be left free to settle down on the farm I was threatening to buy the last time I saw you in Pittsfield.[211] Oh you don't know how Im spoiling for a place to do anything I like to the trees on. I havent put the least bit of interest into my duties here. I've practically done nothing for anyone and I feel like an ingrate.

Ever yours

R. F.

---

209. In 1916 the Philippine Autonomy Act, passed by United States Congress during the Wilson Administration, promised Filipinos greater control of their government and eventual independence. Full independence, however, would not be granted until the Treaty of Manila was ratified in 1946.

210. Before devoting himself exclusively to writing, Untermeyer worked in the family jewelry business.

211. In addition to his ten weeks a year at Amherst, RF would often spend several weeks at Dartmouth, Bowdoin, and Wesleyan.

[To John Bartlett. The first page of the letter is now missing; we rely upon Margaret Bartlett Anderson's transcription in RFJB to complete it. Anderson expurgated the last portion of paragraph 1 and the entirety of paragraphs 3 and 4 from her transcription of the original letter. Text taken from RFJB appears within brackets. ALS. UVA.]

[Ann Arbor, MI]

[May 26, 1926]

[Dear John:]

[Let's see if I can remember what all has happened since the flurry last fall about transporting Carol to Colorado for his health.[212] I was skeptical about prying him loose from his attachments to the South Shaftsbury farm. He's getting more and more dug in there with every tree and bush he makes a hole for. Right now he is adding a hundred Astrachan trees[213] to the dwarf orchard—dwarf so as to get them sooner for the roadside market. He's putting in some sixty of] Miss White's (of Whitesbog N. J.) cultivated high-bush blueberries.[214] And a lot of roses. The process is the dragnet process. You try everything and throw away what you dont like. He and Lillian sold a hundred dollars worth of sweet peas last summer with a small hand painted sign. Theres a new girls college just starting at Bennington[215] four miles away on which he builds some hope of a more or less flowery kind of farming. It may come to a hot house in the end. And it may not. He lost one of his great big workhorses a week or so ago. Farming has hard setbacks. In that loss went about all he had earned in teaming in the woods all winter. He's such a worker as I was never suspected of being though I may have been: so don't be too ready to grin you low-minded Rockingham County Mephistopheles. Speaking of the devil as impersonated by yourself in those golden days, do you remember the Comus, Kenneth Miller[216] whom Mr Bingham trusted

---

212. Carol Frost had been struggling to recover from a difficult respiratory illness. See also RF to Bartlett, December 11, 1925.

213. The Red Astrachan is an apple cultivar.

214. In 1911, Elizabeth Coleman White (1871–1954) began a collaboration with Dr. Frederick V. Coville to develop a highbush blueberry suitable for cultivation. By 1912 they had succeeded in establishing a selection from the wild "Rubel" that produced an ample crop of sweet fruit. They released fifteen successful cultivars by 1937.

215. Although Bennington College did not open its doors until 1932, planning for its establishment had been under way since 1923.

216. Kenneth Lund Miller (1892–1976) graduated from Pinkerton Academy in 1912, and had taken part (with Bartlett) in the production of John Milton's masque *Comus*, which RF staged in 1910, while a teacher at Pinkerton (see *CPRF*, 76, 257, 259). Bartlett—a

with the church communion set for the banqueting scene in Circes Palace.[217] Well I all but saw him in Grand Rapids. He was looking for me but missed me. He is something in the business end of furniture. Then I ran onto [*sic*] another Pinkertonian in a strange way in one of the trust companies in Wall St.—Charles Williams—you may not have known him. He went from Pinkerton to Haverford. He only had his senior year with us.[218]

We're going east again said the pendulum. This was no go this year, or rather it was too much go and what wasnt go was come. Marjorie's long illness (means more than sickness) kept Elinor with her in Pittsfield Mass and me commuting for months. Every week or so I would run the water out of the pipes and leave the house here to freeze. It wasnt exactly in the contract that I should be away all the time and I wasn't quite all. I'm not going to try to keep it up here with the children back there and such things likely to happen again. And anyway I want a farm. It's all arranged so you neednt exclaim a protest about such whiffling. Amherst, Dartmouth, Bowdoin and Connecticut Wesleyan are going to give me a living next year for a couple of weeks in each of them.[219] The rest of the time I shall be clear away from the academic feeding pigeons hens dogs or anything you advise for the pleasure or profit in it. The only thing that worries me is that Bennington College coming in on our pastoral serenity. I ran away from two colleges in succession once and they took revenge by flattering me back to teach in college.[220] Now I am running away again and it looks as if they would come

native of Rockingham County, New Hampshire—had played Mephistopheles in Christopher Marlowe's *Faustus* in the same series (other plays staged included Richard Brinsley Sheridan's *The Rivals,* and W. B. Yeats's *The Land of Heart's Desire* and *Cathleen ni Houlihan*).

217. The immediate reference is to the banquet scene in *Comus* (lines 659–958). Circe figures in the masque as Comus's mother. In Homer's *Odyssey,* Circe—the enchantress with whom Odysseus resides for a year—transforms Odysseus' crew into swine as they feast during an elaborate banquet (a tale alluded to in Milton's masque). The Reverend George Washington Bingham (1838–1918) served as principal of Pinkerton Academy from 1885 to 1909 and also taught English and Latin. The editors thank Mark Mastromarino, archivist at Pinkerton Academy, and Derry historian Rick Holmes for their help.

218. Charles Williams, an underclassman, had been center on the football team and vice president of the Philomathean Society.

219. RF's contract with Amherst stipulated that he offer one ten-week seminar a year (from January to March); at the other colleges here named he regularly spent short residencies.

220. RF had briefly attended Dartmouth and Harvard but graduated from neither.

after me. I'll probably end with one of the ponderous things in bed with me on my chest like an incubus. Look out or the same fate will overtake you, or so I begin to fear from what you tell me about the friendliness of your university out there. [221] We may both live to be sorry we didnt go through school in the regular course of nature and get it over with.

I havent taken out insurance with Carl Ladd yet.[222] Isnt he like a Hearst Newspaper or something?[223] I should think you would think he was funny. You ought to have seen him on the piazza wondering all the time he wheedled away if I had forgotten the time he wheedled me into buying a life of pens or an encyclopedia from him. His rascality is so shallow it seems burlesque in these bad days. I suppose you mind him because he got under your skin when you were young together.

Spring probably is weeks ahead with you of what it is with us. Lilacs are exactly half in bloom. I'm burning wood in the fireplace tonight, May 26–27 (that is to say midnight).

You've got adopted and adapted out there. But me, I'm sort of a Yank from New England. I want to get back, if its just the same to everybody. Nothing's invidious about my preference. I like Michigan people and I like Michigan. Only only.

Best love to you all.

Ever yours in everything
Robert Frost

---

221. The University of Colorado–Boulder. As for Bartlett: in the fall of 1910, he had enrolled at Middlebury College, but his debilitating asthma forced him to leave before completing his first semester.

222. For Carl M. Ladd, another Pinkerton Academy alumnus, see RF to Bartlett, circa January 1, 1926.

223. The media magnate William Randolph Hearst published newspapers in thirty major cities around the country.

[To Kenneth C. M. Sills (1879–1954), president of Bowdoin College. The year is not given; internal evidence suggests 1926. ALS. Bowdoin.]

Ann Arbor [MI]

June 9 [1926]

Dear Mr Sills:

It will be a pleasure to be with you and Mrs Sills again[224]—a pleasure and, as it were, a recommencement of New England.[225] We are winding up the affair here. Mrs Frost is sorry not to be able to come. She is full of the care of the daughter who has been ill all winter.

Always yours

Robert Frost

---

224. Edith Lansing Koon Sills (1988–1978). RF had given a lecture, "Vocal Imagination," on May 4, 1925, at Bowdoin's Institute of Modern Literature.

225. At its commencement, in June 1926, Bowdoin College awarded RF an honorary LittD.

5

Ten Weeks a Year in Amherst, Fourteen Once in Europe

June 1926–December 1928

*You know how acute our homesickness always is: and to what
mental turns it spurs us. I suppose our realest anguish ensues from
our being caught on what looks like touring at all. We ought not to
be in France after all we have said from the platform and the throne
against tourism literal and metaphorical. By metaphorical I mean
in Survey courses in education. . . . Think of me sightseeing in spite
of all the protective laziness I have developed on principle against
it. I deserve to be punished. Upon my soul I never saw anything to
match this summer Paris for ugliness not even a White Mountain
resort. We're catching it. But never mind. As I say we deserve it.
You may say another time we'll know better. Not necessarily. We're
not the kind that can be taught. We know instinctively all we are
going to know from birth and inexperience.*

—Robert Frost to his daughter Lesley, September 1, 1928

[To Wilbur Rowell. ALS. UVA.]

South Shaftsbury Vermont
July 4 1926

Dear Mr Rowell:

This letter from Dr Tyson makes me surer than ever that we ought to do something to make my sister's money available to pay her expenses in the Augusta State Hospital.[1] If I haven't followed you up in the matter it is because at times I have had a glimmer of hope that she might some day come out; in which case she would be as well off to have left her money where it is gathering interest and waiting for her. But she probably never will come out. We may as well face the fact and provide accordingly. As I see it the best use the money can be put to is to give her the comfort of feeling that she is not altogether dependent. Such comfort as it might be! Isn't it a wretched business? I havent the courage to take hold of it nor the conscience (or whatever you call it) to let it alone.

Always yours sincerely
Robert Frost

---

1. Forrest Clark Tyson, who had been named superintendent of the Maine Insane Asylum (in Augusta) in January 1914. RF had committed his sister, Jeanie, to the institution in April 1920.

[*To Flora M. Lamb (1869–1949), executive secretary in the Portland, Maine, publishing house of Thomas B. Mosher, the Mosher Press. After Mosher's death in 1923, she continued to manage the press until her retirement in 1938. ALS. UVA.*]

South Shaftsbury Vermont
July 10 1926

My dear Miss Lamb:

Forgive my not answering sooner. We have been on the move and I have not had where to lay a sheet of paper for writing on. Of course use Reluctance.[2] I have a special feeling for that poem from the way it bound me in friendship to Tom Mosher. You might be so kind as to make your acknowledgement in form to Henry Holt and Co.

I hope all goes well with you in the little shop up off the street.

Sincerely yours
Robert Frost

[*To Edgar Gilbert (1875–1964), a friend and workmate of RF's in his youth, later an industrial chemist. ALS photostat. DCL.*]

July 10 1926
South Shaftsbury

Dear Ed:

I dont suppose we think those days in the mill ever hurt or hindered us a mite.[3] I often speak of them not to say brag of them when I want to set up as an authority on what kind of people work with their hands what they earn or used to earn how they take themselves what they do with their leisure and what becomes of them. There were Hoffman, Brackett, Lang, George, Gilbert, and Frost. You are accounted for and so am I. It seems to me I heard a year or two ago that Billy Golden was still in the Arlington Mills: which would

---

2. "Reluctance" first appeared in *The Youth's Companion*, November 7, 1912, and was later collected as the last poem in *ABW*. Flora Lamb included the poem in her posthumous tribute to Thomas Mosher, *Amphora: A Second Collection of Prose and Verse Chosen by the Editor of the Bibelot* (Portland, ME: Mosher Press, 1926).

3. RF had worked at the Arlington Woolen Mill in Lawrence, Massachusetts, during the winter of 1893–1894. Poems referring to this period of his life include "The Mill City," "When the Speed Comes," "The Parlor Joke" (see RF to Untermeyer, March 21, 1920), and, most notably, "A Lone Striker" (collected in *AFR*).

make some people say "Just think of it." I wonder if Horace Hoffman is still courting Billy Golden's sister.[4] The last I knew they had been engaged for some time with no definite marriage intentions.

I remember the Shakespeare and the wrestling and the bulb throwing and the talks over in your quiet dynamo room and John's large family and the carbon dust and the ladders we slid on one leg ahead of us along the well-oiled floors.[5] I learned a lot of things in those days that have been of no particular use to me since but one thing I never learned was to stand over going machinery on the top step of a step-ladder with nothing to hold on to or brace a shin against and unsling an arc lamp from the ceiling for repairs. It always scared me irresponsible. Once after having used a broom to shut the current off at the switch, I carefully but timidly dropped the broom right across all the threads to (or from) a jackspool.[6] I cut every thread. Before I could get down from my high perch I had been danced at gesticulated at and sworn at by a boss and an overseer. Mea culpa!

4. Horace Hoffman had in fact married Agnes Golden (one of William "Billy" Golden's sisters); he worked in the mills until the 1930s, as did Golden. We have been unable to identify the other men named.

5. In 1937 Gilbert supplied Robert Newdick with the following account of his and RF's friendship: "Bob and I were work mates and had been brought up in the same neck of the woods. He lived in Salem while I was in Methuen, then he in Methuen while I in Salem, then both in Lawrence, and working together, later I teaching in Methuen and he in Pinkerton Academy just beyond Salem. . . . We read Shakespeare's thunders to the hammer of the heavy machinery of the electric power plant, and sang his sonnets to the purr of the brushes on the big dynamos." See *Newdick's Season of Frost: An Interrupted Biography of Robert Frost* (Albany: State University of New York Press, 1976), 327. In a later note to a friend—dated July 27, 1949, and enclosing the photostat of RF's letter—Gilbert recalls more of "the Shakespeare": "Up here [on a raised portion of the roof above the main dynamo room] Bob would huddle in a corner for hours, when not busy with work, reading a pocket edition of Shakespeare which he sometimes carried. The Boss also had a Shakespeare in the book cabinet, a large unexpurgated edition of the complete works, lavishly and suggestively illustrated, in the grand manner of the early printers. I would sometimes take the night shift, to supply lights to the mill when it was running nights, and Bob would be my teammate. Then often we would get out the real book, and spend hours, partly reading aloud but mostly discussing. We sagely decided it was about as easy to fall into the style of lingo of Cassius, Antonio or even Portia as to adopt the speech of the Canuck who happened to work near us" (letter held now at DCL).

6. A large wooden spool used in the manufacture of woolens.

It wasn't ball,[7] but football between Methuen High and Pinkerton that last time we met. You had a delayed pass or something you beat us with.

Last year I wasn't at Amherst,[8] but I was the year before and shall be next year again—at least for the ten weeks of the winter term (We divide the year in three at Amherst.) So if you're visiting Mount Holyoke do look me up for a good old talk.[9]

It was fine to hear from you.

> Always yours
> Robert Frost

[*To Harriet Monroe. ALS. Chicago.*]

> South Shaftsbury Vermont
> July 10 1926

Dear Miss Monroe:

I just haven't the courage to undertake it. August is my nadir month. I never have any luck of any kind in August, especially if I am in clothes. The only way I outwit the jinx is by staying strictly in overalls and one shirt—absolutely coatless.

It is a sad admission to make, but the reason for this is not half as mysterious poetical and spiritual as I wish it were: it is flatly physical. In August I am given up to hay-fever and my refuge is in the very opposite direction from Philadelphia.[10] Why in the name of Liberty are we poets invited to Philadelphia in August anyway? Because we are sure not to come or because we are sure not to have any audience and then the editors can all say they told us so—poetry is no longer a factor in life—or because all the other months are preempted for science religion business and politics?

---

7. That is, baseball.

8. He was Fellow in Letters at the University of Michigan.

9. Mount Holyoke College, in South Hadley, Massachusetts, approximately six miles from Amherst. Gilbert had a daughter studying there (likely one Virginia Gilbert, who graduated in 1928). While visiting her, Gilbert tried to look up RF in Amherst; failing to find him, he sent the note that prompted the present letter.

10. The Frosts spent late summer (and this time early autumn) at the Fobes place in Sugar Hill, New Hampshire, near Franconia.

Seriousness aside, I shall have to let this honor pass. I appreciate your having thought of me and wish I could meet you half way. Twas ever thus from childhoods hour[11] I never had a chance that I proved equal to.

We hope you are in for a good summer. I see you have been doing the West and all the poets in their habitats. It sounds as if you had liked some of them* and had a good time.[12]

> Always yours faithfully
> Robert Frost

*Lew Sarett is worth the lot of them.[13]

[To Lincoln MacVeagh. The letter is undated, but MacVeagh penciled in "Aug 1" at the top right-hand corner of the first page; internal evidence provides the year. ALS. Jones.]

> South Shaftsbury Vt
> [August 1, 1926]

Dear Lincoln:

Haven't happened to tell you have I? We have had two hospital cases this spring and summer. First it was Marjorie all cut up and then it was Lillian.[14] Lillian seems to have profited by it more than Marjorie. So if I havent had you up or been down you wont think anything. I almost went down the other day on an impulse to see a ball game with you and talk about your little volumes

---

11. From *Lalla Rookh,* by Thomas Moore:

> 'Twas bright, 'twas heav'nly, but 'tis past!
> Oh! ever thus, from childhood's hour,
>   I've seen my fondest hopes decay;
> I never lov'd a tree or flow'r,
>   But 'twas the first to fade away.

12. The June 1926 issue of *Poetry* featured an essay by Monroe about her travels and encounters with poets on a trip that took her to New Orleans, Tucson, San Diego, Seattle, Spokane, North Dakota, and Minneapolis, among other places ("A Travel Tale," 150–157).

13. Lew Sarett, the poet, woodsman, forest ranger, and professor of speech at Northwestern University in Evanston, Illinois. RF met him while giving a reading there on December 10, 1921.

14. Lillian Labatt Frost, the wife of Carol Frost, underwent surgery in July 1926. Marjorie was still recovering from the appendectomy she had in March 1926.

of verse,[15] but my heart, strength or prejudices werent in it and after riding in the train a while I thought better of it, let my ticket go as wasted and turned back to see if anything had gone wrong in the family since I left. What's that scare poem of Wordsworths about Lucy?[16] Well. It would save a lot of writing if we could reduce communication to just referring each other to poems that way. We'd have to know many poems. But you and I do. You do anyway. Thats what distinguishes you from any other publisher I know. Which flattery is preliminary to asking you if you would think it too far to come to visit us at Franconia for a few days this summer. I have some heavy suggestions to make you re[17] the little volumes of verse and then I want to loaf around with you. It costs a little more in money to come up there but no more really in time. It is one sleep in a sleeper in either case. I'd say come here now but we are off for Sugar Hill on Friday or Saturday. Our address up there will be Sugar Hill N.H.[18]

Its important you should come. Bring your tennis things on the off chance that we should want to rest from talking some of the time. My best to all.[19]

> Ever yours
> Robert Frost

---

15. MacVeagh had recently launched, at the Dial Press, a series called "The Little Books of New Poetry," some with as few as twenty pages. See, for example, Jacques Le Clercq, *The Sorbonne of the Hinterland* (New York: Dial Press, 1926), and Bennett Weaver, *Sussex Poems* (New York: Dial Press, 1926).

16. William Wordsworth wrote and published his five "Lucy" poems between 1798 and 1801: "A slumber did my spirit seal," "Strange fits of passion have I known," "She dwelt among untrodden ways," "I traveled among unknown men," and "Three years she grew in sun and shower." RF refers, here, to the second:

> *What fond and wayward thoughts will slide*
> *Into a lover's head!*
> *'O mercy!' to myself I cried,*
> *'If Lucy should be dead!'*

17. "regarding"

18. In the 1920s, the White Mountain region of New Hampshire (around Franconia, Sugar Hill, and adjacent towns) underwent a boom in tourism, with expanded railway service in the summer, grand hotels, country clubs (and tennis courts).

19. MacVeagh and his wife, Margaret Charlton MacVeagh, née Lewis. Their daughter Margaret Ewen was then six years old.

[*To Richard H. Thornton. Date derived from postmark. ALS. DCL.*]

[South Shaftsbury, VT]

[August 2, 1926]

Dear Mr Thornton:

My notion is that it will be good advertising to indulge Conrad Aiken—and good friendship too. Conrad is a critic whose backing I value.

I almost visited New York on your recommendation the other day. I got on to the train for New York but got off again a few stations below here and came back to the woods. I charged the waste of carfare up to impulsiveness.

They sent me three New Hampshires instead of the three Mountain Intervals I ordered. Has some one a grudge against Mountain Intervals? Please try again.

Best wishes and thanks for all.

Sincerely yours

Robert Frost

[*To Flora M. Lamb. ALS. UVA.*]

South Shaftsbury Vermont

August 6 1926

My dear Miss Lamb:

I believe I haven't answered your last inquiry yet. It is quite all right about the Reluctance poem.[20] I assume the responsibility. Merely make acknowledgement to Henry Holt and Company as you said you would and all forms will be complied with.

Sincerely yours

Robert Frost

---

20. See RF to Lamb, July 10, 1926.

[*To Mark Sullivan (1874–1952), journalist and historian. ALS. BU.*]

Sugar Hill N.H.

August 15 1926

Dear Mr Sullivan:

A letter was to have gone with that book; but I am a laggard at letters. The book was not very strictly a first edition, was it? It may have been a first class edition plastered as it was with all my addenda in script. But speaking of first editions and speaking of satisfactions, I think I know where I can lay my hand on a couple of the former (real ones) that it would give me many of the latter to confer on the daughter of the author of The Turn of the Century.[21] They should have her name written into them, if you will supply it.[22]

You'll not suppose me insensible of what it will mean to me to have you single out a poem of mine for notice. (I might rather have Calvin Coolidge and then again in the long run I might not.) If I am not saying much, it is partly because I am overcome with surprise and pleasure that a person of your large preoccupations should have been able to name a poem of mine by name. Really and truly! I was born to journalism and politics. My father was an editor and party-worker in San Francisco in the eighties.[23] One of my earliest childhood recollections is seeing him off at Oakland when he went as a delegate to the Cincinnatti [*sic*] Convention that nominated Hancock in 1880.[24] I have followed you in your political writing as a matter of course. I should have followed you any way whatever my beginnings. As good Americans we all keep track of the important Washingtonians. From nothing in my experience of newspapermen and politicians however would I expect you to have kept track of me. One of the most distinguished Boston editors you and I know gets as far in poetry as Edgar Guest and gets no farther.[25] Only lately I had the

---

21. Sullivan's *The Turn of the Century*, published in 1926, was volume 1 of his six-volume work, *Our Times: The United States 1900–1925* (New York: Charles Scribner's Sons, 1926–1935).

22. Mark Sullivan and Marie McMechen Buchanan Sullivan's daughter Sydney was born in 1910.

23. RF's father, William Prescott Frost, also wrote *William Starke Rosecrans: His Life and Public Services: Reasons Why He Should Be Elected to the Congress* (San Francisco: Democratic Congressional Committee, 1880).

24. General Winfield Scott Hancock (1824–1886) topped the Democratic ticket that year.

25. Edgar Guest (1881–1959) English-born American poet of great popularity often called "the people's poet." We've been unable to identify the "Boston editor."

wierdest [*sic*] adventure with a Senator from Ohio.[26] But I see from your book you are not as the others; you are a person many interests meet in. Sometime we must convene and then after you have given me three guesses as to what Calvin said about putting me on the map you will tell me the answer.[27] I can foresee now what my first guess will be: "How'd I look asettin up as an arbiter poetarum?"[28] All the same I am in favor of Calvin. On the fur [*sic*] side of the Green Mountain (sing.), that is, in Western Vermont where I live we have a word for things on the nigh side (reckoning always from Boston) that I like to use on Calvin. We speak of an overthemountain smock, an overthemountain wagon, an overthemountain hayrack. Well he has an overthemountain nature.

Where are you in the summer? I dont suppose within striking distance of us at Sugar Hill N.H. in the White Mountains.

> Sincerely yours
> Robert Frost

[*To Conrad Aiken (1889–1973), in England at the time. Date derived from postmark. ALS. Morgan.*]

> [Sugar Hill, NH]
> [August 28, 1926]

Dear Conrad

My publishers tell me they have given you our joint permission.[29]

Someday I mean to haul off and write you a long letter—either that or get over there and play you a game of tennis. Tennis is neither my vocation

---

26. Incident unknown. At the time, Simeon D. Fess and Frank B. Willis, both Republicans, represented Ohio in the U.S. Senate.

27. Sullivan corresponded with Calvin Coolidge; the letters are on deposit now at the Library of Congress, as a part of the Mark Sullivan Papers. He also wrote of a conversation with Coolidge he once had about New England poets. See Sullivan, *Our Times*, volume 6, *The Twenties* (New York: Charles Scriber's Sons, 1935), 438–439. See also *YT*, 257–258.

28. "Arbiter of poets."

29. Permission from RF and Henry Holt and Company to reprint, in Aiken's *Modern American Poetry* (New York: Modern Library, 1927), "The Road Not Taken," "Home Burial," "The Wood-Pile," "The Fear," "Birches," "The Sound of the Trees," "Hyla Brook," and "The Oven Bird."

nor my avocation: it is my weakness and I am very weak at it, but I will not desist. Would I have to land in English clothes to avoid being insulted on account of the War Debt?[30] Or could I wait till I got ashore to buy them cheaper than I could buy them here. I am sensitive to a number of things but to nothing more than to being held accountable for the United States. You'll notice what that's not saying.

I have recently had an entire reinflamation [*sic*] of my ambition to be a great letter writer. A Mr Hamlin Garland came by here claiming that unless you deliberately wrote literary letters like Van Wyck Brooks with a view to post-humous publication you couldnt be considered for admission to the inner circle of the American Academy. The simile was all his. It's the first I ever heard of Van Wycks [*sic*] writing such letters. I see where hes the next to get taken in out of the cold to succeed Stuart Sherman.[31] I asked Hamlin not to do anything till I found out if it wasnt true as reported that you and Louis Untermeyer were given to exchanging elaborate letters with fine old fashioned passages exemplifying narrative description exposition and ar-gumentation. I'll tell you what I'll do: Later I'll take you on for a stately correspondence such as that of Adams and Jefferson in their old age. Not now but later when we have nothing to gain or lose by it—when we have retired from politics I mean—when we are less of this world than of the next one.

Speaking of Louis, my daughter found someone turning the books over in her bookshop in Pittsfield in the Berkshires the other day, a frail little man not the least martial or retributive-looking. He had very heavy weights in both his coat pockets such as a diver might use to carry him under. These weren't books he had been lifting and they werent bottles and they weren't just stones my daughter was pretty sure. He said he was looking for Virginia Moore.[32] Her Works? No her self [*sic*]. He was her father.[33] What would he do if he found her? Oh nothing—to her. It seems she has gone with the Gaberlunzie

---

30. During World War I, Great Britain's national debt rose from £650m to more than £7.4b in 1919.

31. Stuart Sherman, editor of the "Books" column for the *New York Herald Tribune,* had died.

32. For details of Untermeyer's relationship with Virginia Moore, see RF's December 2, 1927, letter to Sandburg.

33. John Allen Moore.

man[34] and we Frosts are supposed to know where they are living and under what nom de plume. It is significant that in his last anthology Louis had two poems by Yeats two by Jean Untermeyer and two by Virginia Moore. That was Louis in transition. In his next I see no reason why he should change the number by Yeats, but he will doubtless have four by Virginia and none by Jean and it will be consummated. But we Frosts dont know where they are living nor under what name. I'd expect to find them disguised as Dante and Beatrice or Louis anyway as Dante from his known pleasure in being said to look like Dante in profile. I may be accessory after the fact to a mans poetry, but thats no reason why I should be assumed to be accessory to his obscratulations [*sic*].[35] The last I saw of Louis he was thinking of a Russian or Mexican divorce, since Jean wouldn't help him to any other.

May I ask if Emily was consulted as to her inclusions.[36]

The first you know you'll see me over there.

Ever yours

Robert Frost

[*To George Henry Sargent, American bibliographer, book collector, and journalist. Sargent had a summer place called Elm Farm, in Warner, New Hampshire. Date derived from postmark. ALS. Jones.*]

Sugar Hill N.H.

August [30] 1926

Dear Sargent:

I was just telling someone the Devil's changes of residence are as hard to keep track of as mine. He used to inhere in playing baseball on Sunday. But if you laid siege to him there, he would have the laugh on you: that hold is empty. I thought I caught the gleam of his eye today through the lattice of the last place in Gods world where any person ordinarily educated would be looking

---

34. "The Gaberlunzie Man" is a Scots ballad attributed to James V, who (like the figure in the ballad) was said to wander the countryside in disguise, enjoying the pleasures of country girls. The ballad appears in two books RF referred to in his notebooks and essays: Thomas Percy's *Reliques of Ancient English Poetry* (1765), and Francis James Child's *English and Scottish Ballads* (vol. 4, 1886).

35. Likely a misspelling of "absquatulation," a nineteenth-century pseudo-Latin neologism meaning "to abscond."

36. Aiken included in his anthology several poems by Emily Dickinson.

for him. Never mind the name of the place. You are too much of a Universalist or Unitarian or stay-at-home Modernist for anything the Devil does to interest you. I was telling this to a Methodist to whom the Devil still means something (thank God). But the point wasnt so much the Devil as it was me. You think I am at Ann Arbor and, aiming a letter at me there, miss me by at least two removes. Or fancying yourself as in the know, you aim one at me at South Shaftsbury and still you are wide of the mark. I am on Sugar Hill. The worst place to address a letter to me is at Franconia because that makes the Postal department the maddest in the person of the postmaster down there who is sick of forwarding letters to me at Amherst to be forwarded to Ann Arbor to be forwarded to South Shaftsbury to be forwarded to Sugar Hill within five miles of Franconia where it started from.

All this is merely an exercise in theology and geography or theologeography to keep your mind engaged till I can get those books of yours out of storage and back into your bookcase. They are still in Ann Arbor with all my furniture. You shall have them inside of six months which is my idea of a short time.[37]

I wish I might see you some fine day this fall, but I dunno—I am all reacted from the intensities of my last year's preaching. We think I had better stay quiet a long time. It is my loss if I let myself be pulled to pieces.

But I must see you some day not too far distant.

Ever yours
Robert Frost

[To Dorothy Canfield Fisher. Date derived from internal evidence. ALS. Vermont.]

[Sugar Hill, NH]
[circa August 30, 1926]

Dear Dorothy

My children and grandchildren (singular) will believe it when you tell them it is an interesting old historical house they live in.[38] If I told them they might put it down to professional poetry. You go just the right way about fostering

---

37. It took rather longer. See RF to Sargent, November 3, 1927.

38. Canfield Fisher had sent RF a draft of a short essay, "Robert Frost's Hilltop," to be published in the December 1926 issue of *The Bookman*. Accompanying the essay were two woodcuts by J. J. Lankes. The Stone House, the subject of the essay, was occupied by Carol

their fondness for the place and perhaps planting the family on it forever. There is no time like the present, right on top of this to start making it the ancestral home of the Frosts. Five years isnt much toward making it so, but five years is more than four.

We can surely stand having our house praised over our heads, if you think our new neighbors the cast off countesses can who have been buying in among us. What you say is balm of compensation to us for having been left out of the articles in The Banner on the historical houses they have been recently taking up in the Shaftsburys.[39]

No but seriousness aside you make the old house and the region live for us with strokes of the pen. What you dont know and what you dont re-member about men things and happenings in our valley wouldnt take one card in a catalogue. And I suppose we neednt think we have any exclusive place in your memory. You doubtless carry round in your head as much of Kansas Ohio and France as of Vermont.[40] Thats what I am always struck with in your stories—the amount of material you swing. And if I don't al-ways like what you make it come to or seem to prove in the working out, I surely like what you make it come to (you make it prove nothing) this time in Mrs Bascomb.[41] You pack her figure full. You lump her and leave her for what she is. I wonder where all you got her. It would be fun to hear you deal with her the way you did with the Crazy Quilt at Ann Arbor and tell what sights and insights she was composited of.[42] I suppose she is just one of your many. I dont know anyone but myself as well as that. I couldnt go as close as you sometimes do there unless by confession.

---

and Lillian Labatt Frost and their son, Prescott, RF's only grandchild so far; having bought the place in 1920, RF gave it to Carol when he married Lillian in 1923.

39. Shaftsbury, Vermont, includes the communities of South Shaftsbury and Shafts-bury Center.

40. Canfield Fisher was born in Lawrence, Kansas and educated at Ohio State Univer-sity (where her father, James Hulme Canfield, was president), but lived most of her adult life in Vermont. She had been active in war-relief work in France in 1917–1918.

41. Mary Bascomb is the central character in Canfield Fisher's novel *Her Son's Wife* (New York: Harcourt, Brace, 1926). Mrs. Bascomb is widowed and not well disposed toward her only son's wife. She struggles, ruthlessly and in the end successfully, for the power to shape the destiny of her granddaughter, Dibs.

42. A reference to Canfield Fisher's most celebrated short story, "The Bedquilt," first published in *Harper's Magazine* in May 1906. She lectured widely. RF had brought her to the University of Michigan for a reading in March 1923. See RF to Canfield Fisher, Jan-uary 28, 1923; see also RF to Elliott, circa October 15, 1924.

I meant to tell you I have been telling the editors of The Dearborn Independent that you were the one to help them turn their magazine literary, as is now their ambition since they have exhausted the Jew.[43] They seem fearfully in earnest about doing something for the arts with a slight pardonable emphasis on the American as distinguished from the New York arts. I shall do what I can for them. Wouldnt it be splendid if they could lead off with a set of short stories from you.

Just two or three slightest suggestions about the article. It makes me feel a little unhappy to come off too much better than the artist in it.[44] Couldnt

you say: "All very well as a picture. The woodcut is $\begin{cases} \text{beautiful} \\ \text{admirable.} \\ \text{masterly} \end{cases}$

But let the artist take care not to lean for effect too far over on the side of the sombre. This here R. Frost is not etc."[45] And it makes me a little sheepish

---

43. The *Dearborn Independent* had been owned by Henry Ford since 1918 and was a mouthpiece for his anti-Semitic fantasies about international affairs (infamously the publication of parts of *The Protocols of the Elders of Zion*). Criticism and legal action, occasioned by articles in the newspaper, led Ford to moderate its contents and aim for a more "respectable" readership. Lawrance Thompson reports that William J. Cameron, editor of the *Independent*, asked RF to assist in acquiring poetry for the magazine while RF was in Ann Arbor during spring 1926. RF declined, owing to the paper's record of anti-Semitism. But when Cameron assured RF that he intended to transform the paper into a proper literary magazine, the poet agreed to help, suggesting that Marjorie and Lesley screen manuscripts (*YT*, 621). RF himself published two poems and one whimsical playlet in the *Independent*: "The Same Leaves" (later titled "In Hardwood Groves"), December 18, 1926; "Spring Pools," April 23, 1927; and the playlet "The Cow's in the Corn," June 18, 1927. Ford closed the paper down in December 1927. See also RF to Tilley, November 26, 1926, and RF to Brown, early December 1926.

44. Again, J. J. Lankes, who had illustrated *NH* and would illustrate *WRB*. Alongside this section of the letter, in the left margin, RF writes the postscript given here at the letter's end.

45. Canfield Fisher seems to have acceded to RF's request, but in a manner more in keeping with its letter than its spirit. This is how, in the published version of the article, she describes the first of Lankes' woodcuts: "To my eye Mr. Lankes's admirable woodcut of the house is like one of those able portraits of people, of which ordinary inartistic relatives complain, to the exasperation of the artist, 'It's all *right*, I suppose, but it doesn't somehow really look like him. Something about the expression.' . . . The woodcut is masterly as a woodcut but there is certainly something about the expression of the house in it which doesn't look natural to me. It has a rather grim, sombre, depressed look, hasn't it?" She does, however, exculpate RF of the charge of excessive somberness.

to get credit for the woodpile and the sweet peas. Wouldnt it be jolly to say, "his son Carols [*sic*] mountainous woodpile," "his daughter Lillian's sweet peas."[46] I'm a hardened case. I accept a lot of praise I dont deserve and then make it right with myself by sacrificing a tithe of it to the Lord. You must connive a little.

I had the tennis court all ready to play John on if you had come. Better come. It's no journey with a car like yours. You could be over and back before you were missed.[47]

Just at this moment (1.30 A.M.) I am interrupted by the bang of an apple on the roof. Another porcupine is up and at it. To arms! Duty and honor call.

With hurried best wishes to you both.

Ever yours
Robert Frost

You do like the woodcut I hope. We must further Lankes.

[To Harry Jacob Salzberg (1893–1979), salesman and book dealer. ALS. BU.]

Sugar Hill N.H. Sept 9 1926

Dear Mr Salzburg [*sic*]:

No manuscript have I seen from you though I have been on the look out for it since your first letter. There's just a chance that it may have got hung up at South Shaftsbury from where my mail is constantly forwarded. I am writing home to enquire.

Sincerely yours
Robert Frost

46. Lillian Labatt Frost was RF's daughter-in-law. Canfield Fisher complied, this time wholeheartedly: responsibility for the sweet peas and firewood is apportioned as RF desired.

47. John Redwood Fisher was Dorothy Canfield's husband; they lived in Arlington, Vermont, just north of South Shaftsbury.

[To Marjorie Martin Blatchford (1892–1979), who worked in a bookstore and stationer's shop in Pittsfield, Massachusetts. Date derived from internal evidence. ALS. BU.]

[Sugar Hill, NH]
[circa October 1, 1926]

Dear Miss Blatchford:

The folder was fine. Can you get us the Will Rogers book they are advertising and Lewis Mumfords Golden Day?[48] I shall be in to see you all some day on my way somewhere. Glad to hear everything is going so well.

Sincerely yours
Robert Frost

Checks enclosed

[To Lewis Chase (1873–1937). ALS. LoC.]

Sugar Hill N.H.
October 1 1926

Dear Chase:

It will take just exactly one book, my New Hampshire, and no more, to put you abreast of me, and I will see that you get a copy of that as soon as I go home.[49]

You are a long way further from where you were than I am from where I was when we first picked each other up out of the air. My actual home, South Shaftsbury Vermont, isnt more than a hundred miles from the house in Franconia NH where you visited me and at this moment as it happens I am staying for a month or so within three miles of the old place.[50] We are looking at the self same range of mountains; only now it is from deeper in the woods. Look at where you have got to.

---

48. Lewis Mumford's *The Golden Day: A Study in American Experience and Culture* (New York: Horace Liveright, 1926) had just appeared. The book by Will Rogers, also out that fall, is likely *Letters of a Self-Made Diplomat to His President* (New York: Albert and Charles Boni, 1926). RF listed *The Golden Day* under the heading "Ten Books" in a notebook entry likely dating to 1926. See the notes to his January 1, 1926, letter to Bartlett.

49. Since he had last seen Chase RF had published only one new book, his first to win a Pulitzer: *NH.*

50. At the Fobes place outside Franconia.

I suppose you have come back a Buddhist or something if you have been all this time Oriented.[51] The next time I have a running brook on my farm I'll have to have you on to ordain set up and set going a prayer mill in it.[52] I have about reached the age of prayer but I am not so far gone that I wouldnt about as soon have my praying done for me by machinery for a while yet. Me for my knees later.

Don't move—hold steady where you are—till I can get you that book sent.

I often speak of you in public as the Rochesterian who emboldened me in my reading aloud to read each poem twice over lest it should fail of its full effect.[53]

It has warmed me to an unwonted length of letter to hear from you again. Good luck to you.

Sincerely yours
Robert Frost

---

51. In July 1926, Chase had written from California and mentioned that he was scheduled to lecture on RF at UCLA, that he had "passed several years in the Orient," and that he hoped RF would "put me up-to-date with Frostiana." The letter is among the Lewis Nathaniel Chase Papers at the Library of Congress.

52. A prayer wheel figures in one of RF's late poems, "An Importer" (*CPPP*, 360):

Mrs. Someone's been to Asia,
What she brought back would amaze ye. . . .
But the best of her exhibit
Was a prayer machine from Tibet
That by brook power in the garden
Kept repeating Pardon, pardon;
And as picturesque machinery
Beat a sundial in the scenery –
The most primitive of engines
Mass producing with a vengeance. . . .

For some of RF's remarks on Buddhism, see "The Prerequisites" (*CPRF*, 173–174; 331).

53. Chase taught at the University of Rochester in 1917–1918.

[To a Miss Meyers, apparently a schoolteacher, whom we have been unable to identify.
ALS. BU.]

Sugar Hill N.H. (till Nov. 1)
October 16 1926

Dear Miss Meyers:

I like to think I put more of myself into my poems than into anything else I write or deliver. Of course I may not, but I like to think I do. I wonder if you wouldn't prefer a poem in script and inscribed to a message in prose from me. You could pick a poem from my published works or leave the choice to me and run the risk of getting one not yet published. Say frankly which it shall be.

I am not where I can lay hands on a photograph at this moment. But I will send you the nearest I can come to a cabinet size just as soon as I get home to South Shaftsbury Vt.

I am glad to do anything I can for a school named after my favorite American.

Sincerely yours
Robert Frost

[To Hubert N. Hart. ALS. ACL.]

Sugar Hill N.H. (till Nov 1)
October 17 1926

Dear Hart:

I got your stories all right and liked one of them particularly much. I didn't say so, for the simple but humiliating reason that I couldn't remember your address. You are going along smoothly and honestly in your own natural voice. I still feel however that the observations you make, what you remark on in life, doesn't [*sic*] quite matter enough. I still feel that you know "inside stuff" that you wont come out with. My suspicion is that you only tell as much of what you know as you can make fit in with the art of certain authors you admire—their art and their attitude toward God and man. Your own material has got to be everything to you and will be yet. You'll never have an art and an attitude of your own except through complete surrender to your own material. But these are matters for conversation. We must thresh them out when we see each other in the winter. Be sure to come up to Amherst. And get my dates right. I shall be at Amherst all the time from January 3 to March 23. You are my best bet.

Ever yours

Robert Frost

I've just happened to notice the postmark date of your letter—Sept 29. Apparently it has been forwarded only after having lain in wait for me for some time at Amherst. I'm pretty well lost to everybody lately and mean to be. I have had to hide to live.

R.F.

[To Otto Manthey-Zorn. On "Sugar Hill" letterhead. Manthey-Zorn dated the letter to 1923, but internal evidence suggests October 1926. Enclosed is a manuscript copy of "What Fifty Said"; underneath the poem RF appends the remark "Only I dont mean a word of it." ALS. ACL.]

[Sugar Hill, NH]

[October 26, 1926]

Dear Otto:

I didn't set the Rockland man on to you.[54] Maybe Mrs Fobes mentioned you as interested when she gave up the idea of buying the Guernsey place herself.[55] I dont really know whether you want it or not. Of course you dont if we arent sure we are coming back here regularly. Our plans are a sight to contemplate. We have found no home yet in South Shaftsbury we are willing to pay the price for. They are all trying to stick us for millionaires down there. So we are staying in suspense ourselves to keep them in suspense. We can wait. We'll see if they can. While we are waiting we may decide to take the long deferred trip abroad. You see it is all "we may, we may." If we go abroad we wont be here next summer anyway. If we dont we probably will be here. After that probably some more. And yet I dont know. I wish I could see you right off for a talk. Wouldnt it be fun if we could find a small pond somewhere out of the hay fever and a cheap piece of land on it that we could divide. Per-

---

54. Either a Rockland, Massachusetts, real estate agent or the owner of the "Guernsey place" for sale; whatever the case, presumably the "Harney" mentioned later in the letter (the 1940 Census lists an Edmund F. Harney [born 1896] as residing in Rockland).

55. Edith Hazard Fobes, widow of J. Warner Fobes.

haps Elliott would like to come in on it.[56] We ought to take a car and go a hunting. Ernest Hocking[57] found a pond over near Conway and bought all the land touching it, two considerable farms, but for more money than would be my idea. I'd like to have a look at a couple of ponds I know of in Craftsbury VT.

For land the Guernsey place would be hard to beat. It has fields, and woods and an A1 view. I doubt if the springs are above the house place. Still I wouldnt count that as fatal. A lot of people use a hand force pump that does the business. If I were you I should tell Harney to give you time to think it over. I'll bet he'll come down on his figure. Tell him you didnt notice any springs above the house. Ask him to mark them on a sketch map. The way I feel I'd buy the place on speculation if I could get it for 600 dollars. Joll him along a little. Tell him you are more or less interested. Have no scruples to bring him down. He's lying about having sold any land to Mrs Fobes and probably about the elevation of the spring.

Have to report Elinor as clean killed by the recent wedding and so forth.[58] I have been meaning to get down—promised Oldsie[59] I was coming this month; but must linger a week or so more to see if Elinor wont come to. It is imperative that she should do nothing for a while not even practise her manners.

It will be fun to hear you on Europe. You probably have all sorts of stuff that never gets into papers. And any way I have kept from looking into the papers lately to see if it wont make something happen

Ourbesttoyouboth[60]
Ever yours
Robert

Dont even know how foot ball is going.

---

56. George R. Elliott, from 1925 a colleague of RF and Manthey-Zorn at Amherst.

57. William Ernest Hocking, professor of natural religion, moral philosophy and civil polity at Harvard, had been a friend of RF's since 1915.

58. Irma Frost married John Cone on October 15, 1926.

59. George Daniel Olds.

60. Otto and his wife, Ethel Manthey-Zorn.

[To Wilbert Snow. ALS. Wesleyan.]

South Shaftsbury Vermont
November 23 1926

Dear Snow:

I couldn't bring myself to haggle about terms beyond a suggestion that I perhaps ought not to be asked to talk all afternoon with the boys on the two days (or is it three) when I am expected to lecture in the evening.[61] So I am afraid you can't have me as free for play as you would like to ideally. After all what are you dreaming? We ought to think of this as an intensive two weeks with the boys. We'll get in some time together. I must go home to the house with you some of the time, though it seems to be thought best for me to have a headquarters at the college too. These things are not in my hands.

We'll talk about your book that is and mine that is next to be.[62]

Elinor will write to Mrs Snow about her coming with me. She cant get away, I am afraid, till toward the end of the first week.

Ever yours
Robert Frost

[To Louis Untermeyer. RF enclosed manuscripts of two poems, "Lodged," and "The Birthplace"; the texts do not substantially vary from those published in WRB. ALS. LoC.]

South Shaftsbury Vermont
November 25 1926

Dear Louis:

This will be my eighth attempt on you since last we met: from which you may judge how hard you have made it for us, my old. The thing of it was to

---

61. During a two-week residency at Wesleyan (November 18–December 12), RF participated in an "Educational Parley," giving a talk on metaphor on November 30, and a talk titled "The Manumitted Student" on December 5. The latter talk was transcribed and published, without RF's oversight, in the *New Student*, January 12, 1927, 5–7, 2. For an extract from the talk, see *CPRF*, 258–259.

62. *The Inner Harbor*, Snow's second volume of poetry, had been published in 1926 (New York: Harcourt, Brace). RF's *WRB* would be published in 1928.

so word myself that by no shade of meaning I could be suspected of wanting to influence your decision.[63] Whatever you did at a time like this, it musn't be the least bit for me. Of course this is only somewhat and not altogether like changing mounts at the halfway house. It is not the same matter of indifference to your friends and I won't say it is. Ladies arent horses any more than cabbages are watches. You yourself didnt make the change without a pang of regret for the girl left behind. It's no fun being cast off. You saw that. In fact you showed a capacity all through for sustained suffering worthy of a Russian novelist. Let's chalk it up to your credit—to the credit of the whole human race—that you didn't find you could do this invidious thing to Jean without turning a hair. Nor will you blame us if we couldn't watch you do it without turning a hair. Our pang of regret was of course less than yours, but so also were our consolations and compensations infinitely less. We hadn't the physical incentives [to] go ahead at all costs. We weren't in the illusion of the flesh. It was an awkward moment and we had to be careful not to speak discordantly. I can say all this now when it is safely too late to do either good or harm. You see I keep off the merits of the case entirely. Come right down to it my theme is nothing more nor less than my own selfish embarrassment in the affair. But if you and Jean don't care enough to be dissociated in Art and the Miscellaney [sic], I don't see why I should care.

I have been getting down on life lately for one reason or another. The bread I cast upon the waters seems all coming home to roost at once.[64] My philosophy staggers in the breach. But what though my button does lack a shirt—never you mind, roll on![65]

---

63. His decision to divorce Jean Starr Untermeyer and marry the poet Virginia Moore (1903–1993), whom he had met the previous summer at the MacDowell Colony.

64. See Ecclesiastes 11:1: "Cast thy bread upon the waters: for thou shalt find it after many days."

65. An allusion to the second stanza of W. S. Gilbert's (1836–1911) "To the Terrestrial Globe":

It's true I've got no shirts to wear,
It's true my butcher's bill is due,
It's true my prospects all look blue,
But don't let that unsettle you!
Never you mind!
Roll on!

About my part in Art and the Miscellaney: I'm in the middle of sprinkling a bare handful right now over the magazines to pay for Irma's marriage into the deserts of Kansas.[66] There's one that has in it a farmer saying

"A sigh for every so many breath
And for every so many sigh a death.
That's what I always tell my wife
Is the multiplication table of life."[67]

I wish you could have that. But you cant—its sold.

I'm in favor of the Flower Boat too. I wish we could get the original version from the Youth's Companion. My memory of the last stanza is a little shaky. My list would be Lodged, The Flower Boat, and The Birthplace. Maybe I can spare the one act play in one New England dialect. I mean the Cow's in the Corn.[68] But let me sell it if I can. I am short and discouraged. I must write you out Lodged and The Birthplace. I enclose 'em.

> Yours ever
> Robert.

[To Morris Tilley. ALS. Michigan.]

> South Shaftsbury Vermont
> November 26 1926

Dear Morris:

I thought of you often this summer especially when I drove down your old street at Bethlehem to play tennis at the Country Club.[69] You were somewhere

---

66. Untermeyer's *A Miscellany of American Poetry 1927* (New York: Harcourt, Brace, 1927) included RF's "Sand Dunes" (published first in *The New Republic*, December 15, 1926), "The Flower Boat" (first in *The Youth's Companion*, May 10, 1909), "The Passing Glimpse" (*New Republic*, April 21, 1926), "Lodged" (*New Republic*, February 6, 1924) and "The Birthplace" (*Dartmouth Bema*, June 1923). All were collected in *WRB*. Irma Frost had followed her new husband, John Paine Cone, to his family's Kansas farm.

67. These lines appear in "The Times Table," first published in the *New Republic*, February 9, 1927 (and collected in *WRB*).

68. Published in the *Dearborn Independent* for June 18, 1927.

69. The Bethlehem New Hampshire Country Club was founded in 1898. Tilley once owned a house in Bethlehem; he and RF first met in summer 1915, when the Frosts lived in nearby Franconia.

looking at water, while I was there again looking at mountains. We were both fugitives from hay-fever. I hope you got as much out of the break in life with the crowd as I got. I'm one of your slow thinkers who have to take time out once in so often to catch up with what is going on around me and on top of me. I should think it likely that you were too. You look to me sometimes as if the jostle of things made you unhappy. That is to say you look as I feel. I'm all right if I can draw off once in a while and put the world in its place. I'm probably a worse sufferer than you from any apparent meaninglessness in affairs, inasmuch as I am slower witted. It takes me most of the time to figure out what it is all about.

We lingered till November up there in a farm house we had on a back road in the woods on Toad Hill which is behind Iron Mountain near the old Franconia iron mine.[70] You wouldnt know exactly where that is. It is about two miles further from Bethlehem than the house you visited us in. We had bears all around us again this year and I wrote a poem about bears caged and uncaged. I made man out like a bear in a cage. When he walks back and forth from the telescope end to the microscope end of his confinement he is a scientist. When he sits back and sways his head from side to side between metaphysical extremes he is a philosopher. So now you know.[71]

I'm enough ahead on the short poems to feel like scattering a few to the magazines. I'm not forgetting my promise to the editor of the Virginia Quarterly your friend.[72] The Dearborn Independent has gone in for one or two rather heavily. You know I sat up a night or two with the Independent when I was out there.[73] One of the young editors became quite a friend. I didn't get in with Henry so's you'd notice any difference in me. The editor of McCall's is giving Lesley $250.00 for one of my sonnets.[74] At that rate a sonnet a

---

70. The Frosts spent nearly four months in Sugar Hill, New Hampshire, during late summer and early fall. Two iron works had been established in Franconia in the nineteenth century, drawing their ore from mines in or near Sugar Hill. Both had ceased operation by the time RF moved to Franconia.

71. See "The Bear," collected first (as were the other poems mentioned or alluded to in this letter) in *WRB*.

72. James Southall Wilson founded *The Virginia Quarterly* in 1925, and served as its editor until 1931, when he was succeeded by Stringfellow Barr. RF's "Acquainted with the Night" first appeared in *VQ* in October 1928.

73. See the notes to RF's August 30, 1926, letter to Canfield Fisher.

74. "A Soldier," published in *McCall's Magazine* in May 1927.

day would keep the sheriff from the door. It is permitted us to brag to a few on the inside.

June July August September October November—six months my isolation has run into. What after all can I expect more? Any one of any speed should produce a book in that time.

November 29th I begin my two weeks at Wesleyan (Connecticut) and the respite is ended. I am not actually going on the road any more but I plan to be a-colleging more or less in my ineffectual way for two or three months. Another year I shall cut it down still further. I think I have worked it out at last so I can get a little writing done. I really need to be far far away by myself in the dead quietness for whole months at a time if I am ever going to do an epic.

We are trying to buy a farm cheap.

My friend Louis Untermeyer has gone to Mexico to buy a divorce cheap. Which makes me less chipper about life than I might otherwise be.[75]

Let's all be reasonably decent—as decent as we can without actually going over to Romanism.

My best to you.

Faithfully yours
Robert Frost

Is the editor of the Virginia Quarterly named Wilson?

[To Sharon Brown. Dated from internal evidence. ALS. BU.]

South Shaftsbury Vermont
[December 1926]

Dear Brown

I got the Dearborn Independent people into it before they were ready; so now let me get them out.[76] We thought my daughter Margery was going to

---

75. For this, the beginning of Untermeyer's complex marital adventures in the mid- to late 1920s, see RF to Untermeyer, November 25, 1926.

76. In spring 1926, the editors of the *Dearborn Independent*—in an effort to transform the magazine from a platform for Henry Ford's anti-Semitic conspiracy mongering into a respectable literary operation—asked RF to help them acquire poetry. Believing they were sincere, RF agreed to help, suggesting that Marjorie and Lesley screen manuscripts (*YT*, 621). This is how several of Brown's poems (discussed in the letter) came into the

undertake finding their poetry for a while, but her health has proved not up to the job. Another daughter may undertake it and then again she may not—she is so very busy with her bookstore at sea and ashore. (She is taking a "branch" of it around the world this winter on the Franconia.[77]) All is uncertainty about our connection with The Independent you see. So I guess you had better have your poems back where they wont feel lost. Margery liked Query best, especially the second stanza of it. On the Death of a Gentlewoman and Alchemy are good too. Tremble tremble hurts Alchemy. It is a little too utterly uttered. Your reader isnt as excited as all that. Look out for the aesthetic. I mean guard against it. It can be the antithesis of art. <u>Can</u> be. Preciosity too is a danger with you. I say this as a personal friend merely. And it is the merest hint of a misgiving. I'm a great believer in you and have been.

Best wishes for your journey abroad.

Always your friend
Robert Frost

[*To John W. Haines. Dated from postmark. Enclosed on a separate sheet is "The Minor Bird" (retitled "A Minor Bird" in* WRB). *ALS. DCL.*]

[South Shaftsbury, VT]
[December 7, 1926]

Dear Jack:

Do you know what you are going to get for being such a good boy ever since first I knew you? I am going to mail you a poem a week or better for the next few weeks till Christmas say, out of my most recent doings so as to keep you as twere abreast of me and prepare you for the kind of person you may expect to meet if I get over there next summer as I hope to.[78] This is at once

---

Frost family hands. None was printed in the *Dearborn Independent* (which shut down in December 1927). See the notes to RF's August 30, 1926, letter to Canfield Fisher.

77. RF's eldest daughter, Lesley, sailed on the SS *Franconia* from New York City on January 12, 1927; she operated a bookstore on board. The store "ashore" was The Open Book, which Lesley and her sister Marjorie had opened in Pittsfield, Massachusetts, in 1924.

78. RF made good on this promise. In an "Open Book" envelope posted from South Shaftsbury on December 30, 1926, he sent typed copies of "Once by the Pacific," "Bereft," and "The Same Leaves" (the last, as "In Hardwood Groves," he would add to the contents of *ABW* for *Collected Poems* [1930]). At the bottom of "Bereft" in RF's handwriting is

your reward and punishment (it is the new fashion to punish people for being good). So be prepared for almost anything. And to begin with is enclosed one called The Minor Bird—with my love to you all three.[79]

Robert

[To Sidney Cox. Dated from postmark. ALS. DCL.]

South Shaftsbury Vermont
[December 22, 1926]

Dear Sidney

I can think of nothing but how glad I am you are at Hanover safely un-hanged. You were too many hours ahead of your time out there on Rocky Mountain Time and there was always danger of its giving you an exaggerated sense of your own importance and so getting you into trouble with the Kew Clucks.[80] Be at peace now and like your opportunities as much as in you lies to like anything human. I wouldnt give a hoot in derision for the difference between the boys in one college and the boys in another. There are the same kinds in all of them, your kind and the other fellow's kind. It will take time of course for your own to gravitate to you. Time is an element, is of the essence, of everything.

Don't count on me to do anything for Dartmouth or any other college—unless it is through my poems. Read those to the boy under you, but dont rub them into him. I understand that my last visit to Hanover was a little worse than wasted. It is as I would have it. I need all the excuse I can muster for desisting from the colleges. They are none of mine. I didnt invent them and I should be a fool to think in my heart I could really make them over. I'm re-

---

"Further confidences." There are minor differences, mostly in punctuation, from the published versions of "Once by the Pacific" and what would later be called "In Hardwood Groves." "Bereft" also exhibits minor differences from the version published, and two somewhat more significant ones: in line 3, "my looking out for" would become "my standing there for"; and in line 6, "Summer was passed and day was passed" would become "Summer was past and day was past."

79. Jack, his wife Dorothy, and their son Robin.

80. The Ku Klux Klan, less of a presence in Hanover, New Hampshire (Cox having recently started work at Dartmouth), than in Missoula, Montana (where he had been living). RF also alludes to the scandal (in Missoula) that Cox got himself into (see RF to Cox, April 8, 1926).

cessive in teaching. I suppose it flattered me to be called back to meddle in a system as teacher that I spurned as pupil. And that's why I yielded to the temptation. I'm vain like some other people. But I dont stay vain over the same folly all the time. I used to want to think I might become a tennis player by the time I was sixty. I draw in. Im willing to leave tennis playing to those who start young and give their selves to it—tennis playing to tennis players and teaching to teachers. I'm a farmer.

On with the excitement as Byron said.[81] You do what you see to do and Dartmouth will come all right for you without my interposition. Aren't we funny fanciers? You think invoking me would save the pieces. Be disenchanted. I've got too much Amherst Wesleyan Bowdoin and Michigan on my conscience as it is. Another year I must be free from all but Amherst and one other. I'm in hopes of a few more poems before Gabriel blows his trumpet. You see I already have quite a start in poetry.

Speaking of starts.

At Williamstown the other day I heard a workman on the college grounds lament the death of a student worth five millions. "Why weep on an uncertainty," I said. "Wasnt there a good chance of the boy's coming into something better in Heaven than five millions?" The workman (evidently French Canadian and so probably Catholic) gave me a curious look to see if he could make out in what sense I said that. "He'd be a pretty lucky boy to get two such starts in succession," was his answer.

"Then for this reason and for a season

Let us be merry before we go." (Curran)[82]

Merry Christmas to you all.

> Ever yours
> Robert Frost

Mrs Irma Cone's address is Rozel Kansas.[83]

---

81. See Byron, *Childe Harold's Pilgrimage* (1816), canto 3, stanza 22: "On with the dance! let joy be unconfined; / No sleep till morn, when Youth and Pleasure meet / To chase the glowing hours with flying feet."

82. The closing lines of "The Deserter's Meditation" (circa 1786) by the Irish poet and orator John Philpot Curran (1750–1817).

83. Home of John Paine Cone, Irma Frost's new husband.

[To John Bartlett. ALS. UVA.]

South Shaftsbury Vt
Dec 23 1926

Dear John

Elinor has been about to send the enclosed to the children every day for the last two weeks. The general family sickness has prevented her. Never mind what it all is. My sickness is with sickness. We'll all survive this time.

We're always thinking of you away out there and meaning to see you when we get round to it. I may someday give in and make a lecture tour of your region. There would now be the extra inducement of Irma who is just down the slope from you a couple of hundred miles at Rozel farming under the married name of Mrs John Paine Cone as I don't know but that you may have been told.

Some time send us separate snapshots of all the kids with character sketches of them in writing on the back.[84] That would help us a lot to keep us acquainted till we can get to you.

I'm sprinkling a few poems around again—just a few, in the New Republic, Yale Review etc.[85] They are my product for the last three years. Most of them have some age on them. Im the same old slow poke.

I heard from John C. Chase[86] out of a clear sky last week after a silence between us of ten years. He seems to be flourishing as President of The Historic Genealogical Society of America to judge by his letter head. He didnt tell much news of Derry though he said he had a lot of it. I must ask him why not Historical Genealogic or Historical Genealogical or Historic Genealogic. I should have to start teasing again to put things on their old familiar footing. Along there in 1910 we had about teased each other out of friendship. He would tease me about unpublished poetry and when he asked how much I would charge for the Pinkerton Catalogue I had written for him I would answer I had nothing to go on but the price I got for poetry when I got any at all which

---

84. Margaret (age three), Richard (five), John Jr. (nine), and Forrest (eleven).

85. In 1926 the *New Republic* published "Sand Dunes" on December 15, and "Once by the Pacific" on December 29, and, in early 1927, "A Winter Eden," "Bereft," "The Cocoon," and "The Times Table." In July 1927, the *Yale Review* published "The Common Fate" (later collected as "A Peck of Gold"), "Tree at My Window," and "The Rose Family."

86. John C. Chase was secretary of the Pinkerton Academy board of trustees and chairman of its executive committee. He also served as president of the New England Historic Genealogical Society, the oldest genealogical society in the United States, for fourteen years.

to be sure wasn't often—five cents a word.[87] He said it looking grim. But after all he was a personality. I liked his story and I liked him.

In another letter connected with Christmas I'll tell you about someone else who turned up from the old days. No one very objectionable. Still not exactly in the Christmas spirit to be reminded of.

We had nearly a week away below zero and enough snow to scare you for your Ford. But now it is raining.

Happy year ahead!

Ever yours
Robert Frost

[To Mark Antony De Wolfe Howe. Date derived from internal evidence. ALS. Harvard.]

[Amherst, MA]
[January 1927]

Dear Howe

Come right down to it, I am not a good person to put on committees because I want too much in this world to expect anything. But look at what has been done to English A while the old skeptic sat surlily out! And what is this about intermissions of three weeks in winter and spring to relieve teachers of some of the burden of teaching and so make them not only better scholars but better teachers?[88] The first thing we know we shall have it granted that the best way to teach students to do original work is for the teacher to do original work

---

87. RF charged Chase $40 to write a description of the English department for the Pinkerton Academy catalogue (see CPRF, 74 76, 256–257).

88. English A had long been a compulsory course for freshmen at Harvard. But that would soon change, as reported in the *Harvard Crimson*, January 4, 1927: "On December 21, 1926, the Faculty of Arts and Sciences passed the vote submitted to them by the Department of English approving the abolition of the present anticipatory examination in English A. As a substitute for this examination, candidates for admission to Harvard College passing the Comprehensive paper in English with a grade of 70 percent or higher will be relieved from the prescribed work in English A. This change will take effect this spring. . . . English A, the prescribed course for Freshmen, has long been one of the largest and most famous courses in the College curriculum. Next year, under the new regulations, its membership is expected to diminish by over one third, which will in many ways change the nature of the course." The new emphasis on scholarship, about which RF remarks, would soon draw to Harvard F. O. Matthiessen (in 1930) and Perry Miller (in 1931).

himself, and in real scholarship as in art, he who lives most to himself lives most for other people, his disciples included. Then there will be nothing more to complain of in American education and it will serve me right.

My hopes and fears are all with Bliss Perry and you.[89]

I see a glimmer of something to suggest in what you have to report about the students having taken their training in oral debate into their own hands to a certain extent. I fear I should be tempted to try if witholding [sic] on them still longer wouldnt make them take it still further into their own hands. It would be just like me sometime to try what witholding the whole subjects of writing and reading for a while would do for literature in college. You won't believe me serious—and that's why I shouldn't dare to come to your committee meetings. I don't mean I should desert the poor children entirely with poetry—for good and all. I just shouldn't be so forward with it as some of us are now. Like Cloe [sic] (was it?) I might not run away so far that I couldnt be overtaken, but I should run away.[90] There never was anything like an artful alternation between refusing and yielding to whet the appetite.

What a long way we have come in our relations since the days when you were an editor and I was your occasional poet.[91]

Sincerely yours
Robert Frost

---

89. Though not a member of the Harvard faculty, Howe had a long association with the university, having obtained his MA degree there in 1888, served as editor of the *Harvard Alumni Bulletin*, and, in 1918, been appointed "Biographer of the Harvard Dead in the War against Germany." Bliss Perry (1860–1954), an American literary critic and educator, was professor of English at Harvard from 1906 to 1930. Harvard's official history of its Department of English—compiled by Stephen Hequembourg and published on-line— notes that "with the arrival of Bliss Perry in 1906 American literature received new emphasis. Perry's concerns were primarily aesthetic rather than historical or philological, and he was eager to teach the modern novel. He gave lectures on *Madame Bovary* over the objections of many to its perceived lewdness, and taught *Moby-Dick* when it was a largely forgotten novel."

90. Presumably a reference to the myth of Demeter (also known as Chloe) and Poseidon. Demeter, in the shape of a mare, fled from Poseidon and hid among the horses of King Onkios. Poseidon took the form of a stallion, pursued her, and found her out.

91. Howe was associate editor of *The Youth's Companion* from 1888 to 1893 and again from 1899 to 1913. During the latter term Howe published two of RF's poems, "October" (in October 1912) and "The Flower Boat" (in May 1909).

[*To Edward Lewis Davison. TG. DCL.*]

AMHERST MASS JAN 24 [1927]

PROF EDWARD DAVISON

SECOND WEEK IN FEBRUARY MOST OPEN CHOOSE ANY DAY BUT TUESDAY AND
SATURDAY FOR LECTURE[92] WILL YOU DO IT FOR A HUNDRED FOR ME WANT BOTH
OF YOU OF COURSE AND WANT YOU FOR AS MANY DAYS AS YOU CAN STAY LOTS TO
TALK ABOUT YOU KNOW[93]

ROBERT FROST

[*To Rita Halle (1885–1871), American socialite and author. ALS. Wellesley.*]

Amherst Mass January 12 1927

My dear Mrs Halle:

I am glad you are going to use my book plate by J. J. Lankes.[94] He is an
artist I am always proud to have my name linked with: and I wish him the
widest recognition. My thanks for both of us for your very kind letter.

Sincerely yours
Robert Frost

[*To Wilfred Davison. ALS. Middlebury.*]

Amherst Mass
January 25 1927

Dear Davison:

You begin to know what I am—begin I say. From year to year I plan to
go back and pay my party call in Europe. If I didnt go last year (much as I

---

92. Davison delivered a lecture at Amherst, "An Approach to Poetry," on Monday,
February 7, 1927.

93. Almost certainly the problems that sprung from RF's decision to have Gorham
Munson, and not Davison, write about him in the "Murray Hill" biography series published by George H. Doran. "Both of you" is Davison and his wife, Natalie.

94. RF enclosed a copy of his bookplate, which bears the legend "Ex Libris Robert
Frost" over a woodcut by Lankes, with whom RF had collaborated since 1923, when
Lankes illustrated "The Star-Splitter."

expected to), all the more probability of my going this. Still I may not go this, next, nor the next after. Do you want to put me down as a visitor on the off chance that my procrastination will carry me safely past at least one more summer?[95] We'll make my contract with you conditional on my staying at home. I leave it to you to say.

Remember me to your President with my best.[96]

Always yours faithfully
Robert Frost.

[*To Elizabeth M. Tarney (1916–1983). In 1927 Tarney was a grade-school student in Manchester, New Hampshire. ALS. UVA.*]

Amherst Mass
January 25 1927

My dear Elizabeth:

That picture was of exactly the trees in ice I had in mind. It looks as if they were trailing not only their hair on the ground but their hands too.[97] You are as much given to noticing nature as I am. The picture shows it and the poems show it. I like particularly in the poems the idea that the spring flood is so deep there are no rough rapids for the fish to fear. Dont you think "rough" would be a better word there than "deep." I merely suggest it.

Thank you for the whole envelope full, letter poems and picture.

Sincerely your friend
Robert Frost

I was one New Hampshire poet. Then you wrote some poems and now there are two of us.

R. F.

---

95. RF did not visit Europe in the summer of 1927 and did in fact, after considerable "procrastination," spend three days at the Bread Loaf School of English (*YT*, 683).

96. Paul Dwight Moody, president of Middlebury College.

97. The language describes the trees in RF's "Birches," first published in the *Atlantic Monthly* in August 1915 and later collected in *MI*.

[To Edward Lewis Davison. Sent to Davison at Vassar. TG. DCL.]

AMHERST MASS JAN 28 1927

PROFESSOR EDWARD DAVISON

FEBRUARY SEVENTH THEN LOOKING FORWARD WILL YOU GIVE US SOME TITLE FOR
LECTURE[98] TERRIBLE OUT-COME FOR UNTERMEYERS SAD WORLD[99]

ROBERT FROST

*[To Margaret P. Porth (1910–1995), at the time a seventeen-year-old high school student
in Mount Clemens, Michigan. ALS. DCL.]*

Amherst Mass

Feb 2 1927

Dear Miss Porth

Isnt it too bad your letter was so long in reaching me here at Amherst Mass?
Now it is too late to help you I dont know that there was much I could have
done anyway. The biographical material is so scattered in various books. One
of the best places to look me up is in Louis Untermeyer's Modern American
Poetry (Harcourt Brace & Co. New York). He tells a good deal and gives a
good number of my poems. Two biographies of me are to appear this year.
The New Republic printed one of the best things about me last year. You could
perhaps find it in the files. Miss E. S. Sergeant wrote it. She is just publishing
it with other papers in a book with Knopf. [100] Probably the book you speak of

---

98. The lecture Davison delivered at Amherst on this date. "An Approach to Poetry."

99. On January 26, Richard Untermeyer, only child of Louis and Jean Starr Unter
meyer (recently divorced after twenty years of marriage), had been discovered hanged in
his room at Yale. Louis Untermeyer initially rejected suicide as a motive, suggesting
Richard's death was the accidental outcome of an experiment "to test the sensations of
strangulation" (Associated Press, January 27, 1927).

100. See Gorham Munson, *Robert Frost: A Study in Sensibility and Good Sense* (New
York: George H. Doran, 1927), and Elizabeth Shepley Sergeant, *Fire Under the Andes: A
Group of North American Portraits* (New York: Alfred A. Knopf, 1927). The chapter devoted
to RF in the latter book derives from Sergeant's article, "Robert Frost, A Good Greek
Out of New England," *The New Republic*, September 30, 1925. Sergeant would later pub-
lish a full-length biography of the poet, *Robert Frost: The Trial by Existence* (New York:
Holt, Rinehart and Winston, 1960).

is Modern Tendencies in American Poetry by Amy Lowell.[101] You might like
to go to The New Republic for some lyrics I have been publishing lately—six
in the last two or three months.[102]

The best thing to do is get hold of some of my own books if you care at all.
You mustn't take too much trouble over me.

Best wishes.

Sincerely yours
Robert Frost

[*To Lewis Gannett (1891–1966), author, journalist, and editor. In 1927 he was on the
editorial staff of* The Nation. *Gannett was best known for his daily book review column
for the* New York Herald Tribune. *ALS. Columbia.*]

Amherst Mass

February 3 1927

Dear Mr Gannett:

There it goes again!—my inability to write reviews making me desperately
unhappy. I have been a great admirer of Mark Van Doren's poetry from the
first.[103] But that, I know, isn't enough. I should want to come out for it. But
I am not the least bit in the way of reviewing. I never wrote a review in my
life. The very thought of reviewing scares me incoherent. I was in the same
predicament over Ridgley [*sic*] Torrences Hebrides—I mean Hesperides: and
I think he was over my last book.[104] I'm sorry to be such an unready in
prose.—Let me not pretend I am any less unready in verse.

Sincerely yours
Robert Frost

---

101. Lowell, *Tendencies in Modern American Poetry* (New York: Macmillan, 1917), 79–138
(on RF).

102. The poems include "Sand Dunes," December 15, 1926; "Once by the Pacific,"
December 29, 1926; "A Winter Eden," January 12, 1927; "Bereft," February 9, 1927; "The
Cocoon," February 9, 1927; "The Times Table," February 9, 1927.

103. Presumably Gannett had asked RF to review Van Doren's recently published
7 P.M. and Other Poems (New York: Albert and Charles Boni, 1926).

104. Ridgely Torrence published his second collection of verse, *Hesperides,* in 1925
(New York: Macmillan). Louis Untermeyer gave it a good review in the *Saturday Review
of Literature,* May 16, 1925. RF's "A Passing Glimpse" (in *WRB*) is a review of sorts, in poetic form, of Torrence's volume. It bears the dedication "To Ridgely Torrence / On Last
Looking into His 'Hesperides.'" RF's "last book" (*NH*) had been reviewed by Robert Lit-

[*To Sidney Cox. Date derived from postmark. ALS. DCL.*]

[Amherst, MA]
[February 7, 1927]

Dear Sidney:

You <u>would</u> exaggerate me into the most conspicuous prose writer in your collection you doting friend and so disqualify me for doing anything to boost the book.[105] I don't care if you don't. A little undeserved praise now and then will only make it up to me in advance or arrears for the undeserved blame I am always getting—or suppose I am always getting—I never look in the reviews to see. You have more to lose by your act than I have. I am estopped from using or recommending for use any anthology in which I am made to shine.[106] But as I dont use any anthologies at all or think of them to mention in my travels perhaps you are not so much out there as you might at first seem to be. I did carry your beautiful book so beautifully printed to my class in philosophy the other day for the dialogue between Hermotimus and Lucien—one of my most favoritest pieces in the known universe.[107] Isnt that a lovely boy in there? Nearly the whole book proved good reading or rereading. And I must say the biocritical forwards are hard to resist. I'm a Fool is probably Anderson's best though to my nerves it scrapes false in a spot or two. Wilbur Daniel Steele's story has lighthouse in it.[108] My only wonder is that you didnt find anything of Sherman's to

---

tell in the *New Republic,* December 5, 1923, 24–26. Torrence was the magazine's poetry editor.

105. Sidney Cox and Edward Freeman, eds., *Prose Preferences* (New York: Harper and Brothers, 1926), containing RF's short essay "The Poetry of Amy Lowell" (see *CPRF,* 88). See also RF to Cox, May 17, 1926. In the book Cox and Freeman call RF, "when he cares to use it, a master of virile, concentrated prose. He is one good foundation for pride in being American" (*RFSC,* 178).

106. "Estop" is a legal term for the prevention of acts that might have unjust or inequitable consequences.

107. *Hermotimus, or Concerning the Sects,* is a dialogue by Lucian of Samosata (circa 125–180 AD), in which Hermotimus' youthful interlocutor, Lycinus, scoffs at the sterility of academic philosophizing.

108. Sherwood Anderson, "I'm a Fool," originally published in *Horses and Men* (New York: B. W. Huebsch, 1923); Wilbur Daniel Steele, "The Woman at Seven Brothers" (in which a lighthouse figures), originally published in *Land's End, and Other Stories* (New York: Grosset and Dunlap, 1918).

bring in.[109] But I can see how you would refuse to be held answerable for inclusiveness. I'm not particularly in favor of covering in my poetry that I know of.

We are still under the cloud of Marjorie's long illness. Our day in the house revolves around her. She reads a little plays the piano a little and plays cards a little: but she has to be kept from doing even such things too much. Sometimes we get fearfully disheartened. More than glimpses of people seem to exhaust her. She cant be left too much by herself. It seems to me it must be something like your sisters [*sic*] case.[110] The doctors now call it nervous prostration. The nervous prostrates I have seen however were set serious. Marj has her ironies and her grins.

Lesley is on one of the winter tours around the world with a branch of her book store.[111] Shes past Samoa by now. The last letter from her was from Honolulu (sp.) With Irma married into Kansas and Carol away in Vermont we feel a pretty scattered family.

I get a little poem out of it now and then. I might include you one or two in this.[112]

Be seeing you soon.

Best to you all.

Robert Frost

→over[113]

---

109. Stuart Pratt Sherman (1881–1926), literary critic and journalist, had died the previous summer.

110. Cox's younger sister, Gertrude, was a lifelong sufferer from neurasthenia (*RFSC*, 9).

111. The Round-the-World Bookshop on the SS *Franconia*.

112. Enclosed are two typed and signed poems, "What Fifty Said" and "A Soldier," together with the two poems noted below.

113. On the reverse of the sheet RF wrote out and initialed fair copies of "The Rose Family" and "The Minor Bird." They are substantially as published in *WRB*. The only significant variation is "peach," instead of "pear" in the published version, in line 5 of "The Rose Family." At the bottom of the sheet containing "The Rose Family" RF notes: "Plenty of others in New. Rep. lately." "Sand Dunes" was published in the *New Republic* on December 15, 1926, "Once by the Pacific" on December 29, and "A Winter Eden" on January 12. All of the poems associated with this letter would appear in *WRB*, although "What Fifty Said" was added to *WRB* only when this volume was incorporated into RF's *Collected Poems* (1930).

[To Alfred Kreymborg (1883–1966), American poet, novelist, playwright, editor, and anthologist. Year derived from internal evidence. ALS. UVA.]

Amherst
Feb 16 [1927]

Dear Alfred:

I guess you'll have to go ahead without me. I can't hope to make up my mind about this play in time.[114] I deserve to be telegraphed after just as much as an unanswering little boy deserves to be shouted at but neither telegraphing nor shouting seem to conduce very much to the collecting of wits and faculties. Elinor says let it be a lesson to me never to mention anything again I have in process. Well I'm sorry but relieved. I can promise anything but my writing. I wish I could see you or you could see me: you would see how honestly distressed I have been. I've been a wreck ever since your telegram came. Have a heart.

I hear [you're] taking Americans to Europe in the summer.[115] I suppose that precludes your coming to Bread Loaf this year. The Dean was going to invite you for the advanced session when I look in for a day or so.[116] You were one of the inducements he offered me.

Now don't you go to imagining nothing.

Ever yours
Robert Frost

[To Wilbur L. Cross. ALS. Yale.]

Amherst February 24 1927

My dear Cross

Is it too much to ask you to read these small poems in hand writing. One of my daughters who do my type writing for me has just married into the deserts of Kansas another is selling books at this moment in Papua or New

---

114. It seems RF had agreed to contribute to *One-Act Plays for Stage and Study, Third Series: Twenty-One Contemporary Plays Never Before Published in Book Form* (New York: Samuel French, 1927), with a preface by Percival Wilde. Though Kreymborg did not edit the book, he was—as were RF's friends Percy MacKaye and Padraic Colum—a contributor. It is unclear whether RF was at work on one of his two surviving unpublished plays: "In An Art Factory" and "The Guardeen" (see *CPPP*, 576–625).

115. Kreymborg and his wife, Dorothy, traveled frequently to Europe during the late 1920s.

116. Wilfred Davison.

Guinea and a third is under doctors orders to do nothing but rest.[117] If I wait for their offices you may never see the poems.

The three I have had chiefly in mind for you would make a good group in this order—dont you think?

The Rose Family
The Minor Bird
My Window Tree

The Investment which I am sending along too would hardly harmonize with the group.[118] It ought to appear alone if at all. But decision with you and Miss McAfee—to whom be the praise if anything is done right in magazines that is done.[119]

> Faithfully yours
> Robert Frost

I find I am still campaigning with Miss McAfees copy of my own last book. Do you suppose that will cloud her judgements of me?

[*To Elizabeth M. Tarney. Date derived from internal evidence. ALS. UVA.*]

> [Amherst, MA]
> [circa February 1927]

Dear Miss Tarney:

You can cut the above autograph out and paste it into your book. It wouldn't be right for me to sign a book so much of your making. Your name should appear on the title page rather than mine. As long as it is a scissor-and-paste book anyway my augraph [*sic*] should be cut and pasted too it seems to me. I

---

117. Irma Frost Cone had settled with her new husband, John, in Rozel, Kansas. On January 12, Lesley Frost set sail (for a round-the-world cruise) on the SS *Franconia,* on which she operated a bookstore called the Round-the-World Bookshop. Marjorie Frost, in frail health since December 1925, was still convalescing.

118. "The Rose Family," "The Minor Bird," and "My Window Tree" (renamed "Tree at My Window" for *WRB*) were published in the *Yale Review* in July 1927, together with "The Common Fate" (renamed "A Peck of Gold" for *WRB*) and "The Investment."

119. Helen Flora McAfee, assistant to Cross at the *Yale Review.*

appreciate all the pains you have been to to make the book complete.[120] You seem to have had a pleasant time.

Always yours friendly
Robert Frost

[*To Mary E. Cooley. ALS. Michigan.*]

Amherst Mass March 5 1927

My dear Mary Cooley:

It is settled that we are coming back to see you in two or three weeks now.[121] I hope that gives you girls plenty of time to get some poems ready for me to read that I can honestly like. I am sick of poems I can only dishonestly like. My dishonesty is getting to be too much of a good thing. Which may sound pretty mixed up in the mind, but if so, all I can ask is who mixed me up? I mean which generation? You think it over. It is the kind of intelligence question you may expect to have to answer more of if you sign up for my one hour-a-week-for-one-week-in-the-year course in creative creation. And by the way dont let the authorities crowd that course out of my schedule. You'd better get after them, you and Sue Grundy Bonner and Dorothy Tyler.[122] I have half a mind to ask Mrs Little to have it at her house since she turns out to be so much one of us.[123]

I'm in earnest about wanting you to have written some poems. My standing order for always is if you haven't written any, write some. The oil is as good

---

120. See RF's January 25, 1927, letter to Tarney. A grade-school student at the time, Miss Tarney sent RF some poems and a picture inspired by RF's poem "Birches." It seems likely that Tarney had then sent RF the completed "book" she had been working on.

121. RF held a weeklong residency at Michigan beginning in late March.

122. Students at Michigan. RF had worked with them (as he had with Cooley) in 1926. Bonner and Cooley were members of Collegiate Sororis (established at Michigan in 1886); Tyler was on the editorial board of the undergraduate literary magazine, *The Inlander,* to which RF contributed "The Minor Bird" in January 1926 (he changed the title to "A Minor Bird" when he brought it into *WRB*). Tyler published her *Poems* in Detroit in 1932. Shortly after RF died, she published a short essay about him, "Remembering Robert Frost" (*Among Friends* no. 29 [Winter 1962–1963]: 1–4).

123. Katherine D. Andrews, who married University of Michigan president Clarence Cook Little in 1911; she had published poems in magazines.

as anything for life and a living.[124] I have no objection to oil for the direct attack. You've got to go at something directly. But the more you know what to do with yourself the more real the poetry that ought to come of it.

Remember me to your mother and father.[125]

Sincerely yours
Robert Frost

[*To Eva A. Speare (née Clough) (1875–1972), a playmate of RF's during his time in Lawrence, Massachusetts, in the mid-1880s. In a 1962 letter (typescript extracts of which are held at DCL) explaining the occasion for this correspondence, Mrs. Speare recalled that some childhood mischief on RF's part had led her grandmother to anathematize him as "That Frost Boy." ALS. DCL.*]

Amherst Mass March 12 1927

My dear Mrs Speare:

What a pity your national meeting comes so late in the season.[126] I end my visit at Ann Arbor this year by April 6th and by June 2nd I shall be where I am afraid it would cost you too much to bring me from. I am pleased and honored, of course, to have been thought of for your great occasion.

I am not so much a deserter of New England as you seem to think. I still spend a large part of the year in Vermont and New Hampshire. I'm doing the itinerant teacher this year at Wesleyan, Amherst, Michigan, Dartmouth, and Bowdoin—two to ten weeks in each. I expect to be ten weeks at Amherst every year from now on. It is a strange relation to colleges I have grown into.

My very best regards to you and Mr Speare.[127]

Always yours sincerely
Robert Frost

---

124. Cooley was then completing her M.S. in geology (with an emphasis on petroleum) at Michigan. See also RF to Cooley, September 19, 1927.

125. Charles Horton Cooley (1864–1929) and his wife Elsie Jones Cooley (1864–1953).

126. Speare was chair of the program for a General Federation Conference of Women's Clubs to be held in June 1927 in Grand Rapids, Michigan.

127. Guy E. Speare (1876–1945), educationalist, graduated from Dartmouth in 1903 and earned an MEd from Harvard in 1926. From 1921 to 1944 he was director of training at Plymouth Normal School, where RF had taught from 1911 to 1912.

[To Alexander Gardiner (1889–1977), a student at Pinkerton Academy when RF taught there (1906–1911). Date derived from postmark. ALS. Brown.]

[Amherst, MA]
[March 14, 1927]

Dear Mr Gardiner

It seems as if I ought to do more than autograph your book under the circumstances. I'll have to write a stanza of verse in it for old sake's sake. Suppose I write a line or two of the poem in A Boys Will that got me my job teaching in Pinkerton Academy.[128] That might mean something to you when it wouldnt to much of anybody else.

I haven't been near the school for some years now. I knew Reynolds held on and thought perhaps Sylvia Clark held on. Horne came after my time. My bosses were Bingham and Silver. I went with Silver to the Normal School at Plymouth where I taught psychology for a year. I suppose John C. Chase is still a trustee.[129] I had a letter from him a week or two ago asking me to look him up when I was in Boston. He was my great friend, though he would tease me about my verse.

I leave here for Ann Arbor on March 23. I stay at Ann Arbor till April 4.[130] After that the best place to reach me with the book would be South Shaftsbury Vermont. My address at Ann Arbor Michigan will be c/o Dean Joseph Bursley.[131] You see I am a shameless wanderer.

---

128. RF refers to "The Tuft of Flowers," but the poem inscribed in Gardiner's copy of *ABW* is "Atmosphere," first published as "Inscription for a Garden Wall" in *The Ladies' Home Journal* (October 1928) and collected in *WRB*. See George Monteiro, "Robert Frost: An Unpublished Letter and an Inscription in a Copy of 'A Boy's Will,'" *Notes and Queries* 40, no. 1 (March 1993): 70.

129. RF's recollections of Derry include Arthur Reynolds, superintendent of Derry schools; Sylvia Clark, of the Pinkerton faculty; John C. Chase, a Pinkerton trustee; and George W. Bingham and Ernest L. Silver, the Pinkerton principals under whom RF worked from 1906 to 1911. Perley L. Horne followed Silver as principal when the latter resigned in 1911 to assume the presidency at Plymouth Normal School (now Plymouth State University), to which, as indicated here, he brought RF.

130. RF returned to the University of Michigan for a week of student conferences and meetings with the faculty, and to give a reading on March 31 at the Mimes Theatre, home to a student dramatic troupe.

131. Joseph A. Bursley served as dean of students at the University of Michigan from 1921 to 1946.

I liked being reminded of Pinkerton. The bookstacks in the library are my favorite memory in it.

Sincerely yours
Robert Frost

[To Louis Untermeyer. Date supplied by Untermeyer. ALS. LoC.]

[South Shaftsbury, VT]
[circa May 3, 1927]

Dear Louis

Jean assumes to ask for you both* if we have thrown you over. Hell no. I was afraid my silence would begin to be misunderstood. If I was more silent with the pen than usual it was because I could think of nothing adequate to say: I was willing to leave consolation and advice to the author of the author of Elmer Gantry, I mean Alfred the Sloganist.[132] You would have only to call him to comfort you with slogans and he would touch your various stops as skillfully as if you were the public and he were just what he is.[133] Cant I just hear him inspiring what I see by the papers you have been free to say on the subject of faith in life.[134] Honestly it sounds like office talk. Om Mani Padmi

---

132. The "consolation" RF refers to concerns the suicide of Louis Untermeyer's son, Richard (for details see the notes to RF to Edward Davison, January 28, 1927). "Alfred the Sloganist" is Alfred Harcourt, the person who broke the news to Untermeyer about Richard's death. Harcourt enthusiastically endorsed Sinclair Lewis's novel *Elmer Gantry* (New York: Harcourt, Brace, 1927), which satirized religious fundamentalism in the United States.

133. See *Hamlet* 3.2, where Hamlet accuses Guildenstern of lying to him: "Why, look you now, how unworthy a thing you make of me! You would play upon me; you would seem to know my stops."

134. On March 10, 1927, the day Harcourt, Brace and Company released *Elmer Gantry,* the front page of the *Brooklyn Daily Eagle* carried an article by William Weer titled "Louis Untermeyer, Baffled by Son's Death, to Crusade against Suicides of the Young." The article, subtitled "Poet Plans Educational Campaign to Bring about Faith in Life Rather than Religious Faith," quoted Untermeyer extensively, as for example here, where he defends a fully secular approach to finding purpose in life: "We today are almost unfitted for religion in the old sense of the word. We are scientific. The scientific interpretation of the world comes to us with our mother's milk. It cannot be avoided. What we want now, in place of religious faith, is a faith in life itself." Ironically, next to Weer's article appeared another, "Sinclair Lewis's Attack on Clergy [in *Elmer Gantry*] is Branded as Nauseating and Untrue."

Hum [*sic*].[135] Which is to say the lotus flower has a center that means something. So has Eugene ONeil's [*sic*] Great God Brown to anybody who prides himself on living in New York.[136] Come to me if you want to hear some small part of the truth. You are not bad except in the sense that I am bad and a lot of others are bad. Dont mistake me as implying there is no such thing as goodness anymore. You will hear it claimed that esthetics is all there is of ethics. Nothing could be worse thinking as I could explain to you in full if I had time. There is such a thing as badness. But as I say you are not bad. You are only in Dutch. You haven't been prospered.[137] I'm sorry for that, and you hold my sympathy just so long as you keep from delivering in obiter dicta to the newsmongers. Dont dont say things like that about faith in life where I can come across them because they simply bust me all up in the seat of philosophy. You are not responsible I know in the circumstances and I wouldnt want you to be responsible. I should think less of you if you were responsible. Only if you love me for Christ's sake find some more poetic way of going irresponsible than in dub sophistries. I'm hard on you—too hard. But youve got to stand this and more from me. I wish we could meet somewhere by ourselves for a twenty-four hour talk. It would have to be outside of New York. How about Albany. I may not know much about God and man but by the hocus pocus I begin to think I know more about you than you do yourself. You're the only person I ever said as much to. On general principals [*sic*] I refuse to set up as an authority on other people. I am no missionary. You may have noticed I gave you no advice when you were in Ann Arbor [138] Perhaps I should have given you advice. There's where I may have failed you. I've boasted

---

135. "Om Padme Mani Hum" is a Sanskrit mantra often inscribed on Buddhist prayer wheels. The mantra implores the speaker to purify the mind and body in an effort to seek compassion and wisdom. "Padme" can be translated as "lotus flower," an ancient symbol of wisdom.

136. Eugene O'Neill's (1888–1953) *The Great God Brown* was produced in New York in 1926. One of the main characters, the artist Dion Anthony, wears a mask of cynicism that inspires Margaret to fall in love with him. Once Dion casts off his mask and reveals his true artistic and religious yearnings, Margaret rejects him and Dion eventually dies. His best friend, Billy Brown, then dons the mask of cynicism and dupes Margaret to fall in love with him.

137. A locution found in commentaries on 1 Corinthians 16:1–2, or in translations of it and in other ecclesiastical contexts: "Let every one of you lay by him in store according as he hath been prospered."

138. In late spring 1926, Untermeyer had visited RF in Michigan to speak about his pending divorce from Jean Starr Untermeyer and subsequent marriage (in 1927) to the poet Virginia Moore.

lately in my teaching relation with boys that I played neither the psycho-
analyst nor the confessor. I've kept at the level of polite conversation. But I
dont know, about my motives. How do I know that I haven't kept from
meddling for the real pleasure I take in seeing humanity go blameless to
Hell. Oh G thinking of it all in these ways brings the woe all back in waves
over me.

Still I'm yours
R.

I'd have you here if it weren't for Marj. And after all I'd like to be alone with
you for a day.

*Seems funny for Jean to be asking for you. How much married to you does
she think she is? Women are too much for me.[139]

[*To Clarence Lee Cline (1905–1998), a 1926 graduate of Baylor University who at the
time of this letter was a first-year graduate student in English and history at the University of Texas. ALS. HRC.*]

South Shaftsbury Vermont
May 9 1927

Dear Mr Cline:

Now if I only could say the word that would help you. If I had my way (and
I mustn't be allowed to have it too much—it wouldnt be good for me or you
either) I would have you see it through where you are in Texas without coming
to eastern schools or going to Oxford. I would have you make it out of where
you are and what you are. If possible I would have you stay away from New
York—without prejudice to New York which is a good place but just one good
place among many.

Then I would have you use your own inmost guidance as to which it should be
with you, criticism or narrative and description. The two are not so far apart.
We have less good of the first than of the second; and that might tempt me to
steer you toward the first. But I won't take the responsibility. The whole country
not just the South and not just Texas need more than almost anything else at the

---

139. RF's footnote confirms Jean Starr Untermeyer's reluctance to accept both the finality and the legality of the divorce, which was effected against her wishes in Mexico.

moment the deliberate long considered critical help of someone who sits apart and judges with no interference [*sic*] from publishers and authors.

But it is less important what you do than the way you do it. You will stand or fall in both cases as you write or dont write literature in all its qualities of idea, insight, thought, metaphor, phrase and speaking likeness—likeness to speaking. You will have to look into this matter very acutely. You will have to make sure you are seeing everything there is to see in what others write and that you are putting everything into what you write yourself. Be afraid you are missing qualities. Look and look again more jealously. The qualities that others have you can assume you have. You have only to find out what they are and come out with them.

The great thing is this: With too many people literature remains a warm cloud in the breast. It has got to be struck across with the chill of intellect to make it fall in showers of idea metaphor and phrase. There is no other way. Get about having ideas metaphors epigrams epithets. Be sure you know what it is to have an idea that is an idea.

The business part of it I dont know how to help you at all about. You know best how soon you have to be earning money. Money can hardly be looked for right away from real writing. It is not safe to count on it. I always think a young writer of what is called pure literature should have something besides literature to depend on for a living. I went farming for eight years so as not to be hurried into bread and butter books. Of course I'm a slow person. You may be quicker to unfold your qualities than I was. You may not mind being driven as much as I did.

There I have written a lot for me. It shows how much affected I was by your story of the way we met in Waco without my knowing it.[140] You have given me additional reason for remembering that afternoon.

Always yours for this
Robert Frost

---

140. RF gave a reading at Baylor University on November 16, 1922, when Cline was a freshman.

[To Stanley Kimmel (1894–1982), editor of New Orleans Life Magazine. ALS. Private.]

South Shaftsbury Vermont
May 9 1927

Dear Mr Kimmel:

For Heaven's sake relieve my suspense at once by telling what poem of mine you have printed without my permission.[141] I can think of not a solitary one that does not belong to someone else—either to my publishers, Henry Holt and Co or some editor I have sold it to for publication presently. I dont believe you have realized the great liberty you have taken. You cant have intended to get me into trouble and then stand by and look on while I squirm out of it. You see these editors are very particular about the rights in a poem they have bought and paid from twenty-five to two hundred and fifty dollars for. I'm hoping this may prove some poem already published in a book. Then the only person's rights infringed on will be Henry Holt and Company; and they can be squared somehow.

I dont see how as a friend you can have done me such a disservice.

Anxiously yours
Robert Frost

[To Wade Van Dore. ALS. BU.]

South Shaftsbury Vermont
May 30 1927

Dear Van Dore:

Two of these last four you sent are thrust home, High Heaven and The Seeker. The Silence and The Moment before and after Moonrise are less merciless.[142] You are finding out. You are going to do it—if you dont let up on yourself—if you dont get too conceited to watch yourself and everybody else who ever attempted it. Dont miss any tricks or arts, traits or ingredients. Look

---

141. The May 1927 issue of *New Orleans Life Magazine* printed, under the title, "A Facsimile of a Poem by Robert Frost," a fair copy of "The Sound of Trees" inscribed by RF to Kimmel.

142. "High Heaven," "The Seeker," and "The Moment Before and After Moonrise" all appear in Van Dore's first book of poems, *Far Lake* (New York: Coward-McCann, 1930), which bears the dedication "To the sunlight on the pines near Far Lake; to the sound of the aspen leaves at Shebandowan Lake; and to Robert Frost."

and then look some more. Its your funeral. Little I can do to help except say 'em as I see 'em. I'm with you and

> Im your friend
> Robert Frost

Keep sending. Keep me informed of your states and locations.

> R.F.

[*To Stanley Kimmel. ALS. Private.*]

> South Shaftsbury Vt
> May 30, 1927

Dear Stanley Kimmel:

Wasn't I awful! But if you knew the troubles I've got myself into with publishers by carelessly scattering manuscript among friends and giving off hand permissions to reprint—

Bless your soul, it wouldnt have been your fault.

Good luck to your editorship.

> Always yours,
> Robert Frost

[*To Gorham Munson (1896–1969). RF is responding to the manuscript of Munson's* Robert Frost: A Study in Sensibility and Good Sense, *which was published late in 1927 by Doran. Dated from internal evidence. ALS. DCL.*]

> [South Shaftsbury, VT]
> [circa June 18, 1927]

Dear Munson:

I dont know how the life on the farm grew into such a hard luck story unless it was as one thing leads to another.[143] I probably started with what we lacked so as to clear the deck for what we had. But I got too much interested in what we lacked for its own sake and never got any further. It is true that we lacked friends. Only three people ever came the twelve miles out of our past to visit us, and they never more than once or twice a year. No neighbors came calling.

---

143. In Derry, New Hampshire. The period RF discusses here extended from 1900 to 1906.

I got acquainted with my neighbors when we "changed works,"[144] mostly in haying time. But lack of company means plenty of solitude. And solitude was what I needed and valued. I had days and days and days to think the least little thought and do the least little thing. That's where I got my sense that I have forever for accomplishment. If I feel timeless and immortal it is from having lost track of time for five or six years there. We gave up winding clocks. Our ideas got untimely from not taking newspapers for a long period. It couldnt have been more perfect if we had planned it or foreseen what we were getting into. It was the luck. It wasn't even instinct that carried us away—just the luck.[145] We didnt even know enough to know how hopelessly lost we must have looked from the outside. We never can recapture that. It was for once in a lifetime. Thats roughly what A Boys Will is about. Life was peremptory and threw me into confusion. I couldnt have held my own and done myself credit unless I had been a quitter. My infant industries needed the protection of a dead space around them.[146] Everybody was too strong for me, but at least I was strong enough not to stay where they were. I'm still much the same. What's room for if it isn't to get away from minds that stop your works? And the room is the most noticable [*sic*] thing in the universe. Even in an atom there's more space than matter—infinitely. The matter in the universe gets together in a few terribly isolated points and sizzles.

In arranging the poems in A Boys Will I tried to plot the curve from blinking people[147] as if they were the sun to being able to face them with my eyes open. But I wasnt escaping. No escape theory will explain me. I was choosing where to deliver battle.—Im just amusing myself with all this retrospection. It may help give you the spirit.

---

144. Refers to integrated, cooperative labor among farmers who, though they could manage most of the work on their family farms, depended upon neighbors to help complete certain tasks.

145. See RF to William Stanley Braithwaite, March 22, 1915: "I kept farm, so to speak for nearly ten years, but less as a farmer than as a fugitive from the world that seemed to me to 'disallow' me. It was all instinctive, but I can see now that I went away to save myself and fix myself before I measured my strength against all creation. I was never really out of the world for good and all. I liked people even when I believed I detested them" (*LRF-1*, 265).

146. The analogy is between RF's early career in poetry—in particular the benefit he now thinks accrued from being shielded from contact with outsiders—and the demand often made in the nineteenth century that American "infant industries" be protected (by tariffs) from foreign competition.

147. "Blinking" is here used in a transitive sense now rare, meaning to evade, to avoid.

We were poorer than anyone around us, but that kept us from taking a birds eye view of Rockingham County.[148]

I botanized a lot. One of my favorite plays was making paths in the woods and bushes. We were showing the country things to the children as they came along.[149] We had apples pears peaches plums cherries grapes black berries raspberries cranberries and blueberries of our own. I settled what was to be my writing. I got horses into my head. I was always afraid of them, but their ways caught me. We had three horses in succession.

We never had more than one warm room in winter. When we wanted to turn it into two, one of them a study for me to write in, I had E[150] turn her back on me so she couldnt see my struggle and I couldnt see her stretching thread.

Them were the days when we knew whether we really liked a book or not. Now we cant always be sure we dont like or dislike it because we know the author. We read whole books of poetry then. Now we peck at them.

We'll look for you then weekend after next. Ill have poured some more on you before then. I am sending the manuscript back with suggestions. We want to get the fact part right for future reference.

You'll be amused to hear that the classicist-scientist I spoke of admiring has been made president of Amherst.[151]

> Well—
> R.F.

[To Marguerite Ogden Bigelow Wilkinson (1883–1928), American poet, anthologist, and critic. RF added postscripts in the left margin and above the heading. ALS. Middlebury.]

> South Shaftsbury Vt
> June 18 1927

Dear Mrs Wilkinson:

Glad to have you use either or both; and that constitutes permission so far as I am concerned.[152]

---

148. In southeastern New Hampshire, where Derry is located.

149. See RF's "The Need of Being Versed in Country Things" (*CPPP*, 233).

150. Elinor.

151. Arthur Stanley Pease was inaugurated on November 4, 1927.

152. The anthology in question was never published. Wilkinson drowned on January 12, 1928.

We hope you and the ether-wave master will come by pretty soon.[153] We have more room than last year, and would like to put you up for the night.

I havent noticed who is on the Bread Loaf program this year. I doubt if I am.[154] Our best to you.

Sincerely yours

Robert Frost

Two Look at Two is a better poem than Good-bye and Keep Cold—I suspect.[155]

Your Frost and Snow paper was kindly received. Be good to us and you will be happy.

[To Jessie Belle Rittenhouse (1869–1948), an American poet and anthologist. From 1905 to 1915 she was poetry reviewer for the New York Times Book Review; *in 1914 she cofounded the Poetry Society of America. ALS. Jones.]*

South Shaftsbury Vt

August 12 1927

My dear Jessie Rittenhouse:

I have just been looking over your charming first little volume that was before I was. This next will be the third.[156] I shall be proud to be in it with the poems you name.

---

153. An invitation to Wilkinson and her husband to stay with the Frosts. James G. Wilkinson was a stockbroker in New York. In 1927, the development of radio technology linking American and British telephone systems was much in the news; it was often spoken of as done via "ether waves." "Ham" radio sets had also become something of a craze, and it would appear that Marguerite's husband was an enthusiast.

154. RF did indeed teach at Bread Loaf, giving a reading and a talk during a stay there from August 5–7.

155. Both poems are collected in *NH.*

156. Rittenhouse's *The Little Book of Modern Verse: A Selection from the Contemporaneous American Poets* (Boston and New York: Houghton Mifflin) came out in 1913. RF's first book, *ABW,* had appeared in the spring of that year, but his renown was secured a year later with the publication of *NB.* Rittenhouse subsequently brought out *The Second Book of Modern Verse* in 1919, and, in 1927, *The Third Book of Modern Verse*—the anthology RF refers to here, which reprints "To Earthward," "Misgiving," "Stopping by Woods on a Snowy Evening," and "The Onset." All are collected in RF's fourth book, *NH.*

And some time when I get my unpoetic license to drive a car Elinor and I will take you at your word and look in on you and Mr Scollard at Kent.[157] Our daughter Lesley's bookshop at Pittsfield will make a convenient halfway station.

I'm particularly glad you noticed To Earthward.

Best wishes to your venture.

Sincerely yours
Robert Frost

[The recipient of this letter is almost certainly James George Leippert (1909–1964), writing under the pseudonym "Edwin Robinson Leippert." Leippert was born in Kent, New York, and attended Columbia from 1929 to 1933, earning a degree in history, with honors. By 1927, when he was eighteen, Leippert had already begun writing to celebrated authors under false names concocted to win favorable responses. In March 1927 he wrote to A. E. Housman under the name Alfred Housman Leippert requesting a photo and advice about writing poetry, and got this reply: "I suppose I must do what I can to acknowledge your father's politeness in naming you after me. I have not had a photo graph taken for many years, but I have looked out an old one of the date when I was writing A Shropshire Lad. *Do not read books about versification: no poet ever learnt it that way. If you are going to be a poet, it will come to you naturally and you will pick up all that you need from reading poetry" (see* The Letters of A. E. Housman, *ed. Archie Burnett [New York: Oxford, 2007], 17). P. G. Naiditch, in* Problems in the Life and Writings of A. E. Housman *(Beverly Hills, CA: Krown and Spellman, 1995) was the first properly to identify "Alfred Housman Leippert." As "J. Ronald Lane-Latimer," Leippert persuaded Wallace Stevens to allow him to publish* Ideas of Order *(1935) and* Owl's Clover *(1936) at the Alcestis Press, which he had established in New York City. Leippert was clever enough not to address RF in 1927 as an eighteen-year-old named "Robert Frost Leippert"(RF's first book had appeared in 1913), so he used, it would appear, a name of comparable resonance in the world of American poetry, Edwin Robinson Leippert. ALS. Jones.]*

South Shaftsbury Vermont
August 27 1927

My dear Edwin:

I see that you are a real follower of the poets and have something more than the usual collector's claim to one of my bookplates. So you are going to get one. J. J. Lankes pinxit.[158]

---

157. Clinton Scollard, Rittenhouse's husband. They lived in Kent, Connecticut, due south of South Shaftsbury along Route 4 (now U.S. Route 7). This road passes through Pittsfield, Massachusetts.

158. Latin for "one painted [this]." Often used in signatures on paintings and related arts. RF's bookplate was illustrated by the woodcut artist J. J. Lankes, who also did illustrations for a number of RF's volumes of poetry.

Dont you believe your given name may partly account for your interest in poetry? I have a poem buried in one of my books that shows what a given name may do to a child.[159] I venture to predict yours will make you a poet yet. I wish you a future in the art.

I'm not having a new book just now. I don't think of books till they are upon me.[160]

Sincerely yours
Robert Frost

[To Laila Adelaide McNeil (1877–1971,) head librarian at Middlebury College. ALS. Middlebury.]

South Shaftsbury Vt
August 28 1927

My dear Miss McNeil:

The possibility that we were going to Europe this fall kept me from accepting your invitation and the probability that we werent going kept me from rejecting it. I trust that doesnt sound too complicated. It now seems settled that we aren't going. So if your invitation is still open after all these days, I should like to accept it. What you proposed would be one of the public things I should like to do.[161] I don't care to do many. You doubtless know something about my terms. In the State I am willing to take one hundred dollars and if anyone thought that too much I should be willing to listen to reason.

Very likely I am too late. At least this letter will serve as an explanation.

Sincerely yours
Robert Frost

---

159. See "Maple," collected in *NH*.

160. RF's next and fifth book, *WRB*, would appear in 1928.

161. In his unpublished chronology (and in *YT*, 683), Lawrance Thompson places RF lecturing at Bread Loaf from August 5–7. And shortly after this letter was written RF joined Elinor and Marjorie at the Sugar Hill, New Hampshire, farm of Edith Fobes, where they remained until late September (in their annual retreat above the hay-fever line). As a result, it is unclear what autumn lecture RF is arranging here (his pay for work at Bread Loaf was a different matter, and arranged by contract with Wilfred Davison, its Dean). RF did embark on a lecture trip in November, which took him as far west as Buffalo, New York.

Ten Weeks a Year in Amherst, Fourteen Once in Europe: 1926–1928   601

[To Mary E. Cooley. ALS. Michigan.]

Sugar Hill N.H.*

September 19 1927

Dear Mary Cooley:

There's nobody I'd rather have a book from than your father.[162] I'm glad it is to be a note book.[163] That sounds like things he has just inevitably thought, let them put together as they will. I'm less and less for systems and system-building in my old age. I'm afraid of too much structure. Some violence is always done to the wisdom you build a philosophy out of. Give us pieces of wisdom like pieces of eight in a buckskin bag. I take my history in letters and diaries, my philosophy in pensées[164] thrown together like the heads of Charles the Bold's army after it was defeated and slain in Switzerland.[165] You may have noticed them there this summer.[166]

I've been your father's great admirer ever since the first time I heard him talk. So he will be sending his book to a very gentle reader. He has the gift of truth.

Going to Chicago this winter doesnt sound like plunging into oil right away.[167]

----

162. That is, from Charles Horton Cooley, professor of sociology at the University of Michigan.

163. Cooley's *Life and the Student: Roadside Notes on Human Nature, Society and Letters* (New York: Alfred Knopf, 1927), described on the dust jacket as a "sequence of Emersonian observations and reflections."

164. In his notebooks, RF places Pascal's *Pensées* on a list headed "Ten Books" (*NBRF*, 265); see the notes to RF's January 1, 1926, letter to Bartlett.

165. Charles the Bold (1433–1477), Duke of Burgundy, 1467–1477. His army was defeated by Swiss forces at the Battle of Morat in June 1476. In *Childe Harold's Pilgrimage*, canto 3, Byron devotes stanzas 63–64 to the battle (the first of which is given here):

> There is a spot should not be passed in vain,—
> Morat! the proud, the patriot field! where man
> May gaze on ghastly trophies of the slain,
> Nor blush for those who conquered on that plain;
> Here Burgundy bequeathed his tombless host,
> A bony heap, through ages to remain,
> Themselves their monument;—the Stygian coast
> Unsepulchred they roamed, and shrieked each wandering ghost.

166. That is, when she was in Europe.

167. Cooley earned an MS degree in geology (with an emphasis on petroleum) at the University of Michigan in 1927 and soon took a post teaching it at the University of

Why dont you write some more poetry?[168] I wouldn't question everyone thus uncautiously.

Sincerely yours
Robert Frost

*But South Shaftsbury Vermont is the place to send the book. We start for there next Monday.

[*To Henry Seidel Canby, professor of English at Yale, editor of the* Yale Review *(1911–1922), and editor and cofounder of the* Saturday Review of Literature. *ALS. Yale.*]

South Shaftsbury Vermont
September 29 1927

Dear Canby:

Here you are back and at 'em. Please be a good man and don't make me publish my private opinion of Amy Lowell.[169] Good ring generals when they are hit too hard, clinch.[170] I ought to get in close before you can deliver me such another blow. I vow I'll come right down to New York, put both arms round your neck, my chin over one of your shoulders and stay there till you abate a little. No but seriously I had rather you rejected twenty poems by me than got yourself into a position where you had to accept one piece of prose. Speaking as author to editor, honestly. Sometime I may write some prose. But as Mussolini says, the time is not opportune for a war in the Balkans.[171] Later, my bullies. Sometime you may even have to cope with me as a drama-drahmatist.[172]

Chicago. She had worked with RF while an undergraduate student in English (during the spring of 1926).

168. See RF to Cooley, March 5, 1927, and November 10, 1924; he had read her poetry before.

169. Canby had apparently asked RF for an article on Lowell. Though he doesn't mention it here, RF had already published some thoughts about her poetry. In May 1925, a few days after Lowell's death, he wrote a brief tribute to her for the *Christian Science Monitor* (see *CPRF*, 88).

170. "Ring generals": experienced boxers.

171. The summer of 1927 had seen a significant worsening of relations between Yugoslavia and Albania, the latter being firmly within Italy's sphere of interest and control.

172. RF borrows a phrase from Thomas Dekker's *The Shoemaker's Holiday* (1600) (5.2), where Hodge says to Firke and Rafe (at the approach of Hammon and his party, whom they expect to fight): "Peace, my bullies; yonder they come" (where "bullies" means pals, comrades, etc.). The comedy in the scene arises, in fact, as threats, and calls to hold back

More seriously still, we must meet somewhere. I'd like to hear what you got out of Europe. What do you think? Shall we overtake them?

I <u>will</u> send you a poem or two before long.

Ever yours

Robert Frost

[*To Frederic Melcher. ALS. UVA.*]

South Shaftsbury Vermont

September 29 1927

Dear Melcher:

Lesley says on the telephone you are coming to Springfield for a lecture. I think we want to see each other about that Scribners business we got started and never finished.[173] How would it be for you to come this much out of your way for a visit and talkover? You could come up from Springfield to Williamstown on the train and I'd meet you there with a car I've learned how to drive. You could go home through Albany. Tell me what day and train if you agree.

I've been wishing we could get together. We did have some idea of getting down to the Cape when you were there.[174] Margery likes the Cape better than anywhere else. But when it came to the time she had one of her set backs and couldnt make it. It might have been different if I had been driving, and then again it might not have. Everything depends on her condition now-adays. But she'll get well.

Always yours

Robert Frost

---

from them, pile up ("Stand toot, my heartes," "Villaines, hands off!," "Villaines? Down with them!," "Hold, my hearts!," "Downe with that creature!," "Hold, foole!," etc.). We thank Mark Scott for bringing the allusion to our attention. As for "drama-drahmatist": Setting aside the two "masques" he published late in life, RF only completed one play, *A Way Out.* It first appeared in *The Seven Arts* in 1917 and would soon be republished, in book form, by the Harbor Press (in 1929, with a brief preface by RF). Around 1920, RF had started work on, but left unfinished, "In an Art Factory." The manuscript of one other play survives, "The Guardeen." See *CPPP*, 565–625.

173. Unidentified.

174. The Melchers regularly vacationed on Cape Cod.

[To Jean Paul Slusser (1886–1991), professor of drawing and painting at the University of Michigan. ALS. UM.]

South Shaftsbury Vt

Sept 29 1927

Dear Mr Slusser:

You know how to make allowances for me or this would be scandalous. It isnt so much that I have kept your money as that I havent shown you a little enthusiasm. The pictures came and for a while we had them all over us. I should have written right then but I didnt write because I didnt. I cant say I'm awful without sounding too complacent about it.

You'll see me or my ghost back haunting Pontiac St—dont worry. I'm glad you stick to it. Your address stirs me to a pleasant melancholy.[175]

You wander don't you?[176] I do and it's become a habit with me, but it hurts—it makes me sad all the time.

Edgar hasnt answered.[177] Im afraid he takes things too hard. Why dont some of his relatives back him to the rest of his education. He hadnt much more to go had he? He seems to be one who is going to feel it if he isnt admitted to the society and occupations of the educated. Its made hard in America for the intelligent but uncolleged.

Best wishes to you and to him (if you should be writing.)

Always yours

Robert Frost

I enclose the 25.[178]

----

175. Slusser lived at 1324 Pontiac Road and had been a neighbor of the Frosts during RF's second and last appointment at Michigan (1925–1926). Slusser would later move down the street into the house the Frost family had rented, at 1223 Pontiac. The cottage was later purchased by Henry Ford and moved to Greenfield Village; see RF to Lurie, February 26, 1925, and the notes thereto.

176. RF refers to Slusser's travels in Italy and elsewhere.

177. Slusser's nephew Edgar W. Slusser, as Slusser points out, in a typed note added to the present letter on February 18, 1963, immediately after RF's death. Edgar, a student in literature during RF's second appointment at Michigan, left without taking a degree to pursue a career in journalism and business.

178. Slusser indicates in his note that the $25 enclosed "was in payment for a portfolio of linoleum cuts entitled 'Five Block Prints of Italy,' which I had done in the autumn of 1925." RF had also bought from him a watercolor, *The Harbor, Syracuse.*

[To Wilfred Davison. The text given here is derived from SL, 343–344. At the time Thompson prepared SL he listed the letter, in the form of a typed copy, as being in the hands of Reginald Cook. We have been unable to locate either the manuscript of this letter or the copy.]

South Shaftsbury, Vermont
October 5, 1927

Dear Davison:

I want to try to tell you the number of times we changed our minds between going to your pond and not going to your pond.[179] In the end the day of starting for home caught us determined to go to it; and we went. On the way we were charmed once on the rather terrible detour with a little farmhouse high up on a banking above the full swift stream of Joe's Brook.[180] Henceforth that will always be one of the spots on earth where we may come to rest from our wanderings. And so might the pond be too if the population around it can be made to fall off a little.[181] For we were charmed with the pond itself. And your cozy house. There's no prettier piece of water in the woods anywhere. I suppose it must be one of the highest-set in New England if not the very highest.[182] We had a beautiful still evening by it and a beautiful morning. And by way of extravagance to express my feelings I walked on up your road a piece and priced the Ewen farm with all the shore and woods thereunto appertaining.[183] So you can see the lengths I went to. We were all of us sorry not to have longer but it was thought best in solemn assembly assembled[184] to get on while Marj was able. We were late anyway and afraid of

---

179. Joe's Pond, which lies between Danville, Vermont (to its east), and Cabot (to its west). Davison grew up in the area, and was schooled in Cabot.

180. Which feeds into Joe's Pond from the north. Joe's Pond and environs are anything but on the way from Middlebury to South Shaftsbury; hence RF's reference to a "terrible detour."

181. Joe's Pond came into considerable favor as a summering place in the 1920s, with numerous cottages being built around it.

182. At an elevation of 1,591 feet, Joe's Pond is not in fact the "highest-set" body of water in New England. Four other lakes and ponds in Vermont alone are above 1,600 feet. Amherst Lake, in Massachusetts, is over 2,000 feet in elevation.

183. A Davidson Drive branches from Route 15 just to the northeast of Joe's Pond. From the top it offers one of the best views of the area. The (Wilbur) Ewen farm was on the opposite, western side of the water.

184. From Joel 1:14: "Sanctify ye a fast, call a solemn assembly, gather the elders and all the inhabitants of the land."

the weather's breaking against us. We wcre all glad we had the night there. We like such things best of all—too well for our poetry, I sometimes fear, which would be more fateful I suppose if it were more about people and less about nature. Elinor is going to ask you down to see us sometime before long.

Thank your mother for her hospitality in absentia.[185] Remember me to your President.[186]

> Always yours
> Robert Frost

[To Raymona E. Hull (1907–1997), American scholar and teacher. The letter is undated, but Library of Congress processing information identifies the recipient as "Ramona" Hull and records a postmark from South Shaftsbury, Vermont, dated October 17, 1927. ALS. LoC.]

> [South Shaftsbury, VT]
> [October 17, 1927]

Dear Miss Hull:

You wouldn't want to see me get tired of life telling my own. If you want advanced information about me to use in an essay, I'll tell you where you can get it ahead of everybody else: in a biography by Gorham B. Munson just this minute being published by George H. Doran Co New York City.[187] There you will find what I think about nearly everything. I may tell you personally that I think modern poetry is probably good. If this isnt much of a letter it is because my four books are my letter to you and better than any other I can write. You'll say they are my letter to everyone.[188] But some of the poems in them must be

---

185. Lillian C. Davison (1859–1936). Wilfred shared a house on South Pleasant Street, Middlebury, with her and his father, Frank P. Davison (1855–1931). Apparently she had been away while the Frosts were in Middlebury.

186. Paul Dwight Moody, president of Middlebury College.

187. Munson's *Robert Frost: A Study in Sensibility and Good Sense.*

188. Perhaps an echo of Emily Dickinson:

This is my letter to the world,
That never wrote to me,—
The simple news that Nature told,
With tender majesty.

Her message is committed
To hands I cannot see;

specially to you if you will hunt them out. Please do hunt them out and encourage a poor poet.

Sincerely yours

Robert Frost.

[To Forman Brown (1901–1996), a member of the class of 1922 at the University of Michigan, where RF met him. ALS. BU.]

South Shaftsbury Vt

October 18 1927

Dear Forman:

You did a grand stroke of what shall I call it?—business or pleasure? I'm jealous, but with a generous kind of jealousy. Why didnt I see that river flat first?[189] You'll have a lovely time there touching it up. You've got everything a mountain-base, an "interval," a spring of water, a river boundary and woods to burn or not burn— not to mention two houses. You'll see us up there looking in on you. We cant keep away from the region. We'll be neighbors now.

I had a good letter from Lawrence.[190] Some of us met out there in your state to stay friends.[191]

Sincerely yours

Robert Frost

For love of her, sweet countrymen,
Judge tenderly of me!

189. Brown had bought a place in Franconia, New Hampshire, where the Frosts had lived from 1915 to 1920, and where they regularly summered in the 1920s, typically in August and September. Brown kept the house in Franconia for a number of years, using it as a summer residence and retreat.

190. Lawrence H. Conrad.

191. Likely a reference to a visit RF made to the University of Michigan earlier in 1927, from March 26 to April 1, during which he met with former colleagues and students and gave a public reading. As for "your state": Brown was a Michigan native, born in Otsego.

[To Franklin Folsom, then a student at the University of Colorado. ALS. BU.]

> South Shaftsbury Vermont
> October 18 1927

My dear boy:

You mistake me. It is one thing to answer a letter now and then on impulse. You seem to appreciate my having answered yours. I dont answer every-body's—I can't. It would be quite another to write an article to order.[192] You will find on enquiry that I have kept from article-writing thus far. Leave article-writing and the rewards thereof to Shorey.[193] I suppose you chose him to represent modern literature on your program—or was it to represent ancient literature?[194] Which is he the author of? Or merely the authority on?

My very best wishes.

> Always yours
> Robert Frost

---

192. Folsom had solicited an article for *The Window,* an undergraduate magazine that he edited.

193. Paul Shorey (1857–1934) was an eminent classical scholar, educator, translator of Plato for the Loeb Classical series, author of numerous articles and books on ancient Greek poetry and other matters. From 1908 until his death he was the editor of the journal *Classical Philology.*

194. RF refers to a volume then in preparation, *The Creative Intelligence and Modern Life* (Boulder: University of Colorado Press, 1928), one of six books published in the University of Colorado's Semi-Centennial Series 1877–1927. George Norlin, president of the university from 1919 to 1939, provided an introduction. Paul Shorey contributed the concluding chapter, "Literature and Modern Life." The other contributors, in order of appearance, were Francis John McConnell ("Religion and Modern Life"), Frederick James Eugene Woodbridge ("Philosophy and Modern Life"), Roscoe Pound ("The Social Order and Modern Life"), Lorado Taft ("Art and Modern Life"), and Robert Andrews Millikan ("Science and Modern Life"). As it happens, Millikan, who won the 1923 Nobel Prize in Physics, turns up by name in a poem RF collected in his penultimate volume, *Steeple Bush* (1947), "A Wish to Comply."

[To Edward Lewis Davison. ALS. DCL.]

South Shaftsbury Vermont
October 20 1927

Dear Ted:

I've been thinking of you lately—disinterested thoughts only. So dont be troubled in the conscience about that biography.[195] Let's not have the biography between us always as our reason for meeting or avoiding each other. Let's consider it dropped. Then if you ever do write the thing, it won't be because I had you where you had to. It can be entirely of your own motion and I can be as surprised and pleased as a kitten is when a spool seems to show signs of life without being pushed or pulled. Is it a vote?

You must be good and home again by this time. Trailing clouds of London of course that I can smell even at this distance above the odor of tobacco smoke on your clothes. It makes me imaginative. It makes me see faces and hear voices. Several times I was on the point of writing to expect us over this summer. We are not going to stay away much longer. Health or no health Marge says she is taking passage for us all for next April so as to catch daffodils in bloom in Jack Haines' country.[196]

I've just found the place for our ultimate school by a lake high in the mountains, a deserted village called Concord Corners that the railroad has undone by making passes back and forward below it two or three miles off in the valley.[197] All thats left is a black Church a ruinous almshouse and half a dozen farm houses. Witches have debauched the church by sucking through it in the wind, in at one empty window socket and out at another. The church could be our lecture hall. We'd keep it black. We'd send you up to rope the bell in the steeple again so we could set it tolling to call fools into a ring. When poetry fails us that's where we'll go and what do. Is it a vote?

---

195. RF had invited Davison to write a book about him but, unhappy with Davison's approach, gave the job instead to Gorham Munson (the book had recently been published).

196. RF, Elinor, and Marjorie did make it over to France and England in 1928, but not until August; Marjorie would spend most of her time in Paris, but RF and Elinor visited Haines and his family in Gloucester.

197. Concord Corner, near Shadow Lake, in Essex County, Vermont. A lumber town, its population decreased every decade after 1880. In 1937 RF would buy a property there for use during hay-fever season, although he stayed only occasionally.

But poetry mustn't fail us. I'll behave very badly if it does. Deny verities! Preach defeatism! Age unvenerably!

You sent me some of a poem I liked. Where's the rest of it? Wheres the mate to it?[198]

> Ever yours
> Robert Frost

Notice how I put a nice little Esq at the last end of your name instead of a Prof at the front end.[199]

[To Harold Rugg. ALS. DCL.]

> South Shaftsbury Vermont
> October 20 1927

Dear Rugg

I'm still bravely holding out against the orders for prose. Lies, false promises, flattery, bribes, prayers, tears, tear gas, malingering, protective coloration, irony, hysterics, change of pace, tact, everything—I have used everything in self-defense. And I think I am justified. Please please dont make me write any prose yet awhile.

You must have had a good look at the world. I shall want to hear more about it when I see you. I missed you when I was up in the spring. It seems a long time since you sat with us here talking Vermont botany.[200] I was out yesterday with the big clippers cutting as long a straight path as I could through a leafless witchhazel copse in full bloom. The habit of that sort of thing grows on me.

Best wishes.

> Sincerely yours
> Robert Frost.

---

198. Unidentified. The reference here may be to a poem or poems that would appear in Davison's next book, *The Ninth Witch and Other Poems,* published in 1932. Possibly it is the title poem, given the joke earlier in this letter about witches.

199. On the envelope, presumably; it hasn't survived.

200. Shortly before he died, Rugg was elected president of the American Fern Society, of which he had been a member since 1906. His interests in botany (like RF's) ranged widely.

[*To Walter Evans Kidd (1901–1990), then a student at the University of Oregon in Eugene. He later earned a PhD in literature at the University of Denver (1943), and taught at the University of Nebraska, among other places. ALS. BU.*]

South Shaftsbury Vermont
October 28 1927

Dear Mr Kidd

The reality of the voice has been my great interest in art since long before I knew what it was or what to call it.[201] Truth to the tones people speak in—dramatic sound—is what we are after, be it in prose or verse,—in drama, of course, but just as much in narrative, in essay, and even in lyric: or so I have always wanted to believe. The first and only marginal notes I ever wrote into a book were single-word descriptions of the tones of the sentences in the first scene or two of Hamlet. That was before I knew what I was doing or what was troubling me. I was remembering only last night how in those old days I was smitten by the way Clara Morris at a certain high moment in Camille said a simple "I cant" and an actor in Herne's Shore Acres a simple "Kinder shy."[202] It was to incur those wounds that I went to the theatre (when I went)

---

201. For other remarks about the "reality of the voice" and related matters, see *LRF-1:* 121–123, 167–168, 173–176, 198–199, 233–235, 265–266, 306–307, 316–317, and 355. See also *CPRF,* 136–139, 299–304.

202. Clara Morris, née Morrison (circa 1864–1925), Canadian-born American actress, celebrated for her performance in the lead role of *Camille,* a play adapted from the 1848 novel of Alexandre Dumas (fils), *La Dame aux camélias.* Morris first played the part in 1874 in New York. RF saw her in a production staged at the Opera House in Lawrence, Massachusetts, on October 9, 1893, when he was working in the Arlington Woolen Mill in Lawrence, and studying Shakespeare in the manner described earlier in the present letter. James A. Herne (1839–1901), American dramatist and actor, published *Shore Acres* in 1893. The play, with Herne in the lead role of Uncle Nat, was staged in Boston in a highly successful run from December 31, 1894, through late January 1895, when RF was in and around the city, during his brief stint as a reporter for the *Lawrence Daily American.* Perhaps he saw it then; in a February 8, 1916, letter to Walter Prichard Eaton, RF reports that he saw Herne perform the role (see *LRF-1,* 424). But the play was staged a number of times in Boston and other cities in Massachusetts in the mid-1890s. RF and his mother, Isabelle ("Belle") Moodie Frost, would have been attracted to *Shore Acres* in part because of its avowed debt to Henry George's widely read *Progress and Poverty* (1879). RF's father and mother met George (1839–1897) in San Francisco when he edited the *San Francisco Evening Post,* for which RF's father, William Prescott Frost Jr., worked in 1875. George later visited RF, his mother, Belle, and his sister, Jeanie, while on a lecture tour in New England in the autumn of 1885.

and for which presently I found I was picking up books. I got them in all sorts of places. They are nowhere more deadly than from some of the records left by Bert Williams.[203] It takes the imagination at its most excited to deliver them. They are to me the chief imaginative element in art you must understand. It is an imaginative triumph when Milton brings in the tone of

> *Hence with denial vain and coy excuse*

or

> *Shall I go on or have I said enough?*[204]

I have been asked often where I got myself, out of what reading, and I have generally answered by naming a list of all the poets I have read in the order in which I read them. You will find such a list in Gorham Munson's off hand biography of me just published by Doran.[205] The question puts too much temptation in my way to surprise people by emphasising books they wouldnt expect me to have been most influenced by. I've rifled a great variety of books for the imaginative element we are talking about. Theres a lot of writing one cant hear the voice speaking in at all. Some we call prosy— simple declarative monotony. Some is sing song. Some better than sing-song is just one romantic sweep of voice that we call eloquent. I speak of these to make clear a distinction. Patmore has some high spots of the real voice.[206] It is not so strange that Chaucer and Browning have for they so much of the

---

203. Bert Williams (1874–1922), an African American comedian, vaudeville performer, singer and composer, was one of the most successful entertainers of his day. His first recordings were released in 1901; by the time he died, he had sold hundreds of thousands of records. He cultivated a highly flexible, partly spoken singing style, and peppered his songs with talk, as in his 1913 hit "Nobody," and also recorded witty monologues such as "Somebody, Not Me" (1919). The Frosts owned a Victrola.

204. The first line quoted is from John Milton's "Lycidas," the second, from *Comus*, a masque RF staged while teaching at Pinkerton Academy in 1910.

205. Munson, *Robert Frost: A Study in Sensibility and Good Sense*. No such list is given in the book, although the poets RF reports first having read are named: William Cullen Bryant, Poe, Shelley (especially *Alastor*), Keats *(Endymion)* and Edward Rowland Sill (29). Elsewhere in the book the importance to RF of Virgil, Plato, Rousseau *(Emile)*, Matthew Arnold ("Sohrab and Rustum"), Twain, Robert Louis Stevenson, Hawthorne ("Mr. Higginbotham's Catastrophe"), Longfellow, and H. G. Wells come in for mention (52–53, 84).

206. Coventry Patmore (1823–1896), English poet and critic whose "Magna est Veritas" RF often cited and quoted.

time are being consciously dramatic. Browning has some quiet ones I like as well as any:

> *That was I you heard last night*
> *When there shone no moon at all.*
> *Nor to pierce the strained and tight*
> *Tent of heaven one planet small.*
> *Life was dead and so was light.*[207] Etc

> *The fancy I had to day—*
> *Fancy that turned to fear!*
> *I swam far out in the bay*
> *Since waves   warm and clear*[208]
>
> *I lay and looked at the sun*
> *The noon sun looked at me Etc.*

Good luck to your thesis away out there in Oregon

> Sincerely yours
> Robert Frost

[*To "Mr. Bridges," an aspiring poet whom we have been unable to identify.*[209] *The document, held at DCL, appears to be a typed copy of what must have been a manuscript. RF had few of his letters typed at this juncture and, when he did, he signed them; here, where a signature might go, we find instead RF's name typed out and placed within quotation marks. TL-C. DCL.*]

> South Shaftsbury, Vt.
> October 31, 1927

Dear Mr. Bridges:

No question—you have put your mind on getting one of the effects of poetry and you have got that effect. You achieve the thingness of things—the

---

207. First stanza of "A Serenade at the Villa," by Robert Browning (1812–1889).

208. The missing word is "laughed." The lines are from the Prologue to Browning's *Fifine at the Fair.*

209. An index card associated with this letter at DCL identifies its recipient (in error) as "BRIDGES [ROBERT?]," poet laureate (in 1926) of England, whom RF had known since 1913. Bridges was eighty-four in 1926.

concreteness—the images. That's fine as far as it goes. It may be as far as you want it to go. You may be satisfied with an itemized list of good details and a simple declarative monotony. Not everybody can get those details—not many can. It is a good deal of the battle. But I want more. I want you to show the imaginativeness that revels in all the vocal ways of the sentence. I don't mean sing song and I don't mean rhetorical eloquence. I mean the sentences that go this way and that way in intonation. Maybe it is the utter half[210] of imagination. You think it over. Go have a look at the books. Dramatic tones are what I mean. And even in narrative and description—and in lyric.

There's no flummery—no waste tissue in these poems. There is a sureness and a hardness. You are aimed right. Send more sometime.

Always your friend
"Robert Frost"

[To William Stanley Braithwaite. ALS. UNH.]

South Shaftsbury Vt
October 31 1927

My dear Braithwaite:

When you ask me to do hard things like acting as judge in an All American Poetry Prize Contest and I dont want to do them, but hate to refuse you, I am apt to put off writing till it's too late to write. But when you ask me something easy like permission to print, I guess I nearly always answer pretty promptly, dont I? I'm glad to have you use The Minor Bird any way you please.

I dont see you often since I came over on the New York side of the Green Mountains to live. Not that I see New Yorkers much more. I keep to the woods. I've been throwing stones all day—into a bottomless peat-bog with the idea of filling it up so we can walk on it unmiraculously. I tell you that to show you how innocently my time is passed.

Best wishes to your book.[211]

Sincerely yours
Robert Frost

---

210. While "utter half" is not lexically impossible, the typist may have mistaken "utter" for "better."

211. Braithwaite's *Anthology of Magazine Verse for 1927, and Yearbook of American Poetry* (Boston: B. J. Brimmer, 1927), which reprinted RF's "A Minor Bird," originally published

[*To Leonidas W. Payne, professor of English at the University of Texas. ALS. HRC.*]

South Shaftsbury Vermont
November 1 1927

Dear Mr Payne:

I remember somebody away off down there at my furthest South asked the question that I was asked in yesterdays mail by a New Yorker: In my Mending Wall was my intention fulfilled with the characters portrayed and the atmosphere of the place? You might be amused by my answer. I should be sorry if a single one of my poems stopped with either of those things—stopped anywhere in fact. My poems—I should suppose everybody's poems—are all set to trip the reader head foremost into the boundless. Ever since infancy I have had the habit of leaving my blocks carts chairs and such like ordinaries where people would be pretty sure to fall forward over them in the dark. Forward, you understand, <u>and</u> in the dark. I may leave my toys in the wrong place and so in vain. It is my intention we are speaking of—my innate mischievousness.

Isn't that the way to answer them, whether in Texas or New York?

The book pleased me   and your kindness to me in it.[212] Lets see I have forgotten whether you are of the Graduate School at Chicago. Nearly everyone out of there seems to make anyone later suffer by comparison with Will Moody.[213] I couldn't find that you had expressed yourself anywhere as sorry none of us were as good as he. Very likely we arent. And then again very likely

---

in 1926 in the University of Michigan's *Inlander* magazine, then in the *Yale Review* (July 1927), and subsequently collected in RF's 1928 volume *WRB*. Also included in the 1927 anthology were RF's "Tree at My Window," "The Times Table," "The Cocoon," and "The Common Fate" (retitled "A Peck of Gold" in *WRB*).

212. A handwritten note in pencil, presumably written by Payne, identifies the book as Payne's *Later American Writers: Part Two of Selections from American Literature* (New York: Rand McNally, 1926), which included "The Pasture," "Mowing," "Mending Wall," "The Code," "The Grindstone," "Nothing Gold Can Stay," and "Birches." In his "Introductory Notes," Payne writes: "If Edwin Arlington Robinson is the greatest living American poet, Robert Frost is a close second. In fact, not a few of our critics would place Frost first. If not so keenly intellectual, he certainly is nearer to the soil, more human, more approachable, more readily comprehensible. Like Robinson, he is the interpreter of the decaying types of New England. He paints the New England scene with a deft and delicate hand, he reproduces the New England rural types with a powerful realism, and he lights up his sombre pictures with a charming sense of humor."

213. Chicago poet and playwright William Vaughn Moody, whose work won wide acclaim in the first years of the twentieth century.

we are. Such comparisons can become unnovel. I hear—What's his name?—that Gilbert Murray of Chicago, has wiped us all off the map with Moody.[214] That ought to be gratifying to my dear friend Mrs Moody.[215] We all come in for some rewards. When one is getting his we can all sit back in a row, the rest of us, and wait for ours. You put the idea into my head of saying something about anthologies next time I go on the tow path.[216]

Some year you and Armstrong must ask me back to the Alamo and San Jacinto. My friend Dwight Morrow has just gone to see if he cant keep us from having another war with Mexico.[217] By the way I suppose you know the chantey that goes

> *General Taylor won the day*
> *On the plains of Mexico*
> *Santa Anna ran away*
> *On the plains of Mexico.*[218]

---

214. Australian-born scholar Gilbert Murray (1886–1957) was a celebrated translator of Greek tragedies. He never taught at the University of Chicago (he taught at Glasgow, Oxford, and Harvard), nor did he ever review Moody. RF may refer to Edwin Herbert Lewis (1866–1938), who taught classics and rhetoric at the University of Chicago. Lewis's *William Vaughn Moody* (Chicago: Privately printed, 1914), a lecture delivered to the Chicago Literary Club in 1912, had nothing but high praise for Moody: "Moody had the lyrical gift, the historical sense, the scientific information, the human sympathy, and the cosmic vision which fitted him to treat this theme [the Promethean theme], not in the grandiose manner, but in the grand manner. Nothing like this can be said of any other American poet."

215. Harriet Moody, widow of William Vaughn Moody.

216. At the time, Payne had also been working on *A Survey of Texas Literature* (New York: Rand McNally, 1928), the first anthology of Texas literature ever published. RF did in fact give lectures on anthologies in the 1930s. See Mark Scott, "Frost and Anthologies," in *Robert Frost in Context*, ed. Mark Richardson (New York: Cambridge University Press, 2014), 107–113.

217. Andrew Joseph Armstrong was chairman of the English Department at Baylor University and had invited RF to read there in November 1922. The Alamo and San Jacinto were both sites of major battles during the Texas Revolution of 1836. As ambassador to Mexico, Dwight Morrow helped mediate a truce between Catholic loyalists and the anticlerical, secular government of Mexico's president, Plutarco Elias Calles. Morrow's efforts in this capacity were aimed at bringing to an end the violent Christero Rebellion (1926–1929) and helping the United States secure oil and irrigation treaties with Mexico.

218. The sea-shanty most commonly known as "Santianna" celebrates the exploits of Mexican General Antonio Lopez de Santa Anna during the 1846–1847 Mexican-American War. In the shanty it is Santa Anna who wins the day and U.S. General (Zachary) Taylor who runs away. RF's patriotic revision is, however, closer to the historical truth of the

Well the English sing that the other way round Santa Anna won the day etc: which shows that ours is not the only country where history is written with prejudice.

We are having a long warm Indian Summer here that Im taking advantage of to build or rebuild a causeway through our bog with hardheads, as we call them.[219]

Remember me to Cunningham if he is still expounding Hegel down there.[220]

Always yours

Robert Frost

[To John Bartlett. ALS. UVA.]

South Shaftsbury VT

Nov 1 1927

Dear John:

You mustnt be terribly sick. I see you the way you were beside the stove that summer night on Patuckaway Mountain.[221] You have a right to be sick if you want to. We haven't all got to be healthy. I refuse to be tyrannized over by doctors. But I dont want you terribly or dangerously sick, Captain. I started cringing at the way you played yourself ragged in the fall and slopped round on wet feet all that last winter in Derry and you have kept me cringing more or less ever since.[222] Well, whats the use of talking.

---

matter; the battles commemorated in the various versions of the shanty were in fact U.S. victories.

219. "Hardheads": large, round stones typically found near the surface of the soil.

220. Gustavus Watts Cunningham (1881–1968) was professor of philosophy at the University of Texas from 1917 to 1927. He is the author of *Thought and Reality in Hegel's System* (New York: Longmans, Green, 1910) and *A Study in the Philosophy of Bergson* (Longmans, Green, 1916).

221. In the summer of 1915, Robert and Elinor had stayed with John and Margaret Bartlett at the Bartlett family summer farm in the Pawtuckaway Mountains of southeastern New Hampshire.

222. Bartlett was captain of the football team at Pinkerton Academy (in Derry, New Hamphsire) when RF taught there; see the notes to RF's June 11, 1922, letter to him.

I wish it was Elinor and I seeing you about now instead of them two irresponsible wastrels our son and daughter hell bent for California.[223] I sometimes come within an ace of taking up with invitations out that way. What decides me against it is the family. I can't leave them for more than a day or two. If they ever get so they will consent to follow me across the prairies, the first place I'll lead them to will be Boulder. Then we will have a good ole talk as in the days that were.

Carol is a curious boy. I wonder if this expedition of his is to spy out a new country to live in. He wouldn't say so if it was and it may not be. He'll have told you he is pretty deeply involved here what with his considerable sweet pea business and his MacIntosh [*sic*] apples in prospect.

I've been playing myself out back in the bog in his absence throwing wheelbarrow after wheelbarrow full of stones off the walls into the mud and peat to rebuild the old causeway to the back pasture. We've been having days I doubt if you could beat in Colorado: the air at a standstill, the leaf gold still holding out on the trees, frost just barely some nights, others none. Me for it. But it cant last or I cant—Ive got to go down to see a President inaugurated at Amherst day after tomorrow. (I ought not to complain. He is somewhat of my choosing.)[224] I'll have to look up my shoes and see if my clothes have improved any by not having been worn lately. A dip in kerosene coal oil will start the rust. Then I can hollystone[225] it off.

The first report I have had on the biographical sketch speaks chiefly of your contribution to it.[226] I aint agoing to thank you. It was an inspiration of mine to give Munson direct access to my past through two or three of my independent friends. I thought it would be fun to take the risk of his hearing something to my discredit. The worst you could was my Indian vindictiveness. Really I am awful there. I am worse than you know. I can never seem to forgive people that scare me within an inch of my life. I am going to try to be good and cease from strife.[227]

---

223. Carol and Lillian Labatt Frost.

224. Arthur Stanley Pease (1881–1964), a Harvard-trained classicist and skilled amateur botanist, served as president of Amherst from 1927 to 1932. RF's claim here is exaggerated. Although RF had met with and spoken favorably of Pease, he had had little to do with Pease's appointment.

225. "Hollystone" or "holystone" is a type of soft sandstone used to scrub ship decks.

226. That is, Bartlett's memories of RF, as recounted in Gorham Munson's *Robert Frost: A Study in Sensibility and Good Sense* (recently published).

227. See Proverbs 20:3: "It is an honour for a man to cease from strife; but every fool will be meddling."

I suppose you will be helping the State University celebrate its hundredth anniversary by going to a football game or a speech by Loredo [*sic*] Taft that manufacturer of sculpture wholesale.[228] Friends of mine complain that he uses a steam drill and an army of assistants. Art is scandalous.

My isnt it a chill to hear how those youngsters of yours are coming up?[229] If they are that old how old must I be? Tell them easy does it. They must be fine children who can be appealed to. You cant so much as grow in this world without affecting somebody to tears. People had better be careful how they grow. There is something invidious about the way the young grow. I'd like to tease them. They look as if they could take care of themselves. I probably couldnt baffle them very much at my crypticest. Never mind I can baffle some people.

It is now 12 PM [*sic*] your time 3 AM mine. I'm wobbly.

Love to you all.

R. F.

[*To George H. Sargent. ALS. Jones.*]

South Shaftsbury Vt[230]

Nov 3 1927

My dear Sargent:

I have refrained from mailing your four books all these years with the idea that sooner or later they might force me to carry them to you at Elm

---

228. In fact, the University of Colorado was then celebrating its semi-centennial (it was founded in 1877), and, on the occasion, awarded an honorary Doctor of Letters degree to Lorado Taft (1860–1936), an American sculptor and writer whose work was commissioned by several American universities (he had done two pieces for the University of Colorado). Taft was one of the first sculptors to take on women apprentices, a practice deemed socially unacceptable at the time. The group of eight women he assembled to help him meet the deadline for his work at the 1893 Columbian Exposition in Chicago was dubbed "the White Rabbits."

229. See notes to RF's December 23, 1926, letter to Bartlett.

230. Actually, RF posted the letter in Pittsfield, Massachusetts, some forty miles south of South Shaftsbury. In the unpublished chronology he prepared while at work on his three-volume biography of RF, Lawrance Thompson reports that on November 3 RF and Elinor attempted to drive to Amherst for the inauguration spoken of in this letter, but were forced to stop as a late-season hurricane moved into New England, causing major floods throughout the region (November 2–5). Eighty-five people died in the

Farm:[231] which shows how very much I must want to visit you. But various things keep me where I am, sickness in the family, agriculture, culture.[232] It sounds bad enough for an excuse, doesnt it? And there is no prospect of its sounding any better immediately. So I am sending the books along un-accompanied, as having no right to withhold your property further on uncertainties.

Things like inaugurations compel my attendance. Why dont you have an inauguration. I'd come to that as of obligation just as I am at this moment running off to the inauguration of a new president at Amherst.[233]

The train whistleth. I go. Farewell. Greetings. Think kindly of me.

Ever yours
Robert Frost

[To John Erskine. Date derived from internal evidence. ALS. Columbia.]

[South Shaftsbury, VT]
[December 1927]

Dear Erskine

The 9th is impossible; I lecture in Salem that day. But I shall be seeing you a few days after that when I shall be down for a lecture at Montclaire [*sic*].[234] And I shall scold you if you have scolded me too much in public about my colloquality[235] which whether it be overdone or done just enough is the very

---

flooding, eighty-four of them in Vermont. For RF's remarks about the event, see his December 10, 1927, letter to Whicher.

231. Sargent's place in Warner, New Hampshire. As for the books: see RF to Sargent, August 30, 1926.

232. RF's daughter Marjorie had fallen seriously ill again in the summer of 1927, suffering from nervous prostration and losing an alarming amount of weight.

233. Arthur Stanley Pease was inaugurated as the tenth president of Amherst on November 4.

234. At the behest of Frederic Melcher, RF gave a talk at Montclair, New Jersey, on January 13, 1928.

235. Compare the phrasing to RF's inscription in a copy of *NB* given to Regis Michuad in 1919: "I am as sure that the colloquial is the root of every good poem as I am that the national is the root of all thought and art. It may shoot up as high as you please and flourish as widely abroad in the air, if only the roots are what and where they should be. One half of individuality is locality: and I was about venturing to say the other half was colloquiality" (*LRF-1*, 646).

essence of me. The thing to say (and very likely you have said it) is that to be myself at all, naturally some of the time I have to overbe myself.

I never wrote you a word about your poem. For reasons I wont go into here, I think you never wrote a better.

You never wrote better lines than the last three in the Innkeeper.[236]

I have had talk from Dwight Morrow about Amherst that was calculated (I couldn't help seeing) to cheer me up. I am sure it was sincere however. He certainly drew a circle that took you in.

Ever yours
Robert Frost

[To Carl Sandburg, for many years seen as RF's chief rival as the representative "American" poet. The letter appears to have been prompted by RF's receipt of a copy of Sandburg's The American Songbag *(Harcourt, Brace, 1927). ALS. Illinois.]*

South Shaftsbury Vt
December 2 1927

Dear Carl:

I see I shall never be able to resist the flattery of being treated as if I knew anything about music and could sing chanteys. Neither will I that of being treated as if I had been an athalete [*sic*] and could still play tennis. Either form simply strikes me dumb with rapture and caution. You can see the need of the caution. If I said much I might give myself away; if I tried to sing at all I might lose the cheese out of my mouth the way I did when I was a crow in the time of Aesop.[237] You may remember. You were possibly there in the capacity of the fox. When the fox finally said

"Hence with denial vain and coy excuse,"[238]

---

236. The lines read:

Knock till you're weary, then, you can't come in,
There's not a bed. What's that you're looking for?
Not sleep! What? Wise men, are you? O, you are!

237. In Aesop's fable "The Fox and the Crow," the crow sits in a tree holding a piece of cheese in its beak. Desiring the cheese, the fox tricks the crow into dropping it by asking the crow if its song is as delightful as the cheese. Usually taken as a cautionary tale about heeding the words of flatterers, the fable is No. 124 in the Perry Index of Aesop's Fables.

238. A line RF often quoted from Milton's "Lycidas."

I was just fool enough to try to favor him with a song. And the cheese, well,

> *The cheese fell out of my mouth and onto the floor*
> *Turned over itself and rolled out of the door*
> *Mopety mopety mo-no.*[239]

It was a lesson to me. Since then when the wiley [sic] tell me I can sing, I listen like a cushat dove—ravished;[240] I roll my eyes like a searchlight but I keep my mouth tight shut like a steel magnate. (Misgiving: Don't I mean a steel trap?) Thus your splendid tome, by taking legitimate advantage of perhaps the greater of my two greatest human weaknesses, gets away to a perfect start in at least one quarter. I have ordered the sale of it pushed in both of our chain book stores. We have two now, or Lesley has, and I suppose two make a chain just as two pearls are said in the adds [sic] to make a necklace to start with.[241]

Wait till we get to a piano. <u>We'll</u> know what to do with ourselves. The tome is an orgy.

I know a subject better than Frankie and Albert[242] all ready to your hand when you get round to writing ballads on your own account, you old ballad-monger.[243] They were all three poets and the girl he left behind him came out

---

239. The source of this nonsense, if it has any, is unclear, although in sixteenth-century usage a "moppet" was a mop typically used to clean the barrel of a cannon.

240. RF adapts the opening line of "Listening," by Christina Rossetti. The poem appears in *Palgrave's Golden Treasury* (second series). RF's interpolation ("ravished") aptly fits the woman described: "She listened like a cushat dove / That listens to its mate alone: / She listened like a cushat dove / That loves but only one. . . ."

241. The first Frost family bookstore was The Open Book (launched by Lesley and Marjorie); the second, the Book and Print Shop, was set up by Lesley in Ann Arbor, Michigan. For details about Lesley's enterprises, see Lesley Lee Francis, *You Come, Too: My Journey with Robert Frost* (University of Virginia, 2015). The author is the younger daughter of Lesley Frost. As for the pearls, "add-a-pearl" advertising campaigns were common in the 1920s; jewelers offered necklaces with one pearl as ideal birthday presents for young women, the idea being to add a second pearl on the subsequent birthday, a third the next year, and so forth.

242. Sandburg collected three versions of the song—"Frankie and Albert," "Frankie and Johnnie," and "Frankie Blues"—in his *American Songbag*. Most music historians agree that the lyrics are based on the murder of Allen Britt (Albert) by Frankie Baker in St. Louis, Missouri in 1899, when she discovered him with another woman. The song has been recorded in one variant or another by more than 250 artists.

243. The literary joke comes at Sandburg's expense. In *Henry IV, Part I* 3.3, Glendower boasts to Hotspur that he had "framed to the harp / Many an English ditty lovely

in a poem in a book published by Macmillan and charged him with having no wool on the top of his head which is just where the wool ought to grow; the other girl came right back at her with a poem in Henry Canby's Saturday Review saying, Well he might not have any hair on his head at his age, but anyway he had hair in his ears—"a thicket of hair in his ears"—so now.[244] Then you could wind up by saying how many people died of laughter in the third degree. There are more things in actual life than it would be humane or in good taste to work up into art—you old ballad monger.

Always yours
Robert

---

well / And gave the tongue a helpful ornament, / A virtue that was never seen in you." To which Hotspur replies:

> *Marry,*
> *And I am glad of it with all my heart:*
> *I had rather be a kitten and cry mew*
> *Than one of these same metre ballad-mongers. . . .*

244. RF refers to the scandal occasioned by Louis Untermeyer's divorce of Jean Starr Untermeyer in 1926 (effected, for speed, in Mexico), and his marriage to Virginia Moore in 1927. He would divorce Moore in 1928 and remarry Jean Starr the same year. All three worked their marital problems into poetry (see *YT*, 349, for a brief account of the matter). In 1927 Macmillan published Jean Starr Untermeyer's *Steep Ascent*. Collected there is her "Ballad for These Days," which begins, "Oh, Mary, my wife, I wish I were dead, / The hair lays so scanty atop of my head." Virginia Moore published her "Marriage" in the *Saturday Review of Literature*, November 5, 1927, in which Untermeyer figures as a faun (hinting, perhaps, at his goatish reputation):

> *Never reproach me and never ask why*
> *Now that I've married a faun:*
> *A tapering thigh, a pitying eye,*
> *And the look of the mountains at dawn.*

> *Measure a man for his ultimate worth*
> *And see how my husband compares:*
> *The language of earth was his language from birth*
> *And his ear is a thicket of hairs. . . .*

For his part, Untermeyer had long since published an autobiographical poem titled "A Marriage" (it appeared in the first *Miscellany of American Poetry* he assembled—with poems by RF, Jean Starr, and a number of others—for Harcourt, Brace and Howe in 1920). See also the final paragraph of RF's May 10, 1926, letter to Whicher (which concerns a 1926 anthology in which Untermeyer printed poems by *both* Jean Starr and Virginia Moore).

[To Edward Lewis Davison. Date derived from internal evidence. ALS. DCL.]

[South Shaftsbury, VT]
[circa December 2, 1927]

Dear Ted:

I've taken all the engagements I can allow myself if I am to reserve any energy for the main interest. Thanks just the same for your intervention. I'd like to see something of those Southerners some time.[245] It was brotherly of you to have me in mind.

You are not serious about my having taken your date at Baltimore?[246] One of my few virtues is the very minor one of never crowding anyone for place, and it is not really a virtue, it is a fault if you like, since it arises from pride.

Re the clipping you sent.[247] I've just been telling old Carl the Ballad-monger, that when he gets tired of collecting other peoples [sic] ballads and turns to writing ballads of his own, I have a subject for him right out of our own level of society that beats Frankie and Albert to a pulp. Three poets make the triangle. The girl he left behind him comes out in a poem in a book published by Macmillan (the best poem she ever wrote) and insults him with having no wool on the top of his head which is just where the wool ought to grow. The other girl comes right back at her in the poem in The Saturday Review of Henry Canby, the burden of which is that it may be true he has no hair on his head at his age, but any way he has hair in his ears, a thicket of hair in his ears—so now! For a man of his sense of humor I should think such goings on would break any spell he was under. I should think it would kill him of laughter in the third degree. Poor man. God send that the worst is over for him.

Always yours
R.F.

I couldnt wire this.

---

245. Likely the "Fugitive" poets associated with Vanderbilt University, whom RF would meet in 1929. See RF to Reeves, December 15, 1928 (and notes).

246. RF had already been to Baltimore once in November, with his wife, Elinor, and daughter Marjorie; the family had consulted physicians at Johns Hopkins regarding Marjorie's health. While in the city, the Frosts were hosted by Mary C. Goodwillie, who, it seems, had arranged for RF to speak. See RF to Goodwillie, December 3, 1923, for previous speaking engagements in Baltimore.

247. No longer extant in the RF-Davison correspondence at DCL.

[To George Whicher. ALS. ACL.]

South Shaftsbury

December 10 1927

Dear George:

It's seriously terrible that after all these years of striving to make a name and address for ourselves we should still be too unimportant for the New Eng Tel & Tel,[248] when it cant find us on one of our telephones, to call us on the other. We pay for two and some of us have been where we could be reached on one or the other or both without interruption for the last month.

I was going to ask you for help. I'd like the freshmen on those terms.[249] Only don't make too much of a point of their being writers. Why couldnt some of them qualify merely as readers who would be reading anyway whether under orders or not. Another thing: no one would object I suppose if sometimes I didnt see them more than once a week. I could call both days mine (Thursday and Saturday) but make them a present of the second now and then for effect—or for relief "touch and remit after the use of kings."[250]

For the rest I'm at your disposal. I know you wont force me on anyone who doesn't want his schedule broken in on or the minds of his students diverted.* I'm very sensitive to cool receptions. Better that I should sit out unintroduced, a more or less forbidding stranger to the boys, than that I should seem to imply

---

248. The New England Telephone and Telegraph Company was then a subsidiary of AT&T.

249. RF's appointment at Amherst required that he offer one ten-week seminar a year, taught in the winter, and with students prescreened. The description of the course in Amherst's catalog reads as follows: "During the winter, between Christmas and spring vacations, Robert Frost will be in residence to conduct special classes in English and hold informal conferences with the students."

250. From the last stanza of Rudyard Kipling's "To the City of Bombay," the dedicatory poem to his 1896 volume *The Seven Seas* (London: Methuen):

And she shall touch and remit
  After the use of kings
(Orderly, ancient, fit)
  My deep-sea plunderings,
And purchase in all lands.
  And this we do for a sign
Her power is over mine,
  And mine I hold at her hands!

that every single day—moment—in some teachers courses wasnt crucial. I can leave a lot to you.

We were in pretty deep that night—clear up over the seats on one side. Our poor car will never be the same car again. It was an Oakland antedeluvianly.[251] It's lucky if it's a Model T Ford now. When we hit the water going full speed and raised it in a solid dome over us it looked like drowning in a pond. But when we found we werent dead and the wreckers had us out and going again in three hours I thought, unrealizing me, that we had come off absurdly well considering. Little I ever know what I am enjoying or suffering at the time of it. The car has had to go through operation after operation for sand on the vitals. A shovelful was taken out of its circulatory system, as much as a spoonful out of its pineal gland. It begins not to seem as funny as it did when we first discovered we weren't drowned. Nothing but praise for the driver. He kept us nose on and right side up and stopped us short of going clear under.

We'll be coming up from Baltimore when we come. We are taking Marj to Johns Hopkins for another examination before sending her south with a friend.[252] I may ask you to meet us at Northampton if it isn't too stormy.

The heart of the nomads turns once again toward Amherst. We want to see you.

> Ever yours
> Robert Frost

*or distracted

---

251. The Oakland Motor Company, a division of General Motors, produced cars in Pontiac, Michigan. RF refers to the heavy rains and flooding that stranded him and his wife, Elinor, on November 3, as they attempted to drive to Amherst for the inauguration of president Arthur Stanley Pease; see the notes to RF's November 3, 1927, letter to Sargent.

252. On the first consultation at Johns Hopkins University Hospital, see RF to Edward Davison, circa December 2, 1927 (and the notes thereto). The Frosts returned to Baltimore on December 28, whereupon Marjorie was admitted to the hospital for a ten-week stay. The family's intention had been to take her to Florida, in the hope that the climate would restore her health. They subsequently decided to take her to France, and would sojourn in Europe in August–November 1928.

[*To Lewis Mumford (1895–1990), American historian, sociologist, and literary critic. ALS. Penn.*]

South Shaftsbury Vermont
December 12 1927

Dear Mr Mumford:

I can't deny that what you say about my books is going to add something, if only the least little bit proportionally, to the great pleasure I have had in your books.[253] Perhaps I ought not to be so susceptible to sympathy, but such on self-examination I find I am, and I may as well admit it, since whatever else it is an offence against, it certainly isnt an offence against you.

You to the rescue of many things I care for more than myself and my own work. I said as much a year ago on reading The Golden Day.[254] And I said, when I heard the way the youngsters were talking about it, that possibly we had taken a turn for the better.

Sincerely yours
Robert Frost

---

253. Presumably remarks made in an incoming letter. Mumford had not published an essay about RF.

254. Mumford's *The Golden Day. A Study in American Experience and Culture* (New York: Horace Liveright) was published in 1926 as a companion work to his *Sticks and Stones: A Study of American Architecture and Civilization* (New York: Boni and Liveright, 1924). See RF to Blatchford, October 1926, for the order RF placed for his copy of *The Golden Day*. Mumford mentions RF in the book's "Envoi": "Entering our own day, one finds the relations of culture and experience a little difficult to trace out. With the forces that have come over from the past, it is fairly easy to reckon: but how these are being modified or supplanted by new efforts of experience and new stores of culture one cannot with any assurance tell. Is Robert Frost the evening star of New England, or the first streak of a new dawn? Will the Dewey who is struggling to step outside his old preoccupations influence the coming generation, or will the more passive and utilitarian thinker continue to dominate? Will our daily activities center more completely in metropolises, for which the rest of the country serves merely as raw material, or will the politics and economics which produce this state give place to programs of regional development? What is the meaning of [Vachel] Lindsay and [Carl] Sandburg and Mrs Mary Austin? What is the promise of regional universities like Nebraska and North Carolina and New Mexico? May we look forward to a steady process of re-settlement; or will the habits of nomadry, expansion, and standardization prevail?" (273).

[To a Miss Carter, whom we've been unable to identify. ALS. Princeton.]

South Shaftsbury Vermont
December 15 1927

My dear Miss Carter:

I can't think of a single anecdote about myself at the moment except that some say I never retouch a poem after the first writing and some say I do. Oh yes and possibly you might regard it as an anecdote that someone has just written to ask me if I believe in symbols in poetry. If what you are after is a joke at my expense, there's one for you!

I've done the best I could for you, for I realize your emergency is desperate.

Hastily yours
Robert Frost

[To Eugene Whiting Gay-Tifft (1899–1982), a Buffalo native and Dartmouth graduate (1923), and bookseller, editor, and translator. The letter was published in 2005.[255] ALS. Private.]

South Shaftsbury Vermont
December 16 1927

Dear Mr Gay-Tifft:

Sometime you <u>must</u> meet him[256] on a quiet hilltop in Vermont (this is an invitation), if only to repay you for taking so much trouble to read and understand him in a school room in Buffalo. By your description of November here, I judge you have been here before. When you come again, look in on me, spend some hours with me heedless of bells or whistles. I dont say this to many, because when I am away by myself I mean to be clear away; and I am clear away more months in the year than you might imagine. I dip into colleges for a few weeks a few times a year. (Thanks for ascribing to me so much generosity in dipping in). But nine months out of twelve I am so free from every duty and responsibility that I am often ashamed of myself.

---

255. See David Sanders, "Fostering the Poet: An Unpublished Robert Frost Letter," *Resources for American Literary Study* 29 (2005).
256. RF speaks of himself in the third person.

And you mustnt be too hard on Buffalo University in your thoughts. You must make allowances for their just being started out there. The room where I was receiving was make-shift. And you have to remember I was a new thing and quite a number wanted their chance at me.[257] I was really just receiving, not teaching, though appearances were against me. The conspiracy I'm in is to deformalize education all I can. I might hope that a city college would be a better subject for my schemes than any other for various reasons, but chiefly because it has less college life and so less disciplinary requirements and less social distraction. It might have real intellectual possibilities. It might, you know. You can help out there by breaking down the wall between college life and real life.* One of the things nearest my heart is to make college students expect as much of themselves as if they were not in college at all but out in a world of ideas and art and science.

This is more letter than I write to anyone. I may never write such another. I have to keep away from letters as well as schools most of the time.

Thanks and best wishes

Faithfully yours

Robert Frost

*Involve them in your magazine and art affairs.[258] I'll be back that way sometime and see what you have done.[259] RF

And I liked your poem. This is the main thing. Nothing else matters but our poetry.

[*To Mark Van Doren (1894–1972), poet, critic, and professor of English at Columbia. ALS. Columbia.*]

Amherst Mass

January 18 1928

Dear Van Doren:

If I seem slow with these things, its not from reluctance to keep my promise of that pleasant hour I had with you and your wife.[260] It takes a long time for

---

257. RF had given a reading and a talk at the University of Buffalo on November 10 and 11, respectively.

258. The *Buffalo Arts Journal,* founded by the Arts Club of Buffalo.

259. RF returned to Buffalo to give a reading on April 1, 1928.

260. The novelist Dorothy Graffe Van Doren (1896–1993).

me to make up my mind to part with a poem, longer to part with more than one: Even now I'm not quite ready to let you have these three if for no better reason than that they dont make up into a set to print together.[261] Why dont you choose one and send the rest back? Blood is in one vein and the others can't very well be in any vein and the figure kept.

We left the daughter, Margery, for the specialists to solve at Johns Hopkins. They've got nowhere in particular with her yet.

It seems as if we folks ought to see more of each other. We must have you up to visit us when we get our new farm. I'd like your son to meet our grandson.[262]

Amherst wont hold me forever. It looks to me as if it were in for a day of small things.[263] I'm hard to please in presidents, I begin to fear.[264] The only excitement we've had is our own chimney on fire by a poem I was throwing away to spare you the reading of it. The fire company turned out and for the moment I felt reconciled with the place. Let them have it as they please—will. Anyway, Let the long contention cease, Geese are swans and swans are geese.[265] Most teaching is mere correcting mistakes just as most loving is mere folly. Lud sing cuccu.[266]

I have no typewriter and I often shrink completely from going to a public stenographer with poetry. Forgive the handwriting.

Sincerely yours
Robert Frost

---

261. Van Doren was compiling *An Anthology of World Poetry*, to be published later that year (New York: Albert and Charles Boni, 1928). One of the poems RF had sent was "Blood" (renamed "The Flood" when included in *WRB*); the identity of the other two cannot be established, but for those that *did* make their way into *An Anthology of World Poetry* see RF to Mark Van Doren, May 17, 1928.

262. William Prescott Frost, son of Carol Frost and Lillian Labatt, was three years three months old at the time; Carl Van Doren (born in 1926) was one year eleven months.

263. Zechariah 4.10: "For who hath despised the day of small things?"

264. Arthur Stanley Pease (of Amherst College). Compare RF's remarks on page 597.

265. Lines from Matthew Arnold, "The Last Word" (1867).

266. "Loudly sing, cuckoo," from "Sumer is Icumen In," a mid-thirteenth-century English song. "Lud" is more commonly spelled "Lhude."

[To Mark Van Doren. ALS. Columbia.]

Amherst January 23 1928

Dear Van Doren:

I must say you know how to make a fellow feel pleased with his own poems. Thanks for the good words.

You'll notice that I hadn't quite parted with [the] poems when I sent them. There were a couple of lines written wrong in Blood. I am still writing them. I hope to have the definitive version before I mail this. Will you see to the alterations in the proof as anxiously as if they were your own?[267]

Ever yours
Robert Frost

Sixty dollars is splendid. All I demand money at all for is to compel respect for poetry in general.

We've had encouragement from Johns Hopkins. I'm hard to elate.[268]

[To Cyril Clemens (1902–1999), a third cousin twice removed of Mark Twain [Samuel Clemens] and founder, in 1923, of the International Mark Twain Society, lifetime memberships in which he offered to famous writers and politicians. He also designated them, from time to time, Knights of Mark Twain. It is unknown whether RF was aware that Clemens had, in 1927, made Benito Mussolini honorary president of the society, which would in 1936 be incorporated as a nonprofit organization as the Mark Twain Memorial Association. ALS-photostat. ACL.]

South Shaftsbury, Vermont
February 9 1928

Dear Mr Clemens:

I am greatly honored. I shall be proud of the association with the name of Mark Twain.[269]

Sincerely yours
Robert Frost

---

267. "Blood" was not in fact included in *An Anthology of World Poetry*. It was published in *The Nation* in February 1928 and as "The Flood" in *WRB* in November.

268. Encouraging news about Marjorie's health had just come in from Baltimore.

269. Filed with the photostat of this autograph letter at ACL is a note inscribed by RF on March 29, 1937, when he traveled to Kirkwood, Missouri, to accept the Mark Twain Gold Medal and one of Cyril Clemens's Mark Twain "Knighthoods": "Nothing American

[*To James Lukens McConaughy (1887–1948), president of Wesleyan from 1925 to 1943. ALS. DCL.*]

Amherst Mass, Feb 16 1928

Dear Mr McConaughy:

I have hesitated to accept your invitation till I should find out how the new semester arrangement here was going to affect me. I was afraid it might make it hard for me to get away in the middle of February. But hard or easy I must manage somehow. Please consider me enlisted.[270] There's nothing I'd be sorrier to miss than the chance to revisit you at Wesleyan. I saw a gentle poem of Bill Snow's in print a week or two ago that made me homesick for the Wesleyan winter landscape.[271]

Remember me to Mrs McConaughy.[272]

Sincerely yours
Robert Frost

[*To Charles Edwin Anson Markham (1852–1940), an American poet, anthologist, and social crusader who wrote under the name Edwin Markham. Markham was born in California and lived there until his move to New York in 1901. He had requested that RF contribute to an anthology of California poetry. ALS. Wagner.*]

Amherst [MA]
February 20 1928

Dear Mr Markham:

Good of you to bring me home thus to my California. I'm always thinking wistfully of the state, but I needed you to send me back to it in poetry before I would run the risk to imagination of going back to it in person. The poems will draw me after them. I can't refuse to follow where they have lead [*sic*]

---

in prose or verse is more lyric to my ear than Mark Twain's The Jumping Frog of Calaveras County. Robert Frost."

270. RF would read at Wesleyan in the Bennett Lectureship series on February 12 and 13, 1929.

271. "January Thaw," in the *Saturday Review of Literature* for January 14, 1928. Charles Wilbert "Bill" Snow had been teaching at Wesleyan since 1922, supported by McConaughy when, as often happened, Snow's outspoken left-wing political views landed him in trouble.

272. Elizabeth McConaughy.

the way. And I can't say how relieved I am to have the thing taken out of my own hands and settled for me.

The family thought you ought to be offered the choice between my only two strictly Californian poems.[273] These two are my property. Take either or both. The rest belong to Henry Holt and Co. You'll have to ask their permission to use them.

I am coming out to see you in the spring.

Faithfully your friend forever[274] for this act of generosity,

Robert Frost

[*To Lewis Mumford. Sent from Amherst, Massachusetts, the telegram does not include the year in the dateline, but "28?" has been inserted in an unidentified hand. TG. Penn.*]

AMHERST MASS

FEB 21 [1928]

LEWIS MUMFORD

4002 LOCUST ST LONG ISLAND CITY NY

NOT DOWN YET EXCEPT FOR NIGHT OF LECTURE MAKING A WEEK OF IT IN NEW YORK FROM ABOUT MARCH FIFTH MUST SEE YOU THEN[275] BEEN THINKING OF YOU A LOT LATELY

ROBERT FROST

---

273. Enclosed with the letter were typed and signed versions of "A Peck of Gold," on a page RF headed "California memory, 1880," and "Once by the Pacific," headed "California memory, 1882." These were included when the anthology was published in 1931. See John Russell McCarthy, ed., *Songs and Stories*, volume six of *California* (Los Angeles: Powell, 1931). The two poems also appear in RF's 1928 volume, *WRB*, issued by Henry Holt and Company in November.

274. Worth noting here is that, in the introduction he wrote for E. A. Robinson's *King Jasper* (1935), RF borrows a phrase, "immedicable woes," from Markham's "The Man with the Hoe": "There is solid satisfaction in a sadness that is not just a fishing for ministration and consolation. Give us immedicable woes—woes that nothing can be done for—woes flat and final. And then to play. The play's the thing. Play's the thing" (*CPRF*, 121–122).

275. We have been unable to date the lecture mentioned here, and it is not clear exactly when RF next saw Mumford. But a May 20, 1928, letter to Mumford indicates that he had in fact visited Mumford at his house in Sunnyside Gardens, Queens.

[*To Wilfred Davison. TG. Middlebury.*]

AMHERST MASS FEB 28 1928

PROF WILFRED DAVISON

MIDDLEBURY COLLEGE MIDDLEBURY VT

PUT ME DOWN WITH UNDERSTANDING THAT IF I MUST GO TO EUROPE YOU WILL
MAKE MY EXCUSES[276] SORRY YOU HAVE BEEN ILL[277] WISH I MIGHT SEE YOU BEST
WISHES

ROBERT FROST

[*To Loring Holmes Dodd. ALS. BU.*]

Amherst
February 29 1928

Dear Mr Dodd:

I don't see how I can possibly do what you ask this year. I'd like very much
the excuse to visit you again, but there are limits I have to set myself both in
the teaching and in the lecturing.[278] The lectures I allow myself take all the
strength I have to spare after Amherst and the two or three other colleges

---

276. RF, with Elinor and Marjorie, did spend late summer and early autumn of 1928 in
France and England. In July, however, shortly before sailing, RF gave a reading at the
Bread Loaf School of English. In late February or early March 1928 RF drafted a telegram
of inquiry to American Merchant Lines in New York, which survives as an inscription at
the foot of an August 24, 1927, letter to RF from Lincoln MacVeagh suggesting possible
dates of departure in September 1927. The Frosts had several times contemplated the trip,
and as many times deferred it. The draft, in RF's hand, reads: "Very much want accomo-
dation [*sic*] for three Mr & Mrs Robert Frost and daughter on some [ship] sailing between
May 15–June 15. If possible staterooms with baths. Please wire prospect collect" (letter
held now at DCL). As it happened, the Frosts sailed out of Montreal, not New York, and
on August 4, 1928.

277. Davison was still a young man, recently turned forty; he would die unexpectedly
in September 1929.

278. Dodd had first invited RF to speak at Clark University in the spring of 1921. RF
wasn't able to come at the time, but he did later speak at the university, again at Dodd's
invitation, on January 5, 1923. RF stayed at Dodd's house while there. During the visit
Dodd showed RF a number of woodcuts J. J. Lankes had done, inspired by RF's poems.
Lankes and RF soon began a long and fruitful collaboration, with Lankes providing
woodcuts for *NH*, *WRB*, and *Collected Poems* (1930).

that have me for a week or so every year.[279] We talked about you at the house of a delightful friend and disciple of yours at Lafayette one night not long ago. Illingworth was his name.[280]

Very best wishes to you and your wife.[281]

Sincerely yours

Robert Frost

[*To Katherine Larned Boggess (1905–1957), whose name RF misspells, and whom he mistakenly took for a man, having only seen, as it appears, "K. Larned Boggess" on the envelope bearing the request for an autograph.*[282] *ALS. Huntington.*]

South Shaftsbury Vermont*

April 9 1928

Dear Mr Beggess:

Subjoined with one autograph and if that isnt enough to satisfy your thirst, I shall be glad to write you another in any book of mine of any edition you will send me. Can friendliness go further?

Faithfully yours

Robert Frost

*My address for next four weeks.

---

279. RF spent one week as poet in residence at the University of Michigan in March 1928.

280. Robert Stanley Illingworth graduated from Clark University with the class of 1917, and would have met Dodd in that connection (Dodd was already on the faculty). Illingworth taught English at Lafayette College in Easton, Pennsylvania.

281. Ruth Esleeck Dodd (1881–1981).

282. This name also appears on the bookplate of a copy of *NB*. See Rare Book 491731 at the Huntington Library, the record for which reads in part: "Armorial bookplate of Katherine Larned Boggess; motto: Esse quam videri. Autographed cover with stamp addressed to Mr. K. Larned Boggess, postmarked Apr 9, 1928 in South Shaftsbury, Vermont mounted on front pastedown. Envelope once contained autograph signed letter from Robert Frost that was transferred to Mss. in June of 1991 (HM 59545). Photocopy of ALS placed in envelope."

[*To Lewis Mumford. ALS. BU.*]

South Shaftsbury Vermont
April 13 1928

Dear Mumford:

Business will keep me from getting back to Amherst to see and hear you. And perhaps it is just as well. I should only feel balked of you in that crowd of indifferent people. We count on having you and your wife up here some-time.[283] If I claim to have earned anything, it is the right to absolute selfish-ness with a few people. I will have them all to myself on ground of my own choosing. So or nohow.

I am going to hunt for you when I am in New York toward the end of week after next.[284]

I am sending Alfred a poem for his Caravan.[285]

Always yours
Robert Frost.

[*To George Lynde Richardson Jr. (1895–1934), American educator and poet. He was an Instructor in English at Phillips Exeter Academy from 1919 to 1932. ALS. Phillips Exeter.*]

South Shaftsbury Vermont
April 13 1928

Dear Mr Richardson:

I look forward to seeing you all again.[286] I shall arrive on some afternoon train Saturday and stay till Monday morning. I'm in your hands to do what

---

283. Mumford married Sophia Wittenberg (1900–1997) in 1920. Their son, Geddes, was born in 1926.

284. For the visit, see RF to Mumford, circa May 20, 1928.

285. With Mumford and Paul Rosenfeld, Alfred Kreymborg was editing *The Second American Caravan: a Yearbook of American Literature* (New York: Macaulay, 1928). It was a massive anthology, coming in at more than eight hundred pages with sixty-one contributors (and including poetry, fiction, and plays). RF contributed "The Walker" (subsequently collected in *WRB* as "The Egg and the Machine"). The first such anthology, which Mumford, Rosenfeld, and Kreymborg edited with Van Wyck Brooks, had appeared in 1927 as *The American Caravan* (New York: Literary Guild of America).

286. Lawrance Thompson in his unpublished chronology places RF at Exeter on Sunday, April 8, 1928. It would appear, on the evidence of this letter, that this is a mistake.

you please with. My only suggestion is that you give me a few fairly quiet hours just before the reading. Once I am safely through that I dont care what I do. I could see the Lantern Club[287] then or Saturday night, just as you choose. I particularly like company just after reading to take my mind off myself. But as I say I am in your friendly hands.

I'll have a few new poems to say for you. Tell the boys.

Sincerely yours
Robert Frost

[*To Arthur Stanley Pease (1881–1964), president of Amherst from 1927 to 1932. ALS. Harvard.*]

South Shaftsbury Vermont
April 23 1928

Dear Mr Pease:

Thanks for the restatement of my position and especially for the gracious addition as to when I may put in my term of residence.[288] I agree with you: ordinarily the position of a full professor shouldn't need restating every time a new president comes into office. But my case was peculiar, and seems to have called for special treatment. My position would have remained a false position as long as you understood it in one way and I in another. It is just as well we had Mr Olds' letter on the subject.

My only unhappiness that lingers is at having been caught holding on too hard to what I had as a gift. Holding on to a gift too hard is as bad as giving it to myself or as acting as if I deserved it. My skepticism goes a long way in that direction. I don't mean to insist on my value anywhere in any capacity. I myself should be willing to put it that I am not hired to visit Amherst: I am allowed to and allowed $5000 a year if I will refrain from teaching classes while

---

The present letter was written on a Friday. RF likely visited Exeter over the weekend of April 21–23. The last time he had lectured there was on December 10, 1923. On April 18, 1928, RF was in Boston, where he received the "Golden Rose" award from the New England Poetry Club.

287. The Lantern Club, the academy's literary society, published *The Monthly,* a magazine of student creative writing.

288. The reference is to the terms of the appointment RF had accepted at Amherst in 1927 under Pease's predecessor, George Olds (mentioned later in the letter).

there.[289] But please don't you put it quite so harshly. I know you won't. Let's forget all this. Thanks for your kind letter.

I should have answered you sooner, but I have been on my travels.[290] I've been seeing friends of yours as I went—and relatives: your sister-in-law at Exeter, Roy Elliot [*sic*] at Cambridge and Bartlett at Ann Arbor.[291] Bartlett had been in captivity for one hour among the head-hunters of Formosa since I saw him last. He had a pretty story of how he lost his heart to them but not his head. He had them all botanizing for him with their long knives. I heard the latest about his primroses. He still pursues the primrose way to knowledge.[292] He asked to be remembered to you.

Faithfully yours
Robert Frost

---

289. Ironic, but not entirely so: the terms of the contract called for RF to "be in residence to conduct special classes in English and to hold informal conferences with the students" for ten weeks between the Christmas and spring holidays. Students for his "special classes" were prescreened by colleagues. No other teacher in Amherst's Department of English had any such arrangement.

290. A series of lecture engagements took RF to Ann Arbor, Buffalo, and Phillips Exeter Academy in New Hampshire from March 25 to April 8.

291. Pease's sister-in-law was Marion B. Otis, née Faxon. At the time, she and her husband, Edward Osgood Otis, lived at 81 Front St. in Exeter. George Roy Elliott taught literature at Amherst. Harley Harris Bartlett (1886–1960), a tropical botanist, chaired the Department of Botany at the University of Michigan and was also director of its Botanical Gardens and Arboretum. In 1927 he undertook an expedition to Southeast Asia on behalf of the United States Rubber Company, one of several he made under the same auspices, working chiefly in Sumatra. He also did field work on Formosa (modern day Taiwan, then under Japanese occupation). His *A Botanical Trip to Formosa* (Washington, DC: Smithsonian) appeared in 1927. In 1929 he published *The Carvings of the Paiwan of Formosa* (Ann Arbor: University of Michigan Press). The Paiwan, indigenous to Formosa, often beheaded their enemies in warfare.

292. See *Hamlet* 1.3, where Ophelia chides her brother, Laertes:

> *But, good my brother,*
> *Do not as some ungracious pastors do,*
> *Show me the steep and thorny way to heaven,*
> *Whiles, like a puff'd and reckless libertine,*
> *Himself the primrose path of dalliance treads*
> *And recks not his own rede.*

Before joining the faculty at Michigan in 1915, Bartlett was a biologist with the Bureau of Soils and Chemistry in the U.S. Department of Agriculture, where he studied genetic

[To Lawrence H. Conrad (1898–1982), whom RF met during his first stint at the University of Michigan (1921–1923). TG. ACL.]

[Bennington, VT]

[April 24, 1928]

VACHEL LINDSAY LECTURES DETROIT APRIL 28 VERY MUCH WANTS ENGAGEMENT
MICHIGAN COULD YOU GET ONE ON SUCH SHORT NOTICE[293] SUPPOSE NOT BEST
WISHES

ROBERT FROST

[To Lewis Mumford. Date derived from internal evidence. A note at the top of the manuscript, presumably in Mumford's hand, indicates that he answered the letter on May 25, 1928. ALS. BU.]

[South Shaftsbury, VT]

[circa May 20, 1928]

Dear Mumford:

The poem in type is the one I sent Alfred before.[294] The one in writing is offered as an alternative. You editors ought to have some choice, however limited. You can't have both the poems, because they wouldn't pair well. Return one. I hope you will like one or the other half as well as I enjoyed my evening in your Utopia, once I was led to it by someone not so long out of it as to have forgotten the way back.[295]

Always yours

Robert Frost

---

mutations in the evening primrose (genus *Oenothera*); he published a dozen scientific papers on the flowers.

293. Conrad was president of the Michigan Authors Association and in that capacity arranged readings for poets. He replied to RF: "Engaged Lindsay yesterday for May first in Ann Arbor" (the reply is written on the telegram in Conrad's hand).

294. Alfred Kreymborg; see RF to Mumford, April 13, 1928, and the notes thereto, for information about the poem and the anthology for which it was intended.

295. An allusion to Mumford's first book, *The Story of Utopias* (New York: Boni and Liveright, 1922), but also to Mumford's house in Sunnyside Gardens, Queens, a community built under the auspices of the Regional Planning Association of America, of which Mumford was a member. See Donald Miller, *Lewis Mumford: A Life* (New York: Weidenfeld and Nicolson, 1989), 201–203. Sunnyside Gardens is now on the National Register of Historic Places as among the earliest planned communities in the nation.

[To Mark Van Doren. Scrawled in the bottom left-hand corner, not in RF's hand, is a list of poems: "The Oven Bird," "Mowing," "An Old Man's Winter Night," "The Tuft of Flowers," "The Pasture." Of these, "The Oven Bird," "An Old Man's Winter Night," and "The Tuft of Flowers" would be included in Van Doren's An Anthology of World Poetry, *together with "The Runaway," whose title in the list may have been given in error as "The Pasture" (the setting of "The Runaway" is a "mountain pasture"). ALS. Columbia.]*

South Shaftsbury Vt
May 17 1928

Dear Van Doren:

I confess a choice so perfunctory and slighting hurts my feelings.[296] It simply hurts them: I dont think it hardens them. If such is the best you naturally do with or for me, what do you say if I stay out of this anthology and turn my thoughts elsewhere?

Sincerely yours
Robert Frost

[To Wade Van Dore. ALS. BU.]

South Shaftsbury Vt
May 21 1928

My dear boy:

I am terribly sorry to put you off, but this would be no year for you to visit here as it turns out. My daughter has come home sick from Kansas and she will be all my son and his wife ought to have on their hands and minds while we are away.[297] It is serious or I shouldnt find it in my heart to ask you to

---

296. RF took affront at how Van Doren proposed to represent him in the anthology. His note eleven days later reveals that what seemed "perfunctory and slighting" was Van Doren's decision to use "Mending Wall." Once the nature of the anthology was clarified, RF apologized, suggesting that Van Doren use four short poems, not the longer but familiar "Mending Wall." Van Doren's agreement resulted in no living American poet having more poems in the book than RF. See RF to Van Doren, May 28, 1928.

297. Irma Frost Cone had just returned, in considerable distress, from Rozel, Kansas, where she and her husband, John Paine Cone, had settled. The two married in 1926 and moved to the Cone family homestead in Kansas, where they soon had a son, John Jr., born on September 29, 1927. Alarmed at the distress of which Irma had been speaking in

change your plans. We are a very mixed-up family just at this minute and I know you wouldnt want to add to our confusion.

I've had another look at the last-sent booklet. It has several fine things. The Last Leap I hadnt noticed before. Very terrible to the imagination. I have just a lingering doubt about the last few lines. They are good in a way but do they quite come out as a conclusion to the idea of the poem? Never rest from the effort to have and bring out the idea. It's with the idea you will prevail. See how you do it in Ice Ages and Tracks and Arrowheads. Wild Ground has a poor first stanza and I dont like dragging in our Mother (Mother Earth) to complicate the figures toward the end. She could be got out.[298]

What do you say if for your amusement you put me together into a similar booklet all the poems you want to preserve—your collected works to date. I'd like to see how it strikes me. I'd like to see how you judge yourself. Do this soon.

It is pleasant to have those folks out there so kind to you. But remember nothing counts but the sheer goodness of your own thought and art. Weight is what you must achieve to make a place for yourself in the ruck of rhymsters. The visitors at the Bread Loaf School of English made a great fuss discovering a certain young Charles Malam last summer and already he is out with a book, the only really good poem in which I enclose you.[299] From that culture spot he might have spread out pretty far. Whats now to prevent his spreading out from his other and worse poems.

---

letters home, her mother, Elinor, brought her back to the Stone House, now the property of Carol Frost and his wife, Lillian Labatt. Irma's husband, John, soon followed, hoping to save the marriage, and RF purchased for them a small farm in nearby Bennington, Vermont. The episode was yet another sign of Irma's descent into mental illness (from which RF's sister Jeanie also suffered). The incidents of spring 1928 only increased RF and his wife's worries as to how the family would fare when they went to Europe in August, accompanied by Marjorie, a trip that was being undertaken partly in the hope it would improve Marjorie's health.

298. All five poems named by RF are collected in Van Dore's first book, *Far Lake* (New York: Coward-McCann, 1930). Van Dore apparently took RF's suggestion as to the conclusion of "Wild Ground"; there is no "mother" in it, and no maternal metaphors.

299. Malam's first book, *Spring Plowing,* had just been published by Doubleday, Doran. The enclosure was separated from the letter.

I'm sorry I'm not going to see you. But the poems are the thing. You have a lonely job.

Always yours

Robert Frost

Don't wrack your brains trying to find out why I gave the prizes as I gave them in the Inlander contest.[300] They were that tantalizingly mediocre kind all of them in the magazine that I can do nothing with. All of them were well enough. Not one of them smote me with either sense or sound. Tis ever thus in these college-taught children. I heard a rather bitter New York critic say with assurance absolutely no poetry could come out of college. If it came out of college it was not poetry. It was pretty extreme but I let her (she was a she) say it.

R.F.

[To Mark Van Doren. ALS. Columbia.]

South Shaftsbury Vermont

May 28 1928

Dear Van Doren:

I'm too touchy—particularly with friends.[301] Treat me well and you'll be expected to treat me better. That's all the pay you'll get for treating _me_ well. Such I am, though I dont usually give myself away or get found out because I live too far off in the country to speak on impulse and I'm too lazy to write.

I could at least have asked you about the idea of your anthology before getting unhappy.

But if this passage at pens[302] hasnt lost me your respect and you still want to further my poetry, why not leave Mending Wall out of an anthology for

---

300. RF had judged a poetry contest for *The Inlander,* a literary magazine edited by students at the University of Michigan. RF had himself given the magazine a poem, "The Minor Bird," for its January 1926 number (the poem was retitled "A Minor Bird" for *WRB*). At the time, Van Dore lived in Detroit and, though not enrolled at Michigan, would have been following *The Inlander.*

301. See RF to Mark Van Doren, May 17, 1928.

302. A pun on the French *pas d'armes,* a formalized challenge issued in defense of a knight's territory.

once in a way and use in its place (of those you name) The Oven Bird, An Old Man's Winter Night and The Tuft of Flowers?[303]

Always yours sincerely

Robert Frost

[To John Bartlett. Dated from internal evidence. ALS. UVA.]

[South Shaftsbury, VT]

[circa June 1, 1928]

Dear John:

Hooray! To think that I shall set eyes on you in twenty days!—you and the only other Pinkerton graduate I ever really thought worth an A.[304] It's longer since I saw her than since I saw you. The last time I saw you, I guess, you were disappearing on foot down the wrong side of the hill into Littleton New Hampshire.[305] That must be ten years ago—one tenth of a lifetime, to put it mildly. The trouble is you wont stay round long enough. The minute you get here you'll begin to threaten to leave for Raymond. Them's Elinor's sentiments and Carol and Lillians too. Gee why can't you put the Bartlett Service on the running board if there isn't room for it in the car with the four children and transplant it to the east.[306] It might not be too old to transplant. And anyway they transplant trees of almost any age now.

Come on!

Imperatively

R.F.

---

303. All these poems were included in Van Doren's *Anthology of World Poetry*.

304. John's wife, Margaret.

305. While visiting RF in Franconia during the summer of 1916, Bartlett had suddenly been summoned home to tend to his ill children in Raymond, New Hampshire. The next year RF sent the Bartletts $50 to help fund their move to Colorado.

306. The Bartlett Syndicate Service, which managed correspondents throughout the West (*RFJB*, 135). "The running board": After one of their most successful years in journalism, the Bartletts had bought a new 1928 Essex sedan (145).

[To Louis Untermeyer. ALS. LoC.]

South Shaftsbury Vermont USA

June 21 1928

Dear Louis:

I've read the book more than I've read most books even by you.[307] It's a good book, at its best in such things as Variations on a Childs Game and Jewish Lullaby, and in such other things as Disenchantment, Positano and a Critique of Pure Rhyme. How the accents bring you back. If hearing were all, the book would be enough. But it seems as if I must see you somewhere soon again either in Europe or America. Are you coming home right away or are you going to wait in Europe till I can look you up there when we get over in August (as we should if our purpose holds).[308]

If I haven't written in a long time, I suppose it is because I haven't found anything very easy to say. My spirit barely moves in letter writing anyway under its burden of laziness and disinclination. The least addition of sorrow or confusion to my load and I stop altogether. Thats an amusing one you call Words Words Words.[309] For a cent I would subscribe to the sentiment. The logic of everything lands you outside of it; the logic of poetry outside of poetry (I neednt tell you how); the logic of religion by nice gradations outside of Catholicism in Protestantism, outside of Protestantism in agnosticism and finally outside of agnosticism in Watsonian behaviorism: the logic of love, outside of love (if it were only by physical exhaustion); the logic of strife, in China.[310] But what leaves the heart in the mystery and the sting in

---

307. Untermeyer's *Burning Bush* (New York: Harcourt, Brace, 1928).

308. After remarrying in New Jersey, Louis and Jean Untermeyer had traveled that summer to the Black Forest on a second honeymoon. Elinor, Marjorie, and Robert Frost set sail for France on August 4 with the idea that Marjorie would remain in France with Marguerite Fischbacher, a friend of Dorothy Canfield Fisher, while Elinor and Robert traveled to England.

309. Collected in *Burning Bush*. Untermeyer borrows his title from *Hamlet* 2.2:

Polonius. . . . What do you read, my lord?
Hamlet. Words, words, words.
Polonius. What is the matter, my lord?
Hamlet. Between who?
Polonius. I mean, the matter that you read, my lord.

310. John Broadus Watson (1878–1958) was the founder of behaviorist psychology. In June 1928, forces loyal to the Republic of China captured Beijing during the Chinese Civil War.

death is the fact that when you have eliminated yourself by logic as clear out as Eenie meenie minie moe, then you are as good as in again. Which is one of several things that has lead [*sic*] great men to suspect time and space and motion (however directed) and thought of being vicious circles—vicious.[311] We are what we are by elimination and by deflection from the straight line. Life is a fight we say and deify the prizefighter. We could go further and say life is a night club and its presiding deity a <u>retired</u> prizefighter or Bouncer, bouncing us forever out.

I was arrested at your Koheleth.[312] You and I think we know each other pretty well. But I wonder if you ever realized (I never did before) that a good way to distinguish between our natures would be in the way you have and I havent searched in books and out of books for rooted convictions. The only time I ever wish I had convictions is when I am asked for the loan of them. I'm afraid all I see in books and going round is ideas to emulate—to try if I cant have the like of. The only thing that can disappoint me in the head is my own failure to learn to make metaphor. My ambition has been to have it said of me He made a few connections. Sounds fearfully humble—the aspiration of mere craftsmanship. Never mind. Its fun to give the show away; My head may be second rate.[313] But I wasnt bidden to have a heart in vain. If my mind isnt bent on convictions my heart seems set on a few human beings. Not many. But that makes my position all the more perilous. Friends and convictions—what's the difference? One ought to go in for neither or both.

---

311. Aristotle, Newton, and Descartes all wrestled with the concepts of time, space, and circular motion. In the early twentieth century, mathematicians such as Bertrand Russell and Henri Poincaré suggested that nonpredictive statements in classical mechanics had culminated in vicious circles of reasoning, in which mathematical definitions and scientific conclusions were reciprocally linked.

312. See "Koheleth" (in *Burning Bush*), stanza 3:

> I searched in the Book
> > For rooted convictions
> Till the badgered brain shook
> > With its own contradictions.

"Koheleth" is the Hebrew word for "gatherer" or "teacher," and also the name taken by the author of Ecclesiastes. In Ecclesiastes, Koheleth considers the meaning of life and decides that it is *hevel*, which can be loosely translated as "transitory" and "meaningless."

313. The semi-colon is in the manuscript.

It does me good to be where I can talk nonsense to you again. Some film has gone off my mind.

Always yours

R.

Speaking of Metaphor[314]

In going from room to room in the dark,
I reached out blindly to save my face,
But neglected to close my arms in an arc.
The old door got inside my guard
And hit me a blow in the head so hard
I got my basic metaphor jarred.
All things still pair in metaphor
But not with the mates they had before.
I hardly know the world any more.

R.

[To Lincoln MacVeagh. ALS. Jones.]

South Shaftsbury Vermont
June 28 1928

Dear Lincoln:

It has been no use: I have had no answer I could give your telegram all week. Our visitors have been the kind that simply couldnt tell us exactly when they were coming or when they were going. They were from the four quarters. Three of them were named John. One had four children with him.[315] One was from New Zealand, my one and only first cousin.[316] I didn't know that I

---

314. Retitled "A Door in the Dark" (and much revised) when RF brought the poem into *WRB*.

315. John and Margaret Bartlett had four children (see RF to Bartlett, December 23, 1926).

316. John Moodie, RF's first cousin and the only son of Thomas Moodie, the sole brother of his mother, Isabelle ("Belle") Moodie Frost. John had visited the family unexpectedly while passing through the United States en route to the United Kingdom. On his return to New Zealand he wrote the first of what would be a number of long letters

had any. I had supposed my mother's only brother died childless when very young in shipwreck. The cousin proved up all right—a regular Scot who seemed to have come all the way from Christchurch to protest severely against my having allowed my biographer to spell my mother's maiden name Moody instead of Moodie. He was so hard on the inaccuracy that I saw at once he was no impostor.[317]

At this writing there is a red-headed Jew from Chicago and his wife hovering in a Bennington hotel all ready to seize me in his talents the minute I drop out of the herd. You can imagine the state Elinor is in.

And yet I must see you soon or forget what I was going to say. I have a good mind to come down Tuesday or Wednesday to settle up with a few of my publishers before I put to sea.[318] I'm mad about something I'll tell you more about when I see you. Would you be where I could have a day with you or are you in Dublin?[319] I wish you could wire collect.

Always yours in any case
Robert Frost

---

to RF (held now at DCL). On the last sheet he sketched out a family tree, which included the members of the Moodie family in Columbus, Ohio, whose household Belle had joined as child, in 1856, after immigrating from Scotland. Worth mentioning are two daughters in the Columbus family: Jeanie and Florence, the namesakes of RF's sister, Jeanie Florence Frost. As for the third "John": Irma's husband John Paine Cone (or perhaps their infant son John Cone Jr.).

317. In *Robert Frost: A Study in Sensibility and Good Sense,* the first book devoted entirely to RF, Gorham Munson indeed misspells Belle's maiden name.

318. Earlier in the year RF had again considered leaving Henry Holt and Company. However, renegotiation of his contract with Holt in May, with highly favorable results for the poet, kept him with the firm. When he wrote MacVeagh, all of the terms were, apparently, yet to be finalized. They would, once settled, call for a monthly stipend of $250 for five years; higher royalties for his next volume, *WRB* (issued in limited and trade editions in November 1928); a new and expanded *Selected Poems* (also issued in November 1928); and, to cap things off, publication, in 1930, of *The Collected Poems of Robert Frost.* See *YT,* 314–315.

319. The MacVeagh family owned a summer estate in Dublin, New Hampshire, named Knollwood; it is now on the National Register of Historic Places. Knollwood was built in 1899–1900 by Lincoln's great-uncle Franklin MacVeagh, who served as secretary of the treasury under William Howard Taft.

[To James R. Wells (1898–1971). Wells ran a number of small boutique presses, including the Fountain Press, the Bowling Green Press, and—as a private venture—the Slide Mountain Press. This letter was addressed to Wells at Crosby Gaige (the publisher). ALS. ACL.]

South Shaftsbury Vermont

July 14 1928

Dear Mr Wells:

I saw the moment I met you you were a real poet's publisher. You would be my friend and helper in whatever you undertook to do with my poetry. You went so far as to say in kindness once that if this contract made me unhappy, I was to tear it up. But your chiefest liberality lay in leaving the book it called for unnamed and undescribed so that I could have it anything I pleased. That was the way to my heart. You must have seen you had me. It simply doesnt seem as if misunderstanding could arise in a relationship like ours, more friendship than business. But certainly a little confusion has arisen that I find very uncomfortable. I wonder if it wouldn't clear the air if I went over some of the plans we have talked about in fulfillment of the contract.

1) The book could be anything I pleased.[320] When you went away after your first visit, it seemed as if you would be satisfied to have it twenty or thirty old poems with a few new ones to set them off. I got the Holts permission to use the old poems. It still stands I assume.

2) The next time you came it was with Mrs Gaige and I could see you were both hoping the poems for the book might be all new.[321] I saw a possibility there if the book needn't be too large. The talk about size was vague, but I gathered forty pages might be enough.

---

320. In the event, the outcome was modest: RF's whimsical (and very short) "One-Act Irish Play," *The Cow's in the Corn*, was published by the Slide Mountain Press in 1929. One of the first ventures of this press was a luxury edition of E. A. Robinson's six-stanza poem *Fortunatus* (Reno, 1928). *The Cow's in the Corn* would be published out of Wells's home in Gaylordsville, Connecticut.

321. Crosby Gaige (1882–1949), New York theater producer and *bon vivant*, had established a publishing house in 1927; this firm was taken over by Wells in 1929. Possibly connected to these developments, and to Wells's visit to RF in the company of Mrs. Gaige, was the breakdown of the Gaige marriage in 1928.

3) The next I knew we were wondering if the Holts wouldn't let you do the special edition of my next book with them.[322] You never talked about getting my next book away from them entirely. You knew I had tried hard to do that for another publisher and failed dismally. I made a bad business of it. The wonder was that I had anybody the least friendly left in the firm. The weakness of my position was that I couldn't bear to go to a new publisher and not take my four old books with me. I've got to keep my books together.

4) There was talk of your taking my future over and making me a Crosby Gaige author at a salary of $4000 a year. I didnt know how serious you were in that. It was a pleasant dream while it lasted.

5) Finally you proposed to do a book of new poems to lead off with this year, a book of snow poems, old ones, next year, a book of metaphysical poems, old ones, the year after and then a couple of books of plays. You thought you could give me about $5000 in the next five years. You speak of this in a recent letter. The Harbor Press started up your interest in the plays. You mustnt grudge Wood that small play. It was his play as much as mine. In his acting days he "created" the chief part in it.[323]

Here is or ought to be enough to figure something from. Do you really want to make a definite contract with me for five specific books in the next five years with royalties at 15% when you have to pay the Holts for any rights, 20% when you have nothing to pay them?

Two things are clear. You dont want to go back to the original idea and take a book of new and old poems mixed. The Holts wont let anybody else have a hand in my immediate next book. I have had enough trouble with them about things. You wont ask me to have any more right now.

The book can be anything I please. But of course it must please you too. We are friends in all this. You want it to be new material you are sure? You think it for the best interests of everybody concerned. I rely on your judgement. The question is must it be new verse. What should you say to one of

---

322. *WRB*, published in November 1928. The limited edition of this volume was designed and printed by D. B. Updike at the Merrymount Press, not by Wells.

323. The play is *A Way Out*, published (in book form) by the Harbor Press (New York) in 1929; the play had first appeared in *The Seven Arts* for February 1917. Roland Wood, an ex-student of RF's at Amherst—and a cofounder of the Harbor Press—had played the role of Asa in the first performance of the play at the Northampton Academy of Music in February 1919 (*LRF-1*, 647).

my fairly long short poems that will go to make a book called Talks Walking when I have enough of the same kind? It may be 150 lines long. It is some folk myth in the making. Then I have a poem in the rough on California. How long could I have to polish it off?[324] It is like my New Hampshire. What should you say to a short play in prose? That is about one of my sculptor friends.[325]

I take it you don't insist on quantity. George Moore's play is short. There arent fifty pages of it nor twenty lines of speech to the page.[326] Wolfs book is shorter.[327]

Let's get something out of all you have thought of and have it over with. I might even dig you out a few of my poems for the book after next on a pinch. Only it would have to be with the written understanding that they wouldnt be precluded from the book after next or some other book with the Holts in the end.

You can straighten things out for me. Help!

Ever yours

Robert Frost

Money is nothing to me.[328] Money is nothing to you. You could have the three hundred dollars back at the word. But that isnt what you want. You want to publish something of mine and I very much want you to.

R.F.

---

324. No poem on California and "like" RF's "New Hampshire" survives.

325. "In an Art Factory," inspired by RF's acquaintance with the sculptors Alfeo Faggi (1885–1966), Lorado Taft (1860–1936), and Aroldo Du Chêne (1883–1961), and the illustrator James Ormsbee Chapin (1887–1975) (*CPPP*, 995). Thompson suggests that Du Chêne was the person RF specifically had in mind (*SL*, 348). RF never published it (for the text, see *CPPP*, 576–578).

326. George Moore (1852–1933), Irish novelist and playwright. Moore's one-act play *The Making of an Immortal* (New York: Bowling Green Press, 1927) runs to fifty-nine pages, with twenty-five lines of dialogue per page.

327. Robert Leopold Wolf (born 1895), New York–based author. His scandalous *Deux Contes* (New York: Isthmus Press, 1928) is just thirty-two pages long.

328. In a letter to Wells dated October 11, 1929 (and held at ACL), RF waived royalties of $61.42 for *The Cow's in the Corn*, saying, "It's only a joke."

[To Groff Conklin (1904–1968), formerly a student at Dartmouth, later to enjoy distinction as an anthologist. No address is given and the envelope has not survived. Dated by the recipient. ALS. ACL.]

[South Shaftsbury, VT]
[July 23, 1928]

My dear Conklin

You have to take me at my own rate of speed.

These are serious poems. Your letter about them is very able. You must know you write good prose. Compared with much going your poems are plenty good enough. Compared with what they might be they leave some things for you to consider. I should think your own ear would tell you the lovely form of The Mortal Sound is terribly marred by the trouble you get into with the accents in the third stanza. I dont think the logical steps are perfectly taken in "I Want I Want." Are the three dots in front of "I prize" an admission of fumbling? What is the special value of a word like "fist" in a poem like Ambition? It is out of the wrong font, your own taste must tell you. You havent quite the courage or the consciousness of what you are about to go through with it thoroughly. Form in the highest sense of the word is your lay—the reference of every part to every other part and no more parts than you can remember every relation of. You are exalted with it at times, but you let down as if you lacked anyone to hold you up to your true self or werent quite sure it was important as you sometimes thought it was. I say it as I see it. You've got much and you've perhaps realized it enough to deserve publication but not quite enough for you or me. Draw yourself up a little firmer.— I've been dipping in again—I'm very sure I'm right.

Sometime we must meet and talk.

Sincerely your friend
Robert Frost.

[To John W. Haines. ALS-photostat. DCL.]

South Shaftsbury Vermont USA
July 29 1928

Dear Jack:

We have the tickets and that is nearer you and England than we have been for thirteen years. The only thing that can keep me from walking a path with you this year will be the failure of Margery to come up to the mark on sailing day. She is not right. We have a nurse in the house conditioning her for the trial by water. We will have to think of her a good deal while over. We plan to put her in charge of a nurse companion in France to see if the interest in picking up French and the society of some one young enough to laugh a lot wont help her case. So we are sailing, if we sail, directly for France. The ship leaves Quebec Canada with or without us on August 4th.[329] Don't set your heart too much on seeing us—and I will try not to set my heart too much on seeing you. I will bring Elinor to your house inside of a few weeks now, though, if it in me lies. You dont care how old we look. Wont it be astonishing to find ourselves again with the three of you.[330]

Always yours

Robert Frost

[To Richard Thornton. Dated from internal evidence. ALS. DCL.]

[South Shaftsbury, VT]

[early August 1928]

My Dear Thornton:

If I seem slow it is not from lack of appreciation of all your kindness and concern. I dont mean to be slow. This is comparatively quick for me.

Im hurrying it off on the noon train. Theres enough to give you the idea. Will you send me some copies in type? By the time you do I shall have the rest ready for you.[331]

Just one thing I think of now. Dont have many pictures. Lankes will understand easily they are not to illustrate but simply decorate with New England subjects of his own choosing. And I am sure they had best be houses and places—<u>not people at all</u>.[332]

---

329. The SS *Montnairn*.
330. Haines, his wife, Dorothy, and their son Robin.
331. *WRB* was being readied for the press.
332. None of J. J. Lankes' woodcuts for *WRB* depicts people.

The West-running Brook poem I name the book for is blank verse oddly enough among all this rhyming.

> Best wishes.
> Yours faithfully
> Robert Frost

[To Herschel Brickell (1889–1952). Date derived from internal evidence. ALS. Alger.]

> [South Shaftsbury, VT]
> [August 2, 1928]

Dear Mr Brickell:

I made the best haste I could with this with twenty visitors on top of me to say farewell. I'm sorry it hasn't caught an earlier train. You'll have to make allowances for me this time. I'll do differently if I ever get round to another book. I mean I'll start a year ahead of the printers to shape up the manuscript.

The sheets for my autograph have come and I shall be at them till the last minute.[333] I ought to know my own name by the time we leave for Montreal at three this afternoon, but I shan't know it. I shan't know which end my head is on.

Well it isnt such bad fun having to do something in a hurry like a man of affairs for once in a way. It makes me feel manly.

You'll be sending me the proof soon I expect. I can see then to anything I have overlooked.

We'll be dropping down the St Lawrence on the Montnairn for Cherbourgh [*sic*] by the time you get this.[334] Our address for a while will be c/o American Express Rue Scribe Paris.

> Best wishes
> Sincerely yours
> Robert Frost

---

333. Presumably, sheets for the signed, limited edition of *WRB*, which Henry Holt and Company would issue in November alongside the trade edition and an expanded edition of RF's *Selected Poems*.

334. On August 4, RF, Elinor and Marjorie boarded the SS *Montnairn*, bound for Cherbourg, France. The *Montnairn* had been launched in 1907 in Gestemunde, Germany, as the SS *Prinz Friedrich Wilhelm*; subsequently she changed hands a number of times. In 1928 the ship regularly made crossings from Quebec to France and to Liverpool.

[To Henry Seidel Canby. ALS. Yale.]

South Shaftsbury Vt
August 3 1928

Dear Canby:

No Yelping Hill for us this year I'm terribly sorry to have to say.[335] Tell your wife to ask us again when we come back from Europe. If she will.

Say—you know—I wish you would have the sand to print a poem I am having Lesley carry to you. It's a harsh one and a hellbender—the best I ever did. You could blank the bad words in it.[336] It isnt a ballad and yet maybe it is. It uses no ballad arcaicisms [*sic*]. It belongs to my next book after the next but one, the title of which will be "You got to care." I hate people that change round without animosity. I want them to shoot and poison each other in the extremity of emotion. Various and sundry tell me your paper called for an aphrodisiac for me in verse once. The fact is I never needed one. Its those whey-juiced anemics that needed it. They wanted one from me or any one who would take pity on their flaccidity. This is it—this Murder poem.

In terrible haste. I'm off down stream from Quebec. Treat me well behind my back. Make any check out to my daughter Lesley Frost in whom I am greatly interested.

Ill send you something else and different from France England or Ireland.

Ever yours
Robert Frost

[To Lesley Frost. ALS. UVA.]

South Shaftsbury Vt
August 3 1928

Dear Lesley:

A few things in parting. The enclosed check is a present to start the History of Literature bookcase in The Open Book. I had the check through Pierce

---

335. Yelping Hill, Connecticut, where in the summer Canby presided over gatherings of artists, writers, and other choice spirits.

336. "The Middletown Murder," published in the *Saturday Review of Books*, October 13, 1928, and not subsequently included in any collection of verse by RF. The errant wife in the poem, Kate, is a "whore" and her lover, Walt, a "galloping bastard."

Cummings for Atmosphere.[337] I am going to send you home some books for that case from the London bookstands. Tell Canby to make out the check to you for The Middletown Murder and send the proof to me. <u>You keep it.</u>[338]

Tell Barbara Young I sent you to make my apologies.[339] Tell her I didnt get her letter till much too late.

Marjorie seems so-so and we are off on the Flyer for Queens Hotel Montreal this afternoon (Friday).[340] The Montnairn starts us down stream at three tomorrow. Too bad we werent educated against seasickness by being lowered suddenly a lot when babes in arms.

I had a fine time at the ball game with Dwight.[341] I didnt quite hold my own on the peanuts and hot dogs. Another time I'll go prepared to eat everything. We didnt arrive in time to make my team win the first game. In fact we seemed to throw them into confusion. I supposed we embarrassed them coming in after they had given us up. We made ourselves felt for good in the second game all right. I thought I could make them win if I put my mind on it.

Goodbye my dear. We'll write from the boat. Don't let Johnny Farrar trouble you.[342] You trouble him. Such a misleader deserves no consideration. I dont forgive him.

The manuscript came all perfected.[343] Be sure to speak to Pat.[344] Tell him he will see me in Dublin.

---

337. "Atmosphere," collected in *WRB* (1928) first appeared in the *Ladies' Home Journal* in October 1928 as "Inscription for a Garden Wall."

338. This phrase appears in the left margin next to the first paragraph.

339. In May, the poet Barbara Young, author of *The Keys of Heaven* (New York: Fleming H. Revell, 1927), and the patron of the arts Frances Randolph announced plans to open Poetry House, a venue for poets and artists on East Tenth Street in Manhattan.

340. The Flyer offered rail service from New York and Boston to Montreal (via southern Vermont).

341. RF attended a doubleheader with Lesley's fiancé, James Dwight Francis, on June 28. The Boston Red Sox lost game one to the Washington Senators (4–3), but won game two (8–7).

342. RF and John Farrar frequently disagreed about the objectives of the Bread Loaf Writers' Conference, with RF arguing that too many of the sessions dealt with commercial publishing advice rather than writing instruction. Tensions between RF and Farrar were further complicated by Lesley Frost's report that she had been slighted by Farrar while under his employ in New York City at the publishing house of Doubleday, Doran.

343. *WRB*, published in November.

344. Irish poet and playwright Padraic Colum.

I'll have to tell you what you can let Davison have. Ask him if he couldnt sell the Middletown Murder to Squier [*sic*] or someone.[345] It doesnt matter except that he seems bent on interceding for me anywhere and everywhere.

Goodbye again. Hold on though. The other enclosed slip is a duplicate list of my wealth in the Bennington First National Bank. Put it in a very safe place. Dont loose [*sic*] it.

> Affectionately
> Papa

[*To Otto Manthey-Zorn. As he explains in the next letter, RF neglected to post the final sheet(s) of this one. The asterisked note explaining that Bellevue is in France is RF's. ALS. ACL.*]

> Bellevue* (*In France)
> Aug [18] 1928

Dear Otto:

I guess I'll write you the first letter from over here just to let you know that our leaving without saying goodbye wasn't a case of desertion. We had said we were going so often to no purpose that we simply made up our minds this time not to say we were going till we went. Never say die till you're dead. Never say you are going to Heaven till you get there. Don't take that as meaning we think Paris is Heaven. It may or may not be, all depending on how much it succeeds in interesting Marj in the French language and how much good it does her. We had a pretty good time the first few days in the small streets we lived in poking around for ourselves and probably we should have done better to let well enough alone and stay there among the lower classes without benefit of butter or milk. But someone's recommendation brought us out here to Bellevue (next to Sèvres) for tranquility—our lifelong pursuit and occasional capture. It seems to be proving the trial ground or trial sky of a firm of avion manufacturers.[346] We shant like that. We are not at all

---

345. Apparently RF wished to place the poem in a British magazine (in addition to placing it in *The Saturday Review*). RF refers to Edward "Ted" Davison, Scottish-American poet, and. Sir John Collings Squire, British poet, critic, and editor of the *London Mercury*.

346. Meudon, where Bellevue is situated, was an early center of the French aviation industry.

sure that we like anything yet. So don't be surprised if the next time you hear we are in England for an outlet to our pent-up powers of speech. We are pretty well cut off from communication just at present and content to be if anything ultimately comes of it. Dammed back in thought long enough we may break out some day in the foreign language that is handiest. Who knows? I ought not to be indulging myself in English at this minute probably. But God have mercy, I cant be expected always to be kept under. Before I shut the doors of pleasure on myself, let me tell one thing I have on my mind. It is the ghost of President Wilson whom I remember your writing about from Germany years ago when you were over doing your book.[347] The Germans said God damn Wilson, you wrote. I am not good enough at French to know what the French now think of the poor man, but they have arranged for his ghost to walk in this city for a long time to come.[348] Here overlooking the whole city is a small treesy park called Place du President Wilson and there's a fine avenue named after him that runs right through the statue of George Washington. He shares the permanence with Washington and Franklin. It must make Teddy jealous in Heaven.[349] It is a sad story—one of the saddest in history. And we saw it happen every step of the way. I hated the sentimental sophistry of his "Too proud to fight" and worse still his "Nothing permanent was ever achieved by force" and I feel as if I was part of the mercilessness that put him down.[350] But I weaken now at the thought of him fallen with a crash almost Napoleonic. He had calibre—he saw as vastly as anyone that ever lived. He was a great something if it was only a great mistake. And he wasnt merely his own mistake. He was the whole world's mistake everybody's at one time there but Henry Cabot Lodge's—as much the whole world's as was Napoleon or Alex-

---

347. *Germany in Travail* (Boston: Marshall Jones, 1922). Amherst had granted Manthey-Zorn leave of absence—from the summer of 1920 to January 1921—so he could do research for the book.

348. President Woodrow Wilson (1856–1924) was the architect of the 1919 Treaty of Versailles, which imposed harsh reparations upon the defeated Germans. Wilson's main efforts in this period were devoted to the establishment of the League of Nations.

349. Theodore Roosevelt (1858–1919), twenty-sixth president of the United States. Among his many objections to Wilson was the latter's pacifist foreign policy during the first three years of the Great War. During the war RF's position had been closer to Roosevelt's than to Wilson's.

350. Wilson, still in office, suffered a serious stroke on October 2, 1919.

ander.[351] Some might think his failure was in missing a mark that someone else to come after him will hit, but I suspect it was worse than that: he missed a mark that wasnt there in nature or human nature. His [. . .][352]

[To Otto Manthey-Zorn. Paris postmark. RF enclosed various advertisements for Parisian postal services, to one of which, depicting a fashionable young woman with one finger to her lips, he added the note "This is our only encounter with the Paris they tell of. It was handed me on the street. It might save going any more to the Am. Ex." ALS. ACL.]

[Sèvres and Paris]

[August 18, 1928]

Dear Otto:

I find lying round what seems to be the end of a letter without a beginning. I guess it must be the end of the letter I mailed this morning. Well, I guess I'll just have to write it another beginning if I can make the joint with it all right.

I ventured into the American Express Office in Paris with my eyes down cast so as not to recognize anybody from home and whom should I run into bodily but young Cohn, Amherst '31.[353] All that sea-sickness just to find Amherst here ahead of me. He was one of those boys I gave an incomplete education to last year in the class I loved and lost. It shows how your sins will come home to roost and your chickens will find you out. I could resolve to keep away from the American Express where they dont treat you very well any way as too common a breed of sight-seer, but I want any mail that may be coming to me and I dont know that the Am. Ex. is much more dangerous than anywhere else. Take Versailles for instance. I was going down the pictures of the great generals from Charles Martel through Tourennes to Napoleon all so foreign when I ran spang into George Washington again.[354]

---

351. Henry Cabot Lodge (1850–1924), a Republican senator whose opposition to ratification of the Treaty of Versailles effectively blocked American entry to the League of Nations.

352. The letter breaks off here. The continuation of the sentence beginning "His" would seem to be "hugeness was an inflated nothing" (see the next letter and the note thereto).

353. George Cohn Jr., Amherst class of 1931 (died 1981).

354. Charles Martel (circa 688–741), general of the Frankish armies in the decisive defeat of Muslim forces at the Battle of Tours in 732. "Tourennes" is RF's mistake for Henri

Everything is American to him who looks with American eyes. Nobody in this house had the American eyes to discover in years what I noticed the moment I walked out to the look-off place that the town is named for, Bellevue. It is the site of the palace where Madame Pompadour kept herself or was kept.[355] The palace was distroyed [*sic*] during the Revolution.[356] The street leading into the place is called the street of the eighteenth of November nineteen hundred and eighteen and the place is called after President Wilson.[357] None of the French would believe it till they went out and looked. It brought me closer to him and increased his stature to find him lost in that corner. His[358] hugeness was an inflated nothing, but it would be impossible to enlarge on it too much while it lasted. It would be a subject for a Hugo to enhuge.[359]

I'm having a new book in the fall, I don't know just how.[360] I started bravely out to prepare the Holts for the idea of letting my next book when it should be ready next year go to another publisher and ended ignominiously but not unprofitably in letting the Holts have it now. It will only be shorter by a few poems for not waiting longer.[361] It will mean ommitting [*sic*] the few I wanted to have round a little longer for a finishing touch. You've seen most if not all that go in.

We didn't dare to make this expedition with Marj as she is and we didnt dare not to make it. The second fear won and we are here. I doubt if we'll be able to stay. At most I hope to see a few friends. Then for sea sickness again and home. The money we'll have spent would have bought a whole New England farm. I'll have to teach on an extra year at Amherst to make up for

---

Vicomte de Turenne (1611–1675), represented both in sculpture and on canvas at the Palace of Versailles.

355. Madame de Pompadour (1721–1764), mistress of Louis XV.

356. Although looted during the Revolution, the Château de Bellevue was not demolished until 1823.

357. Avenue du 11 (not 18) Novembre 1918 in Meudon runs into the Place du Président Wilson.

358. This marks the end of the second sheet of the letter (see note 352). All that follows should be considered a continuation of the first letter RF had mailed, incomplete, earlier the same day.

359. Victor Hugo (1802–1885), French novelist.

360. *WRB*.

361. Poems added to *WRB* in the 1930 *Collected Poems* were "The Lovely Shall Be Choosers," "What Fifty Said," and "The Egg and the Machine."

the losses. Nevertheless the Louvre is good. And I'll be glad to see Haines, de la Mare, and Squier [*sic*].[362]

Did you hear that Scotty Buchanan had done one of the best books in philosophy lately?[363]

> Our best to you.
> Faithfully yours
> Robert Frost

Owing to the uncertainty of human affairs you cant address us better than in care of the American Express 11 Rue Scribe Paris. They'll send anything back home to us that comes too late.

[*To Lesley Frost. ALS. UVA.*]

> Paris
> August 21 1928

Dear Lesley:

I don't believe this can last long the way it is going. The French are at their worst, I should imagine, at this time of year with the Americans all over them. We have to try too hard to be fair to them. All we can say is countries never love each other. The detestable thing is the greedy leer and wink everybody has for us and our money. You neednt publish it at home, but what we are most aware of is not the beauty of Paris, but the deceitful hate all round us. Even in Dorothy's friends, the Fishbashers.[364] They are more or less secretly annoyed at our lack of French and I cant blame them for that, as why should we be here incommunicado? But it goes deeper down still. I suppose it has something to do with the debt—at any rate with our being rich and their being poor, the franc worth four cents that was worth twenty and our dollar as good as it ever was. The question is who is to blame for instituting the comparison. I suppose we are by our presence in their country. The girl usher at the the-

---

362. John "Jack" Haines, Walter de la Mare, and John "Jack" Collings Squire.

363. Scott Milross Buchanan (1895–1968), philosopher and educationalist, an early convert to Alexander Meiklejohn's radical pedagogy. RF is referring to Buchanan's first book, *Possibility* (London: Kegan Paul Trench and Trubner, 1927).

364. Dorothy Canfield Fisher had arranged for Elinor, Marjorie, and Robert Frost to reside in the Sèvres home of Marguerite Fischbacher. Marjorie would stay on there while RF and Elinor traveled to England.

atre the other night ran off with the stubbs [*sic*] of our tickets instead of taking the trouble to hand them to us when we were in our seats and the office sent someone else back to us with them and a demand for more money for the favor—an actual demand before everybody in the audience. I paid. We went to church at the Madeleine on Sunday.[365] The usher there led us to seats and then insolently blocked the entrance with his foot hard down till I had slipped some money into his underhand. Then someone else prowling the congregation with a fist full of paper money, a woman, descended on us and demanded more money. We paid to avoid making a scene when the priests were marching countermarching bobbing and genuflecting up in front. It was loathsome even to me who part with my money too easily. Outside yelling worse than I ever heard them anywhere, the news boys insulted us personally by coming right at us with New York and London papers. "Latest news from Oshkosh and Minnehaha," was their line. As I say our effect on them is bad. We degrade them in some way. I have no doubt among themselves they are like any other nation. Probably their success in the war hurt them somewhat too. The most prominent of the new statuary in the Tuilleries [*sic*] Gardens shows a great falling off in taste and greatness. It is a puffed up strutting piece of bombast called Victory.[366] I don't believe that as a people they are in a very admirable state. They need to be left to themselves for a while. And I think we will leave them. We'll see how much more themselves the English appear.

I wish you had told us more of the marvelous escape you had in the automobile wreck. There were three cars in the collision, you say. You only speak of two after it. I suppose the third disappeared into thin air—ceased to exist. I think you'll have to do something to break yourself of the habit of being in automobile wrecks. It makes me nervous.

Fine about the store! Isn't Mrs Crane's friendship counting?[367] You got the check I sent to start the new case of old but not necessarily rare books? My heart has always secretly been in the Pittsfield bookstore. I could give it up

365. Le Madeleine, a Roman Catholic cathedral dating from 1182, was rebuilt in 1807 to serve as a monument to Napoleon's army.

366. RF likely refers to *Paris 1914–1918* by Albert Bartholomé. When placed in the Tuileries in 1921, it occasioned controversy and bad press. The statue is of a be-skirted but bare-breasted woman, nose in the air, striking a pose indeed like "strutting."

367. Josephine Boardman Crane, the Cleveland-born educator and philanthropist. For another reference to her, see RF to Edward Davison, January 7, 1926.

any time it seemed really best. But the least turn for the better and it rouses my ambition for it only less than it rouses yours.

Keep us posted.

Affectionately

R.

[*To John W. Haines. ALS-photostat. DCL.*]

The Castille

Rue Gambon

Paris

August 28 1928

Dear Jack:

Thus far I have nothing to report of this expedition but bad. We came to France in the hope that it might improve our invalid Marjorie by awakening an interest in her to learn the French language. That hope has failed and the disappointment has been almost too much for Elinor on top of everything else she has had to bear for the last two years. I cant tell you how she has lost courage and strength as I have watched her. She is in a serious condition— much more serious at this moment than Marjorie. We ought by right to abandon our campaign and baggage and retreat to America. But that seems too cruel to contemplate with nothing done, none of our friends seen that we wanted to see and have been wanting to see so long. I have one last resource. I am going to try to find a sort of travelling-companion-nurse for Marjorie to take her off her mother's hands for a few weeks. A young (but not too young) companion would be much better for Marj than we would be and if she were the right kind could give her a much better time. Then I am going to ask you to help me about Elinor. She must be put on her feet again before we attempt any going around visiting people in England. You must know some rest place where she and I could be taken in and taken care of for a while. I wish it could be somewhere near you, not more than a short run by train or automobile, so you and I could be together as much as possible. For of course it is to see you more than anything else that I made this desperate journey across the Atlantic in our old age and worn–out condition. Elinor has had too much on her. I'm afraid it will take her a long time to recover. Something radical will have to be done for her, and I will have to be the one to do it. She is in a state past doing anything for herself.

In my impatience to be off I have already bought tickets for London that are only good for a few days more here. You cant reach me with an answer, I mean, before we start. I'll tell you how we'll arrange. You be thinking what can be done and I'll ask you by wire from London. You folks mustn't be too much put about for us. Just do the one thing: conjure us up a rest place for the nervously prostrated in lovely country on the shore or inland, but near you.

Ever yours
Robert Frost

[*To Lesley Frost. Dated from internal evidence. ALS. UVA.*]

[Paris]
[circa September 1, 1928]

Dear Lesley:

Business first. Will you have Ted Davison arrange it for me to meet the right person in Longmans for an official talk?[368] I feel as if I wanted to use the opening at this time when I am over here rather to get all my books together than merely to bring out another stray book under a new publisher. Longmans might be willing if Davison put in a word and I had a word too to hold off on me for a year and then do my collected poems simultaneously with Holts in America. That would mean a lot to me and I think it is what Jack Squier [*sic*] has had in mind all along. You might read this much of my letter to Davison over the telephone. Or no you might not because I have called him Davison in it instead of Ted. Just tell him about it in your own words.

Marjorie has been off all afternoon on the Seine and in a gallery looking at Monet's water lilies[369] with Marise Fishbasher and another girl and she reports absolutely on their authority that the French hate us as nationals though they may like us here or there in special cases as individuals. She didnt mention the debt. She blamed our childish behaviour on the boulevards over-pleased with ourselves for having reached furthest Paris and making fun of

---

368. RF was planning a new, "collected" edition of his five books to date. Longmans, Green did indeed issue *The Collected Poems of Robert Frost* in London in 1930 (Henry Holt and Company published the American edition).

369. Among Claude Monet's (1840–1926) most famous paintings are those in his water lilies series.

them and their poor depreciated money. She is an educated young lady, you have to remember, of a clever family: yet she is free to maintain that three Americans have been mobbed and killed in Paris for their frank insolence— or insolence with the frank. One man rode all over Paris with his car pasted all over with hundred-frank notes. She herself has seen Americans tearing up hundred frank notes (4 dollars) and throwing them into post office waste baskets for show. Let her tell it. At least she thinks she has seen these atrocities. It doesnt matter for the purposes of psychology whether she has or not. I have heard at least two loud Americans making fun of the money. They are too insensitive to know that to the French their money is sad—a ruin—the poor old impoverished frank. Marise knew what she was saying. She speaks very good English. So you see what chance we have to be passing friends with the generality. If it werent for the Fishbashers and more especially the Feuillerats[370] and their daughter and son-in-law Mrs and Dr Charles Broquet, not all our philosophy not all our conviction that all nations are alike would have kept us from thinking France was a little worse than America. They have made it up to us for everything. Nevertheless it is a pity we came here at this time of year when the races were both at their terriblest in each others embraces. I saw ten girls come breathless out of one stocking store to consult a moment on the curb before plunging headlong into another. What was their asperation [*sic*]? To be Paris in Ann Arbor. I'll bet it would be a coincidence if it was Ann Arbor, but I'll bet it. I'll bet they were Alpha Phis.[371] No it is no good to any of us. We were in the wrong boat coming over and we are in the wrong boat still. We throw it off with what health and vitality we have; but it is a mistake from the taxi men to the hags that demand money of you for ushering you into your seat in the opera. The taxi man drives up asking And how far are you going? He tells you to walk if he thinks the distance wont pay him. Mama was tired from the Louvre today and I asked four taxi men in vain to take us home. The fifth consented without a murmer [*sic*]. The distance was ten cents. I tipped him fifty and told him why in a mixture of bad English bad French and gestures.

---

370. Albert Fueillerat (1874–1952) and his wife, Fanny, were friends of the Fischbachers. Feuillerat was a literary critic who specialized in Renaissance literature. During his distinguished career he taught at the Sorbonne, Columbia, Harvard, and Yale. RF had met Feuillerat in New Haven.

371. See RF to Moody, February 21, 1922 (for more on Lesley and the Alpha Phi sorority).

Speaking of the Louvre. That's as redeeming as the Feuillerats of course. We'll remember the good things when we look back. As always. You know how acute our homesickness always is: and to what mental turns it spurs us. I suppose our realest anguish ensues from our being caught on what looks like touring at all. We ought not to be in France after all we have said from the platform and the throne against tourism literal and metaphorical. By metaphorical I mean in Survey courses in education. We had business in England and Ireland. We had a right to go there. We had no business at all here after our plans failed to keep appointments with Babbitt[372] and the others earlier in the year. We have ourselves to blame for weakly having come just because we had got headed and impulsed. Let it amuse you. Have anything you please, preferably some more books for the bookstore, on us.

You dont tell me what Canby says to my vindictive poem.[373] Dont press it on him.

I havent brought myself to see the Untermeyers yet in France Germany or No mans Land.[374] It wouldnt do to have them here shell-shocking Marj. Pas encore.

Mama is only so so but stoutly denying it. After this folly, rest. I'm all pent up things to do. What the Hell am I so far out of my balliwick [sic] for anyway. Elinor needs a place of quiet to rest in and I need one to write in. So what's this expedition all about? May be Marj. But she doesnt praise it very highly. We could have bought a farm for the price of it. Aint I going strong?

I like your news.[375]

We've had a lot of opera both at the Opera and Opera Comique.[376] There's more good I forgot to mention. We like French bread. The wine doesnt mean much to us. The newspapers such as Le Matin and Le Figaro beat any we ever

---

372. Presumably literary critic Irving Babbitt (1865–1933), who frequently traveled to Paris to lecture at the Sorbonne.

373. "The Middletown Murder," which Henry Seidel Canby did in fact accept for publication in the *Saturday Review of Literature*.

374. Louis and Jean Untermeyer, on their second honeymoon, were at the time traveling through France and the Black Forest in Germany.

375. Lesley Frost had recently become engaged to James Dwight Francis (1897–1988), the son of a wealthy industrialist. The two would soon marry.

376. The Opéra-Comique was a populist theater company founded in 1714. Although its productions were as a rule lighthearted, some bordered on the tragic. The upstart company was often viewed as a rival to the established national opera and theater companies.

read for interests of the mind. Signed editorials on ideas are treated as news on the front page.

We shall go along in a few days now—probably on Tuesday or Wednesday. Use J. W. Haines house Midhurst Hucclecote Gloucester England as our next address.[377] We dont know just what order we shall follow in visiting places. London may come first.

Think of me sightseeing in spite of all the protective laziness I have developed on principle against it. I deserve to be punished. Upon my soul I never saw anything to match this summer Paris for ugliness not even a White Mountain resort. We're catching it. But never mind. As I say we deserve it. You may say another time we'll know better. Not necessarily. We're not the kind that can be taught. We know instinctively all we are going to know from birth and inexperience.

No mail from any body at home for more than a week.

Marj found in a more or less secret building full of eight great pictures of water lilies by Monet what seems to suit her fastidiousness. I think the absence of Americans in the place helped—and tip-exacting Frenchmen.

I've got my writing bag along for fear I shall think of something I want to do. I think of enough, but it is not the right kind. The bag is a reproach.

I picked up one of the biographical fragments you say are going out. This one is called LaFayette by Deltiel [sic] 1928.[378] You'll see it in translation yet. It begins well by saying LaFayette was own [sic] brother to Jean D'Arc and then quoting LaFayette's boast that he conquered the King of England in his might the King of France in his glory and the mob in their fury. It calls him the founder of two republics France and America. So far so fine and Gallic. Thence it goes on to do the regular thing from the laboratories of Vienna by asserting that the eighteenth century asperation [sic] for liberty was sexual. And we are in up to our ankles again head first. No no nothing will do. Mine be a cot beside a rill[379]—or at worst an appartment [sic] with no telephone in a back street in N. Y. C. That is contemplatable.

---

377. RF and Elinor sailed for England on September 5 and, shortly after arriving, visited Jack Haines in Gloucester.

378. In 1928, Joseph Delteil's *Lafayette* was published in French by Grasset (Paris), and, in the English translation of Jacques Le Clercq, by Minton, Balch in New York.

379. RF borrows a line from "A Dreamer's Paradise," by Scottish poet Alexander Anderson (1845–1909), which is itself adapted from "A Wish," by English poet Samuel Rogers (1763–1855):

You'll say this is a long letter and more or less unified by mood, though it shows joints of being added to from time to time.

Remember me to Dwight. I notice the Giants rose to the surface like a dreg on a bubble got dropped by the bubble when it broke and are now going down to hitch onto another.[380]

Affectionately

R. F.

[*To John Freeman. ALS. HRC.*]

Paris

September 3 1928

Dear Freeman:

I seem to have it somewhere on my conscience that I owe you a letter. But expect nothing very literal from me in this world: this is going to be no more of a letter than it takes to tell you that instead of writing I am coming. I shall be in London day after tomorrow and wanting to see you. It's a long time since we met in some coffee house in some street Ive forgotten the name of. Was

---

'Mine be a cot beside a rill,'
Where books would be my only lodgers;
(The first line's from another quill,
So kindly put it down to Rogers).
'Beside a rill'—the rill itself
Would still its grassy banks be flouting,
With here and there a rocky shelf,
Suggestive of successful trouting.

Rogers' "A Wish"—which RF would have known from Arthur Quiller-Couch's 1912 *Oxford Book of Victorian Verse*, one of his favorite anthologies—begins:

Mine be a cot beside the hill;
A bee-hive's hum shall soothe my ear;
A willowy brook, that turns a mill,
With many a fall shall linger near.

380. The New York Giants, who in 1928 boasted a record of 93–61, fell two games short of the St. Louis Cardinals for the National League pennant.

the coffee house called St George's?[381] Too much has happened since then. Much too much.

The Haineses mention the Vandyke [sic] Hotel, Cromwell Road, Kensington S.W.[382] We shall start there if they will take us in. We'd be grateful for any help out of hotels into—guest lodgings. The great thing is to sit again with two or three of you British.

Always yours
Robert Frost

[*To Lesley Frost. Dated from postmark. ALS. UVA.*]

Midhurst, Hucclecote, Glos.
[September 11, 1928]

Dear Lesley:

We don't seem to have had evidence yet that you have had any letter from us. If the stream keeps on flowing, most of it may sink into the ground and be lost, but some at least must come through sometime to the sea. Be sure to let us know when you are reached.

I've seen a few of the English, J. C. Squier [sic], John Freeman, and the Haineses—not to mention the not least mentionable Badnee or Mrs Hyatt [sic] of Ryton Dymock Gloucestershire. She's all sole alone there now (rent free I suppose by the kindness of the farmer her husband was shepherd for.)[383] The people at the Gallows are at enmity with the neighborhood and drove us off when we tried to look the old place over. Probably they were ashamed of the

---

381. The St. George Restaurant, on St. Martin's Lane near Trafalgar Square. A sign outside the place declared it "the famous house for coffee." There, in 1913, RF was introduced to Edward Thomas, whose death in 1917 he appears to have in mind ("Too much has happened . . ."). Freeman knew Thomas well. See also *LRF-1*, 144 (note 178).

382. John and Dolly Haines had recommended the Van Dyk Hotel, owned by the German photographer Carl Van Dyk.

383. Elizabeth Hyett, resident of Gallows Cottage in Ryton, which was opposite The Gallows, the thatched-roof cottage the Frosts shared with the family of the English poet Lascelles Abercrombie from autumn 1914 until they returned to America in February 1915. Hyett's husband, Sidney Hyett (died 1918), had almost certainly worked as a shepherd for the Chew family, owners of the Callow Farm near Ryton. Bad(k)nee was a nickname bestowed upon Elizabeth by Lascelles Abercrombie's son David (1909–1992)—later in life professor of phonetics at Edinburgh University—in commemoration of her suffering from water on the knee. The editors thank Jeff Cooper for help with these matters.

run-down condition of the property—everything overgrown and the thatch rotted and fallen in. The people at Little Iddens were glad to show us in.[384] That place is better than when we left it. The woods have moved away from the big house.

The Gibsons live at Letchworth where the children can have the advantages of the Quaker schools.[385] Gibson's stock as a poet is quoted very low right now. How he lives is a puzzle to his friends. His third of the income from Rupert Brook's [sic] books may still be a big help.[386]

De la Mare is not yet well from an operation that nearly killed him. He is the most prominent one of them all, getting out with both prose and verse to even the unliterary reader. W. H. Davies[387] suffers his worst pangs of jelousy [sic] over de la Mare. Davies spends a good deal of his time talking about his own relative deserts. Everyone agrees or concedes that he still writes his best. He has married a very young wild thing of no definable class, but partly gypsy.

John Freeman, a well to do head of an insurance firm, has climbed into some poetic prominence. He is so dull that I am tempted again to say my poetry to please me must be sensational. Freeman asked me with too obvious eagerness what I should say Hugh Walpoles[388] article in "Books" on him

---

384. From April to September 1914, the Frosts had resided in Little Iddens, a country home near the Malvern Hills.

385. Wilfrid Gibson and Rupert Brooke (mentioned in the next sentence) were among the so-called Dymock poets, with whom RF lived and worked in Gloucestershire in 1914.

386. Before leaving England in February 1915, as part of the British Mediterranean Expeditionary Force, Brooke had given instructions that royalties from the poems he had recently published in the magazine *New Numbers*—including what was to become his most famous work, "The Soldier"—should in the event of his death be bequeathed to Wilfrid Gibson, Lascelles Abercrombie, and Walter de la Mare.

387. W. H. Davies, the Welsh poet famous for having lived for several years as a hobo in both England and America. His eccentricities had by turns exasperated and entertained RF in 1914 (see *LRF-1*, 180–181, 192–193).

388. Hugh Walpole (1884–1941), a prolific English novelist, art collector, and essayist, summarized his assessment of the best poetry books of 1920 in "Awarding the 1920 Prizes in Literature," in the February 21, 1921, issue of *Vanity Fair*: "The finest new poetic work of the year is, I think, Masefield's 'Right Royal,' and the most interesting new poet Edmund Blunden, the author of 'The Waggoner.' Other important publications have been the collected poems of John Freeman, Walter de la Mare, and Edward Thomas."

rating him among the first six was likely to do for him in America. I told him almost anything: which is no more nor less than the truth. He wrote the article about me in The Mercury and I ought to be grateful.[389]

There's nobody new to take our place as the younger poets: or so I heard them lamenting with a false note in the Mercury office. The Sitwells and T. S. Elliott [sic] were pointedly left out of count.[390]

Laselles [sic] has been too busy and recently too ill to write poetry. Theres a play of his that raised a howl a year or two ago for its immorality.[391] The beginning raised my gorge at its stilted vernacular. I got no further. He has several more children than when we last heard.

Flint is I dont know where.[392] Monro has moved his book shop. I happened to see on his desk a letter signed by Marion Dodd. He is just getting asked to America by Fekins [sic].[393] About time, he says. He has wondered at not having been asked long since. He treated me very shabily [sic]. He always resented my being.

Haines knows and entertains them all now. He may be as much remembered as any. He is full of them all and rich in all their books. He is his whole law firm now and works hard but finds time for correspondence in all directions.

---

389. John Freeman's article "Contemporary American Authors: Robert Frost" appeared in the December 1925 edition of the *London Mercury*.

390. English writers Edith Sitwell (1887–1964), Osbert Sitwell (1892–1969), and Sacheverell Sitwell (1897–1988) and American poet T. S. Eliot (1888–1965).

391. Most likely *Phoenix* (London: Martin Secker, 1923), whose characters are Amyntor (the king), his wife (the queen), his son Phoenix (the prince), and two soldiers who lust after Rhodope, a "bought woman."

392. The poet F. S. Flint, whom RF met in London in 1913; the two men exchanged a number of letters about poets and poetics (see *LRF-1*).

393. Marion Elza Dodd (1883–1961) was the founder of the Hampshire Bookshop in Northampton, Massachusetts, and mentor to Lesley Frost. Harold Monro, proprietor of the Poetry Bookshop in London, where RF met many of the Georgian poets he would later live with in Gloucestershire. William B. Feakins (1872–1946), president of the William B. Feakins Lecture Bureau in New York City, had a long and distinguished career managing lectures by a wide array of intellectuals and writers, including RF's acquaintances Lincoln Steffens, Alfred Noyes, Vachel Lindsay, and Vilhjalmur Stefansson.

Mrs Helen Thomas hasnt been heard from yet. She has entirely new friends. She plans more books about Edward. Nobody blames her too hard for that first one.[394]

> Affectionately
>
> R F.

[*To Padraic Colum. Colum, who was then living in New York City and would be sailing back to the United States in a few days, did indeed escort RF around Dublin for a day; he also arranged for RF to stay in the home of Irish poet Constantine P. Curran. ALS. UVA.*]

> The Imperial Hotel Russell Square
> London England
> September 18 1928

Dear Padraic:

You may be clear out of Dublin, you may even have gone back to New York; but I am not going to give you up without another trial (I made one by telegraph a few days ago.) I dont want to miss the chance of being introduced to Ireland by the right person. I may still decide to look into Dublin if you are not there, but it will not be the same thing and I should be sorry if our rendezvous came to nothing. Nobody ever talked Ireland to me as intimately as you did that day lying by the side of a road in Pelham (near Amherst) ten years ago.[395]

Our invasion hasn't gone as planned. We were a long time getting Marjorie settled in France for her French and Elinor has steadily worn down with the effort of travel. Last week we were lying up for her health in Gloucester. She wouldnt be able to come with me to Dublin: I should be alone.[396]

You would have to promise not to let me burden you. I should only stay a day or two. You would tell me a decent hotel to go to.

---

394 *As It Was* (1926), Helen Thomas's memoir of her and Edward's courtship and marriage.

395. Colum had moved to New York City in 1914 and had visited RF in Amherst on several occasions. In November of 1923, he taught one of RF's classes at Amherst.

396. In September, RF stayed by himself in Ireland for five days and, along with Colum, met with the Irish poets George Russell, William Butler Yeats, and Constantine Curran.

The address you seem to have given me is The Irish Statesman.[397] My address the rest of this week will be the Imperial Hotel, Russell Square, London, England. God grant that I hear from you.

> Yours always
> Robert Frost

[To Lesley Frost. The letter celebrates Lesley's marriage, on September 3, to James Dwight Francis. ALS. UVA.]

> London England
> September 18 1928

Dear Lesley:

I celebrated your news by intending a song, and I should have sung it if my harp hadnt been hanging in a willow tree in a strange land.[398] As it was I could not be kept from smiling. So I smiled for a day in honor of the occasion—not because I rejoice more over marriage than over any other step in love, but because it is about the only step in anybody else's love that is any of my business. My smiling will have to do for the present. If I ever get to singing again, you may be sure it will be partly due to your happiness and so a tribute to your happiness.

I told you the last time I saw you how much I liked Dwight. I was just beginning to understand him. We sensitive people wound each other with our shields.[399]

> Affectionately
> R.F.

---

397. The *Irish Statesman* was a Dublin-based journal that was founded in 1919 to advocate dominion status for Ireland. RF's friend George Russell edited the journal from 1922 until its final issue in 1930.

398. RF alludes to Psalm 137 in which the Jews have been cast out of Zion and weep "by the rivers of Babylon": "We hanged our harps upon the willows in the midst thereof."

399. See RF's remarks in "Education by Poetry" (1931): "The first little metaphor. . . . Take some of the trivial ones. I would rather have trivial ones of my own to live by than the big ones of other people. I remember a boy saying, 'He is the kind of person that wounds with his shield.' That may be a slender one, of course. It goes a good way in character description. It has poetic grace. 'He is the kind that wounds with his shield.' The shield reminds me—just to linger a minute—the shield reminds me of the inverted shield spoken of in one of the books of the *Odyssey,* the book that tells about the longest swim on

[*To Sidney Cox. Date derived from postmark; RF has incorrectly written "1927." ALS. DCL.*]

[London]

Oct 11 [1928]

Sidney, Sidney,

It won't do. You'll say I've been long enough coming to that brief conclu-sion. I practically had to wait till I had grown into another person so I could see the problem presented with the eyes of an outsider. Looking in on it from another country and from another time with all the disinterestedness possible I find I'm against the book—at least in my lifetime: when I'm off the scene you can decide for yourself.[400] My greatest objection to the book is that it doesnt put you and me in the right personal relation. I think you would re-alize that if you took time. Your repeated insistence on the fact that you never came to see me except when summoned has the very opposite effect from what you intend. Instead of making us out equals in friendship as I should have thought we were, it puts you in a position of a convenience used and sent for whenever I had anything for you to set down for posterity. I dont like the picture it makes of either of us. It isnt a true picture either. I can't remember exactly when you asked my permission to keep a record of the best of our talks. But Im sure it was late in our lives. I invited you to visit me and I wrote to you many times before you could have been so self conscious about it all. I might have to search myself for my reason in singling you out for a conversa-tion a year. I can tell you off hand I never chose you as a Boswell. Maybe I liked your awkwardness naiveté and spirituality. We wont strain for an answer.

Meeting Helen Thomas fresh from her experiment in reminiscences of someone else has probably helped me to my decision. You probably read her "As It Was" between her and Edward Thomas—suppressed in Boston.[401] It's

---

record. I forget how long it lasted—several days, was it?—but at last as Odysseus came near the coast of Phaeacia, he saw it on the horizon 'like an inverted shield'" (*CPRF*, 108).

400. Cox had proposed a study of RF, variously titled *"Time to Talk" with Robert Frost* and *Walks and Talks with Robert Frost*, in which he initially planned to include extracts from their correspondence. Cox had sounded out Elinor Frost, with some nervousness, in May 1928. She had not been amenable to the publication of anything smacking of "per-sonal revelation." Cox sent a draft chapter to RF himself in July 1928 (*RFSC*, 185–89).

401. Thomas's memoir, *As It Was*, was indeed suppressed in Boston bookstores. Its successor volume, *World Without End* (London and New York: Harper and Brothers, 1931), was not, despite duplicating material from the first.

a good piece of work in a way, but it took a good [deal] of squirming on her part to justify it. I wondered if she wasnt in danger of making E T look ridiculous in the innocence she credited him with. Mightn't men laugh a manly laugh? E T was distinguished at his college at Oxford for the ribald folk songs he could entertain with—not to say smutty. Worse than As It Was are some other chapters in his life she has been undressing to the public since. In one she has him invite to the house a girl he has met and come home full of admiration of. She gives her self away by calling the girl "this paragon of women." But she finds the minute she sees her (how homely she is) that she can conquer her with magnanimity or conquer her jealousy of her with magnanimity. All women are sisters that the same man loves, she tries to make herself think. Once in the woods listening to a nightingale in the dark E says to the two of them We are knowing, but the nightingale knows all. Then he kisses his wife and to keep the score even his wife makes him kiss the other woman.[402] She pretends to think that is large and lovely, but I happen to know it was a dose she was giving him and rubbing in. These things are hard to do sincerely. And unridiculously. In another chapter she has him carry her off to bed on his last leave of absence before going to the front. It reminds me of Schnitzler's Whatsername.[403]

No you'll have to forgive me and be as good friends as if nothing had ever happened, but it wont do. You'll have to reason our relationship onto a better footing than it has apparently been on lately. Lets not be too damned literary. Really faithfully yours

Robert Frost

London Eng now: but I'll be home in S. Shaftsbury early in November. Want to see you.

---

402. Eleanor Farjeon, who in the years before World War I was drawn into relations of intense emotional dependency upon both Edward and Helen Thomas. Eleanor's relative lack of physical attractions, touched upon by RF here, was a sore point and probably prevented her relationship with Edward Thomas from being consummated.

403. Arthur Schnitzler (1862–1931) Austrian author and dramatist noted for his depiction of sexual themes. The opening scene of his best-known play, *Reigen* (1900; translated as *Hands Around* in 1917), features an encounter between a soldier and a "whore." If RF is referring to this work he is being distinctly uncomplimentary to Helen Thomas.

[*To Edward Lewis Davison. ALS. DCL.*]

> Georgian House
> Bury St
> London S.W.1
> October 11 1928.

Dear Ted:

I'm over here from France among all your friends, though one thing and another has kept me from seeing very much of them. First Elinor was sick and tired of what she had been through in the last two years (she ought never to have made the expedition this year) and now I am sick in bed with a grippe cold. I have seen Squier [*sic*], Freeman, and Shanks of those you would expect.[404] We have been at Freeman's house in Annerly [*sic*] twice for a night.[405] Freeman is one of the amiable kind. It is extraordinary to find him as prominent in business (insurance) as he is in literature. I liked Shanks—what I saw of him. Squier and I haven't been able as yet to agree on a time together. We plan a motor trip to Tiverton where my ancestors came from. I dont know what struck him this way, but he seemed to like the idea of my having originated in Devon.[406] He says we must make the most of it—celebrate it by going down there and looking up the family records in the regulation American fashion. Maybe I'll find I have a coat of arms. Then it wont matter what I do to earn a living any more.

All these people are your true friends who will hold you to what you have led them to expect of you. I remember your blue talk in my hotel room that night. That was just one night of course. I mustnt judge you by it. Ten to one you haven't been as blue since. And I'm blue myself sometimes. Blueblack. But you must get about your writing—not an epic like Benet Henderson and Robison [*sic*] (doesn't it look as if we were in for a period of neo epicism like that of the eighteenth century?) but something your individual own not too much in the mode and obviously out to catch the public.[407]

---

404. Edward Shanks (1892–1953), a minor World War I poet and a contributor to the *London Mercury* (which J. C. Squire, a friend of John Freeman, edited).

405. Anerley, an area of Southeast London adjoining Penge, of cultural interest as the site of the relocated Crystal Palace, and home, until 1925, of Freeman's and RF's friend Walter de la Mare.

406. RF's father was of "old Devonshire stock"; see RF to Freeman, November 5, 1925.

407. Steven Vincent Benét, whose book-length *John Brown's Body* was published in 1928; Walter Brooks Drayton Henderson, Jamaican-born poet, and a teacher at

You'll understand my objections to having the Longmans do West Running Brook. I want to save the goodwill you have procured for me there for my collected poems next year.[408] It would be just thrown away on a little book—another beginning, a fourth or fifth since my beginning in 1913. The Longmans will be my fourth or fifth publishers over here. I loath being scattered around like that. It will take all the good will in the world to put me together again.

Davies was the same old Davies.[409] The minute Elinor and I got there he rose and presented us with an autographed poem as a "souvenir of our visit." He hasn't aged a hair. Still harping on why he isnt read in America. Wants to come over lecturing.

De la Mare is one of the best of the best. We had a night of poetry at his house. He and Squier are the ones I seem least to have lost touch with—I suppose partly from their having been over visiting us, but much more from congeniality of age and temper.

I talked four days and nights on end with A.E.[410] That was a real bout. It was like the late war you couldn't tell who was to blame for it or who was most exhausted by it. Anyway there's another man I like to think of.

Some things have disappointed us as much as we were afraid everything might (we were prepared for the worst); but De la Mare, A.E., Squier, and Freeman havent a bit. Quite the contrary, whatever the contrary is.

Gibson was funny. He was utterly friendly like the sweet thing he is—friendly and forgiving where there was much to forgive. But he addressed a poem to me personally the very next day in excuse for the war's having aged

---

Dartmouth, had also written an epic poem, *The New Argonautica,* published in 1928. It describes an interstellar voyage undertaken by the shades of various Elizabethan nautical luminaries disgusted by the spectacle of World War I. RF discussed this work several years before its publication, either with Brooks Henderson himself or with colleagues at Dartmouth (see RF to Sidney Cox, May 17, 1926.) E. A. Robinson, arguably RF's most serious rival in the 1920s, was increasingly devoting his time to epic poems in unrhymed blank verse. His *Tristram* (New York: Macmillan) had been one of the publishing sensations of 1927.

408. Longmans, Green did not publish *WRB*. As intimated here, the firm did publish the British edition of the *Collected Poems of Robert Frost* (1930).

409. W. H. Davies.

410. Pseudonym of George William Russell (1867–1935), writer, mystic, and Irish nationalist, whom RF saw in Dublin.

us all so horribly.[411] It was a left handed compliment we had to take humorously if at all.

I havent seen Abercrombie yet—nor Monro—nor the Sitwells—nor T. S. Elliott [*sic*]. Monro says I am to see Elliott and him after I read for him at his shop next week. Then I am coming home to the farm.

If I have forgotten anything or anyone it is not invidiously. Oh yes there was Yates [*sic*]. He was the best I ever saw him—quite seemed to see me in the room. I had been scared by stories I had heard about his senatorial greatness.[412]

I'll want to see you when I get back. Dont think we havent had a pretty good time in spite of what you may have heard of our bad beginning in France. England is a relief. I think she is happier and better in many ways than before the war. Anyway she isn't whining and sullen like France. That is to say she isnt unaware of her gains and blessings.

I hope this pencilling wont rub too much in transit. I happened to have a pencil in bed when I started this on impulse and just kept on going.

Remember me to Natalie and the international baby.[413]

Ever yours

Robert Frost

[*To John W. Haines. ALS-photostat. DCL.*]

Georgian House Bury St

London S.W.1.

October 11 1928.

Dear Jack:

I'm sick with a cold too. I grant at once, though, that yours is worse than mine. So don't be roused to jealousy and argument. Such is my indolence cowardice or both that I will grant anything you please rather than run the risk

---

411. Neither Gibson nor RF was a combatant. Gibson attempted to enlist four times and was rejected on each occasion as unfit for service (he had bad eyesight amongst other ailments).

412. W. B. Yeats had been a member of the Irish Senate since its inception in 1922.

413. Peter Davison, in later life a distinguished publisher and poet, had been born to Edward and Natalie Davison on June 27, 1928. Natalie was American.

of argument. Who am I, anyway, to set up to be sicker than another? I was always an unpretentious invalid not seeking to excel in symptoms. I'm proud to be sick at all. Not for me to be sick to the point of distinction or extinction.

Speaking of argument I had an encounter with your papist friend Kerr that woke me from my lethargy at Freeman's the other night.[414] He came at me hurtling. He defied me to doubt lost causes and unread books were best. He blamed us puritans for having overthrown civilization in England and having established it in the southern states of America. There he delivered himself into my hands. But my work was still all before me to bend the slippery muscular porpoise round so as to make the two ends of his argument meet and stick his tail down his throat. I'm afraid he surprised me into an unwonted severity, bless his vigourosity. At this point I remembered your story of the way he had offended Abercrombie and took a resolution not to mind him. And from then on I kept it through onslaught after onslaught on my country with weapons supplied chiefly by my fellow countrymen. His sentences took the form of regret that we seemed to be what Menken [*sic*] and Sink Lewis said we were.[415] My position held fairly calmly after I got my balance was that I didnt know what we were except that we had evidently grown so important that a really good country like England preferred our friendship and alliance to that of France. He knows a lot and if he doesnt know how to use it logically his intentions are of the best. We have to make allowance for all converts, especially to Romanism.

We saw Helen Thomas and that ended one passage in our lives. She delivered herself of several choice things. The reason she didn't want Edwards letters published was because he wasnt interesting in his letters. She sometimes rejoiced he wasnt alive to see the state England was in. She neednt be afraid I shall ever publish his letters to me. She may be right about the state of England. It seems a poor sort of country where a woman has to give up living with a man married to someone else for fear of losing her pension. I decided

---

414. William Kerr was a contributor to *Georgian Poetry 1920–22,* ed. Edward Howard Marsh (London: Poetry Bookshop, 1922), and author of *The Apple-Tree* (Leeds: Swan Press, 1927). One of Kerr's better-known poems, "Past and Present," is about cricket, and later in this letter RF reports a conversation at Freeman's party on the subject of the great game.

415. "Sink Lewis" is Sinclair Lewis (1885–1951), American novelist. Both he and H. L. Mencken were noted for withering observations about the ignorance, conservatism, and cupidity of the American people.

before I had listened to her long that Edward had worse enemies to his memory than poor old simple Wilfred [*sic*].[416] It needed only that decision to make it easy to visit Wilfred at Letchworth. He has since sent me a poem to me in which he stoutly excuses us all for looking so horribly old after such a terrible war. I couldn't see that he had aged much. He must have meant his wife and us. I dont want to be excused for looking horribly old. I want it denied I look horribly old—at least in all complimentary verse here after indited. Thats how I caught cold.

The time draws nigh for going to Marj in France and thence home across the sea-sickness. But first I must see you three again for a day and if possible Lascelles in Leeds.[417] On the eighteenth I read for Monro[418] (I haven't seen him yet) and on the Monday following I meet the Pen Club.[419] That must end it I am afraid. There's much to do still but some of it will have to be left undone. I must get up to see Bridges and a few of my own American children at Oxford.[420]

You and A E have been the great successes of the expedition. I've liked the Freemans very much. Freeman talks sense. His only lapse from sense was when he backed Kerr in saying your game of cricket was not a game but a ritual like what do you suppose? Like the ballet. They were trying to make me see how much more important form was than victory—the duffers. I don't believe they ever played the game. What a picture it makes, all those grown-up athletes in an outdoor ballet! Ever yours

Robert Frost

---

416. Wilfrid Gibson and Edward Thomas had been friends, but Thomas in reviews of Gibson's work had often not been complimentary.

417. Lascelles Abercrombie had been professor of English at the University of Leeds since 1922.

418. Harold Monro, proprietor of the Poetry Bookshop.

419. PEN, the international association of authors established in London in 1921 by the poet Catharine Amy Dawson Scott, and thriving under the presidency of the novelist John Galsworthy.

420. Robert Bridges (1844–1930), poet laureate, living at this time at Boar's Hill, near Oxford (RF visited him on the weekend of November 11–12). One of the "American children" is likely James Notopoulos (1905–1967), an Amherst graduate who had just taken up a two-year scholarship at Jesus College, Oxford.

[To Louis Untermeyer. RF has placed a note in the left margin of the first page, affixed by asterisk to the address: "We are going back to Paris for the first week of November. Address American Express 11 Rue Scribe Paris." ALS. LoC.]

Georgian House Bury St. London
S.W1*
October 11 1928

Dear Louis

Irma mentions your just having looked in on Carol at South Shaftsbury Vermont on your way to a farm of your own in the Adirondacs [sic].[421] And I was thinking of you and Jean as buried deep in the Black Forest of Germany. In fact I had written you a letter there that probably came too late but even so may reach you by forwarding to America sooner than this. It was one of my sad mocking letters (with a picture of me by Watteau in it) and wont do you any good if you read it more than once.[422] So disregard it and listen to me now saying seriously:

How much better if you had been a staid orthodox Jew and never had run wild after a super wisdom that doesnt exist. You are back now where you started from and not one bit improved in mind or spirit. The whole experiment has been a waste of time and energy. You havent found out anything that you didn't know before—that we didnt all know before: and I wont listen to you if you say you have. That's the one thing I cant stand from a person in your predicament. For my sake if you still care for me, dont talk about having been chastened or having profited in any way. You've lost—time if nothing else. I've lost. We've all lost. Having admitted that, let's say no more on the subject. I'd impose it as a penalty on you that you shouldnt wax literary on what you have been through—turn it to account in any way. I wont if you wont. It must be kept away down under the surface where the great griefs belong. I dont mean you must stop writing, but you must confine yourself to everything else in the world but your own personal experience. I beg of you. Honestly. The thought would be too much for me of all three of you putting up a holler in verse about it all. The decencies forbid you should score off it.

---

421. Louis and Jean Untermeyer (recently remarried) had bought a 160-acre farm in the Adirondacks near Elizabethtown, New York.

422. Jean-Antoine Watteau (1684–1721) was a French painter credited with inventing the genre of *fêtes galantes* ("courtship parties"), a style that featured richly dressed men and women cavorting in idyllic, bucolic settings.

Write a court drama of the IVth Dynasty.[423] I should think this was the point where you have almost got to leave off being a subjective poet. That is if you care for me.

I'm coming back in a few weeks now and the first thing I'll do will be to look you up for a good talk—not about the past but about the future. Gee it has been hideous—like going round and round you with a gun trying to shoot an animal at your throat on top of you, but not daring to put a shot in for fear of killing you. You had people like Alfred who knew what to say to you.[424] I didn't know what to say then and I hardly do now. I think you and Jean on a farm <u>most</u> of the time would be a good idea. But you ought to work hard out-doors and in to keep from talking. I wish I knew a subject to assign you for a book and one for Jean too—a real labor like a Benet Robinson Henderson epic—but it neednt be as heavy as that—though heavy.[425]

I'd have struck off to see you in the Black Forest—only only only. There was Marj, none too well. I couldnt have her too much disturbed in the mind. I was in no position to act. Things are looking up for us a little now. Marj seems not unhappy with the Fischbashers [sic] at Sevres. And Elinor gains a little as she cheers up. Both she and Marj have been in a serious condition.

I impose penalties. I'd almost like to prescribe a remedy. Thought on, in these bookish ways our lives go every which way. Dont look into books to see yourself reflected. Avoid the mirror of books. Be as ordinary as you can till I can get there. This is first aid in the emergency! But you dont know what Im talking about. I'll tell you when I come.

Ever yours
Robert

---

423. The Fourth Dynasty of Egypt (2613–2494 BCE) is often referred to as the Golden Age of ancient Egypt, an epoch of peace and prosperity.

424. Alfred Harcourt, who had helped establish RF's relationship with Henry Holt, was Untermeyer's friend and the owner of Harcourt, Brace.

425. See RF to Edward Davison, October 11, 1928.

[*To Louis Untermeyer. Date and mailing address supplied by Untermeyer. ALS. LoC.*]

> Midhurst
> Huccleclote
> Gloucester, England
> [circa October 24, 1928]

Dear Louis:

I've been thinking my fastest about you lately with some renewal of hope to overtake your affairs as they begin to slow down. I almost feel at this moment as if I were abreast of you. Probably Im not, but let me state you as I seem to have you now. By the time you get this letter very likely you'll have scooted like a rocket and left me as far behind as the eighteenth century. Experience ought to have taught me to be careful what I say about your women from a distance that gives too much time for things to happen before my letter reaches you. It takes courage to talk about relationships that are changing as fast as yours.

My judgement on you is that you have wronged yourself in all this business of alternating between two wives. You have been acting against your nature under pressure of the bad smart talk you have listened to and learned to share in in the society you have cultivated in your own New York salons (so to call them.) I've heard the mocking when I have been there and heard you lend yourself to it till I was ready to bet what would happen. None of it was right or wise or real. What I dread most now is that you will go on the assumption that though it was folly and landed you in tragedy it was on the way somewhere and somehow prepared you for greater and fuller life. Shut up. To hell with such comforts. It was all time and energy lost as I have said before.

You have merely talked yourself out of your senses. I refuse to admit you were ravished out of your senses. You talked yourself out of them in your own parlor. For I heard you. Now you are yourself again by sheer weight of the honesty in your bones. Talk no more—unless you can talk unclever unsophicated [*sic*] simple goodness. You tempt me to soak you in milk to renew your innocence. The funny positions people can talk themselves into in a lifetime of try-it-on talk.

Someone you know said to me in drink the other day:[426]

---

426. RF's dialogue is fiction.

Dyou blieve in marriage? After miwife died I got mixtup with a woman wanted me tmarry her. Ver attractive woman yunderstan. Had a child by her. Wouldnt marry her. Didnt want to. Think I ought to marry her?

Does she still want you to

Shdoes—innaway. Dyou think ought to have married her before

Has it caused her much pain your not marrying her?

Sidible

Well we have to consider whether decent marriage isnt a provision of the ages for causing the least possible pain between the sexes. The least possible is all I say.

Shwants to marry someone elsenow.

I thought you said she wanted to marry you.

Shwants to marry me first. Then get divorce 'n marry nother man.

I dont understand yet.

Marry me make tall reglar. Xplain it to him sos she wont have tell him. Thinks he'll like it better.

Wants you to marry her for his sake.

Sbout it.

Louis Louis very few people that leave the good old folk ways can keep from getting all mixed up in the mind. We can make raids and excursions into the wild but it has to be from well kept strongholds. I think you think so now. Lets drop the whole subject.

> Always yours
> Robertus

[*To John W. Haines. ALS-photostat. DCL.*]

> [London]
> [November 2, 1928][427]

Dear Jack:

I am going to have to ask a last favor of you for the time being. I want to write you a personal check for five hundred dollars to buy me a London draft with at your bank in Gloucester. I may have to have it in a hurry so will you tend to it right off? I can see the money I have isnt going to last me and there

---

427. Haines supplies the date of *receipt* in a note. The letter may have been written on November 1.

wont be time to get any more from home before we sail. The news from Marj or about Marj from Elinor in France is no good. This may as well end the expedition. It has been too much of a strain anyway. I wish I could promise to see you again. But it wouldnt be honest as things are. I've made Elinor unhappier keeping her on than I think I ever made her before. She's too sick for a jaunting party and I shouldnt have dragged her out of her home. You've had more of us than any one else and if it isnt enough you know what you can do. You can come to America to our house next year or the year after or any time you get ready—only make it soon.

I'm going to Scotland for a night, taking in Abercrombie on the way. After that we shall see—but probably I shall go straight to France and then waveringly home to New York City, Lesleys apartment.

Will you send the draft in poundshillingpence to me at the Georgian House Bury St St James. ~~After Saturday send any mail that comes to Elinor at Villa Jules Janin 12 Avenue Jules Janin~~ Paris 16ᵃ France till I write again.[428] These closing rites (writes) are mournful. Never mind, we arent women and children.

Ever yours
Robert Frost

Later: After Saturday send all mail to Hotel Imperial Russell Square London. I shall sleep one night there en route.

[To John Freeman. RF composed the letter, on White Star Line stationery, en route from Southampton, via Cherbourg, France, to the United States. ALS. HRC.]

On Board S. S. "Olympic."
November 19 1928

Dear Freeman:

It had to be sometime if it was ever going to be. So we bought a boat on the evening of one day and took the cold plunge into the Atlantic on the morning of the next. The abruptness made it easier to break with you all. And we had got it up for a new superstition that it would be good luck not to be too long about picking and choosing the boat. We took the first boat we happened on and when we looked at her bows she proved to be the Olympic—of

---

428. RF has struck these lines out (and completed his thought at the foot of the letter).

46000 tons burthen. After all we don't know yet what is or isnt lucky. We ran right out of Cherbourgh [sic] into a hundred-and-fifty mile gale that knocked her nose in and brought us to a standstill for three hours a thousand miles from anywhere among some of the biggest waves they say you ever see. It was the same gale that seems to have been killing people in England. (I trust it didn't even hurt any of you or your family indoors or out in your big or little car.) It scared the sea sickness out of us to lie so mysteriously dead in those wind-flayed hills and hollows. We wondered if we had stopped at the port of missing ships and if all the strange pale faces appearing from everywhere weren't ghosts that had come on board.[429] Friday and thirteen are u̲n̲lucky. Someone asked if it was lucky to pray. We hadn't thought. Someone else remarked that at any rate he knew it was unlucky to laugh at sacred things. A lot of people in the world were always doing just that thing—laughing at sacred things? Yes and look at the result. Look at the world as a whole, how unlucky it was. We all relapsed into sea-sickness from the depressing effect of sustained thinking. All that was days ago. We are now knotting along at the rate of 500 a day about off Nova Scotia, and shall soon be on the farm in Vermont with a falalalala. It will be too late to see my water lily leaves before they go under water for the winter. That is a good deal your fault old man and you will have to answer for it by coming over to see us soon in the Richest Country and bringing with you all the family. Seriously you must. You and I knew how to talk to each other.[430] You bound me to England with new ties for some of the old that proved to have broken.

> And I'm ever yours
> Robert Frost

---

429. RF refers to John Randolph Spears's story collection *The Port of Missing Ships and Other Stories of the Sea* (New York: Macmillan, 1897).

430. RF and Elinor had spent two nights with John Freeman and his wife, Gertrude, in their home on 29 Weighton Road, Anerley.

[To Henrietta Kendrick Reeves (1871–1968), a prominent figure in Nashville, where she established a poetry society and brought a number of writers and artists to lecture under the aegis of the Centennial Club. In 1919, she was elected to membership in the Poetry Society of America. ALS. Tennessee State Library.]

South Shaftsbury Vermont
December 15 1928

My dear Mrs Reeves:

If I am not too late for your programme, would you choose a date as close as possible to the three days when I have to be in Pittsburg [sic], Penna, namely April 15 to 17 inclusive.[431] I suppose I could get from Pittsburg to Nashville for a reading in the evening of the 18th. But if you much preferred the week preceding my Pittsburg engagement, how would Friday the 12th or Saturday the 13th suit you?

We have both been fairly hard to reach this summer. You were wandering in Europe and so were we. Our letters were always weeks old when we got them. We are just back in our own house this week. I appreciate the interest that has kept you in pursuit all this time.

My fee would be $225 for the one engagement in a town.

Sincerely yours
Robert Frost

[To Richard Thornton. ALS. DCL.]

South Shaftsbury Vermont
Dec 16 1928

Dear Mr Thornton:

I got home from everything and everywhere tired and dazed.[432] I dont know what I was thinking of for a few days there. Not much, I guess. When I

---

431. As logged in Lawrance Thompson's unpublished chronology, RF's spring 1929 lecture tour took him to Philadelphia (April 3–5), Chicago (April 5–9), Nashville (April 12–13), Pittsburgh (April 17), and Charlottesville (April 18). Present for his reading in Nashville were (among others) John Crowe Ransom, Donald Davie, and Merrill Moore (all poets of the "Fugitive School" associated with Vanderbilt University). RF would later consult Moore, a psychiatrist in addition to a poet, about his son Carol and his daughter Irma (both of whom suffered from severe mental illness).

432. On arriving back in the United States from Europe, RF had given talks in Baltimore and Greensboro, North Carolina, before returning to South Shaftsbury on December 7.

came to I found I had still the check for one fifty in my pocket book.[433] You'll have to forgive me for not sending it till now. It is in this letter.

I'm back posing in front of the chopping block in old Vermont, though it doesnt seem to be the old block which I fear someone has mistaken for fire-wood and split the way of the pieces I used to split upon it.

You've done everything for us and my book[434] and I hope you all realize my gratitude. I ought to settle down in contentment to what comes next from my ink bottle.

I must write you out a bit of the places I am going to in the winter. Let's see, two of them are Wesleyan Middletown Conn February 11 and Norfolk Conn February 26.[435]

I could use two more of the special edition if they are to be had.[436]

> Ever yours
> Robert Frost

[*To Sidney Cox. Dated from postmark. ALS. DCL.*]

> [North Bennington, VT]
> [December 17, 1928]

Dear Sidney:

I'm home from almost everywhere somewhat dazed. But that ought not to prevent me from telling you you did all right the second time. You did better than I deserve, but we wont let it trouble us. We'll accept unscrupulously the luck of the draw. You dig in with a stiff-lipped scoop.

Dont make me write any more now. Im sick with my third overlapping cold since the fog settled down on London. And I dont know exactly where I am, out with a new book or at home with the family.

---

433. We have not been able to elucidate this matter.

434. *WRB*, published by Henry Holt and Company on November 19, 1928.

435. In fact, RF would visit Middletown for two performances at Wesleyan on February 12 and 13, 1929; there is no record of his visiting Norfolk, Connecticut, at this time.

436. The one-thousand-copy signed and limited edition of *WRB*, printed for Henry Holt and Company by the Merrymount Press.

I'll want to see you soon.

> Ever yours
> Robert Frost

You knew Brickel [*sic*] was going to make a book out of your article.[437] It made them all look at me with fresh eyes down there.

[To Hilda Wright (1906–2013). She graduated, in 1929, from Bryn Mawr, where she was editor of The Lantern, *the college literary magazine, for three years. ALS. Bryn Mawr.]*

> South Shaftsbury Vermont
> December 18 1928

Dear Miss Wright:

Your letter has been to England and back on my trail. If I am not too late in receiving and answering it, let me say that I should be glad to read the poems for you.[438] You are right in assuming my special friendship for Bryn Mawr whose young poetesses I began cultivating the acquaintance of almost before I did anything else around the colleges.[439]

> Sincerely yours
> Robert Frost

---

437. Herschel Brickell, head of the trade department at Henry Holt and Company. The book in question was published by Henry Holt as *Robert Frost: Original "Ordinary Man"* in 1929. Following RF's firm discouragement of Cox's plans to write a book called *"Time to Talk" with Robert Frost* (see RF to Sidney Cox, October 11, 1928), Cox had sent an "essay" (that took a different tack) to Richard Thornton, which evidently met with approval at Henry Holt, and with RF.

438. The reading likely occurred in early April (RF was in and around Philadelphia from April 3–5), at the start of a series of lectures that would take him to four states.

439. Among those literary young women RF had met during one of his earliest visits to the college in 1920 was Kathleen Johnston (later Kay Morrison), whose literary club had invited him to the campus. He had subsequently spoken at Bryn Mawr on numerous occasions.

[*To J. J. Lankes. ALS. HRC.*]

South Shaftsbury
December 22 1928
Happy New Year.

Dear Lankes:

You mean to say them there benefactors never sent you no copy of West-Running Brook that disarming Book? What's the reason you didnt kick? Our young four-year-old got for a pre-Christmas present the other day a pair of zipper overshoes that he seems to get more kick out of than out of anything he has had for a long time.[440] You better buy yourself a pair of zipper over-shoes and see if you dont get a kick out of them. A mule wouldnt want to keep on kicking if there was nothing left to kick about. But the thing of it is there always is something left to kick about. I just got a letter from Gardner Jackson an old boy of mine and late chairman of the Sacco Vanzetti Defense Committee calling on me in the name of justice to review the Sacco Vanzetti Letters and register my kick against the way such obviously meditative thinkers were treated by the state of Massa What-do-you-call-it.[441] Will you illustrate my review if I write one. Justice is a very important thing and injustice is a very important thing to kick against. I wish there were no injustice and I should like nothing better than to join the crusade against it but it will be under the banner and transparencies of a greater than Sacco or even Vanzetti. I shall choose my leader not for the injustices he has suffered so much as for the high and deep thoughts he has had on the subject of justice I'm afraid. There was a badly treated Peasant back in the third or forth [*sic*] dynasty who said such wonderful things about justice under the lash

---

440. RF's grandson, Prescott Frost.

441. The Amherst alumnus Gardner Jackson (1896–1965) became secretary for the Sacco-Vanzetti Defense Committee and coeditor, with Marion Denman Frankfurter, of *The Letters of Sacco and Vanzetti* (New York: Viking Press, 1928). Two Italian-born anarchists, Nicola Sacco (1891–1927) and Bartolomeo Vanzetti (1888–1927), were convicted of murdering two men outside the Slater-Morrill Shoe Company in Braintree, Massachusetts, in 1920. The ensuing trial became one of the greatest causes célèbres of the century, with many writers and politicians claiming the two men were being unfairly tried because of a pervasive anti-Italian sentiment in the Boston area and aversion to their political beliefs. The Sacco-Vanzetti Defense Committee raised substantial funds to appeal a guilty verdict, but was ultimately unsuccessful. Proclaiming their innocence until the end, Sacco and Vanzetti were executed by the state of Massachusetts on August 23, 1927.

that the Pharaoh had the lashings continued for ten days so as to get a ten-chapter book out of him for distribution to the judges and governors of the Kingdom.[442]

What you doing away off down there in a part of the state of Virginia that God alone can picture you in. I hear (from you) that you have gone over to the unreconstructed Secessionists: which if true would seem to indicate that you were stealing my singularity and the next thing you will be saying your initials J. J. stand for Joe Johnson [*sic*] the same as mine (RL.) authentically do for Robert Lee.[443] That wont be tolerated. I'm the only original northern Southerner wishing I was on horseback when I'm not and advocating States Rights for Women and Children First. My people were Copperheads and suffered martyrdom for resisting the draught, I mean, draft. One thousand were killed in one day resisting it in New York City alone.[444] You can ask anybody.

What I started to kick about was why you insist on staying away off down there to Hell and Gone in the insipid climate where I keep having to write you a long letter once in so often. Why dont you come up here nearer your friends and markets? Stephanson [*sic*] says the coughs begin at one in an audience in Montreal and increase to ten thousand in an audience by the time he

---

442. RF refers to Khunianupu (circa 2100 BC), the "Eloquent Peasant," who, after being robbed of his donkeys and goods by a wealthy government official, pleads his case in nine written petitions to Pharaoh Khety II, who orders the peasant to be beaten. Eventually the Pharaoh is so moved by the peasant's ruminations on honor and justice that he grants the peasant a generous judgment and heralds him as a sage. See Margaret Bunson, *Encyclopedia of Ancient Egypt*, rev. ed. (New York: Facts on File, 2002), 204.

443. Confederate Army commanders Joseph Eggleston Johnston (1807–1891) and Robert E. Lee (1807–1870).

444. William Prescott Frost Jr., RF's father, was a "Copperhead"—a northerner who sympathized with the Southern cause during the Civil War. He named his son Robert Lee Frost after the great Virginia general. He was also a heavy drinker; hence the joke about resisting the "draught." The New York City "Draft Riots" took place on July 13–16, 1863. After Lincoln issued the Emancipation Proclamation on January 1, the United States Congress passed the Enrollment (or "Draft") Act (March 3), which declared men between the ages of twenty and forty-five eligible for conscription into the Grand Army of the Republic. Those who could afford to pay a $300 commutation fee were exempted. Initially a protest by the working class against the draft, the riots devolved into race riots, which had to be quelled by federal troops fresh from the fighting at Gettysburg. Scholars estimate that 120 people were killed, including 11 black men who were lynched and mutilated, and that over 2,000 people were injured.

gets to New Orealeans [*sic*] thereby impressing me with the size of his audiences and with how rapidly an international cold spreads once it gets started.[445]

Im in earnest about your living so far away. Those are four beautiful pictures you did for the book—the one of the dead-alive tree especially—and they attach me to you and make me wish for your society.[446] If an abandoned farm or something could be found for you in our neighborhood couldnt you all pack off up here for a summer some year. We'll have to talk this up. I'm in need of a cheap farm myself at this moment. I'm practically homeless since I made way for Carol when he got married and all forlorn.[447] It serves me right to be out of doors for some irreverent thing I am said to have said about home.[448] But I have payed [*sic*] enough. It is time I had a little peace and pleasure in life again. I ain't the Wandering Jew am I? Well then.

We devoted or sacrificed this summer to circumventing the Atlantic or however you express crossing it twice once one way and once the other. The Captain or admiral on the bridge stopped the boat on us right in the middle of a 120 mile gale while he thought what to do with us (we were only second class anyway.) Would he sink the ship and make the first class suffer for the class deficiencies of the second class? There we swung in the biggest Conradly waves one thousand miles from France and England while he considered whether the British merchant marine could stand the reproach and what proportion of us were American nationals.[449] The nobler nature within him stirred and after mending the prow of the ship a little (she was the Olympic) he proceeded on his way to Quarantine N.Y. I'm practicing to write some sea tales: so pay no attention to me. I mean dont try to separate truth from fic-

---

445. Most likely a reference to Vilhjalmur Stefansson (1879–1962), a Canadian-born Arctic explorer whom RF mentions in his poem "New Hampshire." As a young man, Stefansson had changed his name from William Stephenson to its Icelandic equivalent when he enrolled at the University of North Dakota. From 1927 to 1930, Stefansson lectured throughout the United States.

446. Among the four prints Lankes created for *WRB* was a woodcut depicting an old, dying sycamore.

447. In 1923, RF had given Carol and Lillian Labatt Frost the Stone House in South Shaftsbury as a wedding present.

448. In "The Death of the Hired Man" (collected in *NB*), where Warren says to Mary: "Home is the place where, when you have to go there, / They have to take you in."

449. The Polish-born Joseph Conrad's experience as a sailor in the French and British merchant marines served as the basis for several vivid fictional and autobiographical accounts of life at sea (which RF read, and commended to his daughter Lesley [*LRF-1*, 631]).

tion. I may say in confidence, however, that that about the Olympic (45000 tons) stopping in the big storm was too true for comfort. I was in Dublin with A. E. and we saw a good deal of de la Mare Stevens [*sic*] Gibson Freeman and the rest. We quite enjoyed some of it—quite as the English say.

Tell <u>me</u> if they don't give you an Updyke [*sic*] special of the book.[450]

Ever yours

Robert Frost

---

450. Daniel Berkeley Updike, of the Merrymount Press, responsible for printing the limited edition of *WRB*.

Biographical Glossary of Correspondents

Abercrombie, Lascelles (1881–1938), was a British poet and literary critic. A major figure among the Georgians, he was also one of the Dymock poets, with whom Frost lived and worked in Gloucester in 1914–1915. Educated at Owens College (now Victoria University of Manchester), he embarked on a successful academic career after World War I that took him from the University of Leeds to a readership at Oxford (1935–1938). His books of poetry include *Interludes and Poems* (1908), *Mary and the Bramble* (1910), *Emblems of Love* (1912), and *Speculative Dialogues* (1913). His *Collected Poems* (1930) was followed by *The Sale of St. Thomas* (1931), a poetic drama. His critical works include *An Essay Towards a Theory of Art* (1922) and *Poetry, Its Music and Meaning* (1932).

Aiken, Conrad Potter (1889–1973), was an American poet, novelist, and critic. Educated at Harvard University, he edited *The Advocate* with T. S. Eliot, with whom he maintained a lifelong friendship, and was mentored by George Santayana. A prolific writer, Aiken published his first volume of poems, *Earth Triumphant,* in 1914; twenty-seven volumes followed. His *Selected Poems* won the Pulitzer Prize in 1930, and he later won the Bollingen Prize for Poetry and a National Book Award. Much of Aiken's work is concerned with depth psychology, and he was deeply influenced by Freud. He also contributed significantly to the recognition of Emily Dickinson's poetic stature in the twentieth century.

Aley, Maxwell (1889–1953), was an American author, editor, publisher, literary agent, and journalist. Born in Indiana and educated at Indiana University (AB 1911), Aley published short stories in *Good Housekeeping, McCalls,* and *Collier's* and a novel, *The Barnstormers* (1912). Relocating to Orono, Maine, where his father, Robert Judson Aley, was president of the University of Maine (1910–1921), he served as editor of the *Bangor Daily Commercial* until 1919, and then as an editor at Henry Holt and Company (1919), as managing editor of *Century Magazine* (1921–1922), and as fiction editor of *Woman's Home Companion* (1922–1929). In 1935 he founded the Aley Literary Agency. At various times he lectured on the short story at New York University. In 1922, he was a primary organizer and founding member of American PEN.

Armstrong, Andrew Joseph (1873–1954), was born in Kentucky and educated at Wabash College (BA 1902) and the University of Pennsylvania (PhD 1908). After teaching briefly at Georgetown College in Kentucky, he joined the faculty at Baylor University where he served as chair of the English Department from 1912 to 1952. Devoted to the poetry of Robert Browning, he donated a small collection of Browning documents to the Baylor Library in 1918. By raising funds and guiding acquisitions, he nurtured the growth of what would become the largest Browning collection in the world. Since 1948, the collection has been housed in the Armstrong Browning Library at Baylor. Throughout his career, Armstrong advanced the university's reputation by attracting prominent writers to Baylor. Along with his wife, Mary Maxwell Armstrong, he established Armstrong Educational Tours in 1912 to provide travel courses to Europe.

Bartlett, John (1892–1941), was an American journalist and editor. A student of Frost's at Pinkerton Academy, from which he graduated in 1909, Bartlett married another Pinkerton graduate, Margaret Abbott, and pursued a journalism career in Vancouver, British Columbia, and then in Colorado. Frost maintained an active and lifelong interest in Bartlett's life and career.

Baxter, Sylvester (1850–1927), was an American journalist, poet, and essayist. In a career working for several Boston newspapers, including the *Boston Herald* and the *Boston Evening Transcript,* he took great interest in urban planning and was instrumental in the creation of Boston's Metropolitan Park System. He served as secretary-treasurer for the board of the Hemenway Southwestern Archaeological Expedition and wrote extensively on architecture and archaeology in the American Southwest. His *The Unseen House and Other Poems* (1917) is a collection of free verse and prose poems, influenced in part by his long friendship with Walt Whitman.

Bayly, Charles Edward, Jr. (1897–1953), was an American fiction writer, translator, editor, and businessman. Born in Colorado and educated at Princeton University (class of 1918), he had a short story, "P'r'aps," included in the *Best College Short Stories (1917–1918).* He served as an ambulance driver in France in 1917 and subsequently as *sous-lieutenant* in the French army. He was an editor at Henry Holt and Company during the 1920s, translating several works from the French and coediting volumes of short fiction. In later life he served as president of the Denver Art Museum and oversaw and expanded Bayly Mfg., the family clothing manufacturing business.

Belden, Charles Francis Dorr (1870–1931), was an American librarian and scholar. A graduate of Harvard University (1898), he served as assistant librarian of Harvard Law School and as state librarian of Massachusetts before becoming chief librarian and director of the Boston Public Library. He was president of the American Library Association in 1925–1926.

Blatchford, Marjorie Martin (1892–1979), was an American businesswoman. Daughter of a Pittsfield, Massachusetts, publisher, bookseller, and stationer, George Blatchford, she graduated from Mt. Holyoke College in 1913. Working as an assistant in her father's business, she remained in Pittsfield and associated with the store after he sold it in 1919. She moved to Cincinnati during the 1930s and worked as a stenographer until retiring to Napa, California. In a letter of condolence to Lesley Frost Ballantine at Frost's death, in 1963, she recalled having typed poems for her father at Lesley's Open Book bookstore (Pittsfield, Massachusetts) in the mid-1920s.

Boggess, Katherine Larned (1905–1957), was an American educator. The daughter of a prominent Louisville, Kentucky, physician, she briefly attended Bradford Academy, in Haverhill, Massachusetts, after high school and then graduated from the Louisville Normal School in 1925. Until her marriage to William T. Brucker in 1934, she worked as a kindergarten teacher in Louisville.

Boyd, Thomas Alexander (1898–1935), was an American novelist and journalist. After an unsettled adolescence, he enlisted as a Marine and during service in France received the Croix de Guerre for actions during a gas attack and was himself a gas victim. In the early 1920s he moved to St. Paul, Minnesota, and worked as a reporter for the *St. Paul Daily News,* launching a literary page, "In a Corner with the Bookworm," which published correspondence and commentary with Sherwood Anderson, Willa Cather, Scott Fitzgerald, and Carl Sandburg, among others. In 1923 he published a novel based on his war experience, *Through the Wheat.* Two other novels followed, *Shadow of the Long Knives* (1928) and *In Time of Peace* (1935), but his novels were less successful than a series of biographies of such figures as Mad Anthony Wayne and Light-Horse Harry Lee. Drawn to socialist causes in the 1930s, he was the Communist Party candidate for governor of Vermont. He died of a stroke in 1935.

Bradford, Gamaliel (1863–1932), was an American biographer, critic, poet, and dramatist. A direct descendant of Governor William Bradford of the Massachusetts Bay Colony, he spent his entire life in and around Wellesley,

Massachusetts. Frail health prevented his completing a degree at Harvard University, and he would be a semi-invalid all his life. He nonetheless established himself as the foremost American biographer of his age by crafting more than a hundred of what he called "psychographies," beginning with *Lee, the American* (1912) and continuing with collections such as *Portraits of Women* (1916) and *Damaged Souls* (1923). His notable volumes of poetry include *A Pageant of Life* (1904) and *Shadow Verses* (1920).

Braithwaite, William Stanley (1878–1962), was an African American poet, literary critic, editor, and anthologist. In addition to writing numerous books of poetry and criticism, he served as literary editor of the *Boston Evening Transcript,* editor of *The Poetry Journal* (Boston), and editor of the annual *Anthology of Magazine Verse and Year Book of American Poetry,* published from 1913 to 1939.

Brennan, Harold Roy (1896–1986), was an American clergyman. Born in Adams Cove, Newfoundland, Brennan immigrated to the United States in 1915 and was naturalized in 1922. He attended Wesleyan University (Middletown, Connecticut), graduating in 1926. He then entered the ministry, serving as pastor for several Methodist congregations over the course of his career, in Bridgeport, Connecticut, in Ann Arbor, Michigan, and then again in Connecticut, this time in Hartford, where he and his wife Mabel P. Brennan (1896–1987) are buried.

Brickell, Henry Herschel (1889–1952), was an American journalist and editor. Born in Mississippi, Brickell edited the *University of Mississippi Magazine* but did not complete a degree before beginning a career in journalism. In 1919, he joined the *New York Post* and in 1923 became book editor. From 1928 until 1933 he was general editor at Henry Holt and Company and edited the *O. Henry Memorial Prize Short Stories* series. As a contributor to the *New York Times,* the *Herald Tribune, The Saturday Review,* and other publications, he was a prominent figure in the literary culture of the 1930s. He worked for the State Department in Colombia during the World War II and later lectured and wrote in Spanish about American literature.

Bromley, Dorothy Dunbar (1896–1986), was an American journalist and author. After graduating from Northwestern University in 1918, she moved to New York and did publicity and editorial work for Henry Holt and Company (1921–1924) while launching a successful career as a freelance magazine writer and later a columnist for a series of New York newspapers. Throughout her career, her books and articles addressed such issues as divorce, birth control, and the status of women in the workplace and the legal system. In the 1930s she wrote regularly about social programs and the political climate in Europe. In 1937 she began long service on the board of the American Civil Liberties Union. In the 1950s she hosted *Report to the People,* a radio program.

Brooks, Van Wyck (1886–1963), was an American literary critic, historian, essayist, and poet. An aspiring poet during his years at Harvard University, Brooks turned to journalism after graduating in 1907 in order to earn a living. In the years before *America's Coming of Age* (1915) established his reputation as a critic, Brooks moved back and forth between London and New York, doing hack work and honing his critical skills in studies such as *The Wine of the Puritans* (1908) and *The Malady of the Ideal* (1913). A prolific writer, Brooks published more than thirty books of criticism, including major studies of Emerson, Twain, Howells, and the literature of New England.

Brown, Forman (1901–1996), was an American entertainer and author. After graduating from the University of Michigan (1922), Forman enjoyed a remarkable career in theater, music, and film, first with the Yale Puppeteers, and then as founder, in 1941, of the Turnabout Theatre in Los Angeles, which attracted to its productions such luminaries as Greta Garbo and Douglas Fairbanks. Brown was also a pioneering figure in gay literature; he wrote, under the pen name Richard Meeker, the 1933 novel *Better Angel* (reprinted in 1951 under the title *Torment*).

Brown, Sharon Osborne (1891–1965), was an American scholar, literary critic, and anthologist. Educated at Brown University (AB 1915), he worked as an instructor in English there before teaching at Phillips Academy Andover and Oregon State University. After serving in the U.S. Army during World War I, he returned to Brown in 1923 as assistant professor of English. He was promoted to full professor in 1945 and retired in 1961. He published *Poetry of Our Times* and *Essays of Our Times* in 1928, and *The Engineer's Manual of English* and *Present Tense* in 1941. His anthology *Two Centuries of Brown Verse* was published in 1965.

Browne, George Henry (1857–1931), was an American educator. After graduating from Harvard University with honors in classics (1878), he founded the Browne and Nichols School in Cambridge, Massachusetts, with his former classmate Edgar H. Nichols. Browne and Frost met in 1915 at Frost's Phi Beta Kappa lecture at Tufts College. From 1915 until 1920, the Browne and Frost families were close, and the Frosts were frequent guests at Browne's farm in Bridgewater, New Hampshire. In addition to a profile of Frost, Browne published a treatise on Shakespeare's versification and a number of works on figure skating.

Burton, Marion LeRoy (1874–1925), was an American educator and Congregational minister. After graduating from Carleton College (1900), Burton served three years as the principal of the Windom Institute before entering Yale University as a divinity student. He earned a BD in 1906 and a PhD in philosophy in 1907. Invited to join the Yale faculty, he taught for one year before accepting a call to the pulpit of the Church of the Pilgrims in Brooklyn, New York. In 1910, Burton was inaugurated as Smith College's second president, but he left Smith in 1917 to assume the presidency of the University of Minnesota. In 1920 he accepted an offer to become president of the University of Michigan, a position he held until his untimely death in 1925. Admired and beloved by faculty and students, Burton successfully oversaw a capital and building campaign at Smith and undertook an even more ambitious program of campus expansion and academic reorganization at Michigan.

Burton, Nina Leona Moses (1875–1966), was an American educator. She married her classmate Marion LeRoy Burton almost immediately after their graduation from Carleton College (with BL degrees) in 1900, and taught at the Windom Institute in Minnesota. The mother of three children, she was active in her role as a university president's wife, establishing the Faculty Women's Club at Michigan in 1921.

Bynner, Harold Witter (1881–1968), was an American poet, writer, and scholar. He was educated at Harvard University (1902), where he was the first member of his class invited to join the literary magazine *The Advocate* by its editor Wallace Stevens. In 1907, he published *Young Harvard,* the first of many volumes of poetry. After a four-year stint at *McClure's Magazine,* he taught for a year at the University of California at Berkeley, but spent the rest of his career as an independent writer and lecturer. In 1920–1921 he traveled to China, where his interest in its literature led to a collaboration with Kiang Kang-hu, a professor of Chinese at Berkeley, on the translation of T'ang Dynasty poems. He settled eventually in Santa Fe, where he hosted many visiting writers over the years. His *Selected Poems* was published in 1936; a late volume, *New Poems 1960,* capped a prolific career.

Canby, Henry Seidel (1878–1961), was an American critic, editor, and educator. After graduating from Yale University in 1899 and completing a PhD in 1905, Canby joined the Yale English faculty. He edited the *Yale Review* (1911–1922) and championed American literature as a field of study. In 1920 he founded the *Literary Review,* a supplement of the *New York Evening Post.* In 1924, Canby and his coeditors, Christopher Morley and William Rose Benét, resigned and founded the *Saturday Review of Literature,* where he was editor until 1936 and chairman of the board of editors until 1958. Beginning in 1926, Canby also chaired the editorial board of the newly launched Book of the Month Club. Notable among his many published works are *Classic Americans* (1931), *Thoreau* (1939), *Whitman* (1943), and *Turn West, Turn East: Mark Twain and Henry James* (1951).

Cass, Edgar David (1865–1939), was an American educator. A graduate of Dartmouth College (BS 1897), Cass was a schoolteacher and principal in Manchester, New Hampshire. President of the New Hampshire Schoolmasters' Club in 1925, he also served on the Council of the Manchester Institute of Arts and Sciences with Frost's friend Carl Burell.

Chase, Lewis Nathaniel (1873–1937), was an American scholar and author. Educated at Columbia University (AB 1895; MA 1898; PhD 1903), he then launched a peripatetic academic career, teaching first at Columbia before moving to Indiana University, Louisville University, and the University of Bordeaux (France). He returned to the United States to teach at the University of Wisconsin (1917–1919) and the University of Rochester (1919–1920), before teaching at universities in India and China (1920–1925). Between 1925 and 1933 he taught at the University of California at Pasadena, Union College (New York), Duke University, and Brown University. His notable works include *The English Heroic Play* (1903) and *Poe and His Poetry* (1913).

Clemens, Cyril (1902–1999), was an American editor, writer, and publicist, and a distant cousin of Samuel Clemens (Mark Twain). He was educated at Georgetown University and Washington University in St. Louis. In 1930 he founded the International Mark Twain Society, and from 1936 was the first editor of the *Mark Twain Quarterly*. In addition to works on Twain—*Mark Twain and Mussolini*, published in 1934, inaugurated a series of studies of Twain in relation to world leaders—Clemens wrote about G. K. Chesterton, Josh Billings, Harry S. Truman, Clement Atlee and A. E. Housman, among others.

Cline, Clarence Lee (1905–1998), was an American scholar and educator. A graduate of Baylor University (1926), Cline earned a PhD in English at the University of Texas in 1938 and enjoyed a distinguished teaching career at Texas, serving two terms as department chair and being named the Ashbel H. Smith Professor of English. His scholarly work centered on nineteenth-century British literature and includes *Byron, Shelley and Their Pisan Circle* (1952) and *The Letters of George Meredith* (1970).

Colum, Padraic (1881–1972), was an Irish poet, novelist, dramatist, folklorist, and author of children's books. Born in County Longford, Colum grew up chiefly in Dublin, where, at the age of seventeen, he became a clerk in the

Irish Railway Clearing House. He kept the job until 1903, by which time he had already begun writing poems. He would soon become acquainted with George Russell (AE), William Butler Yeats, James Joyce, and other prominent figures in the Irish Literary Renaissance. His first book, *Wild Earth* (1907), was dedicated to AE. In 1912, Colum married literary critic and editor Mary Gunning McGuire. In 1914, the couple moved to New York City, where they remained for eight years, before travelling to Hawaii in 1923 (where Colum did work on native folklore). In 1930 the couple moved again, this time to France, where they renewed their friendship with Joyce (Colum assisted in the transcription of *Finnegan's Wake*). In New York again, after World War II, Colum and his wife taught at Columbia University and elsewhere. After Mary McGuire Colum died in 1957, her husband divided his time between Dublin and New York. He died at the age of ninety in Enfield, Connecticut, having authored more than sixty books; his body was removed to Dublin for burial (alongside his wife) in St. Fintan's Cemetery.

Conklin, Edward Groff (1904–1968), was an American editor and anthologist. He attended Dartmouth College and Harvard University, and graduated from Columbia University in 1927. He enjoyed distinction as an anthologist, first of New York literary fiction (his *Smart Set Anthology,* coedited with Burton Rascoe, appeared in 1934), and then of writing generally (his *New Republic Anthology: 1915–1935,* edited with Bruce Bliven, appeared in 1936). He was notable also as a science fiction anthologist, editing more than forty volumes in that genre.

Conkling, Grace Hazard (1878–1958), was an American poet and educator. After earning a BL from Smith College in 1899, she pursued musical studies in Europe until forced by illness to return home and to abandon plans for a musical career. In 1905 she married Roscoe Conkling and settled on a ranch near Tampico, Mexico. After their divorce in 1914, she joined the faculty at Smith, where she remained until retirement in 1947. Her first volume of poems, *Afternoons of April,* was published in 1915 and was followed by *Wilderness Songs* (1920), *Ship's Log and Other Poems* (1924), *Flying Fish: A Book of Songs and Sonnets* (1926), and *Witch and Other Poems* (1928).

Conrad, Lawrence Henry (1898–1982), was an American author and educator. Educated at the University of Michigan (BA 1923; MA 1927), he taught rhetoric there from 1923 to 1928 before joining the English faculty at the New Jersey State Teachers College in Montclair (now Montclair State University) in 1930. He remained there until 1963, focusing on American literature and creative writing. From 1967 to 1970 he worked at the University of San Diego in the

Educational Development Center. Conrad published one novel, *Temper* (1924), and several nonfiction books, including *The Author's Mind* (1925), *Descriptive and Narrative Writing* (1927), and *Teaching Creative Writing* (1937).

Cooley, Mary Elizabeth (1904–1978), was an American scientist and educator. The daughter of Charles Horton Cooley (1864–1929), professor of sociology at the University of Michigan, she completed both a BA in English in 1926 and an MS in geology in 1927 at Michigan. After serving as an instructor in geology at the University of Chicago, Antioch College, and Mt. Holyoke College, she returned to Michigan in 1940 as secretary for the Hopwood Awards program (creative writing scholarships) and counselor general to student writers. She received a Hopwood herself in 1941 for an essay entitled "Charles Wilkes and the U.S. Exploring Expedition."

Cox, Sidney Hayes (1889–1951), was an American scholar and critic who was educated at Bates College (AB 1911) and the University of Illinois (AM 1913). His work toward a doctorate at Columbia University was interrupted by the war. Cox met Frost in 1911 when Cox was teaching high school English in Plymouth, New Hampshire. Cox went on to teach English and creative writing at the University of Montana before joining the Dartmouth College faculty in 1926. He had a distinguished forty-year teaching career at Dartmouth, during which he wrote two books about Frost: *Robert Frost: Original "Ordinary Man"* (1929) and *A Swinger of Birches* (1957). His other works include *The Teaching of English: Avowals and Ventures* (1928), *Indirections for Those Who Want to Write* (1947), and a popular anthology-textbook, *Prose Preferences* (1926).

Cross, Wilbur Lucius (1862–1948), was an American literary scholar, editor, professor, and politician. After earning a BA (1885) and a PhD (1889) from Yale University, Cross taught in the Yale English Department from 1894 until 1916, when he became dean of the Yale Graduate School. After retiring from Yale in 1930, Cross was elected the fifty-sixth governor of Connecticut and held the office from 1931 until 1939. In 1911 he became the editor of the *Yale Review,* and continued in that role, despite changes in position and responsibility, until 1941. As a scholar his focus was primarily on eighteenth-century British literature; noteworthy among his books are *The Life and Times of Laurence Sterne* (1909) and *The History of Henry Fielding* (1918).

Davison, Edward Lewis "Ted" (1898–1970), was a Scottish-born American poet, lecturer, critic, and educator. After serving in the British navy in World War I, he studied at Cambridge University and published the first of his eight volumes of poetry in 1920. He emigrated to the United States in 1925, joined the faculty at Vassar College, and wrote for the *Saturday Review of Literature*. After receiving a Guggenheim fellowship, and teaching at the University of Miami, he joined the faculty at the University of Colorado, where he established the Rocky Mountain Writers' Conference. After military service in World War II, as a lieutenant colonel in charge of the reeducation of German prisoners of war, he served as dean at Washington and Jefferson College and Hunter College

Davison, Wilfred Edward (1887–1929), was an American scholar and educator. After graduating from Middlebury College (1913), he studied German in Berlin, attended the Curry School of Expression in Boston, and took graduate courses at Harvard University and Columbia University. He joined the Middlebury faculty as instructor in German, but started to teach English in 1918. He was instrumental in the formation of Middlebury's Department of American Literature, in 1923, and he was the first dean of Middlebury's Bread Loaf School of English, serving from 1921 to 1929.

Dilliard, Irving Lee (1899–2002), was an American journalist and editor. A native of Collinsville, Illinois, Dilliard took a job as a local correspondent for the *St. Louis Post-Dispatch* in 1924. He subsequently attended the University of Illinois, graduating in 1927, after which he was again hired by the *Post-Dispatch,* this time as a staff reporter. During World War II, Dilliard rose to the rank of lieutenant colonel, serving as a specialist in psychological warfare on the staff of Gen. Dwight D. Eisenhower. After the war, Dilliard rejoined the *St. Louis Post-Dispatch,* this time as a columnist, devoting his attentions chiefly to legal matters, the Supreme Court, and the Constitution. In 1954 (the year the French were defeated at Dien Ben Phu), Dilliard launched a series of editorials opposing American involvement in Indochina. After leaving the newspaper business, Dilliard turned to teaching. He was a Ferris Professor of Journalism at Princeton University from 1963–1973, and a number of universities and colleges awarded him honorary degrees. His books include *Building the Constitution* (1937), *The Development of a Free Press in Germany: An Aspect of American Military Government* (1949), and *The Spirit of Liberty* (1952).

Dodd, Loring Holmes (1879–1968), was an American scholar, art critic, and poet. Educated at Dartmouth College (AB 1900), Columbia University (AM 1901), and Yale University (PhD 1907), he joined the English faculty at Clark University in 1910, becoming a professor of both English and Art and the chairman of both departments. He retired in 1949. Trained as a medievalist, he published *A Glossary of Wulfstan's Homilies* in 1908, but much of his later work focused on American art, notably *The Golden Age of American Sculpture* (1936), *With an Eye on the Gallery: American Painters in Oil* (1956), and *A Generation of Illustrators and Etchers* (1960).

Dodd, Marion Elza (1883–1961), was an American bibliophile, businesswoman, and writer. Granddaughter of the founder of Dodd, Mead Publishing Company, she graduated from Smith College (1906) and attended Columbia University School of Library Science (1908–1909). In 1916, with Mary Byers, she cofounded the Hampshire Bookshop in Northampton, Massachusetts. Dodd was a member of the executive board of the American Booksellers' Association for twenty-five years and its first woman officer; she contributed to such publications as *Yankee Magazine, Publishers' Weekly,* and the *Atlantic Monthly,* and also taught courses about the history of the book and bookselling at Columbia's School of Library Science and at Smith.

Eaton, Walter Prichard (1878–1957), was an American drama critic and author. After graduating from Harvard University, Eaton worked as a drama critic at the *New York Tribune* (1902–1907), the *New York Sun* (1907–1908), and *American Magazine* (1909–1918). He was professor of playwriting at Yale University from 1933–1947. In addition to writing about literature and theatre history, Eaton wrote extensively and successfully about nature and the outdoor life (RF particularly admired his 1913 book *Barn Doors and Byways* [see LRF-1, 328]).

Elliott, George Roy (1883–1963), was a Canadian American scholar and educator. After earning an AB at the University of Toronto (1904) and a PhD at Friedrich Schiller University of Jena (1908), he taught at the University of Wisconsin (1909–1913), Bowdoin College (1913–1925), and Amherst College (1925–1950). Notable among his many published works are *The Cycle of Modern Poetry* (1929), *Humanism and Imagination* (1938), and *Church, College, and Nation* (1945).

Erskine, John (1879–1951), was an American writer, scholar, educator, and musician. Educated at Columbia University (BA 1900; PhD 1903), he taught at Amherst College before returning to Columbia to join the English faculty, where he taught from 1909 until 1937. He is credited with starting the system of General Education at Columbia called General Honors, through his Great Books Program. A prolific writer in a variety of genres, he is best known for *The Moral Obligation to Be Intelligent and Other Essays* (1915) and the novel *The Private Life of Helen of Troy* (1925). Having trained early as a pianist, Erskine returned to music in the 1920s and performed as a soloist with the New York

Symphony. He was president of the Juilliard School of Music from 1928 to 1937, editor of *A Musical Companion* (1935), and author of a number of books about music.

Farson, Mary Elizabeth (1851–1935), was an American educator. Educated at Illinois Normal University, she rose through the Chicago school system as a teacher, principal, and assistant superintendent. She was widely acknowledged for innovative instructional and curricular practices, among which was the use of creative literature to teach science and ethics.

Firuski, Maurice (1894–1978), was an American bookseller and collector. Born in New York, he graduated from Yale University in 1916 and served in the U.S. Navy during World War I. In the early 1920s he owned the Dunster House Bookshop in Cambridge, Massachusetts, before moving to Salisbury, Connecticut, where he ran the Housatonuc bookstore for forty-seven years. A well-known man of letters and adviser to book collectors, he enjoyed friendships with a number of prominent literary figures and was considered an authority on Herman Melville.

Fisher, Dorothy Canfield (1879–1958), was an American author, educator, and social activist. Educated at Ohio State University (AB 1899), the University of Paris, and Columbia University (PhD 1904), she trained for an academic career teaching modern languages, but after her marriage to John Fisher in 1907 she turned to writing. When John Fisher volunteered for ambulance duty in France, she and their children relocated to France and she spent the war years doing relief work; she remained committed to such work throughout her life. In Rome, in 1912, she met Maria Montessori and developed an interest in educational theory. She published several books on education and child-rearing, and served on the Vermont State Board of Education. She also published numerous novels and short-story collections, and over twenty works of nonfiction, including, toward the end of her life, contributions to Vermont history. From 1925 to 1951 she served as a member of the Book of the Month Club selection committee. Throughout her life she was a tireless advocate of women's rights, racial equality, and other progressive causes.

Fisher, John Redwood (1883–1959), was an American educator, politician, and editor. While a student at Columbia University (AB 1904), he was a class president, captain of the football team, and a roommate of Alfred Harcourt. An aspiring writer and critic, he married Dorothy Canfield in 1907 and they settled in Arlington, Vermont. As her writing career flourished, he served as her editor and agent. He volunteered for ambulance service in France in 1915 and served later as lieutenant with the U.S. Medical Corps and captain with the U.S.

Army Ambulance Service. He served two terms in the Vermont General Assembly (1925, 1937) and was named to the State Board of Education in 1939, chairing it from 1941 to 1949.

Fletcher, John Gould (1886–1950), was an American poet and essayist. He attended Harvard University but left in 1908 without graduating. Of independent means, he settled in London and was among the original group of imagist poets, although his poems were included in imagist anthologies only after Amy Lowell assumed editorship of them, beginning with *Some Imagist Poets,* in 1917. He published two volumes of imagist poems, *Irradiations: Sand and Spray* (1915) and *Goblins and Pagodas* (1916). His poetry moved toward social criticism in the 1920s and from 1927 until 1932 he was closely aligned with the Southern Agrarian movement and the Fugitive poets. *Selected Poems* (1938) was awarded a Pulitzer Prize, but later and more formal works, *South Star* (1941) and *The Burning Mountain* (1946), were not widely reviewed.

Foerster, Norman (1887–1972), was an American literary scholar and a prominent figure in the New Humanist movement. Foerster was born in Pittsburgh, Pennsylvania, educated at Harvard University (class of 1910), and at the University of Wisconsin, where he completed an MA in 1912. After working as an instructor at Wisconsin, he enjoyed a successful teaching career at the University of North Carolina, the University of Iowa (where he directed the School of Letters from 1930–1944), Duke University, and elsewhere. He was awarded honorary degrees by the University of the South, Grinnell College, and the University of North Carolina. Foerster published scores of essays about literature, art, and education, and authored a number of books, including *The Chief American Prose Writers* (1916), *Nature in American Literature* (1923), and, with RF's friend George R. Elliott as his co-editor, *English Poetry of the Nineteenth Century: A Connected Representation of Poetic Art and Thought from 1798 to 1914* (1923).

Folsom, Franklin B. (1907–1995), was an American author and scholar. Educated at the University of Colorado (BA 1928), Folsom taught English at Swarthmore College. In 1930 he won a Rhodes Scholarship. During a long career as a writer, he published many works on American social history from a progressive viewpoint as well as a number of fictional and historical works for juvenile audiences. The year before he died, Folsom published a memoir of his days in the League of American Writers, founded by the Communist Party USA in 1935 *(Days of Anger, Days of Hope).* When called before the House Committee on Un-American Activities in 1956, he refused to testify.

Folsom married the writer Mary Elting, with whom he cowrote several children's books.

Forbes, Anita Prentice (1889–1965), was an American educator and editor. Educated at Radcliffe College (AB 1910; MA 1912), she was an instructor in English at Mt. Holyoke College before taking a faculty position at Weaver High School in Hartford, Connecticut. Her anthology of *Modern Verse, British and American* (New York: Henry Holt, 1921) became a standard high school text. Forbes is perhaps best remembered for her strictures, in a speech to the National Education Association, against the pernicious effects of pulp magazine fiction on the minds of teenage readers.

Freeman, John Frederick (1880–1929), was a British poet, novelist, critic, essayist, and businessman. Associated with the Georgians, he published numerous volumes of poetry, including *Twenty Poems* (1909), *Poems New and Old* (1920; it won the Hawthornden Prize), and *Collected Poems* (1928).

Frink, Maurice Mahurin (1895–1972), was an American journalist, historian, author, and educator. A graduate of the Columbia University School of Journalism (1919), he had a thirty-year career as a journalist in Elkhart, Indiana, and later taught journalism at the University of Colorado in Boulder (1951–1954). Subsequently he served as executive director of the Colorado Historical Society and Museum in Denver. He published extensively on the history of the American West, most notably *Cow Country Cavalcade* (1954), and was a collector of Native American materials.

Gallishaw, Alonzo John "Jack" (1891–1968), was a Canadian-born American author and educator. After leaving school at age fourteen and working at a variety of jobs, he entered Harvard University as a special student in 1914, but enlisted in the Canadian army the same year. After training, he requested a discharge and joined the Newfoundland Regiment of the British Army. Wounded at Gallipoli, he was discharged and returned to Harvard. He published a well-received account of the campaign, *Trenching at Gallipoli* (1916), and in 1917 became a U.S. citizen and married Eleanor Browne. He joined the U.S. Army in 1918 and was gassed during action at the Marne. He returned to Harvard and served as an assistant dean with the task of assisting returning veterans to reintegrate, but left for reasons of health without having earned a degree. He earned a degree in journalism from the University of California, Berkeley (1923), completed a degree in English at Harvard, and founded a school of creative writing in 1924. Between 1924 and 1937 he published three books on teaching fiction writing. In 1937 he went to Hollywood on contract to Metro-Goldwyn-Mayer to teach scriptwriting, and later worked as a consultant. In 1958, he moved to Hawaii and taught briefly at the University of Hawaii.

Gannett, Lewis (1891–1966), was an American author, journalist, and editor. Educated at Harvard University (BA 1913; MA 1915), he was a reporter and foreign correspondent for *The (New York) World* (1916–1919) and then joined the staff of *The Nation* (1919–1928). As editor and columnist at the *New York Herald-Tribune* (1928–1956), he wrote the influential daily book review column "Books and Things." Among his notable publications are *Young China* (1927), *I Saw It Happen: Eyewitness Accounts of the War* (1942), *Cream Hill: Discoveries of a Week-End Countryman* (1949), and *The Family Book of Verse* (1961). The son of the reformer and suffragist Mary Thorn Lewis Gannett, he was a social activist and served on the board of directors of the NAACP.

Gardiner, Alexander (1889–1977), was an American journalist and editor. A student at Pinkerton Academy while Frost taught there, he graduated from Brown University in 1914 and worked briefly as a newspaper editor before becoming editor at the *American Legion Monthly*.

Garland, Hannibal Hamlin (1860–1940), was an American novelist, short story writer, essayist, reformer, and philanthropist. Having grown up on midwestern farms, he moved to Boston to become a writer and educated himself at the Boston Public Library. His first success came with *Main-Travelled Roads* (1891). Notable among his forty-six published books are *Crumbling Idols* (1894), a collection of essays about contemporary literature; *A Son of the Middle Border* (1917) and the Pulitzer Prize–winning *A Daughter of the Middle Border* (1921), the first two volumes of his autobiography; and *The Book of the American Indian* (1923), a collection of stories about Native American culture in transition.

Gay-Tifft, Eugene Whiting (1899–1982), was an American bookseller, editor, and translator. Gay-Tifft, a native of Buffalo, New York, was educated at Dartmouth College (class of 1923). He married Lola Olzewski (1900–1987), also a native of Buffalo, where the couple spent most of their lives. Gay-Tifft is perhaps best known as the translator of Norwegian novelist Knut Hamsun (1859–1952), winner of the Nobel Prize for Literature in 1920; of the Danish novelist Aksel Sandemose (1899–1965), a finalist for Nobel Prize in Literature in 1963; and of Helge Ingstad (1899–2001), the Norwegian explorer of Canada's Northwest territories (and elsewhere), whose books about his travels won him a wide readership in Norway and beyond.

Gibney, Sheridan de Raismes (1903–1988), was an American theatrical writer and producer. Educated at Phillips Academy Exeter and Amherst College (1925), he taught briefly at Hobart College. He achieved his first success writing plays, including *Merry Madness* (1929) and *Calico Wedding* (1931), but is best known for his work in film. His extensive list of screenplays includes *I Am a Fugitive from a Chain Gang* (1932), *Anthony Adverse* (1936), and *The Story of Louis Pasteur* (1936), for which he won Oscars for Best Original Story and Best Screenplay. Between 1930 and 1941, and again in 1947–1948, he was president of the Screen Writers Guild. In late career he wrote for a number of popular television series.

Gilbert, Edgar (1875–1964), was an American chemist, businessman, and educator. After graduating from Dartmouth College (AB 1905), he taught science and mathematics at Methuen (Massachusetts) High School for five years, before becoming general manager of the Lyster Chemical Company in New York. In the mid-1920s he established Gilbert Laboratories in Morristown, New Jersey—a chemical manufacturing firm in which his son Frederick eventually joined him—and later the Gilbert Research Institute for cancer research.

Gilchrist, Halley Phillips (1876–1944), was an American poet. A lifelong resident of Vermont, she trained in elocution and public speaking, completing a two-year program at the School of Expression in Boston in 1897. During the 1920s she toured eastern cities with a program of readings in modern poetry. She was later house mother for Smith College's Hubbard House. She served as vice-president and secretary of the Southern Vermont Poetry Society.

Glass, Everett William (1891–1966), was an American actor, theater director, and playwright. After graduating from Amherst College in 1914, Glass became one of the original members of the Greenwich Village Theater Company, in 1917. After success on the stage in New York and California, he directed at the Berkeley Playhouse and managed the Wheeler Hall Plays series at the University of California, Berkeley. In 1948 Glass began a film acting career and appeared in dozens of notable character roles in movies and television series in the 1950s and 1960s.

Goodwillie, Mary C. (1870–1949), was an American philanthropist. Active in a variety of social and charitable organizations in Baltimore, she was chair of the Southern District of Federated Charities, president of the Baltimore Social Service Exchange from 1924–1945, and president of the Friends of the Johns Hopkins University Library. She was instrumental in establishing the Baltimore Poetry Society. In 1940 Johns Hopkins University awarded her an honorary master's degree.

Greenslet, Ferris Lowell (1875–1959), was an American author and editor. Educated at Wesleyan University (AB 1897) and Columbia University (MS, PhD 1900), he worked briefly at the Boston Public Library before becoming an associate editor at the *Atlantic Monthly*. In 1910 he took a position as literary adviser and director at the publisher Houghton Mifflin, where he remained for the rest of his career. Notable among his written works are *James Russell Lowell: His Life and Work* (1905), *The Life of Thomas Bailey Aldrich* (1908), and *The Lowells and Their Seven Worlds* (1946).

Haines, John Wilton "Jack" (1875–1966), was a British solicitor, poet, and botanist. After graduating from Cheltenham College, where he twice won the Iredell Prize for Literature, he trained as a solicitor and in 1899 joined the family law firm, Haines and Sumner. He was friend, legal adviser, and patron to many of the Georgian poets. He published one volume of poetry, *Poems*, in 1921.

Halle, Rita Sulzbacher (1885–1971), was an American socialite and author. Educated at Wellesley College (BA 1907) and married first to the statesman and scholar Louis Joseph Halle in 1908 and then to the banker Arthur Susman Kleeman in 1934, she was a family friend of the Roosevelts and the author of *Young Franklin Roosevelt* (1945)—a biography for young readers—and *Gracious Lady* (1935), about Sara Delano Roosevelt. A regular contributor to magazines and newspapers, she was a member of the Writers War Board from 1941 to 1945 and a director and later trustee of PEN; she also chaired the Western Hemisphere Solidarity Committee of the National Council of Women.

Hallowell, Charlotte Louise Rudyard (1882–1972), was an American writer and editor. A graduate of Vassar College (1904), she worked briefly at the *Brooklyn Daily Eagle* before becoming an assistant editor at *Harper's* in 1907. In 1914 she was one of the six original editors of the *New Republic* but resigned in 1916 after marrying the magazine's business manager, Robert Hallowell.

Harcourt, Alfred (1881–1954), was an American publisher. After graduating from Columbia University in 1904, Harcourt worked for Henry Holt and Company until 1919, when he founded, with his classmate and colleague, Donald Brace, and fellow editor Will D. Howe, the publishing firm of Harcourt, Brace and Howe. After Howe's departure in 1921, the firm became Harcourt, Brace and Company.

Hart, Hubert Nichols (1904–1986), was an American educator. A graduate of Amherst College (AB 1925), he later studied English literature and education at Columbia University and taught at New York University and Brooklyn College before joining the faculty at C. W. Post College.

Heyward, Edwin DuBose (1885–1940), was an American novelist, playwright, and poet. Frequently ill when young, he had no formal schooling beyond a year of high school but had an avid interest in literature. In 1919 he formed a close friendship with Hervey Allen and they founded the Poetry Society of South Carolina. In 1922 they jointly published *Carolina Chansons: Legends of the Low Country* and edited an issue of *Poetry* featuring southern poets. After publishing *Jasbo Brown and Other Poems* (1924), Heyward turned to fiction, and *Porgy* was published in 1926. In collaboration with his wife, Dorothy Kuhns Heyward, he adapted it for the stage in 1927, and he later wrote the libretto for George Gershwin's musical adaptation, *Porgy and Bess* (1935).

Hillyer, Robert Silliman (1895–1961), was an American poet. Educated at Harvard and at the University of Copenhagen, he won the Garrison Prize for poetry at Harvard while a student there and was on the editorial board of the Harvard *Advocate*. Hillyer served as an ambulance driver in the French Army at Verdun, for which he received a citation. From 1919 to 1926 he was Instructor in English at Harvard. After a short term at Trinity College, he returned to Harvard in 1928, and, in 1937, was named Boylston Professor of Rhetoric and Oratory. He received the Pulitzer Prize for his *Collected Verse of Robert Hillyer* (New York: Knopf, 1933). Hillyer was president of The New England Poetry Club (1923–1925) and president of The Poetry Society of America (in 1949, and again in 1951–1953). He retired from Harvard in 1944, but held posts, in his later years, at Kenyon College and at the University of Delaware.

Hocking, William Ernest (1873–1966), was an American philosopher and educator. Intending a career as a civil engineer, he attended the Iowa State College of Agriculture and Mechanical Arts until reading William James led him to philosophy. He completed an MA at Harvard University in 1901, studied for two years in Germany, and returned to Harvard for the PhD (1904). After teaching at Andover Theological Seminary and The University of California, Berkeley, he joined the faculty at Yale University in 1908. He returned to Harvard in 1912 and, after war service as a civil engineer at the front, remained there for the rest of his career. Having studied with Josiah Royce, Hocking elucidated his own version of idealist philosophy and developed what he called "negative pragmatism" in two major works: *The Meaning of God in Human Experience* (1912) and *Morale and Its Enemies* (1918). Although his primary interest was in the philosophy of religion, Hocking also wrote extensively on issues of political philosophy. Hocking married Agnes O'Reilly, daughter of the journalist and poet John Boyle O'Reilly.

Holden, Raymond Peckham (1894–1972), was an American poet, novelist, essayist, and editor. After graduating from Princeton University in 1915, he served for two years in the National Guard and the Office of Naval Information before beginning a career in publishing that included stints at the *New Yorker, Fortune, Newsweek,* and *Reader's Digest.* His first collection of poems, *Granite and Alabaster,* was published by Macmillan in 1922. His other poetry collections include *Natural History* (1938), *The Arrow at the Heel* (1940), and *The Reminding Salt* (1964). After his 1917 marriage to Grace Ansley Badger ended, Holden married the poet Louise Bogan in 1925; they divorced in 1937.

Holt, Roland (1867–1931), was an American theater critic and publisher. Son of the publisher Henry Holt, he began his literary career while still in college as an editor of the *Yale Courant* and as a drama critic at the *New Haven Daily Palladium.* He graduated from Yale University in 1890 and began working for Henry Holt and Company, serving as vice-president from 1903 to 1924.

Howe, Mark Antony DeWolfe (1864–1960), was an American editor and author. After graduating from Lehigh University (1886) and completing an AM at Harvard University (1888), he served as associate editor of the *Youth's Companion* (1888–1893; 1899–1913), assistant editor of the *Atlantic Monthly* (1893–1895), and vice-president of the Atlantic Monthly Company (1911–1929). Prolific as both editor and author, he edited the Beacon Biographies (31 volumes, 1899–1910), *The Memory of Lincoln* (1889), and *Home Letters of General Sherman* (1909); he wrote volumes on Boston and regional history and biographies of Phillips Brooks, George Bancroft, Bishop Hare, and others, winning the Pulitzer Prize for Biography in 1925 for *Wendell Barrett and His Letters.* He also published two volumes of poetry, *Shadows* (1897) and *Harmonics* (1909).

Hubble, Jay Broadus (1885–1979), was an American scholar and editor. Educated at Richmond College (BA 1905), Harvard University (MA 1908), and Columbia University (PhD 1922), he was a professor of English at Southern Methodist University from 1915 to 1927 and served as an artillery lieutenant in World War I. He joined the faculty at Duke University in 1928 and the next year founded the journal *American Literature,* chairing its editorial board until retirement in 1954. A significant figure in the establishment of American literary study as a discipline, he published *The Enjoyment of Literature* (1929) and *Southern Life in Fiction* (1960); his anthology *American Life in Literature* (1936) was reprinted many times.

Hull, Raymona Elsie (1907–1997), was an American educator and scholar. After graduating from Flora Stone Mather College at Case Western University in 1929, she taught high school before earning an MA at Cornell University in 1933. She joined the faculty at the State University of New York at Canton and in 1951 earned an EdD from Columbia University. From 1958 to 1975 she taught at Indiana State College in Indiana, Pennsylvania. She was a founding member of the Hawthorne Society and published *Nathaniel Hawthorne: The English Experience, 1853–1864* in 1980.

Johnson, Henry Reynolds (1868–1959), was an American bookseller. Along with his brother, the writer Clifton Johnson, he owned and operated Johnson's Bookstore in Springfield, Massachusetts.

Jones, Llewellyn (1884–1961), was a British-born American editor and literary critic. Born on the Isle of Man, he was educated at King William's College and the Douglas School of Science. He was the literary editor of the *Chicago Evening Post* from 1914 until 1932. During the 1920s he also taught creative writing classes at the University of Chicago and at Northwestern University. He was editor for Willett, Clark and Company, a Chicago publishing firm, until moving to Boston in 1937 as editor of the *Christian Register,* from which he resigned in 1941. His books include *First Impressions: Essays on Poetry, Criticism, and Prosody* (1925); *How to Criticize Books* (1928); and *How to Read Books* (1930).

Kidd, Walter Evans (1901–1990), was an American poet, fiction writer, and scholar. He was educated at the University of Oregon (BA 1926; MA 1935), where the creative writing program is named for him. After years of teaching high school in Portland, he earned a PhD at the University of Denver (1943) and held teaching posts at the University of Nebraska; Stephen F. Austin State College, in Texas; Fresno State College; and, as a visiting professor, at the University of Michigan. He published four books of poetry and two scholarly works. Many of his works were published under the pseudonym Conrad Pendleton.

Kimmel, Stanley Preston (1894–1982), was an American novelist, journalist, musician, poet, and playwright. He attended the University of Southern California for three years but left for France in 1914, at the outbreak of World War I, to drive an ambulance for the French army. He returned to the United States in 1917 to train as an aviator in the U.S. Navy and then returned to Europe.

He lived in Paris among writers of the "Lost Generation" before moving to Chicago, where he worked as a reporter for the *Chicago Post*. In the late 1920s he was the editor of *New Orleans Life* magazine. During the 1940s he worked under Nelson Rockefeller at the Office of Inter-American Affairs. From 1972 to 1980 he was author in residence at the University of Tampa. Among his notable works are *Poems and Fantasies* (1916), *Crucifixion* (1922), *The Mad Booths of Maryland* (1940), *Mr. Lincoln's Washington* (1957), and *Mr. Davis's Richmond* (1958).

Kreymborg, Alfred Francis (1883–1966), was an American poet, novelist, playwright, editor, chess master, and anthologist. Although a prolific and widely published poet, he figures more significantly in literary history as the founder and editor of three literary magazines: *The Glebe* (1913–1914), *Others* (1915–1919), and *Broom, An International Magazine of the Arts* (1921–1924). A prominent figure in Greenwich Village and closely associated with the photographer Alfred Stieglitz, he was instrumental in advancing the careers of many modernist poets. His notable books include *Apostrophes* (1910), *Mushrooms* (1916), *Manhattan Men* (1929), *Ten American Ballads* (1942), and *No More War and Other Poems* (1950). He published an autobiography, *Troubadour*, in 1925, and a history of American poetry, *Our Singing Strength*, in 1929.

Lamb, Flora MacDonald (1869–1949), was an American clerical worker and businesswoman. Born and educated in Windham, Maine, she graduated from Shaw's Business College in Portland, Maine. Having worked as a bookkeeper and stenographer, she began a forty-year association with Thomas B. Mosher's publishing house in 1897. By the time of Mosher's death in 1923, she had served as executive secretary for a number of years, and his will stipulated that she was to assume direction of the press. After two decades of astute management, she oversaw the sale of the business to Williams Book Store of Boston in 1941. In September 1925, Lamb was featured in "The Shorthand Short Cut to Fame," an article in *Collier's, The National Weekly* about secretaries and stenographers who had risen to positions of prominence.

Lankes, Julius John "J. J." (1884–1960), was an American illustrator, woodcut print artist, author, and educator. After graduating from the Buffalo (New York) Commercial and Electro-Mechanical Institute in 1902, he worked as a draftsman specializing in patent drawings before continuing his art studies at the Art Students' League of Buffalo and the Boston Museum of Fine Arts. He produced the first of his more than 1,300 woodcuts in 1917; his most significant early illustration was done for *The Liberator,* at which he was listed as contributing editor (1918–1920), and for *Century Magazine* (1921–1922). In 1923 he illustrated Frost's *New Hampshire,* and the two began a lifelong friendship. He was to enjoy a similar professional and personal relationship with Sherwood Anderson. Relocating to Virginia in 1925, he published *Virginia Woodcuts* in 1930 and *A Woodcut Manual* in 1932. Encouraged by Frost to accept a visiting professorship at Wells College in Aurora, New York, in 1933, he remained on the faculty until 1939. During World War II he joined the National Advisory Committee for Aeronautics as head of technical illustrating at the Langley Memorial Aeronautical Laboratory.

Latham, Minnie Alice Strong (1865–1945), was an American clubwoman. Born in Connecticut, she married the businessman Charles Latham; their son was Harold Strong Latham (1887–1969), editor-in-chief at Macmillan Publishers. Active in social and cultural affairs, she participated in the Chautauqua Literary and Scientific Circle (1892), chaired the Press Committee of the New Jersey Federation of Women's Clubs, and served as president general of the National Society of the Daughters of the American Revolution.

Leippert, James George (1909–1964), was an American editor, publisher, and poet. Educated at Columbia University (BA 1933), he won the Philolexian Award for Poetry at Columbia in 1931 and was editor of the university literary magazine *Lion and Crown* (formerly *New Broom*) in 1932–1933. He founded the Alcestis Press and *Alcestis: A Poetry Quarterly* in 1934 and began to correspond with Wallace Stevens under the name Ronald Lane Latimer, which became his legal name in 1935. He had for years previously written under assumed names (for instance, Edwin Robinson Leippert; Alfred Housman Leippert) to prominent authors requesting autographs. *Alcestis* published seven poems by Stevens, including, in the first issue, "The Idea of Order at Key West." The Alcestis Press later published works by both Stevens and William Carlos Williams. In the online poetry magazine *Jacket2,* Alan Filreis described Leippert as "Columbia student, publisher-communist, then Buddhist in flowing robes in New Mexico, then expatriate in Japan, finally Episcopal priest in Florida" ("A Soul Collected," June 1, 2009).

Lewis, Edward Morgan "Ted" (1872–1936), was a Welsh-born American professional baseball player, educator, and academic administrator. After graduating from Williams College (AB 1896), he pitched four seasons for the Boston Beaneaters (National League) and one for the Boston Americans (American League) while completing an MA at Williams (1899). He taught for two years at Columbia University (1901–1903) before returning to Williams as assistant professor of public speaking (1903–1911). Joining the English faculty at the Massachusetts State Agricultural College (now the University of Massachusetts Amherst), he served as dean of languages and literature, acting president (1913–1914, 1918–1919, 1924–1926) and president (1926–1927). He was president of the University of New Hampshire from 1927 until his death in 1936.

Lloyd, Alfred Henry (1864–1927), was an American philosopher, educator, and academic administrator. After graduating from Harvard University (AB 1886), he spent two years in Göttingen, Berlin, and Heidelberg as Walker Fellow of Philosophy before earning his MA (1888) and PhD (1893) from Harvard. He joined the University of Michigan's philosophy faculty in 1891, became full professor in 1906, and dean of the graduate school in 1915. He served as acting president of the university from February to October of 1925. His major publications include *Citizenship and Salvation* (1897), *Dynamic Idealism* (1898), *Philosophy of History* (1899), and *The Will to Doubt* (1907).

Lovell, Mabel B. Brackett (1870–1942), was an American clubwoman and poet. A longtime resident of Cranford, New Jersey, she was active in its Woman's Club and placed poems in *A Book of Verses by New Jersey Clubwomen* (1929) and in *Homespun: An Anthology of Poetry by the General Federation of Women's Clubs* (1936).

Lowell, Amy (1874–1925), was an American poet, critic, anthologist, and collector who did much to advance the cause of poetry in modern America. Born into the prominent Lowell family of Brookline, Massachusetts, she published her first volume of poetry in 1912. Its title, *A Dome of Many-Coloured Glass*, suggests her abiding interest in Keats, of whom she would publish a two-volume biography in 1925, shortly before her death. Her second volume, *Sword Blades and Poppy Seed* (1914), was written in free verse and "polyphonic prose" and revealed her immersion in the aesthetics of imagism, whose emergence in the United States she facilitated through *Some Imagist Poets,* an annual anthology published in 1915, 1916, and 1917. Although a champion of free verse, she wrote a laudatory review of *North of Boston* and devoted a chapter to Frost in her *Tendencies in Modern American Poetry* (1917).

Lowes, John Livingston (1867–1945), was an American scholar and critic. After completing a PhD at Harvard University (1905), he taught English at Swarthmore College (1905–1909) and Washington University in Saint Louis (1909–1918) before joining the faculty at Harvard, from which he retired in 1939. Noteworthy among his many publications are *Convention and Revolt in Poetry* (1919), *The Road to Xanadu* (1927), two books on Chaucer (1931, 1934), and two collections of essays, *Of Reading Books and Other Essays* (1930) and *Essays in Appreciation* (1936).

Lurie, Helen Bernice Stewart (1891–1982), was an American journalist. Educated at the University of Michigan (BA 1915), she worked for the *Detroit Free Press* until her marriage in 1922 to the sociologist Harry Lawrence Lurie (1892–1973), who in 1922–1923 was an instructor in the Economics Department at Michigan. Their daughter, Alison Lurie, is a Pulitzer Prize–winning novelist and a professor of American literature at Cornell University.

MacKaye, Percy Wallace (1875–1956), was an American dramatist and poet. After graduating from Harvard University in 1897, MacKaye spent several years in Europe, and then taught in New York, before joining an artists' colony in Cornish, New Hampshire, and devoting himself to writing drama. Between 1903 and 1919 he published fourteen plays, including the two works, *The Canterbury Pilgrims* (1903) and *The Scarecrow* (1908), upon which his reputation as a dramatist rests. MacKaye also published three volumes of poetry between 1912 and 1915. In 1920, Miami (Ohio) University made MacKaye the first American poet in residence, an appointment he held until 1924.

MacVeagh, Lincoln (1890–1972), was an American soldier, diplomat, editor, publisher, and archaeologist. After graduating from Harvard University in 1913 and studying languages at the Sorbonne, he served with distinction as a major in World War I. He joined Henry Holt and Company after the war and left in 1923 to establish the Dial Press. Between 1933 and 1953, MacVeagh served the Roosevelt and Truman administrations as ambassador to Greece, Iceland, South Africa, and Spain. During his years in Greece, he conducted excavations beneath the Acropolis and made contributions to the National Archaeological Museum of Athens.

Makielski, Leon A. (1885–1974), was an American painter. Born in Pennsylvania and reared in Indiana, he studied at the Art Institute of Chicago between 1903 and 1909. After four years in Europe, including two years in Paris at the Académie Julian and the Académie de la Grande Chaumière, he returned to the United States in 1913, settled in Ann Arbor, and taught at the University of Michigan from 1915 until 1927. For a number of years he worked at painting portraits of fellow faculty members and their families. After leaving the university, he divided his time between studios in Detroit and Ann Arbor. Although he produced a number of highly regarded impressionistic landscapes, he is primarily known as a portrait painter. His portrait of Frost is in the University of Michigan Art Museum

Manthey-Zorn, Otto (1879–1964), was an American scholar and educator. After graduating from Western Reserve University (1901), he completed a PhD at the University of Leipzig (1904). He joined the Amherst faculty in 1906 and retired as professor of German in 1955. In 1907 he married Ethel K. Bray, a Canadian. Among his notable works are *Germany in Travail* (1922) and *Dionysus: The Tragedy of Nietzsche* (1956).

Markham, Charles Edwin Anson (1852–1940), was an American poet, anthologist, educator, and social reformer who wrote under the name Edwin Markham. Born in Oregon City, Oregon, to a ranching family, Markham grew up in California, near San Francisco. In his youth he worked as a ranch hand and a cowboy. He was educated at California College (Vacaville, California), San Jose State Normal School, and Christian College (Santa Rosa, California). Markham then began a career in teaching and administration, all the while publishing poems in such magazines as *The Overland Monthly, Century Magazine,* and *Scribner's Monthly.* In 1898, he published his most celebrated poem, "The Man with the Hoe" (inspired by Jean-François Millet's painting, *L'homme à la houe*). The poem was collected in his first book, *The Man with the Hoe and Other Poems* (1899), which launched his literary career. With his third wife, Anna Catherine Murphy (and their son Virgil), Markham moved to New York in 1901, eventually settling in Staten Island. He published four additional volumes of verse, but none won him the acclaim accorded his first. Upon his death, Markham's immense private library, and his papers, were bequeathed to Morgan College (Staten Island), where they still reside at the Horrmann Library.

McAfee, Helen Flora (1884–1956), was an American scholar and editor. Educated at Smith College (BA 1903; MA 1914), she did additional graduate study at Yale and taught briefly in Turkey. She was assistant editor and later managing editor at the *Yale Review,* and with Wilbur Cross coedited a number of anthologies comprised of selections from that publication. In 1916 she published *Pepys on the Restoration Stage.*

McConaughy, James L. (1887–1948), was an American educator and politician. Educated at Yale University (AB 1909) and Bowdoin College (MA 1911), he completed a PhD at Columbia University in 1913. He taught English and education at Bowdoin from 1909 to 1915 and was professor of education at Dartmouth from 1918 to 1925. He served as president of Knox College in Illinois and Wesleyan University from 1925 to 1943. McConaughy entered politics in 1938 when he was elected lieutenant governor of Connecticut, an office he held until 1941. During World War II he served as civilian deputy of the Office of Strategic Services from 1943 to 1945. Elected governor of Connecticut in 1946, he died before completing his term.

McNeil, Laila Adelaide (1877–1971), was an American librarian. Born in Burke, Vermont, McNeil attended high school at nearby St. Johnsbury Academy.

She graduated from Wellesley College in 1901. She began a career as a librarian in Brookline, Massachusetts, and later became head librarian at Middlebury College. She never married. McNeil died in Caledonia County, Vermont, where she had been born, at the age of ninety-three.

Mearns, William Hughes (1875–1965), was an American educator and poet. Educated at Illinois Wesleyan (PhB 1899) and Harvard University (AB 1902), he was for a number of years an English professor at the Philadelphia School of Pedagogy. In 1920 he became head of the Lincoln School, a laboratory school conducted by the Teachers College of Columbia University and dedicated to the application of John Dewey's educational theory. By introducing "creative writing" to the middle-school curriculum, he helped to shape future educational practice. He developed these principles in two books, *Creative Youth: How a School Environment Set Free the Creative Spirit* (1925) and *Creative Power: The Education of Youth in Creative Arts* (1929). As a poet he is best remembered for "Antigonish" (1899), which was adapted as a popular song titled "The Little Man Who Wasn't There" in 1939.

Meigs, Henry Tunis (1855–1932), was an American farmer, the proprietor of The Maples farm in Romney, Indiana. He attended Wabash College, in Crawfordsville, Indiana, in 1872–1873.

Melcher, Frederic Gershom (1879–1963), was an American publisher, editor, and bookseller. Although he had planned to attend MIT, financial circumstances led him to accept a job in the mailroom of Estes and Lauriat Bookstore in Boston. Moving into sales, he developed what would be a lifetime commitment to children's books. After managing a bookstore in Indianapolis, he assumed the editorship of *Publishers' Weekly* in 1918. At the death of R. R. Bowker in 1933, he became president of the firm. In 1959 he resigned to become chairman of the board of directors. Throughout his career, he not only served the bookselling profession as head of many trade associations and programs but also advanced the field of library science and nurtured the development of children's literature. He established the Newberry Medal in 1922 and the Caldecott Medal in 1937.

Miller, Benjamin De Mier (1856–1934), was an American businessman, sportsman, and poetry enthusiast. Born in Virginia, Miller attended Columbian University (now Georgetown University) in Washington, D.C., as a member of the class of 1874, but there is no record of his having completed a degree. Married to Frances Maddox in 1885, he prospered as a lumber merchant. A member of the Sons of the American Revolution and an officer in the Washington chapter of the General Society of Colonial Wars, he was also a noted amateur golfer and an active participant in several art and literary societies. He and his wife, and later their daughter Frances, received regular mention in the society pages of Washington, D.C., newspapers.

Mitchell, Robert Stewart (1892–1957), was an American editor, poet, and historian. Educated at Harvard University (AB 1915; MA 1916), he served for two years in World War I as an artilleryman before becoming managing editor of *The Dial* (1919–1920). After completing a PhD in history at Harvard (1928), he became editor of the *New England Quarterly* (1928–1937). In 1917, a selection of Mitchell's poems appeared in *Eight Harvard Poets* along with those of E. E. Cummings, Robert Hillyer, and John Dos Passos. In addition to his work as editor, he wrote *Poems* (1921) and *Horatio Seymour of New York* (1938) and edited *New Letters of Abigail Adams* (1947).

Monro, Harold (1879–1932), was a British poet and the proprietor of the Poetry Bookshop in London, which served as a gathering place and reading venue and even provided temporary housing for many modern poets. Monro also founded and edited two magazines, *Poetry and Drama* and the *Poetry Review,* and was involved in the publication of the *Georgian Poetry* anthologies.

Monroe, Harriet (1860–1936), was an American poet, editor, publisher, and critic. While working as a freelance correspondent and art critic for the *Chicago Tribune,* Monroe convinced one hundred prominent Chicago business leaders to sponsor a magazine devoted to the new poetry. After founding *Poetry: A Magazine of Verse* in 1912, she served as its editor until 1936.

Moody, Harriet Brainard (1857–1932), was an American teacher, entrepreneur, and patron of the arts. Born Harriet Tilden, the daughter of a wealthy Chicago businessman, she graduated from Cornell University (1876) and completed a year of study at the Women's Medical College in Philadelphia before leaving to enter Chicago society. Her first marriage, to Edwin Brainard, a Chicago lawyer, ended in divorce. The death of her father led her in 1889 to seek employment as a high school English teacher. Supporting an invalid mother, she supplemented her income by launching a gourmet delicacies business, which flourished until 1929. In 1909, after a ten-year friendship-turned-courtship, she married the poet William Vaughn Moody, who died suddenly in 1910. In her later years, she maintained a residence in Chicago and an apartment in Greenwich Village, and opened both to a host of younger writers and poets to whom she offered encouragement, friendship, and support.

Morin, Richard Wedge (1902–1988), was an American educator and diplomat. After graduating from Dartmouth College in 1924, he studied at New College, Oxford, and completed a law degree at Harvard University in 1928. From 1928 to 1932 he served as U.S. vice-consul in Paris; from 1932 to 1935 and again from 1942 to 1945 he was a foreign service officer for the State Department, practicing law in the interval. In 1948 he became executive officer of Dartmouth, and served as the college librarian from 1950 to 1968. He was the editor of the *Dartmouth Bema,* an arts magazine that ran in the mid-1920s. In later life he was a skilled watercolorist.

Morton, David H. (1886–1957), was an American journalist, poet and educator. He was born in Elkton, Kentucky, and educated at Vanderbilt University in Nashville. He taught high school in Louisville, Kentucky, and soon began writing for the Associated Press, the *Louisville Evening Post,* and the *Louisville Courier Journal.* G. P. Putnam published his first volume of poetry, *Ships in Harbor,* in 1921. Four years later, Morton took a position in the Department of English at Amherst College, where he worked for the remainder of his career. His wife was Elizabeth Merrick Morton.

Moult, Thomas (1893–1974), was a British journalist, novelist, poet, and editor. A graduate of the University of Manchester, he was associated with the Georgians and published his first volume of poems, *Down Here the Hawthorn,* in 1921. A versatile writer, he was the music critic for the *Manchester Guardian* and the art and drama critic for the *Athenaeum* and the *English Review,* as well as a sportswriter for English and Australian journals. From 1922 to 1943 he edited a series of anthologies of the best British and American poems of the year. From 1952 to 1962 he was president of the Poetry Society (UK) and chairman of the editorial board of *Poetry Review.* Among his critical works are studies of Mary Webb, J. M. Barrie, and W. H. Davies.

Mumford, Lewis (1895–1990), was an American historian, sociologist, urban planner, architectural critic, and literary scholar. He studied at the City College of New York and the New School for Social Research, but withdrew for reasons of health and never finished his degree. After serving as a radio electrician during World War I, he became associate editor of *The Dial.* In the course of his career he edited the *Sociological Review,* wrote for *The Freeman* and the *New Yorker,* and cofounded the *American Caravan.* He served for brief periods on the faculties of Dartmouth College, Stanford University, the University of California at Berkeley, and the University of Pennsylvania. Notable among his many books, written across a wide variety of subjects, are *The Golden Day* (1926), *Herman Melville* (1929), *Technics and Civilization*

(1934), *The Culture of Cities* (1938), *The Condition of Man* (1944), *The Conduct of Life* (1951), *The City in History* (1961)—for which he won the National Book Award—and *Sketches from Life* (1982), an autobiography.

Munson, Gorham Bockhaven (1896–1969), was an American literary critic, social historian, editor, and educator. After graduating from Wesleyan University (BA 1917), he came to prominence as part of the avant-garde literary culture of Greenwich Village. In 1922 he cofounded with Matthew Josephson and Kenneth Burke the short-lived but influential journal *Secession.* He published *Waldo Frank: A Study* in 1923; among the works that swiftly followed were *Robert Frost: A Study in Sensibility and Good Sense* (1927), *Destinations: A Canvas of American Literature Since 1900* (1928), *Style and Form in American Prose* (1929), and *The Dilemma of the Liberated: An Interpretation of Twentieth Century Humanism* (1930). In 1931, having taught frequently at the Bread Loaf School of English, he offered a writers' workshop class at the New School for Social Research that proved so popular that he taught it annually for nearly three decades. His guide, *The Written Word: How to Write Readable Prose* (1949), was a standard in the field. Beginning in the 1930s, he became a leading advocate for the social credit movement in the United States and a disciple of George Gurdjieff's "fourth way" philosophy. In late career he held prestigious appointments at Wesleyan and at Hartford University. *The Awakening Twenties: A Memoir-History of a Literary Period* was published posthumously in 1985.

Nicholl, Louise Townsend (1890–1981), was an American poet, fiction writer, and editor. A graduate of Smith College (1913), she was a literary editor for the *New York Evening Post,* an editor at *Contemporary Verse,* and one of the founding editors of *Measure* (1921–1925). She later worked as an editor for E. P. Dutton. She published seven volumes of poetry, beginning with *Water and Light,* in 1939.

Palmer, George Herbert (1842–1933), was an American scholar, translator, and philosopher. Educated at Harvard University (1864), he began his teaching career there as a tutor in Greek and was Alford professor of natural religion, moral philosophy, and civil polity from 1889 to 1913. A translator of Homer, he also authored studies of the works of George Herbert and Shakespeare. His important philosophical works include *The Field of Ethics* (1901), *The Nature of Goodness* (1904), and *Altruism: Its Nature and Varieties* (1919).

Park, Marion Edwards (1875–1960), was an American scholar and academic administrator. After graduating from Bryn Mawr first in her class (AB 1898; AM 1899), she spent a year at the University of Chicago in 1900 and two years at the American School of Classical Studies in Athens. From 1902 to 1906 she was an instructor in classics at Colorado State University. She was acting dean at Bryn Mawr from 1911 until 1913 and then returned to Colorado State as assistant professor in 1913–1914 and associate professor in 1914–1915. Having pursued additional graduate study at Bryn Mawr and at Johns Hopkins University from 1912 to 1917, she earned a PhD in classics from Bryn Mawr in 1918. She served as dean of Simmons College from 1918 to 1921 and of Radcliffe from 1921 to 1922 before being named president of Bryn Mawr, a position she held until 1942.

Patton, Julia (1873–1953), was an American scholar. After graduating from Oberlin College (1895), she taught at Cornell College in Iowa (1904–1907). She earned an AM (1908) and PhD (1918) from Columbia University. She was a member of the English faculty at Vassar College from 1908 to 1915 and at Russell Sage College in Troy, New York, from 1916 until retirement. Her most notable work was *The English Village: A Literary Study, 1750–1850* (1919); she also published a history of Russell Sage College in 1941.

Payne, Leonidas Warren, Jr. (1873–1945), was an American linguist and literary scholar. Educated at the Alabama Polytechnic Institute (BA 1892; MA 1893), he taught English at Southwest Alabama Agricultural School, the State Normal School, and the University of Pennsylvania, where he earned his PhD in 1904. Associate editor of Worcester's *Dictionary of the English Language* for two years, he accepted a faculty position at the University of Texas in 1906. He was made full professor in 1919 and retired in 1943. Cofounder and the first president of the Texas Folklore Society and the author of *History of American Literature* (1919), he published the first anthology of Texas writing, *A Survey of Texas Literature* (1928) and *Texas Poems* (1936).

Pease, Arthur Stanley (1881–1964), was an American scholar and academic administrator. Educated at Harvard University (AB 1902; AM 1903; PhD 1905), he taught Latin at Harvard (1906–1909) before joining the faculty at the University of Illinois (1909–1924). Three years after coming to Amherst College, in 1924, he was named president in 1927 and resigned in 1932 to return to the faculty at Harvard. He was appointed Pope Professor of Latin in 1942 and retired in 1950. Although an accomplished classicist, Pease is best remembered for his amateur contributions to New England botany and has had four species of plants named for him; he donated an herbarium of more than twelve thousand specimens to Harvard.

Penniman, Helen Alison Fraser (1882–1964), was an American theater critic, artist, and socialite. The daughter of a British diplomat, Gilbert Fraser, she married Nicholas Penniman, a wealthy Baltimore manufacturer. A talented painter, she was also a theater critic and for forty years the moving force behind the Vagabond Players amateur theater company. Established in 1916, today the company holds the distinction of being America's oldest little theater in continuous operation.

Piercy, Josephine Ketcham (1895–1995), was an American scholar. Educated at Western College (Ohio) and Indiana University (AB 1918; MA 1919), she became an instructor in the English Department at Indiana University. She earned a second MA in literature at Columbia University in 1922 and taught at the University of Illinois before returning to Indiana in 1926. In 1928 she entered the PhD program at Yale University and completed the degree in 1937. She spent twenty-seven additional years on the Indiana University faculty and was made full professor in 1964. She published *Modern Writers at Work* in 1930, having corresponded with each of the eighty-five writers profiled in the book, and *Studies in Literary Types in Seventeenth Century America* in 1939.

Pohl, Frederick Julius (1889–1991), was an American playwright, literary critic, editor, and author. After graduating from Amherst College in 1911, he completed an MA at Columbia University in 1914. A prolific writer, he is best known for his books espousing speculative and controversial historical theories of pre-Columbian transoceanic contact by Europeans, especially the Vikings. In 1923, he published an open letter in the *New York Times* urging liberals at Amherst College to organize. He taught English for many years at Boys High School in Brooklyn and after retirement at Ohio Wesleyan College.

Porter, Charlotte Endymion (1857–1942), born Helen Charlotte Porter, was an American poet, editor, and translator. Educated at Wells College (AB 1875), she was the cofounder and editor of *Poet Lore* (1889–1903) and the editor of *Shakespeariana*. She also published editions of the works of Shakespeare, Robert Browning, and Elizabeth Barrett Browning.

Porth, Margaret P. (1910–1995), was an American clerical worker. Born in Clinton, Michigan, and educated at Mt. Clemens High School, she worked as a saleswoman and clerk in Lansing, MI. She married Gerald Conrad in 1934 and was divorced from him in 1940.

Pratt, Ralph Farman (1878–1961), was an American painter and children's book illustrator. Trained at the Cowles Art School and the Museum of Fine Arts in Boston, he lived in Warner, New Hampshire, and specialized in White Mountains landscapes. His principal works include *Echo Lake*, *Franconia Notch*, *Mt. Washington from Intervale*, *Mt. Lafayette*, and *Moosilauke in October*.

Quinn, Arthur Hobson (1875–1960), was an American scholar. Educated at the University of Pennsylvania (BS 1894; PhD 1899), he joined the English faculty as an instructor in 1895 and was later named Welsh Professor of History and English. He served as dean of the college from 1912 to 1922. Among his notable publications are *A History of the American Drama* (1927), *Edgar Allan Poe: A Critical Biography* (1941), and *The Literature of the American People* (1951).

Rankin, Thomas Ernest (1872–1953), was an American scholar and critic. Educated at the University of Michigan (AB 1898; AM 1905), he served as a faculty member in the Department of Rhetoric at Michigan from 1905 until 1928. He was the author of numerous works on composition and rhetoric and, with Wilford Aikin, two critical surveys: *English Literature* (1917) and *American Literature* (1922). After leaving Michigan, he was a professor of English at Carleton College.

Rascoe, Arthur Burton (1892–1957), was an American journalist, editor, and literary critic. While a student at the University of Chicago (1911–1913), he began to write for the *Chicago Tribune* and remained there until 1920. From 1922 to 1929 he was literary editor of the *New York Tribune*. At various times over the next two decades, he was associated with *The Bookman, Arts and Decorations, Esquire, Newsweek, American Mercury,* and two New York newspapers, *The Sun* and the *World-Telegram*. Notable among his books are *Theodore Dreiser* (1925), *The Titans of Literature* (1932), *Before I Forget* (1936), and *The Joys of Reading* (1937).

Reeves, Henrietta Kendrick (1871–1968), was a prominent figure in the social and cultural life of Nashville, Tennessee, the city of her birth. She was educated at Peabody College and Vanderbilt University, and married John Herriford Reeves (1862–1921), a successful Tennessee businessman, in 1891. After serving as president of the Centennial Club (in Nashville), she also chaired its literary department, and in that capacity brought a number of writers and artists to speak in Nashville (RF among them). Reeves, a poet and a musician, was also an amateur scholar of French and a popular local lecturer. In 1919, she was elected to membership in the Poetry Society of America. Her papers are held now at the Tennessee State Library and Archives in Nashville.

Richardson, George Lynde, Jr. (1895–1934), was an American educator and poet. Though born in Bennington, Vermont (the son of an Episcopal minister), Richardson grew up chiefly in Philadelphia. He was educated at Williams College, from which he graduated in 1917. After a year-long stint in the Army, Richardson took a post, in 1919, as Instructor in English at Phillips Exeter Academy (New Hampshire), where he remained until 1932. He died in Exeter at the age of thirty-nine, survived by his wife Ellen Search Richardson and their two children.

Ridge, Rose Emily "Lola" (1873–1941), was an Irish-born American poet and editor. After a childhood in Dublin, she moved to New Zealand in 1887 and lived there and in Australia for twenty years. Briefly married (1895) in New Zealand, she left to study painting at Trinity College in Sydney. She emigrated to the United States in 1907. In April 1918, the *New Republic* devoted three pages to "The Ghetto," a sequence of poems that would form the core of *The Ghetto, and Other Poems,* published later in the same year. Additional volumes of poetry followed: *Sun-Up, and Other Poems* (1920), *Red Flag* (1927), *Firehead* (1929), and *Dance of Fire* (1935). She was a contributor, publicist, and editor at two avant-garde literary magazines, *Others* (1918–1919) and *Broom* (1922–1923).

Rittenhouse, Jessie Belle (1869–1948), was an American poet and anthologist. After teaching school and working as a reporter in Rochester, New York, she moved to Boston in 1899 and then New York, where from 1905–1915 she was poetry reviewer for the *New York Times Book Review.* In 1914 Rittenhouse helped to found the Poetry Society of America, of which she was secretary until 1924. Active on the lecture and reading circuit, she published four books of poems—*The Door of Dreams* (1918), *The Lifted Cup* (1921), *The Secret Bird* (1930), and *Moving Tide: New and Selected Lyrics* (1939)—and edited a series of influential anthologies, including *Little Book of Modern Verse* (1913), *Little Book of American Poets* (1915), and *Second Book of Modern Verse* (1919). In 1930 she was the first recipient of the Poetry Society of America's Robert Frost Medal.

Robbins, Frank Eggleston (1884–1963), was an American scholar and academic administrator. A graduate of Wesleyan University (BA 1906; MA 1907), he earned a PhD in classics at the University of Chicago (1911) and joined the faculty at the University of Michigan in 1912 as professor of Greek. In 1921 he accepted a position as assistant to the president and continued in it until retirement in 1953. He was director of the University of Michigan Press (1930–1953) and editor of the *Michigan Quarterly Review.* He authored a number of scholarly papers on classical astronomy and mathematics.

Root, Edward Merrill (1895–1973), was an American poet, essayist, and educator. After graduating from Amherst College (1917), he went to France as a member of the American Friends Service Committee and returned to study at Andover Theological Seminary. In 1920 he joined the English faculty at Earlham College and taught there until retirement in 1960. In the late 1930s his position had shifted from Quaker pacifism to extreme conservatism. *Collectivism on the Campus* (1954) and *Brainwashing in the High Schools* (1958) were vitriolic condemnations of American liberalism and proclamations that communism was rampant in American education. In retirement, Root became an editor of *American Opinion,* the bimonthly magazine of the John Birch Society. Among his volumes of poetry are *Dawn Is Forever* (1938), *Before the Swallow Dares* (1947), and *Ulysses to Penelope* (1952), a sonnet sequence.

Rowell, Wilbur Everett (1862–1946), was an American attorney. Educated at Wesleyan University (AB 1885; AM 1888) and Harvard Law School (1888), he was a prominent lawyer (Rowell and Gray), banker, district court judge in Lawrence, Massachusetts, and executor of the estate of William P. Frost, RF's grandfather. In 1912, he published an article in *The Survey* condemning the Lawrence textile strike. He served as a trustee of the Lawrence Public Library and of the White Fund (local education).

Rugg, Harold Goddard (1883–1957), was an American librarian, historian, naturalist, and collector. A graduate of Dartmouth College (1906), he began his career as a library secretary in 1906, became executive assistant to the librarian in 1912, and was promoted to assistant librarian in 1919. He also held a faculty position in the Art Department, offering courses on the history of book design and printing. From 1914 until retirement in 1953, he served as the literary editor of the *Dartmouth Alumni Magazine.*

Salzberg, Harry Jacob (1893–1979), was an Austrian-born American salesman and book dealer. A naturalized citizen, having moved to the United States as a child in 1901, Salzberg lived nearly all his life in the Bronx, New York. His formal education ended after the fifth grade, but by the early 1920s, he was managing the sales department of Boni and Liveright. In 1922, seeking to establish himself as a bookseller, he offered a mail-order list of presentation copies and first editions—books inscribed to him by such writers as Theodore Dreiser and Upton Sinclair can still be found in the market—and took over the operation of the Book Stall at the Greenwich Village Theater. By 1927, he was the east coast sales representative for the Chicago-based Regan Publishing Corporation. His later career was in commercial stationery sales.

Sandburg, Carl August (1878–1967), was an American poet, journalist, and author. Having left school at the age of thirteen and worked a variety of jobs (driver, porter, bricklayer, farmhand), he joined the army during the Spanish-American War but did not see combat. In 1898, he enrolled at Lombard College in Galesburg, Illinois, but left in his senior year without completing a degree. Over several years he worked as a salesman and political organizer and wrote three volumes of poetry that were published privately. He began his public writing career as a reporter for the *Chicago Daily News* in 1908. The appearance of several poems in *Poetry* in 1914 was followed by the publication of *Chicago Poems* in 1916 and *Cornhuskers* in 1918. Upon the success of *Rootabaga Stories* (1922), a collection of children's tales, he was encouraged by Alfred Harcourt to write a biography of Abraham Lincoln for young readers. Years of research resulted instead in the two-volume *Abraham Lincoln: The Prairie Years* (1926), a critical and financial success, and the four-volume *Abraham Lincoln: The War Years* (1940), for which he won the Pulitzer Prize. During a prolific career, he published more than a dozen books of poetry and of nonfiction, a novel, and seven collections for children. He won a second Pulitzer in 1951 for *Complete Poems*.

Sanford, Albert Hart (1866–1956), was an American historian and educator. After graduating from the Wisconsin State Normal School (Platteville) in 1886, he taught high school before earning a BA at the University of Wisconsin (1891) and an AM at Harvard University (1894). He taught at the State Normal School at Stevens Point until 1909 and then at the State College at La Crosse until retirement in 1936. Joint author of several high school history textbooks, he was active in the Wisconsin Historical Society and served a term as its president.

Sarett, Lew R. (1888–1954), was an American poet, scholar, and public speaker. Born Lewis Saretsky, he was educated at the University of Michigan (1907–1908), Beloit College (BA 1911), Harvard Law School (1911–1912) and the University of Illinois Law School (LLB 1916). From 1912 to 1920 Sarett taught English and public speaking at the University of Illinois. He published the first of his six volumes of poetry, *Many Many Moons,* in 1920. He became an advisory editor of *Poetry* magazine in 1921 and won the Levinson Poetry Prize in 1921 and the Poetry Society of America's annual prize in 1925. As professor of speech at Northwestern University from 1920 until 1953, Sarett became famous for his dual lifestyle, teaching for one semester and living in the Wisconsin wilderness for the remainder of the year. He was widely successful as a lecturer on wilderness topics.

Sargent, George Henry (1867–1931), was an American bibliographer, book collector, and journalist. A native of Warner, New Hampshire, he began a career in journalism as a reporter at and then the city editor (1890–1895) of the *St. Paul Daily Pioneer Press.* He was a literary editor for the *Boston Evening Transcript* from 1895 until 1931 and the author of a column about rare books called "The Bibliographer." Among his published works are *Amy Lowell, A Mosaic* (1926) and *A Busted Bibliophile and His Books* (1928). A semi-invalid in his later years, Sargent wrote his column while residing at his ancestral home, The Elm Farm, in Warner.

Scoggin, Gilbert Campbell (1881–1947), was an American scholar, translator, author, and professor of classics. After earning an AB and an AM from

Vanderbilt University (1902) and a PhD from Harvard University (1906), he became professor of Greek at the University of Missouri (1908–1920) and an editor of the *Classical Journal*. After serving on the faculty of Case Western Reserve University and on the editorial board of the *Encyclopedia Britannica*, he was chief librarian at the American School of Classical Studies at Athens from 1925 until 1931.

Scott, Marjorie Dawson (1899–1989), was a British author. The daughter of the poet Catherine Amy Dawson Scott, who founded PEN, she served as secretary of the society. In 1926 she married Arthur Watts, an illustrator whose work appeared regularly in *Punch*. She published an account of the society's origins, *P.E.N. The Early Years, 1921–1926,* in 1971 and a study of her mother's life, *Mrs. Sappho: The Life of C. A. Dawson Scott,* in 1987.

Sills, Kenneth Charles Morton (1879–1954), was a Canadian-born American educator, academic administrator, and poet. After graduating from Bowdoin College (1901), he earned an AM from Harvard University in 1903 and joined the Bowdoin College faculty as an instructor in English and the classics. With the exception of one year as a tutor in English at Columbia University (1904–1905), he remained at Bowdoin until retirement in 1952. From 1907 to 1946 he was Winkley Professor of Latin Language and Literature, and he served successively as dean (1910–1918), acting president (1917–1918), and president (1918–1952). He was chairman of the board of the Carnegie Foundation from 1939 to 1941. He published *The First American and Other Poems,* a volume of poems and translations, in 1911.

Skinner, Burrhus Frederic (1904–1990), was an American psychologist and novelist, and pioneer of the science of behaviorism. After graduating from Hamilton College (BA 1926), he briefly pursued a career as a writer and then enrolled at Harvard University (MA 1930; PhD 1931) to study psychology. He taught at the University of Minnesota (1936–1945) and chaired the Psychology Department at Indiana University (1945–1947), before returning to Harvard in 1948. He was Edgar Pierce Professor of Psychology there from 1958 until retirement in 1974. His major works include *The Behavior of Organisms* (1938), *Walden Two* (1948), *The Technology of Teaching* (1968), *Beyond Freedom and Dignity* (1971), and *About Behaviorism* (1974).

Slusser, Jean Paul (1886–1991), was an American artist, art critic, museum director, and educator. Educated at the University of Michigan (AB 1909; AM 1911), he studied further at the University of Munich (1909–1910), the Museum of Fine Arts School in Boston (1913–1915), the Art Students League of New York (summers 1914–1917), and the Hans Hofmann Schule in Munich (1924–1925).

Before joining the art faculty at Michigan in 1927 as assistant professor of drawing and painting, he worked as art critic for the *Boston Herald* (1913–1915) and assistant art critic for the *New York Herald* (1921–1923). Made full professor in 1944, he served as director of the University of Michigan Art Museum from 1947 until retirement in 1957. An accomplished painter, his works were frequently exhibited and widely collected.

Smith, Marion Nora Parris (1879–1964), was an American economist, educator, and feminist. Educated at Bryn Mawr College (AB 1901; PhD 1908), she did post-graduate work in economics at the University of Vienna. She joined the faculty at Bryn Mawr, eventually rising to the rank of full professor. In 1912, she married William Roy Smith, a Bryn Mawr history professor. She was instrumental in the successful establishment of Bryn Mawr's Graduate Department of Social Economy and Social Research; as author and teacher, she examined social problems in the modern state and the role of ethics in economic theory. Among the many students she influenced was poet Marianne Moore. During the Depression, she consulted on activities of the National Recovery Administration in Pennsylvania, and she was named to the Pennsylvania Education Board in 1936. Her notable publications include *Total Utility and the Economic Judgment Compared with Their Ethical Counterparts* (Philadelphia: John C. Winston, 1909) and *What Constitutes a Liberal Democracy?* (Philadelphia: n.p., 1925).

Snow, Charles Wilbert "Bill" (1884–1977), was an American poet, educator, and politician. Born in Maine and educated at Bowdoin College (BA 1907) and Columbia University (MA 1910), he held academic appointments briefly at Williams College, Miami (Ohio) University, the University of Utah, and Indiana University, but was considered too far left in his politics to be retained. After serving as an artillery officer and instructor during World War I, he joined the faculty at Wesleyan University and, despite many political contretemps, remained there until retirement in 1952. Active in Democratic politics, he was elected lieutenant governor of Connecticut in 1944 and served thirteen days as governor in 1946–1947. Notable among his volumes of poetry are *Maine Coast* (1923), *The Inner Harbor* (1926), *Down East* (1932), and *Spruce Head* (1959). *Collected Poems* was published in 1963 and an autobiography, *Codline's Child*, in 1974.

Speare, Eva Augusta Clough (1875–1972), was an American educator and author. Born and reared in Lawrence Massachusetts, she married Guy Edwin Speare in 1903 and lived most of her life in Plymouth, New Hampshire, where her husband was superintendent of schools. In addition to her civic work and lifelong association with the New Hampshire Federation of Women's Clubs, she published a number of local histories, most notably *New Hampshire Folk Tales* (1932) and *Twenty Decades in Plymouth, New Hampshire* (1963). Published posthumously, her last book, *Stories of New Hampshire* (1973), collected her work as a columnist for the Manchester *Union Leader,* which she undertook at the age of ninety-four.

Squire, Sir John Collings (1884–1958), was a British poet, critic, and literary editor. After taking a history degree at St. John's College, Cambridge, in 1905, he worked for a newspaper in Plymouth before moving to London in 1907 and worked as a parliamentary reporter for the National Press Agency until 1912. A regular contributor to *New Age,* he cofounded a publishing company, Howard Latimer, which issued his first collection of poems, *The Three Hills,* in 1913, the year he became the literary editor of the *New Statesman.* His book of poems *The Survival of the Fittest* (1916) was a protest against World War I and was reprinted several times. In 1919 he established the *London Mercury* and, as its editor until 1934, played an influential role in British literary culture. He worked as a reviewer for *The Observer* until 1937 and for the *Illustrated London News* until his death. The last decades of his life were marked by struggles with alcohol, the dissolution of his marriage and family life, a flirtation with fascism, and bankruptcy. His *Collected Poems* was published in 1959.

Stork, Charles Wharton (1881–1971), was an American poet, playwright, editor, critic, and translator. Educated at Haverford College (AB 1902), Harvard University (AM 1903), and the University of Pennsylvania (PhD 1905), he taught at the University of Pennsylvania from 1908 to 1916, before resigning to devote himself to literary work. He was the editor of *Contemporary Verse* from 1917 to 1925. In addition to volumes of his own verse, drama, and criticism, he published translations of Norwegian, Danish, and Swedish writers and compiled anthologies of poetry translated from those languages.

Strauss, Louis Abraham (1872–1938), was an American literary scholar. Educated at the University of Michigan (BL 1893; PhM 1894; PhD 1900), he spent forty-five years on the English faculty there, rising to full professor in 1911 and serving as department chair from 1920 to 1937. Strauss edited George Farquhar's *A Discourse Upon Comedy, The Recruiting Officer and The Beaux Stratagem* (Boston and London: D. C. Heath, 1915); the edition, with a long introduction and extensive notes, drew considerable notice for its contribution to scholarship on Restoration drama.

Sullivan, Mark (1874–1952), was an American journalist, political columnist, and historian. After graduating from the West Chester (Pennsylvania) Normal School and working as a reporter, he enrolled at Harvard University and completed an AB degree in 1900 and a law degree in 1903. Freelance work as a progressive journalist led to staff positions at *McClure's Magazine* and then *Collier's,* which sent him to Washington, D.C., in 1912. After positions at two New York newspapers, the *Evening Post* and the *Herald Tribune,* he began a syndicated column that appeared three days a week in more than a hundred newspapers. Between 1926 and 1935 he wrote the six-volume social history *Our Times: The United States, 1900–1925.* His autobiography, *The Education of an American,* was published in 1938.

Tarney, Elizabeth Mackenzie (1916 1983), was an American educator. Not long after her birth in Milwaukee, Wisconsin, the Tarney family moved to Goffstown, New Hampshire, where Elizabeth attended high school. She earned a degree from Middlebury College in 1938, and a doctorate at the University of Massachusetts in 1940—the same year she married Jason Peter Sikoski in Hinsdale, New Hampshire. Tarney-Sikoski then embarked on a long career in education, teaching English, history, and French at Hinsdale High School (1947–1962), and then at a high school in Greenfield, Massachusetts (1962–1980), where she died at the age of sixty-seven.

Tewson, William Orton (1877–1947), was a British-born American journalist, critic, and radio personality. He joined the staff of the *New York Times* in 1907 and subsequently served as its London correspondent. From 1912 to 1916 he was editor in chief of the Hearst newspapers and agencies in Europe. He returned to the United States to become the literary editor of the *Philadelphia Public Ledger* and was editor of the *New York Evening Post's* literary review from 1921 to 1926. Between 1928 and 1934 he was heard regularly on WNYC. He wrote "An Attic Salt Shaker," a syndicated book column, from 1921 until his death.

Thornton, Richard Hurt (1889–1977), was an American educator, editor, and publisher. A graduate of Lynchburg (Virginia) College (1907), he completed an MA at Columbia University (1914) and a PhD at the University of Chicago (1926). After serving as a Navy ensign in World War I, he taught English and journalism at the University of North Carolina and was on the faculty of the Women's College of North Carolina at Greensboro. He joined Henry Holt and Company in 1924 as head of the foreign-language department and served as president of the company from 1932 to 1938. From 1939 until retirement, in 1955, he was editor of college publications and a director of Ginn and Company.

Tietjens, Eunice (1884–1944) was an American poet, novelist, journalist, and editor. Born Eunice Strong Hammond in Chicago, she was educated in Europe. From 1904 to 1914 she was married to the composer Paul Tietjens. In 1913, she began a twenty-five year association with *Poetry* magazine as an associate editor, and she was the *Chicago Daily News* correspondent in France during World War I. In 1920 she married the playwright and director Cloyd Head. In addition to children's books, translations from Spanish and French, a novel, and a memoir, she published four volumes of poetry that reveal a sustained interest in Asian cultures: *Profiles of China* (1917), *Body and Raiment* (1919), *Leaves in Windy Weather* (1929), and *China* (1930).

Tilley, Morris Palmer (1876–1947), was an American scholar and teacher. A student of both literature and language, he earned a BA (1897) and an MA (1899) in English from the University of Virginia, and a PhD in German language and literature from the University of Leipzig in 1902. His most notable scholarly work while he was a professor of English at the University of Michigan, from 1906 to 1946, was *A Dictionary of the Proverbs in England in the Sixteenth and Seventeenth Centuries* (1950).

Tittle, Walter Ernest (1883–1966), was an American illustrator and portrait painter. Born in Ohio, he studied art in New York under William Merritt Chase and became a regular contributor of illustrations and articles to *Harper's, The Century, Life,* and other magazines. Working in both England and the United States, a member of both the Royal Society of Arts and the Society of American Etchers, he was a prolific portraitist working in various media (etching, lithography, and painting). His subjects included writers, artists, actors, and statesmen, and he is particularly remembered for his portraits of Joseph Conrad. He often interviewed and wrote profiles of those he painted, most expansively in his *Roosevelt as an Artist Saw Him,* in 1948. His work is represented in the National Gallery, the Art Institute of Chicago, the British Museum, and the National Portrait Gallery, London.

Torrence, Frederic Ridgely (1874–1950), was an American poet, playwright, and editor. After attending Miami (Ohio) University and Princeton University, he worked as a librarian in New York (1897–1903), as an assistant editor for *The Critic* (1903–1905), and as fiction editor for *Cosmopolitan* (1905–1907) before serving as poetry editor for the *New Republic* from 1920 to 1933. His first poetry collection, *The House of a Hundred Lights* (1900), was followed by *Hesperides* (1925), and *Poems* (1941). His *Three Plays for a Negro Theater* (1917), the first

Broadway production by a white author to use an all-black cast, was a break-through in the way that African Americans were depicted onstage.

Towle, Clifton Augustus (1876–1963), was an American educator and academic administrator. Educated at Bowdoin College (AB 1899), he taught science at Worcester (Massachusetts) Academy from 1903 to 1910 and served as assistant to the principal from 1910 until he was named superintendent of schools in Exeter, New Hampshire, in 1919, a position he held until retirement in 1945. In 1922–1923 he was the New Hampshire director for the National Education Association. In 1938 he published *The Public Schools of Exeter, New Hampshire.* He was a longtime member of the Appalachian Mountain Club, a conservation organization.

Trolle-Steenstrup, Svend Herluf (1883–?), was a Danish-born American educator and author. Born in Copenhagen, he came to the United States in 1915, settled in Providence, and worked as a music teacher. He became a citizen in 1921. He published a popular autobiographical account for young readers, *When I Was a Boy in Denmark,* in 1923.

Untermeyer, Louis (1885–1977), was an American poet, anthologist, critic, and editor. Having left high school to work in his father's jewelry firm, Untermeyer published his first book of poems in 1911. Sympathetic to socialist causes, he wrote for many of the radical magazines of the time, including *The Masses* and *The Liberator.* In 1923 he left business to devote himself to writing. Over the next fifty years he wrote, edited, or translated more than one hundred books, including several volumes of his own poetry. His anthologies, notably *Modern American Poetry* (1919) and *Modern British Poetry* (1920), were regularly reissued and became classroom standards. As anthologist and critic he was an influential figure in the creation of a modern poetry canon. One of the original panelists on *What's My Line?,* he was blacklisted from television in 1951 under suspicion of being a Communist sympathizer. In 1956 Untermeyer was awarded a Gold Medal by the Poetry Society of America. He was the consultant in poetry for the Library of Congress from 1961 until 1963.

Van Dore, Wade Kivel (1889–1989), was an American poet and environmentalist. Born in Detroit, he left school in the tenth grade and labored at a variety of jobs, including carpenter, ice harvester, gardener, and farmhand. His books of poetry include *Far Lake* (1930) and *Verse with a Vengeance, a Volley of Epigrams for the Gratification of Honestly Educated Men* (1961). His poetry appeared not only in prestige publications such as the *Atlantic Monthly,* the *New Republic,* and the *New Yorker* but also in ecology journals such as *The Land* and *Nature*. In 1950 he was poet in residence at Marlboro College, in Vermont. He was elected to membership in the Poetry Society of America in 1968, the same year in which he cofounded the Thoreau Fellowship. He would later serve as poetry editor for the *Thoreau Journal Quarterly*. In addition to several essays about Frost, he published occasional monographs, including *Walden as the American Bible: A Gospel of Ecology* (1971) and *Richard Eberhart: Poet of Life in Death* (1982). *Robert Frost and Wade Van Dore: The Life of the Hired Man,* an autobiographical narrative edited by Thomas Wetmore, was published in 1986.

Van Doren, Carl Clinton (1885–1950), was an American critic and biographer. After completing a PhD at Columbia in 1911, he joined the faculty and taught there until 1930. The managing editor of *The Cambridge History of American Literature* from 1917 to 1921, Van Doren was the literary editor of *The Nation* (1919–1922) and of *Century Magazine* (1922–1925). His major works include *The American Novel* (1921, 1940) and *Benjamin Franklin* (1939), a Pulitzer Prize–winning biography. He was the brother of the poet Mark Van Doren.

Van Doren, Mark (1894–1972), was an American poet, novelist, critic, and scholar. After graduating from the University of Illinois (BA 1914), he completed a PhD at Columbia University in 1920 and joined the English Department, where he taught with great distinction until retirement in 1955. Van Doren was a highly influential teacher and critic, mentoring, inter alia, John Berryman, Allen Ginsberg, Jack Kerouac, Lionel Trilling, and Donald Keene. In 1940 he was awarded the Pulitzer Prize for Poetry for his *Collected Poems: 1922–1938.* In addition to numerous books of poetry he published three novels, a volume of short stories, and studies of Thoreau, Dryden, Shakespeare, Hawthorne, and E. A. Robinson. His 1943 book, *A Liberal Education,* is still often cited in debates over the role of the humanities in education.

Ward, Herbert Dickinson (1861–1932), was an American journalist and author. Educated at Phillips Academy Andover and Amherst College (BA 1884; MA 1887), he taught briefly at Catawba College (North Carolina) before studying for the ministry at Union Theological Seminary (1885–1887) and Andover Theological Seminary (1887–1888). Licensed to preach but never ordained, he pursued a literary career. His marriage in 1888 to Elizabeth Stuart Phelps (1844–1911) raised interest because of the age discrepancy between them. His first two books, *A Lost Hero* (1889) and *The Master of the Magicians* (1890), were fictionalizations of biblical stories coauthored with Elizabeth Phelps.

Ward's own *The New Senior at Andover* appeared in 1890, and thereafter he published prolifically. He was the son of William Hayes Ward and the nephew of Susan Hayes Ward, editor and poetry editor, respectively, of *The (New York) Independent*.

Weaver, John Van Alstyne (1893–1938), was an American journalist, poet, and screenwriter. After studying at Hamilton College and at Harvard University, Weaver served in World War I, and held editorial positions at the *Chicago Daily News* and the *Brooklyn Daily Eagle* before moving to Los Angeles in the mid-1920s to write for the screen. Weaver published several books of vernacular poetry in the early 1920s, beginning with *In American* (1921). Weaver's complete poems were later published in a volume under the same title, with a preface by H. L. Mencken, in 1939.

Wells, James R. (1898–1971), was an American publisher. Wells ran a number of small boutique presses, including Crosby Gaige, the Fountain Press, the Bowling Green Press, and, as a private venture, the Slide Mountain Press. Wells's particular remit was to organize the publication, in the United States, of luxury editions of British and European writers. To these ends he corresponded with James Joyce, T. S. Eliot, Virginia Woolf, George Moore, and many others.

Wenley, Robert Mark (1861–1929), was a Scottish philosopher and educator. Educated at Glasgow University (AM 1884; PhD 1895) and Edinburgh University (DSc 1891), he was assistant professor of Logic at Glasgow (1885–1893) and lecturer on logic and moral philosophy and dean of the Arts Department of Queen Margaret College, Glasgow (1886–1895). He came to the University of Michigan in 1896 and chaired the Department of Philosophy until his death in 1929. Notable among his many publications are *Socrates and Christ* (1889), *Aspects of Pessimism* (1897), *The Preparation for Christianity in the Ancient World* (1898), *Kant and His Philosophical Revolution* (1910), *The Anarchist Ideal and Other Essays* (1913), and *The Life and Work of George Sylvester Morris* (1917). He was a Fellow of the Royal Society of Edinburgh, and of the Royal Society of Literature.

Whicher, George Frisbie (1889–1954), was an American scholar and educator. After graduating from Amherst College (1910), he completed his MA (1911) and PhD at Columbia University (1915). He was professor of English at Amherst from 1915 to 1954. Notable among his many publications are *This Was a Poet: A Critical Biography of Emily Dickinson* (1938), *The Goliard Poets* (1949), and *Poetry and Civilization* (1955).

White, Albert Beebe (1871–1952), was an American historian and educator. Educated at Yale University (BA 1893; PhD 1898), he joined the history faculty at the University of Minnesota in 1898 and became full professor in 1907. He spent the 1921–1922 academic year at the University of Michigan. An authority on English constitutional law, he published widely, most notably *The Making of the English Constitution* (1908) and (with Wallace Notestein) *Source Problems in English History* (1915).

Wilkinson, Marguerite Ogden Bigelow (1883–1928), was an American poet, anthologist, and critic. Canadian-born, she grew up in Evanston, Illinois, and attended Northwestern University as a special student (1906–1908). Between 1910 and 1925 she published three volumes of poetry (*In Vivid Gardens*, 1911; *Bluestone*, 1920; and *The Great Dream*, 1923); a book of essays on contemporary poetry (*New Voices*, 1919); and an anthology (*Contemporary Poetry Prior to 1915*, 1923). She was a regular contributor of poems, reviews, and essays to *Touchstone* and other journals, and lectured widely on modern poetry.

Wright, Hilda (1906–2013), was an American educator. She graduated from Bryn Mawr College in 1929, having edited the literary magazine, *The Lantern*, for four years. She then taught at Oldfield's School in Baltimore and at the Madeira School in Fairfax, Virginia, before marrying an attorney, William L. Broad, in 1937. She lived the remainder of her life in Fayetteville, New York.

Yates, Crystine Ruth (1904–1983), was an American educator. After earning a BS (1935) and an MA at George Peabody College for Teachers (Nashville), she taught for many years in the Nashville public school system. She married Aubrey Soyars in 1936. After retirement, she earned an AB in religion from Trevecca Nazarene University (Nashville) in 1965.

Young, Charles Lowell (1865–1937), was an American scholar and teacher. Educated at Harvard University (AB 1893), he joined the faculty at Wellesley College in 1898 and retired as professor of American literature in 1933. His most notable scholarly work, *Emerson's Montaigne*, was published posthumously in 1941.

Chronology: February 1920–December 1928

1920 RF resigns position at Amherst College in early February over disagreements with President Alexander Meiklejohn. In the Franconia, New Hampshire, farmhouse he bought in 1915, RF and family weather the Great Winter Storm of 1920 (February 4–7), which leaves the family snowbound, except for his eldest daughter, Lesley, who is a student at Barnard College in New York, which would also soon be paralyzed by the storm. RF wrote to Lesley: "Rescuing parties have been by with teams of six and eight horses, but these are merely local and neighborly: they are satisfied if they push the snow a little from our doors: they are not intended to establish communication with the outside world. Everybody is frightened but Marjorie . . . who doesn't know enough, isn't, I fear, tall enough to appreciate the seriousness of snow actually half way up our windows. She coolly, nay freezing coldly, calls for paints and brushes and sits down at a window, that has to be shoveled open for her, to do [Mt.] Lafayette in oils." Delivers lecture at the University of Pennsylvania on February 13, hosted by Professor Arthur Quinn. In March, determines to purchase a farmhouse farther south in New England, Franconia winters having proved perilous to the health of his son Carol, and Franconia summers having proved too short even for modest farming. On March 8, writes to George Roy Elliott, professor of English at Bowdoin, marking the start of what would become a lifelong friendship. Elliott had invited RF to speak at Bowdoin and had published an essay on RF in *The Nation*, of which RF wrote: "What you wrote for me in The Nation made me feel that I had formed a new tie in the world." Daughter Lesley assists RF in preparing typescripts of poems for publication in magazines. RF enjoys sugaring with his son, Carol, in Franconia. "The sap started yesterday," he writes to Lesley in mid-March. "Some of the buckets are nearly full. Carol and I principally Carol are going to do one mans share of the sugaring this year. You can stock up with sugar and hand the girls [at Barnard] cakes of it in place of arguements [*sic*] for or against God." Advises Baltimore's Vagabond Players in a letter as to how best to stage his play *A Way Out*. At this point RF intended to write additional plays, and to see them staged, but ultimately he would not pursue the matter. Learns on March 31 that his younger sister Jeanie Florence Frost, who has exhibited symptoms of paranoia and instability for years, had been arrested in Portland, Maine, on March 25 for disturbing the peace, and had been pronounced insane by an attending physician. RF writes to Louis Untermeyer: "The police picked her up in Portland Maine the other day insane as nearly as we can make out on the subject of the war. She took the police for German officers carrying her off for immoral use. She took me for someone else when she saw me. She shouted to me by name to save her from whoever she thought I was in person." Spends the first week of April in Portland, where he commits Jeanie to the state mental hospital at Augusta, Maine. (RF would continue to visit her in the hospital, occasionally, until her death in 1929.) While in Maine, visits George Roy Elliot and the publisher and bibliophile Thomas Bird Mosher. Negotiates the sale of the remainder of his property in Franconia to Raymond Holden, who had bought part of it in 1919. In April, publishes poem "To E.T." in memory of Edward Thomas in the *Yale Review.* Visits Jeanie in Augusta, Maine, again on May 1. Continues to worry that his affairs with David Nutt, the London publisher of his first two books, are not in order. The matter would be resolved for good only when the firm went into bankruptcy, and, through the offices of Maurice Firuski and Jack Haines, RF saw to the disposition of the remaining unsold copies of the British editions of *A Boy's Will* and *North of Boston.* In May, scouts out farms for purchase in Connecticut and writes to Untermeyer, "I have three or four houses on the possible list—one at Monson Mass, one at West Springfield Mass, one at Winsted Conn and one at New Milford," but holds off buying. Visits Jeanie twice more during the spring. Publishes four poems in *Harper's* in July (they would all be collected in RF's fourth book, *New Hampshire,* in 1923). Elinor continues house hunting, as RF stays on at Franconia. Writes George Browne on July 28: "To-day she may be in Arlington, Vermont tomorrow in Milford, New Hampshire. Such enterprise for this time of year! May it not have to be its own only reward. Any other prayer would seem heartless." Alfred Harcourt, RF's editor at Henry Holt and Company, having left Henry Holt to found his own publisher, tries to persuade RF to follow him. Lincoln MacVeagh, RF's new editor at Henry Holt, convinces RF to stay on. In late summer, RF decides to purchase an eighteenth-century farmhouse, the Stone House, in South Shaftsbury, Vermont, near the homes of family friends Sarah Cleghorn and Dorothy Canfield Fisher. In September, Elinor and their children go to Arlington, Vermont, to wait for the house in nearby South Shaftsbury to be renovated. RF stays on in Franconia, seeing to the sale of the farm there, then joins Elinor, Irma,

Carol, and Marjorie in Arlington in early October. Writes English friend Jack Haines on October 10: "I have been leaving Franconia, New Hampshire (a German English combination of names) to go and live in South Shaftsbury Vermont (an English French combination). Our notions for making the change are not poetical, however, but agricultural. We ask a better place to farm and especially grow apples. Franconia winter-killed apple trees and some years even in July and August frosted gardens. The beautiful White Mountains were too near for warmth. A hundred miles further south and out of the higher peaks as we shall be, we think we ought to be safer." His daughter Irma goes to New York to study at the Arts Students League; Lesley arranges for housing. RF follows the presidential race, writing to George Roy Elliott on October 23: "I depose . . . that I dislike the poetic style of Mr. Harding and that I shall vote for Jimmie Cox if I can persuade myself I dislike his poetic style any less. If I complain of this pair as too much for me on such short notice, you wont think it is from a habit of finding fault with what is set before me. I saw the greatness of Cleaveland Roosevelt and Wilson in time to vote for them. And Wilson was a great man. The incalculable hypocracy in all this talk against him for having tried courageously to be a complete leader. Blame him for having failed to be a complete leader but not for having tried to be one." Takes a trip to New York City with the family in early November, and, on their return to Vermont, moves into the Stone House. Lesley remains in New York, where she had taken a job as a writer and publicist for the National Association of Book Publishers, headed by Frederic Melcher. In mid-November, RF begins serving as consulting editor for Henry Holt on a stipend of $100 per month. He writes to Elliott: "I owe this under Heaven to Lincoln MacVeagh a younger member of the firm. The pay will be small but large for a poet and the work between you and me will be nothing but seeing MacVeagh once in a while in friendship as I would see you." On December 1, gives eulogy at a memorial service for a family friend, J. Warner Fobes. The Frosts met Fobes and his wife, Edith, in 1915, and throughout the 1920s often stayed on the Fobes place, in Sugar Hill, New Hampshire, in September, seeking refuge from hay fever. On December 9, gives first of three seminars in writing to students at Bryn Mawr, then goes to New York City, where he meets Ridgely Torrence, the poetry editor of the *New Republic,* and the poet and dramatist Percy MacKaye, who in 1921 would help RF obtain an appointment as Fellow in Creative Arts at the University of Michigan. *Harper's* publishes four more poems by RF (all of them wound up in *New Hampshire*). On December 19, RF writes Wilfred Davison about what would in 1921 become the Bread Loaf School of English at

Middlebury, initiating a relationship with the school that would last throughout the poet's life. He writes: "I have been a good deal interested in your new Summer School from afar off. I have been wondering if what is behind it may not be what has been troubling me lately, namely, the suspicion that we aren't getting enough American literature out of our colleges to pay for the hard teaching that goes into them. . . . I might fit into your summer plan with a course on the Responsibilities of Teachers of Composition—to their country to help make what is sure to be the greatest nation in wealth the greatest in art also. I should particularly like to encounter the teachers who refuse to expect of human nature more than a correct business letter." Spends first Christmas with his family at the Stone House.

1921 In January, publishes four more poems, this time in the *Yale Review* (later collected in *New Hampshire*). On January 17, begins discussions with Percy MacKaye about an appointment as Fellow in Creative Arts at Michigan: "Your letter finds me in a good frame of mind to listen to any proposal to rescue me from the public lecture platform for a living. I have had to interrupt one of my best spells of writing to go out talking this winter. I'm just home now from one lecture trip and about to go out on another; and I'm rather sad about it. Not that I don't always do more than enough writing to keep from being pitied as the father of a family in spite of everything." In late January, writes his English friend Jack Haines of his affection for Edward Thomas, killed at the Battle of Arras in 1917: "You and I cared for him in a different way from the rest of them. We didn't have to wait till he was dead to find out how much we loved him. . . . I don't know what he looked for from me in his black days when I first met him. All he ever got was admiration for the poet in him before he had written a line of poetry. It is hard to speak of him as I want to yet." Illness keeps RF in bed during late January and early February, preventing him from attending a memorial service held in New York to honor William Dean Howells, who had died in May 1920. Writes Hamlin Garland: "Howells himself sent me The Mother and the Father after he saw my North of Boston. It is beautiful blank verse, just what I should have known from his prose he would write. My obligation to him however is not for the particular things he did in verse form, but for the perennial poetry of all his writing in all forms. I learned from him a long time ago that the loveliest theme of poetry was the voices of people. No one ever had a more observing ear or clearer imagination for the tones of those voices. No one ever brought them more freshly to book." Accepts appointment as honorary member of the Poetry Society of

Southern Vermont, writing to its secretary: "You come pretty near being right in your guess that I think poetry societies a rather roundabout way of producing American poetry. I can't find however that Plato who was opposed to poets was opposed to poetry societies." On March 4, delivers his (and John Livingston Lowes's) verdict as to who should win a poetry contest prize organized by the editor of *Contemporary Verse*: "Here then, since you must be ready to listen to it without further delay, is the decision of your judges in the contest for the three prizes . . . : that the first shall go to Miss Sara Teasdale, the second to Mr David Morton, the third to Mr. Stephen Benét." On February 17 and March 10, offers his second and third seminars in writing at Bryn Mawr, completing the series he began in December 1920. He stays at the residence of the Pennsylvania supreme court justice Robert von Moschzisker, a family friend. Gives two readings in New York in February, where he and Elinor stay at the Waverly Place residence of Harriet Moody, and a third in Princeton in March. Spends a week in late March as poet in residence at Queens University, Kingston, Ontario. Publishes four poems in the *New Republic* in March and April; all of them would also appear in *New Hampshire*. Reads in Syracuse on April 15. Writes to Untermeyer about the fiction he's been reading—by Dorothy Canfield Fisher, Sherwood Anderson, Howells, Sinclair Lewis, Waldo Frank, Floyd Dell, Zona Gale, and Willa Cather. Singles out Cather's "Coming Aphrodite," collected in *Youth and the Bright Medusa*, for praise: "The best writing of all is Coming Aphrodite. Now I'm envious. We have had no such short story. You must agree with me. Every stroke of it to the very last. I wept for the sheer perfection." Henry Holt and Company issues a second edition of *Mountain Interval* in April, featuring as the frontispiece a photograph of Aroldo Du Chêne's bust of the poet. On May 31, RF reads as Phi Beta Kappa poet at Columbia University. The poem, with which RF was disappointed, doesn't survive, but descriptions show that it was an early version of what would become "Build Soil," which RF read, again as the Phi Beta Kappa poet, at Columbia in 1932. Plants apple orchard and pine trees with Carol. Reads at the Boston Public Library on June 23 as a part of the American Library Association's Swampscott Conference (June 20–27, 1921). Now regularly receives $100 per lecture or reading (about $1,300 in 2016 dollars). On June 25, writes Percy MacKaye that he will "gladly accept" the offer to serve as Fellow in Creative Arts at the University of Michigan; writes formal letter of agreement to President Marion LeRoy Burton on July 7: "You had my telegram accepting your offer. It remains for me to thank you for having chosen me to be a representative of creative literature in this way at Michigan University. We'll waive the question of whether you might not better have chosen someone else for the honor. I should have thanked you almost as much if you had. The important thing is that you should have chosen anyone. I dont know why I am so gratified unless it is because I am somewhat surprised when men of your executive authority . . . see it as a part of their duty to the state to encourage the arts." Arranges for his son, Carol, to undertake a rock-hunting expedition in Vermont and New Hampshire with Ralph Walter Stone, of the U.S. Geological Survey. The London firm of David Nutt, publisher of RF's first two books, and now bankrupt, attempts to collect royalties RF was paid for the books he published with Henry Holt and Company in 1915 and 1916. RF would rely on his British friend Jack Haines and the Cambridge, Massachusetts, book dealer Maurice Firuski to see to the disposition of some 900 copies of the two Nutt editions, *A Boy's Will* and *North of Boston,* which had been left unsold when the firm went into receivership. *Harper's* publishes four more poems by RF in its July number (all collected in *New Hampshire*). Reads in July at the newly established Bread Loaf School of English in Ripton, Vermont. Writes to publicist at Henry Holt and Company: "I have just been to lecture at the Middlebury Summer School of English on the prospects of what I may call the studio method in teaching English. The experienced older painter allows inexperienced younger painters to set up their easels alongside of his for what they can get out of his example, stimulation, and shop-talk. So the experienced writer might receive inexperienced, but promising, or at any rate ambitious, writers into companionship." In August retreats with his family to Franconia, New Hampshire, to escape hay-fever season. With Charles Lowell Young, a family friend who is a professor of English at Wellesley, takes a five-day (September 12–17) hike from Upton, Maine, to Lake Willoughby, Vermont. For Henry Holt, reviews manuscripts by Helen Hoyt, Edwin Ford Piper, and Babette Deutsch; recommends that Henry Holt publish only Deutsch. Having accepted the one-year, $5,000 Fellow in Creative Arts appointment at the University of Michigan, moves with family in early October to Ann Arbor (Marjorie remains in high school in Bennington). Though no specific duties are assigned, finds schedule busy with advising students, especially the ones associated with the Whimsies, an undergraduate literary society. On November 22, is honored, along with Edgar A. Guest, at a dinner in Detroit. In early to mid- December, gives a series of talks in Oshkosh, Wisconsin, at the University of Wisconsin–Madison, at Northwestern University, and in Detroit and Chicago. Spends Christmas in Ann Arbor.

1922 "The Witch of Coös" is published in the January issue of *Poetry*. In January and February, RF reads at Ohio State University; before a meeting of the Women's Club in Terre Haute, Indiana; at the University of Wisconsin–La Crosse; at Mankato State Teachers College, in Mankato, Minnesota; and at the University of Chicago. Advises a former Amherst colleague, George Whicher, as to what he should expect of a teacher at the Bread Loaf School of English: "The strength of the teacher's position lies in his waiting till he is come after. His society and audience are a privilege—and that is no pose. On the rare occasions when he goes after the pupils it will be to show them up not for what they aren't but for what they are. He will invade them to show them how much more they contain than they can write down; to show them their subject matter in where they came from and what in the last twenty years they have been doing." Arranges successful lecture series at University of Michigan, in which Padraic Colum, Carl Sandburg, Louis Untermeyer, Amy Lowell, and Vachel Lindsay all appear; the series extends from March 1 through May 24. Named Poet Laureate of Vermont by the state League of Women's Clubs in early June, only to find himself made sport of in an editorial in the *New York Times,* which pointed out that the new laureate was born in San Francisco, attended Dartmouth and Harvard, had lived for some years in Franconia, and had taught at Amherst, before adding (in error) that *North of Boston* was a book of "free verse." In a letter to the editor, Halley Phillips Gilchrist, a member of the Vermont State League of Women's Clubs, defends the laureateship, certifying that RF has been a registered voter in Vermont since 1920, and has never written free verse. On June 19, RF awarded an honorary MA by the University of Michigan at its commencement ceremony. Back in South Shaftsbury on June 24, writes the first of many letters to Wade Van Dore, an aspiring poet whom RF would befriend and encourage throughout the 1920s: "First about Thoreau: I like him as well as you do. In one book [*Walden*] he surpasses everything we have had in America. You have found this out for yourself without my having told you; I have found it out for myself without your having told me. Isn't it beautiful that there can be such concert without collusion? That's the kind of 'getting together' I can endure." On a single night in mid-July, writes a draft of "New Hampshire" and then pens "Stopping by Woods on a Snowy Evening" at dawn. Arranges for Heinemann to be his new London publisher (the firm will release the English edition of his *Selected Poems* in 1923). Writes Wilbur Rowell, the family's attorney, about his sister Jeanie: "Jean is still where she was. We have been on the point of seeing if some provision couldn't be made for her in the country where she could have a more individual existence not herded in an institution. . . . But in spite of the fact that she enjoys longer and longer lucid intervals in which she talks and writes like anyone else, she hasn't a real grip on herself and just when it begins to look as if she could be counted on, goes all to pieces again. . . . It is all too much for me." Approves a plan at Henry Holt and Company to offer a discount to public schools wishing to buy his books. In late August, with his daughters Lesley and Marjorie, their friend Lillian Labatt, and his son, Carol, embarks on a hike up the Long Trail through the Green Mountains of Vermont. Lesley, Carol, Lillian, and Marjorie succeed in walking the 220 miles—and along the way, Carol and Lillian fall in love—but RF is forced to drop out early, owing to exhaustion and blisters on his feet. He writes Untermeyer: "Here I am out at St Johnsbury [Vermont] that famous town for St Johnswort, having for my part achieved peace without victory. The children made a record for the two hundred and twenty miles of Vermont from Mass to Canada. I am content that it is all in the family though as for me personally the laurels wither on my brow as of course they were bound to sooner or later." On October 8, RF accepts the renewal of his fellowship at the University of Michigan for 1922–1923; attends official reception on October 11, then returns to New England to fulfill lecture engagements. Reads in Rutland, Vermont, on October 18, in Boston on October 23, and at Wellesley on October 24. Back in South Shaftsbury on November 1, RF learns that *Poetry* has awarded him its $200 Levinson Prize for "The Witch of Coös." Travels by train from New York to New Orleans (November 8–9), where he speaks at Tulane on November 10. Over the next six days gives readings at the University of Texas, at Temple College in Temple, Texas, and in San Antonio, Fort Worth, Dallas, and Waco, before returning, with a stop at the University of Missouri along the way, to Ann Arbor on November 20, exhausted and seriously ill. Is confined to bed for several weeks. Writes Lincoln MacVeagh about a meeting planned for New York City: "I could have telegraphed 'Can't keep appointment. Expect to die November 25th. Sorry.' But one doesnt like to make gloomy predictions about one's health. It looks too cowardly. It furnishes the Christian Scientists with too much to go on." In early December is beset by doubts as to the propriety of Henry Holt and Company's issuing his *Selected Poems* the coming March and writes to MacVeagh: "I want the field clear for my new books. It is going to break my heart to have this old dead horse talked about and reviewed as if it were my present bid for notice." But subsequently is pleased at the outcome. On December 22, writes the Cambridge bookseller Maurice Firuski the first of series of letters concerning Firuski's efforts, through Jack Haines in England, to obtain unsold copies of the London editions of his first two books. Returns to South Shaftsbury to spend Christmas with his family. Reads T. S. Eliot's *The Waste Land,* published in December 1922.

1923 RF and his wife, Elinor, spend a week in New York from January 6 to 13, visiting friends, meeting with RF's publisher, and also with Carl Van Doren, who is preparing a feature on RF for *Century Magazine.* RF also meets the critic and journalist Burton Rascoe, who angers RF by publishing an account of their conversation about modern poetry. RF writes but doesn't send a scathing letter in reply: "Save yourself trouble by presenting my side of the argument for me, would you? . . . Interview me without letting me know I was being interviewed, would you? . . . I'm sure you made a platitudinous mess of my talk." Jokes about Eliot's *Waste Land:* "One American poet living in England has made an Anthology of the Best Lines in Poetry. He has run the lines loosely together in a sort of narrative and copyrighted them so that anyone using them again will have to enclose them in double quotation marks." When preparing his own 1923 volume, *New Hampshire: A Poem with Notes and Grace Notes,* for the press, RF devises a series of footnotes to the title poem, linking it to other poems and lines in poems elsewhere in the book, partly (perhaps) in answer to the notes Eliot added to the Boni and Liveright edition of *The Waste Land,* but chiefly for reasons of his own. Writes to Untermeyer: "It might be a good idea to call the explanatory poems Notes. I'm pretty sure to call the book New Hampshire. The Notes will be The Witch of Coos, The Census-taker, Paul's Wife, Wild Grapes, The Grindstone, The Ax-helve, The Star-splitter, Maple, The Witch of Grafton (praps), The Gold Hesperidee (praps) and anything else I can think of or may write before summer. I'll go further and say that I may even bring out a volume of lyrics at the same time and refer to it in New Hampshire as The Star in the Stone-boat. I'm in a larking mood. I'll do almost anything for the sake of contraption." Returns to Ann Arbor on January 31. Van Doren's essay on RF, "The Soil of the Puritans: Robert Frost, Quintessence and Subsoil," appears in the February 23 issue of *Century Magazine.* RF brings Hamlin Garland, Dorothy Canfield Fisher, and Louis Untermeyer to Michigan as guest lecturers in a series that runs from February to April. "Stopping by Woods on a Snowy Evening" appears on March 7 in the *New Republic.* Henry Holt and Company issues *The Selected Poems of Robert Frost* on March 15 (Heinemann publishes it in London). RF suffers another bout of influenza like the one he had in November 1922. In April, continues negotiations with Maurice Firuski to secure, through Jack Haines, the remaining unsold copies of David Nutt's editions of his first two books. Returns to South Shaftsbury during the first week of April. With Lincoln MacVeagh, at Henry Holt and Company, settles on an agreement to issue his fourth book of new poems, *New Hampshire,* late in the year. On April 30, writes to Marion Eliza Dodd, owner of the Hampshire Bookshop in Northampton, to arrange for an internship for his daughter Lesley, who plans to open a bookstore with her sister Marjorie. In a May 2 letter to Untermeyer, refers to "Stopping by Woods" as his "best bid for remembrance." At his Amherst colleague George Whicher's request, agrees to lecture again at the Bread Loaf School of English (he had skipped its 1922 session): "I only ask one thing of you and that is that you will absolutely protect me from cameras and such like adulation. Just give it out at announcement-time that I don't want anybody to pay any attention to me at all except when I am lecturing and then I want everybody to pay attention to me and to hurrah for me like Hell." Returns to Ann Arbor on May 15; gives readings at the University of Michigan on May 29 and May 31. In mid-June, travels to Burlington, Vermont, where he stays with Henry Holt, the founder of the press, and now retired; is awarded honorary LHD (doctor of humane letters) by the University of Vermont on June 18. In July, arranges, with Lincoln MacVeagh, for the preparation of a working typescript of *New Hampshire:* "Theres fun in the book and there's some beauty. We'll say that now beforehand and we wont be scared out of it by anything that happens"; is pleased that the book will feature woodcuts by J. J. Lankes. Accepts appointment as professor of English at Amherst after President Alexander Meiklejohn is dismissed by the Board of Trustees; teaches at the Bread Loaf School of English. In early August visits Lincoln MacVeagh and his family at their summer place in Dublin, New Hampshire. Writes Lankes to arrange the woodcuts for the new book: "Just as most friendship is feigning, so is most liking a mere tacit understanding between A and B that A shall like B's work as much and as long as B likes A's. In our case I see good circumstantial evidence that there was no such sordid bargain. I liked your work before I knew you liked mine; you apparently liked mine somewhat before you knew I liked yours. Such a coincidence of taste can never be forgotten." In part at the behest of George Olds, the incoming president of Amherst, RF tries to secure replacements for the faculty members who had resigned in protest when Meiklejohn was dismissed. In late August, goes camping in Maine and visits his sister Jeanie in the Maine Insane Asylum in Augusta, where she remains confined. When the Harvard professor of philosophy Ernest Hocking is unavailable, RF decides to teach one course at Amherst in the fall term, on "philosophical judgments," and another course in literature. In the latter, he will assign readings from Melville, Thoreau, Emerson, Gibbon, George Borrow, Benvenuto Cellini, and Christina Rossetti. Discusses quantum theory with the Danish physicist Niels Bohr when Bohr lectures at Amherst in October. "Nature's First Green" ("Nothing Gold Can Stay"), "To Earthward," and "I will Sing You One-O" appear together in the October issue of the *Yale Review* (all would soon be collected in *New Hampshire*). Gives his son, Carol, now twenty-one, the South Shaftsbury farm as a wedding present when he marries Lillian LaBatt on November 3. Writes to MacVeagh: "Carol's marriage was only a little of a surprise. He and Lillian had been engaged for some time. They were such children that I didn't want to commit them to each other by taking much notice of the affair or saying much about it. I doubt if I thought it would survive Lillian's first year at college. But it turned out in a way to show that I was no judge of the intensity of children. Lillian's first year at college it was that didn't survive. She quit, homesick, and Carol went right to her mother and got her. It was all done in a week. I may be frosty, but I rather like to look on at such things. And I like children to be terribly in love." *New Hampshire: A Poem with Notes and Grace Notes,* with woodcuts by J. J. Lankes, is published by Henry Holt and Company on November 15, even as Lincoln MacVeagh decides to leave the firm to found the Dial Press. RF writes him on November 19: "The only move you would have to seek my approval of before you made it would be getting out and leaving me alone with the heirs of Henry Holt. I'll bet that is what you are contemplating; but if I thought at all seriously, I would come right down to New York to talk you out of it." In a letter enclosed with a copy of *New Hampshire* (which he dedicated to Vermont and Michigan), RF explains his decision to accept the new appointment at Amherst to his University of Michigan friend Morris Tilley: "You must wonder at my coming to Amherst after what I said to you about coming back to Michigan. But if you stop to consider you will see no great inconsistency. Michigan on year-to-year contract and no prospect of settling down and making myself at home was out of the question. I may not have made myself clear enough on that point when you felt me out on our walk that day. I was too homeless for my age out there." Grieved at the rapid decline in health of Susan Hayes Ward (the first editor ever to accept a poem of his, "My Butterfly," which appeared in *The Independent* in 1894), RF writes to her nephew on December 27: "I knew your father and both your aunts so well (they were the first friends of my poetry) that I could almost feel that I had always known you too. I am greatly pained by what has overtaken Miss Susan. I had just been thinking I must get to South Berwick [Maine] again while she was still of this world. And now I am too late. I don't suppose she would know me if she saw me or would get any pleasure out of a letter. We had a grand talk about poetry the last time I went to South Berwick. . . . My wife and I both cared for her more than I can tell you." Ward would die some six weeks later, on February 5.

1924 Resumes teaching at Amherst on January 4, but begins to weary of the demands it makes on him. Writes Jack Haines in February: "I'm teaching too hard this year. I suppose it is good for me in the eyes of the inscrutable." Eldest daughter, Lesley, publishes (as "Leslie Field") a short story in *The Bookman* in February. RF advises Untermeyer: "You did not err. The story in the Bookman was Lesley's. But be more truthful than common. You never recognized it from any family resemblance. You had many clues to help you. . . . You mustn't tell her any more that she repeats her father. The charge is dangerous to her further development. She has been held back long enough by our discretion and her own. It's time she let out in prose and verse." Considers a trip to France and England for the summer, but defers it (the voyage wouldn't occur until 1928). Spends four days in Ann Arbor in the spring. Gives a reading, attends events held in his honor, and meets with the Whimsies, the undergraduate literary society he had worked with in 1921–1922. Writes to Morris Tilley, an English professor at Michigan and a family friend: "My time with you will extend from Sunday afternoon March 30 to early Thursday morning April 3, and you may act upon me accordingly. It will be fun to see several of you again. I got to be a good deal more Ann Arboreal than I should suppose I could have at my age." Spends a week in April helping his son, Carol, lay out an apple orchard at the Stone Cottage in South Shaftsbury. Spends May 13–17 in New York with his wife, Elinor; gives a reading and accepts at a dinner an honorary membership in PEN. Other attendees and RF appear in a caricature drawn by Wyncie King for the *New York Times Book Review* on June 1. Awarded the Pulitzer Prize for *New Hampshire* in May. On May 29, visits Pittsfield, Massachusetts, to help daughters Lesley and Marjorie launch their new bookstore, The Open Book. Receives Honorary Litt.D. degrees from Middlebury College and Yale University in June. Spends a week at the Bread Loaf School of English in July. Confesses his dissatisfaction with teaching, writing to George Roy Elliott on July 26: "One year more of little Amherst and then surcease of that particular sorrow. I like to teach, but I don't like to teach more than once a week now. I'm become a spoiled child of fortune. I may be drawn back to Michigan or I may take to the woods." In August, advises Frank Robbins, assistant to the president at the University of Michigan, as to possible candidates for the Fellowship in Creative Arts that RF himself held from 1921 to 1923: "Jesse Lynch Williams would mean more to the undergraduates than anyone else dramatic you have named. He wouldn't be cold water on their prejudices. He is a practical playwright who has held himself in ideals well above the ruck of Broadway. . . . He is all alive to the America of the moment." Spends September above the hay-fever line in Sugar Hill, New Hampshire, near Franconia, in a guest cottage on land owned by a family friend, Edith Fobes. In early October, RF accepts the offer of a permanent appointment as Fellow in Letters (with no teaching duties) at the University of Michigan, to begin in fall 1925; defers public announcement until November. Grandson, William Prescott Frost, son of Carol and Lillian, is born on October 15. RF helps George Roy Elliott select speakers for the Bowdoin Institute of Modern Literature, to be held in May 1925: "Willa Cather is A No 1. You <u>must</u> have her, and you may tell her I said so. Besides being a real figure in letters, she's both thinker and speaker. [Edna St. Vincent] Millay is a great audience-killer. Boys and girls equally fall for her charm. She loses nothing of course with them by her reputation for dainty promiscuity. . . . I dont have to tell you how much I admire her less flippant verse. She will succeed anywhere. . . . And don't forget Amy [Lowell]. She's a shining lecturer, whatever else you may or may not grant she is." In November, writes to a number of Ann Arbor friends about the new appointment; says to Morris Tilley: "Well, old friend, we are going to be where we shall see a lot of each other again. I shall count on you more than on anyone else to help me find out how to make the most of what the University has given me. We must conspire to manage me with the wisdom of the serpent." Arranges to be made his sister Jeanie's guardian, writing to Wilbur Rowell: "I'm sure Jean wants me made her guardian now. So if you <u>would</u> help me in the matter, I should be grateful. I don't see how we could claim a residence for her anywhere in particular. But, as you say, the estate is in Essex County and her share of it might well be paid from there. . . . She will be easier in her mind, I'm sure, when she is using her own money to pay her expenses." Spends Christmas with his family in South Shaftsbury.

1925 On January 3, speaks and reads before the Saturday Club in Boston, founded in 1855 by Ralph Waldo Emerson and others. In mid-January, Frederick

Melcher proposes that RF be honored with a birthday dinner in March, and RF accepts: "I won't say I dont like to be made of by the right sort of friends. I am going to let you give me that triumphal dinner on my fiftieth birthday if it is understood beforehand that I dont much deserve it and that I don't necessarily have to look or act exactly the age" (at the time RF was still unaware that he was born in 1874, not 1875). On January 28, reads at annual reception for seniors at Amherst. Begins arranging for housing in Ann Arbor in late February, writing a Michigan friend: "We think that that small house would be just the thing to complete and save the poem—if poem our life is going to be out there. Your description of it is by implication an appreciation of me such as few have written." On February 23, entertains Amy Lowell in Amherst; she had come to give a talk and reading. On February 28, does the same for the Irish poet and novelist James Stephens. In March embarks on a reading-lecture junket that takes him to Philadelphia on March 5, Franklin and Marshall College on March 6, and Chambersburg and Abington, Pennsylvania on March 9 and 12. On March 26, in New York, attends "Fiftieth Birthday Dinner"; among the attendees are Untermeyer, Dorothy Canfield Fisher, Frederic Melcher, Willa Cather, Irita and Carl Van Doren, Elinor Wylie, and Wilbur L. Cross. Reads and lectures in Lawrence, Massachusetts, on March 31. On May 1 speaks at memorial services held in Ann Arbor for Marion LeRoy Burton. On May 4 speaks on "vocal imagination" at the Bowdoin Institute for Modern Literature. Writes a brief obituary tribute to Amy Lowell for the *Christian Science Monitor* (published on May 16), and addresses an assembly of students at Amherst about her poetry and legacy on May 14. Speaks at Vassar on May 22. With his wife, Elinor, visits his sister Jeanie at the Maine Insane Asylum; reports to Wilbur Rowell on June 27: "Elinor and I went to see [Jeanie] a few weeks ago and found her fairly well. I was surprised at the personal interest Dr [Forrest Clark] Tyson, the Superintendent, showed in her and the special account he was able to give of her case. I am sure she has the best care and is at least as happy as I have seen her for years. That's not happy enough to smile much. I just mean she has her satisfactions from day to day almost like a normal person." Spends most of June and July in South Shaftsbury; spends most of August and September with his wife and daughter Irma at the Fobes place in Sugar Hill, New Hampshire; writes Witter Bynner on August 29: "This is Sugar Hill N.H. on a back road. But dont tell anybody. I am feigning to be in Canada a fugitive from injustice. I have hardly more than cheeped in verse this summer." Goes to Ann Arbor in late September to begin new appointment at Michigan, despite Elinor's concerns about their children's health;

Marjorie and Lesley remain in Pittsfield, and Carol, in South Shaftsbury. On October 18, addresses the New Hampshire Schoolmasters' Club in Manchester; on October 26 gives a talk and reading in Philadelphia. Gives additional talks in late October and early November in Chicago and in Grand Rapids, Michigan. On November 5, in response to a request, outlines some of his ideas about poetry in a letter to John Freeman: "Sentences may have the greatest monotony to the eye in length and structure and yet the greatest variety to the ear in the tones of voice they carry. . . . The imagination of the ear flags first as the spirit dies down in writing. The 'voices' fail you. . . . The actor's gift is to execute the vocal image at the mouth. The writer's is to implicate the vocal image in a sentence and fasten it printed to the page." Consoles longtime friend Sidney Cox when his first son, named for RF, dies at the age of two; writes on December 5: "I just think it is too terrible. There are absolutely no consoling thoughts about it—not of this world anyway. It is the worst form of balked desire. Let it die down if you want to. Talk will help it die down of course. Some people encourage talk for that reason. But dont let it die down if you dont want to. We have a right to keep any memory we please even to soul sickness." On December 16, Elinor departs Ann Arbor for Pittsfield, where Marjorie has fallen ill with pneumonia, a pericardiac infection, appendicitis, and nervous exhaustion; RF writes to his Amherst friend Otto Manthey-Zorn the next day: "Elinor went to Pittsfield last night to see Marj who is in the hospital there with influenza or something. I may follow if she gives the word. It wouldnt be long anyway before we began to think of heading for Amherst. But I rather wanted to stay still where I was for a few weeks. Elinor may bring Marj out here if she is well enough to move. I'm weary of this scattered way of living. Either I mean to become an explorer and live homeless entirely or to settle down and raise chickens with a single post office address." RF follows Elinor several days later, and the two remain in and around Pittsfield through the holidays.

1926 Begins the New Year by writing long letters to his old friends Sidney Cox and John Bartlett. To Cox he writes: "You're a better teacher than I ever was or will be now. But I'd like to put it to you while you are still young and developing your procedure if you dont think a lot of things could be found to do in class besides debate and disagree. Clash is all very well for coming lawyers politicians and theologians. But I should think there must be a whole realm or plane above that—all sight and insight, perception, intuition, rapture. Narrative is a fearfully safe place to spend your time. Having ideas that are neither pro nor con is the happy thing." To Bartlett: "You and Margaret were my favorite kids at Pinkerton [Academy] you know whether taken singly or as a pair. So it wont be anything on me particularly if you happen to come out right. . . . Mind you though, I dont insist on success. Feel perfectly free to come out any way you please. Lose if you think it will get you in better with God. I shall still write you letters oftener than I do anyone else except my very own children." In early January begins correspondence and friendship with the Scottish-born poet Edward Davison, whom RF would bring to the faculty at Bread Loaf. Marjorie's illness darkens the prospect of the departure for Michigan; RF writes an Ann Arbor friend from Pittsfield on January 11: "We have made very bad work of our divided life so far this year. This attempt (bold at our age) to be about equally eastern and western may defeat itself like trying to sit on more than thirteen to fifteen eggs at once. It may addle the eggs and give the hen a nervous breakdown. Life has never been a choice for me. I can honestly say I have seen but one thing presented to do at a time. Until now anyway." Returns to Ann Arbor in early February after spending two weeks in residency at Amherst and giving talks at Bryn Mawr and Union College, in Schenectady. Joined in March by Elinor, Marjorie, and Irma; the latter had quit art school in New York. Lectures in Iowa City on March 25 and at the University of Illinois at Urbana-Champaign on March 29; returns to Ann Arbor ill and, on April 5, writes Witter Bynner, who had solicited a preface from him: "For my part, my daughter, the best poet in the family, has been dangerously ill for twelve weeks now, my wife is prostrated and my heart indisposed to prefaces. . . . In the last homecoming to roost, the exigencies of the irresponsible are more ruthless than the most military of law and order. But I forgive you them even as I hope to be forgiven a murder I once did. The question is what am I going to do for you. I'm damned if I see in my confusion. I havent had a metaphor for months. This is the twilight of the mind— before God it is. I'll go out to grass at a word in the wrong key. Aren't we in a terrible mess?" On April 7, writes long letter to B. F. Skinner about a book of short stories Skinner was working on. Meets with the aspiring poet Wade Van Dore, a Michigan native, in April to discuss his work, writing him on March 23: "Can't you put off coming till Sunday after next. I've been thinking about you and I want to see you soon again. It is great if by anything I have done you have gained time. Only don't be betrayed into taking art easy. I know you wont be. So why am I advising? Spread out spread out and look into all the corners of your own mind and nature now—and into all the ends of literature to see what it is in its fullness. Look over fences into what you are not sure is any concern of yours even. I mean read all sorts of things with a writer's eye." When George Daniel Olds, the president of Amherst, visits Ann Arbor on or about May 1, RF accepts his offer to rejoin the faculty as a professor of English, with a salary of $5,000 a year and no obligation to teach formal classes (RF would offer only informal seminars of ten weeks, to be held each year from January to March). Writes Untermeyer on May 3: "I accept school just as I accept the sonnet form or any other social convention: only it seems to be in me to want to make the school as un-schoollike [*sic*] as possible. . . . But let not God consider me. I know damn well the subtle ways he turns and passes and turns again. . . . Teaching will be teaching after I have done my prettiest to translate it to an Elysian Academe. I don't pretend not to be a fool. Teaching is not really where I live anyway, come to think of it." Awarded honorary Litt.D. by Bowdoin College on June 14; while in Maine, RF visits his sister Jeanie at the Maine Insane Asylum and confers with her doctor, Forrest Clark Tyson. Returns to South Shaftsbury in late-June. On August 15, participates in inaugural session of the Bread Loaf Writers' Conference. With Elinor, spends late August, September, and October in Sugar Hill, New Hampshire, writing George Sargent on August 30: "The worst place to address a letter to me is at Franconia because that makes the Postal department the maddest in the person of the postmaster down there who is sick of forwarding letters to me at Amherst to be forwarded to Ann Arbor to be forwarded to South Shaftsbury to be forwarded to Sugar Hill within five miles of Franconia where it started from." Daughter Irma marries John Paine Cone in Franconia on October 15. RF counsels a young writer, Hubert Hart, who had been a student of his at Amherst: "You are going along smoothly and honestly in your own natural voice. I still feel however that the observations you make, what you remark on in life, doesn't quite matter enough. I still feel that you know 'inside stuff' that you wont come out with. My suspicion is that you only tell as much of what you know as you can make fit in with the art of certain authors you admire—their art and their attitude toward God and man. Your own material has got to be everything to you and will be yet. You'll never have an art and an attitude of your own except through complete surrender to your own material." Returns to South Shaftsbury in November, before decamping for a two-week residency at Wesleyan College, November 18 to December 12. Undertakes (ultimately without success) to help rehabilitate *The Dearborn Independent* as a proper literary magazine; it had long been tainted by Henry Ford's anti-Semitism. Provides financial assistance to Irma and her new husband as they resettle on the Cone family farm in Rozel,

Kansas. In a holiday mood, sends fair copies of four poems to his English friend John W. Haines; three of them would be collected in *West-Running Brook* (1928).

1927 Moves to Amherst in January, where he teaches for ten weeks. The description in the course catalogue reads: "During the winter term Professor Robert Frost will be in residence to conduct special classes in English and to hold informal conferences with students." On January 12, sees his daughter Lesley off as she sets sail from New York on the SS *Franconia* for a round-the-world cruise. During the cruise she operates a bookstore. RF arranges for Edward Davison to lecture at Amherst on February 7, easing the strain on their friendship that attended RF's withdrawal of an invitation for Davison to write a biography of him (Gorham Munson was assigned the job instead). Writes his friend Sidney Cox about his family worries: "We are still under the cloud of Marjorie's long illness. Our day in the house revolves around her. She reads a little plays the piano a little and plays cards a little: but she has to be kept from doing even such things too much. Sometimes we get fearfully disheartened. More than glimpses of people seem to exhaust her. . . . The doctors now call it nervous prostration. The nervous prostrates I have seen however were set serious. Marj has her ironies and her grins. Lesley is on one of the winter tours around the world with a branch of her book store. Shes past Samoa by now. The last letter from her was from Honolulu (sp.) With Irma married into Kansas and Carol away in Vermont we feel a pretty scattered family." Arranges for Harriet Monroe to read at Amherst on March 7, and for Gorham Munson to lecture on March 18. RF lectures and reads at the Museum of Art in Toledo, Ohio, on March 25, then spends a week in residence at the University of Michigan, March 26 to April 1. In April moves from Amherst back to South Shaftsbury. In early May, several months after Untermeyer's son, Richard, had committed suicide, RF writes to Untermeyer: "I was afraid my silence would begin to be misunderstood. If I was more silent with the pen than usual it was because I could think of nothing adequate to say. . . . Come to me if you want to hear some small part of the truth." On May 9, moves with Elinor and Marjorie out of the South Shaftsbury house and into the Shingled Cottage in nearby North Bennington. Counsels an aspiring writer, then a graduate student at the University of Texas: "I would have you use your own inmost guidance as to which it should be with you, criticism or narrative and description. . . . But it is less important what you do than the way you do it. You will stand or fall in both cases as you write or dont write literature in all its qualities of idea, insight, thought, metaphor, phrase and speaking likeness— likeness to speaking. You will have to look into this matter very acutely." On

May 30, writes Wade Van Dore (whose poetry RF had been reading in manuscript, and whose first book RF would help put together): "Two of these last
four you sent are thrust home, High Heaven and The Seeker. The Silence and
The Moment before and after Moonrise are less merciless. You are finding
out. You are going to do it—if you dont let up on yourself—if you dont get
too conceited to watch yourself and everybody else who ever attempted it.
Dont miss any tricks or arts, traits or ingredients. Look and then look some
more. . . . I'm with you and Im your friend. . . . Keep sending." In a long June
letter, gives an account of his years on the Derry farm (1900–1909) to Gorham
Munson, then at work on the first biography of RF ever published. Gives
readings and a talk at the Bread Loaf School of English (August 5–7). With
Elinor and Marjorie, takes up his yearly retreat in Sugar Hill, New Hampshire from August 21 to September 26. On September 8, lectures at Wells
College, in Aurora, New York. Grandson John "Jack" Cone Jr. is born to Irma
and John Cone on September 29 in Larned, Kansas. On October 28, in reply
to a query from a graduate student at the University of Oregon, again lays
out his ideas about art: "The reality of the voice has been my great interest in
art since long before I knew what it was or what to call it. Truth to the tones
people speak in—dramatic sound—is what we are after, be it in prose or
verse,—in drama, of course, but just as much in narrative, in essay, and even
in lyric: or so I have always wanted to believe. . . . I was remembering only
last night how in those old days I was smitten by the way Clara Morris at a
certain high moment in Camille said a simple 'I cant' and an actor in Herne's
Shore Acres a simple 'Kinder shy.' It was to incur those wounds that I went to
the theatre (when I went) and for which presently I found I was picking up
books. I got them in all sorts of places. They are nowhere more deadly than
from some of the records left by [the singer, comedian, and vaudevillian]
Bert Williams." On November 3, as they attempt to drive to Amherst for
the inauguration of the incoming president, Arthur Stanley Pease, RF and
Elinor are stranded in floodwaters from a late-season hurricane: "We were
in pretty deep that night—clear up over the seats on one side. Our poor car
will never be the same car again. It was an Oakland antedeluvianly. It's
lucky if it's a Model T Ford now. When we hit the water going full speed
and raised it in a solid dome over us it looked like drowning in a pond."
In November, travels with Elinor and Marjorie to Baltimore to consult
with doctors at Johns Hopkins Hospital regarding Marjorie's health; returns to Baltimore in late December. On December 28 Marjorie is admitted
to the hospital for six weeks of observation. RF returns with Elinor to
Amherst.

1928 On January 2, RF begins his ten-week seminar at Amherst College, taking leave to lecture in Salem, Massachusetts, on January 9, and in Montclair, New Jersey, on January 13. Gives a public reading at the Jones Library, Amherst, on February 5. Winds up his duties at Amherst in March, then embarks on a lecture trip from March 25 to April 8 that takes him to Ann Arbor, Buffalo, and Phillips Academy Andover; returns to South Shaftsbury with Elinor on April 9. Travels to Boston to receive, on May 1, the Golden Rose award from the New England Poetry Club. Later in May, spends a week in New York City with Elinor; during which stay they visit Lewis Mumford. Dismayed by Irma's letters from Rozel, Kansas, where she had settled with her husband, John Cone, in mid-May Elinor travels to the Kansas farm and brings Irma and her infant son, John Cone Jr., back to South Shaftsbury. When Irma's husband follows her, hoping to save the marriage, RF buys them a small farm in North Bennington, Vermont. On May 21, writes Wade Van Dore about the latter's poems (in 1930 RF would help the young poet bring them into print as *Far Lake*): "I've had another look at the last-sent booklet. It has several fine things. The Last Leap I hadnt noticed before. Very terrible to the imagination. I have just a lingering doubt about the last few lines. They are good in a way but do they quite come out as a conclusion to the idea of the poem? Never rest from the effort to have and bring out the idea. It's with the idea you will prevail. . . . What do you say if for your amusement you put me together into a similar booklet all the poems you want to preserve—your collected works to date. I'd like to see how it strikes me. I'd like to see how you judge yourself." The confusion in South Shaftsbury—resulting from resettling Irma, and also from Marjorie's continued illness—is compounded in June, when RF entertains his former students and old friends John and Margaret Bartlett and their four children, who drive east from Boulder, Colorado, where they had established the Bartlett Syndicate Service. RF also entertains a first cousin he did not know he had, John Moodie of New Zealand, then on a trip, via Canada and the United States, to Britain. The meeting begins an acquaintance that would survive via letters for some twenty years. Writes Lincoln MacVeagh on June 28: "Our visitors have been the kind that simply couldnt tell us exactly when they were coming or when they were going. They were from the four quarters. Three of them were named John [John Cone, John Moodie, and John Bartlett]. One had four children with him [Bartlett]. One was from New Zealand, my one and only first cousin. I didn't know that I had any. I had supposed my mother's only brother died childless when very young in shipwreck. The cousin proved up all right—a regular Scot who seemed to have come all the way from

Christchurch to protest severely against my having allowed my biographer [Gorham Munson] to spell my mother's maiden name Moody instead of Moodie. He was so hard on the inaccuracy that I saw at once he was no impostor." Meets Lesley's fiancé, James Dwight Francis. On July 21, reads in Bennington before the Poetry Society of Southern Vermont; on July 23 gives a talk and reading at Bread Loaf. Makes arrangements with Henry Holt and Company for *West-Running Brook,* scheduled for release in the fall, with woodcuts by J. J. Lankes. Hoping to restore Marjorie's health, and wishing to see old friends in England, RF sails for France, from Montreal, on August 4, with Elinor and Marjorie. On August 18, writes his Amherst friend Otto Manthey-Zorn from France: "I'll write you the first letter from over here just to let you know that our leaving without saying goodbye wasn't a case of desertion. We had said we were going so often to no purpose that we simply made up our minds this time not to say we were going till we went. Never say die till you're dead. Never say you are going to Heaven till you get there. Don't take that as meaning we think Paris is Heaven. It may or may not be, all depending on how much it succeeds in interesting Marj in the French language and how much good it does her." Writes to daughter Lesley on September 1: "We've had a lot of opera both at the Opera and Opera Comique. There's more good I forgot to mention. We like French bread. The wine doesnt mean much to us. The newspapers such as Le Matin and Le Figaro beat any we ever read for interests of the mind. Signed editorials on ideas are treated as news on the front page. We shall go along in a few days now—probably on Tuesday or Wednesday. Use J. W. Haines house Midhurst Hucclecote Gloucester England as our next address." On September 5, leaves Marjorie with friends of Dorothy Canfield Fisher in Sèvres and travels to England with Elinor. Spends early to mid-September in Gloucestershire with his barrister-botanist friend Haines, revisiting places they had explored in 1914 with Edward Thomas. In mid- to late September sees old literary friends in London, where, by mail, he gets word of Lesley's (September 3) marriage to Dwight Francis. On September 18 writes her a note of congratulation: "I celebrated your news by intending a song, and I should have sung it if my harp hadnt been hanging in a willow tree in a strange land. As it was I could not be kept from smiling. So I smiled for a day in honor of the occasion—not because I rejoice more over marriage than over any other step in love, but because it is about the only step in anybody else's love that is any of my business. . . . I told you the last time I saw you how much I liked Dwight. I was just beginning to understand him. We sensitive people wound each other with our shields." On September 29, RF travels alone to Dublin, spending four days with Padraic Colum and George

Russell ("AE"); also sees William Butler Yeats again. Writes Edward Davison on October 11: "[W. H.] Davies was the same old Davies. The minute Elinor and I got there he rose and presented us with an autographed poem as a 'souvenir of our visit.' He hasn't aged a hair. Still harping on why he isnt read in America. Wants to come over lecturing. [Walter] De la Mare is one of the best of the best. We had a night of poetry at his house. He and [J. C.] Squire are the ones I seem least to have lost touch with—I suppose partly from their having been over visiting us, but much more from congeniality of age and temper. I talked four days and nights on end with A. E. That was a real bout. It was like the late war you couldn't tell who was to blame for it or who was most exhausted by it. Anyway there's another man I like to think of." Meets with Helen Thomas (widow of Edward) in early October. On October 18, reads in London at Harold Monro's bookstore and on October 19, through Monro, meets T. S. Eliot for the first time. Meets with Frank S. Flint in London on November 2 (meanwhile Elinor goes to France to bring Marjorie to England, arriving in London on November 3). RF spends several days with friends in Leeds (Lascelles Abercrombie and family) and in Edinburgh (with the family of James Cruickshank Smith), and then again with Jack Haines in Gloucester. On November 11, RF visits poet laureate Robert Bridges at Boars Hill, Oxford. On November 14, RF sets sail with Elinor and Marjorie from Southampton (via Cherbourg) for New York City (where they arrive on the 21st). Back in the United States, learns that Lesley, who had married Dwight Francis in September, is already unhappy and considering divorce. On November 19 Henry Holt and Company publishes *West-Running Brook,* with woodcuts by J. J. Lankes; the firm also brings out an expanded edition of RF's *Selected Poems.* RF signs new contract with Henry Holt providing for an increase in royalties from 15 to 20 percent after 5,000 copies of a book are sold, as well as a $2,000 advance, and regular monthly payments of $250 for the next five years. On November 30, RF reads in Baltimore before a convention of the National Council for Teachers of English. In early December he reads at the North Carolina College for Women, in Greensboro, before returning on December 7 to South Shaftsbury. On December 22, writes a year-end letter to J. J. Lankes, who illustrated both the trade and limited editions of *West-Running Brook:* "Those are four beautiful pictures you did for the book—the one of the dead-alive tree especially—and they attach me to you and make me wish for your society. If an abandoned farm or something could be found for you in our neighborhood couldnt you all pack off up here for a summer some year. We'll have to talk this up." Spends the holidays with his family in South Shaftsbury.

Acknowledgments

The melancholy of having to count souls
Where they grow fewer and fewer every year
Is extreme where they shrink to none at all.
It must be I want life to go on living.

  —Frost, "The Census Taker" (1923)

Many people, in many different places, have generously worked with us not only to bring *The Letters of Robert Frost* to life but also to help it "go on living." Kindred spirits in either a devoted admiration of Frost's poetry or an admirable devotion to the shared enterprise of primary scholarship—or both—they have allowed us to benefit from their time, effort, and expertise in collecting Frost's far-flung correspondence and preparing this scholarly edition. At the end of this section, by the institutions with which they are affiliated, is a list of the many librarians, curators, archivists, executors, and technical support personnel whose invaluable assistance we wish with deep gratitude to acknowledge. Our work in locating and acquiring copies of the letters suitable for transcription would have been impossible without their help.

Our greatest debt, of course, is to the Estate of Robert Lee Frost for permission to publish the letters. To Peter A. Gilbert, Executor, we are additionally indebted for his enthusiasm, assistance, and advice. We are deeply grateful to the Frost family, in particular to Lesley Lee Francis, Elinor Wilbur, Robin Hudnut, and to John P. Cone Jr., for their interest and encouragement. Patrick Alger not only granted us full access to his substantial Frost collection, but also provided welcome guidance in matters related to contemporary collectors and collecting. Jack Hagstrom generously shared his first-hand knowledge of the assembly and eventual disposition of early Frost collections. In locating materials and navigating the intricacies of catalogs and archives, we enjoyed the benefits of frequent consultation with John Lancaster and Daria D'Arienzo, librarian-archivists extraordinaire (about whom all things gold do stay). Alex Gouttefangeas rendered invaluable assistance—as much for volume 2 as he did for volume 1—helping to ready, and verify by voice-checking, transcriptions of a great many letters. Thanks also to William Briggeman of Allegheny College for patient assistance in voice-checking. At various points along the way, we have benefitted greatly from the expertise and generosity of Jeff Cooper, Welford Taylor, Carole Thompson, Dan Toomey, Shanshan Wang, and Setsuko Yokoyama. We owe a special thanks for cordiality and patience to a few special collections librarians to whom we turned repeatedly, and often urgently, for help: Jay Satterfield at Dartmouth College, Alice Staples at Plymouth State University, Mike Kelley at Amherst College, Heather Riser at the University of Virginia, Cynthia Harbeson at the Jones Library, Amherst, and Rebekah Irwin at Middlebury College. These, and the many other people we have consulted, good souls all, and hardly few in number, have many a time forestalled the melancholy weariness that might otherwise have attended our taking census of Frost's surviving letters.

Preparation of this edition of Frost's letters was supported by a National Endowment for the Humanities We the People grant (2006). Additional support was provided by the Japanese Ministry of Education (MEXT/JSPS) through two *kakenhi* grants (numbers 19520273 and 23520341). For this support, and for that of Edinboro University of Pennsylvania and Doshisha University (Kyoto), we are grateful. In all matters related to the publication of this volume we have depended upon the professionalism and patience of the staff at Harvard University Press: Lindsay Waters, Executive Editor for the Humanities, Amanda Peery, Assistant Editor, Stephanie Vyce, Director of Intellectual Property and Subsidiary Rights, Tim Jones, Director of Design and Production, and Anne Zarrella, Editorial Department Administrator. We are thankful as well to Debbie Masi, Production Supervisor, Editorial Services, and Katherine Scott, Copyeditor, for the efficient expertise with which our detailed and always evolving typescript was readied for publication at Westchester Publishing Services.

Finally, we wish to acknowledge the personal as well as professional investment in the quality of this volume made by Mark Scott. A poet and a scholar, he brought to a reading of the work as it developed a unique perspective, an extraordinary acuteness of perception, and a deep knowledge of Frost. His contributions and corrections, small and great, have improved the quality of the annotations throughout. For his solicitous attention to the content of this volume we thank him. For his solicitude in regard to the morale of the editors we cannot thank him enough.

*   *   *

Estate of Edward Thomas
Richard Emeny, Executor, Rosemary Vellender

Estate of Laurence Binyon
Edmund Gray, Executor

Greenaway Family
David Greenaway III; Malcolm Greenaway

Makielski Family
Larry Elder, Elder Gallery

Agnes Scott College, McCain Library
Marianne Bradley, Library Administrative Coordinator

Amherst College Library
T. Michael Kelly, Head, Archives and Special Collections; Margaret R.
Dakin, Archives and Special Collections Specialist; Peter A. Nelson,
Assistant Archivist

University of Arkansas Library
Tim Nutt, Head, Special Collections; Andrea Cantrell, Head, Research
Services

Augustana College Library
Harry F. Thompson, Director of Research Collections and Publications,
Center for Western Studies

Bates College Library, Edmund Muskie Archives and Special
Collections
Elaine Ardia, Archives Supervisor

Baylor University, Armstrong Browning Library
Rita S. Patteson, Director/Curator of Manuscripts; Jennifer Borderud,
Associate Director

Baylor University, Texas Collection
John S. Wilson, Director and Associate Dean for Special Libraries; Benna
Vaughan, Special Collections and Manuscripts Archivist

Boston Athenaeum
Stanley Ellis Cushing, Curator of Rare Books and Manuscripts

Boston University Library, Howard Gotlieb Archival Research Center
Vita Paladino, Director; Ryan Hendrickson, Assistant Director for
Manuscripts

Bowdoin College Library, George. J. Mitchell Department of Special
Collections and Archives
Richard Lindemann, Director; Daniel Hope, Assistant; Caroline Moseley,
Archivist

Brandeis University Library, Robert D. Farber University Archives and
Special Collections
Sarah Shoemaker, Special Collections Librarian

Brigham Young University Library
Russ Taylor, Supervisor of Reference Services

British Library (UK)
Rachel Foss, Curator of Modern Literary Manuscripts

Brown University, John Hay Library
Thomas Horrocks, Director of Special Collections; Timothy Engels, Senior
Library Specialist

Bryn Mawr College Library
Marianne Hansen, Special Collections Librarian; Evan McGonagill, Acting
College Archivist

University of California at Berkeley, Bancroft Library
Elaine Tennant, Director; David Kessler, Archivist

University of California at Los Angeles Library
Thomas Hyry, Director, Library Special Collections; Robert D. Montoya,
Operations Manager, Public Services Division

University of California at Santa Barbara Library
David Seubert, Head of Special Collections; Yolanda Blue, Special Collections Librarian

Cambridge University (UK), King's College Archives
Patricia McGuire, Archivist

Cardiff University (UK) Library
Peter Keelan, Head of Special Collections and Archives

University of Chicago Library, Special Collections Research Center
Daniel Meyer, Director, Special Collections Research Center, University
Archivist, University of Chicago Library; Christine Colburn, Reader
Services Manager

Coe College, Stewart Memorial Library
Jill Jack, Head of Reference; Sara Pitcher, Archives Assistant

Coker College Library
Alexa E. Bartel, Director

University of Colorado Boulder Libraries
Deborah Hollis, Associate Professor
Special Collections and Archives

Columbia College, J. Drake Edens Library
Jane P. Tuttle, Head Research and Instruction Librarian

Columbia University Library
Michael Ryan, Curator of Manuscripts, Rare Books and Manuscript Library,
Tara C. Craig, Reference Services Supervisor

Connecticut College Library, Linda Lear Center for Special Collections and
Archives
Benjamin Panciera, Director of Special Collections

Dartmouth College Library
Jay Satterfield, Special Collections Librarian

Derry (NH) Museum of History
Richard Holmes, Director and Town Historian

Duke University, David M. Rubenstein Rare Book and Manuscript Library
Naomi Nelson, Director; David Strader, Library Assistant

Emory University Library
Kathy Shoemaker, Research Services Associate Archivist

University of Florida, George A. Smathers Library
Carl Van Ness, Curator of Manuscripts and Archives

Franconia Heritage Museum
Barbara Holt

George Washington University Library
Christopher Walker, Archives and Manuscript Specialist

Georgetown Un iversity Library
Nicholas Scheetz, Manuscripts Librarian; Scott S. Taylor, Manuscripts
Processor; Ted Jackson, Manuscripts Archivist

University of Georgia, Hargrett Library
Mary Linnemann, Digital Imaging Coordinator

Gloucestershire (UK) Archives
Mick Heath, Archives Assistant, Gloucestershire Archives

Goddard College
David Hale, Archivist

Hamilton College
Katherine Collett, Archivist

Harvard University, Houghton Library
Leslie Morris, Curator of Modern Books and Manuscripts, Houghton
Library, Harvard University; Heather G. Cole, Assistant Curator; Emilie L.
Hardman, Public Services Assistant; Pamela Madsen, Curatorial Assistant,
Harvard Theatre Collection

Harvard University, Schlesinger Library, Radcliffe Institute for Advanced
Study
Sarah Hutcheon, Reference Librarian

Haverford College Library
Diana Franzusoff Peterson, Manuscripts Librarian and College Archivist

HistoryMiami Archives and Research Center
Dawn Hugh, Archives Manager

Hofstra University Library
Geri Solomon, Assistant Dean of Special Collections

Houghton Mifflin Harcourt
Susan Steinway, Archivist

Huntington Library
Sara S. (Sue) Hodson, Curator, Literary Manuscripts

University of Illinois Library
Chatham Ewing, Curator of Special Collections

Indiana University Library, Ruth Lilly Special Collections and Archives
Joel Silver, Director; Rebecca Cape, former Head of Reference and Public
Services

Indiana University of Pennsylvania
Harrison Wick, Special Collections Librarian and University Archivist

Johns Hopkins University Library, Special Collections and Archives
Gabrielle Dean, Curator of Modern Literary Rare Books and Manuscripts;
Kelly Betts, Assistant Curator of Manuscripts

Jones Library, Amherst (MA)
Cynthia Harbeson, Curator, Special Collections; Kate Boyle, Assistant
Curator

Lasell College
Allison Bjorndahl-McCarter, Reference Librarian and Archivist

Library of Congress
Jeffrey M. Flannery, Head, Reference and Reader Services Section, Manuscript Division; Lewis Wyman, Reference Librarian

Manchester (NH) Historic Association
Ben Baker, Library Assistant

University of Maryland Library
Beth (Ruth M.) Alvarez, Curator of Literary Manuscripts

Massachusetts Historical Society
Tracy Potter, Assistant Reference Librarian

Miami (OH) University Library, Walter Havighurst Special Collections
Elizabeth Brice, Assistant Dean for Technical Services and Head,
Special Collections and Archives; Janet Stuckey, former Head, Special
Collections

University of Miami, Otto G. Richter Library
Cristina Favretto, Head of Special Collections; Laura Capell, Research
Services Assistant; Cory Czajkowski, Senior Library Assistant

University of Michigan Library
Martha O'Hara Conway, Director, Special Collections; Kate Hutchens, Reader and Reference Services Librarian, Nancy Bartlett, Head, University Archives and Records; Malgosia Myc, Lead Reference Archivist

Middlebury College Library
Rebekah Irwin, Director and Curator, Special Collections and Archives; Mikaela Taylor Postgraduate Fellow

Milton Academy
Diane Pierce-Williams, Staff Assistant, Cox Library

University of Minnesota Archives
Elmer L. Andersen Library Erin George, Assistant Archivist

University of Montana, Mansfield Library
Donna McCrea, Head of Archives and Special Collections; Steve Bingo, Adjunct Archivist; Mark Fritch, Archives Photo Specialist

The Morgan Library and Museum
Declan Kiely, Curator and Department Head, Literary and Historical Manuscripts

The Newberry Library
Alison Hinderliter, Manuscripts and Archives Librarian

University of New Hampshire Library, Douglas and Helena Milne Special Collections and Archives
Roland Goodbody, Manuscripts Curator; Nancy Mason, Special Collections Assistant

University of New Orleans, Earl K. Long Library, Louisiana and Special Collections
Connie L. Phelps, Services Department, Chair

New York Public Library
Isaac Gewirtz, Curator, Henry W. and Albert A. Berg Collection of English and American Literature; Laura Ruttum, Reference Archivist; Laura Slezak Karas, Archivist

New York University, The Fales Library and Special Collections
Marvin J. Taylor, Director; Kelsi Evans, Assistant

State University of New York at Buffalo
Michael Basinski, Curator, The Poetry Collection

University of North Carolina Library
Walter C. (Tim) West, Curator of Manuscripts and Director of the Southern
Historical Collection; Robin Davies Chen, Assistant Manuscripts Reference
Librarian

Northwestern University Library
Kevin B. Leonard, University Archivist; Janet C. Olson, Assistant Archivist

Ohio State University Library
Rebecca Jewett, Assistant Curator, Rare Books and Manuscripts

University of Pennsylvania, Rare Book and Manuscript Library
Nancy Shawcross, Curator of Manuscripts

Pennsylvania State University Library
Sandra Stelts, Curator of Rare Books and Manuscripts

Phillips Academy Andover
Ruth Quattlebaum, former Academy Archivist

Phillips Academy Exeter, Edouard L. Desrochers, Assistant Librarian and
Academy Archivist

Pinkerton Academy
Mark Mastromarino, Archivist; Anne Massa Parker, Director of Alumni
Relations; Laura Burnham, Assistant Librarian

University of Pittsburgh Library System
Charles E. Aston Jr., Curator, Rare Books, Prints, and Exhibits, Special
Collections Department

Plymouth State University Library, Alice P. Staples, Archives/Special
Collections Librarian; Susan Jarosz, Archives Assistant

Princeton University Library
Don C. Skemer, Curator of Manuscripts; AnnaLee Pauls, Special Collections Assistant III; Sandra Bossert, Special Collections Assistant

Rollins College, Olin Library
Wenxian Zhang, Head of Archives and Special Collections

St. Lawrence University
Mark McMurray, Curator of Special Collections and University Archivist;
Darlene Leonard, former Archives Assistant

South Carolina Historical Society
Mary Jo Fairchild, Senior Archivist

Town of South Shaftsbury (VT)
Judy Stratton, Town Clerk

University of Southern California, Doheny Memorial Library
Melinda Hayes, Head, Special Collections; Claude Zachary, University
Archivist and Manuscript Librarian

Southern Illinois University Edwardsville, Lovejoy Library
Stephen Kerber, University Archivist and Special Collections Librarian

Stanford University Library
Polly Armstrong, Public Services Manager, Special Collections and University Archives

University of Tampa, Macdonald-Kelce Library
Art Bagley, Special Collections Librarian

Tennessee State Library and Archives
Jay Richiuso, Assistant Director for Manuscripts Services

University of Texas at Austin, Harry Ransom Center
Rick Watson, Head of Reference Services; Elspeth Healey, Public Services
Intern

University of Toledo, Ward M. Canaday Center for Special Collections
Kimberly Brownlee, Manuscripts Librarian and Assistant University
Archivist

Trinity College, Watkinson Library
Richard J. Ring, Head Curator

Tufts University Library
Laura Cutter, Archives and Research Assistant

University of Tulsa, McFarlin Library
Marc Carlson, Librarian of Special Collections and University Archives;
Kristen Leatherwood Marangoni, former Assistant

University College Dublin
Seamus Helferty, Principal Archivist

Vassar College Library, Catherine Pelton Durrell Archives and Special
Collections
Dean M. Rogers, Special Collections Assistant

University of Vermont, Bailey/Howe Library
Chris Burns, Curator of Manuscripts and University Archivist

Vermont Historical Society
Paul Carnahan, Librarian

University of Virginia, Albert and Shirley Small Special Collections
Library
Molly Schwartzburg, Curator; Heather Riser, Head, Reference and Re-
search Services; Christina Deane, Head, Digitization Services

Wagner College
Lisa Holland, Archivist

Wellesley College, Margaret Clap Library
Ruth R. Rogers, Special Collections Librarian; Mariana S. Oller, Special
Collections Research and Instruction Specialist

Wesleyan University, Olin Library
Suzy Taraba, Director of Special Collections and Archives; Jennifer Hadley,
Assistant

University of Wisconsin–La Crosse, Murphy Library
Laura M. Godden, Librarian; Megan Gosse, Library Assistant, Special
Collections

Wisconsin Historical Society
Harry Miller, Reference Archivist

Wofford College, Sandor Teszler Library
Phillip Stone, Archivist

Yale University, Beinecke Library
Nancy Kuhl, Curator, Poetry, Yale Collection of American Literature;
Moira Fitzgerald, Public Services Staff, Manuscripts and Archives

———————

Eldred's Auction Gallery
Deborah Gaile Clemence

Quill and Brush
Beth Fisher

Index